MW01015361

AMERICAN REGIONAL COOKING

A Culinary Journey

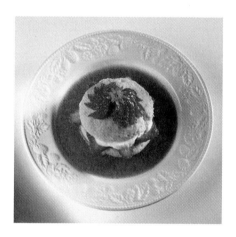

Patricia A. Heyman

Recipes and Wine Pairings by Alan H. Roer

PEARSON

Prentice
Hall

Upper Saddle River, New Jersey
Columbus, Ohio

Library of Congress Cataloging-in-Publication Data

Heyman, Patricia A.
  American regional cooking: a culinary journey / Patricia A. Heyman;
recipes and wine pairings by Alan H. Roer.
      p. cm.
  Includes bibliographical references and index.
  ISBN-13: 978-0-13-170856-3 (casebound)
  ISBN-10: 0-13-170856-2 (casebound)
  1. Cookery, American—History.   2. Cookery, American.   I. Roer, Alan H.
II. Title.
  TX715.H5748 2009
  641.5973—dc22

                                    2008022387

Editor in Chief: Vernon Anthony
Acquisitions Editor: William Lawrensen
Editorial Assistant: Lara Dimmick
Production Coordination: Thistle Hill Publishing Services, LLC
Associate Managing Editor: Alexandrina Benedicto Wolf
Project Manager: Alicia Ritchey
Operations Specialist: Deidra Schwartz
Art Director: Diane Ernsberger
Interior and Cover Design: Candace Rowley
Cover Image: Image Bank
Director, Image Resource Center: Melinda Patelli
Manager, Rights and Permissions: Zina Arabia
Manager, Cover Visual Research and Permissions: Karen Sanatar
Image Permission Coordinator: Kathy Gavilanes
Director of Marketing: David Gesell
Marketing Manager: Leigh Ann Sims
Marketing Assistant: Les Roberts
Copyeditor: Rebecca M. Bobb

This book was set in TradeGothic by Aptara®, Inc., and was printed and bound by Quebecor World
Color/Versailles. The cover was printed by Phoenix Color.

Pearson Education Ltd., London
Pearson Education Singapore Pte. Ltd.
Pearson Education Canada, Inc.
Pearson Education—Japan

Pearson Education Australia Pty. Limited
Pearson Education North Asia, Ltd., Hong Kong
Pearson Educación de Mexico, S.A. de C.V.
Pearson Education Malaysia Pte. Ltd.

10 9 8 7 6 5 4 3 2 1
ISBN-13: 978-0-13-170856-3
ISBN-10:   0-13-170856-2

For much appreciated support and tasting many recipes, I send unlimited love and thanks to my mother, Lisa Heyman; my stepchildren—Samantha Roer, my daughter, and David and Jason Roer, my sons; and, of course, to my husband, Alan Roer, for everything!

Always in my heart and thoughts, Julius Heyman, Irving Roer, and Emma Frank.

CONTENTS

Preface   vii

A Few Words on Wine   x

Acknowledgments   xiii

Web Sites   xv

CHAPTER 1   History   2

CHAPTER 2   New England   18
Maine, Vermont, New Hampshire, Massachusetts, Connecticut, and Rhode Island

CHAPTER 3   Middle Atlantic States   54
New York, New Jersey, Pennsylvania, Delaware, and Maryland

CHAPTER 4   Southern States   92
Virginia, West Virginia, North Carolina, South Carolina, Kentucky, Tennessee, Georgia,
Alabama, Mississippi, and Arkansas

CHAPTER 5   Florida   126

CHAPTER 6   Louisiana   158

CHAPTER 7   Midwestern States   186
Michigan, Wisconsin, Minnesota, Ohio, Indiana, Illinois, Iowa, and Missouri

CHAPTER 8   Plains States   220
North Dakota, South Dakota, Nebraska, Kansas, and Oklahoma

CHAPTER 9   Southwestern States   248
Texas, New Mexico, and Arizona

CHAPTER 10   Mountain States   284
Montana, Idaho, Wyoming, Colorado, Utah, and Nevada

CHAPTER 11   Pacific Northwest, Alaska, and Hawaii   316
Washington, Oregon, Alaska, and Hawaii

CHAPTER 12   California   354

CHAPTER 13   The Melting Pot   384

GLOSSARY   417

BIBLIOGRAPHY   421

INDEX   425

PREFACE

After exploring international cookery and writing the book, *International Cooking: A Culinary Journey*, the next logical step was writing the companion, *American Regional Cooking: A Culinary Journey*. The international book provides an excellent foundation for this American regional book for two reasons. First, permanent settlements in the United States by non-Native Americans did not begin until the sixteenth century, which is quite recent in terms of world history. Second, most of the ethnic groups that settled in the United States emigrated from areas discussed in the international book, so their cuisines are already familiar.

Every student majoring in culinary arts needs to study American regional cooking as well as international cooking. The combination of these two courses provides a comprehensive explanation of the evolution and development of many cuisines from around the globe. Hopefully, these companion textbooks make learning this enormous topic easier.

Researching American regional cooking, I discovered an unfolding history where immigrant after immigrant came to this new land in search of religious or political refuge, economic opportunity, escape from famine and starvation, and/or the chance to create a better life for themselves and their families. With relatively few Native Americans, most Americans trace at least part of their heritage to one or more countries in Europe, Africa, Asia, or Central and South America. The United States formed as a country of immigrants from every continent, which makes the culinary history of this nation different from most others.

Like countries throughout the world, the regional cuisines of the United States did not develop by coincidence or in a random way. Each cuisine developed and evolved based on the history of the region, the culinary traits of those who settled in the area as well as those who already lived there, the climate and topography of the region, and what crops and animals thrived in that particular region.

Stretching from the Atlantic Ocean to the Pacific and even into the Pacific Ocean (Hawaii), the United States encompasses a very large and diverse landmass. In the beginning, settlers landed on the east coast, but gradually they moved to the west. Finding an incredible variety of climates, terrains, and growing conditions, immigrants chose to settle in a location based on any number of criteria, including the availability of land to farm or jobs, what crops and animals flourished or were indigenous to the region, the number of people of the same ethnic group who lived there, and/or the similarity of the climate and terrain to their homeland.

Besides the climate, topography, and what grew or was raised in any given area, the regional cuisines developed from layers of culinary influences by immigrants from around the world. When people immigrated, they brought their culinary heritage with them. Although they moved into new neighborhoods in new towns and cities in a new country, they continued to cook the familiar foods and recipes from their homeland. In the absence of necessary ingredients for their recipes, they substituted. Tasting dishes from their friends and neighbors, they soon added those recipes to their own repertoire. As a result, the melting pot containing ingredients from the culinary heritages of countless ethnic groups grew, simmered, and eventually created its own unique cuisine in each area/region. As the years passed, more and more people from various ethnicities moved into the United States. All brought their culinary past with them. Even today, the changes continue, and the cuisines of each region remain a fascinating work in progress.

GOAL OF THIS BOOK

This book presents a comprehensive explanation of the development and evolution of American regional cookery. Through this book, we show the culinary history of this country and how the history, climate and topography, growing conditions, indigenous foods, and the groups of people who moved into different locations molded each region's cuisine. Along with an understanding of the reasons and benefits for many ethnic groups immigrating to this country, students should realize that the settlers did not allow two groups, the Native Americans and the African slaves, to decide where they lived. They forced the Native Americans to keep moving west to lands considered uninhabitable, and they imported Africans against their will to work as slaves. For most immigrants, the move to this country represented dreamed-about freedom and opportunity.

ORGANIZATION OF THIS BOOK

Like its companion textbook, *International Cooking: A Culinary Journey,* each chapter is divided into six sections: history, topography, common food ingredients, cooking methods, individual information about the states constituting the region, and general characteristics of the cuisine. Understanding the information in each of these sections makes the development of the cuisine apparent. Following these six sections, each chapter contains a chart summarizing the material covered in the chapter, review questions, a glossary, and an assortment of recipes characteristic to the region that represents all segments of a menu.

The collection of recipes at the end of each chapter contains at least one first course, soup, salad, vegetable, starch, and bread, at least two desserts, and a minimum of four entrées representing meat, poultry, and fish or seafood. With this assortment of recipes, the student can prepare a buffet representing the cuisine of each region. While the recipes reflect traditional dishes and/or ingredients commonly seen in the region, a working chef from many of the regions contributed one or more recipes that reflect a contemporary twist on a classic or traditional dish. Hopefully, these chefs' recipes show the student how to transform a traditional recipe into a new, interesting, innovative dish. This book contains almost 220 recipes that Alan Roer or I have tested. The contributing chefs tested their own recipes.

Both Alan Roer and I strongly believe that wine and food pairing play a crucial role in today's culinary education. A suggestion for the style of wine and a specific wine example from the region accompanies each appropriate recipe. Having taught a course in wine appreciation at the State University of New York at Cobleskill for more than 15 years, Alan wrote the wine pairings for this book.

Cooking methods used in each recipe appear at the top. Regardless of the origin of the recipe or what ingredients and flavorings it contains, my former colleague Bob Chapman always taught students that there are only five methods of cooking. To cook any dish involves one or more of the following cooking methods: braise, bake/roast, grill/broil, boil/simmer/poach/steam, sauté/pan-fry/deep-fry. Regardless of what spices, flavorings, or other ingredients surround the food items, there is only one way to roast, one method of braising, and one way to fry. Hopefully, this removes the fear of trying any recipe.

Like its companion, this textbook includes a list of Web sites to help explore all aspects of American regional cooking or to find more recipes. Of course, any listing of Web sites is constantly changing, and I am sure by the time this book is printed, some sites will be moved or gone. Use a search engine to find Web sites and check links on these sites. The available information seems limitless, so just consider this list as a starting point for exploring American regional cooking through the Web.

OUR HOPE

Between the two of us, we have worked in food operations or taught culinary classes for over 50 years! Needless to say, we believe in the value of culinary education. We fervently hope this textbook helps you understand and appreciate American regional cooking. Furthermore, we hope this textbook is easy to use and proves a good guide through the cookery found throughout the United States.

PATRICIA A. HEYMAN

A FEW WORDS ON WINE

The United States has developed into one of the most important wine-producing nations in the world. Starting from humble beginnings, the current industry grew. In a short period of time, this country moved from Prohibition to one that produces quality wines that rival those of France, Italy, and Spain. Each of the 50 states produces some type of wines.

Historians trace the first mention of grapes and wine in the United States to Leif Eriksson, who landed in the vicinity of New England around 1003 AD. Eriksson discovered grapevines of the *Vitis labrusca* species that include Concord, Delaware, and Niagara grapes. Still growing in the eastern United States, these grapes contain aromas and flavors described by many as "foxy" or "musky."

Indigenous to the South, native grapes called the "muscadines" flourished in the warm, humid conditions. This unique variety is still grown throughout the Southern states, and wine is produced from it. Among the grapes found in the *Vitis rotundifolia* family, Muscadine and Scuppernong are the most familiar. While the quality of the wines produced from these grapes disappointed the early settlers, in the nineteenth century they introduced the European *Vitis vinifera* varieties, including Chardonnay, Cabernet Sauvignon, Pinot Noir, and Riesling. With these new varieties, the quality of American wines began to improve.

Many call the third president of the United States, Thomas Jefferson, the most knowledgeable wine connoisseur of his age. When he served as ambassador to France, Jefferson developed enormous interest in both food and wine. Furthermore, he planted grapes in his gardens at Monticello and served wines with dinners at the White House when he became president.

On October 28, 1919, Congress passed the Eighteenth Amendment, which prohibited the manufacture, sale, and transportation of alcoholic beverages, and Prohibition began. Although some wineries produced sacramental wines or sold grapes for home winemaking during Prohibition, most ceased operating. The American wine industry basically stopped. In 1933, this amendment was repealed, and the vintners began producing wine again.

When he started Boordy Vineyards in Maryland in 1945, Philip Wagner planted French hybrids in his vineyard. Mixing French and native American varieties of grapes, vintners propagated hybrids that thrived in the harsh climates found in the East. Seyval Blanc, Vignoles, Chancellor, and Baco Noir are all examples of French-American hybrids. The hybrids still thrive, and vintners in several regions make wine from these grapes.

With commitment and technology, winemakers survived Prohibition, the spread of phylloxera (a root-feeding insect that destroys the entire plant), the Depression, and the Second World War. The American wine industry owes a great deal to technology, which helped make this country's wine industry one of the most important in the world. With renowned programs in oenology, people at the University of California at Davis and Fresno State University constantly research and work to improve the wine industry. Many advancements to the wine industry came from technological innovations, such as cloning, T-budding, malolactic fermentation, trellising and canopy management, pruning techniques, and cool stainless steel fermenting procedures, along with new ideas concerning varietals, hybrids, and the attention to *terrior*. A French term, *terrior* refers to the soil, temperature, and climate of an area and how they affect the growing grapes and ultimately the wine.

The most significant growth in the American wine industry began during the 1960s when most of the technological advances occurred. With the ongoing evolution and interest in American cooking led by people like Julia Child, Alice Waters, James Beard, and Emeril Lagasse, the popularity of American wines continues to grow.

What does the future hold for the American wine industry? From new insect infestations, to legal requirements, to the popularity of foreign countries' wines, the future holds endless challenges for the wine industry. In the last 30 years, American vintners raised the standards for American wines and created many that successfully compete with excellent wines from around the world. The industry will continue to face challenges, find solutions, and survive by realizing what changes are needed and implementing them. The future of the American wine industry rests with our entrepreneurial vision, marketing expertise, and technology.

IMPORTANT LEADERS AND DEFINING MOMENTS OF THE AMERICAN WINE INDUSTRY

- Leif Eriksson: Norse explorer reached North America around AD 1000 and christened the land "Vinland" because of all the vines he found there.
- Father Junipero Serra: Franciscan monk introduced the Mission grape to the Mission San Diego de Alcada, the first of 21 missions established throughout California.
- Jean-Louis Vignes: Introduced vinifera grapes to California.
- Agoston Haraszthy: Known as the Father of California wine, he brought 100,000 grapevines, representing hundreds of grape varieties that he obtained from France, Spain, Italy, Switzerland, and Germany to California. Haraszthy adapted many European methods of winemaking at his Buena Vista winery in Sonoma.
- Phillip Wagner: The first to bring French-American hybrids such as Vignoles and Seyval Blanc to the United States. Started Boordy Vineyards in Maryland.
- Charles Fournier: Before becoming president of Gold Seal Vineyards in New York, he managed the famous champagne maker Veuve Clicquot-Ponsardin in France. With this experience, Fournier produced some excellent sparkling wines in New York.
- André Tchelistcheff: Born in Russia and trained in France, Tchelistcheff produced great Cabernets and Pinot Noirs at Beaulieu Vineyards in California.
- Dr. Konstantin Frank: His experiments with vinifera varieties in New York during the 1960s ranks as one of the finest wine achievements in New York wines.
- Robert Mondavi: After leaving his family's Charles Krug Winery, Mondavi started his own winery and became a driving force in California's wine industry.
- Steven Spurrier: An Englishman who organized a blind tasting of wines in Paris in 1976 where American wines scored higher than French wines for the first time.
- French Paradox: In 1991, a nationwide television program linked red wine to reduced levels of heart disease in France. This initiated the first public awareness of the potential health benefits of wine.
- Phylloxera: In 1995, this root-feeding insect attacked the vineyards of California, killing acres of grapevines for the second time.

FOOD AND WINE PAIRINGS

Americans are an adventuresome group of people. From the beginning, the settlers and immigrants traveled from the east to the west, over mountains and difficult terrain, and they adapted to whatever they found. They learned to prepare the available foods and developed wines to drink.

In approaching the wine pairings for this book, I tried to keep this adventuresome spirit alive. Although I often recommend traditional wine pairings, many times I suggest nontraditional wine and food pairings. Traditionally, red wines match well with red meats and white wines match well with seafood. In breaking with tradition, I might recommend a light Pinot Noir with salmon or Gewürztraminer with spicy oriental beef.

I believe that letting people drink any wine they like encourages them to drink and enjoy wine. If an individual prefers dry red wines and wants to pair that with a delicate fish entrée, great. If someone serves a full-bodied Chardonnay with steak, enjoy! Usual recommended pairings are based on traditional criteria such as dry wines before sweet wines, sparkling wines before still, younger before older, and light before heavy wines. Others prefer to stretch the boundaries as our forefathers did.

It is my hope that you will try many different wines with a wide variety of dishes. Remember what is important: enjoy the food and wine that you consume. Salute!

ALAN H. ROER

ACKNOWLEDGMENTS

My heartfelt thanks go to many friends and relatives for caring and sharing. Thank you Alan Roer, Lisa Heyman, Samantha Roer, David Roer, Bobby and Stephanie, Arlene, Laraine, Stephanie, Sandy, Judy, Marisa, Bonnie and Charlie, and BJ and Ellen. You all share my joy at completing this book and especially that I will quit obsessing about it.

My sincere appreciation goes to the chefs who contributed to this textbook. With an idea, I wrote and explained my thoughts to many chefs across the country, and six miraculously agreed to help me with the project. I believe that students will learn a lot from seeing a working chef's contemporary twist on a traditional recipe. Hopefully, this will demonstrate how to work with a recipe and transform it. The fact that any of these busy chefs would expend the time and energy "just to help" is yet another example of how many in our profession "give back" so freely. To help future cooks and chefs, this group of culinary professionals submitted recipes for this book and answered many questions and e-mails from me until the recipe seemed completely clear. With great admiration, I thank Todd English and Gina Gargano from the Olive Group in Boston; Charlie Palmer and Anthony Aiazzi from Eatwell Enterprises in New York City; Kathy Cary from Lilly's and Le Peche in Louisville, Kentucky; Mark Militello and Francy Deskin from Mark's four restaurants in southeastern Florida; Todd Slossberg from the Hotel Jerome in Aspen, Colorado; and Peter Merriman and Sheena from Merriman's restaurants in Hawaii.

I send thanks to Kevin Keith and Robot Coupe for the use of a fabulous new food processor. My first Robot Coupe is still running after 23 years! Thanks to Alain LeNôtre of the Culinary Institute Alain and Marie LeNôtre in Houston.

Special thanks to Jillian, Tom, and all the other reference librarians at the Guilderland Public Library in Guilderland, New York, for helping me obtain books locally and throughout the country. Also thanks to the reference librarians at the Gulf Gate and Selby Libraries in Sarasota, Florida. Please know that I really appreciate all of your help and know how fortunate we are to have public libraries. Lots of heartfelt gratitude to my former colleague, Bob Chapman, for countless ideas, great ideals, being a role model I will never forget, and many wonderful years of working together!

Many people at manufacturers, promotion or marketing boards, and other organizations allowed me to use their photographs in this book. I thank Pat Weed from Land O' Lakes, Sherri Coleman and Gerry Unrau from CanolaInfo, Rae Maestas from the American Lamb Board, David Goldenberg from the California Salmon Council, Don Odiorne from the Idaho Potato Commission, Christy Marr from the National Turkey Federation, Shaily Jariwala from the USA Rice Federation, Jami Yanoski from the National Honey Board, Leah Garcia-Busick from the Florida Tomato Committee, Carma Rogers from the National Pork Board, Leslie Wagner from the Peanut Advisory Board, Kim Reddin from the National Onion Association, Elisa E'Amico from the American Egg Board, Lonna Severson and Polly Owen from the Hazelnut Marketing Board, Megan Livingston from the American Dry Bean Board, Allison Rogers at King Arthur Flour, and Barbara Getz and Laurie Harrsen at McCormick Spices. Besides these people, many others offered suggestions of people to contact when they did not have the photograph I needed. Thanks to all of you; I hope I did not forget anyone!

Many thanks to the reviewers for their comments and suggestions: Richard Grigsby, Florida Community College at Jacksonville; Brian Hay, Austin Community College; Christian Kefauver, West Virginia Northern Community College; Pam Lewis, University of

Southern Mississippi; Odette Smith-Ransome, Art Institute of Pittsburgh; David Weir, Orlando Culinary Academy; and Jeffrey Yourdon, Lenior Community College.

Finally, thanks to all the people at Prentice Hall who worked on this book, both those I know and those whose names I never even heard. I send a special thanks and appreciation to Vern Anthony, who supported me through two books. With your promotion, I will miss your being "my" editor.

WEB SITES

A world of information exists on the Web, but obtaining that information often presents a formidable challenge. After much searching, I have compiled a list of Web sites that should augment the information discussed in this book, including various regions, food products, and recipes. There are literally thousands of Web sites with information and/or recipes. This list represents just a small portion of the sites available in "cyberland."

When beginning to research any topic, start with any search engine like Google or Yahoo. Access the search engine, e.g., www.google.com. Type the subject into the search box, hit the Enter button, and choose to search from thousands or even millions of available sites. If the information is not quite right, reword the subject in the search box and try again. In my experience, the information is out there, but sometimes the tricky part is finding it. The key lies in the wording of the search. When exploring a site, check its links; that often leads to other good sources.

A disclaimer—Web sites come and go, so realize that this list changes constantly, and some of these sites may disappear. I view this merely as a start for further research.

Regions and/or States:

Check the tourism site for each state. Many contain a section on history.

www.ct.gov	Connecticut
www.ndtourism.com	North Dakota
www.travelsd.com	South Dakota
www.accesskansas.org	Kansas
www.gti.net.mocolib1/kid/foodfaq4.html	state recipes, an assortment
www.state.nj.us/jerseyfresh/recipes/index.html	New Jersey Department of Agriculture, recipes
www.recipelink.com/rcpusa.html	recipes—regional America
www.sciencebulletins.amnh.org	information on Georges Banks
www.keyingredients.org	foods through American history
www.cuisinenet.com/digest/contents/region.shtml	information on regional cooking
www.whatscookingamerica.net	all sorts of information
www.isu.edu/%7Etrinmich/allabout.html	Oregon Trail
www.mdarchives.state.md.us	Chesapeake Bay information
www.usahistory.info/colonies	information on colonies
www.californiadigitallibrary.org	click on University of California digital collections, then food or desired topic
www.cdfa.ca.gov	information on California agriculture
http://www.historylink.org/essays/output.cfm?file_id = 400	history of Donation Land Law
www.vcnevada.com	Virginia City, Nevada, and Comstock Lode
www.washingtonpost.com/wp-srv/national/longterm/meltingpot/melt0222.htm	information on melting pot
www.homepages.uhwo.hawaii.edu	Hawaii
www.hawaiischoolreports.com	Hawaii and various ethnic groups; click on "people" and explore links; also "ethnic food glossary" under "people"

www.bostonfamilyhistory.com	Boston immigration
www.crt.state.la.us	Louisiana
www.louisianatravel.com	Louisiana
www.traveloregon.com	Oregon

Cheese and Dairy Products:

www.cheesenet.info	information
www.cheese.com	information
www.realcaliforniacheese.com	information
www.gotmilk.com	recipes
www.landolakes.com	recipes

Meats, Poultry, and Seafood:

www.eatturkey.com	turkey, National Turkey Federation
www.beef.org	beef and veal
www.americanlambboard.org	lamb
www.californialamb.com	lamb
www.otherwhitemeat.com	pork
www.nationalchickencouncil.com	National Chicken Council
www.eatchicken.com	chicken
www.aboutseafood.com	National Fisheries Institute, seafood
www.virginiaseafood.org	seafood
www.catfishinstitute.com	catfish
www.alaskaseafood.org	Alaska seafood
www.calkingsalmon.org	California salmon

Legumes:

www.pea-lentil.com	legumes
www.americanbean.org	legumes
www.aboutpeanuts.com	peanuts
www.peanut-institute.org	peanuts

Fruits, Vegetables, and Grains:

www.chinaranch.com	dates
www.apples-ne.com	New England apples
www.nyapplecountry.com	New York apples
www.appleofyourpie.com	apple information
www.agmkt.state.ny.us/agfacts.html	New York agriculture
www.vegparadise.com	various vegetables
www.floridatomatoes.org	tomato recipes
www.tomato.org	tomato recipes
www.avocado.org	avocado recipes
www.florida-agriculture.com	Florida agriculture
www.onions-usa.org	onions
www.calstrawberry.com	strawberries
www.idahopotato.com	potato recipes
www.kikkoman.com	Kikkoman soy sauce
www.usapears.com	pears
www.mushroominfo.com	mushrooms
www.mushroomcouncil.org	mushrooms
www.usarice.com	rice

Miscellaneous:

www.inventors.about.com	information about various inventors
www.foodtimeline.org	timeline and information of many foods
www.whatscookingamerica.net	information on variety of foods
www.delmonicosny.com	Delmonico's Restaurant
www.thefurtrapper.com	information and history of Mountain Men
http://memory.loc.gov/learn/features/immig/introduction.html	Library of Congress info on immigrants to the United States
http://www.rapidimmigration.com/usa/1_eng_immigration_facts.html	immigration information
http://www.expo-comida-latina.com/2005/market.shtml	information on Hispanic immigration
www.bergen.org/aast/projects/immigration	immigration information
www.ellisisland.com	information on Ellis Island
www.honey.com	honey information and recipes
www.nhb.org	honey
www.homebaking.org	baking recipes
www.aeb.org	egg recipes and information
www.canolainfo.org	canola oil information and recipes
www.nuthealth.org	nuts
www.oregonhazelnuts.org	hazelnuts
www.walnuts.org	walnuts
www.heb.com	list of Web sites for food promotion groups
www.kingarthurflour.com	baking recipes
www.mccormick.com	all sorts of recipes

AMERICAN REGIONAL COOKING

A Culinary Journey

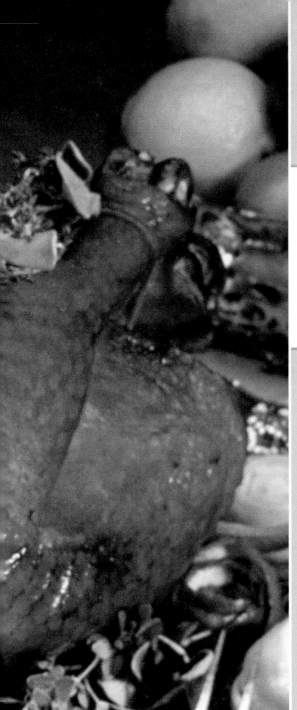

1

History

OBJECTIVES

By the end of this chapter, you will be able to

- Discuss factors that molded cuisines in the United States
- Explain the role of the Native Americans in the survival of the European settlers
- Discuss the nationalities of the early Europeans who immigrated to the United States
- Discuss the reasons most chose to settle in this new land
- Explain the impact of the railroad and waterways on the development of this country
- Explain the development of the Industrial Revolution
- Identify food products indigenous to the United States

OVERVIEW

In the beginning, American regional cookery developed when the settlers combined influences from their homeland with what they learned from the Native Americans (Indians). The settlers joined their culinary heritage cooking techniques, and recipes with indigenous foods found in each region and the cooking techniques and recipes learned from the Native Americans. When the first settlers landed, they established colonies near the Atlantic Ocean at various sites stretching from Maine to Georgia. The survival of these settlers/immigrants hinged on the available foods found in each location and the information they learned from the people who already inhabited this country, the Native Americans.

Later, as more immigrants came to America, settlers began moving west in search of more land and/or greater opportunity. Again, the cuisine evolved when the native cookery, traditions, and culinary heritage of the settlers melded with the cookery of the people who already lived in the new area. As they moved to the west, settlers found Native Americans and various groups of people who already had migrated to the region. As the westward expansion continued, the population increased, and more and more ethnic groups factored into each region's cookery. This resulted in a cuisine with many ethnic layers. From the start, this new land became a melting pot. Today, American regional cookery remains a work in progress, continually evolving as more immigrants move to the United States.

BRIEF HISTORY

According to archaeologists, Alaska and Asia were connected many thousands of years ago, and the first Indians migrated from Asia to North America about 15,000 years ago. Long before the white men arrived, many different tribes of Indians inhabited the land that would become the United States.

The first Native Americans came from three distinct groups, Inuit (Eskimos), Hawaiians, and Indians. Inhabiting Alaska, the Inuit remained in the cold northern areas near the Arctic Circle, the Hawaiians settled in Hawaii, and the Indians occupied most of the continental United States. While the Indians and Inuit trace their ancestry to Asia, the Hawaiians migrated from the Polynesian Islands.

Native Americans survived on foods they gathered, hunted, and planted. Neighboring tribes often traded for various foods depending on their excesses and their needs. Game, birds, fish, and/or seafood provided most of the protein while berries, fruits, vegetables, seeds, and nuts indigenous to the area constituted much of their diet. Nuts and seeds fulfilled an important role in the diet because the Native Americans ate them raw, dried them for the winter, and ground them into meal to thicken stews or prepare breads. Cooking techniques remained simple: grilling, boiling, and steaming over an open fire, as well as baking and steaming in a pit of hot stones or embers. By smoking, drying, or salting any excess foods, the Native Americans provided sustenance during the lean times like winter, bad weather, or drought.

Because many tribes of Native Americans lived across the diverse regions of this vast land, the characteristics of each tribe strongly reflected the region they inhabited. The climate, topography, and indigenous plants and animals found in each region determined how the Native Americans lived, what they ate, and how they prepared their food. In the East, the Narragansett, Penobscot, Wampanoags, and others introduced the settlers to baked beans and the clambake. Creating ovens, they dug pits to contain the fire used to cook their foods. The tribes of the South such as the Cherokees, Seminoles, Creek, and Powhatan raised a wide variety of crops in the long, hot, humid growing season. The Cheyenne, Sioux, Comanche, and Dakota tribes lived a nomadic life on the Plains that centered on the buffalo. With all parts of the buffalo being used, this animal provided food, shelter, and clothing. In the Southwest, the Pueblos, Hopi, Zuñi, and Papago tribes consumed ample amounts of chili peppers, beans, squash, tomatoes, and avocados. Native American tribes of the Northwest like the Tlingit, Salish, and Kwakiutl survived on the bounty of fish and seafood, especially salmon obtained from the Pacific Ocean and the rivers. Usually, they simply broiled, steamed, or simmered the fish.

While each group of Native Americans developed its own cuisine based on available ingredients, corn reigned as the one food grown in every region. Even though the recipes and the form of corn (ground, dried, fresh) varied greatly throughout the regions, corn served as a mainstay in the Native American diet.

Archaeologists believe Vikings landed in North America just south of Cape Cod, Massachusetts, around 1000. Although they reported huge numbers of birds flying overhead and abundant wild grapes and corn growing in this new land, these first white inhabitants did not stay long. About 500 years after the Vikings, Christopher Columbus landed in San Salvador.

While searching for a passage to the Pacific Ocean and the Spice Islands, Christopher Columbus landed in America by mistake. Instead of finding the waterway that led to Asia, Columbus discovered the New World in 1492. Until his death in 1506, Columbus believed he had sailed to the Orient as opposed to the Western Hemisphere.

In 1526, the Spanish landed somewhere along the Atlantic coast in what became the southern United States, but that settlement lasted only one year. The Spanish established the city of St. Augustine (now in Florida) in 1565. After discovering Mexico, the Spanish entered the southwestern United States by traveling north from Mexico. Soon, the Spanish built missions throughout the Southwest and California, where they planted grapes to make wine in addition to orchards and crops, including figs, dates, citrus fruits, and much more. In 1598, the Spanish brought sheep to the lands they controlled, and they also introduced cattle, pigs, goats, fowl, and seeds for peaches, apples, apricots, pears, and wheat, as well as tools like spades, plows, and hoes. Even today, strong Spanish influence remains throughout the Southwest and California.

Founded in 1607, Jamestown, Virginia, near the Chesapeake Bay, became the first permanent British settlement in this new land. Although those early settlers came in search of gold and treasure, they found hardship, starvation, and illness. To survive their first winter, they ate the animals they brought for breeding. A few years later, colonists brought cows to Jamestown, opening the way for dairy products in this new land. In those early years, tobacco served as their main crop for export to England.

Carrying 100 passengers seeking religious freedom, the Mayflower landed on Cape Cod in the fall of 1620, then crossed the bay and settled in a deserted Indian village in Plymouth, Massachusetts. Because of the bounty of fish, seafood, and especially cod off the coast of New England, they stayed there after landing. In addition to seafood, the colonists found abundant game in the forests and a staggering number of birds filling the skies. With help from the Native Americans, these Pilgrims from England survived by hunting, fishing, and planting corn, beans, and squash. Since most of the Pilgrims were Puritans, morals played a large role in both their religion and their life. The Puritans valued a life filled with thrift, purity, and simplicity, and they strictly avoided excess. Their food reflects this simplicity and austerity.

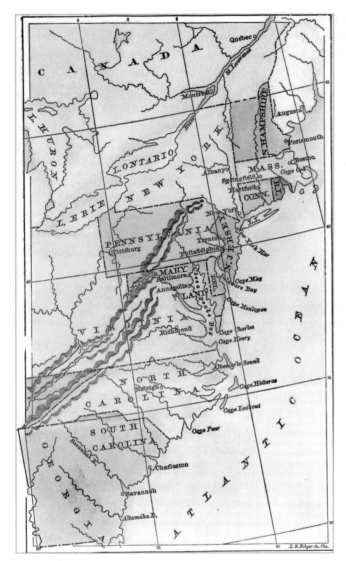

Original American Colonies

For several reasons, before 1700, most colonists prepared entrées in a single pot over the fire, so stews and soups usually served as the main dish. First of all, both men and women filled their days taking care of the countless tasks necessary for survival. They needed to clear land, grow and raise food, build and maintain their shelter, make clothing and quilts, bear and raise children, tend to animals, plant crops and gardens, and much more. With no free time and an endless list of necessary chores, a one-pot meal hanging above the fire or nestled in the coals solved one problem by providing a meal. First, the pot cooked slowly without requiring attention. A second advantage was that they could add any assortment of ingredients and/or scraps to the pot and create a flavorful soup or stew.

After 1700, the settlers established many more homesteads and raised more farm animals to provide meat. The additional meat enabled women (or whoever prepared the food for the household) to sometimes cook roasts and other cuts of meat. Most settlers raised chickens, some cows that provided milk, and hogs that roamed freely and ate whatever they found. Settlers made butter and cheese with the milk.

By the middle of the eighteenth century, the original thirteen colonies existed. Spanning from current-day Maine in the north to Georgia in the south, the colonies stretched through New England, the Middle Atlantic, and the South. Although initially settled by the British, each colony had its own legislature and a governor who reported directly to the British government. By the middle of the 1760s, trouble brewed between the colonists and the British. While the colonists expected the same treatment as British citizens, the British government desperately needed more money to offset the tremendous losses incurred in the French and Indian War that ended in 1763. In 1764, the British tried to generate extra money from the colonies by initiating several new taxes on goods imported to the colonies, particularly sugar. One year later, the British levied the Stamp Act without consulting the colonists. The Stamp Act taxed all printed paper such as legal documents, marriage licenses, newspapers, and playing cards. Although the British said the money raised from the Stamp Act would fund the British troops protecting America, the enraged colonists agreed to boycott British goods until they repealed the Stamp Act.

Following a change in leadership, the British passed the Townsend Act in 1766. This resulted in new taxes imposed on many imported goods, including tea, paper, glass, lead, and paint. Responding to the furious colonists, in 1770 they repealed the Townsend Act except for the tax on tea. In December 1773, a number of revolutionaries, including Paul Revere and Samuel Adams, retaliated with the Boston Tea Party when they dumped all of the tea from British ships into the Boston Harbor. The colonists remained disgruntled with the British and their rule; however, the British continued passing laws that restricted the colonists' freedom. Finally, in April 1775, the British attacked the colonists in Massachusetts, and the Revolutionary War began.

The Revolutionary War lasted from 1775 until 1782. On July 4, 1776, a group of men signed the Declaration of Independence, which declared the thirteen American colonies

STATES ADMITTED TO THE UNION

Year	State(s)
1787	Delaware, Pennsylvania, New Jersey
1788	Georgia, Connecticut, Massachusetts, Maryland, South Carolina, New Hampshire, Virginia, New York
1789	North Carolina
1790	Rhode Island
1791	Vermont
1792	Kentucky
1796	Tennessee
1803	Ohio
1812	Louisiana
1816	Indiana
1817	Mississippi
1818	Illinois
1819	Alabama
1820	Maine
1821	Missouri
1836	Arkansas
1837	Michigan
1845	Florida, Texas
1846	Iowa
1847	Wisconsin
1850	California
1858	Minnesota
1859	Oregon
1861	Kansas
1863	West Virginia
1864	Nevada
1867	Nebraska
1876	Colorado
1889	North Dakota, South Dakota, Montana, Washington
1890	Idaho, Wyoming
1896	Utah
1907	Oklahoma
1912	New Mexico, Arizona
1959	Alaska, Hawaii

Because such a large number of people came to this country to escape persecution and/or to find religious freedom, the writers of the Constitution of the United States addressed this major issue at the beginning of the document. In fact, the First Amendment guarantees freedom of speech and religious freedom to every American.

as states and announced their independence from England. According to the Treaty of Paris signed in 1783, the United States consisted of the land bordered by the Great Lakes on the north, the Atlantic Ocean on the east, Florida on the south, and the Mississippi River on the west. As stated in the Articles of Confederation of 1781, each state was sovereign, meaning each state governed itself. Finally, with the ratification of the Constitution in 1788, the United States of America became official as a group of states with one central government.

Prior to the late 1800s, most immigrants came from western and northern European countries, including Britain, Ireland, Spain, France, Germany, the Netherlands, and Scandinavia. Although some Spanish settled in the western portion of the United States and Florida in the 1500s, the larger settlements developed along the eastern coast when the British arrived. French, Dutch, Scandinavian, and German immigrants also settled along the eastern coast.

Between 1770 and 1870, more than eleven million emigrants sailed from the British Isles to the United States. Crossing the Atlantic Ocean proved a long and arduous trip, and many did not survive the rough voyage. While crossing the ocean, the food often spoiled, became invaded by mold, or infested by maggots. Meager supplies of food and fresh water, poor living conditions, and treacherous, turbulent waters meant some passengers starved to death or contracted deadly diseases. Others drowned after being swept overboard during storms.

The early settlers who survived the trip to the United States tried to recreate the lifestyle of their European homelands. While that proved somewhat possible for the wealthy or those who lived in towns, the remaining immigrants, such as poor people and those who migrated farther west, faced daily survival issues like the weather, building shelter, and how to make do with any available food and supplies. They used maple syrup or molasses to flavor many dishes and consumed cornmeal mush instead of the wheat or rye bread they ate in their native homeland. After the Europeans brought cows, pigs, sheep, horses, chickens, and donkeys to the new land, the settlers could prepare many recipes from their culinary heritage.

Throughout the history of the United States, many groups, including Puritans, Roman Catholics, Quakers, French Protestants (Huguenots), Jews, Lutherans, and other German Protestants, came to this new land seeking religious freedom and/or political tolerance. Usually moving to a specific location, numerous Puritans settled in New England, Roman Catholics in Maryland, and Quakers in Pennsylvania. Ironically, many of these same people who immigrated to this new land to escape from persecution drove the Native Americans from their land and destroyed the wild buffalo that provided their main source of food.

Because of the opportunity to obtain land for free or a low price, many chose to immigrate for economic reasons and the chance to own land. The rich and/or the royalty owned most of the land in Europe, so few people could purchase land there in the seventeenth and eighteenth centuries. Also, periods of famine and severe unemployment encouraged many to seek a better life in the New World.

On a more somber note, many immigrants came against their will. Beginning in 1619, Europeans brought Africans to America to serve as slaves; in fact, reports estimate 500,000 slaves from Africa came to this country prior to 1807. Importing slaves from Africa continued for more than half of the nineteenth century. In addition, many British and Irish prisoners were exported to the New World to relieve the overcrowded prisons.

Of course, the Native Americans wielded a huge influence over the culinary development in the early days. The colonists tried to raise the foods of their native homeland, but most of those crops failed in the different climate found in this new land. Finally, the starving

- corn
- beans
- squash
- Jerusalem artichokes
- turkey
- chili peppers
- pumpkins
- tomatoes
- avocados
- potatoes
- wild rice
- Concord grapes
- blueberries
- cranberries
- pecans
- black walnuts

Known as the sunchoke, Jerusalem artichokes grew wild along the coastal areas from Nova Scotia to Georgia. Native Americans called them "sun roots" and ate them raw and cooked. Jerusalem artichokes actually belong to the sunflower family, and they are not related to the globe artichoke that appears more commonly today. In fact, globe artichokes are not indigenous to the United States.

Corn used for popping contains a high ratio of protein to starch. Because high protein holds more moisture, the husk (outside covering) breaks apart when the kernel is heated, causing the flesh inside to explode.

The Native Americans made popcorn by tossing dried kernels into the fire and catching the popped corn as it shot out of the fire. For a treat, they mixed the popped corn with maple syrup and formed it into balls—the forerunner of Cracker Jack even before the white settlers arrived in America!

colonists turned to the Native Americans to learn about indigenous foods, the plants that grew well here, and how to prepare those foreign foods.

Although unknown in Europe, corn soon became a staple for the settlers in America. The Native Americans valued every part of the sacred corn plant, cooking fresh and dried corn kernels in all sorts of recipes, wrapping foods in the husks for steaming, and feeding the corn stalks to the animals. They served dishes containing corn for every segment of the menu from appetizer to dessert. The settlers learned several preparations for cornbread from the Native Americans including ashcake, a disk of cornmeal baked in the ashes of the fire, and corn pone, baked in the fire but not covered with ashes.

The Shawnee tribes of the Northeast originated a flat cornmeal cake called johnny-cake. Since travelers carried them on their journeys, some think the name derived from "journey cakes." As more and more people traveled to the West, many recipes for johnny-cakes appeared, each claiming to be the original.

The Native Americans created spoonbread from porridge made from corn. Eaten with a spoon, spoonbread resembles loose cornbread or a cornmeal soufflé. Spoonbread is still served in the South.

The colonists learned of another corn product, hominy, from the Native Americans. Hominy is corn with the husks and germ removed. To make hominy, Native Americans boiled corn with wood ashes until it swelled. The settlers made hominy by soaking corn in a lye solution, then removing the hulls, thoroughly washing the corn, and boiling it until tender. Still a favorite in the South, grits are prepared from ground hominy.

Before roasting fresh corn on the cob, the Native Americans soaked the corn, including the silks and the husk, in water for a couple of hours and then placed it in the ashes of the fire. After slowly roasting the corn for a long time, they removed the husk and silks, revealing corn with a nutty flavor created from the caramelization of the natural sugars in the corn.

To survive the winter, Native Americans left corn on the stalk to dry and then stored it for later use. They cooked whole dried corn in stews and ground it into different sizes, including coarse (grits), medium (cornmeal), and fine (flour). Besides providing food during lean times, dried corn was compact for traveling and did not spoil.

The Native Americans were excellent gardeners and cultivated a variety of crops. Besides beans, pumpkins, melons, and squash, the various tribes produced a dozen varieties of corn. Depending on the region, Native Americans grew many different types of squash. Traditionally, the men cleared the land, and left the planting and care of the garden to the women.

The Native Americans used a wide variety of chili peppers; in fact, chilies replaced salt as the most popular seasoning. Like corn, all excess chili peppers were dried for use during the winter.

Another food prized by the Native Americans in areas where it grew, wild rice is actually aquatic grass, not rice. The Sioux and Chippewa tribes fought battles over control of the land where wild rice grew.

Native Americans introduced the settlers to the turkey. The word "turkey" probably derived from the Indian word for this bird, *furkee*. Of course, turkey served as one of the entrées for the Pilgrims' first Thanksgiving banquet.

Depending on the climatic conditions in each region, the Native Americans taught the white settlers the best ways to preserve meat for the lean months. Preservation methods included pickling, salting, drying, and/or smoking. The Native Americans also prepared jerky by cutting meat into strips, seasoning it with salt and pepper, and then drying it. A versatile food, jerky became important in pioneer days since they carried it on long journeys, ate it as is, cooked the jerky in stews, or added it to a sauce and served it over cornbread or biscuits.

In the early days, Europeans who made the journey to America were amazed to discover such a huge area of land, very few inhabitants, and the diversity of topography and climate. Depending on the region, they trapped and consumed a variety of animals such as bear, deer, possum, woodchuck, raccoon, assorted fowl, fish, and seafood. Also, the Native Americans taught the pioneers and settlers to heal wounds and cure illnesses using medicinal herbs and plants.

The new inhabitants quickly learned to survive on the bounty of indigenous foods they found growing. All sorts of berries grew wild, and the early settlers discovered varieties unknown in their native countries. For example, the pioneers thought the quick-spreading, thorn-filled branches of blackberries were weeds until they discovered the value of the fruit and ate it. Soon, blackberry recipes became part of the settlers' repertoire. Although the early inhabitants had no sugar, they relied on molasses and maple syrup to sweeten recipes. Those early inhabitants truly survived with whatever was available.

Smoking Jerky

Generally, cooking took place over an open fire. When settlers built homes in New England, they placed the hearth in the center of the home where it provided warmth in addition to cooking. In the South, they often detached the kitchen from the main part of the house to avoid adding heat to the house in the warm climate. Regardless of the placement of the hearth, cooks used similar cooking methods. They grilled on a spit, boiled in a pot suspended over the fire, and baked by nestling the closed pot in embers of the fire and placing more embers on the lid so heat penetrated the pot from the top and the bottom. The thick cast iron pots proved ideal because they conducted heat evenly. "Spider pots" had three legs that elevated the bottom of the pot from the embers when baking. Some hearths contained a crane, which allowed the cook to easily lower or raise a pot.

For a number of different reasons, the pioneers eventually began moving west to discover new lands. Some sought greater freedom, others went in search of adventure, and some migrated to find better social or economic status, to make a fortune, or simply to obtain more. Not knowing about crop rotation or other ways to replenish the soil, after years of planting the same crops in the same location, many left their depleted farmland in search of fertile soil. Because land equaled wealth, land passed through families, usually inherited by the oldest son. As a result, acquiring more land increased the wealth of the family. Like the original immigrants who came to the New World, most immigrated to the west looking for a better life for themselves, their children, and their families.

Serving as the minister to France from 1784 to 1789, Thomas Jefferson became enthralled with French food, wine, and their elegance. After returning from France, Jefferson introduced the pasta maker, waffle iron, Parmesan cheese, Italian rice, anchovies, Dijon mustard, olive oil, vanilla, and several varieties of figs. Passionate about fine dining, Jefferson enjoyed a wide variety of international dishes. He introduced macaroni and cheese, but not the orange type prepared with cheddar cheese. Rather, his version consisted of pasta mixed with butter and Parmesan cheese and then baked. Possessing a great fondness for wine, Jefferson brought French and Italian wines to this country. Because of his concern with all aspects of dining, Jefferson initiated the use of round and oval tables instead of rectangular ones in the White House so guests could converse more easily.

Jefferson's genuine passion for food involved both growing it and dining. In the extensive gardens at Monticello, his home in Virginia, he propagated and grew an astounding number of fruits and vegetables. For example, he grew more than fifty varieties of peas. During his travels, Jefferson gathered the seeds and plants of foods he wanted to cultivate in this country, including grapevines that he planted at Monticello. While he served as the third President of the United States, the cooks in the White House used much of the produce from his garden at Monticello.

Because of his enchantment with French food, Jefferson hired a French chef to cook in the White House. This further promoted an infatuation with French cooking in the United States that already existed among the wealthy. Prominent southern families often sent their cooks to France for cookery classes.

When the French Revolution occurred in the late 1700s, many French chefs and cooks employed by the aristocracy lost their jobs. While a number of these chefs and cooks opened restaurants in France, a lot of these skilled cooks emigrated. Some made their way to the United States, where they found work cooking or procured other types of work. As a result, the French cuisine again impacted the cookery of this country with the introduction of fine dining, fondue, fricassee, bonbons, and many French dishes.

Map of the United States Expansion

During the 1800s, many people became intrigued with the opulent lifestyle of England's Queen Victoria. This fascination resulted in the popularity of serving pieces, like silver platters and utensils.

After acquiring the Louisiana Purchase from France, Jefferson sent Meriwether Lewis and William Clark to explore the area in 1804. They began their voyage from St. Louis, Missouri, and proceeded to explore the Plains States, the Rocky Mountains, and much of the western United States. During their exploration that lasted more than two years, they meticulously documented the details of their journey, the land they traveled, and their observations.

After designating a large parcel of land as worthless desert and suitable for the Native Americans, Congress set up "Permanent Indian Frontier" in the land west of an imaginary line from Lake Superior to Louisiana around 1825. Until Brigham Young reached the Salt Lake Valley in Utah with a group of Mormon followers in 1846, no one wanted this "worthless" land. The Mormons irrigated the land, planted crops, and transformed this barren soil into fertile farmland. Some crossed this once-barren land while traveling the Oregon Trail on their way to the Northwest; others traveled through it on their way to Texas. After the discovery of gold in California in 1849, hordes of settlers crossed this "desert" en route to California, stopping at the Mormon settlements to replenish their supplies. After seeing the Mormons' transformation of barren land to fertile soil, many realized the potential of this land and, again, moved in and took the Native Americans' land. Soon, they confined the Native Americans to small parcels of land called reservations in areas that used to belong to them.

Arriving in three distinct waves, more than 30 million immigrants moved to the United States between 1820 and 1919. Between 1815 and 1859, eight and one-half million Germans and Austrians, four million Irish, two million English, many Russian Jews, and smaller numbers from Eastern Europe, Belgium, China, Japan, Africa, and India immigrated here. The next wave poured in between 1860 and 1890; the last and largest group of about 15 million immigrants entered between 1890 and 1920. While many of these people farmed in their native homeland, many left farming and took any available jobs in factories, mines, or industry, as laborers for the railroad, building roads, or digging canals. Generally, people of a nationality or ethnicity settled with others from the same background. As a result, Chicago attracted many Polish, Hungarians, and Bohemians; numerous Italian and Jewish immigrants settled in New York City; and San Francisco and Los Angeles drew a large Japanese and Chinese population.

In 1846, the Potato Famine began when fungus attacked the potato, the mainstay of the Irish diet. Famine swept through Ireland, causing more than two million Irish citizens to flee their homeland to escape starvation and death between 1846 and 1855. Many of the Irish coming to the United States settled in Boston or New York. Although many of these immigrants initially found work as domestic servants, by 1900 close to one-third of these now Irish Americans owned their own homes.

German immigrants introduced the custom of having a Christmas tree in the home.

Fleeing from several years of failed crops, starvation, or religious persecution, millions of Germans immigrated to the United States. The first groups settled in Pennsylvania and formed enclaves of farming centered on their religion (Mennonite, Amish, or other religious sects). Later waves of German immigrants established homes in the Midwest and Texas.

Approximately two million Scandinavians moved to the United States between 1820 and 1914. Since many of these immigrants left farms in Scandinavia, they sought farmland in their new country. The similar cold climate and lots of lakes resembling their homeland enticed a large number of Scandinavians to settle in Michigan, Minnesota, and Wisconsin. Later, Scandinavian immigrants went to the Plains, Oregon, and Texas.

To escape religious persecution, the first Jewish immigrants came from Curaçao in 1654. Sephardic Jews from Spain and Portugal comprised the next group of immigrants. Around 1848, large numbers of German refugees fled from the political unrest in their homeland and sought freedom in the United States. Between 1880 and 1927, millions of Jewish people left Russia and other Eastern European countries to avoid persecution. Unlike many of the other European immigrants, these people often had no background in farming. Many settled in cities and found work as merchants and bankers. Still more Jews flooded to this country in the 1930s to escape persecution under Hitler's rule and the Nazis. The large number of Jewish immigrants from all over Europe brought many ethnic foods, including chopped chicken liver, bagels, matzo ball soup, kreplach, and blintzes, as well as the delicatessen.

Beginning around 1870 and continuing through the twentieth century, many Polish people came to the United States. To escape the political persecution in their homeland, they settled in large cities to work in factories, homesteaded in the Plains States and the West, and occupied farms. Because the Polish immigrants were hard workers, they established themselves in their communities, prospered in their new homeland, and cooked the dishes from their culinary heritage such as sausages like *kielbasa*, stuffed cabbage leaves, *pierogi* (turnovers filled with meat, cottage cheese, mushrooms, potatoes, or sauerkraut), and a wide assortment of pastries.

After the decline of the citrus industry in southern Italy, many Italians relocated to the United States to find work. The Italian culinary impact remains huge throughout this country as seen with wines, cheeses, pasta dishes, sauces, pizza, and much more.

Most Greek immigrants arrived in the twentieth century. Although many found work in restaurants, groceries, or hotels, the Greeks stayed rather isolated as an ethnic group. Their cookery penetrated into the American cuisine with dishes like *moussaka*, *souvlaki*, gyros, and baklava. Even today, Greek Americans own many of the diners found in the Northeast.

With the Gold Rush of 1849 attracting prospectors to California and the West, Chinese immigrants poured into these states as a way of escaping the political and economic turmoil in their native country. With limited opportunities available to them, many worked manual jobs like building the railroad, washing laundry, or cooking. Although their culture seemed very foreign to the majority of citizens of European heritage, their foods, cooking techniques, and customs penetrated into the American culture in areas like San Francisco, where many Chinese immigrants settled. Today, Chinese restaurants, stir-fry dishes, soy sauce, chopsticks, and woks commonly appear in most areas of the country.

Many Japanese immigrated to Hawaii to work in the sugar plantations. Japanese impact remains very strong on the cookery there.

After the Civil War, in the late 1800s, the flow of immigrants leaving countries throughout Europe and Asia seeking their dreams and/or freedom in America continued. Since many immigrants lived in ethnic pockets in cities and rural areas, the United States became a melting pot of traditions, customs, and, of course, culinary heritages of numerous ethnic groups.

Communities developed, and recipes and cooking techniques passed from one family to the next. Through church suppers, barn raisings, community suppers, quilting bees, and taking care of sick or troubled neighbors, families exchanged recipes and adopted favorites from their neighbors. Later, they recorded the recipes in cookbooks, and the exchange continued. Each immigrant family learned from others, and the culinary melting pot grew.

The Homestead Act of 1862 guaranteed between 80 and 160 acres of free land to citizens who lived on that land for five years. The first wave of settlers to take advantage of this offer moved to Kansas and Nebraska. The next groups settled in North and South Dakota and Oklahoma. Initially, these settlers encountered enormous problems with isolation, the difficulty of clearing the tough prairie grasses that covered the land so they could plant crops, and the lack of wood for fuel and building material. They resorted to building houses out of sod and burning buffalo chips (dried buffalo manure). Later, other difficulties like tornadoes, windy conditions on the Plains, droughts, and insect infestations threatened the lives of the homesteaders. After some time, the isolation resolved with the increasing number of settlers, who cleared the fields of the tough grasses, grew crops and raised animals, and imported wood from areas to the east.

Many farmers chose to raise livestock and/or farm grain in Texas, Wyoming, the Midwest, and the Plains States. From the ranches scattered throughout those states, cowboys herded the cattle to the slaughterhouses and meat processing plants in Kansas City and Chicago. An entirely different type of cookery developed for feeding the cowboys on the trail while transporting the cattle. The cook, called "cookie," needed to bring all foods in addition to cooking utensils for preparing meals over an open fire. Of course, the location of the "kitchen" changed daily as the group traveled. Standard fare prepared on the trail included stews, dumplings, one-pot dishes, and breads and biscuits leavened with sourdough starter.

Initially, the development in this country depended on waterways. People and goods entered by ship, and they stayed near their entry point. The search for land to farm encouraged the settlers to move away from the ports, but the ports remained intrinsic to importing and exporting goods. Through much of the 1700s, it was easier to travel between cities by ship in the Atlantic than over land. That situation changed in the late eighteenth century when roads were built to connect the cities, and travel by horse and buggy became

From the time of the early settlers, Americans liked beer. Around 1840, they switched from preferring the heavy ales and porters common in the British Isles to lighter lagers.

With the signing of the Land Grant Act in 1862, President Abraham Lincoln designated colleges specializing in the science of agriculture. These colleges conducted research in many areas of agriculture and made numerous discoveries, including the development of hybrid plants.

possible. Soon, building roads became a major undertaking and the connecting of the United States continued. Around the same time, construction of canals began to connect major waterways. The completion of the Erie Canal in 1825 allowed travel by water from the Hudson River to the Great Lakes. The building of roads and canals created many jobs, which attracted myriad immigrants to this country.

Between 1820 and 1890, hordes of immigrants from countries throughout the world found work building canals, railroads, and roads that would connect all parts of the United States. More and more ethnic groups moved here, and each brought its culinary heritage along. Within each region, the culinary traits of the various groups melded together and eventually formed the distinct cuisine found in that region.

After the Civil War, the railroads expanded to the west, opening the country for major westward migration of both people and goods. Because of this greater accessibility, much land was converted into farmland for raising grain. In 1869, the railroad joined in Promontory Point, Utah, and connected the entire United States. With the country connected by railroads, canals, and roads, travel and transportation became easier and the country opened for coast-to-coast commerce. Herding cattle to the major centers became unnecessary with trains connecting the smaller towns to Chicago, Omaha, and Kansas City. In addition, refrigerated railcars allowed the transportation of perishable foods from one region to another. This changed the way Americans ate because it allowed people to obtain meats, seafood, fruits, and vegetables in locations other than where they were caught, raised, or grown. In addition, all sorts of imported products became available throughout the United States instead of only in port cities. Gradually, the horses used for farming were replaced with an array of farm equipment that was developed to make planting, caring for crops, and harvesting easier, more efficient, and less labor intensive. Less labor meant fewer people needed to farm. At that point, the Industrial Revolution began.

Prior to the middle of the 1800s, the preservation of foods meant salting, pickling, drying, or smoking. In addition, hearty fruits and vegetables like apples, carrots, potatoes, cabbage, and parsnips kept for months in the root cellar. To dry fruits and vegetables, people sliced or left them whole and dried them in the sun or an oven to remove moisture and prevent rotting. To preserve perishable products, they turned apple juice into vinegar or cider, and they made excess milk into cheese. Although most methods of preserving foods took a lot of time and effort, this began to change around the time of the Industrial Revolution, when the many inventions changed life for the farmer and the homemaker. Machines advanced from being powered by men to powered by horses, then steam, and finally gasoline. Each generation of power greatly reduced the amount of time needed to accomplish tasks. For example, harvesting one acre of wheat required 56 hours of work for a man with a sickle in 1800. Today, harvesting that acre takes only ten minutes.

Around the same time, advances in equipment for the kitchen simplified the life of the homemaker, too. Born in Massachusetts in the middle 1700s, Benjamin Thompson, also known as Count Rumford, experimented and made several significant inventions. His work revolved around the exploration of heat, theories involving friction, and the creation of heat. This led to his finding better ways to heat a home and cook food. Thompson designed a cooking range, improved the chimney, and invented the pressure cooker, the drip coffeepot, and more.

Canning began around 1820, but when John Mason invented the glass canning jar in 1858, the homemakers' job of preserving food changed drastically. Instead of the time-consuming drying, pickling, or salting of foods, now they processed many foods by packing them in a jar and cooking the jars of canned foods in a kettle of boiling water

In 1900, no gas or electric stoves existed. Cooks still used stoves fueled with oil, wood, or some other material. Although the first refrigerator replaced the icebox around 1916, this appliance did not reach an affordable price until the early 1940s. Around that time, the freezer for home use became a reality.

Named because it is "food fit for the angels," angel food cake is white, light, and airy. Containing no egg yolks, this cake requires stiffly beaten egg whites for leavening. Many think the thrifty Pennsylvania Dutch created angel food cake to use the egg whites that remained after making noodles. Recipes for angel food cake first appeared in cookbooks in the late nineteenth century. Traditionally, this cake is baked in a tube pan (a pan with a hole in the center).

known as a hot water bath. The next advancement in canning came in the early 1900s when the pressure canner became available. The pressure canner removed air from the jars under pressure, which proved a much safer and faster method for canning. After World War I, freezers allowed storage for frozen foods, which eliminated much of the need for canning.

The Industrial Revolution brought a major population shift. Leaving rural life behind, many moved away from farms and into cities. The cities offered conveniences that made life easier. For example, a farmers' market developed in most cities where farmers sold fresh produce and often meat, and fishermen brought their catch for sale. Instead of hunting, fishing, raising animals, and growing produce, the farmers' markets offered the opportunity to buy these products. In addition, bakeries in the cities sold bread, freeing the inhabitants from the need to bake their own.

This move to the cities impacted the normal meal pattern, too. Prior to the Industrial Revolution most lived on farms and consumed the main meal of the day at noon. With the migration to the city and jobs in factories, mills, and other venues, many people could not return home for a large midday meal. Representing a significant change in people's culinary schedule, the evening meal became the main meal of the day.

The introduction of stoves during the Industrial Revolution drastically altered cooking in all of the regions of the United States. By the 1840s, the mass-produced cast-iron range with two burners fueled by wood or coal replaced the open hearth in middle and upper class kitchens throughout the country. With the disappearance of the hearth (open fire for cooking and spit roasting) and the brick oven used for baking, cooking changed both in its execution (for the person cooking) and the flavor and texture of the finished product. With the increased ability to regulate the temperature, cooking and baking became much simpler and produced dishes with more consistent results.

Soon, commercially canned foods, processed foods, and mass-produced foods appeared. William Kellogg and Charles Post developed packaged cereals, Henry Heinz canned pickles and condiments, and Joseph Campbell invented and canned condensed soups. These timesaving "conveniences" dramatically decreased the workload of the household cook.

Around 1900, many Mexicans started crossing the border to find work and a better life in this country. In Mexico, they experienced political unrest, and most of the people lived in poverty, so they sought work in the states of the Southwest that border Mexico. As more Mexicans continued to migrate, they started relocating to Chicago and other large cities to find work. Today, many cities contain a large Mexican population, and Mexican food permeates menus around the country.

In sharp contrast to the poverty of many immigrants and the hard-working middle class in the beginning of the twentieth century, the wealthy feasted on extravagant 12-course meals. For example, one of these sumptuous meals began with oysters followed by clear broth, then an array of other foods including poached salmon, beef, lamb chops, creamed chicken, roasted fowl, boiled potatoes, asparagus, dessert, tea, and coffee. Wine accompanied each course. Obviously, great diversity marked this country's culinary history.

In the first half of the nineteenth century, chocolate cake meant yellow or spice cake accompanied by hot chocolate or cocoa. By the latter half of the 1800s, chocolate cake became yellow or spice cake frosted with chocolate icing. Cakes incorporating chocolate in the batter did not appear until the late 1800s. When Walter Baker processed unsweetened chocolate into one-ounce squares in 1904, baking with chocolate became simple for

1940—James Beard published his first cookbook, *Hors d'Oeuvre and Canapés*

1946—James Beard established the first television cooking show in the United States

1954—TV dinners introduced

1960s—packaged foods flood the market

1960s—fast food entered the United States with eateries like McDonalds and Kentucky Fried Chicken

1961—Julia Child, Simone Beck, and Louisette Berthold published *Mastering the Art of French Cooking*

1962—Julia Child began the television cooking show *The French Chef* on PBS

1970s—food and wine viewed as stylish

1970s—Julia Child's cooking shows on television garner much public attention

1971—Alice Waters opened the restaurant Chez Panisse in Berkeley, California

1990—California Organic Food Acts established

1990s—annual sales of salsa surpass catsup sales

1990s—genetically engineered plants are raised

1993—Food Network begins on television

1999—Restaurant Nora in Washington, D.C., is named first organic restaurant

2006—New York City is the first city in the United States to ban trans fats in restaurants

Swanson Company produced the first TV dinner in 1954. The Swanson Company decided on the name "TV dinner" because the aluminum tray that held the food resembled the newly

(Continued)

the home cook. At that time, Fannie Farmer and the Boston Cooking School developed a recipe for brownies, and an American dessert was born.

Another major influence on the food world occurred in 1920, when the Constitutional amendment prohibiting alcohol went into effect. Because of that law, people could no longer drink alcohol in public places. As a result, drinking moved from bars and restaurants into the private home. Suddenly, people served "cocktail food," and the concept of "finger food" blossomed. The Prohibition lasted until 1933, but "cocktail food" continued.

After the stock market crash in 1929, this country plunged into an economic depression. Many lost jobs, the value of money decreased, and food became scarce for many. The opulent times ended, and cooks again learned to extend any available foods.

As Thomas Jefferson's time living in France altered his culinary world, many men and women who left the United States to fight wars came home with a different culinary perspective. Often, their exposure to foods in foreign lands impacted the recipes prepared in their homes after their return. World Wars I and II definitely brought many European dishes to American tables. For example, pizza, submarine sandwiches, and other Italian specialties were served in Italian communities in this country before the war, but they gained much popularity throughout the United States after the soldiers returned from World War II.

By 1923, Americans owned about 20,000 refrigerators; however, twenty years later, most kitchens contained a refrigerator as well as a gas or electric stove. Again, the workload of the cook changed dramatically. These two appliances eliminated the need to can and preserve foods at home or keep a fire burning to cook. Now the cook could buy ingredients, take them home, and prepare the dish, or purchase the food in advance and store it in the refrigerator or the freezer until needed.

Throughout the twentieth century, changes continually brewed in the kitchens of America. After World War II, the use of convenience foods—including frozen, canned, and packaged—flourished. With more women working outside of the home, time became a major factor in cooking meals. As a result, frozen items and packaged mixes became widely accepted and popular.

Instead of shopping at individual stores like the produce market and the butcher shop for different items, food shopping became consolidated at the supermarket. This allowed the household cook to make one stop and purchase all the food and household supplies needed.

During the 1950s, the casserole became a mainstay on the dinner table. To prepare a casserole, cooks combined two or more foods in a baking dish for the oven or in a pan for cooking on the stove. Often, they assembled casseroles ahead of time, stored them in the refrigerator, and then cooked the dish when desired. Conversely, the quick preparation for the casserole enabled women to make this dish after returning from work.

Starting in the late 1950s, Americans developed a fascination with space travel and subsequently with the freeze-dried foods consumed on voyages through space. Around the 1960s, Tang, a powdered orange drink, became popular.

In the 1990s, new concerns about foods arose since few people raised and grew their own. Many worried about the use of pesticides, herbicides, what farm animals consumed, and methods of raising farm animals. Debate raged over issues like genetically modified foods, food irradiation, feeding antibiotics and hormones to farm animals, and whether to confine farm animals or allow them to roam freely. As a result, the market for organically raised food products developed and grew.

(Continued)

popular televisions. People mistakenly thought the name meant they should eat the food while watching TV, so they did! To accommodate microwave ovens, manufacturers replaced the aluminum tray in 1984.

In 1948, Julia Child moved to Paris because her husband was transferred there. Not knowing how to cook at the age of 36, she enrolled in classes at the Cordon Bleu in Paris. Of course, she went on to become an extremely popular cooking teacher, television personality, and cookbook author. Most credit her with introducing French cooking to modern home cooks.

When household cooks became full-time workers outside of the home, restaurants flourished. Even with time-saving cooking equipment and shopping, cooking a meal after a long day of work meant more work. With increased income, many chose to dine out one or more times each week. As a result, the number and types of restaurants increased dramatically, and dining in a restaurant moved beyond the grasp of only the wealthy, the traveler, or someone indulging in a "special treat."

The flow of immigrants into the United States continues. In the 1950s, Hungarians fleeing Communist rule sought freedom in this country. The 1960s brought Czechoslovakian, Korean, and Vietnamese immigrants. Haitians and Cubans fled to Florida, while Mexicans filled the Southwest and California. Whether to avoid starvation, escape religious or political persecution, own land, seek the chance to accumulate wealth, and/or to find a better life, immigrants continue to come to the United States to establish a new home as they did throughout this country's history. The constant influx of new immigrants means the continual changing of the cookery and cuisine of each region.

REVIEW QUESTIONS

1. Describe the contributing factors that caused the cuisine to develop as it did.
2. What ethnic groups first settled in this new land? Where did they settle and why?
3. What prompted most foreigners to immigrate to this new land?
4. Discuss the role of the Native Americans in the survival of the early settlers.
5. What events led to and created the Industrial Revolution?
6. Discuss Thomas Jefferson's contributions to the cuisine of the United States.

GLOSSARY

ashcake – disk of cornmeal baked in the ashes of the fire

corn pone – bread made from cornmeal, baked in the fire but not covered with ashes

furkee – Indian word for turkey

grits – ground hominy

hominy – corn product made by Indians by boiling corn with wood ashes until it swelled; the settlers made hominy by soaking corn in a lye solution, then removing it from the hulls, washing it, and boiling it until tender

Huguenots – French Protestants; many immigrated to the New World in search of religious freedom

Inuit – early group of people known as Eskimos who migrated to North America, inhabited Alaska and stayed in the cold northern areas near the Arctic Circle

kielbasa – type of Polish sausage

pierogi – Polish turnover filled with meat, cottage cheese, mushroom, potato, or sauerkraut

spoonbread – loose cornbread resembling a soufflé, eaten with a spoon, developed from porridge made from corn that the Indians ate; still served in the South

2

New England

OBJECTIVES

By the end of this chapter, you will be able to

- Discuss the early settlers, including their reasons for immigrating, their heritage, and how they survived in New England
- Describe the Native American influence on the cuisine of New England
- Discuss the British influence on the cuisine of New England
- Explain how the topography and climate affected the cookery that developed in New England
- Identify food products prevalent in New England
- Prepare a variety of dishes indicative of the cuisine of New England

States included in New England:

- Maine
- Vermont
- New Hampshire
- Massachusetts
- Connecticut
- Rhode Island

HISTORY

Initially, the cuisine of New England developed from the combination of British cookery with that of the Native Americans (also called Indians). The first group to establish a permanent colony in New England, Puritans left Great Britain by ship in search of religious freedom. Carrying 102 passengers (50 men, 20 women, and 32 children), the Mayflower landed on Cape Cod in November of 1620. One month later, they crossed the bay and settled in a deserted Native American village at the site of today's Plymouth, Massachusetts. The Pilgrims wanted to grow the foods that flourished in their homeland and cook dishes from their British heritage, so they planted the crops that thrived in Britain in their new home. Due to the harsh weather and the rocky soil found in New England, their gardens failed. Half of the colonists died that first winter. The other half survived only because of help from the Native Americans. Besides starvation, diseases claimed the lives of many of these early settlers.

Because most of the Pilgrims worked as tradesmen or craftsmen in Britain, they knew little about hunting or catching fish. The Native Americans who had inhabited this area for about 3,000 years prevented the settlers from starving by teaching them to hunt, fish, gather indigenous plants, and grow foods that thrived in New England. The Pilgrims received enormous help from Squanto, a Native American living in Plymouth who apparently learned English while living in England. Acting as a translator, Squanto educated the settlers about the indigenous plants and animals, how to find and gather wild plants, and how to plant and cook foods they had never seen. Furthermore, he introduced the settlers to corn, beans, squash, pumpkins, cranberries, maple syrup, and turkeys. The Native Americans also instructed the colonists on preserving foods to sustain them through the long, cold winters of New England. In the end, the settlers prepared recipes from their homeland by substituting indigenous foods for unavailable ingredients.

Since most of the Pilgrims were Puritans, morals played a huge role in both their religion and their lives. They admired traits like thrift, purity, and simplicity; the Puritans strictly avoided excess. Following this philosophy, the Pilgrims chose very simple cookery.

In 1621, the Pilgrims and the Wampanoag tribe led by Chief Massasoit celebrated the first Thanksgiving, which lasted for three days. Some say the menu at that first Thanksgiving included lobster, goose, cod, duck, turkey, rabbit, venison, stew, pumpkin, corn pudding, fruits, and Dutch cheeses. While the actual origins of this holiday remain a mystery, theories abound. Some think this banquet commemorated the harvest, others believe the festival marked a day of thanks for the help of the Indians, and still others say that it was a combination of the two. Regardless of its beginnings, today Thanksgiving remains a day to give thanks for our rich bounty.

A favorite Native American contribution to the cuisine of New England, the clambake marked celebrations and festivals from the time of the colonists until now. Along the shores of New England, clambakes did and still commemorate all sorts of events ranging from weddings to political elections. To create the clambake, people dig a pit in the sand, line it with stones, and top the stones with wood. After the wood burns for about an hour, the stones become red-hot. At that point, the cooks remove the ash and remaining fire and then lay seaweed over the hot stones. After placing clams on the seaweed, they cover the pit with wet animal hide (in the Pilgrims' day) or wet canvas (in modern times) that is anchored to the ground with stones so the steam stays inside the canvas. Although the heat radiating from the stones cooks all ingredients, the canvas must remain moist to ensure proper steaming of the foods. Now, most prepare the famous New England clambake by stacking alternating layers of seaweed and foods such as an assortment of clams,

Called the "three sisters" by the Native Americans, corn, beans, and squash formed the basis of the diet for both the Native Americans and the Pilgrims. The Native Americans taught the Pilgrims to plant the seeds for these three plants in the same hole. The beans twisted around the corn plants for support while the large squash leaves shaded the ground around the roots of all three plants and kept them from drying too quickly. Additionally, the beans added nitrogen to the soil that the corn depleted. Today, most gardeners place stakes in the ground to support bean vines.

In 1863, President Abraham Lincoln declared Thanksgiving a national holiday.

lobsters, unpeeled potatoes, and corn in the husk. Some also add sausages, chicken, and other types of fish. After arranging all of the food items between the layers of seaweed, they cover it with wet canvas to steam as in colonial times.

Because of their close proximity, numerous French Canadians moved into New England, and the French influence on the cuisine still prevails. The Canadians cooked many French inspired dishes like *tourtiére*, savory pie. Until 1759, the French occupied Vermont and part of New Hampshire. In addition to very cold winters and the difficult terrain of mountains and dense forest that inhibited travel to this area, the French and the Indians kept most of the settlers away from this part of New England.

After the French and Indian War ended in 1763, major trouble began between the colonists and the British. The British needed money after that long war, and they tapped the colonists to fulfill this need. Although the colonists expected the same treatment as British citizens, the British monarchy saw things differently and gave the colonists no voice in regards to taxation. Through much of the 1760s, the disgruntled colonists experienced repeated tax levies from their British rulers. The notion of equality for the colonists failed, and the Boston Tea Party erupted in December 1773 as a reaction to yet another taxation—this one on tea. The British retaliated and attacked the colonists in 1775, which marked the beginning of the Revolutionary War. With the signing of the Treaty of Paris in 1783, this eight-year war finally ended. The signing of the Declaration of Independence in 1776 proclaimed independence from Britain for the thirteen colonies comprising the United States of America. See Chapter 1 (History) for more explanation.

Around this time, successful farmers grew corn, oats, rye, wheat, vegetables, herbs, berries, apples, peaches, and plums. They raised chickens for their meat and eggs, cows for dairy and beef, sheep that provided lamb, mutton, and fleece, and hogs that yielded meat and lard. Foraging for acorns, nuts, seeds, and any available food on their own, hogs thrived with little care from the farmer.

During the 1800s, immigrants from Ireland, Portugal, and Italy arrived in New England. While many Irish fled to America to escape the Potato Famine, Portuguese fishermen immigrated because of the rich bounty in the oceans off the shores of New England. With its thriving whaling industry, New Bedford, Massachusetts, attracted many Portuguese. Whether these people came to the New World seeking religious or political freedom, escape from famine, better job possibilities, or greater opportunity for their children, the one thing all the immigrants shared was their desire for a better life. Each group of immigrants brought recipes and culinary traditions from its native homeland, and that heritage influenced the cuisine of New England.

TOPOGRAPHY AND CLIMATE

With the Atlantic Ocean forming the eastern border of New England, the colonists found abundant fish and seafood for eating as well as exporting. In addition to supplying food, the waterways provided excellent transportation. Numerous rivers allowed travel to other areas within the United States while the Atlantic gave access to the Caribbean and Europe.

Long, cold winters and cool summers prevail in New England, and the harsh winters created survival problems for the early immigrants. They preserved foods by salting, drying, smoking, and pickling to provide sustenance for the winter months. In addition, the settlers planted gardens full of cold weather vegetables like cabbage, several varieties of winter squash, carrots, beets, turnips, parsnips, and potatoes to stock their root cellars, insuring food during the long winter. As a result, the cuisine of New England featured hearty foods, which matched the robust weather found there.

> In the 1700s, ninety percent of the colonists were farmers. Although land was cheap or even free at that time, much hard work was required to clear the land and prepare it for planting crops and building a homestead.

While the area in New England lying near the Atlantic Ocean forms low-lying coast, forested plains run from the Atlantic Ocean to the Appalachian Mountains. Abundant forests supplied material for building shelters and ships as well as plentiful game such as bear, deer, rabbit, quail, pheasant, duck, pigeon, and wild turkey. The game served as an important source of food for the early settlers. Moose roamed and supplied additional meat for the colonists in northern New England.

When the glaciers melted, the land in New England contained much granite. The hilly terrain and rocky soil created difficult farming conditions for the early settlers. As a result, the land proved most suitable for raising livestock. Soon, most farmers had at least a few cows and chickens, and they turned the excess milk into cheese. In the early days, they produced enough to feed their family and trade for other goods. Today, large and small dairy farms thrive in New England, producing endless varieties of cheeses and other dairy products.

The retreating glaciers created a huge impact on the topography of Maine, the most northern state in New England. Leaving a jagged coastline and myriad islands, harbors, bays, and inlets, the glaciers also carved large and small lakes throughout the state that contain freshwater fish like salmon, trout, bass, and perch. Mountains rise in the central and western part of the state, with the White Mountains running through Maine and New Hampshire. Today, forests containing plenty of game cover about 90 percent of Maine. Substantial crops of potatoes come from this state's fertile plateau.

New Hampshire and Vermont lie south and west of Maine. In addition to rocky soil that made farming difficult for the early settlers, both states contain many lakes, forests, and a mountain range. The Connecticut River forms the border between New Hampshire and Vermont. The White Mountains lie in central New Hampshire; the Green Mountains run north to south through much of Vermont. Both of these mountain chains primarily con- sist of round-topped, "old" mountains. Although the mountains made travel difficult for the early settlers, they yielded ample game, providing food.

Ranked as the largest lake in New England, Lake Champlain lies in the northwestern part of Vermont. Vermont is the only state in New England that does not border the ocean. Lying to the east of Vermont, New Hampshire contains only 18 miles of Atlantic coastline. Although small in size, New Hampshire claims diverse climate, landscape, and terrain. Meadows and farmland lie near the Connecticut River, but much of the rest of the state consists of rocky soil and forests.

Situated south of Vermont and New Hampshire, Massachusetts is bordered on the east by the Atlantic Ocean. The site of the Mayflower's initial landing in 1620, the penin- sula of Cape Cod juts into the Atlantic. In sharp contrast to the rocky, jagged coastline found in the northern parts of New England, sand dunes form the gentle coast along Cape Cod. Cranberries thrive in the bogs of the low-lying coastal areas; in fact, southeastern Massachusetts claims more than 13,000 acres of cranberry bogs. The western part of the state contains hills and forests. The Connecticut River flows north to south through Massachusetts, and its fertile valleys form valuable farmland.

Connecticut and the tiny state of Rhode Island lie south of Massachusetts. The Atlantic Ocean borders the south and east of Rhode Island and the southern side of Connecticut. Both of these states experience more temperate weather than the rest of New England, with cool winters and warm summers.

While the coastal plain and the central valley consist of fairly flat land, hilly terrain makes up the remainder of Connecticut. The northern and western portions of the state contain steep hills and rivers. The Connecticut River flows through the center of the state, creating valleys. Forests, hills, and rivers make up the east. Numerous lakes that remained after the glaciers retreated mark Connecticut's countryside. Primarily a farming state in the early days, the fertile soil here still yields a cornucopia of fruits and vegetables. A Connecticut claims a large production of eggs.

The smallest state in the United States, Rhode Island consists of just 1,213 square miles. Most of it lies at or near sea level and is classified as lowlands, and only the northwestern part of the state is hilly. Besides bays, inlets, and harbors, lakes abound. Miles of coastline provide access to fish and seafood.

Ingredients and foods commonly used throughout the cuisine of New England include

- many varieties of fish and shellfish, including cod, scrod, salmon, mackerel, bluefish, shad, halibut, bass, swordfish, pollock, lobster, scallops, clams, crabs, and oysters
- all sorts of game, such as deer, rabbit, wild turkey, quail, duck, pheasant, and more
- turkey
- dairy, milk, and cheeses
- beans, corn, squash, and pumpkin
- cold weather vegetables like beets, cabbage, winter squash, turnips, parsnips, carrots, and potatoes
- wild mushrooms
- cranberries and blueberries
- apples
- maple syrup

COOKING METHODS

Exhibiting a preference for simple cooking methods, the settlers of New England prepared many foods by boiling, baking, grilling, or steaming. Like the Native Americans, the settlers boiled any available ingredients in one pot, steamed, and grilled (or barbecued) over an open fire. Of course, the Native Americans taught the colonists about the clambake, which steamed the foods in a pit containing hot stones covered with wet animal hide. In essence, this created an oven that steamed any variety and amount of foods at one time.

With abundant fresh fish and shellfish from the ocean, rivers, and lakes available throughout New England, the usual choice of preparation included frying, grilling, baking, boiling, or steaming with the size, flavor, and fat content of the fish determining the preferred cooking method. The early New Englanders relied on the very fresh taste of the seafood since they seasoned it with few or no herbs and spices. Lobster preparation usually consisted of boiling lobsters in a pot or steaming them in the clambake.

Boiling ranked as the most popular cooking method for several reasons. First, Native Americans boiled many foods. Secondly, the British boiled many foods, so the colonists were accustomed to boiled foods.

With many months of cold weather, a fire usually burned in the hearth to warm the house. Since the fire burned anyway, an iron kettle of food buried in the embers or a pot of soup or stew hanging over the fire cooked with little extra effort from the people. The colonists worked from morning until night just to take care of basic survival needs: hunting and fishing for food, tending the animals and crops, planting and caring for a garden,

...created the ...h, a fish soup ...wder, with the ...m the water-ways. Evolving from a French dish, the early chowders contained no milk or potatoes, because those two ingredients were not yet available in New England.

Never use soap to clean a cast iron pot because the soap clogs the pores of the pot and the food sticks. If soap is used on a cast iron pot, it can be seasoned again. Instead of using soap, clean cast iron vessels by scrubbing with salt (which acts as an abrasive) to remove cooked-on particles.

Just as the settlers baked pies on the floor of the oven, in today's ovens, it is preferable to bake pies with the rack placed in the lower half of the oven so the bottom crust receives more heat.

Cooking took place in the fireplace until the wood-burning cook stove became available around the 1850s.

chopping wood for the fire, making clothing, building and maintaining shelters, and more. No one had time to stir the pot too often. As a result, food that "cooked on its own" was almost a necessity. For example, Boston brown bread steamed for a couple of hours in a pot of simmering water and baked beans cooked for at least five hours in the embers of the fire. For this reason, a multitude of dishes requiring long slow cooking simmered or braised over the fire and filled menus throughout the long winter.

Soups and chowders are another example of one-pot cookery that enjoyed great popularity in the early days. The most famous soup from this region was clam chowder, which received its name from the French word for a large copper pot, *la chaudière*.

In New England, chowder usually referred to a fish or seafood soup. Early versions combined fish and/or seafood, some sort of pork for flavoring, hardtack (very hard crackers), and water. Although chowder recipes are documented from the first half of the 1700s, clams did not appear in written recipes until the 1830s.

While countless clam chowder recipes exist, they contain two crucial ingredients: salt pork or bacon and clams. Today, recipes add any number of other foods, but traditional New England clam chowder includes potatoes and milk or cream. With the influx of Irish immigrants in the 1840s, potatoes joined the ingredient list of many chowder recipes. New England clam chowder features a milk-laden broth; however, water and tomatoes form the base for Manhattan clam chowder.

Braising—slow cooking in liquid—tenderized tough meats like wild game and extended any available food ingredients. This cooking method resulted in stews and other one-pot meals. One example, New England boiled dinner, features several foods in a single pot of simmering liquid. To make this dish, corned beef simmers for several hours until almost tender, then vegetables are added to the meat and cooked until done.

Containing the hearth, the kitchen formed the center of the New England home with the other rooms radiating from it. This arrangement helped warm the whole house because heat from the hearth circulated throughout the home.

The colonists used an assortment of pots for cooking including the spider, a pot perched on three legs that kept the bottom of the pot above the embers. In the early days, they mostly used cooking pots made of cast iron because of its advantages as a cooking medium. The thick cast iron conducted heat well, so foods cooked evenly. In addition, cast iron pots were "seasoned" by coating the inside of the pot with fat and then cooking or baking the pot over low heat. This process caused the fat to penetrate the pores of the cast iron and diminished foods sticking to the pots. To enable the cook to choose the pots' placement in relation to the fire and move them easily, pots hung over the fire suspended from a chain attached to a crane.

In addition to the crane, many hearths were equipped with a spit for grilling meat or birds. Also, a brick-lined oven stood next to the hearth for baking breads and pies once or twice each week. As a rule, pies went into the oven after the breads were baked. Placing them on the floor of the oven ensured that the most intense heat radiated through the bottom of the pie, helping to cook the bottom crust thoroughly and prevent soggy pies.

Whether baking in the oven or in a covered pot set in the embers of the fire, regulating the temperature proved extremely difficult in the days before the invention of stoves with a controllable source of heat and a thermostat. As a result, baking breads and pastries presented quite a challenge to the colonists, and the quality of baked goods often was inconsistent.

The harsh winters made preserving food a necessity, and the Native Americans shared their knowledge of preserving foods. With cod and sea salt readily available from the Atlantic Ocean, salt cod became a staple in the New England diet. In addition to cod, the colonists salted any extra meat and fish, including pork and venison. Although it was an important ingredient for preserving, salt remained very expensive until 1800. With plenty of wood available from forests, smoking served as another common method of preserving. Colonists also pickled numerous foods to preserve them. Corned beef and New England boiled dinner appeared frequently because they used pickled beef.

Dried fruits and vegetables, preserves, relishes, and pickled vegetables preserved produce and provided ingredients for soups, stews, and desserts through the months when no garden grew. The settlers pickled almost any produce including cucumbers, watermelon rind, beans, onions, mushrooms, corn, green tomatoes, cabbage, and more.

STATES

Of course, the cuisine of New England reflects the culinary heritage of the immigrants who settled there. Maine, New Hampshire, and Vermont became home to immigrants from Scotland and Wales who cooked items like meat pies and scones from their native country. When Germans settled in Maine and Massachusetts, they brought sausages and sauerkraut. Meanwhile, the Portuguese in Massachusetts and Rhode Island prepared their traditional recipes for fish and seafood dishes as well as kale soup. Throughout New England, the French introduced dishes like *cassoulet*, a casserole of beans, various meats, and sausages. Italians cooked all sorts of pasta dishes.

The bounty of seafood flourishing along the coast of Maine attracted the early settlers, and they stayed there, joining the Penobscot tribes who inhabited Maine. Initially, the settlers caught mainly cod, but lobster, clams, shrimp, scallops, mussels, mackerel, herring, sardines, haddock, flounder, bass, tuna, pollock, and salmon also proliferated in these cold waters. While smoking fish for the winter months served as the usual method of preservation in the early days, later canning fish and seafood became common.

Since Maine is known for abundant lobsters, a wide variety of dishes featuring this crustacean appear on menus throughout the state. Lobster is cloaked in cream sauce, prepared as a salad, served on a roll, or simply boiled and accompanied by melted butter for dipping.

Several crops, including potatoes, beans, wild blueberries, and cultivated blueberries, flourish in Maine. Inhabitants prized the intense, concentrated flavor of tiny wild blueberries for eating and cooking in colonial times as well as today. The settlers planted numerous apple orchards that still thrive. Today, farmers in Maine raise dairy cattle, poultry, and eggs.

Besides the Native Americans, most of the early inhabitants of Maine were British or French Canadian. Initially, they settled along the coasts, but as more people immigrated and claimed the land near the Atlantic, they staked land further to the west. In the middle 1700s, Germans moved to Maine.

With no coastline, harsh winters, and a terrain of mountains and forests, Vermont attracted fewer people. In fact, Vermont's population still remains small. Game and wild mushrooms thrive in the mountains. The forests contain many sugar maple trees that yield Vermont maple syrup. The abundant wild turkeys of the early days gave way to domesticated turkeys, which remain a flourishing industry today. Although the many lakes and streams contain freshwater fish like trout and bass, the early inhabitants ate more meat than any other New England state because they had no access to the ocean. Numerous dairy farms provide cheese and milk throughout the state, and Vermont is well known for its dairy industry and cheese production, particularly cheddar. With many sheep grazing, the settlers spun wool, wove it, and consumed plenty of lamb. Many French Canadians immigrated to Vermont in the 1800s. English, Irish, and Scottish immigrants also settled here and left their mark on the cuisine.

Since the topography of New Hampshire resembles that of Vermont, many of the same food ingredients appear in both states. With abundant game and wild mushrooms in

Because of the copious amounts of cod in the waters around the peninsula jutting from Massachusetts, Bartholomew Gosnold dubbed it "Cape of Cod." Today, we call that peninsula Cape Cod.

Governor John Endicott of Plymouth, Massachusetts planted the first apple seed in this new land in the early 1600s. With help from the Native Americans who quickly adopted this tree, the planting of apple trees spread throughout the United States. In 1625, clergyman William Blaxton of Massachusetts planted the first apple orchard. He later moved to Rhode Island where he continued planting apples, and in 1635, Blaxton developed the Sweet Rhode Island Greening, the first variety of American apples.

The English liking for spices from India brought the use of cinnamon, nutmeg, mace, cloves, and ginger to New England. Even today, those spices flavor traditional pies like apple and pumpkin. In contrast, the Puritans used few spices because of their desire for simplicity. With seeds they brought from Europe, the colonists planted herbs such as lavender, mint, parsley, savory, anise, wormwood, pennyroyal, and more in their gardens. They learned to gather herbs like sorrel and yarrow from the Native Americans. The colonists used herbs for flavoring foods, for medicinal purposes, and for household uses like pennyroyal and wormwood to control fleas.

In the 1760s, the first chocolate factory in the United States opened in Dorchester, Massachusetts. Harvard

(Continued)

the mountains and forests, the early settlers hunted and gathered food and traded furs. The coastal lowlands and the river valleys contain fertile farmland. Numerous dairy farms flourish throughout the state. Many lakes dot the landscape and contain freshwater fish like trout, bass, and salmon. The Connecticut River flows north to south between New Hampshire and Vermont and provides fertile valleys for agriculture. Unlike Vermont, New Hampshire borders the ocean on the southeast. This gave the colonists easier transportation, access to the land, and plenty of available seafood and fish like lobster, clams, oysters, shrimp, cod, tuna, and bluefish.

In the early part of the eighteenth century, many Scotch-Irish families immigrated to New Hampshire. They brought the potato, and its popularity spread throughout New England. Meanwhile, French Canadians contributed French influence to the cookery. The English settlers first planted turnips, a popular cold weather root vegetable. Apple orchards still thrive in both Vermont and New Hampshire.

Of course, Massachusetts was the site of the first permanent New England settlement. The abundant cod became the mainstay in the diet of early inhabitants in Massachusetts with countless recipes using both fresh and salted cod, including chowders, hash, cod cakes, and boiled dinners. Cod appeared as the entrée at any meal, including breakfast.

In addition to the ubiquitous cod, large amounts of fish and seafood like haddock, lobster, clams, oysters, tuna, and swordfish came from the Atlantic Ocean. The lakes and rivers yielded bass, trout, and perch that also provided food for the settlers in Massachusetts.

Boston thrived as a major entry port for immigrants in the 1800s. At that time, Irish immigrants flooded into the United States to escape poverty, famine, and/or starvation. As a result, many Bostonians claim Irish ancestry. Because of the Irish fondness for potatoes, the cuisine of New England soon included potatoes in many dishes such as chowders and stews, and as a popular side dish.

Attracted by the lucrative fishing and whaling industries, many Portuguese seamen immigrated to the coastal towns of Massachusetts seeking a better life. These fisherman and their families contributed many traits from their native cookery to New England's cuisine, including Portuguese sweet bread, fish soup, and sausage and kale soup. With items like spicy sausages and an assortment of spices, Portuguese cooking was quite a contrast to the bland English and Irish foods. Soon the cookery of New England added Portuguese traits.

The coast of Massachusetts had several port towns/cities besides Boston. Ships left the ports loaded with exports and returned filled with all sorts of products like spices, rum, and molasses from the Caribbean and coffee from Brazil. Starting in the port cities, many of these new foods entered the cuisine of New England.

In Connecticut, the Connecticut River provided the settlers with fish for food and rich valleys for farmland. The fertile soil attracted English and Dutch immigrants to this area, where they found a more temperate climate than in the rest of New England and planted crops like rye, a wide variety of vegetables, and berries, as well as fruit orchards. In addition, they raised cattle for both dairy and meat.

With miles of coastline along the Atlantic Ocean, Connecticut residents obtained ample fish and seafood. Freshwater fish swam in the rivers and lakes. The settlers feasted on clams, lobsters, scallops, oysters, shad, trout, flounder, and more. As in Massachusetts, Portuguese fisherman immigrated to Connecticut and settled along the coast, and, of course, they brought their culinary influence to the area.

Rhode Island contains many miles of coastline, providing access to plenty of seafood including flounder, cod, bluefish, bass, mackerel, tuna, swordfish, oysters, lobster, and several varieties of clams such as quahogs, cherrystones, and littlenecks. The lakes and

(Continued)
graduate Dr. James Baker and his Irish partner John Hannon produced squares of unsweetened chocolate. That invention made baking chocolate available to the home baker, which undoubtedly changed the course of baking in America.

Simply called Toll House cookies, the first chocolate chip cookie was made at the Toll House Inn in Whitman, Massachusetts, in 1930. This well-known American cookie remains an icon.

Amelia Simmons of Connecticut wrote *American Cookery*, the first American cookbook, which was published in the United States in 1796. This book contained both English and Native American recipes.

Around 1900, the first hamburger in a bun was served in New Haven, Connecticut. Created as a way to use excess meat, the ground steak trimmings were formed into patties and broiled. A customer in a hurry asked for the patty inside a roll so he could eat it without a fork and knife, and the hamburger in a bun was born!

New Haven, Connecticut, claims to be the home of the first lollipop in 1908.

In the nineteenth century, clams and lobsters weighing between 16 and 25 pounds and six-inch oysters still inhabited the waters. Incredibly, some of those lobsters measured five to six feet wide from the tip of one claw to the tip of the other!

rivers supply bass, trout, and perch. In addition to numerous chicken and turkey farms producing poultry and eggs, apples and potatoes grow well here.

Founded as a free state by Puritans from Massachusetts, Rhode Island attracted many immigrants including English, Irish, Portuguese, French Canadian, French Huguenots, Polish, Italian, and Eastern Europeans. Each group brought their culinary heritage with them to their new home.

CHARACTERISTICS OF THE CUISINE

Fish and seafood served as a mainstay in colonial New England life. The wide assortment of seafood became a significant part of the diet and a major industry for the region. In fact, some say that when the colonists arrived, the ocean and waterways teemed with such an abundance of fish and seafood that they could be caught with bare hands. Supposedly, lobster was so plentiful that the Native Americans used it as bait to catch fish rather than eating it. If the colonists resorted to serving lobster to guests, they apologized for providing such meager fare!

From the middle 1600s, cod functioned as one of the main sources of protein for the settlers. They dried and salted excess cod for their own use during the winter as well as for exporting. In fact, it is said that the colonists dried more than 300,000 cod in 1640. Unfortunately, overfishing and pollution greatly diminished the number of fish and shellfish available, and, in some cases, pollution concerns have impacted the market for various local fish and shellfish.

Scrod, young cod weighing less than two pounds, and halibut appeared often in New England cookery. Other popular fish like bluefish, mackerel, striped bass, swordfish, and pollock also thrived in these cold waters.

A series of shoals (shallow plateaus) lie in the Atlantic Ocean, stretching from Newfoundland to southern New England. Lying in the southwest portion of those shoals, Georges Banks was home to the plankton, algae, krill, and other plants and animals that fish eat. As a prime breeding and feeding ground for a wide range of fish and seafood, this area attracted many fishermen in colonial days as well as earlier times. This incredibly rich shoal once teemed with cod, bluefish, haddock, halibut, mackerel, and much more. According to historians, Basque fisherman sailed there around 1000, but they managed to keep this excellent fishing spot a secret for almost 500 years! Around 1500, the English and Italians discovered this fertile area in the sea. Due to overfishing, Georges Banks became almost devoid of fish. Today it is a restricted fishing area in hopes that it will once again become a fertile ground for sea life.

While many different types of scallops inhabit the waters of New England, the bay scallop remains the most popular. Many claim the bay scallop is sweeter and more tender than other varieties. This small scallop is prevalent around Cape Cod and southern New England.

QUAHOG (HARD-SHELLED) CLAMS FOUND IN NEW ENGLAND	
Type	Size
Littleneck	smallest; measure less than two inches across
Cherrystone	slightly larger than littlenecks; medium size; less than three inches across
Quahog	largest; usually chopped and used in recipes like chowder because they are tough; sometimes called chowder clams

Whether made from leftover fresh fish, salted fish, or a combination of the two and mixed with mashed potatoes, fried fish cakes served as a breakfast staple in colonial times. Fish cakes for breakfast had two advantages: they used leftovers, and they provided plenty of necessary calories for the day's work. Today, fish cakes often appear as an appetizer or entrée at lunch or dinner.

Like many dishes prepared in this area of the country, the New England boiled dinner used the meats preserved for winter. This dish featured corned beef, cured spiced beef cooked with an assortment of winter vegetables like cabbage, carrots, and/or beets and parsnips. From the Irish influence, New England cooks later added potatoes to this dish.

Popular red flannel hash developed from the need to use leftover New England boiled dinner. All ingredients remaining from the New England boiled dinner are chopped and then fried to prepare this hash. Its name, "red flannel hash," reflected the reddish color the beets gave to the dish.

Since New England experienced long, harsh winters, menus featured all kinds of soups such as chowders, vegetable soup, pumpkin soup, bean soup, squash soup, and pea soup. Preparing soups had several advantages for early New Englanders. As mentioned earlier, soups incorporated any available ingredients, including all remaining foods or scraps. Also, since a fire burned all day in the hearth during the winter, the soup pot simmering over the fire for hours wasted no additional energy. Last but not least, the hot soup warmed the people eating it.

The early settlers missed the beef and dairy products so common in England, but in 1624, cows arrived at Plymouth, Massachusetts. Because dense forests covered much of the countryside, land for grazing was scarce at first. Fifteen years later, plentiful cattle ensured the availability of butter, milk, cheese, and beef for New England cooks. Vermont remains particularly well known for excellent quality dairy products.

When traders from New England emptied their ships' cargo in other ports, they returned loaded with foods from those places. Some of these new foods included citrus fruits from the Mediterranean areas and molasses from the West Indies. Molasses became an ingredient in many New England recipes and played an important role in this region's history. It was a necessary ingredient in rum, and New Englanders made rum to drink as well as to trade for slaves in Africa.

The Puritans served Boston baked beans on their Sabbath each week for their Saturday night dinner and Sunday morning breakfast. Baked beans consisted of ingredients available to the early settlers: dried beans, salt pork, and flavorings, including maple syrup. When regular trade with the West Indies developed, molasses replaced maple syrup in the baked beans. To avoid working (cooking) on their Sabbath, the Puritans prepared this bean dish before the Sabbath began. The dish simmered for hours in the embers of the fire. Sometimes, they took the prepared beans to the local baker, who cooked the beans and returned it to the home for Saturday night dinner. Traditionally, Boston brown bread, dense steamed or baked bread flavored with molasses, accompanied these beans.

Settlers at Plymouth Rock learned of succotash, a mixture of corn and beans, from the Narragansett Indians. In the summer, they made this dish with fresh beans and fresh corn, but succotash consisted of long-simmered dried corn and dried beans in the winter. The original dish combined corn with kidney or lima beans, but today, succotash usually means corn cooked with lima beans.

Since wheat did not grow well in New England, the settlers relied on corn for a significant portion of their diet. Dried corn sustained them through the winter and provided the settlers with both whole grain and ground meal or flour. The settlers reconstituted dried whole grain and dried beans through long cooking. With ground dried corn or hominy, the settlers prepared two dishes: samp, cornmeal porridge, and cornmeal mush, known as

The Puritan Sabbath began at sundown on Saturday night and ended at sundown on Sunday. Baked beans served with Boston brown bread became the customary Sabbath meal because the preparation was completed in advance and the dish adapted well to long, slow cooking in a fireplace. This culinary tradition resembles the cooking of *cholent*, an Eastern European dish of meats and dried beans that cooked slowly overnight for serving on the Jewish Sabbath.

From the Puritan tradition of serving baked beans and brown bread for Saturday night dinner, Boston became known as "Bean Town."

Harvesting Cranberries in Bog

Native Americans taught the settlers to make a bread, originally called "journey cakes," from a mixture of ground corn (cornmeal) and water. After shaping the dough into a patty, they cooked it over an open fire. Most think the name "journey cakes" derived because the cornbread was easy to prepare while traveling. They were standard fare in the diet of migrating settlers. No one knows why or when the name "journey cake" changed to "johnnycake."

hasty pudding. Cornmeal porridge was a breakfast staple in colonial times. Similar to Italian polenta, the cooled leftover cornmeal mush was later sliced and fried.

To prepare hominy, settlers soaked corn in lye to dissolve the outer skin, washed it repeatedly in fresh water, and then cooked the corn for hours. Hominy was served plain with a seasoning of butter or other fat (bear fat in the early days), salt, and pepper. They also combined hominy with other foods and baked it like a casserole.

The New England garden played an important role in the colonists' survival. Besides supplying ample amounts of produce in the summer, the hearty vegetables grown in the garden provided food throughout the winter. Known as cold weather vegetables, pumpkins, several varieties of winter squash like butternut and acorn squash, cabbage, white potatoes, carrots, parsnips, turnips, and/or beets filled the settlers' root cellars. These supplied necessary food and vitamins through the long winter. Other vegetables cultivated by the early settlers included a variety of salad greens, parsley, chervil, sorrel, savory, sage, radishes, asparagus, cucumbers, Brussels sprouts, kale, and more. The settlers collected wild watercress (called Indian cress), and they grew it. By the 1760s, sweet potatoes came to New England from Virginia.

The bogs found in some of the coastal areas of Massachusetts provided an ideal habitat for the indigenous wild cranberries that thrived in sandy soil and wet conditions. The Native Americans and early settlers ate both raw and cooked cranberries. To prepare this acidic fruit, they boiled the berries with sugar to make a sauce to accompany meats, or they added cranberries to pemmican. Resembling jerky, pemmican consisted of salt-dried game pulverized with cranberries and fat, then stuffed into animal casing. Besides storing well, pemmican provided sustenance through the winter and/or when traveling. Cranberries' high vitamin C content made pemmican valuable in preventing scurvy, so sailors took it on their voyages across the seas. The Native Americans also used cranberries for medicinal purposes and as dye.

Although wild grapes grew abundantly in New England, their poor taste inhibited their use. In the middle 1800s, Ephraim Bull of Concord, Massachusetts, developed the Concord grape, and the production of wine, grape juice, and grape jelly dramatically increased with this new American grape.

Prior to the late 1700s, the settlers created leavening from yeast or by incorporating air into the batter through vigorous beating. Around that time, the settlers discovered pearlash, a form of potash that worked as a leavening agent. Like leavening agents commonly used today, pearlash released carbon dioxide. The carbon dioxide formed bubbles that rose through the dough, and during baking, the dough or batter solidified around the trapped bubbles of carbon dioxide, creating tiny air spaces. This chemical reaction causes breads and cakes "to rise" and results in baked goods with a light, airy texture. In 1792, America exported 8,000 tons of pearlash to Europe. Americans developed baking powder in the 1850s, and first produced it commercially in Boston. With the use of baking powder, baked goods rose much more consistently.

Started from seeds the colonists brought with them from their European homelands, apples flourished throughout New England. As settlers moved west, they took apple seeds and saplings with them and planted them in many regions. The apples grew well, thriving in all but the warmest climates. Providing food for lean times, the hardy apples kept for long periods of time when stored in cool conditions like a root cellar. As a result, people

Cranberries, blueberries, and Concord grapes are fruits indigenous to the United States.

Better known as Johnny Appleseed, the legendary John Chapman was born in 1774 in Massachusetts. According to folklore, he planted countless apple seeds that grew into trees and orchards as he traveled west, particularly in Ohio and Indiana. Also, he gave thousands of apple seeds to strangers so they would plant apple trees in new sites when they migrated to the west.

Reflected in the expression "as American as apple pie," apples became an American icon.

Betty—layers of fruit alternated with bread crumbs, bread cubes, or buttered slices of bread
Cobbler—baked confection of biscuit dough, either on top or bottom of fruit
Crisp—fruit topped with crumbly topping, usually containing oats, then baked
Crumble—fruit topped with crumbly topping, then baked
Grunt—fruit dessert consisting of dumplings dropped into hot berries, then steamed
Pandowdy—fruit dessert composed of fruit covered with pastry dough, then baked
Slump—fruit dessert featuring cooked fruit topped with biscuit dough, then baked

Note: Often, there is discrepancy in the definition of these terms.

Besides its use in traditional dishes like winter squash or Indian pudding, maple syrup is used in countless ways today. Cooks might add it to

(Continued)

enjoyed apple pie, pandowdy, cobbler, crisp, crumble, and brown betty throughout the fall and winter.

In addition to apples, many other fruits and berries thrived in New England. By drying, pickling, or preparing jam, marmalade, or jelly, the settlers preserved any excess berries, fruits, and vegetables that would not store well in the root cellar. All sorts of fruit pies were enormously popular, but the early New England residents also prepared cobblers, crisps, slumps, grunts, and pandowdies. With some variations, all of these resemble the cobbler of today. Fresh fruits in the summer and dried fruits in the winter filled these confections.

Since the Native Americans and early settlers consumed pumpkin, traditional Thanksgiving desserts include pumpkin pie. Some say the early inhabitants cut the top off the pumpkin, removed seeds and strings, filled the pumpkin with spices and milk, and baked it in the fire. Other pumpkin recipes featured it as a soup or side dish. Pumpkins originally came from Central America. They stored well in the root cellar. In addition to cutting the flesh of the pumpkin into strips and drying it for later use, the Native Americans used pumpkin for medicinal purposes.

Mincemeat—consisting of a blend of meat, sugar, raisins, citron, suet, and any other preferred ingredients, such as dried fruits, candied fruit rinds, and spices—kept well in a crock stored in a cool place. Mincemeat confections appeared frequently in the days of the colonists.

Early cookbooks record recipes for cream pies; however, these were actually cakes rather than pies. They consisted of layers of cake separated with a filling of custard, pastry cream, or a number of different flavorings. Boston cream pie features yellow cake sandwiched with vanilla custard and topped with chocolate icing.

Prepared by either boiling or baking, Indian pudding combines cornmeal, milk, and molasses. If available, added eggs helped make the mixture richer, and later versions incorporated raisins and other flavorings. Hard or soft gingerbread was another popular dessert prepared in colonial times that contained molasses. Gingerbread referred to either a cookie or more of a cake-type confection.

Savory as well as sweet puddings and pies appeared frequently in New England cookery and reflected the British heritage. All sorts of meat pies like beef, veal, and chicken graced menus. Puddings also contained a wide variety of ingredients. If wheat flour was unavailable, colonists prepared pies without a crust. In fact, early renditions of pumpkin pie featured the spiced filling without a crust. While pies require baking, puddings are steamed. Since it was easier to steam than bake over an open fire, puddings appeared frequently in the early days.

For dessert puddings, the colonists combined almost any available ingredients together, flavoring it with butter and sugar, maple syrup, or molasses. The simple yet popular hasty pudding consisted of the ubiquitous cornmeal, boiled in water then topped with butter and maple syrup.

From the Indians, the settlers learned to collect the sap of the sugar maple tree in the early spring and boil it to evaporate most of the liquid, which concentrated the sap and reduced it into maple syrup. Making maple syrup proved to be a huge undertaking because 35 gallons of sap yields just one gallon of syrup. Maple syrup and maple sugar served as the sweeteners available to the early inhabitants until they imported molasses from the West Indies. With about one-third of the maple syrup made in the United States coming from Vermont, maple syrup still remains a large industry in Vermont and in other New England states. Makers of maple syrup grade the product by color, with light considered the best, followed by amber, and finally dark that is used mostly in baking or cooking.

(Continued)
a marinade or sauce for meat, fowl, fish or seafood; use maple syrup to sweeten glazed carrots; or bake a maple syrup crème brûlée.

Alcoholic beverages arrived in New England with the Pilgrims on the Mayflower. Beer or cider usually accompanied meals, especially since the colonists thought the water in their new homeland contained diseases. When available, the colonists consumed rum imported from the Caribbean and/or wine made from local grapes.

CHEESES OF NEW ENGLAND

**Cheddar—one of the first cheeses produced in the United States; ranges from mild to extra sharp flavor; firm texture
Colby—close to cheddar but more moist, softer, and less acidic; a mild cheese with smooth texture; semi-hard
Goat cheese—many varieties produced in New England
Monterey Jack—bland, buttery, semi-soft; originally made in California, now made in New England
Mozzarella—mild flavor, soft texture, melts well, originally from southern Italy**

NEW ENGLAND APPLE VARIETIES AND USES

Cortland	sweet with tart	excellent baking and eating
Crispin (Mutsu)	sweet	excellent baking and eating
Empire	sweet with mild tartness	excellent eating, fair for baking
IdaRed	sweet with tart	excellent baking, good eating
Jonagold	sweet	excellent eating, fair for baking
Macoun	sweet	excellent eating
McIntosh	sweet with mild tartness	excellent eating, fair for baking
New England Red Delicious	sweet	excellent eating
PaulaRed	tart	excellent eating
Rome	mildly tart	excellent baking and eating

Area	Weather	Topography	Foods
Maine most northern state; Atlantic on north, south, east, and west; New Hampshire to west	cold winters, cool summers	rocky, jagged coast; inlets; harbors; islands; lakes; bays; coastline; forests; rocky land; mountains central and west; White Mountains; fertile plateau	abundant seafood and fish including lobster, scallops, clams, shrimp, mussels, cod, salmon, mackerel, herring, sardines, haddock, trout, flounder, bass, perch, tuna, pollock; game, deer, moose, potatoes, beans, apples, wild and cultivated blueberries
Vermont Canada to north, New Hampshire to east, Massachusetts to south, New York to west	cold winters, cool summers	no coast, rocky soil, forests, lakes, rivers, Green Mountains running north to south, Connecticut River on eastern border, Lake Champlain in northwest	game, cattle, lamb, turkey, deer, freshwater fish, trout, bass, dairy products, cheese, milk, wild mushrooms, apples, maple syrup
New Hampshire Canada to north, Maine and Atlantic Ocean to east, Massachusetts to south, Vermont to west	cold winters, cool summers	rocky soil, forests, meadows, 18 miles of coast in southeast, farmland, lakes, meadows, White Mountains in central, Connecticut River on western border, lowlands near coast	freshwater and saltwater fish and seafood, trout, salmon, bass, lobster, clams, oysters, shrimp, cod, tuna, bluefish, game, deer, dairy, cheese, milk, wild mushrooms, turnips, potatoes, apples
Massachusetts Vermont and New Hampshire to north, Atlantic to east, Rhode Island and Connecticut to south, New York to west	cold winters, cool summers	Cape Cod peninsula on east, coast on east, lowlands near coasts, hills and forests in west, rivers, lakes, harbors, fertile valleys, Connecticut River flows north to south	fish and seafood, cod, clams, bluefish, lobster, scallops, oysters, haddock, swordfish, tuna, bass, trout, perch, game, deer, pumpkins, squash, beans, corn, succotash, potatoes, Boston brown bread, cranberries, Concord grapes, apples

(Continued)

(Continued)

Area	Weather	Topography	Foods
Connecticut Massachusetts to north, Rhode Island to east, Atlantic Ocean to south, New York to west	cool winters, warm summers, temperate	coast on south; farmland, fertile soil, lakes, Connecticut River through center of state; rivers, hills, valleys in north and west; forest, hills, and rivers in east	fresh and saltwater fish, seafood, shad, lobster, clams, oysters, scallops, flounder, trout, cattle, game, beef, dairy products, eggs, rye, apples, many fruits and vegetables, berries
Rhode Island Massachusetts to north and east, Atlantic Ocean to east and south, Connecticut to west	cold winters but temperate, cool summers	coast on east and south; bays, harbors, inlets, islands, lowlands except in hilly northwest; lakes, forests	fresh and saltwater fish; seafood; quahog, cherrystone, and more clams; oysters; lobster; cod; flounder; tuna; mackerel; bluefish; perch; swordfish; bass; trout; game; chicken; turkey; eggs; corn; potatoes; apples

REVIEW QUESTIONS

1. Name six foods the Native Americans introduced to the colonists.
2. Discuss the problems the colonists endured raising food during their first winter in New England. How did they solve these problems?
3. In terms of the topography of New England, name one advantage and one disadvantage the colonists faced when settling the area.
4. What three vegetables formed the basis of the Native Americans' diet?
5. Discuss protein sources available to the settlers in different areas of New England.
6. What two ethnic groups influenced the early colonists and formed the foundation of New England cookery? Discuss the influence from each group.

GLOSSARY

cassoulet—casserole of beans, various meats, and sausages originating in France

corned beef—cured spiced beef

hasty pudding—cornmeal mush resembling English porridge topped with butter and maple syrup, often served for breakfast in colonial times

hominy—corn soaked in lye to dissolve the outer skin, rinsed several times in fresh water to remove husks and lye, then boiled for hours until tender

mincemeat—mixture made of meat, sugar, raisins, citron, suet, and any preferred dried fruits, candied fruit rinds, and spices; generally used as a filling for pie; stored well in a crock in a cool place like the root cellar

New England boiled dinner—one-pot dish consisting of corned beef boiled with an assortment of winter vegetables, including cabbage, carrots, potatoes, and/or beets and parsnips

pearlash—a form of potash discovered as a leavening agent in the late 1700s, replaced by baking powder in the mid-1800s

pemmican—like jerky; consisted of cranberries pulverized with salt-dried meat, usually venison, then mixed with animal fat and placed in an animal casing

red flannel hash—dish made from chopping and frying leftover New England boiled dinner; red color of the dish came from the color of the beets

samp—porridge prepared from cornmeal

scrod—young cod weighing less than two pounds

spider—a pan with three legs, which elevated it above the embers in the hearth

tourtiére—savory pie prepared by French Canadians

CODFISH CAKES

Codfish Cakes
photo by David Murray and Jules Selmes © Dorling Kindersley

Since the salt cod needs to soak in water overnight, begin preparation for this recipe the day before serving.

The early settlers fried codfish cakes in bear, deer, or pork grease.

To make this recipe more contemporary, add finely diced green or red pepper and a little cayenne pepper for a spicier version.

NUMBER OF SERVINGS:
  12 appetizers or 6 entrée portions
COOKING METHOD:
  Fry
SERVING SIZE:
  1 each 3-oz patty for appetizer
  2 each 3-oz patties for entrée
TOTAL YIELD:
  2 lbs, 5¼ oz

Wine Style: Light, delicate Pinot Grigio, Chenin Blanc, or Sauvignon Blanc
Example: Pinot Grigio—Cape Cod Winery, East Falmouth, MA. Delicate notes of pear and pineapple with a fresh citrus finish. This wine has floral and fruit aromas.

INGREDIENTS	WEIGHT	VOLUME
salt cod	1 lb	
potatoes, mashed	1 lb, 5¾ oz	3 cups
butter, melted	1 oz	2 tablespoons
half-and-half	½ oz	1 tablespoon
eggs, beaten	3½ oz	2 each
pepper		½ teaspoon
dry mustard		1 teaspoon
Worcestershire sauce		2 teaspoons
oil, for frying		
GARNISH:		
parsley, minced		
tartar sauce, *optional*		

1. Soak codfish in refrigerator in bowl of cold water at least 10 hours, preferably overnight. Change water several times.
2. Place cod in pan covered by 1 inch of water; simmer until fish flakes, about 10 to 15 minutes.
3. Drain fish, finely flake it, remove any bones and skin. Place fish in bowl.
4. Add potatoes, butter, half-and-half, eggs, pepper, dry mustard, and Worcestershire sauce. Mix well.
5. Form into 3-oz patties, cover, and refrigerate until needed.
6. Place about ¼ inch oil in heavy skillet; heat until hot.
7. Fry patties until golden brown; drain on absorbent paper.
8. Serve, garnished with parsley and accompanied by tartar sauce, if desired.

BAKED STUFFED CLAMS

Baked Stuffed Clams

Make these with cherrystone clams, if available. Cherrystones are hard-shelled, medium-sized clams that proliferate off the coasts of New England.

NUMBER OF SERVINGS: 12
COOKING METHOD:
  Bake
SERVING SIZE:
  2 clams
TOTAL YIELD:
  24 clams on the half shell
  uncooked filling yields 4 lbs

Wine Style: Sauvignon Blanc, Seyval Blanc, or dry Riesling
Example: Seyval Blanc—Boyden Valley Winery, Cambridge, VT. This wine is a dry German-style wine; very crisp with a flowery bouquet.

INGREDIENTS	WEIGHT	VOLUME
clams, cherrystone, live, scrubbed		24 each
butter	6 oz	¾ cup or 1½ sticks
onion, small dice	2½ oz	½ cup
green pepper and red pepper mixture, small dice	2½ oz	½ cup
mushrooms, white, small dice	1 lb, 2½ oz	20 medium, 6 cups
dry mustard		½ teaspoon
garlic powder		½ teaspoon
oregano		2 teaspoons
salt		½ teaspoon
pepper		½ teaspoon
cayenne pepper		¼ teaspoon
Worcestershire sauce		2 teaspoons
paprika		½ teaspoon
parsley, fresh, minced	¼ oz	2 tablespoons
clam juice or water, if needed	12 oz	1½ cups
bread crumbs, dried	8½ oz	2½ cups

GARNISH:

paprika

parsley, minced

lemon wedges

1. Steam or bake clams until shells begin to open. To steam clams, cook over, *not in*, small amount of water just until they open, about 5 minutes. To bake clams, place on pan and bake at 350 degrees just until they open.
2. Preheat oven to 350 degrees.
3. Remove clams from shells, chop into medium dice; reserve clam liquor. If steamed, reserve steaming water.
4. Melt butter in pan; add onion, green and red pepper, and mushrooms; sauté until tender.
5. Add clams, mustard, garlic powder, oregano, salt, pepper, cayenne, Worcestershire sauce, paprika, and parsley. Stir in clam juice and any necessary water to make amount (12 oz or 1½ cups), bring to boil, and stir in bread crumbs.
6. Divide stuffing evenly among 24 scrubbed half clamshells (about 2½ to 2¾ oz each).
7. Sprinkle with paprika and parsley. Bake 10 to 12 minutes. Serve immediately with lemon wedges.

CLAM CHOWDER

NUMBER OF SERVINGS: 8
COOKING METHOD:
 Boil
SERVING SIZE:
 8 oz
TOTAL YIELD:
 4 lbs, 4½ oz

Clam Chowder
photo © Dorling Kindersley

INGREDIENTS	WEIGHT	VOLUME
salt pork, cut into 1/4-inch dice	4 oz	
onion, small dice	5 oz	1 cup
water	1 lb	2 cups
potatoes, cut into 1/4-inch dice	1 lb, 6 oz	4 cups
clams, chopped, fresh or canned, drained; reserve clam juice	1 lb	
clam juice	8 oz	1 cup
half-and-half	1 lb	2 cups
thyme		1/8 teaspoon
salt	to taste	
pepper	to taste	

GARNISH:

paprika

parsley, minced

crackers

1. Stirring constantly, sauté salt pork over high heat until layer of fat covers pan.
2. Lower heat to medium, add onions, and sauté until golden, about 5 minutes.
3. Add water and potatoes; bring to boil, lower heat, and simmer until potatoes are tender, about 12 to 15 minutes.
4. Add clams, clam juice, half-and-half, and thyme. Heat until hot but not boiling.
5. Add salt and pepper to taste.
6. Correct seasonings. Serve, garnished with paprika and/or parsley, and accompanied by crackers.

COD CAKE AND FIVE CLAM CHOWDER WITH CHORIZO AIOLI AND CELERY SALT

This dish marries my New England background with my love for Spanish cooking. Cod has a light, flaky flesh that pairs beautifully with the bold, smoky chorizo, and the celery salt really brings out the freshness and flavor of the shellfish. I love to serve the cod cake in the soup because it acts as a crouton and absorbs all of the wonderful richness of the chowder.

—Todd English

NUMBER OF SERVINGS: 8
SERVING SIZE:
  10 oz
TOTAL YIELD:
  5 lb

Wine Style: Light, delicate Pinot Grigio, Chenin Blanc, Sauvignon Blanc, or Riesling
Example: Riesling—Turtle Creek Winery, Lincoln, MA. This dry wine is fermented in stainless steel and has a wonderful crisp flavor and finish.

INGREDIENTS	WEIGHT	VOLUME
CHORIZO AIOLI:		
grapeseed oil	5$\frac{1}{2}$ oz	$\frac{2}{3}$ cup
chorizo, small dice	3 oz	
egg yolk	$\frac{3}{4}$ oz	1 each
lemon juice, fresh		$\frac{1}{2}$ each
Dijon mustard		1 teaspoon
salt	to taste	
pepper	to taste	
CELERY SALT:		
celery leaves		1 bunch
coarse sea salt	1 oz	
COD CAKE:		
fresh cod	1 lb	
milk	8 oz	1 cup
leeks, cleaned, diced	6 oz	
peppercorns		4 each
garlic cloves	$\frac{1}{4}$ oz	2 each
bay leaf		1 each
Idaho potatoes, cooked, hot	4 oz	
parsley, chopped	$\frac{1}{2}$ oz	$\frac{1}{4}$ cup
extra virgin olive oil	1 oz	2 tablespoons
eggs, beaten	6$\frac{3}{4}$ oz	4 each
Panko bread crumbs	as needed	
flour, all purpose	as needed	
grapeseed oil	1 oz	2 tablespoons
CHOWDER:		
grapeseed oil	1$\frac{1}{2}$ oz	3 tablespoons
bacon, diced	8 oz	
Quahog clams, washed	5 lbs	
white wine	6 oz	$\frac{3}{4}$ cup
chicken stock	10 oz	1$\frac{1}{4}$ cup
half-and-half	1 lb	2 cups
heavy cream	8 oz	1 cup
bay leaf		1 each
thyme sprigs		2 each
Idaho potatoes, diced	1 lb	
onion, diced	4 oz	1 medium
carrot, diced	2 oz	$\frac{1}{3}$ cup
celery, diced	2 oz	$\frac{1}{3}$ cup
Cockle clams		8 each
Littleneck clams		8 each
Razor clams		8 each
Manilla clams		8 each

For Chorizo Aioli:

1. Coat warm sauté pan with 1 ounce (2 tablespoons) grapeseed oil. Add chorizo, sauté until fat is rendered, then remove chorizo from pan.

2. Purée chorizo in food processor; add egg yolk, lemon juice, and mustard. Process until paste. Continue processing while very slowly adding remaining grapeseed oil through feed tube.

3. Season to taste with salt and pepper.

For Celery Salt:

1. Place leaves on a paper towel–lined microwave-safe plate. Microwave for approximately 2 minutes or until dried.

2. Place dried leaves and salt in bowl of food processor fitted with knife blade. Pulverize until well mixed.

For Cod Cake:

1. In a shallow sauté pan over low heat, poach cod in milk with leeks, peppercorns, garlic, and bay leaf until flaky, about 6 to 8 minutes. Cool and reserve.

2. Preheat oven to 350 degrees. Put warm potatoes through food mill and into bowl.

3. Flake cod into potatoes; add parsley, olive oil, and half the eggs (3$\frac{1}{2}$ oz or 2 each). Form into 8 cakes.

4. Dust with flour, coat with remaining egg, and then dredge with bread crumbs.

5. In ovenproof sauté pan, heat grapeseed oil. Sauté cod cakes over medium heat until browned. Turn cod cakes and place pan in oven for approximately 3 minutes or until browned.

For Chowder:

1. In large pot, warm grapeseed oil. Add bacon and cook until rendered.

2. Add Quahog clams and wine, bring to a boil, then add chicken stock, half-and-half, heavy cream, bay leaf, and thyme sprigs. Cook until clams open and are tender, approximately 10 minutes. Strain and reserve liquid with bacon.

3. Place potatoes, onions, carrots, and celery in liquid and bring to boil. Simmer until potatoes are tender, approximately 20 to 25 minutes.

4. Add cockles, littlenecks, razors, and manillas. Simmer until all clams open, approximately 5 minutes.

To Assemble:

1. Divide the chowder into 8 bowls.

2. Spoon chorizo aioli onto cod cake, and place cake in the center of the bowl.

3. Arrange clams around the cod cake, and finish with a sprinkling of celery salt.

Chef Todd English has enjoyed a staggering number of accolades during his remarkable career. He has been recognized by several of the food industry's most prestigious publications and has established one of the best-known restaurant brands in the nation with locations in Boston, New York City, Seattle, Washington, D.C., Las Vegas, Aspen, Orlando, Connecticut, Tokyo, and on Cunard's majestic Queen Mary. In addition to his extensive television credits, he has published three cookbooks: *The Olives Table*, *The Figs Table*, and *The Olives Dessert Table*.

- 1991—James Beard Foundation National Rising Star Chef
- 1994—James Beard Foundation Best Chef in the Northeast
- 1999—one of the "Top 50 Tastemakers" by *Nation's Restaurant News*
- 2001—*Bon Appetit's* Restaurateur of the Year award
- recently named in James Beard Foundation's *Who's Who in Food and Beverage in America*

At 15, English began his cooking career in a professional kitchen, and at 20, he attended the Culinary Institute of America, where he graduated with honors in 1982. He continued his education working with Jean Jacques Rachou at New York's *La Cote Basque,* and then relocated to Italy, where he apprenticed at the well-established *Dal Pescatore* in Canto Sull O'lio and *Paraccuchi* in Locando D'Angello.

English is involved with several local and national charities, including Men With Heart, the Anthony Spinazzola Foundation, Community Servings, Share Our Strength, the Boys and Girls Clubs, and City Year.

PORTUGUESE SAUSAGE AND KALE SOUP

Hailing from the influence of the many Portuguese immigrants in New England, this soup is a variation of Portugal's popular caldo verde. *If Portuguese sausage is unavailable, substitute Italian hot and Italian sweet sausage for the two Portuguese sausages.*

Start soaking the peas for this soup the day before cooking. If that is not possible, bring pot of water to boil, add peas, turn off water, and soak the peas for a couple of hours.

NUMBER OF SERVINGS: 14
COOKING METHOD:
  Boil
SERVING SIZE:
  9 oz
TOTAL YIELD:
  7 lbs, 15 oz

Portuguese Sausage and
Kale Soup
photo © 2008 StockFood

INGREDIENTS	WEIGHT	VOLUME
pea beans (small white beans), dried	7 oz	1 cup
stock, beef or chicken	6 lbs	3 qts
sausage, Portuguese like *chouriço*, thickly sliced	15 oz	
sausage, Portuguese like *lingüiça*, thickly sliced	15 oz	
onion, small dice	5 oz	1 cup
potatoes, peeled, cut into 1-inch cubes	15½ oz	4 medium
kale, fresh, stems removed, shredded	1 lb	2 bunches
beer	8 oz	1 cup
salt	to taste	
pepper		½ teaspoon

1. Soak peas in water overnight.
2. Bring stock to boil, add peas, cover and cook over low heat until peas are almost soft, about one hour.
3. Meanwhile, sauté both sausages with onion until sausage browns and onion softens. Drain any excess fat from pan. Refrigerate until needed.
4. When peas are almost soft, add potatoes. Cook about 10 minutes.
5. Add sausage and onions, kale, and beer. Cook for about 15 minutes, until potatoes are tender.
6. Season with salt and pepper, correct seasonings. Serve.

BEET AND APPLE SALAD

Beet and Apple Salad

Because they grow in cool weather and store well in a root cellar through the winter, beets appear often on New England menus.

If desired, replace honey with maple syrup.

Chill plates in advance for plating this recipe.

NUMBER OF SERVINGS: 8
COOKING METHOD:
  Boil (beets)
SERVING SIZE:
  1¼ oz (1 cup) romaine with
  remaining ingredients
TOTAL YIELD:
  3 lbs, 14 oz finished salad
  vinaigrette yields 15½ oz

INGREDIENTS	WEIGHT	VOLUME
VINAIGRETTE:		
oil, salad or olive	4 oz	½ cup
white or red wine vinegar	4 oz	½ cup
orange juice	3 oz	6 tablespoons
honey	½ oz	1 tablespoon
orange zest, minced	½ oz	1 tablespoon
green onions, sliced, include about 1 inch of green	2 oz	6 tablespoons, about 4 each
mint, fresh, minced	¾ oz	3 tablespoons
salt	to taste	
pepper	to taste	
SALAD:		
beets, fresh cooked or canned, julienne	2 lbs	6 medium
romaine lettuce, washed, torn into bite-sized pieces	11 oz	8 cups
apple, tart like Granny Smith, core removed, diced	1 lb	2 each
GARNISH:		
mint, fresh		

For Vinaigrette:

1. Place all ingredients in bowl or jar with lid.
2. Mix well. In bowl, mix with whisk. In jar, shake vigorously. Correct seasonings. Refrigerate until needed.

For Salad:

1. Place beets in bowl, pour half of vinaigrette over them, and mix gently. Cover and refrigerate at least 2 hours or as long as overnight.
2. Combine romaine and apple in bowl. Gently mix with enough remaining vinaigrette to coat thoroughly.
3. Place romaine mixture on chilled plate, top with beets, serve. If desired, garnish with fresh mint.

CRANBERRY RELISH

Cranberry Relish

photo courtesy of National Turkey Federation. For more cooking tips and recipe ideas, visit www.eatturkey.com

The sweetness of this sweet/tart relish depends on the tartness of the cranberries as well as personal preference. If this is not sweet enough, add a little more sugar.

NUMBER OF SERVINGS: 9
SERVING SIZE:
  3 oz
TOTAL YIELD:
  1 lb, 11½ oz

INGREDIENTS	WEIGHT	VOLUME
orange, cut into quarters	5¼ oz	1 small to medium
almonds, any type	4¼ oz	¾ cup
cranberries, washed, drained	12 oz	1 each 12-oz bag
sugar	5¾ oz	¾ cup

1. With food processor running, drop orange through feed tube. Pulse a few times to begin to pulverize.
2. Add almonds; pulse until chopped into pieces no larger than peas.
3. Add cranberries; pulse a few times.
4. Add sugar; pulse until coarsely chopped relish.
5. Taste and add more sugar, if needed. Cover and store in refrigerator until needed. Serve cold.

NEW ENGLAND BOILED DINNER

New England Boiled Dinner

photo © Dorling Kindersley

Serve accompanied by mustard or horseradish sauce.

NOTES:
- *Corned round of beef can be substituted for brisket. Round contains less fat than brisket.*
- *The vegetables vary from recipe to recipe. Many also include parsnips.*
- *Some like to cook each vegetable separately to maintain individual flavors instead of cooking in liquid containing brine.*

NUMBER OF SERVINGS: 9
COOKING METHOD:
  Boil
SERVING SIZE:
  5 oz meat
TOTAL YIELD:
  3 lbs meat

Wine Style: Medium-bodied Cabernet Sauvignon, Zinfandel, or Merlot
Example: Cabernet Sauvignon/Viognier—Chicama Vineyards, Martha's Vineyard, MA. This wine is a distinctive fusion of oak-aged Cabernet Sauvignon and subtly flavored Viognier.

INGREDIENTS	WEIGHT	VOLUME
corned beef brisket	5 lbs	
onions, small, white, peeled	13½ oz	12 each
carrots, peeled	12 oz	6 small
turnips, scrubbed	1 lb, 8 oz	6 small
potatoes, red new, peeled	2 lbs, 2 oz	12 each
beets, scrubbed, trimmed	1 lb, 12 oz	8 small
cabbage, green, cored, quartered	3 lb, 13 oz	1 medium

GARNISH:

parsley, chopped

mustard or horseradish sauce

1. Rinse corned beef under cold water to remove brine. Place in pot of cold water.

2. Bring to boil, removing scum that rises to the surface, as necessary.

3. Cover; simmer for 50 minutes per pound, until tender (approximately 4 hours for 5 lb meat).

4. About 45 minutes before meat is done (after 3 hours, 15 minutes, meat should be almost tender), add onions, carrots, turnips, and potatoes. Raise heat to return to simmer, then lower heat to maintain simmer.

5. In separate pan, place beets, cover with cold water, bring to boil, lower heat, and simmer approximately 30 to 40 minutes, until tender. Drain; place in warm oven to hold until serving time.

6. Remove meat and vegetables from liquid, slice meat, and place in warm oven to hold until serving time.

7. Meanwhile, bring cooking liquid to boil, add cabbage, and cook about 10 minutes, until tender.

8. Remove from liquid. Arrange all meat and vegetables on serving dish.

9. Sprinkle with parsley and serve, accompanied by mustard or horseradish sauce.

YANKEE POT ROAST

Yankee Pot Roast
photo © Dorling Kindersley

This dish can be cooked on top of the stove as well as in the oven.

To remove more fat from the gravy, cook meat until the point of adding the vegetables, refrigerate overnight, and then remove solidified fat.

NUMBER OF SERVINGS: 8
COOKING METHOD:
  Braise
SERVING SIZE:
  5 oz meat
TOTAL YIELD:
  7 lbs, 9 oz
  2 lbs, 10 oz meat

Wine Style: Wide variety: Enjoy the wine of your choice, such as Merlot, Cabernet Sauvignon, Pinot Noir, or Cabernet Franc
Example: Cabernet Franc—Taylor Brooke Winery, Woodstock, CT. This wine is full of violets and raspberries, bright berry fruit, and green pepper notes.

INGREDIENTS	WEIGHT	VOLUME
salt pork, 1/4-inch dice	2 oz	
salt		1/2 teaspoon
pepper		1/2 teaspoon
beef, boneless, chuck,	4 lb to	
brisket, or bottom round,	4 lb, 8 oz	
washed		
flour, for dredging	as needed	
onions, peeled, halved	15 oz	6 small
celery, 1-inch pieces	5 1/4 oz	3 stalks
water	1 lb	2 cups
bay leaf		1 each
garlic, cloves, minced	1/4 oz	2 each
thyme	1/4 oz	2 teaspoons
carrots, peeled, 1-inch pieces	12 oz	6 each
turnip, peeled, 1/2-inch dice	9 1/4 oz	1 large
potatoes, cut into thirds	1 lb, 7 oz	6 each
flour, optional	1/2 oz	2 tablespoons

1. Preheat oven to 325 degrees.
2. Heat Dutch oven or large ovenproof pot, sauté salt pork until brown, then remove cracklings.
3. Salt and pepper meat, dredge in flour, then sauté meat in fat on all sides until brown.
4. Add onions, celery, water, bay leaf, garlic, and thyme; cover and bake for 2 hours.
5. Add carrots and turnips; return to oven for 30 minutes.
6. Add potatoes; cook until potatoes are tender.
7. Remove meat and vegetables to platter; keep warm. Skim as much fat as possible from meat liquid. Correct seasonings.
8. If thicker gravy is desired, mix 1/2 oz (2 tablespoons) flour with a few tablespoons cold water to form thin paste. Whisk into liquid from meat; bring to boil, whisking often, and cook until desired thickness.
9. Slice meat; place on platter with vegetables. Serve, accompanied by gravy.

ROASTED TURKEY WITH GRAVY

Roast Turkey with Gravy
photo courtesy of National Turkey Federation. For more cooking tips and recipe ideas, visit www.eatturkey.com

According to the National Turkey Federation, whole turkey with skin yields about 53 percent of its weight, while turkey breast with skin yields 62 percent. A 12 lb turkey yields 5.64 lbs of edible meat without the skin.

The amount of gravy depends on personal preference and which foods require gravy. Since it might be used on turkey, stuffing, and/or potatoes, the amount will vary.

Remember, when consulting yield charts for turkey, that some of the meat might be removed as small pieces, particularly on legs. Some of that might not be served in a restaurant as sliced turkey; however, those scraps flavor soup or make dishes like turkey á la king.

NUMBER OF SERVINGS:
  turkey: about 12
COOKING METHOD:
  Bake, Sauté
GRAVY:
  25 each 1-oz or 12 each 2-oz
SERVING SIZE:
  4 oz turkey, about 1 oz gravy for turkey
TOTAL YIELD:
  1 lb, 9 oz or 3 cups gravy

Wine Style: Wide Variety—Chardonnay, Viognier, Pinot Blanc, Pinot Gris, Grenache, or light Zinfandel
Example: Estate Chardonnay—Sakonnet Vineyard, Little Compton, RI. This soft and elegant wine has citrus lime, green apple, and peach aromas with a wide arrangement of subtle flavors.

INGREDIENTS	WEIGHT	VOLUME
turkey, washed, giblets and neck removed from cavity	12 lbs, 6 oz	
GRAVY:		
reserved liquid from roasting pan		
flour, all purpose	1¼ oz	5 tablespoons
turkey or chicken stock, hot	1 lb, 8 oz	3 cups
dry white wine	4 oz	½ cup

1. Move rack to middle of oven. Preheat oven to 325 degrees.
2. Place turkey on rack in pan, breast side down. Bake for 1 hour.
3. Turn turkey so breast side faces up. Bake another 2 hours, 30 minutes, until correct internal temperature. Baste occasionally.
4. Remove turkey from oven and pan; cover with foil to keep warm while preparing gravy. Let turkey rest at least 20 minutes before carving so juices retreat into turkey.

To Prepare Gravy:

1. Remove all liquid from pan except 11 oz (1⅓ cups). Heat the remaining 11 oz (1⅓ cups) to boiling.
2. Whisking constantly, sprinkle in flour. Cook for 2 to 3 minutes.
3. Whisk in stock, then add wine. Deglaze by scraping all bits from bottom of pan.
4. Cook, stirring constantly, until thickened.
5. Strain gravy through China cap or sieve. Correct seasonings. Serve immediately to accompany turkey and stuffing (*recipe later in this chapter*).

BROILED STUFFED COD

Broiled Stuffed Cod
photo © 2008 Jupiterimages Corporation

Make sure all ingredients are measured and ready before starting because the stuffing is assembled after the fish goes into the oven.

The rule of thumb is that fish cooks 10 minutes per inch of thickness. While some cod fillets are quite thick, others are thin. Judge cooking time according to the thickness of the ones being prepared.

NUMBER OF SERVINGS: 8
COOKING METHOD:
  Broil
SERVING SIZE:
  7 oz
TOTAL YIELD:
  8 servings each with
  7 oz raw fish

Wine Style: Light- to medium-bodied dry white wines such as Seyval Blanc, Chardonnay, Sauvignon Blanc, or Semillon
Example: Sanctuary—Newport Vineyards, Middletown, RI. This blend of Seyval Blanc and Chardonnay is dry and oak-aged with hints of apple and pear, similar to a white Bordeaux.

INGREDIENTS	WEIGHT	VOLUME
cod or scrod fillets, cut into 7-oz pieces	3 lbs, 8 oz	
butter, melted	4 oz	1 stick or ½ cup
salt	to taste	
pepper	to taste	
bread crumbs	9¼ oz	2 cups
onion, minced	1¼ oz	3 tablespoons
green pepper, small dice	1½ oz	¼ cup
Dijon mustard	½ oz	1 tablespoon
Worcestershire sauce		1 teaspoon
hot pepper sauce like Tabasco	few drops, to taste	
lemon juice	2 oz	¼ cup
parsley, fresh, minced		1 teaspoon
paprika	sprinkling	
GARNISH:		
lemon wedges		

1. Preheat broiler.
2. Dip fillets in butter (reserve all remaining butter), season with salt and pepper, and place on pan with skin side down. Broil for 5 minutes. Turn fish over.
3. Meanwhile, combine remaining butter, bread crumbs, onion, green pepper, Dijon mustard, Worcestershire sauce, hot pepper sauce, lemon juice, and parsley in bowl. Mix.
4. Divide bread crumb mixture equally over fish fillets. Sprinkle lightly with paprika.
5. Broil 5 to 8 minutes or until fish flakes and crust is slightly brown. *Note: If fish is more than 1 inch thick, it will need more time. If topping becomes too brown, tent with aluminum foil and continue broiling. To tent, place large sheet of foil over fish making sure foil is puffed up in center so that it does not touch surface of the fish and disturb the crumb topping.*
6. Serve immediately, garnished with lemon wedge if desired.

SCALLOPS AU GRATIN

Scallops au Gratin
photo © 2008 Jupiterimages Corporation

Accompany Scallops au Gratin with Duchess potatoes piped around the serving dish before broiling, or serve this dish with rice on the side.

If bay scallops are unavailable, substitute sea scallops but cut them in half for use in this recipe.

NUMBER OF SERVINGS: 9
COOKING METHOD:
  Sauté, Boil, Broil
SERVING SIZE:
  8 oz
TOTAL YIELD:
  4 lbs, 9 oz

Wine Style: Light- to medium-bodied Pinot Blanc, Chardonnay, Viognier, or Gewürztraminer
Example: Traminette—Jewell Towne Vineyards, South Hampton, NH. Traminette is a hybrid of Gewürztraminer, the noblest grape of Alsace and Germany.

INGREDIENTS	WEIGHT	VOLUME
SAUCE:		
butter	2 oz	4 tablespoons, ¼ cup, or ½ stick
onion, small dice	5 oz	1 medium
flour, all purpose	1½ oz	6 tablespoons
milk, hot	1 lb, 8 oz	3 cups
salt		½ teaspoon
white pepper		½ teaspoon
cloves, whole		6 each
peppercorns, whole		6 each
bay leaf		1 large
thyme		¼ teaspoon
cayenne pepper		⅛ teaspoon
nutmeg		¼ teaspoon
cheddar cheese, extra sharp, grated	8 oz	3 cups
ASSEMBLY:		
butter or oil	½ oz	1 tablespoon
bay scallops, washed, drained thoroughly	3 lbs	
paprika	for sprinkling	
cheddar cheese, extra sharp, grated	6¾ oz or as needed ¾ oz per serving	about 2½ cups 3 tablespoons per serving

For Sauce:

1. Melt 2 oz (4 tablespoons) butter over medium flame; add onion and sauté until onion softens, about 3 or 4 minutes.
2. Sprinkle in flour; whisk until white to blonde roux, about 2 minutes.
3. Turn heat to low and slowly whisk in hot milk, adding a little at a time.
4. Add salt, white pepper, cloves, peppercorns, bay leaf, thyme, cayenne, and nutmeg.
5. Whisking frequently to avoid sticking, let sauce cook about 12 to 17 minutes, until quite thick.
6. Strain through sieve into separate bowl; press on ingredients in sieve to extract all liquid. Discard ingredients remaining in sieve.
7. Add 8 oz (3 cups) cheddar to hot sauce; stir to dissolve. Correct seasonings. Set sauce aside until needed. Cool, cover, and refrigerate sauce if not needed immediately.

Assembly:

1. Preheat broiler.
2. Heat ½ oz (1 tablespoon) butter or oil in large skillet until hot.
3. Add scallops, sauté about 1 or 2 minutes, to release excess liquid.
4. Drain thoroughly; combine scallops with hot sauce. If sauce is not hot, heat it, then add scallops.
5. Transfer scallop mixture to ovenproof individual serving dishes.
6. Sprinkle top of each dish with paprika, then sprinkle ¾ oz (3 tablespoons) cheddar cheese on top.
7. Broil until starting to brown, about 2 minutes. Serve immediately.

BOSTON BAKED BEANS

Boston Baked Beans

photo courtesy of National Pork Board

Begin preparation for this dish the day before serving so the beans can soak overnight. If that is not possible, bring pot of water to boil, add beans, turn off water, and soak the beans for a couple of hours.

NUMBER OF SERVINGS: 10
COOKING METHOD:
  Bake
SERVING SIZE:
  6 oz
TOTAL YIELD:
  3 lbs, 15 oz

INGREDIENTS	WEIGHT	VOLUME
beans, Great Northern or navy, dried	1 lb	2 cups
water	to cover beans by 2 inches	
salt pork, with rind, in one piece	8 oz	
onion, stuck with 2 whole cloves, cut into quarters	4 oz	1 medium
molasses	4 oz	1/3 cup
dark brown sugar	3 oz	1/2 cup
dry mustard		1 teaspoon
pepper		1 teaspoon
salt, *optional*	to taste	

1. Wash beans, cover with water, refrigerate and soak overnight.
2. Drain beans, cover with fresh water, bring to boil, cover and simmer one hour.
3. Drain and reserve cooking liquid.
4. Preheat oven to 250 degrees.
5. Cut salt pork in half. Leave one half whole and score top through rind with 1/2-inch cuts in both directions to form checkerboard pattern. Cut other half into 1/2-inch cubes. Place cubes in bottom of bean pot.
6. Place onion in pot, top with beans.
7. In bowl, combine molasses, brown sugar, mustard, pepper, and 1 lb, 2 oz (2 1/4 cups) reserved bean liquid. If there is not enough bean liquid, add water to make 1 lb, 2 oz (2 1/4 cups).
8. Pour liquid mixture over beans, making sure they are covered by 1/2 inch. Place scored salt pork on top, cover tightly, and bake for 5 hours.
9. Uncover and bake for another 30 to 45 minutes.
10. Correct seasonings; serve.

SUCCOTASH

Succotash

photo © Dorling Kindersley

Red pepper is not traditional, but it adds a welcome dash of color to the dish. To stay authentic, eliminate it from the recipe.

NUMBER OF SERVINGS: 10
COOKING METHOD:
  Boil
SERVING SIZE:
  4 oz
TOTAL YIELD:
  2 lbs, 11 oz

INGREDIENTS	WEIGHT	VOLUME
heavy cream, cold	8 oz	1 cup
flour, all purpose		1 teaspoon
corn kernels, fresh or frozen	1 lb, 4 oz	4 cups
lima beans, fresh or frozen	1 lb, 4 oz	4 cups
salt	1/4 oz	1 teaspoon
pepper	to taste	
paprika		1/4 teaspoon
red pepper, small dice	2 oz	1/2 each

1. Mix cold cream and flour together.
2. Place corn and lima beans in saucepan. Add cream mixture, salt, pepper, and paprika.
3. Cook over medium heat about 5 minutes, stirring frequently.
4. Add red pepper; cook another 5 minutes until vegetables are tender.
5. Correct seasonings; serve.

GLAZED CARROTS AND PEAS

Cutting Carrots on the Diagonal

NUMBER OF SERVINGS: 11
COOKING METHOD:
 Boil
SERVING SIZE:
 4 oz
TOTAL YIELD:
 2 lbs, 15 1/2 oz

INGREDIENTS	WEIGHT	VOLUME
carrots, peeled, sliced on diagonal 1/8-inch thick	2 lb	12 each
maple syrup	2 3/4 oz	1/4 cup
butter	2 oz	1/4 cup or 4 tablespoons
salt		3/4 teaspoon
pepper		1/4 teaspoon
peas, frozen	1 lb	4 cups

1. Steam carrots (or boil in a little water) until cooked about three-quarters done. Drain any excess water and return carrots to pan.
2. Add maple syrup and butter to carrots. Turn gently to melt butter and coat.
3. Add salt, pepper, and peas. Mix gently and cook until peas are hot and carrots are done.
4. Correct seasonings. Serve.

ACORN SQUASH WITH MAPLE SYRUP

Acorn Squash with
Maple Syrup

photo © Dorling Kindersley

This recipe produces a very fragrant, sweet squash.

NUMBER OF SERVINGS: 8
COOKING METHOD:
 Bake
SERVING SIZE:
 1/2 squash or 9 oz
TOTAL YIELD:
 4 lbs, 81/2 oz

INGREDIENTS	WEIGHT	VOLUME
acorn squash, halved, seeds and fibers removed	4 lb, 101/2 oz	4 each
brown sugar, firmly packed	31/2 oz	1/2 cup
coriander		1/2 teaspoon
nutmeg		1/2 teaspoon
cinnamon		1 teaspoon
cloves or allspice		1/4 teaspoon
salt		1/2 teaspoon
pepper		1/4 teaspoon
maple syrup	51/4 oz	1/2 cup

1. Preheat oven to 350 degrees. Place squash skin side up in baking dish. Pour 1/2 inch water into baking dish.
2. Bake for 30 minutes. Remove from oven and discard water. Turn squash over so cut side faces up.
3. While squash bakes, combine brown sugar, coriander, nutmeg, cinnamon, cloves, salt, and pepper.
4. Divide sugar mixture equally and place one portion in center of each squash. Add 3/4 oz (1 tablespoon) maple syrup to center of each squash.
5. Bake another 15 minutes, until tender, basting every 5 minutes. Remove from oven, serve.

HERB STUFFING

Herb Stuffing

photo courtesy of McCormick Spices

Countless variations of stuffing recipes abound. Some cooks add oysters, others include roasted chestnut pieces and/or chopped dried fruits, and still others prefer sausage in their stuffing. In addition, many people choose cornbread instead of plain bread for the basis of their stuffing. Generally, peoples' preferences reflect their family's traditions as well as the region they inhabit. All in all, possible additions and variations on stuffing are endless, limited only by the imagination.

NUMBER OF SERVINGS: 15
COOKING METHOD:
 Sauté, Bake
SERVING SIZE:
 4 oz
TOTAL YIELD:
 3 lbs, 13 oz

INGREDIENTS	WEIGHT	VOLUME
butter	8 oz	2 sticks or 1 cup
onion, small dice	10 oz	2 cups or 2 large
celery, small dice	6 oz	1 1/3 cups
bread cubes, dried, 3/4-inch	1 lb, 2 1/2 oz	15 cups
marjoram		2 teaspoons
sage		2 teaspoons
thyme		2 teaspoons
rosemary		2 teaspoons
parsley, fresh, minced	1 oz	1/2 cup
salt	1/2 oz	2 teaspoons
pepper		1 teaspoon
chicken stock	2 lbs	4 cups or 1 qt

1. Pan-spray ovenproof baking dish. Preheat oven to 350 degrees. Melt butter in pan over medium heat. Sauté onion and celery for 3 to 4 minutes.
2. In large bowl, combine bread cubes, marjoram, sage, thyme, rosemary, parsley, salt, pepper, and sautéed onions and celery.
3. Slowly add stock, stir gently to moisten. Correct seasonings.
4. Transfer to prepared baking dish. Cover and bake 30 minutes. Uncover and continue baking another 30 minutes, until thoroughly heated.

BOSTON BROWN BREAD

NUMBER OF SERVINGS: 7
COOKING METHOD:
  Steam
SERVING SIZE:
  1 slice 3/4-inch thick
TOTAL YIELD:
  1 loaf baked in 12 oz coffee can (4-inch diameter, 5 1/2 inches tall)

Boston Brown Bread
photo courtesy of King Arthur Flour

INGREDIENTS	WEIGHT	VOLUME
whole wheat flour	2 oz	1/2 cup
rye flour	2 1/2 oz	1/2 cup
cornmeal	2 1/2 oz	1/2 cup
baking soda		1/2 teaspoon
salt		1/2 teaspoon
buttermilk	15 1/2 oz	2 cups
molasses	4 oz	1/3 cup
raisins	2 oz	1/3 cup

1. Butter inside of coffee can. Butter piece of parchment paper or waxed paper large enough to generously cover opening of can.
2. Fill pot large enough to accommodate coffee can with enough water to reach three-quarters up coffee can. Bring to boil.
3. Meanwhile, sift whole wheat flour, rye flour, cornmeal, soda, and salt into bowl.
4. Add buttermilk and molasses. Mix just to combine.
5. Stir in raisins. Mix just to combine.
6. Pour batter into prepared can, making sure to leave at least 1-inch headroom at top. Cover top with parchment paper, buttered side down (facing batter). Cover with aluminum foil, leaving plenty of headroom for bread to expand (foil should be puffed about one inch over top of can). Secure foil with kitchen twine.
7. Place coffee can in pan of water, return to boil, reduce heat, cover pot, and simmer for 2 to 2 1/2 hours. Remove can from pan.
8. Remove bread from can and cut into 3/4-inch slices. If desired, cut each slice in half, and serve warm, accompanied by butter.

BLUEBERRY MUFFINS

Portioning Blueberry
Muffin Batter

Blueberry Muffins
photo courtesy of Land O' Lakes, Inc.

If available, make these muffins with wild blueberries. Besides having a more intense flavor, the tiny wild blueberries spread throughout the batter more evenly.

The flavor of these muffins actually improves after sitting for a few hours.

NUMBER OF SERVINGS: 15
  each 2¹/₂-inch muffins *or* 30
  each 1³/₄-inch miniature
  muffins
COOKING METHOD:
  Bake
SCALING:
  2 oz batter for 2¹/₂-inch
  muffins
  1 oz batter for
  1³/₄-inch muffins
TOTAL YIELD:
  1 lb, 15 oz batter

INGREDIENTS	WEIGHT	VOLUME
flour, all purpose, sifted	8¹/₄ oz	2 cups
baking powder	¹/₄ oz	2 teaspoons
baking soda		¹/₄ teaspoon
salt		¹/₄ teaspoon
sugar	3³/₄ oz	¹/₂ cup
buttermilk	7³/₄ oz	1 cup
egg	1³/₄ oz	1 each
butter, unsalted, melted, cooled	2¹/₂ oz	5 tablespoons
vanilla		1 teaspoon
lemon rind, finely grated		1 teaspoon
blueberries, fresh, washed, dried, or frozen	7¹/₂ oz	1¹/₂ cups

1. Place rack in center of oven. Grease or pan-spray muffin tins. Preheat oven to 400 degrees.

2. Sift together flour, baking powder, baking soda, salt, and sugar in medium bowl. Form a well or indentation in center of flour mixture.

3. With fork or whisk, combine buttermilk, egg, butter, and vanilla.

4. Add lemon rind and buttermilk mixture into well of flour. Quickly mix together with fork until barely combined. *Do not overmix* or muffins will have poor texture and/or be tough.

5. Gently fold in blueberries.

6. Spoon mixture into prepared muffin tins, filling until almost full.

7. Bake until lightly browned with springy tops, about 15 minutes for 1³/₄-inch muffins and about 20 minutes for 2¹/₂-inch muffins.

8. Let sit in pans a few minutes, then remove gently. Cool completely before wrapping.

INDIAN PUDDING

Native Americans introduced the settlers to this confection consisting of cornmeal mush sweetened with maple syrup. As time passed and more ingredients became available for this traditional colonial dessert, molasses replaced the maple syrup, eggs enriched the recipe, and cooks added spices and any variety of available dried fruit. Jazz up this rather plain dessert by topping it with a dollop of whipped cream or ice cream.

NUMBER OF SERVINGS: 14
COOKING METHOD:
  Bake
SERVING SIZE:
  4 oz
TOTAL YIELD:
  3 lbs, 10 oz

Indian Pudding
photo by Clive Streeter © Dorling Kindersley

INGREDIENTS	WEIGHT	VOLUME
milk	2 lb, 8 oz	5 cups
cornmeal	4 oz	2/3 cup
butter, unsalted	2 oz	4 table-spoons or 1/2 stick
eggs, beaten	6³/4 oz	4 each
molasses	6 oz	1/2 cup
dark brown sugar, firmly packed	2¹/2 oz	1/2 cup
salt		1/2 teaspoon
cinnamon		2 teaspoons
ginger, ground		1 teaspoon
nutmeg, ground		1 teaspoon
dried fruit, diced, raisins, apples, apricots, mixed, or combination	6 oz (depends on type of fruit)	1 cup

GARNISH:

whipped cream, lightly sweetened

or

ice cream

nutmeg or cinnamon

1. Preheat oven to 325 degrees. Butter or pan-spray 2 each 1-qt ovenproof dishes.
2. Combine 1 lb (2 cups) milk, cornmeal, and butter in saucepan. Whisking constantly, bring to boil.
3. Reduce heat to low, cover, and cook for 5 minutes. Meanwhile, combine eggs and remaining 1 lb, 8 oz (3 cups) milk.
4. Remove from heat; whisk in molasses, brown sugar, salt, cinnamon, ginger, nutmeg, and egg/milk mixture. Add dried fruit.
5. Pour into prepared dishes. Bake for 1 hour and 15 minutes, until knife inserted into pudding comes out clean.
6. Serve warm or chilled, accompanied by a dollop of whipped cream or ice cream and topped with a sprinkling of cinnamon and/or nutmeg.

PUMPKIN PIE

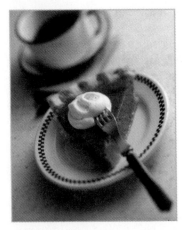

In the early colonial days, the absence of wheat meant no pie dough; however, colonists cooked or steamed pumpkin without dough. Pumpkin pie probably consisted of pumpkin simply cooked with molasses or maple sugar for sweetening. Spices and sugar came later when ships brought these imported ingredients to New England.

Use any desired recipe for pie dough or the one provided after the pumpkin pie recipe.

NUMBER OF SERVINGS: 8
COOKING METHOD:
  Bake
SERVING SIZE:
  1 slice, 1/8 of pie
TOTAL YIELD:
  1 each 9-inch pie

Pumpkin Pie
photo courtesy of Land O' Lakes, Inc.

INGREDIENTS	WEIGHT	VOLUME
pie shell, partially baked, *recipe follows*		
FILLING:		
pumpkin puree, fresh cooked or canned	1 lb	2 cups
brown sugar	2 1/4 oz	1/3 cup
white sugar	2 1/4 oz	1/4 cup
molasses	1/2 oz	1 1/2 teaspoons
cinnamon	1/4 oz	1 teaspoon
nutmeg		1/4 teaspoon
ginger		1/2 teaspoon
cloves, ground		1/8 teaspoon
salt		pinch
eggs, beaten	3 1/2 oz	2 each
cream, heavy	6 oz	3/4 cup
rum	1/2 oz	1 tablespoon
GARNISH:		
whipped cream, slightly		
or		
sweetened ice cream		

1. Place rack in lower third of oven. Preheat oven to 400 degrees.
2. Place all filling ingredients into bowl. Mix well with whisk.
3. Pour into prepared partially baked pie shell. Bake for 10 minutes.
4. Reduce temperature to 350 degrees. Bake another 25 to 30 minutes, until filling appears set (except for about 2 inches at center) when gently shaking pie. If necessary, tent pie with aluminum foil if crust of pie becomes too brown before filling sets. To tent, place large sheet of foil over pie, making sure foil is puffed up in center so that foil does *not* touch surface of pie (to prevent marring smooth surface of pie).
5. Remove pie from oven and cool completely on rack.
6. Serve, garnished with slightly sweetened whipped cream or ice cream, if desired.

PIE DOUGH

Dough After Pulsing in Butter or Shortening
photo by David Murray and Jules Selmes
© Dorling Kindersley

Ball of Pie Dough
photo by David Murray and Jules Selmes
© Dorling Kindersley

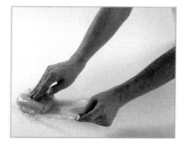

Wrapping Ball of Pie Dough for Chilling
photo by David Murray © Dorling Kindersley

Rolling Dough into Circle
photo by David Murray and Jules Selmes
© Dorling Kindersley

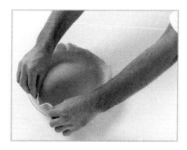

Easing Dough into Pie Pan
photo by David Murray and Jules Selmes
© Dorling Kindersley

Pressing Pie Dough into Pan
photo by David Murray and Jules Selmes
© Dorling Kindersley

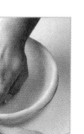

Fluting Pie Dough
photo © Dorling Kindersley

Brushing egg white on the bottom crust helps seal the dough from the moisture of the filling.

SERVING SIZE: About 11 oz for
  9-inch tart
TOTAL YIELD:
  13 oz pie dough

INGREDIENTS	WEIGHT	VOLUME
flour, all purpose	6³/4 oz	1¹/2 cups
salt		¹/2 teaspoon
butter, lard, or shortening, cold, cut into pieces	4³/4 oz	¹/2 cup + 1¹/2 tablespoons
cold water	1³/4 oz	3¹/2 tablespoons
egg white, slightly beaten, *optional*	1 oz	1 each

For Pie Dough in Food Processor:

1. Place flour and salt in bowl of food processor. Pulse to mix.
2. Cut cold butter or shortening into small pieces, about half-tablespoon size. Place on top of dry ingredients and pulse several times, until butter is pea-sized.
3. With motor running, add water through feed tube. Pulse until dough comes together into several big pieces or ball.
4. Remove from bowl; knead once or twice to form ball.
5. Cover and refrigerate for several hours or overnight. If time for refrigeration is short, flatten wrapped ball of dough into disk and place in freezer until cold.

(Continued)

For Pie Dough by Hand:

1. Place flour and salt in bowl; place butter pieces on top.
2. With fingertips, two knives, or pastry mixer, cut in butter or shortening until evenly mixed into pieces no larger than peas.
3. Add water, stir quickly with fork to moisten evenly, and knead a couple of times to make ball. Add a few drops water if too dry; add sprinkling of flour if too wet.
4. Cover and refrigerate for several hours or overnight. If time for refrigeration is short, flatten wrapped ball of dough into disk and place in freezer until cold.

To Roll Dough:

1. Place chilled ball on table. If using butter, dough will be stiff. With rolling pin, hit ball to flatten into disk about one inch thick. Lightly flour table and rolling pin, if needed.
2. Roll dough, from middle to sides, releasing dough from table with icing spatula every few rolls. Turn dough one-quarter turn to keep dough even and roll into circle until desired thickness, between 1/8 and 1/4 inch.
3. Release from table with spatula. Fold gently in half. Lift and position dough over pan so it covers pan when unfolded.
4. Press dough into all corners of pan. Either flute edges or cut flush with top of pan.
5. If possible, chill thoroughly before baking.

To Partially Bake:

1. Place rack in bottom half of oven. Preheat oven to 375 degrees. Line inside of pie shell with aluminum foil with shiny side down (to prevent dough from buckling). Make sure foil reaches into all "corner" seams (where sides and bottom of pan join).
2. Bake for about 8 minutes, until just set. Remove from oven; remove foil.
3. If desired, brush bottom crust with egg white. Return to oven for a few minutes to thoroughly bake egg white. Remove from oven when crust is partially cooked.

CHOCOLATE CHIP COOKIES

Chocolate Chip Cookies
photo by Getty Images, Inc.

Invented at the Toll House Inn in Massachusetts by Ruth Wakefield in 1930, chocolate chip cookies became an American icon. Countless variations exist: some use more brown sugar and less white sugar, some decrease the butter, many omit the nuts, and on and on. This recipe produces a buttery, flat cookie with a crisp texture. If a softer, chewy cookie is desired, increase the amount of flour slightly. Also, if the butter is too warm or whipped too much, the resulting cookie will spread more during baking.

TOTAL YIELD:
  3 lbs, 3¾ oz batter
  68 cookies about 2 inches
  wide
COOKING METHOD:
  Bake

INGREDIENTS	WEIGHT	VOLUME
flour, all purpose, sifted	10$\frac{1}{4}$ oz	2$\frac{1}{4}$ cups
baking soda	$\frac{1}{4}$ oz	1 teaspoon
salt		$\frac{1}{8}$ teaspoon
butter, unsalted, softened	8 oz	1 cup or 2 sticks
sugar	5$\frac{1}{4}$ oz	$\frac{3}{4}$ cup
brown sugar, firmly packed	6$\frac{1}{2}$ oz	$\frac{3}{4}$ cup
eggs	3$\frac{1}{2}$ oz	2 each
vanilla		1 teaspoon
semisweet chocolate chips	12 oz	2 cups
nuts of choice, chopped, lightly toasted if desired	5$\frac{1}{2}$ oz	1 cup

1. Place oven rack in middle or slightly above middle of oven. Preheat oven to 375 degrees.
2. Sift flour, baking soda, and salt together in bowl. Set aside until needed.
3. Cream butter and both sugars at medium speed until fluffy, using flat beater, if available.
4. Add eggs, one at a time, beating after each addition. Add vanilla.
5. Add flour; combine on lowest speed until just incorporated.
6. Stir in chocolate chips and nuts.
7. Drop $\frac{3}{4}$ oz (one teaspoon) on sheet pan, leaving at least 1$\frac{1}{2}$ inches between cookies.
8. Bake for 8 to 10 minutes, until lightly brown. Let cool 30 seconds or a minute, then remove from pan with spatula.
9. Cool on rack completely before wrapping for storage.

APPLE CRANBERRY BETTY

While the "Betty" is an old-fashioned dessert prepared with bread and any available fruits, this more modern variation combines two fruits from New England, apples and cranberries.

NUMBER OF SERVINGS: 15
COOKING METHOD:
  Bake
SERVING SIZE:
  6 oz
TOTAL YIELD:
  5 lbs, 10$\frac{1}{2}$ oz

Apple Cranberry Betty
photo courtesy of Land O' Lakes, Inc.

INGREDIENTS	WEIGHT	VOLUME
bread, cut into $\frac{1}{2}$-inch cubes	1 lb	8 cups or 2 qts
butter, unsalted, melted	12 oz	3 sticks
apples, variety of choice, peeled, cored, sliced	2 lb, 1$\frac{1}{2}$ oz	6 large
cranberries, coarsely chopped	8$\frac{1}{2}$ oz	2 cups
raisins	5 oz	1 cup
brown sugar	11$\frac{1}{2}$ oz	1$\frac{1}{2}$ cups
sugar	8 oz	1 cup
cinnamon	$\frac{1}{2}$ oz	1 tablespoon
nutmeg		1 teaspoon
cloves		$\frac{1}{2}$ teaspoon
salt		$\frac{1}{2}$ teaspoon
lemon rind, grated	$\frac{1}{2}$ oz	1$\frac{1}{2}$ tablespoons
vanilla	$\frac{1}{2}$ oz	1 tablespoon

1. Grease or pan-spray 4-quart baking dish. Preheat oven to 375 degrees.
2. Combine bread cubes and melted butter in bowl; mix gently. Set aside until needed.
3. Place apples, cranberries, raisins, brown sugar, sugar, cinnamon, nutmeg, cloves, salt, lemon rind, and vanilla in separate bowl. Mix gently to combine thoroughly.
4. Evenly place one-third of bread cubes in prepared dish, top with one-half of apple mixture.
5. Place one-half of remaining bread cubes over apples, then top with remaining apples. Sprinkle remaining bread cubes over top.
6. Bake for 30 minutes, until apples are tender. Cool slightly; serve plain or with ice cream, heavy cream, whipped cream, or custard sauce.

3

Middle Atlantic States

OBJECTIVES

By the end of this chapter, you will be able to

- Discuss the early settlers, including their reasons for immigrating to the Middle Atlantic region, their heritage, and how that heritage impacted the cuisine
- Explain how the topography and climate of the Middle Atlantic region affected the cookery
- Discuss the role of the Chesapeake Bay in the development of the Middle Atlantic region
- Identify food products prevalent in the Middle Atlantic region
- Prepare a variety of dishes indicative of the cuisine of the Middle Atlantic region

States included in the Middle Atlantic:

- New York
- New Jersey
- Pennsylvania
- Delaware
- Maryland

HISTORY

Prior to the arrival of the white settlers, Algonquian and Iroquois tribes inhabited the land comprising the Middle Atlantic region. As in New England, the Native Americans helped the early settlers survive by teaching them how to plant the triumvirate of beans, corn, and squash; how to use indigenous foods; how to hunt game for meat and furs; and techniques for catching fish and shellfish in the rivers, lakes, bays, and ocean. While the waterways provided seemingly unlimited amounts of seafood, fish, and fowl, such as crabs, lobsters, clams, oysters, turtles, shad, bass, perch, ducks, and geese, the many forests yielded plentiful game, including deer, rabbit, squirrel, wild turkey, pigeons, and partridges. The colonists found a bounty of foods in this new region.

The Middle Atlantic attracted immigrants from England, Germany, Holland, and Sweden. They particularly liked pork and desserts such as pies and coffeecakes. The Dutch introduced the cookie in this region. Both the English and the Dutch used spices like cinnamon, cloves, nutmeg, ginger, and allspice in desserts.

After moving to Virginia, Maryland, and Delaware, the more affluent English settlers built grand estates, imported slaves, and enjoyed aristocratic foods. They planted orchards and grew large gardens containing substantial amounts and varieties of vegetables, fruits, and herbs. These wealthy settlers raised chickens for meat and eggs, hogs for pork and lard, cows for beef and dairy products, and sheep for lamb and wool. The slaves brought cooking methods, recipes, and foods from both the South and their native countries, and these melded with the foods available in the Middle Atlantic region. With a preference for spicy foods, the slaves used plenty of chili peppers and black pepper. Often they prepared the settlers' usual foods in new ways. For example, they replaced plain boiled crab with deviled crab.

In 1614, the first immigrants from Holland arrived in the area now called New York. By 1624, these Dutch settlers had imported dairy cows for milk and cheese, horses, hogs, sheep, poultry, and seeds for a variety of crops. They planted fields of grains, including wheat, rye, barley, and buckwheat, so they could make the hearty whole grain breads from their native land. In 1625, the Dutch bought Manhattan Island from the Native Americans for $24.00 and named it New Amsterdam.

In sharp contrast to the early settlers in Jamestown and New England, the founders of New Amsterdam planned for their survival through the winter. Before the fall ended, the Dutch filled their root cellars. They also smoked, dried, and preserved a wide assortment of foods. In 1664, the English gained control of Manhattan and changed the name to New York.

In the latter 1600s, many seeking religious freedom, including sects of Mennonites, Amish, Quakers, and Moravians, moved to Pennsylvania. Since many spoke German (*Deutsch* is the German word for "German"), they became known as the Pennsylvania Dutch. Reflecting their German and Dutch heritage, these settlers prepared the foods and dishes from their homeland. Having chosen a simple lifestyle, most of the Pennsylvania Dutch were hardworking farmers and preferred simple, hearty, and filling food.

Accurately describing the Chesapeake Bay, the Native American word *chesapeake* means "great shellfish bay." Oysters served as a mainstay in the diet of the Native Americans, and the settlers adopted oysters into their diet, too. To prepare for the lean times, the Native Americans smoked or dried any excess seafood.

Emigrating from Manchester, England, in 1774, Shakers settled in Waterveliet and later Mount Lebanon, New York. The industrious Shakers planted gardens and orchards, experimented with plants, soils, and fertilizers, created new varieties of fruits, started nurseries, and sold seeds for fruits, vegetables, herbs, and spices. Some of their many

Stocking their cellars for the winter, the Dutch stored kegs of hard cider, barrels of apples, clams stored in cornmeal and sawdust that they drenched with saltwater from the ocean twice each week, a variety of pickled and preserved foods, and much more.

accomplishments included the invention of several machines and tools to make farming and/or processing foods easier and more efficient. Some of the inventions include the flat broom, the circular saw, a machine to shell peas, a machine to core and cut apples, a threshing machine, a revolving oven, and an improved washing machine. With the community owning everything, Shakers lived in communes. Known for their excellent cooking, the Shakers prepared food for their community in three separate, huge kitchens. They used one kitchen for cooking, one for baking, and another for canning. The Shakers wrote precise recipes, cooked food in a wholesome, healthful manner, and placed great emphasis on sanitation in food handling and preparation. Fruits and vegetables played a major role in their diet; as a matter of fact, they developed numerous vegetarian dishes incorporating grains, nuts, seeds, dairy products, fruits, and/or vegetables. Besides seasoning their dishes with generous amounts of herbs and spices, the Shakers also relied on herbs and spices for medicinal purposes. Because Shakers believed in remaining celibate, their communities depended on converts for survival.

In 1825, the completion of the 350-mile Erie Canal connected Buffalo to Albany, New York. The completion of this canal meat that waterways linked the Atlantic Ocean to the Great Lakes, facilitating travel to the West for both people and goods. By 1875, railroads connected many cities and towns, eliminating the dependence on the waterways for travel. To accommodate travelers, hotels and restaurants opened throughout the settled portions of the country. Trains added a dining car in the late 1860s, which made train travel more comfortable, convenient, and luxurious.

Looking for a better life for themselves and their families, immigrants flocked to the United States in the middle 1800s to work in factories, mills, or mines, or with the railroad. Typically, these people filled the cities and settled into ethnic neighborhoods. As the populations of New York, Philadelphia, and Baltimore swelled, they grew from towns into large cities.

In 1873, New York merchant Ed McGrath visited China. Impressed with the large Pekin duck, he arranged to transport nine duck eggs to New York. Four of the nine eggs survived and hatched, and these ducks proliferated. They adapted well to the humid climate, sandy soil, and abundant water available on Long Island, and soon, many farms produced Long Island ducklings. When land on Long Island became very valuable and expensive around 1950, most of the duck farms closed, and many relocated in the Midwest. Still known for their excellent quality, Long Island ducks remain in demand.

To escape persecution and/or seek a better life, more than two million Jewish people immigrated to the United States from Germany and Eastern Europe between 1880 and 1924. These immigrants came from a number of different countries and brought recipes from diverse culinary heritages. In spite of varying culinary backgrounds, the Jewish immigrants shared their religion, and many of these people followed kosher dietary laws. *Kugel*, noodle or potato pudding; kasha, buckwheat groats; matzo ball soup; and many other dishes became common foods in New York City, where a large number of the Jewish immigrants settled.

TOPOGRAPHY AND CLIMATE

Lying southwest of New England, the Middle Atlantic region experiences a much more temperate climate than that found in New England. With the exception of upper New York, cold but not harsh winters dominate the Middle Atlantic region.

The Atlantic Ocean borders on the east, and many bays, inlets, and harbors define the jagged coastline. Of particularly importance, the Chesapeake Bay in Maryland ranks as the largest estuary in North America. A partially enclosed body of water, an estuary forms when fresh water sources meet with salt water. More than 100 rivers and streams, including the Susquehanna, Potomac, Patuxent, York, Appomattox, and James Rivers, flow into the Chesapeake Bay, which connects to the Atlantic Ocean. This combining of fresh and salt waters creates a unique environment because the water near the ocean is saltier than the water farther away from the opening to the ocean. As a result, the Chesapeake Bay was home to an amazing variety of fish and shellfish including crabs, oysters, striped bass (also called rockfish), and much more. Unfortunately, due to overfishing, pollution, and disease, the supply of fish and seafood in the Chesapeake Bay diminished drastically. Today, the area is best known for the prized blue crab, although the number of these crabs also has decreased greatly. Attempts to restore the conditions of the bay have increased the numbers of some varieties a little, but not others. Ongoing environmental work on this problem focuses on refurbishing marine life in the Chesapeake Bay.

Because deepwater harbors along the Atlantic facilitated trade, industry developed in this region. The many available jobs enticed people to move here. Several large cities with harbors, including Philadelphia, New York, and Baltimore, became major trade centers. Numerous towns and cities grew along the shores of the Chesapeake Bay, including Baltimore, Annapolis, Washington, Norfolk, and Newport News. From these ports, ships loaded with goods from the United States left for destinations all over the world. Those same ships returned filled with items from wherever they went. This gave people in the port cities access to a wider range of food products, and it exposed them to new foods and/or ingredients from distant lands.

Most inland areas in this region contain rolling hills, fertile plains, forests, mountains, rivers, valleys, and lakes. The rich soil surrounding the river valleys provided fertile farmland for bountiful agriculture.

Canada lies north of New York; Vermont, Massachusetts, and Connecticut are situated to the east; New Jersey and Pennsylvania border on the south; Lakes Erie and Ontario lie to the west. New Jersey actually lies to the west of New York City and Long Island. Although the New York City area experiences temperate winters, the bitter winters of the central and northern regions of New York resemble the frigid ones found in New England. Mild summers prevail.

New York is a very large state with diverse topography. The northern part of the state contains forests, mountains, and many lakes. Flat terrain and harsh, windy winters with lots of snow dominate the western region, which borders Lake Erie and Lake Ontario. In fact, abundant snowfall results from the moisture and conditions associated with the Great Lakes. Glaciers formed the numerous long narrow lakes in western New York known as the Finger Lakes. With row after row of grapevines, wine production flourishes in the western part of the state. While northern New York consists of forests and mountains, the remainder of the state contains rivers, valleys, hills, and the Catskill Mountains, until the terrain becomes flat near the ocean.

Stretching 315 miles, the Hudson River begins in the Adirondack Mountains in northern New York and runs south to New York City. For thousands of years before settlers came, Native Americans lived in this area, hunted, gathered food, and planted crops in the fertile valleys around the Hudson River. At that time, the Hudson River teemed with salmon and sturgeon. These valleys later provided the Dutch and English settlers with rich land for dairy farms and crops. Roaming the Adirondack Mountains in the north and the Catskill Mountains in the south, abundant game supplied still more food for the early inhabitants.

Located in central New York in the foothills just south of the Adirondacks, Saratoga Springs attracted Native Americans many years before settlers arrived. The natural

Many dairy farms still thrive in the fertile river valleys of New York, and these areas are known for the production of cheese. Apples and grapes top the list of fruits that flourish in New York.

A famous resort town known for its mineral springs, Saratoga Springs claims the origination of potato chips in the middle 1800s. Supposedly, a customer complained about the thick potatoes, so the chef sliced the potatoes very thinly and deep-fried them. The satisfied customer loved them and the chef invented potato chips!

mineral springs found in Saratoga Springs and their healing powers lured the Native Americans to this area.

New York lies to the north and east of New Jersey, the Atlantic borders New Jersey on its east and south, and the Delaware Bay lies to the southwest and separates New Jersey from Delaware to the west. Pennsylvania also neighbors New Jersey on the west. The ample coastline yields plenty of seafood, including scallops, clams, oysters, crabs, and lobster. The sandy soil of the coastal plains near the ocean is excellent for growing berries and many other crops. New Jersey has warm to hot summers and cold but not harsh winters.

The initial settlements in New Jersey developed around the Hudson River on the eastern side and the Delaware River on the west. For a couple of reasons, these two rivers claim major importance in New Jersey's history. First, both rivers provide fertile river valleys for growing a multitude of crops. Second, the Hudson River divides New Jersey from New York on the east, and the Delaware River forms the western border with Pennsylvania. This provided easy access to New York City and Philadelphia. The swampy central portion of New Jersey remained unsettled for quite a while. Rolling land describes the terrain of both western New Jersey and eastern Pennsylvania. New Jersey also contains mountains, forests, and lakes and rivers with shad, bluefish, sturgeon, pike, and bass.

Pennsylvania consists of mountains, hills, plateaus, rivers, streams, forests, and fertile farmland. New York lies to its north and east, New Jersey to its east, Maryland and West Virginia to the south, and West Virginia and Ohio border on the west. Part of the Appalachian Mountain chain, the Allegheny Mountains run through Pennsylvania from the north central section to the south and southeast. With the Delaware River bordering on the southeastern corner and Lake Erie lying in the northwest, these two areas contain flat terrain. Vegetables and fruits including grapes thrive in the sandy soil near Lake Erie. The northeast and northwest contain dairy farms, many types of mushrooms flourish in the southeast, and a variety of fruits such as apples, peaches, berries, cherries, and grapes come from the mountain valleys. Fertile soil and rich farmland yielding crops of corn, buckwheat, oats, fruits, and vegetables make up the area around Lancaster in the southern part of the state. While the Ohio River runs through western Pennsylvania, the Delaware River flows in the eastern and central part of the state. Cold winters and warm summers prevail in the humid climate.

Surrounded by bays, a 200-mile-long peninsula runs through the states of Delaware, Maryland, and Virginia. The bays keep the climate temperate and humid. This area is known for abundant seafood as well as chicken production.

Connected to Pennsylvania and Maryland on the north and Virginia on the south, much of Delaware borders water. Providing fish and seafood, the Atlantic Ocean and Delaware Bay lie to the east while the Chesapeake Bay is situated on the west. Most of Delaware consists of flat, low coastal plains where agriculture thrives. Only the northern section of the state contains hills and valleys. The Delaware River flows through the state.

The Chesapeake Bay divides Maryland into an eastern and western section. Flat, low terrain forms the coastal plains that make up the east. Hills, valleys, mountains, plateaus, forests, and fertile farmland describe the west. Many inlets and harbors define the coastline. Pennsylvania lies to the north; Delaware and the Atlantic Ocean border on the east; the Potomac River and Virginia lie to the south; and Washington, D.C., Virginia, and West Virginia are situated on the west of Maryland. The Potomac River forms the western border. The Patuxent River runs through southeastern Maryland and empties into the Chesapeake Bay, as does the Potomac River. Humid conditions with mild winters and hot summers describe the climate.

A port city lying inland, Pittsburgh developed where the Allegheny and Monongahela rivers join. The two rivers meet to form the Ohio River.

Settled by Quakers from England, Philadelphia was the site of the signing of the Declaration of Independence and meetings of the Continental Congress. Also, Philadelphia served as the first capital of the United States until 1785, when New York City became the capital. Although New York City was the capital for only five years, the inauguration of George Washington took place there. In 1790, the capital moved to Washington, D.C., where it remains today.

Ingredients and foods commonly used throughout the cuisine of the Middle Atlantic include

- fresh and saltwater shellfish and fish, including crabs, clams, oysters, shrimp, lobsters, scallops, shad, cod, flounder, sturgeon, trout, pike, bass, rockfish, perch, and bluefish
- game, including deer, wild turkey, duck, and geese
- pork, including all parts of the animal, lard, salt pork, sausages, and meat
- chicken and Long Island ducks
- dairy products, including milk, cheese, butter, and ice cream
- root vegetables, including carrots, potatoes, and sweet potatoes
- many other vegetables, including asparagus, lettuce, corn, cabbage, and tomatoes
- apples, peaches, plums, pears, cherries, strawberries, and blueberries
- grapes and wine

COOKING METHODS

Many oysters came from this region, and they appeared on menus in homes and restaurants. Although oysters no longer flourish in the Chesapeake Bay, they remain a popular menu item. As a result, oysters are imported from other areas. Oyster preparations include broiling, baking, frying, and steaming or boiling. Residents of the Middle Atlantic States eat raw oysters, prepare scalloped oysters, and add them to stuffing, omelets, and more. Another favorite shellfish, crab appears in almost any form imaginable using any cooking method that fits, including soup, deviled crab, and crab cakes. Frying remains the most common cooking method for soft-shelled crabs.

In the early days, boiled foods appeared often. Examples are soups and stews as well as several varieties of dumplings and noodles. The Pennsylvania Dutch had a special fondness for noodles and dumplings.

Whether deep-fried, pan-fried, or sautéed, many fried foods graced tables in this region. From meats, chicken, and seafood to fritters, vegetables, potatoes, noodles, pancakes, and waffles, the skillet and some lard or butter fried all kinds of foods throughout the Middle Atlantic States. In many areas, lard served as the standard fat for frying.

Oily fish like bluefish was usually baked or broiled (grilled). In addition, oily fish held up well to smoking.

Large ovens accommodated the hearty breads and many pies served here. Popular coffeecakes, cinnamon buns, and sticky buns (that originated in Philadelphia) required baking.

To preserve foods for the winter, the settlers prepared excess fish, meat, vegetables, and fruits by salting, smoking, and drying. In addition, they transformed fruits and vegetables into pickles, relish, and jam.

STATES

Searching for a northwest passage to the Spice Islands in the early 1600s, Henry Hudson, an English explorer working for the Dutch East India Company, came to the river in New York that would bear his name, the Hudson River. Soon, the Dutch settled in the areas now called Albany, New York, New York City, New Jersey, Delaware, and Connecticut. In 1614,

An American derivation of the hearty Dutch stew called *Hutspot*, meaning hodgepodge, contained cornmeal porridge, corned beef, and an assortment of winter vegetables from the root cellar.

Around 1964, Buffalo chicken wings made their first appearance at the Anchor Bar in Buffalo, New York. Traditionally, celery sticks and blue cheese dressing accompany these spicy wings.

The sandwich called beef on weck originated in Buffalo. This sandwich features lots of thinly sliced rare roast beef on a *kummelwek* roll, a hard roll topped with coarse salt and caraway seeds. Traditionally, horseradish and pan juices from the roast beef (*au jus*) accompany a beef on weck.

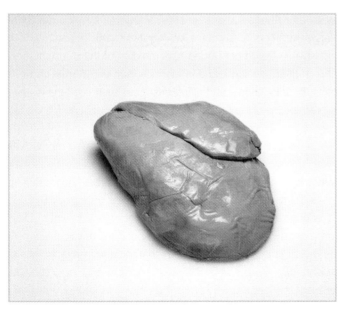

Foie Gras

they established Fort Orange (around Albany) that was the most northern post of their settlements. About ten years later in 1625, thirty Dutch families settled New Amsterdam. Because Dutch settlers brought dairy cows and planted fields of grain in their new homeland, they could prepare pancakes, dumplings, waffles, breads, cookies, and cakes, which became an intrinsic part of the cuisine here.

Finding lobsters that measured five or six feet across and huge one-foot oysters swimming in these waters, people in this region enjoyed the bounty of fish and shellfish from the ocean, bays, and rivers in New York. For use during the winter, they dried and salted copious amounts of excess shad caught in the Hudson River. Another rich source of food, the forests teemed with game and birds. As in Holland, the settlers' diet and cookery included plenty of cheese, butter, and milk. Hearty foods like split pea soup cooked with a ham hock and filling stews dominated the menus. With cabbage available from the root cellar, coleslaw, from the Dutch word *koolslaa*, appeared often. The Dutch settlers frequently ate goose, duck, and pork.

Supplying both freshwater and saltwater fish as well as transportation, waterways played an important role in New York. The Great Lakes border on the west, many lakes mark the landscape of New York, several rivers run through the state, and, of course, the Atlantic Ocean provides New York City with an excellent deep harbor that enabled the city to become a major trading center.

Because huge numbers of immigrants arrived through the port in New York City, many ethnic groups settled in New York City and throughout the state of New York. The Mohawk Valley attracted Germans, while many Eastern Europeans made their home in Buffalo in western New York. Meanwhile, French Canadians migrated south and settled in northern New York. Of course, the cookery in each area reflected the culinary heritage of those who settled there.

Lying east of Manhattan, Long Island today is known for ducks and its production of grapes and wine. In earlier days, the bounty of fruits and vegetables grown on Long Island supplied New York City with produce. Surrounded by the Atlantic Ocean, both Manhattan and Long Island had access to seafood such as oysters, clams, scallops, shad, bluefish, swordfish, striped bass, and more.

Throughout New York's history, the Hudson Valley was prized as a rich agricultural area. Today, the Hudson Valley yields herbs, spices, fruits, vegetables, and many specialty crops like miniature vegetables. While blueberries, strawberries, and grapes are indigenous to this area, the Dutch introduced peaches, apples, pears, cherries, apricots, currants, and gooseberries.

In addition to the shad that swam up the Hudson to spawn, sturgeon, varieties of bass, bluefish, trout, and more lived in the Hudson and its tributaries. Producing artisan cheeses made from the milk of goats, sheep, and cows, numerous dairy farms are located in this valley today. In addition, the Hudson Valley is well known for another specialty, *foie gras*, the enlarged liver from goose or duck. To enlarge the liver, farmers feed the birds large amounts of food. Often, they confine the birds, so they fatten more quickly. Many people object to this procedure because they feel it is inhumane.

Stretching from the east to the west through central New York, apple orchards dominate acres of land today. Growers produce numerous varieties of apples, with McIntosh,

In an effort to find a safer, more sanitary way to keep milk from spoiling, inventor Gail Borden created condensed milk in the middle 1800s and patented it in 1853. Although the product was developed in the South, Borden did not have the money to market the milk until a wholesale grocer with a New York factory became his partner. By 1860, they produced up to 5,000 gallons of condensed milk daily. Later, the factory changed its name to Borden Inc. In addition to its many uses for the Army and Navy, condensed milk became a mainstay in the devastated South after the Civil War when fresh milk was not available.

Cream cheese, Jell-O, and Knox gelatin were invented in New York.

Although farmers raise many varieties of apples, only a few sell commercially throughout the country. They only export varieties that travel well, are versatile in terms of their uses, and are widely known.

Throughout the regions where apple orchards thrive, people go to orchards in the fall to pick their own apples. After picking, many children and adults enjoy apple cider and apple cider donuts, which are prepared and sold at many of the orchards. These donuts reflect both the Dutch heritage and the foods prevalent in the region.

In 1847, two brothers, John and Adam Exeter, invented the oyster cracker in New Jersey. The 1¼- by ½-inch crisp cracker proved the perfect accompaniment for oysters and oyster stew.

Empire, Rome, Idared, Cortland, Golden Delicious, and Red Delicious apples ranking as the most prevalent. Depending on the conditions and the size of the apple harvest, the apple industry in New York brings in more than $100 million in revenue annually.

In addition, ample amounts of maple syrup come from central and northern New York as well as Pennsylvania. As in New England, the early spring means the tapping of sugar maple trees. After gathering the sap, producers boil it to reduce the liquid, leaving thick maple syrup. Today, evaporators replace boiling kettles of syrup placed over the fire.

A cornucopia of produce comes from New Jersey, which is called the "Garden State." With different soils existing in various parts of the state, crops of asparagus, corn, beans, root vegetables, spinach, squash, tomatoes, apples, peaches, strawberries, blueberries, and more thrive here. Besides agriculture, New Jersey claims an abundance of fish and shellfish from the Atlantic Ocean such as monkfish, mackerel, tuna, squid, sea bass, oysters, scallops, and crabs.

Initially, New Jersey consisted of two settlements. The Dutch, English, Scottish, and French Huguenots settled in the east along the Hudson River, while Quakers developed the settlement in the west along the Delaware River. Both became agricultural centers with close proximity to large cities where they sold their produce—New York City for the eastern settlement and Philadelphia for the settlement in the west.

In 1681, King Charles II of England gave William Penn the land that became Pennsylvania. Named for his father, the state name literally means "Penn's forest." The Quakers from England were the first group to immigrate to Pennsylvania. They settled near the area that became Philadelphia. The Quakers made friends with the Native Americans, who taught them about corn, indigenous fruits and vegetables, how to hunt game like elk, deer, wild turkey, and wild birds, as well as how to survive in this area.

At the invitation of the Quakers, Germans from other religious sects came seeking the religious freedom that the Quakers found in this new land. Many Mennonites and Amish moved to Pennsylvania; in fact, their population remains large today. The Mennonites and Amish still live in closely knit communities where neighbors help each other.

In compliance with their religious beliefs, members of both of these groups chose a life of simplicity and rejected many worldly goods. Reflecting their heritage, the cookery displays strong German, Swiss, and Alsatian characteristics. Many still speak a dialect of German. After 1710, even larger numbers of Germans immigrated to this region.

The cuisine of the Pennsylvania Dutch developed as a melding of their German heritage, the ingredients available in their new land, and influences from other American settlers and the Native Americans. Simple, hearty, and filling describes their cookery. Instead of serving different courses, a traditional Pennsylvania Dutch meal brought all the dishes to the table at the same time.

Regardless of their religion, most Pennsylvania Dutch families supported themselves by farming. Each family grew a large garden and raised hogs, cattle, and chickens on their farm. As a result, they consumed plenty of produce and prepared pork, beef, and chicken dishes. On most farms, they built a separate smokehouse for smoking excess meat. Each family canned and/or dried enough produce for consumption through the winter. Days began early on the farm, and a hearty breakfast started the day of hard physical labor. At noon, the family gathered for the large main meal of the day that included meat, potatoes, noodles, vegetables, and dessert.

Reigning as the favorite meat, pork was served often. Pigs provided lard for frying and making pie crusts; salt pork and ham hocks for flavoring soups, stews, and vegetables; assorted parts and scraps for sausages; and meat for the entrée at meals. To preserve food for the winter months, they smoked hams and excess meat. The members of all of the religious sects who settled in Pennsylvania shared one value: thrift. They wasted nothing. Besides salting and/or smoking any extra meat, they used all remaining parts and scraps after slaughtering hogs and cattle. They prepared dishes like sauerkraut with pigs' knuckles and made a wide variety of sausages, including bologna, salami, souse, and numerous others. Today, factories in Pennsylvania produce all sorts of sausages and ship them to destinations throughout the United States.

Representing a combination of German and Native American influences, scrapple consists of pork scraps, cornmeal, and spices simmered together until it forms cornmeal mush. Cooks then place the mush in a pan to cool, then slice it and sauté the slices. Scrapple frequently accompanies the traditional hearty Pennsylvania Dutch breakfast.

In addition to pork, beef and chicken often graced tables. The Pennsylvania Dutch served traditional German dishes like *Sauerbraten*, sweet and sour marinated beef, as well as chicken pot pie.

Like meals in Germany, Pennsylvania Dutch meals included ample amounts of starches such as dumplings, noodles, and potatoes. Dumplings topped many stews and meat dishes or served as a side dish. Prepared in countless ways, potatoes and noodles regularly accompanied meals.

Baked goods leavened with yeast frequently incorporated mashed potatoes or the water left from cooking potatoes to add extra leavening and create lighter baked goods. Using the many egg whites remaining after making noodles, angel food cakes appeared often in the 1800s and later.

Following the German culinary tradition, Pennsylvania Dutch meals included a variety of sweet and sour foods. In fact, the custom states that each meal should contain seven sweets and seven sours. Examples of sweets are pickled pears, crabapples, spiced apples, relishes, jams, and preserves. Sour foods include sauerkraut, coleslaw (in a vinegar dressing), and pickled cucumbers or other vegetables.

A wealth of fruits and berries flourished throughout Pennsylvania. People stocked their root cellars with fresh apples, and they dried countless apples for use during the winter months in dishes ranging from entrées to pies. By substituting apples for plums, many made apple butter, which resembled the plum jam commonly served in Germany. The Quakers found peaches growing in Pennsylvania. It is believed the Native Americans brought them from Florida. Although the colonists transported pear seeds to their new land, they discovered the Seckel pear on a farm in Pennsylvania shortly after the Revolutionary War. Blueberries thrived here, and today they are eaten plain, frozen for winter use, made into jam, and added to muffins, pancakes, pies, cakes, and cobblers.

With an apple orchard growing on almost every farm, each year the farmers pressed the first of the apples for cider. After crushing the apples, they allowed the natural yeasts to ferment the juice. In addition, they sometimes used pears or peaches to make cider.

Soups and stews served as a mainstay for the early settlers in Pennsylvania as well as throughout the Middle Atlantic region. Available from the rivers, turtle appeared in both soups and stews. Another popular soup, the hearty Philadelphia pepper pot consisted of tripe, peppercorns, bones, and many scraps, herbs, and spices. Philadelphia pepper pot was created during the Revolutionary War from any and all available food products.

A frequently served one-pot dish, pigs' knuckles with sauerkraut dumplings (dumplings cooked in sauerkraut) reflected the strong German heritage. *Schnitz un knepp* consisted of smoked ham boiled with dried apples and then topped with dumplings. Hearty soups accompanied by fruit sometimes served as supper rather

(Continued)

and a strong sense of community guided the lives of the Amish. They carefully chose which "modern conveniences" to accept and formed self-sufficient communities where most families lived on farms producing what they needed. Today, many Amish still choose to live without many modern conveniences and travel in horse-drawn buggies instead of cars.

The German immigrants brought pretzels to Pennsylvania. Prior to the late 1600s, the soft texture of the pretzel resembled a roll rather than a cracker. Some time after that, a Pennsylvania baker supposedly fell asleep while tending the hearth—with most of their moisture gone, crisp pretzels emerged and soon became popular. In 1861, the first commercial pretzel bakery opened in Lititz, Pennsylvania.

In 1905, congealed salads thickened with gelatin appeared in Pennsylvania. The American population embraced this dish, and it remained popular until the middle to late 1900s. Although congealed salads were usually a sweet dish, some served savory congealed salads like tomato aspic. Because congealed salads require cold conditions to set, all of their preparation was completed in advance. This freed the cook for other tasks near the time of service.

In 1869, Henry Heinz opened a processing plant for horseradish near Pittsburgh. Although he declared bankruptcy in 1875, the plant soon reopened, and workers began preparing pickles, vinegar, sauerkraut, and

(Continued)

than as a first course. To make the soup more filling, cooks added dumplings, noodles, bread, or rivels, small dumplings made from flour and eggs. Rivels resemble German *spaetzel,* which is a cross between a noodle and a dumpling. Other well-liked soups in Pennsylvania Dutch country include potato soup and bean soup, as well as chicken and corn soup.

Cabbage played a significant role in the diet. Because this versatile winter vegetable thrived here, it filled root cellars for use throughout the winter as a salad (coleslaw), as a vegetable served on the side, or as an ingredient in soup or stew. In addition, settlers pickled cabbage and stored it as sauerkraut. The Dutch settlers introduced coleslaw, consisting of shredded cabbage in the dressing of choice, to this country. Today, coleslaw recipes abound, with some coating the shredded cabbage with a mayonnaise-based dressing, others preferring a dressing of vinegar and oil, and still others preparing a cooked dressing.

Settlers gathered a bounty of mushrooms from the many forests in Pennsylvania, and they appeared in numerous recipes including soups and entrées. Even recipes for chicken pot pies usually contained mushrooms in this area. About 1920, Pennsylvanians began growing mushrooms in caves and selling them throughout the United States. Mushrooms remain an important crop in Pennsylvania.

A hen house on each farm supplied eggs for breakfast as well as for making noodles and all sorts of desserts. In many communities, noodles accompanied at least one meal daily and dessert followed the main meal of the day. The dessert of choice in Pennsylvania Dutch communities, pies were baked in a wide variety of flavors: fresh fruits in the summer, dried fruits in the winter, and shoofly, buttermilk, or vinegar pie when no fruits were available. Although recipes for shoofly pie abound, all contain molasses, flour, and spices. The name derives from the necessity of shooing flies away from the baked pie. Because cooks had plenty of eggs, cakes and puddings also concluded many meals.

Pat and Harry Olivieri invented the Philadelphia steak sandwich around 1930. At their hot dog stand near the Italian section in south Philadelphia, Pat decided to make a beef sandwich for lunch instead of having a hot dog. He thinly sliced some steak, cooked it with onions, and put it on a roll. A taxi driver stopped for a hot dog, but after smelling the steak sandwich, asked for one. After tasting it, he told Olivieri to forget about hot dogs and sell the steak sandwiches. Twenty years later, an employee added cheese to the steak sandwich and the Philadelphia cheese steak sandwich was born. Today, the sandwich is ordered "wit," meaning with fried onions, or "witout."

A precursor to the vending machine, the first automat appeared in the early 1900s in Philadelphia and later in New York City. Like a combination of a food vending machine and a cafeteria, the automat dispensed plates of food from a vending machine after money was inserted. Before making their purchase, customers could see the enclosed food through a glass door. The first drip-brewed coffee was served in automats. Replaced by fast food restaurants, automats went out of business in the 1970s.

Initially, Swedish and Dutch immigrants settled Delaware, and they planted fields of wheat and rye. Before long, England gained control, and the cuisine of Delaware soon resembled the cookery of the English with Germanic overtones. More prevalent German influence appears in northern Delaware because it borders Pennsylvania, which contains strong German heritage.

The early settlers in Delaware found plenty to eat: venison, oysters, shrimp, crabs (including the prized blue crabs), turtles, more seafood, wild fruits, and berries. The Scandinavians planted peaches, plums, and cherries. After the Civil War, farmers started

(Continued)

catsup in addition to horseradish. Heinz obtained the patent for printed labels in 1897. Because of his excellent advertising and marketing skills, Heinz 57 became a household phrase. Soon Heinz plants opened in several locations near areas of fertile farmland within the United States. Their product line increased to include baby food, soups, and much more. Of course, the business still thrives today.

Founded in 1730, the oldest, still operating public market in the United States is located in Lancaster, Pennsylvania. Since Lancaster County is the center for the Amish and Mennonite communities, they sell all sorts of fruits and vegetables, meats, sausages, eggs, cheeses, herbs and spices, baked goods, fresh and dried flowers, crafts, and more at this market.

Philadelphia claims to be the home of the ice cream soda. In 1874, a salesman selling soda fountains ran out of cream for his usual demonstration product, consisting of sweet cream mixed with syrup and carbonated water. He substituted ice cream for the sweet cream and created the first ice cream soda.

Ice cream was promoted at the Philadelphia Exposition held in 1876, and Philadelphia became known for it. Today, many ice cream producers operate factories in or near Philadelphia and use dairy products from the numerous farms in this area.

commercially raising chickens for their eggs. The poultry industry still flourishes in Delaware with high production of eggs and broilers.

Lured by the promise of 100 acres in this new land, the first settlers from England arrived in Maryland in 1634. They planted orchards and grew extensive gardens containing many herbs, spices, and vegetables. Apples, tomatoes, and a wide range of fruits and vegetables thrived in Maryland's moderate climate. At first, the settlers wanted to prepare dishes from their native homeland like puddings and pies, but their English culinary background soon melded with two other factors: cooking traits from African slaves they imported to work the plantations and the indigenous foods found in Maryland.

While the English settlers remained in the southern and eastern portions near the Chesapeake Bay, the western regions of Maryland filled with people of German heritage who migrated from Pennsylvania. Of course, the cooking in each region reflected the influence of the people who settled there. The early settlers consumed ample amounts of game, and those living near rivers and bays feasted on the bounty of seafood. They also consumed much pork. Both fresh and cured ham appeared often. In Maryland, country hams aged for two to three years, resulting in a rich, smoky taste. As in several states in the Middle Atlantic region, dairy and chicken farms flourish throughout Maryland today.

When the early settlers first arrived at the Chesapeake Bay on the eastern side of Maryland, they discovered waters teeming with crab, oysters, clams, and many other varieties of fish and shellfish. In addition to seafood, bountiful wild ducks, geese, and other fowl in this coastal area provided more food for the early settlers. Although no longer abundant in the Chesapeake Bay, oysters and crabs prepared in countless ways still dominate menus in this region.

Crab imperial remains a popular and elegant entrée. Usually baked and served in individual casserole dishes, this dish features crab, diced sweet peppers, and mushrooms in a creamy, spicy sauce. Crab cakes reign as another favorite signature dish for Maryland. Whether fried, baked, spicy, or bland, most restaurants offer their own version of the "best crab cake" served in Maryland.

In the late 1700s and 1800s, the Germans planted wheat in the western part of the state, and it became an important crop in Maryland. With the wheat, they prepared the breads from Germany instead of the quick breads based on corn that prevailed throughout eastern and southern Maryland.

CHARACTERISTICS OF THE CUISINE

Simple and hearty describes the cookery of the Middle Atlantic States. Basically, the cuisine of this region resembles the cooking of New England with significant German and Dutch influence. This translates into a culinary combination of German, Dutch, English, and Native American cooking.

Since wheat and other grains grew better in the Middle Atlantic region than in New England, these settlers prepared a wide variety of breads, dumplings, noodles, pancakes, waffles, cakes, cookies, pies, and doughnuts from wheat, buckwheat, and rye. For grinding grains, they established mills along the rivers and used the flowing water to turn the mills.

To use leftover pieces of bread dough, the English boiled any remaining bits of dough for dumplings while the Dutch fried the balls of dough in grease. The Dutch called the fried dough *olykoeks*, oil cakes. Later, Dutch settlers in New York added currants or raisins to their *olykoeks* and called these rolled balls of dough "dough nuts." In the late 1700s, they formed the dough into a circle and removed the center to expedite the cooking, which spawned the modern doughnut.

As in New England, the settlers discovered a wealth of seafood such as oysters, crab, turtle, clams, and many varieties of fish in the ocean, bays, rivers, streams, and lakes found in the Middle Atlantic region. As a result, seafood and fish played a major role in the diet of the settlers and later inhabitants. While New England is known for the clambake, the oyster roast became the seafood event in the Middle Atlantic region. Roasted oysters served as the introduction for any large meal; in fact, settlers often consumed the plentiful oysters at breakfast, lunch, and dinner! They served them broiled, baked, stewed, scalloped, and raw.

A great fondness for cheese and dairy products emerged from their Dutch heritage. The early settlers raised dairy cows and made cheese, butter, and ice cream from the milk and cream. Like farmers in neighboring Vermont, New York farmers/cheesemakers produced excellent cheddar cheese. One of the few cheeses developed in the United States, Liederkranz cheese was first made in Monroe, New York, in 1892. It was named for the Liederkranz Club in New York. The Quakers in Pennsylvania also imported cows and produced cheese. Although first made in New York, cream cheese is associated with Philadelphia.

Soups, chowders, and stews frequented menus throughout the Middle Atlantic region. While soups and chowders served as a starter course for the meals of the wealthy, they were dinner for the poor. Any available ingredients entered the soup pot, including seafood, poultry, meat, and vegetables. Abundant in the Chesapeake and Delaware Bays in the early days, turtle and terrapin found their way into many soup pots as well as becoming an entrée. Cooks made snapper soup from snapping turtles in Philadelphia. Throughout the region, oyster stew and crab soup appeared on many menus.

Through the years, controversy surrounded clam chowder. The people in New England claimed the only "real" clam chowder contained milk or cream; in fact, the state legislature in Maine outlawed the combining of clams and tomatoes in clam chowder. Quite unlike the creamy clam chowder served throughout New England, a spicy tomato broth forms the base of Manhattan clam chowder. Still other versions of clam chowder exist, and in Maryland, clam chowder often contains chicken and vegetables in addition to seafood.

To fill the root cellars for winter consumption, the settlers' gardens produced hearty vegetables like cabbage, potatoes, carrots, and sweet potatoes. They also raised corn, berries, and many fruits that they dried, pickled, or made into preserves for the winter.

Throughout the East, people cherished all sorts of pies. Fruit pies remained the first choice, but when fruit was unavailable, they prepared all sorts of other pies featuring nut, buttermilk, or sugar fillings.

The Native Americans introduced the settlers to strawberries that grew larger than the varieties found in Europe. The settlers soon developed recipes for strawberry shortcake. This popular dessert consisted of sugared strawberries sandwiched between biscuit halves and topped with whipped cream.

Many varieties of apples thrive in the Middle Atlantic region, particularly in New York. Besides making hard cider and applejack (apple brandy) from them, cooks used apples in all sorts of savory and sweet dishes. Cooks made fresh and dried apples into a wide range of desserts like pies, cobblers, pandowdy, betty, crunch, crisps, cakes, and dumplings.

(Continued)

lifetime. **Already forming another shell underneath when its shell splits, the crab sheds the old shell and the new shell begins hardening right away. Crabs at this stage are called "soft-shell" crabs. Because the new shell is already in place, soft-shell crabs must be caught within 24 hours of molting while the shell is still soft enough to eat. A significant problem for soft-shelled crabs in their natural habitat is other crabs or predators eating the "defenseless" shell-less crab. Today, people place crabs ready to molt in pools to make it easier to spot the molting crabs and eliminate predators. In the meantime, attempts to develop viable methods for raising crabs to obtain soft-shell crabs continue.**

Cortland	sweet with tart	excellent baking and eating
Golden Delicious	sweet and juicy	good all purpose
Jonagold (cross between a Jonathan and a Golden Delicious)	sweet	excellent eating, fair for baking
Jonathan	moderately tart	good eating and baking
McIntosh	sweet but slightly tart	excellent eating, good baking
Northern Spy	tart	good all purpose
Rambo (oldest Pennsylvania apple)	tangy	excellent baking
Red Delicious	sweet and juicy	excellent eating, poor baking
Rhode Island Greening	tart	excellent baking
Rome Beauty	slightly tart	excellent baking
Stayman	sweet and tart	all purpose
Winesap	mildly tart	good eating

In 1851, the first cheddar cheese in this country was produced in Rome, New York. Of British origin, cheddar soon became one of the most popular cheeses in the United States.

First prepared near the Smoky Mountains, stack cake consisted of six or eight thin layers of molasses-flavored cake sandwiched with an apple or applesauce filling. Depending on the time of year, the filling contained fresh or dried apples.

Grapes still flourish in this region. New York ranks second to California in wine production, with most of the wine coming from the western part of the state, the Hudson River Valley, and Long Island. Pennsylvania, New Jersey, and Maryland produce wine, too.

As settlers moved west and south, they built railroads to connect all of the populated areas. The railroad facilitated the transportation of produce, meats, seafood, building materials, industrial products, and passengers throughout the country. Because this increased transportation helped many businesses, some men and their families amassed great wealth. With the creation of wealth came the demand for fine food and service.

In 1827, Swiss brothers Giovanni and Pietro Del-Monico opened their first restaurant, a cafe serving pastries, coffee, and wine in New York City. They expanded their business and started a French restaurant with an *a la carte* menu in 1830. Delmonico's became the first fine-dining restaurant not attached to a hotel in this country. According to accounts, Delmonico's wine cellar contained 16,000 bottles of wine in 1837, and, in 1838, their menu consisted of 100 pages! Beginning in 1862 and for more than thirty years, the creative French chef Charles Ranhofer ran the kitchen and developed a number of memorable dishes. Besides preparing classical dishes, Ranhofer used the bounty of American products and recipes for his menus. Furthermore, Ranhofer created a precedent by listing all items on the menu in both French and English.

Some of the dishes created at Delmonico's include lobster Newburg, a rich mixture of lobster, cream, sherry, and eggs; chicken à la king, creamed chicken and vegetables served over toast points; eggs Benedict, English muffins topped with Canadian bacon, poached eggs, and Hollandaise sauce; and baked Alaska. Originally called Alaska-Florida, the baked Alaska consisted of a core of ice cream placed on a foundation of cake, then covered with meringue. The cake and meringue insulated the ice cream while the meringue quickly browned in a very hot oven, resulting in a warm pastry hiding a cold surprise of ice cream inside.

In the early 1900s, French Chef Louis Diat first made *crème vichyssoise glacée* at the Ritz-Carlton Hotel in New York. Based on one of his mother's recipes, Diat's original recipe for this cold soup consisted of leeks, onions, potatoes, and cream puréed to form a smooth soup.

In 1872, Walter Scott of Providence, Rhode Island, parked a horse-drawn wagon outside of a newspaper office and sold food to the workers at night. His lunch wagon business was successful, and other people opened similar operations. In the 1890s, some moved their lunch wagon into out-of-commission trolley cars, and the lunch wagon became the diner. After adding a kitchen, booths, and tables, the trolley-turned-restaurant was ready for business. Regardless of the work shift, lunch wagons parked outside of factories and businesses to sell food to workers during their meal break. When the lunch wagons turned into diners, the business was no longer mobile. On the other hand, diners usually offered a large menu featuring breakfast, lunch, and dinner with a wide selection of choices at inexpensive or moderate prices. Since many people of Greek descent own diners, Greek specialties frequently appear on diner menus. For example, two commonly served Greek dishes are *souvlaki*, marinated lamb or chicken served in pita bread with a sour cream, garlic, and mint sauce, and *gyros*, rotisserie roasted lamb thinly sliced and served in pita bread with onions.

Known as the "deli," the delicatessen remains popular in New York City and many cities throughout the United States. Beginning in the late 1800s, the delicatessen began as a business selling foods from the native countries of various ethnic groups. In the beginning, Germans and Alsatians operated the delicatessens in this country. Later, Italians, Eastern Europeans, and people from different ethnicities opened them. The "typical" deli features a wide variety of sandwiches filled with combinations of smoked or cured meats and fish as well as soups, salads, condiments, and more. Sometimes, bowls of crunchy kosher dill pickles and pickled green tomatoes sit on the table as condiments in Jewish delis. Many feature combination sandwiches with amusing names or sandwiches named after someone. Since delicatessens originally opened as a haven for Jewish/Eastern European foods, deli menus frequently offer dishes like *blintzes*, cheese-filled crepes; *knishes*, potato- or meat-filled potato pastry; chicken soup with matzo balls; gefilte fish, a fish dumpling; *latkes*, potato pancakes; Reuben, sautéed sandwich filled with corned beef, sauerkraut, Swiss cheese, and Thousand Island dressing; and rye bread sandwiches piled high with pastrami, corned beef, tongue, salami, chopped liver, or other meats. Measuring about 3 to 4 inches tall, the famous New York–style cheesecake remains a popular deli dessert.

The colonists thought the water in their new land carried diseases, so fermented cider or beer accompanied meals in colonial days. Both cider and beer contained about six to eight percent alcohol. Colonists began making beer at home soon after arriving, but they used corn or other available grains in the absence of malted barley and hops. William Penn and his colonists began a brewery in Pennsylvania in 1683, but, according to some reports, they made beer with unusual ingredients like molasses, sassafras, and pine because traditional beer ingredients were limited. Cider ranked as the beverage of choice until the middle 1800s, when the availability of grains grown in the Midwest enabled the people to make traditional beer. At that time, beer replaced cider as the favorite alcoholic beverage.

Area	Weather	Topography	Foods
New York Canada to north, Vermont, Massachusetts, and Connecticut to east, New Jersey and Pennsylvania to south, Lake Erie and Lake Ontario to west; New Jersey west of New York City	harsh winters and cool summers in north; temperate, cool winters and warm summers in south	north: forests, mountains, many lakes, fertile valleys east: Hudson River, fertile valleys, hills south: Manhattan and Long Island; flat west: flat terrain; Finger Lakes, Lake Ontario, Lake Erie	cattle, game, geese, ducks, cod, shad, haddock, bluefish, striped bass, swordfish, flounder, oysters, scallops, clams, *foie gras*, sheep, cows, dairy, milk, cheese, apples, many fruits and vegetables, cherries, apricots, pears, blueberries, strawberries, grapes, wine, maple syrup
New Jersey New York and Pennsylvania to north, New York and Atlantic Ocean to east, Delaware and Atlantic to south, Delaware and Pennsylvania to west	temperate; cool winters, warm hot summers	Delaware River in west; Hudson River in east; swamp in central; Delaware Bay to southwest; forests, coastal plains, lakes, fertile valleys, rolling land, mountains	seafood, monkfish, mackerel, tuna, sea bass, squid, oysters, scallops, lobster, clams, crabs, shad, bluefish, bass, sturgeon, pike, dairy, eggs, many fruits and vegetables, corn, asparagus, lettuce, cabbage, carrots, potatoes, tomatoes, spinach, squash, beans, sweet potatoes, apples, peaches, strawberries, blueberries
Pennsylvania New York to north and east, New Jersey to east, Atlantic Ocean at southeast corner, Maryland and West Virginia to south, West Virginia and Ohio to west, Lake Erie to northwest	temperate; humid, cool winters, warm summers	mountains, hills, plateaus, rivers, streams, forests, fertile farmland; Allegheny Mountains north central to south and southeast, Delaware River east and central, Ohio River in west	pork, game, beef, sausage, chicken, milk, eggs, dairy, scrapple, noodles, dumplings, corn, buckwheat, oats, sauerkraut, cabbage, carrots, mushrooms, sweet potatoes, potatoes, pickles, peaches, apples, cherries, grapes, blueberries, strawberries, pears, many fruits and vegetables, pies, ice cream
Delaware Pennsylvania and Maryland to north, Atlantic and Delaware Bay to east, Virginia to south, Maryland to west	temperate; humid, cool winters, hot summers	Atlantic and Delaware Bay to east; Chesapeake to west; low flat coastal plains, Delaware River, hills and valleys in north; forests	seafood, oysters, crabs, shrimp, clams, shad, bass, turtle, venison, chicken, eggs, wheat, rye, horseradish, peaches, plums, cherries, wild fruits, berries
Maryland Pennsylvania to north, Delaware and Atlantic to east, Virginia on south and west, West Virginia and Washington, D.C., on west	temperate; humid, mild winters, hot summers	Chesapeake Bay in middle, Patuxent River runs through southeast, Potomac River on southern border east: low, flat plains west: hills, valleys, mountains, plateaus, fertile farmland, forests, coast, inlets, harbors	seafood, oysters, crabs, clams, striped bass, turtle, game, pork, ham, ducks, geese, chicken, dairy, eggs, wheat, corn, biscuits, cornbread, many fruits and vegetables, tomatoes, apples

REVIEW QUESTIONS

1. Discuss the people who settled in Pennsylvania, including the countries they left, why they wanted to emigrate, and the effect of those heritages on the cuisine.

2. Name and describe, if needed, at least five dishes commonly served by the Pennsylvania Dutch.

3. Discuss the topography of the Chesapeake Bay and why the colonists settled there.

4. What is a soft-shell crab and how does it come into being?

5. Explain why New Jersey is called the "Garden State."

6. Describe the settling of eastern New Jersey and western New Jersey, including who settled there and how they managed financially.

applejack—apple brandy

baked Alaska—originally called Alaska-Florida, the baked Alaska contains a core of ice cream placed on a foundation of cake, and then covered with meringue. The cake and meringue insulate the ice cream while the meringue quickly cooks in a very hot oven. Delmonico's Restaurant in New York City first served the baked Alaska to celebrate the purchase of Alaska.

blintzes—cheese-filled crepes

chicken à la king—creamed chicken and vegetables served over toast points, from the menu of Delmonico's Restaurant

eggs Benedict—English muffins topped with Canadian bacon, poached eggs, and Hollandaise sauce, created and served at Delmonico's Restaurant

estuary—partially enclosed body of water that forms when fresh water sources meet with salt water

foie gras—the enlarged liver from goose or duck; to enlarge the liver, the birds are fed large amounts of food

gefilte fish—a fish dumpling

hutspot—meaning hodgepodge, a hearty Dutch stew made in colonial America containing cornmeal porridge, corned beef, and winter vegetables from the root cellar

kasha—buckwheat groats

knishes—potato- or meat-filled potato pastry

koolslaa—the Dutch word for coleslaw, this salad consisted of shredded cabbage and a dressing, often prepared in the winter months since cabbage stored well in a root cellar

kugel—noodle or potato pudding

latkes—potato pancakes

lobster Newburg—a rich mixture of lobster, cream, sherry, and eggs, created and served at Delmonico's Restaurant

olykoeks—oil cakes, prepared by the Dutch settlers in New York by dropping rolled balls of dough, "dough nuts," into hot fat. In the late 1700s, they shaped the dough into a circle and removed the center (creating a hole) to expedite the cooking, resulting in the modern doughnut.

rivels—made from flour and eggs, they resemble German *spaetzel*, which is a cross between a noodle and a dumpling

Reuben—sautéed sandwich filled with corned beef, sauerkraut, Swiss cheese, and Thousand Island dressing

Sauerbraten—sweet and sour marinated beef originally from Germany

sauerkraut dumplings—dumplings cooked in sauerkraut

Schnitz un knepp—Pennsylvania Dutch dish consisting of smoked ham boiled with dried apples and topped with dumplings

Souvlaki—Greek preparation of marinated lamb or chicken, usually served in pita bread and accompanied by sour cream, garlic, and mint sauce

CRAB CAKES

Crab Cakes

photo courtesy of McCormick Spices

Crab cakes can be deep-fried, broiled, or baked instead of pan-fried, if desired. If serving as an entrée, just double the serving size.

NUMBER OF SERVINGS: 14
COOKING METHOD:
  Pan-fry or deep-fry
SERVING SIZE:
  1 each 3-oz crab cake
TOTAL YIELD:
  2 lb, 12 oz raw mixture
  14 each 3-oz crab cakes

Wine Style: Sauvignon Blanc, Pinot Blanc, Pinot Gris, or Chenin Blanc
Example: Fumé Blanc—Cove Point Winery, Lusby, MD. Sauvignon Blanc grapes fermented in Hungarian oak deliver a wine with crisp acidity, hints of green apples and melons, and a light citrus finish.

INGREDIENTS	WEIGHT	VOLUME
crab meat, lump	2 lb	
mayonnaise	2 oz	1/4 cup
dry mustard	1/2 oz	1 tablespoon + 1 teaspoon
seafood seasoning like Old Bay	1/2 oz	2 teaspoons
Worcestershire sauce	1 oz	2 tablespoons
Tabasco or hot pepper sauce		1 1/2 teaspoons
cracker crumbs	4 1/2 oz	1 1/2 cups
egg	3 1/2 oz	2 each
salt	to taste	
pepper	to taste	
parsley, minced	1 oz	1/4 cup
fat for frying		

GARNISH:
lemon wedges
tartar sauce, cocktail sauce, or sauce of choice

1. Gently mix crab meat, mayonnaise, mustard, Old Bay seasoning, Worcestershire sauce, hot pepper sauce, cracker crumbs, egg, salt, pepper, and parsley in bowl. Be careful not to break up pieces of crab meat by mixing too much.

2. Gently form 3 oz of mixture into 3- to 4-inch cake. Keep crab cake as loose as possible; do not firmly pack crab mixture together.

3. Place about 1/2 inch oil or butter in skillet; heat until hot.

4. Fry crab cakes until golden brown on each side; remove to absorbent paper to drain. If necessary, keep warm in oven while frying others.

5. Serve immediately, accompanied by lemon wedges and tartar sauce, cocktail sauce, or sauce of choice.

CRISP CRAB CAKES WITH CELERI AND FENNEL SLAW

Recipe by Charlie Palmer

Chef and restaurateur Charlie Palmer from New York City contributed the following recipe. Begin slaw preparation six hours ahead or the day before needed.

NUMBER OF SERVINGS: 12
COOKING METHOD:
  Bake, Deep-fry or Pan-fry
SERVING SIZE:
  Crab cake: 1 each
  Slaw: 2¼ oz
  Tartar sauce: 2¼ oz
TOTAL YIELD:
  Crab cake: 4 lbs, 12 oz
  Slaw: 1 lb, 12 oz
  Tartar sauce: 1 lb, 13 oz

Wine Style: Sauvignon Blanc, Pinot Blanc, Pinot Gris, Chenin Blanc, Seyval Blanc, or Chardonnay
Example: Seyval-Vidal-Chardonnay—Boordy Vineyards, Hydes, MD. This mouth-watering grape trio produces a wine with aromas of melon and herbs, a fresh flavor, and a crisp finish.

INGREDIENTS	WEIGHT	VOLUME
CRAB CAKES:		
Béchamel Sauce:		
butter	4 oz	½ cup or 1 stick
celery, small dice or minced	5 oz	1 cup
red onion, small dice or minced	5 oz	1 cup
garlic, minced	1½ oz	2 tablespoons
Old Bay seasoning	1½ oz	¼ cup
flour, all purpose, sifted	3 oz	½ cup
milk, hot	1 lb	2 cups
cod	12 oz	
olive oil	for brushing	
salt	to taste	
white pepper	to taste	
crab meat, lump	1 lb, 8 oz	
Dijon mustard	2 oz	¼ cup
chives, minced	1 oz	¼ cup
BREADING:		
flour	as needed	
egg, beaten	as needed	
Panko bread crumbs	as needed	
SLAW:		
fennel, trimmed of fronds, cut in half	1 lb	2 heads
celeri root, peeled	1 lb	2 medium
white wine vinegar	1lb, 8 oz	3 cups
sugar	1 lb, 6½ oz	3 cups

For Crab Cakes:

To Prepare Béchamel Sauce:

1. Melt butter in heavy-bottomed pan. Add celery, onion, and garlic; sauté for about 5 minutes.

2. Add Old Bay seasoning; continue cooking 1 to 2 minutes. Whisk in flour and cook over moderate heat, whisking constantly until flour combines with butter.

3. Slowly whisk milk into flour mixture. Reduce heat to low; stir often and cook for about 5 minutes. Remove from heat, cool, cover and refrigerate until needed.

To Continue Crab Cakes:

1. Preheat oven to 350 degrees. Pan-spray baking sheet. Brush cod with olive oil; sprinkle with salt and white pepper.

2. Cook until cod flakes, about 10 minutes for each inch of thickness. Remove from oven, cool, and gently flake cod into bowl.

3. Add crab, chilled béchamel, mustard, and chives to bowl. Fold in *very* gently so fish stays in chunks and does not break into little pieces.

4. Correct seasonings; divide mixture evenly and form into 6-oz patties.

5. Using standard breading procedure, dredge each fish cake with flour, dip in egg, then coat with Panko bread crumbs. Place on pan or plate, cover, and store in refrigerator until needed.

For Slaw:

1. Using mandoline if available, thinly slice fennel. Finely julienne celeri root. Place in bowl together.

2. Add vinegar, sugar, and salt; mix to combine. Cover and refrigerate at least 6 hours or overnight.

3. Place vegetables in clean kitchen towel; squeeze to remove all excess moisture. Roughly chop vegetables and return to bowl.

4. Mix in mayonnaise, salt, and white pepper. Correct seasonings. Cover and refrigerate until needed.

INGREDIENTS	WEIGHT	VOLUME
salt	1 oz	1 tablespoon + 1 teaspoon
mayonnaise	12½ oz	1½ cup
salt	to taste	
white pepper	to taste	

AVOCADO TARTAR SAUCE:

avocado, peeled, seed removed, medium dice	12 oz	2 each
lime juice	2 oz	¼ cup
shallot, minced	1 oz	2 tablespoons
cornichon, minced	1½ oz	3 tablespoons
capers, chopped	1½ oz	3 tablespoons
dill, minced	1 oz	¼ cup
crème fraîche, whipped	7 oz	2 cups
salt	to taste	
white pepper	to taste	
oil for frying		

GARNISHES:

dill oil	4 oz	½ cup
yellow and red bell pepper, roasted, puréed	1 lb	4 each yellow
dill sprigs, fresh		and 4 each red

For Tartar Sauce:

1. Carefully fold all ingredients together in bowl. Season with salt and white pepper.
2. Cover tightly with plastic film; refrigerate until needed.

For Assembly:

1. Preferably, deep-fry crab cakes, but if desired, pan fry in ½ inch oil. Heat oil to 350 degrees in skillet over medium-high heat or deep-fryer.
2. Add crab cakes, a few at a time so oil temperature does not drop too much. Fry until golden, turn, fry other side. Remove from pan, drain on absorbent toweling, and keep warm until needed.
3. Using 4-inch ring as guide, place thin 4-inch disk of slaw on room temperature plate.
4. Place one crab cake on top of the slaw, and place large quenelle (oval dollop) of tartar sauce on top of crab cake.
5. Decorate plate with dill oil and dots of roasted pepper purée. Garnish with sprigs of dill. Serve immediately.

Copyright Charlie Palmer

CHARLIE PALMER
Executive Chef & Restaurateur

In 1988, at the age of 28, Charlie Palmer opened Aureole, his first restaurant in New York City. Initially serving as chef and proprietor of Aureole, Palmer now owns ten restaurants and catering operations in various locations including New York, Washington, D.C., Las Vegas, Los Angeles, and Sonoma. With a continually expanding resume, he has made many television appearances, designed over 200 recipes for use on the Seabourn Cruise Lines, received several James Beard awards as well as numerous other honors and accolades, and is the author of several cookbooks.

Palmer is known for his signature "Progressive American" cuisine. This style reinterprets classic European cooking using American artisanal products and small farm producers. Commenting on his culinary philosophy, Palmer says, "I realized that American cuisine was just in its infancy and I spent a lot of time thinking about what the idea of American cooking really meant to me as a chef."

Highly influenced by his childhood on a farm in upstate New York and the time spent at Georges Blanc in France, Palmer says of Georges Blanc, "One artisanal producer would bring all of his perfectly made goat cheese to the doorstep of our kitchen—that had a strong impact on me." He began to research small American producers and to support them in an effort to use the best raw products available at his restaurant, Aureole. He credits this with inspiring his creativity and helping to define his style. Palmer is a graduate of the Culinary Institute of America.

FOIE GRAS WITH APPLES

Foie Gras with Apples

NUMBER OF SERVINGS: 8
COOKING METHOD:
  Boil, Sauté
SERVING SIZE:
  2 oz *foie gras*, 2 oz apples,
  3/4 oz (1 1/2 tablespoons)
  sauce

Wine Style: Sparkling wines, Rieslings, or rich, full-bodied Chardonnays
Example: Chateau Frank Brut Champagne—Dr. Konstantin Frank Winery, Hammondsport, NY. A great balance between the fruity Pinot Noir and the acidity of Chardonnay results in a long clean finish. This wine has great complexity with citrus flavors and mineral characteristics.

INGREDIENTS	WEIGHT	VOLUME
apples, tart like Granny Smith, peeled, cores removed, sliced 1/2-inch thick	1 lb	
brandy	2 oz	1/4 cup
apple cider or juice	8 oz	1 cup
flour, all purpose	1 1/2 oz	6 tablespoons
salt		1/2 teaspoon
pepper		1/4 teaspoon
foie gras, 1/2-inch thick	1 lb	8 each 2-oz slices
butter	1/2 oz	1 tablespoon
brandy	2 oz	1/4 cup
apple cider or juice	4 oz	1/2 cup
white wine	1 oz	2 tablespoons
nutmeg		1/2 teaspoon

1. Place apple slices, 2 oz (1/4 cup) brandy, and 8 oz (1 cup) apple cider in pot. Bring to boil, reduce heat, and poach until just tender, no more than 5 minutes. Remove apples, reserve.
2. Stirring occasionally, continue boiling liquid until reduced to 2 oz (1/4 cup). Reserve.
3. Mix flour, salt, and pepper on plate. Dredge *foie gras* in flour mixture.
4. Heat butter in skillet until hot. Sauté *foie gras* until brown on both sides, 1 to 2 minutes per side. Remove *foie gras* and reserve.
5. Discard all except 1 oz (2 tablespoons) of fat. Add 2 oz (1/4 cup) brandy, 4 oz (1/2 cup) apple cider, white wine, nutmeg, and reserved liquid from apples. Stirring occasionally, boil to reduce until about 3 oz (6 tablespoons).
6. Arrange or fan 2 oz apple slices on plate. Top with *foie gras* and 3/4 oz (1 1/2 tablespoons) sauce.

CHICKEN CORN SOUP WITH RIVELS

Forming Rivels with Two Teaspoons over Pot of Soup

Chicken Corn Soup with Rivels

A cross between noodles and dumplings, rivels make this soup a filling enough dish to easily serve as an entrée. If desired, prepare the soup without the addition of rivels or substitute egg noodles for them.

NUMBER OF SERVINGS: 13
COOKING METHOD:
  Boil
SERVING SIZE:
  9 oz
TOTAL YIELD:
  7 lbs, 6 1/2 oz

INGREDIENTS	WEIGHT	VOLUME
RIVELS:		
flour, all purpose	11½ oz	2½ cups
egg	3½ oz	2 each
milk	4 oz	½ cup
SOUP:		
butter	6 oz	12 tablespoons or 1½ sticks
onion, small dice	6 oz	1⅓ cups or 1 medium to large
celery, small dice	13½ oz	3 cups or about 7 ribs
carrot, small dice	4 oz	2 small
flour, all purpose	3½ oz	¾ cup
chicken stock, strong, hot	6 lbs	3 qts
corn, removed from cob fresh or frozen	1 lb, 2½ oz	4 cups
half-and-half	1 lb, 8 oz	3 cups
parsley, minced	½ oz	¼ cup
nutmeg, grated		¾ teaspoon
white pepper	¼ oz	1½ teaspoons
poultry seasoning		1 teaspoon
chicken, cooked, diced or shredded, ¾-inch pieces	1 lb, 8½ oz	6 cups

For Rivels:

1. Place flour in bowl; make well in center.
2. Beat eggs to mix. Pour eggs into well in flour; mix with fork until just combined.
3. Add milk. Mix dough with fingertips until pieces the size of peas.
4. Add additional flour if dough is too thin. Cover; set aside until needed.

For Soup:

1. Melt butter in large pot. Add onions, celery, and carrots. Sauté for about 3 minutes, until softened.
2. Whisk in flour; sauté a few minutes until blonde roux.
3. Slowly add chicken stock, whisking constantly. Bring to boil; add corn, half-and-half, parsley, nutmeg, white pepper, poultry seasoning, and chicken. Reduce heat and simmer about 5 to 10 minutes, until slightly thickened.
4. Bring back to boil; add rivels into boiling liquid. To form rivels, use two teaspoons. Fill one teaspoon with dough; use other spoon to scoot pea-sized pieces off spoon and into soup.
5. Cook another 8 to 10 minutes, until rivels are done.
6. Correct seasonings. Serve.

CRAB BISQUE

Crab Bisque
photo by Clive Streeter © Dorling Kindersley

NUMBER OF SERVINGS: 10
COOKING METHOD:
  Boil
SERVING SIZE:
  8 oz
TOTAL YIELD:
  5 lbs, 7¾ oz

INGREDIENTS	WEIGHT	VOLUME
butter	4 oz	½ cup or 1 stick
onion, medium dice	2 oz	½ small
carrot, peeled, medium dice	2 oz	1 small
celery, medium dice	2 oz	1 rib
garlic, minced	¼ oz	1 large or 2 small cloves
flour, all purpose	4 oz	⅞ cup
fish, shrimp, crab, or lobster stock, hot	4 lbs	2 qts
tomato paste	1 oz	1½ tablespoons
sherry, dry	2 oz	¼ cup
white wine	4 oz	½ cup
SACHET:		
bay leaf		1 each
peppercorns, crushed		¼ teaspoon
thyme		½ teaspoon
parsley stems		4 each
heavy cream	8 oz	1 cup
salt	¼ oz	1 teaspoon
white pepper		¼ teaspoon
Old Bay seasoning		½ teaspoon
nutmeg, grated		½ teaspoon
cayenne pepper, ground		⅛ teaspoon or to taste
crabmeat, lump	1 lb	
GARNISH:		
chives, chopped		
paprika		

1. Melt butter in saucepan. Sauté onion, carrot, and celery until tender.
2. Add garlic, cook a minute, then sprinkle flour over vegetables. Whisk for about two minutes, until blonde roux.
3. Over low heat, slowly whisk in hot fish stock, adding a little at a time. Raise heat; bring mixture to boil, whisking occasionally.
4. Reduce heat to simmer. Add tomato paste, sherry, white wine, and sachet bag containing bay leaf, peppercorns, thyme, and parsley. Simmer for 45 minutes.
5. Strain through sieve lined with dampened cheesecloth.
6. Return to heat; add cream, salt, white pepper, Old Bay seasoning, nutmeg, cayenne, and crab. Bring to simmer.
7. Correct seasonings, serve garnished with chopped chives and/or paprika.

WALDORF SALAD

Waldorf Salad
photo by Dave King © Dorling Kindersley

Endless variations of this salad exist. Supposedly, the original contained apples, celery, nuts, and mayonnaise. Many add grapes, others use raisins, and still others replace some or all of the mayonnaise with plain unflavored yogurt to create a version with fewer calories.

NUMBER OF SERVINGS: 13
SERVING SIZE:
  4 oz
TOTAL YIELD:
  3 lbs, 5½ oz

INGREDIENTS	WEIGHT	VOLUME
apples, peeled, cored, medium dice	1 lb, 3½ oz	4 cups
celery, medium dice	9 oz	2 cups
walnuts, chopped, toasted	8 oz	2 cups
grapes, seedless, cut in half	11 oz	2 cups
mayonnaise	8½ oz	1 cup

GARNISH:

lettuce leaves, whole or chiffonade

1. Place all ingredients in bowl. Mix gently to combine well.
2. Cover and chill until serving time.
3. Serve on lettuce leaf or bed of lettuce.

CREAMY COLESLAW

Creamy Coleslaw
photo © 2008 StockFood

NUMBER OF SERVINGS: 8
SERVING SIZE:
  4 oz
TOTAL YIELD:
  2 lbs

INGREDIENTS	WEIGHT	VOLUME
cabbage, shredded	1 lb	1 small head or 8 cups
carrot, peeled, shredded	4½ oz	2 small
green pepper, small dice	3 oz	½ medium
DRESSING:		
mayonnaise	7½ oz	¾ cup
sugar	1¼ oz	3 tablespoons
vinegar, cider	1 oz	2 tablespoons
celery seed		½ teaspoon
Worcestershire sauce		½ teaspoon
Dijon mustard		½ teaspoon
salt		½ teaspoon

1. Mix cabbage, carrot, and green pepper in bowl.
2. In separate bowl, combine all dressing ingredients; mix well.
3. Combine dressing mixture and cabbage mixture, mixing well to coat all vegetables with dressing.
4. Correct seasonings. Cover and refrigerate until serving time.

CHICKEN POT PIE

Chicken Pot Pie

photo courtesy of National Turkey Federation. For more cooking tips and recipe ideas, visit www.eatturkey.com

If possible, make chicken stock for this dish the day before so the fat has time to congeal on the refrigerated stock, making it easy to remove. Use strong chicken stock for filling! Also, the pie dough can be prepared a day or two in advance.

For buffets or steam table service, this recipe can be prepared in a 9- by 13-inch pan or steam table pan, if desired. If holding this dish on a steam table, add 8 oz to 1 lb (1 to 2 cups) extra chicken stock to the filling to create a looser sauce because filling ingredients will absorb the sauce while sitting.

NUMBER OF SERVINGS: 13
COOKING METHOD:
  Boil, Sauté, Bake
SERVING SIZE:
  1 each au gratin dish
  8 oz filling and 3 oz dough
TOTAL YIELD:
  2 lb, 7¹/₂ oz pie dough
  6 lb, 10¹/₂ oz filling

Wine Style: Light- to medium-bodied Chenin Blanc, Pinot Gris, or Sauvignon Blanc
Example: Sauvignon Blanc—Duck Walk Vineyards, Southampton, NY. This wine is crisp and fresh with a natural herbaceous character.

INGREDIENTS	WEIGHT	VOLUME
STOCK:		
chicken, whole or combination of breasts, legs, and thighs, washed	about 5 to 5¹/₂ lbs	
onion, peeled, cut in half	8 oz	1 large
carrots, peeled, cut in half	7¹/₄ oz	3 medium
celery, cut into 3-inch pieces	5¹/₂ oz	2 ribs
bay leaf		1 each
water	to cover	
PIE DOUGH:		
flour, all purpose	1 lb, 4 oz	4¹/₃ cups
salt	¹/₄ oz	1 teaspoon
butter, lard, or shortening, cold, cut into pieces	13³/₄ oz	1²/₃ cups
cold water	6³/₄ oz	³/₄ cup + 1¹/₂ tablespoons
FILLING:		
butter	2 oz	¹/₄ cup or ¹/₂ stick or 4 tablespoons
onion, medium dice	4¹/₂ oz	1 medium
flour, all purpose	2 oz	¹/₃ cup + 1¹/₂ tablespoons
chicken stock, strong, hot	2 lbs, 8 oz	5 cups or 1 qt + 1 cup
light cream	4 oz	¹/₂ cup
chicken, cooked, skinned, boned, diced into 1-inch pieces	1 lb, 15 oz	6 cups

For Stock:

1. Combine chicken, onion, carrots, celery, and bay leaf in large pot. Fill with water, covering chicken by 2 inches.
2. Cover, bring to boil, lower heat, and simmer for one hour or until chicken is done.
3. Remove chicken; cool until it can be handled. Remove skin, bones, and cartilage.
4. Strain stock. Reserve carrots for filling. Let stock cool, then refrigerate overnight if possible, and remove solidified fat from top the next day.

For Pie Dough in Food Processor:

1. Place flour and salt in bowl of food processor; pulse to mix.
2. Place butter pieces on top; pulse until size of peas.
3. With motor running, add water through feed tube. Pulse until dough comes together into several big pieces or ball.
4. Remove from bowl; knead once or twice to form ball.
5. Cover and refrigerate for several hours or overnight. If time for refrigeration is short, flatten wrapped ball of dough into disk and place in freezer until cold.

For Pie Dough by Hand:

1. Place flour and salt in bowl. Place butter pieces on top.
2. With finger tips, two knives, or pastry mixer, cut in butter until evenly mixed into pieces no larger than peas.
3. Add water; stir quickly with fork to moisten evenly. Knead a couple of times to make ball. Add a few drops water if too dry; add sprinkling of flour if too wet.
4. Cover and refrigerate for several hours or overnight. If time for refrigeration is short, flatten wrapped ball of dough into disk and place in freezer until cold.

For Filling:

1. Melt butter in large pot over medium heat; add onion and sauté until translucent, about 3 minutes.

INGREDIENTS	WEIGHT	VOLUME
carrots, cooked, reserved from stock preparation, medium dice	7¼ oz	3 medium
potatoes, medium dice	1 lb, 2¼ oz	3 cups, about 3 medium
mustard, ground		½ teaspoon
white pepper		½ teaspoon
nutmeg, grated		½ teaspoon
thyme, dried		1½ teaspoons
salt	¼ oz	1 teaspoon
Worcestershire sauce		½ teaspoon
parsley, fresh, minced	½ oz	¼ cup
peas, fresh or frozen	10 oz	2 cups

2. Whisk in flour; cook about 2 to 3 minutes for blonde roux.
3. Gradually whisk in hot chicken stock, letting flour absorb each addition.
4. Whisk in cream; simmer about 20 minutes, until mixture thickens slightly.
5. Add chicken, carrots, potatoes, mustard, white pepper, nutmeg, thyme, salt, and Worcestershire sauce. Mix to combine; correct seasonings.
6. Add parsley and peas.

For Assembly:

1. Position oven rack in top half of oven. Preheat oven to 350 degrees.
2. Pour 8 oz filling into serving dishes.
3. Roll pie dough to desired thickness, about ⅛ inch. About 3 oz dough will cover standard au gratin dish.
4. Cover top of dish with pie dough; crimp edges on dish. Cut 2 slits into crust so steam can escape.
5. Bake for 30 to 40 minutes, until crust is golden.
6. Remove from oven, cool about 5 to 10 minutes, and serve.

DUCK WITH GRAPES

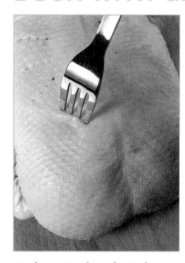

Sticking Duck with Fork
photo by Dave King © Dorling Kindersley

Duck with Grapes

For crisp duck, place duck in broiler while deglazing the pan. Broil until crisp and golden on both sides.

NUMBER OF SERVINGS:
  8 or 4
COOKING METHOD:
  Bake
SERVING SIZE:
  ¼ duck or ½ duck
SAUCE:
  2 oz for ¼ duck, 4 oz for ½ duck
TOTAL YIELD:
  5 lbs, 8½ oz
SAUCE:
  1 lb, ½ oz

Wine Style: Light- to medium-bodied Riesling, Gewürztraminer, Grenache, Pinot Noir, mild Shiraz, or Zinfandel
Example: Pinot Noir—Castello di Borghese/Hargrave Vineyards, Cutchogue, NY. This classic Pinot Noir contains exotic aromas of black cherry, roses, and currants.

INGREDIENTS	WEIGHT	VOLUME
ducks, washed, giblets removed from neck cavity	8 lb, 1½ oz	2 each
salt		to taste
pepper		to taste
bay leaf		2 each
onion, peeled, halved	6 oz	2 small
water	8 oz	1 cup
SAUCE:		
red wine	4 oz	½ cup
brandy	2 oz	¼ cup
chicken or duck stock, strong	8 oz	1 cup
cornstarch		1 teaspoon
water, cold	½ oz	1 tablespoon
grapes, red, seedless, washed	8 oz	1½ cups

1. Preheat oven to 425 degrees.
2. Season inside cavity of each duck with salt, pepper, and bay leaf, and place halved small onion (3 oz) inside cavity.
3. Place duck on rack in roasting pan, breast side up. Pierce duck all over with fork to allow fat to drain.
4. Roast for 5 minutes; reduce oven temperature to 375 degrees.
5. Drain fat from pan after 30 minutes. Turn duck over on breast; pierce duck all over with fork.
6. Cook another 30 minutes, drain fat, and turn duck breast side up; pierce duck all over with fork.
7. Continue baking, draining fat occasionally, until duck reaches proper internal temperature, about 2 hours total.
8. Remove duck from pan. Keep warm while making sauce in pan used for roasting duck. If crisp duck is desired, while preparing sauce, place duck under broiler until crisp and golden on both sides. Keep warm until ready to serve.

For Sauce:
1. Remove as much fat as possible from roasting pan.
2. Add wine, brandy, and stock. Deglaze pan over high heat by scraping any bits from bottom of pan while liquid reduces for two minutes.
3. Mix cornstarch with cold water until smooth paste. Reduce heat to medium, whisk cornstarch into stock mixture, and return to boil, whisking constantly.
4. Add grapes.
5. Continue cooking, stirring often, until sauce thickens and coats spoon. If it becomes too thick, add a little stock and/or wine.

For Assembly:
1. Cut duck into desired serving size (quarter or half).
2. Ladle sauce (2 oz for ¼ duck, 4 oz for ½ duck) over duck. Serve immediately.

MUSHROOM STUFFED MEATLOAF

Mushroom Stuffed Meatloaf
photo courtesy of Mushroom Information Center

This recipe produces extra sauce, so if increasing the recipe size, adjust sauce measurements as needed.

NUMBER OF SERVINGS: 10
COOKING METHOD:
  Bake
SERVING SIZE:
  7 oz meat, 1½ to 2 oz sauce
TOTAL YIELD:
  4 lbs, 11 oz raw meat mixture
  4 lbs, 12 oz cooked meat loaf
  1 lb, 10 oz sauce

Wine Style: Medium- to full-bodied dry red wines, Cabernet Franc, Cabernet Sauvignon, or Shiraz
Example: Cabernet Franc—Millbrook Vineyards and Winery, Millbrook, NY. This wine has fruity aromas with hints of red currant, black cherry, and cinnamon. It contains soft tannins and a smooth finish.

INGREDIENTS	WEIGHT	VOLUME
STUFFING:		
butter	2 oz	4 tablespoons or 1/2 stick
onion, minced	10 oz	2 cups
mushrooms, sliced 1/8-inch	8 oz	3 cups
sour cream	81/2 oz	1 cup
MEAT:		
ground beef	1 lb, 8 oz	
ground pork	1 lb, 8 oz	
eggs	63/4 oz	4 each
bread crumbs	6 oz	11/2 cups
milk	8 oz	1 cup
catsup	3 oz	1/4 cup
Worcestershire sauce		2 teaspoons
brown sugar	1 oz	2 tablespoons
salt	1 oz	1 tablespoon + 1 teaspoon
water, cold	3 oz	6 tablespoons
bacon	31/2 oz	4 strips
SAUCE:		
butter	1 oz	2 tablespoons
mushrooms, sliced 1/8 inch	101/2 oz	4 cups
sour cream	1 lb, 1 oz	2 cups
horseradish	1 oz	1 tablespoon
Dijon mustard	1/2 oz	2 teaspoons
nutmeg		1/2 teaspoon
salt	1/4 oz	1 teaspoon
white pepper		1/2 teaspoon

For Stuffing:

1. Melt butter in skillet. Add onion and mushrooms; sauté until wilted.
2. Remove from heat; stir in sour cream. Set aside until needed.

For Meat and Assembly:

1. Preheat oven to 350 degrees.
2. Combine beef, pork, eggs, bread crumbs, milk, catsup, Worcestershire sauce, brown sugar, salt, and water in bowl. Mix thoroughly.
3. Divide half of meat mixture between 2 each 9- by 5- by 3-inch (2 qt) loaf pans. Make trough or indentation down center of each loaf.
4. Place half of stuffing mixture into each trough.
5. Top each with remaining meat, making sure stuffing mixture is covered and edges are sealed.
6. Place 2 strips of bacon over each meatloaf. Bake for 1 hour.
7. Remove from oven; let stand about 5 minutes before removing from pan. Let stand another few minutes to firm before slicing.

For Sauce:

1. While meatloaf bakes, prepare sauce. Melt butter in skillet, add mushrooms, and sauté until lightly brown.
2. Add remaining sauce ingredients; stir over low heat.
3. Correct seasonings.

To Finish:

1. Slice meatloaf into 1/2-inch slices. Place 7 oz of meat slices on plate.
2. Spoon sauce over meatloaf slices. Serve immediately.

SCHNITZ UND KNEPP

Schnitz und Knepp

Schnitz is from the German word for cut and refers to the apple slices (cut apples) and knepp *refers to dumplings.*

NUMBER OF SERVINGS: 8
COOKING METHOD:
  Boil
SERVING SIZE:
  10 oz
TOTAL YIELD:
  5 lbs, 4 oz

Wine Style: Light- to medium-bodied reds, Merlot, Gamay, Grenache, or Pinot Noir
Example: Merlot—Laurel Mountain Winery, Falls Creek, PA. This wine is medium-bodied with nice soft tannins and a smooth taste.

INGREDIENTS	WEIGHT	VOLUME
cured or smoked ham or smoked pork picnic	2 lbs	
water	to cover	
dried apples, rings cut in half	5 oz	2 cups
brown sugar, firmly packed	2¼ oz	¼ cup
DUMPLINGS:		
flour, all purpose, unsifted	9 oz	2 cups
baking powder	½ oz	1 tablespoon + 1½ teaspoons
salt		½ teaspoon
egg	1¾ oz	1 each
milk	6 oz	¾ cup
butter, melted	1 oz	2 tablespoons

1. Place pork in pot; cover with water. Bring to boil, cover, reduce heat, and simmer 30 to 40 minutes.
2. Add apples and brown sugar, cover, and simmer another hour. Remove meat, cut into 1- to 1½-inch cubes, and return to pan.
3. Meanwhile, make dumplings. Combine flour, baking powder, and salt in bowl.
4. In separate bowl, beat egg with milk and butter.
5. Add liquid mixture to flour mixture; stir quickly until just incorporated.
6. Drop tablespoons of dough into simmering ham and apple mixture, using all dough.
7. Cover tightly. Cook without lifting lid for 15 to 20 minutes, until dumplings are done; toothpick inserted into dumpling comes out clean.
8. Serve immediately, portioning pork, apples, dumplings, and sauce for each plate.

FLOUNDER STUFFED WITH CRABMEAT

Flounder with Crabmeat

If desired, substitute sole or any flat white fish fillet for the flounder.

NUMBER OF SERVINGS: 12
COOKING METHOD:
  Sauté, Bake
SERVING SIZE:
  7 oz or 2 fillets
TOTAL YIELD:
  5 lbs, 9 oz

Wine Style: Wide variety—Pinot Grigio, Sauvignon Blanc, Chardonnay, soft Reds, or Grenache
Example: Chardonnay—Elk Run Vineyards and Winery, Mt. Airy, MD. This Chardonnay is aged in French oak and put through malolactic fermentation, which gives it a rich butter flavor with hints of melon and vanilla.

INGREDIENTS	WEIGHT	VOLUME
butter	6 oz	12 tablespoons or 1½ sticks
onion, small dice	4 oz	1 small
celery, small dice	2½ oz	½ cup or 2 stalks
red pepper, small dice	2½ oz	½ cup
green pepper, small dice	2½ oz	½ cup
garlic, minced	½ oz	2 large cloves
parsley, minced	½ oz	¼ cup
bread crumbs	3½ oz	1 cup
salt		½ teaspoon
pepper		½ teaspoon
seafood seasoning like Old Bay		½ teaspoon
lemon juice	1 oz	2 tablespoons
Dijon mustard	1 oz	2 tablespoons
crab meat, backfin, picked over to remove shells and cartilage	1 lb	
flounder fillets, washed, dried	4 lb, 4 oz	24 fillets, about 2½- to 3½-oz each

GARNISH:

paprika

parsley, minced

lemon wedges

1. Line sheet pan with parchment paper or pan-spray. Preheat oven to 400 degrees.
2. Melt half the butter (3 oz or 6 tablespoons) in skillet; add onion, celery, red and green pepper, garlic, and parsley. Sauté until tender, about 5 to 6 minutes.
3. Add bread crumbs, salt, pepper, Old Bay seasoning, lemon juice, Dijon mustard, and crab meat. Stir gently to combine.
4. Lay each fillet down with dark side up. Place 1½ oz filling on each fillet and roll (like a jellyroll) into paupiette. (Divide filling evenly among the fillets.) Place paupiettes seam side down on prepared pan.
5. Melt remaining 3 oz (6 tablespoons) butter. Brush on fish fillets. Sprinkle with paprika and extra minced parsley.
6. Bake 20 minutes, until fish is done and flakes easily. Serve immediately, accompanied by lemon wedges.

AMISH GREEN BEANS WITH MUSTARD SAUCE

NUMBER OF SERVINGS: 9
COOKING METHOD:
  Sauté, Boil
SERVING SIZE:
  4 oz
TOTAL YIELD:
  2 lbs, 7 oz

INGREDIENTS	WEIGHT	VOLUME
green beans, washed, stems and strings removed	2 lbs	
butter	1½ oz	3 tablespoons
onion, minced	3 oz	½ cup
light brown sugar, firmly packed	2 oz	3 tablespoons
prepared mustard	2½ oz	¼ cup
lemon juice	1 oz	2 tablespoons
cider vinegar	1½ oz	3 tablespoons
dill		1 teaspoon
salt		½ teaspoon
pepper		½ teaspoon
parsley, fresh, minced	1 oz	½ cup

1. Cook green beans in about ¾ inch water until tender but still slightly crisp. Drain excess water.
2. Meanwhile, melt butter in skillet, add onion, and cook until wilted, about 5 minutes.
3. Add brown sugar, mustard, lemon juice, vinegar, dill, salt, and pepper. Cook a few minutes over medium heat, stirring frequently.
4. Pour sauce over hot green beans. Add parsley. Mix thoroughly.
5. Correct seasonings. Serve immediately.

SAUERKRAUT WITH APPLES

NUMBER OF SERVINGS: 8
COOKING METHOD:
 Braise
SERVING SIZE:
 4 oz
TOTAL YIELD:
 2 lbs, 2½ oz

INGREDIENTS	WEIGHT	VOLUME
butter	1 oz	2 tablespoons
bacon, cut in ½ inch pieces	2 oz	2 slices
onion, thinly sliced, ¼ inch thick	2½ oz	½ medium
apples, tart like Granny Smith, peeled, cored, thinly sliced, ¼ inch thick	7 oz	2 small
sauerkraut, drained	1 lb, 8 oz	
beer, flat	6 oz	¾ cup
caraway seeds	¼ oz	1 teaspoon
pepper		¼ teaspoon
dry mustard		½ teaspoon

1. Melt butter in pot; add bacon and cook until bacon is almost crisp.
2. Add onion and apple; sauté until onion is translucent, about 3 to 4 minutes.
3. Add sauerkraut, beer, caraway seeds, pepper, and mustard. Cover and simmer about 40 minutes.
4. Correct seasonings, serve.

NOODLES WITH A CRUMB TOPPING

Variation: omit the crumb topping and serve these noodles sautéed with the onion, parsley, and poppy seeds; however, add butter used in crumb topping to the noodles.

NUMBER OF SERVINGS: 12
COOKING METHOD:
 Boil, Sauté
SERVING SIZE:
 4 oz
TOTAL YIELD:
 3 lbs, 2 oz

INGREDIENTS	WEIGHT	VOLUME
NOODLES:		
flour, all purpose	11¼ oz	2½ cups
egg yolks	3½ oz	5 each
salt		¾ teaspoon
water	4 oz	½ cup
ASSEMBLY:		
butter	4 oz	8 tablespoons or 1 stick
onion, small dice	7¼ oz	1 medium to large
noodles from preceding recipe, cut into ½- by 3-inch strips	1 lb, 2¾ oz	
parsley, fresh, minced	¼ oz	3 tablespoons
poppy seeds	½ oz	1½ tablespoons
salt		½ teaspoon or to taste
pepper		½ teaspoon or to taste
cracker crumbs and/or bread crumbs	5½ oz	1½ cups
GARNISH:		
paprika		

For Noodles:

1. Mix flour, egg yolks, salt, and water in bowl until well combined and not sticky. Dough should be somewhat soft but not sticking to hands when kneaded. Knead one or two turns to make sure of consistency. Add a few drops water if too firm; knead in more flour by the teaspoon if sticky.

2. Divide into three portions; cover well and let rest for about one hour.

3. Roll dough by hand or through pasta machine until 1/16 inch thick.

4. Cut noodles ½ inch wide and 3 inches long or desired size. To store, place on floured parchment paper, cover, and let dry until needed. May be refrigerated and stored one day.

5. When ready to cook, bring large pot of water to boil. Add noodles; cook until *al dente*, about 3 minutes. Pour into colander; cool by running cold water over noodles. Drain until needed.

For Assembly:

1. Melt half the butter (2 oz or 4 tablespoons) in pan.

2. Add onion; sauté until translucent, about 3 to 4 minutes.

3. Add noodles, parsley, poppy seeds, salt, and pepper. Stirring constantly, sauté until hot. Correct seasonings.

4. In separate skillet, melt remaining 2 oz (4 tablespoons) butter. Add bread crumbs; sauté until crumbs turn golden brown.

5. Place noodles in serving dish, top with bread crumbs, and garnish with sprinkling of paprika. Serve.

SOFT PRETZELS

Shaping Pretzel
photo by Ian O'Leary © Dorling Kindersley

Soft Pretzel
photo © Dorling Kindersley

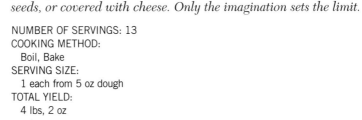

While this recipe looks like it contains a lot of instruction, it is really no more difficult than any yeast bread or roll.

Although the traditional Philadelphia soft pretzel is topped with coarse salt, some people prefer these pretzels sprinkled with cinnamon and sugar, poppy seeds, or sesame seeds, or covered with cheese. Only the imagination sets the limit.

NUMBER OF SERVINGS: 13
COOKING METHOD:
  Boil, Bake
SERVING SIZE:
  1 each from 5 oz dough
TOTAL YIELD:
  4 lbs, 2 oz

INGREDIENTS	WEIGHT	VOLUME
milk	12 oz	1½ cups
water	12 oz	1½ cups
sugar	1¾ oz	¼ cup
oil	2 oz	¼ cup
yeast, dry, granulated	½ oz	1 tablespoon
salt	½ oz	2 teaspoons
flour, all purpose	about 1 lb, 2 oz	about 4 cups

POACHING SOLUTION:

water	2 lbs	1 qt or 4 cups
baking soda	1½ oz	2 tablespoons
egg white	2 oz	2 each
water	1 oz	2 tablespoons
kosher salt	as needed for sprinkling	

GARNISH:

mustard, yellow or variety of choice

1. Heat milk, water, sugar, and oil until lukewarm, about 110 degrees. Remove from heat.

2. Sprinkle yeast over liquid, stir to combine, and allow to sit until foamy.

3. Meanwhile, combine salt and 15¾ oz (3½ cups) flour in mixing bowl. Slowly add yeast mixture, stirring at low speed with dough hook, if available.

4. When thoroughly mixed, turn dough out onto floured table and knead, adding flour as needed, until dough is smooth and elastic.

5. Cover; let rise until doubled, about 1 hour, 15 minutes.

6. Punch dough down; scale into 5-oz portions. Roll each piece into rope about 25 to 30 inches long.

7. Form into pretzel shape by making loop in center of rope and twisting each end around to form another loop. Attach ends firmly. Place on baking sheet, cover, and let rest a few minutes while preparing poaching bath. Place rack in middle of oven. Preheat oven to 500 degrees.

8. Combine water and baking soda in large skillet. Bring to boil; reduce heat to simmer.

9. Add pretzels a few at a time, so temperature of water does not drop drastically. Poach for 30 to 40 seconds on each side. Remove from water, pat dry, and place on parchment-lined baking sheet.

10. Blend egg white with water; brush mixture on pretzels. Lightly sprinkle with kosher salt. Bake for about 8 minutes, until golden brown.

11. Serve hot, accompanied by mustard if desired.

SHOOFLY PIE

Shoofly Pie

Many versions of shoofly pie exist. Some result in a gooey pie; others are dry with a crumb topping. This one falls somewhere in the middle.

NUMBER OF SERVINGS: 8
COOKING METHOD:
  Bake
SERVING SIZE:
  ⅛ wedge of pie
TOTAL YIELD:
  1 each 9-inch pie

INGREDIENTS	WEIGHT	VOLUME
Pastry for single pie crust		

For pie dough recipe, see recipe for pie dough with pumpkin pie in Chapter 2 or use any pie dough recipe desired.

flour, all purpose	4½ oz	1 cup
brown sugar, firmly packed	5 oz	⅔ cup
butter, cold, cut into pieces	2½ oz	5 tablespoons
egg	1¾ oz	1 each
molasses	5¾ oz	½ cup
water, cold	6 oz	¾ cup
baking soda	¼ oz	1 teaspoon
water, warm	2 oz	¼ cup

GARNISH:

ice cream

whipped cream, lightly sweetened

To Roll Dough:

1. Place ball of dough on table. With rolling pan, hit ball to flatten into disk about one inch thick. Lightly flour table and rolling pin, if needed.

2. Roll dough from middle to sides, releasing dough from table with icing spatula every few rolls. Turn dough one-quarter turn to keep dough even; roll into circle until desired thickness.

3. Release from table with spatula. Fold gently in half. Lift and move dough to pan. Position dough over pan so it covers pan when unfolded.

4. Press dough into pan. Either flute edges or cut flush with top of pan.

5. Chill for one hour before baking, if possible.

6. Place oven rack in bottom half of oven. Preheat oven to 375 degrees.

7. Place piece of aluminum foil with shiny side down firmly over pie dough. This prevents it from buckling. Bake until dough is set, about 10 minutes. Remove from oven.

For Filling:

1. Raise oven temperature to 425 degrees.

2. Place flour and brown sugar in bowl of food processor. Pulse to combine.

3. Add butter; pulse to mix until the size of peas.

4. Reserve ½ cup of mixture for top of pie.

5. Lightly beat egg in bowl; add molasses and cold water. Blend just to combine. Do not beat too much or air bubbles will form in pie.

6. Mix baking soda with warm water in separate container; add to molasses mixture.

7. Add flour mixture (not the reserved ½ cup) to molasses mixture. Mix to combine thoroughly.

8. Pour into prepared pie shell; top with reserved flour mixture. Bake for 5 minutes, then lower temperature to 350 degrees. Bake about 30 minutes, until almost firm and lightly brown. Pie continues to firm as it cools.

9. Cool completely. Serve accompanied by ice cream or lightly sweetened whipped cream.

STRAWBERRY SHORTCAKE

Pouring Sugar on Strawberries

photo by David Murray © Dorling Kindersley

Cutting Biscuits for Shortcake

photo by David Murray © Dorling Kindersley

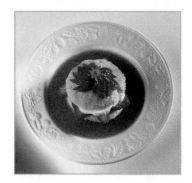

Strawberry Shortcake

photo by David Murray © Dorling Kindersley

NUMBER OF SERVINGS: 10
COOKING METHOD:
  Bake
SERVING SIZE:
  1 each 3-inch biscuit, 4³/4 oz
  (³/4 cup) strawberries, dollop
  about ³/4 oz (3 tablespoons)
  whipped cream
TOTAL YIELD:
  10 each 3-inch biscuits, 3 lb,
  1 oz (2 qts) strawberries,
  8¹/4 oz (2 cups) whipped
  cream

If strawberries lack flavor, add a little lemon juice and extra sugar. The amount of sugar will depend on the sweetness of the berries and the desired sweetness of the finished dessert. For a very sweet dessert, add a little more sugar to the whipping cream.

INGREDIENTS	WEIGHT	VOLUME
STRAWBERRIES:		
strawberries, washed, dried, stems removed, cut in half	3 lbs	2 qt
sugar	2³/4 oz or to taste	¹/3 cup or to taste
BISCUITS:		
flour, all purpose	1 lb, 2 oz	4 cups
baking powder	¹/2 oz	1 tablespoon + 1 teaspoon
baking soda		¹/2 teaspoon
sugar	³/4 oz	1 tablespoon + 1 teaspoon
salt		¹/2 teaspoon
butter, unsalted, cold, cut into pieces	6 oz	³/4 cup or 1¹/2 sticks
buttermilk	10 oz	1¹/3 cups
CHANTILLY CREAM:		
heavy cream, cold	8 oz	1 cup
confectioners' sugar	¹/4 oz or to taste	1 tablespoon or to taste
vanilla		¹/2 teaspoon

For Strawberries:

1. Place strawberries in bowl. Add sugar; mix gently.

2. Let stand at room temperature if only an hour before serving or refrigerate a few hours until serving time. Strawberry mixture will form sugar syrup; the longer the sugared strawberries stand, the more syrup they form.

For Biscuits with Food Processor:

1. Place oven rack in upper third of oven. Line baking sheet with parchment paper. Preheat oven to 425 degrees.

2. Place flour, baking powder, baking soda, sugar, and salt in bowl of food processor. Pulse a few times to mix well and aerate.

3. Place butter pieces on top of flour mixture. Pulse to mix until butter is size of peas.

4. With processor running, add buttermilk through feed tube. Pulse until dough starts to come together into ball.

5. Remove from processor. Knead about 8 or 10 times; roll or pat dough until 1 inch thick.

6. Cut biscuits using 3-inch cutter or desired size. Place on prepared baking sheet. Bake for 10 to 12 minutes until lightly browned on top and bottom.

7. Cool completely on cooling racks.

For Biscuits without Food Processor:

1. Place oven rack in upper third of oven. Line baking sheet with parchment paper. Preheat oven to 425 degrees.

2. Sift flour, baking powder, baking soda, sugar, and salt into bowl.

3. Place butter pieces on top of flour mixture. Working quickly so butter does not become soft, cut butter into flour with two knives or fingertips until butter is size of peas.

4. Make well in flour. Pour buttermilk into well and mix with fork until just incorporated.

5. Remove from bowl. Knead about 8 or 10 times; roll or pat dough until 1 inch thick.

6. Cut biscuits using 3-inch cutter or desired size. Place on prepared baking sheet. Bake for 10 to 12 minutes until lightly browned on top and bottom.

7. Cool completely on cooling racks.

For Chantilly Cream:

1. Chill mixing bowl and beaters. Pour cream into bowl.

2. Beat with mixer on medium speed for about 30 seconds to 1 minute. Turn mixer to high speed and beat until just starting to form peaks.

3. Sift confectioners' sugar. Add confectioners' sugar and vanilla to cream. Beat until soft peaks. Correct flavoring.

4. Refrigerate until serving time.

To Assemble:

1. Using serrated knife, cut biscuits in half horizontally. Place bottom on serving plate.

2. Top biscuit with about 4¾ oz (¾ cup) strawberries and juice. Strawberries should rest on biscuit and around the biscuit on plate.

3. Place top half of biscuit over berries directly on bottom half or set at angle over bottom half (with edge of biscuit on plate and leaning against bottom half).

4. Place whipped cream on top of biscuit. Garnish top of whipped cream with strawberry piece(s) and some juice.

5. Serve immediately.

NEW YORK CHEESECAKE

New York Cheesecake
photo courtesy of American Egg Board

While there are hundreds of cheesecake recipes from around the world, the New York cheesecake forms a class of its own. Always a tall, dense cheesecake, the "original" Lindy's Restaurant version contains lemon and orange rind.

Originally, a pie dough crust encased New York cheesecake, but today most use a crust made of crushed graham crackers or cookie crumbs.

Although this cheesecake is delicious served plain, if desired, top with a fruit topping like strawberry, cherry, or blueberry.

NUMBER OF SERVINGS: 16
COOKING METHOD:
  Bake
SERVING SIZE:
  1 wedge ¹/₁₆ of cake
TOTAL YIELD:
  1 each 9-inch cake

INGREDIENTS	WEIGHT	VOLUME
CRUST:		
graham cracker crumbs, finely crushed	5¼ oz	1½ cups
sugar	1½ oz	3 tablespoons
cinnamon		1 teaspoon
butter, unsalted, melted	2½ oz	5 tablespoons
FILLING:		
cornstarch	¾ oz	2 tablespoons
sugar	7½ oz	1 cup
cream cheese, softened	2 lbs	
salt	pinch	
orange rind, grated	¼ oz	1½ teaspoons
lemon rind, grated	¼ oz	1½ teaspoons
vanilla		1 teaspoon
eggs	10 oz	6 each
egg yolks	1½ oz	2 each
sour cream	3 oz	¼ cup

For Crust:

1. Place graham cracker crumbs, sugar, and cinnamon in bowl; mix together. Add butter; mix thoroughly with fingertips.

2. Place mixture in 9-inch springform pan with 3-inch sides. Using back of fingers, press crumb mixture on sides of pan. Press remaining crumbs on bottom of pan. Be careful that the bottom seam/edge (where sides join bottom of pan) is not thicker than the rest.

For Filling:

1. Preheat oven to 475 degrees.

2. Sift cornstarch and sugar together. Using paddle attachment, if available, beat cream cheese with sugar and cornstarch at medium speed until fluffy, about 3 minutes. Add salt, orange rind, lemon rind, and vanilla. Mix to combine.

3. Add eggs and egg yolks, one at a time, beating after each addition until just incorporated.

4. Add sour cream; mix until just incorporated.

5. Pour into prepared pan; bake for 12 minutes. Lower heat to 200 degrees; bake for 1 hour.

6. Turn off oven, prop door open with wooden spoon, and leave in oven for another hour.

7. Remove from oven; cool completely on rack. Cover tightly and refrigerate at least overnight if not one or two days.

8. Remove rim of pan; release from bottom with flexible blade spatula (icing spatula). Transfer to serving plate or cardboard round. Cut with clean knife or unflavored dental floss into 16 pieces. (Clean knife after each cut to prevent knife from dragging through cake.)

4

Southern States

OBJECTIVES

By the end of this chapter, you will be able to

- Describe the early settlers, including their heritage and why they settled in the South
- Explain the effect of the climate and topography on the cuisine that developed in this region
- Discuss the role of the slaves and their impact on cooking and the cuisine of the South
- Discuss how the Civil War affected the cookery of the South
- Identify food products prevalent in the South
- Prepare a variety of dishes indicative of the cuisine of the South

States included in the South:
- Virginia
- West Virginia
- North Carolina
- South Carolina
- Kentucky
- Tennessee
- Georgia
- Alabama
- Mississippi
- Arkansas

HISTORY

In 1585, the English established the first colony on Roanoke Island, but by 1590, all of the 100 inhabitants of that colony had disappeared mysteriously. Today that settlement is known as the *Lost Colony*.

In their quest for religious freedom, immigrants from Great Britain founded the first permanent British settlement at Jamestown, Virginia, near the Chesapeake Bay in 1607. When the settlers arrived, they discovered a land teeming with fish, game, and produce; however, the foods they found in this new land did not resemble the foods from their native homeland. The Powhatans taught the colonists about game, fish, seafood, and plants available here. With help from the Native Americans, the settlers hunted venison, bear, raccoons, pheasant, quail, wild turkeys, and ducks; fished for sturgeon, turtle, and oysters; and planted squash, beans, corn, sweet potatoes, and pumpkins. In addition, the Native Americans also instructed the settlers about the preparation of these foods.

When farming depleted the rich land in Jamestown of its nutrients, settlers migrated to the west in search of new, fertile land. After crossing the Blue Ridge Mountains and the lush Shenandoah Valley in the western portion of Virginia, they entered the territory that later became West Virginia. Around the same time, settlers of German heritage living in Pennsylvania migrated south into Virginia and West Virginia in their search for fertile farmland. Meanwhile, Scottish inhabitants from Ireland fled to the hills and mountains of Virginia, North Carolina, West Virginia, Kentucky, and Tennessee in pursuit of religious freedom. Since many settled in isolated mountainous regions, strong remnants of their culinary heritage remain.

In the Carolinas, the Catawba and Cherokee Indians taught the early settlers to preserve foods by drying them in the smoke of the fire, which was the foundation for barbecue. Even today, practically every region in the United States creates its own barbecue. While most prefer wet and saucy barbecue, some start with a flavoring rub and the barbecued food remains dry.

Initially, barbecue sauces contained no tomato or ketchup. In the early days, vinegar and/or butter and water served as the base for the sauce while smoky flavor from the smoldering wood permeated the meat. Today, the predominant flavors found in barbecue sauce vary widely from vinegar to catsup to mustard to smoky. Regardless of the recipe, most barbecue sauces incorporate salt, sweet, sour, and hot into the seasoning. Even the type of meat used for barbecue differs from area to area. While most Southerners prefer pork for their barbecue, Texans and many in the cattle country of the Southwest want beef. The version served in Owensboro, Kentucky, starts with mutton.

Native Americans in the South enjoyed a profusion of foods: sweet potatoes, corn, squash, beans, melons, wild berries, nuts, and game, including deer, rabbit, bear, wild turkey, and squirrel. Of course, those who lived near coasts and rivers feasted on a variety of fish and seafood. As in other regions, the Native Americans introduced the settlers to corn and showed them many ways to use it. Soon, corn became a mainstay in the Southern diet.

Southern cooking combines elements from the cooking of Native Americans and the cookery found in the various countries of Europe and Africa. Although the cuisine of the South exhibits influence from the Spanish and French, characteristic "Southern cooking" primarily combines traits from English and African cookery. The basis for the cooking came from the English who initially settled this coastal area. They prepared dishes from their British heritage like stews, pies, puddings, roasted meats, and boiled vegetables.

In spite of the overwhelming English influence, characteristics from French cookery show up in numerous areas in the South. Settling along the coasts from Charleston, South Carolina,

---

Early Virginia inhabitants introduced the turkey to Europe when they sent a coop containing turkeys back to England.

BARBECUE TERMINOLOGY

pulled meat—shredded, pulled in long strands

chopped meat—cut into cubes

wet—prepared with a sauce

dry—seasoned with a spice rub instead of a liquid sauce

to Mobile, Alabama, the Huguenots (French Protestants) introduced sauces and gratins. In the 1700s, many French immigrants moved to the capital of the Louisiana Territory, Mobile. With the founding of New Orleans, many French moved from Mobile to New Orleans. Today, the French impact on the cuisine in both of these cities remains strong. The Spanish brought rice pilaf and fruits such as peaches and figs to areas they settled.

In 1612, colonists began growing tobacco for export. In addition to tobacco, other labor-intensive crops like sugar and rice became the main money-producing crops grown in the South. Plantation owners needed cheap labor to produce these labor-intensive crops. At first, Native Americans worked the plantations, but they soon refused. Slaves from Africa filled the need, so the colonists imported many, many slaves. In 1619, the first African slaves arrived in Jamestown on a Dutch ship. Because the warm climate of the South resembled their homeland, the slaves planted the foods that grew in Africa and prepared their native dishes. Slaves cooked in all but the poorest Southern homes, so the cuisine soon adopted many typical African foods and dishes, such as a wide variety of greens, yams, sweet potatoes, sesame seeds, okra, peas and beans, eggplant, watermelon, peanuts, sorghum, and an abundance of fried foods. Later, peanuts grew wild throughout the South and provided the basis for stews and soups during times of scarce meat.

The first and third presidents of the United States, George Washington and Thomas Jefferson, had several things in common. Both came from Virginia, possessed a passion for food and dining, and were avid gardeners. During their terms as president, White House dinners incorporated many foods from their gardens. Also, they shared an affinity for serving their guests dishes containing in-season produce and foods indigenous to the United States.

While serving as an ambassador to France, Thomas Jefferson lived in France and developed a fine appreciation for French food. In 1801, he hired a French chef to cook at the White House. Much of the produce served at Jefferson's lavish parties came from the extensive gardens at his estate, Monticello. In his gardens, he planted all sorts of vegetables and fruits, such as peas, corn, beans, squash, asparagus, cabbage, onions, eggplant, salsify, endive, spinach, artichokes, radishes, cucumbers, carrots, tomatoes, many varieties of lettuce, apples, peaches, cherries, plums, strawberries, raspberries, dewberries, mulberries, cloudberries, oranges, watermelons, grapes, olives, and almonds. Besides growing vegetables and fruits that he tasted while traveling in Europe, Jefferson experimented with planting numerous varieties to see which type grew best and contained the best flavor. On one of his trips to Italy, he smuggled a pocketful of Italian rice into this country, which, according to some, led to the thriving rice industry that developed in the Carolinas. Having acquired a love for wine while in France, Jefferson planted grapes in his garden and made his own wine from those grapes. During his term as president, Jefferson served wine regularly at the White House.

While small farmers settled in the western part of Virginia, plantation owners dominated the eastern portion of the state. Of course, the plantation owners needed slaves, and their support of slavery created dissent with the farmers in the west when the Civil War began. Led by the plantation owners, Virginia seceded from the Union. Since many Virginians in the western part of the state opposed joining the Confederacy, they divided Virginia and formed the state of West Virginia, which remained with the Union.

In 1670, colonists settled the Carolinas. With a continual influx of people, the number of colonies in North Carolina swelled dramatically by the latter part of the seventeenth century. From the Carolinas, the settlers moved westward and crossed the Appalachian Mountains. To connect the developing south to the established east, the Great Philadelphia Wagon Road ran between Philadelphia and South Carolina. Offshoots of that road led to Georgia, Alabama, and Mississippi.

Sesame seeds, known as benne, appeared in all sorts of recipes including biscuits, cakes, candy, and cookies. Even their oil was extracted, providing sesame oil for cooking and salads.

Thomas Jefferson liked sesame oil and added it to his recipe for Monticello dressing.

At the age of 33, Jefferson signed the Declaration of Independence.

Four of the first five presidents of the United States came from Virginia. They were George Washington, Thomas Jefferson, James Madison, and James Monroe.

The resplendent cooking that developed on plantations in the South lasted until the Civil War. Known as the War Between the States in the South, this devastating war brought major changes to the cookery of the South for the rich and the poor.

In the opulent days of plenty before the Civil War, the slaves received paltry amounts of food that included all of the unwanted foods and scraps from the plantation kitchen. After the war, the tables turned and the upper class had little food. Now, all of the inhabitants of the South faced starvation. The former slave owners lived with the meager rations they provided their slaves in earlier times, and they resorted to the slaves' "soul food" cooking to survive on the sparse amount of available food. The lack of meat led to extensive seasoning with ham hocks, salt pork, fatback, or just bacon grease. The Civil War changed the South in many ways!

When the Civil War ended, the South was devastated both economically and emotionally. The economy was in shambles, and the social structure of the South was wrecked. Many of the men died in the war or returned home unable to work because of serious injuries. In the absence of slaves, the women had to take over the kitchen and farming duties, as well as manage the farms and plantations. These new responsibilities left the overburdened women with neither the time nor energy to create interesting new dishes from their meager food supplies. The era of sumptuous meals served on southern tables for the past two centuries ended.

Some states remained divided on whether to join the North or the South in the Civil War, so they stayed uncommitted to either side. Residents of these so-called Border States could choose to support the North or the South or remain neutral. The result was sometimes divided families with brothers fighting their brothers. Delaware, Maryland, Missouri, and Kentucky became Border States.

TOPOGRAPHY AND CLIMATE

The Atlantic Ocean borders Virginia, North Carolina, South Carolina, and Georgia on the east. To the south of Alabama and Mississippi lies the Gulf of Mexico. Much of the land near these two bodies of water consists of low-lying marshland that created excellent conditions for oysters, shrimp, and other shellfish that thrived here.

The Mississippi River meanders down the western side of Kentucky, Tennessee, and Mississippi and the eastern side of Arkansas. That river contains abundant catfish, which quickly became a staple in the areas near the Mississippi River. Running north to south, this river served as an important means of transportation in the early days. It functioned as a major waterway for moving people as well as goods through the country. As a result, numerous towns grew up along the Mississippi River, and several, such as Natchez, Mississippi, developed into thriving transportation centers. To link towns not situated on the river, the Natchez Trace was built to connect Natchez at the Mississippi River with Nashville, Tennessee. The Natchez Trace stretched for more than 400 miles.

The Appalachian Mountain chain basically runs north to south diagonally, beginning in Tennessee, then curving through Kentucky, West Virginia, and Virginia, and continuing through Pennsylvania. This mountain range is known as Allegheny Mountains in West Virginia and Pennsylvania, Blue Ridge Mountains in West Virginia, Virginia, and North Carolina, Smoky Mountains in Tennessee, and Cumberland Mountains in Kentucky. Although the Appalachians are an old chain with round-topped mountains, they create a colder climate than the surrounding area and provide fertile valleys for planting crops. Also part of the Appalachian Mountains, the Ozarks run through Missouri and Arkansas. A bounty of game flourishes in all of these mountainous areas.

Short, mild winters and hot, humid summers prevail throughout the South, providing a long growing season conducive for growing a multitude of crops. Eggplants, corn, tomatoes, sweet potatoes, okra, and peanuts are just a few of the many fruits and vegetables that thrive throughout this region.

Flat coastal plain dominates eastern Virginia from the coast to the west. This plain encompasses 100 miles of lowlands, marshes, swamps, bays, and inlets. This area is called the Tidewater because tidal waters back up over much of this land. Also situated in this region, the Chesapeake Bay provided abundant seafood, including a bounty of crabs, oysters, scallops, clams, flounder, shad, and mackerel in the early days.

Piedmont defines central Virginia with rivers, streams, and waterfalls dotting the landscape. Freshwater fish like pike, perch, bass, and trout swim in the rivers and streams. The terrain in the western part of Virginia consists of the Blue Ridge Mountains, many valleys including the fertile Shenandoah Valley, gorges, and plateaus. About 60 percent of the land in Virginia remains forest. This area provided plenty of fish and game, including deer, rabbits, turkey, duck, geese, quail, and more for the settlers.

Maryland lies north of Virginia, the Atlantic Ocean borders on the east, North Carolina and Tennessee are situated to the south, and Kentucky and West Virginia are on the west. Mild climate with temperate winters and hot, humid summers prevails. Although the mountainous western half experiences a cooler climate, the eastern half remains warmer with temperatures moderated by the ocean.

Basically, rugged describes the topography of West Virginia. The eastern portion of the state contains mountains, rivers, valleys, and forests, and the western section consists of steep hills, rolling hills, valleys, and rivers. Game flourishes in the forests of both the Blue Ridge Mountains and Allegheny Mountains running through this state. Separating West Virginia from Ohio, the Ohio River defines West Virginia's western border.

Pennsylvania and Ohio lie to the north of West Virginia, Virginia is situated to the east and south, and Ohio and Kentucky border on the west. The climate consists of warm summers and temperately cold winters.

Bordered on the north by Virginia, the east by the Atlantic Ocean, the south by South Carolina, and the west by Tennessee, North Carolina contains coastal plains in the east, piedmont in the central section, and mountains in the west. Flat terrain, reefs, islands, low-lying land, swamps, marshes, and fertile farmland (in the western part of the coastal region) define the land found in the east. Some of the fish, seafood, and fowl flourishing here include ducks, geese, flounder, crabs, shrimp, and clams. While hills and rivers make up the piedmont region in the central section, mountains, forests, and fertile valleys define the west. Ample game thrives in the forests that cover two-thirds of the state. Rivers and mountain streams teem with trout and bass. Although the mountainous areas have significantly cooler temperatures in both winter and summer, hot, humid summers and mild winters define the piedmont and coastal areas.

North Carolina lies to the north of South Carolina, the Atlantic borders on the east, and Georgia is situated to the south and west. Lying along the Atlantic Ocean, coastal plains called the Low Country comprise the southeastern two-thirds of South Carolina. A number of rivers traverse the swamps and marshland west of the ocean, providing plenty moist soil.

Because of the many bays, harbors, inlets, and islands, this flat and often low-lying land actually contains almost 2,900 miles of coastline. The waters in the Low Country yield all sorts of fish and seafood, such as oysters, shrimp, crabs, clams, crawfish, bass, mullet, mackerel, flounder, catfish, grouper, turtle, and more. In addition, waterfowl like ducks, turkey, quail, and pheasant live here.

Oysters became a mainstay in the diet of the people who first settled South Carolina. They are the featured food in an oyster roast, a gathering resembling the clambake of New

Because of the hot climate that dominated the South, settlers usually built the kitchen and smokehouse as separate buildings detached from the main house on a plantation. While New England kitchens were in the center of the house to utilize the heat generated by cooking to heat the house during the many months of winter, the southern plan of detaching the kitchen avoided adding excess heat into the house from cooking. Detaching the kitchen also ensured that any fire that started in the kitchen did not spread to the house.

Different types of rock compose the Allegheny Mountains and Blue Ridge Mountains although both are part of the Appalachian Mountain chain.

England. To prepare the oyster roast, cooks first threw the tightly closed-shell oysters into the fire and then covered them with burlap. As the shells opened (which indicates a cooked oyster), they removed the oysters from the fire with a shovel and placed them directly on the table for eating. Equipped with an oyster knife for shucking the oysters, diners ate their fill. (Note that oysters are cooked when the shell relaxes. Unlike some other shellfish whose shells open widely when cooked, oyster shells open one-quarter to one-half inch.)

Known as the Up Country, the remainder of South Carolina consists of the central piedmont, hills, and mountains of the west. Like Virginia and North Carolina, hills and rivers make up the piedmont, and the west contains mountains, hills, valleys, forests, and rivers. Part of the Blue Ridge Mountains runs through South Carolina's western portion. Many fish, including trout and bass, thrive in the rivers of this region.

Forming Kentucky's northern border, the Ohio River separates this state from Ohio, Indiana, and Illinois. On the western side of Kentucky, the Ohio River flows into the Mississippi River. Ohio and Indiana lie to the north of Kentucky, West Virginia and Virginia to the east, Tennessee to the south, and Illinois and Missouri to the west. The Cumberland Mountains, plateaus, valleys, rivers, and streams compose the eastern part of the state. The central section consists of rolling hills. Plains and low hills fill the flat western portion of Kentucky. Known as the Bluegrass, the rolling hills of the central region yield ample crops of corn and tobacco and provide pastures for horses to graze. The horse farms of Kentucky lie in this region. Rich, fertile farmland fills the areas near the Ohio River and the Mississippi River. Forests cover about half of the state.

Kentucky and Virginia lie to the north of Tennessee, North Carolina to the east, Georgia, Alabama, and Mississippi to the south, and Arkansas and Missouri to the west. Diverse topography defines this state. The Blue Ridge Mountains, with fertile valleys, forests, rivers, and streams, rise in the east. The central portion of the state comprises rolling hills, forests, rivers, and streams. Although not bordering an ocean, the west tapers to coastal plains and lowlands leading to the Mississippi River. Fertile farmland surrounds the Mississippi River. Hot, humid summers and temperate winters describe the climate in most of Tennessee.

The largest state east of the Mississippi River, Georgia is situated with Tennessee and North Carolina to the north, South Carolina and the Atlantic Ocean to the east, Florida to the south, and Alabama to the west. The northern part of the state contains Appalachian Mountains, fertile valleys, ridges, plateaus, and forests. The mountainous north tapers to rolling hills and piedmont in the central region, and the southern half of Georgia consists of coastal plains and lowlands. While the sandy soil found near the Atlantic in Georgia's southeast yields watermelons, peanuts, sweet potatoes, and onions, the richer soil of the southwest produces more crops, including peanuts and soybeans. Numerous islands dot the coastal area.

Tennessee lies to the north of Alabama, Georgia to its east, Florida and the Gulf of Mexico to the south, and Mississippi to the west. With forests, hills, and rivers making up the north, the southern two-thirds of Alabama contains forests, low hills, rivers, and low-lands. Swamps and bayous describe the terrain found in the lower southern section near the Mobile River and the Gulf of Mexico. Typical of the South, Alabama experiences hot, humid summers and mild winters.

Tennessee is situated north of Mississippi, Alabama lies to its east, and the Gulf of Mexico and Louisiana to its south. The Mississippi River forms its western border, separating Mississippi from Arkansas and Louisiana to the west. Fertile plains make up the western part of the state near the Mississippi River. The rest of Mississippi consists of rolling hills, forests, prairies, lowlands, rivers, and lakes. Long, hot, humid summers and short, mild winters dominate the climate here.

The Ozark Mountains, valleys, gorges, plateaus, streams, and rolling hills with fruit orchards fill the northern section of Arkansas, which resembles the land found in the

Midwest. Eastern Arkansas consists of lowlands; the Mississippi River, which forms its eastern border; and fertile delta plains. Lowlands and coastal plains make up the south. Low-lying land and swamps fill the area between the Mississippi and Arkansas Rivers in southeastern Arkansas. Rice actually grows well in this area. As in the northern section of Arkansas, mountains, valleys, plateaus, and rivers fill much of the west. While the hills provide abundant game, a bounty of fish, including bass and catfish, as well as ducks come from the many lakes. Seemingly endless plains are found in some of the western part of the state. Numerous natural springs and hot springs throughout Arkansas draw many people with hopes of a cure for their ailments.

Missouri borders Arkansas on the north, Tennessee and Mississippi lie to the east, Louisiana is on the south, and Oklahoma and Texas are situated to the west. The fertile land and hot climate supports the growth of a multitude of fruits and vegetables. Hot, humid summers and cool winters prevail, with cooler temperatures in the mountainous areas.

Ingredients and foods commonly used throughout the cuisine of the South include

- pork and pork products, including ham, sausage, and country ham
- freshwater and saltwater fish and seafood, including pompano, red snapper, grouper, mullet, shrimp, crab, oysters, crayfish, clams, catfish, trout, and bass
- chicken
- barbecue
- fried foods like fried chicken, croquettes, and fritters
- corn, cornbread, grits, and hush puppies
- rice
- all sorts of greens, including collards, mustard, beet, turnip, and kale
- sweet potatoes and yams
- peanuts and pecans
- beans and peas
- many vegetables, fruits, and berries

COOKING METHODS

The cookery of the South uses all cooking methods: frying, boiling and steaming, braising, grilling, and baking. The slaves fried many foods, and Southerners still prepare a wide range of fried foods, including meats, poultry, fish and seafood, vegetables, fruits, and fritters. Fried chicken, fried fish, fried okra, fried green tomatoes, hush puppies, fried pies (actually fried turnovers), and fried almost anything often appear on menus in homes and restaurants. Hog fat rendered into lard and oil from the palm trees growing in the southern parts of this region provided plenty of fat for frying.

There are countless recipes for fried chicken. While some cooks simply dredge the chicken in seasoned flour before frying, others soak the chicken in buttermilk before coating with flour. Still others use the standard breading procedure and dredge the chicken in flour, dip it into egg, and then coat it again with flour, cornflake crumbs, or the coating of choice. The next debate surrounding fried chicken involves whether or not to cover the frying pan. While some swear by cooking the chicken in a covered pan, others adamantly disagree. Regardless of the cooking and breading technique, deep-fried chicken remains an intrinsic part of Southern cooking.

Vegetable preparations often involve boiling. Traditionally, Southerners simmered vegetables for hours with fatback or ham hocks for flavoring, producing very soft, limp vegetables. For example, green beans and greens (a mixture of assorted leaves such as turnip greens, collard, mustard greens, and/or kale) usually received this treatment.

By canning, pickling, or drying, settlers preserved any excess vegetables and fruits. In the days before refrigeration, excess meat from slaughtered animals needed preserving to prevent its spoiling during the hot weather. Like the Native Americans, the settlers preserved meat by salting and smoking. A smokehouse where they smoked all sorts of meats, including pork, game, and sausages, stood on every plantation and many farms. After smoking, the meats were often hung for aging. Pork ranked as the most popular meat. Settlers smoked and cured a whole piece of pork like ham or "parts" like pigs' feet, hocks, or sausage. Pigs transformed into valuable protein as fresh and cured meat, country ham, bacon, sausage, and other products that served as staples throughout the South.

To preserve meats by salting, Southerners used one of two methods. They either soaked the meat in salt brine or dry salt cured it. To dry salt cure, they rubbed the pork with salt (dry) and allowed it to cure for a couple of days. After that curing, the meat was rubbed with more salt and any desired spices and hung to air-dry. Regardless of the method used, the heavily salted hams hung to age, which allowed them to lose moisture. The longer the hams hung to cure, the more moisture they lost. Hams with less moisture have a stronger, more intense flavor. The well-known Virginia country hams are an example of strongly flavored cured hams with long aging. If desired, the hams could be slowly smoked over hickory, applewood, or another wood of choice after aging. Some people liked their hams smoked; others preferred them not smoked.

As people migrated to the west, they moved these curing processes with them into Kentucky, Tennessee, and other southern states. Recipes changed and residents of each area produced their own version of country ham. Of course, each group insisted that their country ham was the best.

Preparation of the very salty cured ham begins with soaking the ham in water. In fact, many cooks soak the ham for a day, changing the water several times to extract as much salt as possible. After eliminating salt through soaking, they scrub the ham with a wire brush to remove any remaining mold. Next, they boil the ham, trim most of its fat, and finally bake the ham.

Red-eyed gravy is a popular sauce that often accompanies country ham. To make red-eyed gravy, add coffee (or water) to the skillet after removing the fried slices of the country ham, deglaze the pan by scraping the bits from the bottom of the skillet, and then reduce the liquid.

STATES

To earn the coveted title "Smithfield ham," the cured ham must be produced in the town of Smithfield, Virginia, and be made from hogs fed on peanuts. To cure a Smithfield ham, it is rubbed with salt and then stacked or hung for weeks so the salt penetrates into the meat. At that point, the ham is rubbed again with salt, scrubbed, covered with pepper, smoked for about six weeks, and then hung in a cool place to age for at least three months.

Hams simply classified as "country ham" originate from anywhere and come from hogs fed on any diet. While pepper is rubbed on the rinds of Smithfield hams, most replace the pepper with sugar on other country hams. In addition, most country hams age for less time than Smithfield hams. Regardless of the choice of seasonings or the aging time, preparation for country hams includes curing, possibly smoking, and aging. Throughout the South, debate still rages over the process of curing a country ham and how to cook the cured ham. Most adamantly claim that their method of curing and/or cooking is best.

Virginians boast that they feed hogs destined to become country hams on a diet of peanuts and acorns. They claim that diet leads to producing the best hams. In Kentucky, farmers feed hogs fated for country ham on grain and clover. Of course, the diet of the hog affects the flavor of the ham.

Today, Virginians commercially raise chickens, cattle, soybeans, peanuts, and a variety of fruits and vegetables, such as apples, potatoes, sweet potatoes, and tomatoes. The fertile valleys in the western half of the state, including the Shenandoah Valley, support abundant agriculture.

Germans from Pennsylvania migrated south and settled in West Virginia. Additionally, many English, Irish, and Scottish settlers came to this area. In the late nineteenth and early twentieth centuries, numerous immigrants arrived seeking work in the coal mines. Each of these ethnic groups influenced the cookery of West Virginia. Discovering a mountainous terrain with forests, rivers, and valleys, the early settlers survived on the bounty of game from the forests, fish from the rivers, and crops planted in the valleys. Today, abundant apple and peach orchards flourish in the eastern part of the state. West Virginians raise cattle, produce dairy products, and grow corn for feed. Numerous chicken and turkey farms generate income.

In the early days, German, Swiss, Irish, and Scottish immigrants moved to North and South Carolina to establish farms. Numerous English settlers left Virginia and went to the Carolinas seeking land and fortune; however, many of the early settlers moving into North Carolina wanted land for small farms instead of the huge plantations found to the north. All of the settlers moving into North and South Carolina came with their culinary heritage and left their mark on the cookery.

Today's farmers in North Carolina raise turkeys, chickens, sweet potatoes, peanuts, apples, peaches, strawberries, and blueberries. With mountains, piedmont, and coastal plains, North Carolina contains a variety of climates, types of soil and terrain, and growing conditions. The diversity of land and conditions leads to a cornucopia of fruits, vegetables, and animals.

South Carolina consists of the Low Country near the ocean and the interior section called the Up Country. While many Germans, Scottish, Irish, and Swiss settled in the Up Country, the Low Country attracted people seeking land and/or religious freedom, including numerous wealthy French Huguenots, Sephardic Jews from Spain and Portugal, and English settlers, as well as slaves from Africa. As a result, Low Country cooking evolved from the mingling of each of these groups with additional influence from the West Indies. Besides abundant fish and seafood in the waterways and marshland, all sorts of birds thrived throughout the Low Country. Ducks, quail, pheasant, turkey, and more provided food for the people who lived in this region.

Since Charleston, South Carolina, is situated along the coast with numerous inlets and bays, the residents caught copious amounts of crabs, oysters, and shrimp. A wide variety of soups, bisques, and entrées featured one or more types of shellfish. Also, many recipes combined locally grown rice with shellfish.

By 1700, countless ships laden with rice sailed from Charleston's port heading for destinations across the seas. The town of Charleston grew quickly, and many residents amassed great wealth through shipping and other ventures. Foods and spices from around the world flowed through Charleston's busy port, and residents assimilated many of these ingredients into the city's cuisine. As a result, curry flavors a number of dishes in Charleston as well as throughout the Low Country, and vinegar forms the basis for barbecue sauce in this region.

Brought to the lowlands of South Carolina at the end of the 1600s, rice thrived in this wet, swampy land with long, hot, humid summers and short, mild winters. According to one account, a ship sailing from Madagascar to England lost its course due to a storm and landed in Charleston. While waiting for the ship to be repaired, the captain gave some rice grains to the governor and the rice industry began. Others believe Thomas Jefferson introduced rice here. Regardless of its origin, settlers planted the rice, and it thrived. Before long, rice crops grew in Mississippi, Arkansas, Louisiana, and Texas.

The labor-intensive rice production continued to flourish in the marshes of South Carolina for almost two centuries until the Civil War, which ended slavery. Without the free labor of slavery, most plantation owners found rice impossible to raise profitably. In the 1880s, a hurricane swept salt water over the rice fields and the rice crops failed, but the final end of growing rice in this area came in the 1940s when the Corps of Engineers dammed the rivers, and the land flooded with salt water.

Known as "Carolina Gold," rice became an important part of the diet and recipes for people living in this area. Numerous dishes prepared in the South included rice as a key ingredient; in fact, numerous renditions of chicken and rice dishes are served throughout many regions of the South. Limping Susan, a combination of okra and rice, hails from South Carolina. Another favorite dish, shrimp pilau, consists of a combination of shrimp, sweet peppers, onion, spices, and rice. Pilafs and rice side dishes still accompany all sorts of foods.

As with the rice crops, the plantation owners imported many slaves to work the labor-intensive cotton crops. When boll weevils destroyed much of the cotton crop in the 1920s, farmers diversified and began growing other crops, such as tobacco, vegetables, corn, and fruits.

Many of the settlers in Kentucky immigrated from Scotland and Ireland. Coming from areas that produced whiskey, scotch, and other liquors, these people helped create the excellent quality bourbon distilled in Kentucky. Still today, they make liquor from the rye, wheat, and corn that grow here.

Burgoo, a stew or thick soup, contained a variety of meats. Originally, burgoo included squirrel, pork, beef, possum, chicken, and/or anything available in addition to vegetables and seasonings. Prepared throughout Kentucky, huge pots of burgoo fed those attending church suppers, political rallies, horse sales, and the Derby.

In 1806, Shakers moved to Pleasant Hill, Kentucky. Because they did not believe in men and women procreating, this Shaker community became extinct around 1910. The Shakers developed many recipes still in use today, particularly in the areas of baking and preserving.

The rivers, lakes, and streams in Kentucky supply catfish, carp, walleye, bluegill, bass, and other fish. With many horse farms for breeding and training thoroughbreds, horse breeding remains an important industry in Kentucky. Farmers raise plenty of grain here. Some is used in distilleries for making liquor, and much becomes feed for the livestock. Ample fruits and vegetables such as corn, popcorn, apples, and peaches thrive in the hot, humid summers.

The many lakes, streams, and rivers found in Tennessee provide plenty of trout, pike, and bass. The forests yield a bounty of game like deer, wild turkeys, and ducks. With a warm climate, many fruits and vegetables, including beans, apples, and peaches, thrive. Beef cattle, hogs, and poultry flourish here with soybeans and corn grown for their feed.

German, Scottish, and Irish immigrants first settled in Georgia. Their culinary heritage combined with the cooking influence from Spanish-ruled Florida lying to Georgia's south to mold the early cuisine in this state.

Lying only 105 miles apart, two bustling port cities, Savannah, Georgia, and Charleston, South Carolina, developed completely different characteristics. The difference between these two cities is rooted in their cultural heritage. Savannah displays pronounced English influences in both cuisine and architecture while Charleston reflects significant West Indian traits.

With long, hot summers and short, mild winters, a bounty of crops thrives in Georgia. In fact, Georgia ranks first in peanut and pecan production in the United States. Vidalia onions are a Georgia specialty with an interesting history. In 1931, Mose Coleman grew onions on his farm near Vidalia, Georgia. To Coleman's surprise, the onions tasted almost

The first shot of the Civil War was fired in Charleston Harbor.

Louisiana and Arkansas now lead the nation in rice production.

With heavy dependence on slaves to work the plantations, South Carolina became the first state to secede from the Union in December 1860.

Established in 1875, the oldest continuously running horse race, the Kentucky Derby is run the first Saturday in May at Churchill Downs in Louisville, Kentucky.

Kaelin's Restaurant in Louisville, Kentucky, claims the creation of the first cheeseburger in 1934.

While having a cup of coffee at the Maxwell House in Nashville, Tennessee, in 1907, Teddy Roosevelt supposedly said "Good to the last drop!" in reference to the coffee. Of course, that expression became the advertising slogan for Maxwell House Coffee.

In 1886, a pharmacist in Atlanta, Georgia, combined extracts from coca leaves and cola nuts to form a remedy for headaches. Someone mistakenly added carbonated water, creating Coca-Cola.

sweet rather than hot and pungent. Coleman did not know that their sweet flavor resulted from the low sulfur level of the soil. Eventually, these onions became quite popular and known as Vidalia sweet onions. Today, Vidalia onions grow in 20 counties in Georgia. In addition to peanuts, pecans, and onions, farmers throughout the state generate significant revenue from peaches, watermelons, sweet potatoes, corn, chickens, and eggs.

Georgia's rivers, streams, and lakes yield much fish, including trout, catfish, and bass. A wide range of seafood and fish such as shrimp, oysters, crab, mullet, and flounder comes from the Atlantic Ocean.

Besides exhibiting heavy influence from the French, Alabama's cuisine displays impact from the early English and Spanish settlers. Today, the Gulf of Mexico supplies southern Alabama with a variety of seafood and fish, while the western and central areas contain rich soil yielding a wide assortment of fruits and vegetables. When the boll weevil destroyed the cotton crop in the late 1800s, the farmers of Alabama diversified their crops. They now grow corn, sweet potatoes, greens, okra, black-eyed peas, beans, cucumbers, tomatoes, strawberries, watermelons, peaches, apples, pears, peanuts, pecans, soybeans, and oats. The forests supply abundant game, and the rivers contain plenty of freshwater fish such as catfish, bass, and mussels. Residents catch flounder, mullet, red snapper, mackerel, shrimp, oysters, crab, and more in the Gulf of Mexico. Raising poultry, eggs, cattle, hogs, and bees for honey remains important business in Alabama.

In 1719, the French brought slaves to Mississippi to work in the fields of tobacco and rice. The French lost control of this land to the British in 1736. Situated on the Mississippi River, Natchez, Mississippi, had abundant cotton plantations. Just prior to the Civil War, Natchez claimed the greatest income per capita of any city in the United States. Because of their wealth, the inhabitants of this city enjoyed an affluent lifestyle with sumptuous dining.

The fertile plains near the Mississippi River support the growth of a multitude of crops. In addition to rice, corn, wheat, peanuts, pecans, sweet potatoes, watermelons, and peaches, farmers in Mississippi raise chickens and livestock. Deer, geese, quail, wild turkeys, and ducks abound in the forests and around the waterways. Freshwater and saltwater fish like catfish, bass, trout, red snapper, mackerel, shrimp, oysters, and crabs come from the many rivers, streams, and the Gulf of Mexico.

France controlled Arkansas in its early history, lost control to Spain, and later regained the leadership. In 1803, the United States annexed Arkansas with the Louisiana Purchase, and Arkansas became a state in 1836. The cookery found in the southern part of the state bordering Louisiana still exhibits strong culinary traits from the South. With many poultry farms raising chickens, turkeys, and eggs, Arkansas leads the states in production of chicken. In addition to poultry, much of the income in this state comes from growing a cornucopia of fruits, vegetables, grains, and nuts, including spinach, tomatoes, beans, corn, potatoes, melons, grapes, peaches, apples, soybeans, rice, and pecans.

With forests covering half of the state, plentiful game exists. The streams and rivers yield catfish, trout, perch, and bass. Farm-raised catfish emerged as a thriving business in Arkansas.

CHARACTERISTICS OF THE CUISINE

Plantations for growing tobacco and cotton thrived in the South. With these two valuable crops producing much of their income, farmers did not use the land for grazing cattle. As a result, beef was not plentiful throughout the South. On the other hand, hogs thrived on scraps from the farm and foraging, which explains why Southern cooking features pork in countless recipes. From the time of the early settlements in Virginia, the settlers brought hogs to their new homeland and the animals flourished. Corn introduced by the Native Americans provided the hogs with plenty of feed. Often served at every meal, pork prevailed as the meat of choice. Pork products like bacon, ham hocks, and fatback served as flavoring for all sorts of dishes throughout the South.

To prevent spoilage, most butchering took place in the cooler temperatures of the fall. Because of the lack of refrigeration in those early days, preserving foods was crucial. Making country hams remains popular throughout the South, particularly in Virginia, Kentucky, Tennessee, North Carolina, and Georgia. As a way of using all parts and scraps of the hog after butchering, they made sausage, which became an intrinsic part of the southern diet.

All sorts of poultry flourished on the plantations, farms, and open land, so chicken, turkey, duck, and a variety of game birds became a large part of the southern diet. Since the butchered fowl yielded food for one or two meals, they did not require any preserving. Whether fried, boiled, braised, baked, or broiled, poultry served as the usual entrée for Sunday dinners in the South. Depending on the particular area, rice or potatoes accompanied it.

Game played a significant role in the diet of the early Southerners. Quail, pigeon, pheasant, wild duck, venison, squirrel, and rabbit contributed to the settlers' protein consumption.

In the Southern region, the Atlantic Ocean borders from North Carolina south to Georgia and the Gulf of Mexico forms the coastline from Georgia west to Mississippi. The coastal waters yield abundant fish and shellfish, including pompano, red snapper, grouper, shrimp, crab, oysters, crayfish, and clams. A number of crab dishes like deviled crab and crab cakes frequently appear on menus. Southerners consume many oyster dishes such as oyster stew, fried oysters, scalloped oysters, and raw oysters. Also, fried shrimp, shrimp and tomato pie, shrimp cocktail, shrimp salad, and many other shrimp dishes grace southern tables.

In general, soups from the South directly reflect the area and the season. Whatever grows in the garden, swims in the waterways, or is hunted shows up in the soup pot. Seafood soups and bisques emerged from all of the coastal areas, and each featured the seafood available in that particular location. Milk and/or cream usually provided the base for these seafood soups. She-crab soup from Charleston, South Carolina, remains well known.

Gumbo, a soup containing okra, also appears regularly. Depending on the available ingredients, gumbo is made from almost any type of meat, fowl, seafood, or combination. Thickening for these soups relied on okra in most of the South, but some preferred thickening with filé, ground sassafras leaves. To thicken with filé, remove soup from the heat, dissolve the filé powder into some liquid from the soup, and then stir the filé mixture into the pot of soup. Eat immediately, but if reheating, do *not* boil or the soup becomes stringy.

In the times of slavery, black women usually cooked for their owners. With a well-stocked kitchen, they prepared sumptuous meals. Freshly made biscuits or cornbread accompanied most meals. Many plantation owners even sent their cooks to Charleston or other large towns to learn recipes and techniques from French and English cooking. Unfortunately, great disparity existed between what the slaves cooked for their masters and what they prepared for their own families. The slaves received the least desirable foods, including pork intestines (chitterlings), pigs' feet, and pigs' skin, which they fried until crisp and called crackling. The slaves simmered beans, black-eyed peas, and/or greens for hours with a ham bone, fatback, or other pork scraps. These ingredients discarded from the "main house" became the basis and major flavoring of "soul food."

Cooks prepared many stews throughout the South. Besides extending any available meat, fish, and seafood, good-tasting stews often contained a variety of these items. Both

Originally, only female blue crabs were used in South Carolina's she-crab soup because the female crabs have a sweeter flavor. Adding the roe gave the soup its pale orange color.

Called "pot likker" throughout the South, a prized liquid remains after removing boiled greens from the pot. Usually served as a soup or ladled over food like gravy, pot likker derives its flavor from some sort of pork, like bacon grease, fatback, or ham hocks.

Brunswick County in North Carolina and Brunswick County in Virginia claim to be the home of Brunswick stew. Regardless of its birthplace, it began as a squirrel stew; however, today most omit the squirrel and prepare it as a stew of chicken, beef, and/ or pork, beans, potatoes, corn, and tomatoes.

Beans also played a major role in the southern diet. All kinds of beans, including black-eyed peas, pinto beans, butter beans, and lima beans, filled the menus in homes and restaurants. Generally, the people living in the northern states of the South preferred pinto and lima beans while those in the Deep South usually prepared black-eyed peas and red beans.

A multitude of fruits and vegetables flourish in the hot, humid weather found in most areas of the South as well as the cooler climate in the mountainous regions. As a result, many vegetables accompany Southern meals. Cabbage, green beans, pole beans, greens, turnips, peas, asparagus, mushrooms, okra, eggplant, corn, tomatoes, cucumbers, sweet and hot peppers, squash, cantaloupes, honeydews, watermelon, peaches, plums, black-berries, strawberries, rhubarb, figs, and apples grow in this region.

Still a popular vegetable, greens consists of one type or any combination of leaves like collards, mustard, kale, turnip, and others cooked with fatback, bacon grease, or other pork flavoring. White potatoes and sweet potatoes also played a large role in the Southern menu.

Hot peppers pickled in vinegar remain a favorite condiment throughout the South. Initially, the easily grown chili peppers replaced black pepper because they were much cheaper. Eventually, this condiment became such a popular flavoring that many restaurants and homes have a bottle of vinegar containing hot peppers standing on the table next to the salt and pepper shakers. Introduced by the English who discovered it in the East Indies, curry became popular in the early colonies. Many areas in the South prepare their own version of chicken country captain, a curried chicken dish.

Regardless of whether it was yeast-based or quick bread, some sort of bread accompanied every meal in the early days. Steaming biscuits, baked or fried cornbread, cornsticks, spoonbread (a soufflé-like version of cornbread), Sally Lunn bread (a very light, airy, rich, yeasted bread), and other freshly baked breads regularly appeared on the table at breakfast, midday dinner, and evening supper. Serving other starches like dressing (stuffing) or dumplings did not eliminate breads with the meal.

Usually made from flour, dumplings were dropped into the boiling liquid from a spoon or were rolled out and cut into strips before being added to the liquid surrounding a variety of foods. Because dumplings cooked in the pot with chicken, beef stew, or greens, they absorbed flavor from the cooking liquid.

Corn and cornmeal appear in countless recipes throughout the South. Corn was served at every meal in earlier days, and today many meals still include corn. As a side dish, it is prepared by boiling, frying, roasting, grilling, or baking.

Grinding dried corn produces cornmeal, the basis for cornbread, corncakes, spoonbread, fritters, and breading used for frying. Whether fried, baked in individual pans, or prepared in a large cast-iron skillet and cut into wedges, cornbread graces many tables. Hush puppies, deep-fried balls of cornmeal mixed with onion, commonly accompany fish.

Hulled corn treated with lye becomes hominy. Prepared from ground, dried hominy and cooked like a cereal, grits serves as a breakfast staple accompanying eggs and sausage or bacon. Although it looks like cream of wheat cereal, Southerners season grits with butter, salt, and pepper, not sugar. Flavored with cheddar or garlic cheese, grits casserole remains a popular brunch dish.

In the early days, breakfast in the South meant a huge meal beginning with a mint julep or brandy. While hash brown potatoes and toast accompany breakfast in the northern

---

A traditional dish served on New Year's Day throughout the South, hoppin' John consists of black-eyed peas and rice. According to folklore, black-eyed peas bring good luck.

In 1865 in Kentucky, Jack Bibb developed Bibb lettuce, a soft, buttery-textured lettuce that grows in small, loose heads. Growing in the early spring, Bibb lettuce is featured in salads served around the time of the Kentucky Derby.

Fried cornbread resembles a pancake.

Served throughout the South, hush puppies are balls of deep-fried cornbread containing minced onions. Supposedly, the first hush puppies were made to quiet the yapping dogs in the kitchen and keep them away from the food while the women cooked. Legend says a cook fried a dollop of cornbread batter in the skillet where the fish cooked, and then said "hush puppy" to the dogs as she fed them the fried cornbread balls. The name stuck, and hush puppies still typically accompany fried fish throughout the South.

Hush Puppies

Grits comes from the Old English word *grytta*, meaning coarse meal, bran, or chaff. After sifting ground corn, the finer ground grain is cornmeal and the coarser grind is grits.

Although diners flourish in the East, the coffee shop reigns in the South. Coffee shop menus feature a wide variety of simple foods.

In order to label liquor "Kentucky bourbon," it must be made from at least 51 percent corn, aged at least two years in charred, new oak barrels in Kentucky, and be no more than 160 proof. Actually, many distillers use 70 percent corn, age the bourbon for four years, and allow no more than 125 proof.

Recipes for the mint julep abound throughout the South, but preparation begins with bourbon poured over ice and then mixed with some sort of sweetness and fresh mint. The Kentucky Derby version adds simple syrup (sugar water) to the bourbon and a crushed sprig of fresh mint. Crushing the mint releases its pungent oils, and the mint sprig garnishes the drink.

Much of the wine made in the South started with Scuppernong grapes or a member of the family of Muscadine grapes. These grapes produced a mildly sweet, fragrant, pungent wine. A number of other varieties of grapes are grown in the South today, producing many types of wines.

states, grits and biscuits are preferred in the South. The traditional Southern breakfast usually consists of eggs, biscuits, and grits with ham, bacon, or sausage. Gravy frequently completes the plate.

Treasuring their desserts, homes and restaurants offer all sorts of confections on their menus. Cloying sweet desserts like pecan pie remain popular. Because of the hot weather, pie dough could be difficult to handle, but that never stopped Southern cooks from preparing countless varieties. Pecan pie, black bottom pie, sweet potato pie, and chess pie; plus pies made with every imaginable fruit, raisins, and green tomatoes; lemon meringue pie; and cream pies including coconut, banana, and chocolate, as well as buttermilk pies appeared at all kinds of events from church socials to christenings, funerals, and home dinners. Also, cakes enjoyed great popularity. The low-gluten flour that grew in the southern soil produced tender cakes and biscuits.

Southerners are known for their "sweet tooth," and sweetened beverages reign throughout the South. Ordering iced tea in a restaurant usually means a glass of already sweetened iced tea. Since the majority of people prefer sweetened tea, they add sugar to the hot tea just after making it, and the sugar completely dissolves. Then they chill the tea. The sugar thoroughly melts in the hot tea, so it requires less sugar to taste sweet, and there are no grains of sugar remaining in the tea. Lemonade ranks as another popular drink in the hot, humid summers. Known for consuming large amounts of soft drinks, many Southerners like their morning caffeine jolt from a cola beverage instead of coffee.

The only liquor actually developed in the United States, bourbon originated in Bourbon County, Kentucky, in the early 1800s. The mash for the bourbon consisted of corn, rye, and barley. In the 1830s, James Crow started aging bourbon in oak barrels, which greatly improved the flavor and the finish of the liquor. Today, most bourbon comes from Kentucky and Tennessee, where it is aged in charred oak barrels. Distilled from sugar cane, rum was also readily available in the South.

Area	Weather	Topography	Foods
Virginia Maryland to north, Atlantic Ocean to east, North Carolina and Tennessee to south, West Virginia and Kentucky to west	temperate winters; hot, humid summers; cooler in mountains	east: coastal plains, lowlands, marshes, inlets, Chesapeake Bay central: piedmont, rivers, streams, waterfalls west: Blue Ridge Mountains, gorges, fertile valleys, Shenandoah Valley, forests, plateaus	pork, country ham, cattle, seafood and fish, oysters, crabs, scallops, clams, shad, flounder, mackerel, pike, perch, bass, trout, chickens, game, deer, rabbits, turkey, duck, geese, quail, soybeans, peanuts, vegetables and fruits, apples, sweet potatoes, potatoes, tomatoes
West Virginia Pennsylvania and Ohio to north, Virginia to east and south, Ohio and Kentucky to west	warm summers, temperately cold winters	east: mountains, rivers, valleys, forests west: steep hills, rolling hills, valleys, rivers, Allegheny and Blue Ridge Mountains, Ohio River on western border	cattle, chickens, turkeys, freshwater fish, game, dairy, corn, apples, peaches
North Carolina Virginia to north, Atlantic Ocean to east, South Carolina to south, Tennessee to west	hot, humid summers and mild winters in east and central; cool summers, moderately cold winters in mountains	east: coastal plains, flat terrain, islands, reefs, low-lying land, swamps, marshes, fertile farmland in western coastal region central: piedmont, hills, rivers west: mountains, rivers, fertile valleys, forests	turkeys, chickens, game, pork, fish, seafood, ducks, geese, trout, flounder, crabs, shrimp, clams, fruits and vegetables, sweet potatoes, peanuts, apples, peaches, strawberries, blueberries
South Carolina North Carolina to north, Atlantic Ocean on east and south, Georgia to south and west	hot, humid summers; mild winters	east: coastal plains, bays, harbors, inlets, islands, coastline, swamps, marshes rivers, fertile land, sandy hills in west central: piedmont, hills, rivers west: mountains, hills, valleys, forests, rivers, Blue Ridge Mountains Low Country: coastal Up Country: interior	fish, seafood, oysters, shrimp, crabs, clams, crawfish, bass, mullet, mackerel, flounder, catfish, grouper, trout, turtle, duck, turkey, quail, pheasant, pork, rice, corn, curry, fruits and vegetables
Kentucky Ohio and Indiana to north, West Virginia and Virginia to east, Tennessee to south, Illinois and Missouri to west	hot, humid summers; cool winters	east: Cumberland Mountains, plateaus, valleys, hills, forests, rivers, streams central: rolling hills, fertile farmland west: plains, low hills Ohio River forms northern border, Mississippi River in west	beef, carp, bass, walleye, bluegill, catfish, corn, rye, wheat, vegetables and fruits, apples, peaches, popcorn, bourbon, whiskey
Tennessee Kentucky and Virginia to north, North Carolina to east, Georgia, Alabama, and Mississippi to south, Arkansas and Missouri to west	hot, humid summers; temperate winters	east: Blue Ridge Mountains, fertile valleys, forests, rivers, streams west: rolling hills, streams, rivers, lowlands and plains in far west, Mississippi River in west	beef, hogs, poultry, game, deer, wild turkeys, ducks, trout, pike, bass, soybeans, corn, beans, apples, peaches, fruits and vegetables
Georgia Tennessee and North Carolina to north, South Carolina and Atlantic Ocean to east, Florida to south, Alabama to west	hot, humid summers; mild winters	north: Appalachian Mountains, plateaus, fertile valleys, forests central: rolling hills, piedmont south: coastal plains	chicken, eggs, shrimp, oysters, crab, mullet, bass, flounder, trout, catfish, soybeans, many fruits and vegetables, peanuts, pecans, sweet potatoes, corn, onions, peaches, watermelon
Alabama Tennessee to north, Georgia to east, Florida and Gulf of Mexico to south, Mississippi to west	hot, humid summers; mild winters	north: forests, hills, rivers southern two-thirds: low hills, forests, lowlands, swamps, bayous, rivers, delta	beef, chickens, eggs, hogs, game, deer, wild turkey, geese, ducks, catfish, bass, flounder, red snapper, mackerel, mullet, shrimp, oysters, crab, soybeans, oats, corn, peanuts, pecans, okra, black-eyed peas, beans, greens, sweet potatoes, cucumbers, tomatoes, watermelons, strawberries, peaches, pears, apples, honey

(Continued)

Area	Weather	Topography	Foods
Mississippi Tennessee to north, Alabama to east, Gulf of Mexico and Louisiana to south, Louisiana and Arkansas to west	hot, humid summers; short, mild winters	west: Mississippi River forms western border, fertile plains remaining: forests, rolling hills, prairies, lowlands, rivers, lakes	chickens, livestock, game, deer, wild turkeys, geese, quail, ducks, catfish, bass, trout, mackerel, red snapper, shrimp, oysters, crabs, wheat, rice, corn, sweet potatoes, peanuts, pecans, peaches, watermelons
Arkansas Missouri to north, Tennessee and Mississippi to east, Louisiana to south, Oklahoma and Texas to west	hot, humid summers; cool winters; cooler climate in mountainous areas	north: plateaus, Ozark Mountains, valleys, gorges, rolling hills, streams east: lowlands, Mississippi River on eastern border, fertile delta plains south: lowlands, coastal plains west: mountains, valleys, plateaus, rivers	chickens, turkeys, livestock, game, ducks, catfish, trout, perch, bass, eggs, wheat, soybeans, corn, rice, fruits and vegetables, spinach, beans, tomatoes, potatoes, melons, peaches, apples, grapes, pecans

REVIEW QUESTIONS

1. How did the Civil War change the cooking found in the South?
2. Explain how and why African influence entered the cookery of the South. Include examples of foods.
3. Discuss the climate and topography of the South and how that influenced the cuisine. Include the growing of rice, fruits, and vegetables, and explain why the raising of cows was limited.
4. Explain the development of "soul food."
5. Define *hominy*, *grits*, and *cornmeal*. Explain the two cooking techniques for preparing cornbread.
6. Describe the process of making and cooking country ham, and tell why country ham developed as an important food in the South.

GLOSSARY

benne—sesame seeds

burgoo—a stew or thick soup containing a variety of meats, originally including squirrel, pork, beef, possum, chicken, or anything available, in addition to vegetables and seasonings; a specialty of Kentucky

chitterlings—pork intestines, part of "soul food" cookery

crackling—pigs' skin fried until crisp; appears extensively in "soul food"

filé—ground sassafras leaves used to thicken gumbo

grits—ground dried hominy, cooked like a cereal; accompanies eggs and sausage or bacon as a breakfast staple

gumbo—soup containing any available ingredients thickened with okra or filé

hominy—hulled corn treated with lye

hush puppies—deep-fried balls of cornmeal mixed with onion; commonly served with fried fish

red-eyed gravy—popular sauce with country ham; prepared by deglazing the pan where the ham was fried with coffee (or water) and then reducing the liquid

spoonbread—a soufflé-like version of cornbread

DEVILED EGGS

To make deviled eggs look professional, pipe filling into egg whites and garnish top of filling attractively and with color. Use capers, red pepper or pimento that is minced or cut into small strips, black olives, or a combination.

NUMBER OF SERVINGS: 12
COOKING METHOD:
  Boil
SERVING SIZE:
  2 each egg halves
TOTAL YIELD:
  24 each egg halves
FILLING: 11¼; oz

Wine Style: Light to medium, semi-dry white wines, Riesling, or Chenin Blanc
Example: White Muscadine—Perdido Vineyards, Perdido, AL. This wine is semi-dry, spicy, with a fragrant bouquet.

Deviled Eggs
photo courtesy of American Egg Board

INGREDIENTS	WEIGHT	VOLUME
eggs, hard-boiled, shells removed	1 lb, 4 oz	12 each
mayonnaise	2¾ oz	⅓ cup
mustard, prepared (yellow)	½ oz	1 tablespoon
onion, minced	¼ oz	1 tablespoon
Worcestershire sauce		½ teaspoon
cayenne		⅛ teaspoon
salt		½ teaspoon
white pepper		½ teaspoon
GARNISH:		
pimento		
capers		
black olives		
paprika		

1. Cut eggs in halves lengthwise. Being careful not to tear whites, remove yolks and place in separate bowl.
2. Mash yolks with fork. Add mayonnaise, mustard, onion, Worcestershire sauce, cayenne, salt, and pepper. Mix well.
3. Correct seasonings. Pipe or spoon yolk mixture into recess of egg whites.
4. Garnish with pieces of pimento, capers, and/or black olives sprinkle with paprika. Serve.

KENTUCKY CATFISH SPRING ROLLS WITH ASIAN DIPPING SAUCE

Chef Kathy Cary uses Wei-Chun brand spring roll wrappers when preparing this recipe.

Available in Asian food stores, Sriracha is an Asian sauce containing chili peppers, sugar, garlic, salt, and vinegar.

—Recipe by Kathy Cary

NUMBER OF SERVINGS: 12
COOKING METHOD:
  Deep-fry
SERVING SIZE:
  1 each spring roll
TOTAL YIELD:
  12 each spring rolls
FILLING:
  2 lb, 3¼ oz

Wine Style: Light- to medium-bodied Chenin Blanc, Pinot Blanc, mild Chardonnay, or White Zinfandel
Example: Chardonnay—Lost Heritage Vineyards, Alexandria, KY. This wine is made in a fruity, citrus style, with light oak and a crisp finish.

INGREDIENTS	WEIGHT	VOLUME
FILLING:		
catfish fillets, fresh skinless	2 lbs	
mint, minced	¾ oz	3 tablespoons
cilantro, minced	½ oz	2 tablespoons
ginger, fresh, peeled, minced	¼ oz	1 tablespoon
scallions, minced	¾ oz	3 tablespoons
Serrano peppers, seeds and ribs removed, minced	½ oz	2 tablespoons
kosher salt	½ oz	2 teaspoons
Sriracha		2 teaspoons
DIPPING SAUCE:		
rice wine vinegar	8 oz	1 cup
fish sauce		1 tablespoon + 1 teaspoon
brown sugar	2 oz	¼ cup
lemon juice	1 oz	2 tablespoons
garlic, minced	½ oz	2 teaspoons
cilantro, minced		1 tablespoon + 1 teaspoon
egg, beaten	1¾ oz	1 each
water for thinning egg		
thin spring roll wrappers		12 each

For Filling:

1. Place catfish in bowl of food processor fitted with steel knife blade. Pulse until finely ground.
2. Remove catfish from processor and place in bowl. Add mint, cilantro, ginger, scallions, peppers, salt, and Sriracha. Combine thoroughly. Cover and refrigerate until needed.

For Dipping Sauce:

1. Combine rice wine vinegar, fish sauce, and brown sugar together in saucepan over medium heat; simmer until reduced by half.
2. Remove from heat; add lemon juice and garlic. Cool to room temperature; add cilantro.

For Assembly:

1. Preheat oil in deep-fryer or skillet to 350 degrees. With fork, mix egg with a few drops water to thin it. Place spring roll wrapper on work surface. Brush outer edge of each wrapper with egg wash.
2. Place about 2 ¾; oz (⅓ cup) catfish mixture in small compact log diagonally across wrapper.
3. Fold ends over filling, then roll wrapper over filling to make tight roll. Repeat with remaining wrappers and filling.
4. Add spring rolls to hot fat, a few at a time, to maintain temperature of oil. Deep-fry until golden, approximately 3½ to 4 minutes.
5. Remove from oil, drain on absorbent paper, and slice into thirds (or smaller sections, if used for passed hors d'oeuvres). Serve, accompanied by hot or room-temperature dipping sauce.

—Copyright Kathy Cary

KATHY CARY

Chef/Owner

Currently the chef/owner of three food businesses in Louisville, Kentucky, Chef Kathy Cary started La Pêche, which includes both a gourmet-to-go store and a catering operation, in 1979. Later, she opened Lilly's, an upscale restaurant with dishes described as French-inspired cooking using traditional Kentucky ingredients with unexpected, contemporary twists.

Cary apprenticed with a Cordon Bleu–trained chef in Washington, D.C. In addition to numerous other commendations, Cary was selected as a James Beard Award Nominee for Best Chef of the Southeast numerous times. She has made many appearances on the Television Food Network.

She places great emphasis on buying fresh produce directly from local farmers and promoting sustainable agriculture. Also, Cary is involved with several charities including a cooking-and-gardening educational program to benefit at-risk inner-city teens, Citymeals-on-Wheels, and Share Our Strength.

SHE-CRAB SOUP

She-Crab Soup

NUMBER OF SERVINGS: 8
COOKING METHOD:
  Boil
SERVING SIZE:
  6 oz
TOTAL YIELD:
  3 lbs, 3¼ oz

INGREDIENTS	WEIGHT	VOLUME
butter	2 oz	4 tablespoons
flour, all purpose	1 oz	¼ cup
half-and-half	2 lbs	1 qt
paprika		¼ teaspoon
nutmeg		½ teaspoon
cayenne pepper		⅛ to ¼ teaspoon, to taste
salt		½ teaspoon
white pepper		½ teaspoon
mace		⅛ teaspoon
sherry	2 oz	¼ cup
Worcestershire sauce		1 teaspoon
crabmeat and roe	1 lb	

GARNISH:
lemon rind
paprika
parsley, minced

1. Melt butter in large pot, whisk in flour, and continue whisking over medium-low heat for about 3 minutes to make white roux.
2. Add half-and-half; whisk constantly until almost boiling and beginning to thicken.
3. Add remaining ingredients. Heat thoroughly but do not allow to boil. Correct seasonings.
4. Serve, garnished with lemon rind, paprika, and parsley.

CREAMY PEANUT SOUP

Creamy Peanut Soup

photo courtesy of Peanut Advisory Board

In pre–Civil War days, the African slaves made peanut soup with sweet potatoes and tomatoes instead of cream. Many people still prefer peanut soup prepared in this way.

NUMBER OF SERVINGS: 12
COOKING METHOD:
 Boil
SERVING SIZE:
 8 oz
TOTAL YIELD:
 6 lbs, 5½ oz

INGREDIENTS	WEIGHT	VOLUME
butter	8 oz	1 cup or 2 sticks
onion, small dice	10 oz	2 medium or 2 cups
celery, small dice	10 oz	2 stalks or 2 cups
flour, all purpose	1 oz	¼ cup
chicken stock, hot	3 lbs	6 cups
heavy cream	1 lb	2 cups
peanut butter, creamy	14½ oz	1½ cups
peanuts, ground	4½ oz	1 cup
lemon juice		1 tablespoon + 1 teaspoon
salt		½ teaspoon
pepper		½ teaspoon
cumin		1 teaspoon
cayenne		¼ teaspoon
GARNISH:		
peanuts, coarsely chopped	2¼ oz	½ cup
parsley, minced		

1. Melt butter in stock pot over medium heat. Sauté onion and celery until it softens, about 3 to 4 minutes.

2. Whisk in flour; cook 1 to 2 minutes. Slowly whisk in stock. Bring to boil to thicken. Remove from heat; cool slightly.

3. Purée mixture in food processor. Return mixture to pot, place over medium-low heat, and add cream, peanut butter, ground peanuts, lemon juice, salt, pepper, cumin, and cayenne.

4. Cook for several minutes, until hot. Correct seasonings. Place in bowl; garnish with chopped peanuts and parsley. Serve.

WILTED SALAD

Wilted Salad

Any greens can replace the romaine in this recipe. More tender greens wilt quicker; tougher greens need more time to wilt.

NUMBER OF SERVINGS: 12
COOKING METHOD:
 Sauté
SERVING SIZE:
 4 oz
TOTAL YIELD:
 3 lbs, 1½ oz

INGREDIENTS	WEIGHT	VOLUME
bacon, chopped	8 oz	
onion, grated	1 oz	2 teaspoons
vinegar, white	4 oz	1/2 cup
water	4 oz	1/2 cup
salt	1/4 oz	1 teaspoon
pepper		1 teaspoon
sugar	1/4 oz	2 teaspoons
romaine, cleaned, coarsely chopped	2 lbs	2 heads

GARNISH:

hard-boiled egg, slices or wedges

1. Heat large skillet or braiser over medium heat; sauté bacon until crisp.
2. Add onion; cook until tender, 1 or 2 minutes. Drain off all but 2 oz (4 tablespoons or 1/4 cup) bacon grease.
3. Add vinegar, water, salt, pepper, and sugar. Stir to mix and bring to boil.
4. Add romaine and stir. Allow to cook until lightly wilted, about 3 to 5 minutes.
5. Serve immediately, garnished with hard-boiled egg.

COLESLAW

Coleslaw
photo by David Murray © Dorling Kindersley

If desired, prepare this slaw a day before serving.

NUMBER OF SERVINGS: 14
SERVING SIZE:
  4 oz
TOTAL YIELD:
  3 lbs, 8½ oz total
DRESSING:
  1 lb, 4 oz or 2¼ cups

INGREDIENTS	WEIGHT	VOLUME
DRESSING:		
oil, variety of choice	5¾ oz	¾ cup
vinegar, apple cider	8 oz	1 cup
sugar	7 oz	1 cup
dry mustard	1/4 oz	2½ teaspoons
celery seed	1/4 oz	2½ teaspoons
salt	1/4 oz	1 teaspoon
pepper		1/2 teaspoon
SALAD:		
cabbage, cored, coarsely shredded	1 lb, 13½ oz	1 large
carrot, peeled, shredded	1¾ oz	1 each
red pepper, minced	6 oz	1 each
onion, minced	1/2 oz	1 tablespoon

1. Mix all dressing ingredients together in saucepan. Bring to boil over medium heat; reduce heat and simmer 5 to 10 minutes.
2. Remove from heat and cool slightly.
3. Place cabbage, carrot, red pepper, and onion in stainless steel or glass bowl; toss to mix. Add dressing; mix well.
4. Correct seasoning; refrigerate until cold.

COUNTRY CAPTAIN CHICKEN

Hailing from South Carolina, this dish originated near the ports where ships returned bearing all sorts of spices from their trading journeys to faraway places. The English acquired a fondness for curry from their colony, India, and they brought this liking for curry to their new land, the United States.

Country Captain Chicken

© 2008 Jupiterimages Corporation

NUMBER OF SERVINGS: 8
COOKING METHOD:
  Braise
SERVING SIZE:
  ¼ chicken
TOTAL YIELD:
  9 lbs, 2½ oz

Wine Style: Soft and fruity Pinot Blanc, Chardonnay, or rich, soft Pinot Noir
Example: Chardonnay—Benjamin Vineyards and Winery, Graham, NC. This well-balanced Chardonnay is aged in American oak to add body and fullness.

INGREDIENTS	WEIGHT	VOLUME
raisins	6 oz	1 cup
flour, all purpose	4½ oz	1 cup
salt		½ teaspoon
pepper		½ teaspoon
paprika		½ teaspoon
chicken, fryer, washed, cut into quarters	5 to 6 lbs	2 each
oil	3 oz	6 tablespoons
onion, medium dice	10 oz	2 cups or 2 large
green pepper	10 oz	2 cups or 2 each
garlic, minced	½ oz	2 teaspoons
tomatoes, canned	1 lb, 13 oz	4 cups
curry powder	½ oz	2 tablespoons

ACCOMPANIMENT:

rice

GARNISH:

almond slices or slivers, toasted	3½ oz	1 cup
chutney		

1. Soak raisins in warm water; set aside.
2. Combine flour, salt, pepper, and paprika. Dredge chicken with this mixture.
3. Heat oil in large skillet over medium-high heat. Brown chicken on both sides. Remove from pan; reserve.
4. Add onion and green pepper. Sauté lightly, until onion is translucent.
5. Add garlic, tomatoes, and curry powder. Bring to boil, add chicken, cover, and simmer for 25 to 30 minutes, until chicken is done.
6. Remove chicken from pan; cover and keep warm.
7. Turn heat to high; reduce sauce until it thickens, approximately 10 minutes.
8. Reduce heat; return chicken to pan, add raisins, and correct seasonings.
9. Serve accompanied by rice, toasted almonds, and chutney.

BRUNSWICK STEW

A word of caution: the large weight on this recipe reflects the sauce, which contains many vegetables as well as liquid.

In earlier days, Brunswick stew contained squirrel and other available meat and game.

NUMBER OF SERVINGS: 8
COOKING METHOD:
  Braise
SERVING SIZE:
  ¼ chicken with sauce
TOTAL YIELD:
  12 lbs, 8 oz

Wine Style: Light- to medium-bodied Chenin Blanc, Pinot Blanc, or mild Chardonnay
Example: Pinot Blanc–Three Sisters Vineyard, Dahlonega, GA. This is a crisp wine with tangerine and grapefruit citrus fruit and notes of pear, honey, and melon.

Brunswick Stew
© 2008 StockFood

INGREDIENTS	WEIGHT	VOLUME
salt	¼ oz	1 teaspoon
pepper		½ teaspoon
paprika		½ teaspoon
chicken, washed, cut into quarters	about 6 lbs	2 each
butter	5 oz	10 tablespoons
onion, thinly sliced	1 lb	4 cups or 2 each large
green pepper, medium dice	10 oz	2 cups or 2 each
celery, medium dice	1 lb, 2½ oz	4 cups or 10 stalks
flour, all purpose	1½ oz	6 tablespoons
chicken stock or water, hot	2 lb, 8 oz or as needed	5 cups or as needed
tomatoes, chopped	2 lbs, 6 oz	4 cups
cayenne		¼ teaspoon
Worcestershire sauce	1 oz	2 tablespoons
lima beans	1 lb, 10 oz	4 cups
corn	1 lb, 4 oz	4 cups

ACCOMPANIMENT:
rice

1. Mix salt, pepper, and paprika together. Sprinkle evenly over chicken.
2. Heat butter in braising pan or ovenproof pan over medium-high heat; brown chicken.
3. Add onion, green pepper, and celery; cook until onion becomes transparent.
4. Reduce heat to medium-low. Whisk in flour and cook another 2 to 3 minutes, for blonde roux.
5. Slowly whisk in chicken stock or water. Add tomatoes, cayenne, and Worcestershire sauce..
6. Add lima beans and corn. Cook another 30 minutes, until chicken is done.
7. Correct seasonings; serve accompanied by rice.

OVEN BARBECUED PULLED PORK

Oven Barbecued Pulled Pork
photo courtesy of National Pork Board

Typically, pulled pork is prepared on a grill with a cover. This recipe calls for cooking in the oven, but if a grill is available, feel free to grill the pork instead of baking it.

NUMBER OF SERVINGS: 10
COOKING METHOD:
  Bake
SERVING SIZE:
  4 oz
TOTAL YIELD:
  2 lbs, 9½ oz total
MEAT:
  1 lb, 15 oz

Wine Style: Soft red hybrids such as Chambourcin, Merlot, or fruity Pinot Noir
Example: Chambourcin—Glen Marie Vineyards and Winery, Burlington, NC. Full-bodied with a taste of black cherries and a spicy finish.

INGREDIENTS	WEIGHT	VOLUME
DRY RUB:		
brown sugar, firmly packed	1½ oz	3 tablespoons
black pepper	¼ oz	1 tablespoon
salt	¾ oz	1 tablespoon
paprika	¼ oz	1 tablespoon
thyme		1 teaspoon
garlic powder	¼ oz	1 teaspoon
rosemary		1 teaspoon
cayenne pepper		⅛ teaspoon
pork shoulder or Boston butt roast, washed, dried	about 4 lbs	
BARBECUE SAUCE:		
vinegar, apple cider	1 lb	2 cups
brown sugar, firmly packed	4½ oz	½ cup
red pepper flakes		½ teaspoon
Worcestershire sauce	1¼ oz	2 tablespoons
salt	¼ oz	1 teaspoon

ACCOMPANIMENTS:
hamburger buns
colesslaw

1. Preheat oven to 350 degrees.

2. Mix all ingredients for dry rub together in small bowl.

3. Line roasting pan with aluminum foil. Place meat in pan; thoroughly rub spice mixture over meat.

4. Cover pan tightly with aluminum foil. Bake for 5 hours until meat is very tender and shreds easily.

5. While meat bakes, prepare barbecue sauce by mixing all ingredients together in bowl. Divide barbecue sauce into 2 portions and set aside until needed.

6. Remove meat from pan and place on cutting board. Shred meat by pulling apart using two forks.

7. Place meat in bowl. Pour half of sauce (one portion) over meat; mix to coat meat.

8. Serve on buns, accompanied by remaining barbecue sauce and cole slaw.

BARBECUED RIBS

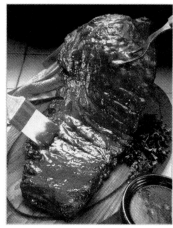

To prepare this recipe without a grill, proceed as instructed in the recipe until preheating the grill. Instead, drain any fat from pan, baste both sides of ribs, and bake in oven for another hour or until done. Baste about every 10 minutes. The total cooking time will depend on the size and thickness of the ribs.

NUMBER OF SERVINGS: 8
COOKING METHOD:
  Braise
SERVING SIZE:
  7 oz
TOTAL YIELD:
  3 lbs, 10 oz

Wine Style: Full-bodied red wines, Cabernet Sauvignon, Syrah, or Zinfandel
Example: Syrah—Horizon Cellars, Siler City, NC. This wine is ripe and soft, with smoky flavors and a long, spicy finish.

Barbecued Ribs
photo courtesy of National Pork Board

INGREDIENTS	WEIGHT	VOLUME
salt		¹/₂ teaspoon
pork spareribs	20 lbs	4 each racks
SAUCE:		
butter	8 oz	2 sticks or 1 cup
onion, small dice	10 oz	2 cups or 2 each medium
garlic, minced	1 oz	4 cloves or 4 teaspoons
vinegar, cider	8 oz	1 cup
water	8 oz	1 cup
hot pepper sauce		¹/₂ teaspoon
catsup	1 lb, 3 oz	4 cups
brown sugar	2¹/₂ oz	6 tablespoons or ¹/₄ cup + 2 tablespoons
salt		¹/₂ teaspoon
pepper		1 teaspoon
dry mustard	¹/₂ oz	2 tablespoons

1. Preheat oven to 350 degrees. Evenly salt ribs with ¹/₂ teaspoon salt. Place ribs on baking sheet; bake for 1 hour to partially cook.
2. Meanwhile, prepare sauce by melting butter in saucepan over medium heat. Add onions and cook 4 to 5 minutes until onion is translucent.
3. Add garlic; cook one more minute. Add remaining sauce ingredients, bring to boil, reduce heat, and simmer 15 minutes.
4. Preheat grill. Baste one side of ribs with sauce. Place ribs on grill, sauce side down.
5. Baste other side with sauce. Turn frequently, basting often until ribs are done, about 30 minutes.

Note: The type of grill (wood, charcoal, or gas) affects the time needed to cook the ribs as well as the flavor of the ribs.

FRIED CATFISH

Fried Catfish
photo © Dorling Kindersley

NUMBER OF SERVINGS: 9
COOKING METHOD:
  Fry
SERVING SIZE:
  6½ oz
TOTAL WEIGHT:
  3 lbs, 11¼ oz

Wine Style: Light-style Chardonnay, Viognier, or soft fruity Semillon
Example: Viognier—Beachaven Vineyards and Winery, Clarksville, TN. This wine has an apricot bouquet that leads into grapefruit and honeysuckle flavors.

INGREDIENTS	WEIGHT	VOLUME
cornmeal	7 oz	1 cup
flour, all purpose	3¼ oz	¾ cup
baking powder		½ teaspoon
salt	¼ oz	1 teaspoon
pepper		1 teaspoon
cayenne		⅛ teaspoon
paprika		¼ teaspoon
egg	1¾ oz	1 each
milk	4 oz	½ cup
oil	for frying	
catfish fillets, rinsed	3 lbs, 4½ oz	9 large or 18 small each

GARNISH:

lemon wedges

tartar sauce

1. Combine cornmeal, flour, baking powder, salt, pepper, cayenne, and paprika in bowl. Set aside until needed.
2. Beat egg and milk together in another bowl. Set aside until needed.
3. Heat ½ inch of oil in skillet to 375 degrees.
4. Dip fish fillets into milk mixture, then dredge both sides in cornmeal mixture.
5. Place fish, a few at a time, into hot oil. Do not add too many at once or temperature of oil will fall too much.
6. Fry until golden and thoroughly cooked, about 2 to 3 minutes on each side.
7. Remove from oil; drain well on absorbent paper. Serve, accompanied by lemon and tartar sauce.

HOT BROWN

Hot Brown
photo courtesy of National Turkey Federation. For more cooking tips and recipe ideas, visit www.eatturkey.com

This open-faced sandwich originated at the Brown Hotel in Louisville, Kentucky. It makes a wonderful luncheon or light dinner entrée. It works well as a passed hors d'oeuvre when prepared on an English muffin and cut into quarters.

NUMBER OF SERVINGS: 8
COOKING METHOD:
  Boil, Broil
SERVING SIZE:
  1 each sandwich containing
  1 slice bread, 2 oz turkey,
  1¾ oz (2 slices) tomato,
  2¼ oz (3 tablespoons)
    Mornay sauce,
  ¼ oz (1 tablespoon)
    Parmesan cheese,
  ¾ oz (2 slices) cooked bacon
TOTAL YIELD:
  Mornay sauce: 1 lb, 4¼ oz
  or 1¾ cups

Wine Style: Crisp Chardonnay, Sauvignon Blanc, Blush, Rose, or Grenache
Example: Chardonnay—Equus Run Vineyards, Midway, KY. This wine has green apple flavors for a crisp mouth feel and a very slight hint of melon followed by a touch of oak finish.

INGREDIENTS	WEIGHT	VOLUME
MORNAY SAUCE:		
butter	1 oz	2 tablespoons
flour, all purpose	3/4 oz	2 tablespoons
milk, warm	12 oz	1 1/2 cups
clove, stuck into onion *below*		1 each
onion		1/2 each
nutmeg		1/4 teaspoon
cayenne		pinch or to taste
sherry, dry	1/2 oz	1 tablespoon
salt		1/4 teaspoon
pepper		1/8 teaspoon
cheddar cheese, extra-sharp, grated	4 oz	1 cup
bread, toasted		8 slices
turkey, sliced, warm	1 lb	
tomato, sliced 1/4-inch	14 oz	16 slices, about 3 medium
Parmesan cheese, grated	2 oz	1/2 cup
bacon, cooked	6 oz	16 slices

For Mornay:

1. Melt butter in saucepan over medium-low heat. Add flour, whisk, and cook about 2 to 3 minutes until blonde roux.
2. Slowly whisk in milk, add clove-studded onion, stir frequently, and cook until thickened, at least 10 minutes.
3. Whisk in nutmeg, cayenne, sherry, salt, pepper, and cheddar cheese. Whisk until cheese melts.
4. Correct seasonings. If not needed immediately, cool, cover, and refrigerate until needed.

For Assembly:

1. Preheat broiler. Place toast on baking pan; top each toast with 2 oz warm turkey.
2. Place 1 3/4 oz (2 slices) tomato on turkey, then spoon 2 3/4 oz (3 tablespoons) hot Mornay sauce over sandwich. Sprinkle with 1/4 oz (1 tablespoon) Parmesan cheese over top.
3. Broil until lightly brown and bubbly. Remove from broiler.
4. Top with 3/4 oz (2 slices) bacon crisscrossed on top. Serve immediately.

GREENS

Greens

Use any combination of greens available and/or desired. Some possibilities include mustard, collard, turnip, and kale.

Be careful to wash away all sand and dirt from greens before cooking.

NUMBER OF SERVINGS: 9
COOKING METHOD:
  Boil
SERVING SIZE:
  4 oz
TOTAL YIELD:
  2 lbs, 6 1/2 oz

INGREDIENTS	WEIGHT	VOLUME
ham hock	10 1/4 oz	1 each
water	2 lbs	1 qt or 4 cups
onion, small dice	5 oz	1 cup or 1 medium
greens, assorted, washed well, drained, chopped	2 lbs	

1. Place ham hock, water, and onions in pan, bring to boil, reduce heat, and simmer for 15 to 20 minutes.
2. Remove ham hock, cut meat from bone, and cut into small dice. Return ham and bone to pot, add greens, and cook for 1 to 2 hours, until tender.
3. Remove bone. Serve greens with some of the cooking juice from pot (called pot likker).

OKRA AND TOMATOES

NUMBER OF SERVINGS: 13
COOKING METHOD:
  Boil
SERVING SIZE:
  4 oz
TOTAL YIELD:
  3 lbs, 4 oz

INGREDIENTS	WEIGHT	VOLUME
bacon, chopped	2³/₄ oz	3 slices
onion, medium dice	15 oz	3 cups or 4 onions
garlic, minced	¹/₂ oz	2 cloves
okra, sliced ¹/₂-inch thick	1 lb, ¹/₂ oz	4 cups
tomatoes, canned, with juice	2 lbs, 3 oz	4 cups
salt	¹/₂ oz	2 teaspoons
pepper		1 teaspoon
cayenne	dash or to taste	

1. Sauté bacon until crisp in saucepan over medium heat. Remove bacon and drain on absorbent paper.
2. Add onion and sauté for 5 minutes, until translucent.
3. Add garlic; cook another minute. Add okra, tomatoes, salt, pepper, and cayenne. Simmer for 20 minutes, until okra is tender.
4. Correct seasonings, top with reserved bacon pieces, and serve.

HOPPIN' JOHN

Hoppin' John

Serve this dish on New Year's Day for good luck!

Begin soaking the peas for this recipe the day before serving, if possible.

NUMBER OF SERVINGS: 14
COOKING METHOD:
  Sauté, Boil
SERVING SIZE:
  6 oz
TOTAL YIELD:
  5 lbs, 7 oz

INGREDIENTS	WEIGHT	VOLUME
black-eyed peas, dried	1 lb	
bacon, small dice	2³/₄ oz	3 slices
onion, small dice	5 oz	1 medium
garlic, minced	¹/₄ oz	1 large clove
liquid from cooking peas	1 lb, 14 oz	3³/₄ cups
rice	13¹/₂ oz	2 cups
bay leaf		1 each
salt		1¹/₂ teaspoons
pepper		¹/₂ teaspoon

1. Rinse peas, place in pot, cover with water allowing 3 inches of water over peas, and soak overnight. (To avoid overnight soaking, bring water to full boil, add peas, turn off heat, and allow to soak for at least a couple of hours.)
2. Drain peas, cover with fresh water, bring to boil, reduce heat, and cook until done, about 30 minutes. Drain and reserve cooking liquid for later use.
3. In separate pot, sauté bacon until crisp. Add onion and sauté about 3 minutes. Add garlic; sauté another minute.
4. Add peas, cooking liquid from peas, rice, bay leaf, salt, and pepper. If not enough liquid, add water until 1 lb, 14 oz (3³/₄ cups).
5. Bring to boil, reduce heat, cover tightly, and simmer for 20 minutes.
6. Correct seasoning; serve immediately.

CHEESE GRITS

Cheese Grits

This dish regularly appears at brunches.

NUMBER OF SERVINGS: 11
COOKING METHOD:
  Boil, Bake
SERVING SIZE:
  4 oz
TOTAL YIELD:
  2 lbs, 14¾ oz

INGREDIENTS	WEIGHT	VOLUME
water	1 lb, 8 oz	3 cups
grits, quick cooking	6½ oz	1 cup
salt		¼ teaspoon
cheddar cheese, sharp, grated	8 oz	2½ cups
butter	4 oz	½ cup or 1 stick
eggs, beaten	5 oz	3 each
milk	2½ oz	5 tablespoons
cayenne		¼ teaspoon or to taste
garlic powder		¼ teaspoon
baking powder		½ teaspoon
Worcestershire sauce		1 teaspoon
paprika		sprinkling

1. Place rack in middle of oven. Lightly grease 2- or 2½-quart baking dish. Preheat oven to 350 degrees.
2. Bring water to boil in saucepan; stir in grits and salt. Reduce heat, cover, and cook for 5 to 7 minutes, until thickened.
3. Remove from heat. Stir in 6 oz (2 cups) cheddar cheese, butter, eggs, milk, cayenne, garlic powder, baking powder, and Worcestershire sauce.
4. Pour grits mixture into prepared pan. Sprinkle remaining 2 oz (½ cup) grated cheddar cheese and paprika over top. Bake for 40 minutes, until firm and cheese browns.

SALLY LUNN

Sally Lunn

Many believe this bread derived its name from a baker living in England during the seventeenth century. This recipe produces a very light, airy bread reminiscent of brioche.

NUMBER OF SERVINGS: 12
COOKING METHOD:
  Bake
SERVING SIZE:
  1 wedge ¹⁄₁₂ of loaf
TOTAL YIELD:
  1 each baked in 10-inch angel food cake pan or Bundt pan

INGREDIENTS	WEIGHT	VOLUME
water, warm, about 105 degrees	2 oz	1/4 cup
sugar		1 teaspoon
yeast, granulated	1/2 oz	1 tablespoon
flour, all purpose	1 lb, 2 oz	4 cups
salt	1/4 oz	1 teaspoon
butter, softened	4 oz	1/2 cup or 1 stick
sugar	3 oz	1/3 cup
eggs	6 3/4 oz	4 each
milk, warm, about 105 degrees	6 oz	3/4 cup
melted butter, *optional*		

1. Place water and sugar (1 teaspoon) in nonreactive bowl; sprinkle yeast on top. Mix. Let stand a few minutes, until bubbly.
2. Combine flour and salt; set aside.
3. Cream butter and sugar (3 oz or 1/3 cup) until fluffy.
4. Add eggs, one at a time, mixing well after each one.
5. Add yeast mixture; mix well.
6. Add one-third of flour mixture; mix thoroughly. Add half of milk; mix thoroughly. Add half of remaining flour; mix well. Add remaining milk; mix well. Add remaining flour.
7. Cover and let rise in warm place for 2 hours.
8. Meanwhile, grease 10-inch angel food cake pan or Bundt pan. Stir batter to deflate; transfer to prepared pan. Cover and let rise until doubled.
9. Meanwhile, position rack in center of oven and preheat to 350 degrees. Place bread in oven and bake for 45 to 55 minutes, until golden. If desired, brush with melted butter after about 40 minutes of baking.
10. Cool on rack. Serve.

PEACH COBBLER

To peel peaches, place peach into boiling water for about 30 seconds. Remove from water, cool until can be handled, then use knife to remove skin from peach. Grab skin between thumb and knife and pull—the skin should slip off easily. If not, the peach needs a bit more time in the boiling water. After removing skin, cut peach in half, remove pit, and cut into slices.

NUMBER OF SERVINGS: 9
COOKING METHOD:
 Bake
SERVING SIZE:
 6 oz
TOTAL YIELD:
 3 lbs, 7 oz

INGREDIENTS	WEIGHT	VOLUME
FILLING:		
butter, unsalted	1 1/2 oz	3 tablespoons
sugar	5 oz	2/3 cup
cornstarch	3/4 oz	2 tablespoons
cinnamon		1/2 teaspoon
nutmeg, grated		1/8 to 1/4 teaspoon, to taste
peaches, peeled, pitted, sliced 1/2-inch thick	2 lb, 6 1/4 oz (about 2 lb, 12 oz before peeling)	7 medium to large
lemon juice	1/2 oz	1 tablespoon
almond extract		1/4 teaspoon
TOPPING:		
flour, all-purpose, unsifted	5 3/4 oz	1 1/4 cups
sugar	1 oz	2 tablespoons
baking powder	1/4 oz	2 teaspoons
salt		1/4 teaspoon
butter, unsalted, cold, cut in pieces	2 oz	4 tablespoons or 1/2 stick
milk	6 oz	3/4 cup
GARNISH:		
ice cream		

For Filling:

1. Place butter in large pot over medium-high heat until melted.
2. Mix sugar, cornstarch, cinnamon, and nutmeg together, add to peaches, then add peaches to melted butter. Stir gently to keep from burning. Cook until boiling.
3. Remove from heat; add lemon juice and almond extract. Set aside while preparing topping.

For Topping in Food Processor:

1. Position rack in center of the oven. Preheat oven to 400 degrees.
2. Place flour, sugar, baking powder, and salt in bowl of food processor fitted with knife blade. Pulse to mix.
3. Place butter on top of flour mixture; pulse to cut in butter until pieces are size of peas.
4. With motor running, add milk through feed tube. Pulse until just combined.

For Topping by Hand:

1. Position rack in center of the oven. Preheat oven to 400 degrees.
2. Mix flour, sugar, baking powder, and salt in bowl.
3. Place butter on top of flour mixture. Using two knives, pastry cutter, or fingertips, quickly mix until pieces are size of peas.
4. Add milk; stir quickly with fork until just combined.

For Assembly:

1. Place hot peach mixture into ungreased 2-qt dish.
2. Spoon topping over peaches. Most of peaches will be covered. If desired, drop spoonfuls of dough over peaches, leaving uncovered space.
3. Bake for about 25 minutes, until golden.
4. Cool on rack for about 10 minutes. Serve warm, accompanied by ice cream.

LEMON CHESS PIE

Lemon Chess Pie
photo courtesy of Land O' Lakes, Inc.

Two theories explain the origin of the name of this pie. One is that the name derives from the pie chest where pies where stored in earlier days, except that the translation from a southern accent emerged as chess *instead of* chest. *The second explanation recounts the tale of a diner asking the waitress what kind of pie was available for dessert. According to lore, her answer was "Jes' pie" (meaning* just pie*), which the diner understood as* chess pie. *No one knows how the name truly originated, but this very sweet pie is a traditional favorite throughout the South. This variation adds lemon for flavoring.*

NUMBER OF SERVINGS: 8
COOKING METHOD:
  Bake
SERVING SIZE:
  ⅛ pie
TOTAL YIELD:
  1 each 9-inch pie

For pie dough recipe, see recipe for pie dough with pumpkin pie in Chapter 2 or use any pie dough recipe desired.

INGREDIENTS	WEIGHT	VOLUME
pastry dough for single crust	about 10 oz	
butter, unsalted, softened	3 oz	6 tablespoons
sugar	13¼ oz	1¾ cups
eggs	6¾ oz	4 each
cornmeal	¼ oz	1 tablespoon
flour, all purpose	¼ oz	1 tablespoon
salt		¼ teaspoon
lemon rind, grated	½ oz	1 tablespoon
lemon juice	2 oz	¼ cup
milk	2 oz	¼ cup

GARNISH:

whipped cream, slightly sweetened

nutmeg

1. Line pie pan with pastry dough; flute edges. Place pie in freezer for 30 minutes to 1 hour.
2. Place rack at lowest level in oven. Preheat oven to 350 degrees.
3. Beat butter with mixer until creamy. Add sugar and beat until fluffy.
4. Add eggs, one at a time, beating well after each addition.
5. Add cornmeal, flour, salt, lemon rind, and lemon juice. Mix well just to combine.
6. Add milk; mix well just to combine.
7. Pour into prepared pie shell, place in oven, and bake 15 minutes.
8. Reduce heat to 325 degrees; bake until set, about 50 minutes.
9. Cool on rack until room temperature. Serve garnished with whipped cream and a grating of nutmeg, if desired.

5

Florida

OBJECTIVES

By the end of this chapter, you will be able to

- Discuss how the Spanish impacted the cookery found in Florida
- Discuss the Caribbean influence on Florida's cuisine
- Explain how the topography and climate of Florida affect the cuisine
- Identify food products prevalent in Florida
- Prepare a variety of dishes indicative of Florida's cuisine

HISTORY

The cuisine of Florida combined flavors and foods indigenous to Florida and the Caribbean, particularly from the islands of Cuba, Jamaica, and the Bahamas. Additional culinary influences came from Spanish settlers, African slaves, and many others who came to Florida. Using the extensive bounty of fish and seafood as well as the multitude of available fresh produce, each of these groups combined the ingredients found in Florida with their native cooking methods, flavorings, and recipes. Eventually, Florida's cuisine emerged.

Archaeologists say Native Americans inhabited Florida at least 10,000 years ago. These Native Americans consumed fish, seafood, game, and indigenous plants including hearts of palm, yucca, and plantains.

In his quest for gold and the Fountain of Youth, Ponce de León discovered Florida on Easter Sunday in 1513 and claimed the land for Spain. He named the area "Pascua Florida" which means "Easter feast of flowers." Before long, the Spanish brought pigs, cattle, and horses to their new land. In the early sixteenth century, Ponce de León became the governor of Florida and Puerto Rico, which established a link between the islands and Florida. The Spanish imported many foods from the Caribbean Islands to Florida, leading to pronounced Caribbean influence on Florida's cuisine. Rum was one of the imports that came to Florida from the islands.

Located in the western portion of Florida's panhandle, Pensacola was established by the Spanish in 1559. This community survived only two years. In 1565, the Spanish founded St. Augustine, which became the first permanent settlement of European explorers in the United States. Spanish influence still permeates the ingredients and the cookery found in St. Augustine.

As the Moors brought rice pilaf to Spain, the Spanish introduced both rice and pilaf to Florida. In addition, they brought and planted orange seeds and saplings in St. Augustine. Since the Spanish did not tend the orange trees, they grew wild all over the countryside and eventually spread throughout the state. Of course, oranges became one of Florida's most important crops and remain a significant source of income. In addition to strong culinary impact from the Spanish, Florida's cuisine shows traces from the cuisines of the many people who migrated to Florida from Spanish-ruled islands in the Caribbean.

In the 1560s, the French arrived in Florida, adding characteristics from their cookery to the existing cuisine. Also, thousands of African slaves arrived in the middle 1500s. They contributed another layer to the cuisine by introducing okra, sweet potatoes, yams, eggplant, sesame seeds, peas, and beans. After the Civil War, many freed slaves moved to Florida, further intensifying the African influence on the cuisine.

While the British settlers in New England and Virginia made friends with the Native Americans, the Spanish conquistadors eliminated them with weapons and the diseases they introduced. Many of the Creeks, Timucuas, Seminoles, and other tribes perished under the Spanish rule, which lasted until 1763. At that time, the Spanish gave the British control of Florida in exchange for Cuba. The British leadership in Florida continued only two decades until the end of the Revolutionary War, and then the Spanish again took the command.

Playing a large role in Florida's history, pirates found ample opportunity for looting or finding treasure and salvage in the many ships sailing in the vicinity as well as numerous wrecked ships lying in the waters near Florida. Although piracy has a long history throughout the world, many pirates lived on the waters around Florida and in the Caribbean, where they successfully attacked ships. The miles of shoreline and many islands provided plenty

After Christopher Columbus introduced sugarcane in the Caribbean Islands, settlers began making rum from molasses and other sugarcane by-products.

Pirates smuggled rum from the Caribbean into this country during times of high taxation on alcohol.

of places for the pirates to disappear. For example, the Florida Keys, located at the southern tip of the United States, proved an ideal, isolated place for pirates and outlaws to hide. Reportedly, the pirates mostly robbed ships of the Spanish Main, which encompassed Spanish-ruled lands in the Caribbean, Central America, and South America. The Spanish found quantities of gold, silver, and other valuables in these lands, and the pirates robbed them while they transported their treasures within these lands or to Spain.

In 1821, the United States obtained Florida from Spain. Passed in 1830, the Removal Law forced the five large Native American tribes of the South to move west into Oklahoma. This law affected the Seminoles who lived in Florida. Great battles ensued, but the Native Americans lost. They relocated to Oklahoma with promises of owning that land forever. By the early 1900s, the Native Americans lost much of their land in Oklahoma and were moved to reservations.

In 1845, Florida became a state. Since Florida aligned strongly with the Confederacy, the Civil War greatly affected northern Florida.

The cuisine of Cuba combines influences from the Spanish, who ruled this island for 500 years, African slaves who worked on the sugar plantations, and the native foods and cookery already on the island. With Cuba lying only 90 miles south of Key West, many Cubans moved to Key West, bringing their culinary heritage with them. From 1950 to the 1980s, an influx of Cubans immigrated to Florida, with many settling in Miami because of its close proximity to Cuba. This migration created a strong Cuban influence on Florida's cuisine, especially in the southern part of the state.

Through the years, many Haitians, Dominicans, and Puerto Ricans fled to Florida in search of freedom. They arrived with their culinary heritage, and each group added traits to the cookery found there. The cuisine of Florida evolved and continues to evolve, as each new wave of immigrants moves there to find freedom and/or a better life.

In 1949, President Truman signed a law creating a facility for testing rockets at Cape Canaveral. The space program began growing dramatically in the late 1950s and 1960s, when the Russians made great strides in space exploration and launched the first astronaut into space. The space program still exists, and Cape Canaveral remains a tourist attraction.

With Disneyland successfully operating in California, Walt Disney decided to build Disney World in Orlando in the 1960s. Situated in the central part of the state, Orlando lies in the area where the orange groves thrive. In the ensuing years, Disney World grew into a tourist destination for children and adults from all over the world, showcasing foods from around the globe.

TOPOGRAPHY AND CLIMATE

With the Gulf of Mexico bordering on the west and the Atlantic Ocean lying to the east, Florida forms a 400-mile-long peninsula with more than 2,000 miles of coastline. Flat terrain dominates the state, except in the northern section. Waterways, including oceans, bays, swamps, rivers, and lakes, profoundly affect the climate, topography, and cuisine of Florida. With such close proximity to numerous bodies of water, both freshwater and saltwater seafood and fish abound.

Warm climate prevails in the "Sunshine State," with long, hot, humid summers and warm winters. While ocean breezes moderate the temperature along the coasts, the inland areas receive hotter summers and colder winters. The southern portion of the state experiences tropical climate that supports a cornucopia of crops like bananas, pineapple, mango, guava, avocado, citrus fruits, strawberries, tomatoes, and more. Because of the warm climate, tropical, subtropical, and cooler-climate fruits and vegetables grow throughout the year with different produce flourishing in the summer and winter. As a result, some varieties of fruits and vegetables are always in season here.

Because Florida borders both the Atlantic Ocean and the Gulf of Mexico, hurricanes sometimes strike the coastal areas. The hurricane season lasts approximately from June through October.

Tropical conditions, in which freezing temperatures rarely occur, prevail in most of Florida. While annual rainfall totals 50 to 65 inches, the daily forecast in the summer season often includes rain while the winter season yields only a moderate amount of rain. Palm trees and tropical plants dominate the foliage; the deciduous trees found in most of the United States grow only in northern Florida.

Called the panhandle, the northern portion of Florida consists of forests, rolling hills, and lakes, and experiences cooler winters than the areas to the south. Cypress and oak trees, draped with Spanish moss, and tall pines dot the landscape in this part of the state. The cuisine in northern Florida resembles that of the southern United States, rather than the Spanish, Cuban, and Caribbean-influenced cuisine found in southern Florida. With 800 miles separating Pensacola from Key West, Florida, there is great diversity in the cookery of these cities as well as the many towns, cities, and regions between them.

Agriculture continues as big business in central Florida. Lying inland, the Indian River area forms the heart of the citrus-producing region and a wide variety of vegetables and fruits grow there. While the Indian River yields shellfish such as clams and oysters, lakes in the central region contain catfish, bass, perch, and other freshwater fish. Game roams the Ocala National Forest, providing deer for venison stew and chili. Cattle are raised in the vast central region, and consumption of meat is much greater here than in the coastal areas, where diets include more fish and seafood.

Encompassing about 730 square miles and ranking as the second-largest freshwater lake in the United States, Lake Okeechobee is situated at the southern end of the central region. Acres of vegetable crops grow around this lake, supplying produce during the winter for inhabitants of many northern states.

Tampa, Sarasota, Fort Meyers, and Naples lie on the western side of the state, which is known as the "Gulf Side" because it is bordered by the Gulf of Mexico. Situated by the Atlantic Ocean on the eastern side of Florida are Cape Canaveral, Daytona, West Palm Beach, Fort Lauderdale, and Miami, which lies at the southeastern end of the state's mainland.

The Everglades and Big Cypress Swamp dominate the southern interior section of the state with northern borders of Naples on the west and Fort Lauderdale on the east. In the early days, the Seminole Indians inhabited this area, which consists of 2,746 square miles of freshwater swamp. Besides teeming with alligators, the Everglades contains countless frogs. Both alligator meat and frog legs played a large role in the diet of those living in this area in earlier times.

Stretching for 150 miles southwest of the Florida peninsula, twenty-five large coral islands and hundreds of small ones compose the Florida Keys. The southernmost point in the contiguous United States, Key West is the last island in this chain of islands. Four miles long and less than two miles wide, Key West lies with the Gulf of Mexico bordering on its western side and the Atlantic Ocean on its east. The railroad connecting Miami to Key West was completed in 1912; however, a hurricane destroyed part of it in 1935. Highway and bridges were built where the railway used to lie, and this highway still links the Keys to each other and to the mainland.

Because of the large number of alligators in this region, the road crossing the state connecting Naples and Fort Lauderdale was called "Alligator Alley." Cutting through the swamp and connecting the western and eastern parts of the state, the Alligator Alley consisted of more than 100 miles of two-lane highway with no stoplights or posted speed limits. Scruffy palm trees, swamp, tall grasses, and an occasional teepee formed the scenery. Some say that mosquitoes, snakes, and other creatures made up most of the population of the Everglades. Now an interstate highway replaces the Alligator Alley.

The famous American writer Ernest Hemingway lived in Key West, Florida. A lover of cats, Hemingway willed that his house be preserved as a home for cats. As a result, countless cats roam the streets of Key West, and, because of inbreeding, some Key West cats have six toes!

Ingredients and foods commonly used throughout the cuisine of Florida include

- freshwater and saltwater seafood and fish, including numerous varieties of snapper, pompano, grouper, mullet, mackerel, tuna, dolphin, catfish, bass, perch, oysters, shrimp, lobster, clams, and stone crab
- citrus fruits, including oranges, lemons, limes, and grapefruit
- palm products, including coconut, hearts of palm, and palm oil
- all sorts of fruits and vegetables, including strawberries, mangoes, tomatoes, avocados, bananas, pineapples, guava, and many more
- honey

COOKING METHODS

Seafood preparations include steaming, broiling, grilling, baking, and frying. A popular cooking technique for fish (or any food), *en papillote* involves encasing the food in parchment paper, placing it in a paper bag, or enveloping it in aluminum foil, and then baking the package. With the ingredients sealed in a wrapper, the food actually steams in its own juices.

Grilling hails from the Arawaks, a group of people who inhabited the Caribbean islands before the European settlers arrived. They cooked over an open fire, holding the food on grids made from green wood. Since green wood contains more moisture, the grids did not burn while the food cooked. The green wood grid became the prototype for today's grill. Called *barbacoa* in Spanish, the word "barbecue" derived from this.

From deep-frying to sautéing, any type of frying remains popular for cooking seafood. Breading choices vary in different regions: cornmeal is preferred in the northern part of the state while flour, nuts, and other ingredients surround the fish and seafood more often in the south.

Oil from palms and other plants provided plenty of fat for deep-frying. From fritters to vegetables and seafood, all sorts of deep-fried foods remain popular and appear on menus both in homes and restaurants.

The settlers often preserved fish by smoking it. The technique of smoking fish came from the Native Americans who preserved any excess fish for lean times or bad weather. Mullet, a strongly flavored oily fish caught in the Gulf of Mexico and the Atlantic, remains a favorite for smoking, particularly on the west coast of Florida. Looking like tiny shacks with a smokestack, smokehouses used to stand behind many fish markets and homes.

Today, alligator farms provide much of the alligator meat. Alligator meat is tough, so it is usually pounded to tenderize it before cooking. Typical preparation methods for alligator include deep-frying, sautéing, roasting, and braising.

Alligators were placed on the endangered species list from 1967 until 1987. At that time, thousands were killed for their skin to make into shoes, handbags, or wallets. Today, the alligator is longer in danger of extinction in Florida.

REGIONS

Some say the hush puppy originated in Tallahassee, situated in northwestern Florida.

In culinary terms, Florida is divided into the north, south, east, west, and central regions. The cookery of the north and much of the central part of the state reflects the cuisine of the southern United States. Cornbread, grits, greens, okra, lots of pork, flavoring with ham hocks, fatback, or bacon grease, and many deep-fried, foods, including fried fish, fried chicken, and hush puppies, appear commonly here.

Although the origin of the term "Cracker" is not certain, many think it refers to the cracking of the whip by the cowboys who drove cattle throughout this area of Florida.

In 1942, Marjorie Kinnan Rawlings published *Cross Creek Cookery*. This Florida cookbook featured cooking from her home near Gainesville, Florida.

A style of cookery unique to Florida, Cracker cooking prevailed throughout the northern and central areas of Florida until the 1900s. Actually a combination of soul food and country cooking, Cracker cooking emerged when African cooking fused with the cookery of the South. It featured foods like turtle, fried chicken, fried steak, pork, greens, biscuits, cornbread, grits, and other dishes characteristic of Southern cooking.

Peanuts, pecans, melons, soybeans, and many fruits and vegetables grow well in the Panhandle of northern Florida. Bordering the northern Gulf of Mexico, this area's bounty of fish and seafood includes mullet, mackerel, grouper, snapper, and more. At the southwest corner of the panhandle lies Apalachicola, home of the excellent Apalachicola Bay oysters. Forests in this northern region supply game.

Large central Florida contains many farms for growing fruits and vegetables as well as raising cattle. As a result, beef is plentiful here. Acres of sugarcane fields and citrus groves flourish in the area around Lake Okeechobee and north of it. Florida claims the largest sugar production of any state in the continental United States.

Hunting provided game such as deer, rabbit, wild hogs, and birds like quail, wild turkey, and duck for inland residents. Those living near the coasts relied on fishing for much of their protein consumption. Inhabitants of the eastern side of Florida caught fish and seafood from the Atlantic Ocean while those near the western coast fished in the warmer waters of the Gulf of Mexico.

Because of labor problems, Vincente Ybor and other cigarmakers of Cuban and Spanish descent moved their operations from Key West to Tampa on the west coast of Florida in 1885. The Ybor City section of Tampa once claimed the largest production of cigars in the world. The cigar-rolling business flourished in Tampa until the 1950s, when machinery replaced people for rolling cigars. With many Cubans living here, frequent use of ingredients like black beans, plantains, and rice and other Cuban influences still appear in many of the dishes and cookery found in Tampa and the surrounding area.

Located on the western coast near Tampa, Tarpon Springs developed a thriving sponge industry toward the end of the 1800s. Familiar with diving for sponges in their native islands, many Greek immigrants moved here in search of a better life. Like most immigrants, they meshed the cookery of their native homeland with the foods available in their new land. As a result, lamb, feta cheese, and dishes flavored with lemon juice, olive oil, garlic, kalamata olives, and/or oregano appear often in this region of Florida.

Many Italian immigrants settled in Naples, Florida, on the southwestern coast. They named Naples after the city with the same name on the coast of southern Italy. Numerous Italians also immigrated to Tampa. In both of these cities, the local cuisine incorporated aspects of Italian cookery.

Since its early days, Miami has remained a melting pot. Located near the southern end of the peninsula, the city attracted immigrants from all of the islands, and the combination of inhabitants from the islands created its own cultural mix. Because various European countries controlled different islands throughout their history, each of the islands contains its own mixture of ethnic backgrounds. For example, Cuba exhibits culinary influence from the native Indians, the Spanish who arrived in the late 1400s, Africans imported as slaves, and the Chinese who came to provide cheap labor. When the Cuban immigrants flooded into Miami, they came with their culinary history. While Jamaica's cuisine reflects British traits acquired when Britain ruled it, the French, Spanish, and Portuguese controlled other islands, and their culinary presence appears prominently on the islands they inhabited. Immigrants from each island moved to Miami bringing their unique culinary heritage, which included the culture and cuisine found on their native island. Truly a melting pot, the cuisine of Miami commonly includes curries from Trinidad; *arepas,* corn cakes

Very popular in Miami and Tampa, the Cuban sandwich is served both hot and room temperature and in endless variations. The original Cuban sandwich consisted of slices of roast pork, ham, cheese, and pickles on Cuban bread. The sandwich is grilled in a press called a *plancha* to make the bread crisp, melt the cheese, and warm the meats. Many use yellow mustard on the Cuban sandwich.

from South America; jerk seasoning from Jamaica; and many other foods and dishes from numerous Latin American countries.

As people discovered its tropical weather and beauty, more and more people came to Miami from destinations around the world. According to the census in 1900, inhabitants from Germany, Sweden, Spain, Great Britain, Russia, China, Caribbean islands, and states throughout the United States lived in Miami. In the 1930s, Miami attracted many Jewish people from the northeast. The 1940s brought returning veterans from World War II. Between 1960 and the 1980s, many refugees from Cuba, Haiti, and other islands relocated to Miami. Today, Spanish is spoken as commonly as English in Miami.

The Keys thrived in the early 1800s. Cigar manufacturing, the mining of salt, and sponge diving flourished, and these industries brought wealth to Key West, the largest city in the Florida Keys. Because so many people with Cuban ancestry reside in the Keys, culinary traits from Cuba remain prominent.

CHARACTERISTICS OF THE CUISINE

With more than 500 varieties of fish and seafood thriving in the oceans and waterways of Florida, seafood and fish remains a staple in the diet. Some of the many varieties include grouper, pompano, swordfish, tuna, red snapper, mackerel, mullet, shrimp, conch, Florida lobster, clams, oysters, crab, turtle, alligator, and frogs.

A popular fish in Florida, pompano is a firm-fleshed, flat fish with a mild, sweet flavor. Pompano is frequently prepared *en papillote*. Shortly after the Civil War, the red snapper industry developed in the Pensacola area. Lean and white-fleshed, cooked red snapper appears cloaked in many guises, including a Spanish sauce containing mushrooms, peas, tomatoes, green peppers, and lemon. Another traditional preparation pairs the snapper with orange rind, orange juice, pepper, and nutmeg.

Much confusion surrounds dolphin the mammal and dolphin the fish. Known as mahi mahi in Hawaii, dolphin fish (often called dolphin) is not a mammal.

FAT CONTENT OF SOME FLORIDA FISH

High Fat	Lean
mackerel	grouper
pompano	snapper
mullet	redfish

SOME FISH FOUND IN WATERS AROUND FLORIDA

cobia	firm texture, mild flavor	also called ling
dolphin fish	thick fish, mild flavor	also called by its Hawaiian name, mahi mahi
flounder	flatfish, fine texture, mild flavor	
grouper	thick fish, firm texture, mild flavor	many varieties, including red, black, warsaw, and more
mackerel	oily fish, strong flavor	many varieties, including Spanish and king
mullet	oily fish, strong flavor	often smoked
pompano	flatfish, mild, sweet flavor, dry texture	one variety
snapper	sweet, mild flavor, tender texture	over 70 varieties in Florida; 12 sold commercially, including red, gray (mangrove), black, and more
tuna	large fish, pink to black meat, firm texture	many varieties, including yellowtail, blackfin, and more

Stone Crab Claws
photo © Dorling Kindersley

Soft-Shell Crab

Florida lobsters differ from the lobsters caught off the coast of Maine. The Florida variety lacks the front claws found on the Maine lobsters; however, the spiny Florida lobster contains more tail meat than its Maine counterpart. Florida's lobster season runs from the end of August until April.

Stone crabs abound in the oceans of southern Florida. To ensure the proliferation of these prized crabs, fishermen remove only one claw and then return the crab to the ocean, where it will grow another claw. Another crab delicacy, soft-shell crabs are available throughout the year in Florida. Soft-shell crabs are not a separate species of crab; they are crabs molting their shells. Within four hours of shedding its old shell, a crab begins to grow its new shell. This leaves a very small window of opportunity to catch the shell-less crabs in the ocean. In Florida, companies raise crabs ready to molt in special tanks, which makes it easier to capture them while they still have a soft shell.

Known for conch dishes, Key West menus frequently feature conch chowder, conch fritters, and/or conch salad. Tasting a little like clams, the tough conch meat is pounded, chopped, and cooked for a long time to make it palatable. Some say the conch resembles a large, saltwater snail. Because so many conchs come from the Keys, natives of Key West are nicknamed "Conchs." Turtle meat also appears in many recipes throughout the Keys as well as in the interior sections of mainland Florida. Traditionally, turtle soup contains an ample amount of spice and pepper, and often sherry or rum flavors it.

In addition to conch chowder and turtle soup, numerous varieties of fish chowder and a wide range of soups appear in different areas of the state. From the Cuban influence, black bean soup graces many menus. With Florida's hot climate, cold soups are served often.

As in Tampa and Miami, strong Cuban influence is evident throughout the Keys. Since many of the Cuban dishes evolved from the Spanish, they often feature chicken, beef, or pork rather than seafood. Some Cuban dishes that are served include *arroz con pollo*, rice with chicken; *arroz con carne*, rice with meat; and *boliche,* eye of beef stuffed with Cuban sausage or ham, green pepper, onions, and pimento-stuffed olives, and flavored with lime juice and cumin. Another Spanish dish, *alcoporado* is beef stew containing raisins, olives, and spicy flavorings. From the island influence where beef was scarce, shredded "tough cuts" appear frequently in meat dishes. Cuban *ropa vieja* and *vaca frita* both use boiled skirt steak or any leftover boiled beef.

An often-used marinade, *adobo* came from the Spanish conquistadors' influence in Cuba and other places where they settled. In the early days in Spain, this marinade consisted of salt and vinegar. Adapting it to their taste, Cubans changed the mixture to salt, garlic, cumin, oregano, and sour orange juice. They frequently use this marinade on fish, seafood, meat, and poultry.

Beginning in the 1990s in southern Florida, chefs created Floribbean cooking. This style of cooking blended the flavors and foods of the Caribbean Islands and Florida with

Southern influences. The emphasis was on fresh ingredients, and it featured foods available in Florida and the Islands. Some of those foods included fish, seafood, poultry, fruits and fruit juices, particularly tropical fruits and citrus, and honey. Spices and herbs prominent in the Islands like allspice, black pepper, cayenne, cilantro, cinnamon, cumin, fennel seeds, ginger, mustard seeds, oregano, turmeric, thyme, and many peppers often appear in Floribbean dishes. Another feature of Floribbean cookery is the use of peppers or spices juxtaposed with tropical fruits and/or honey, which create a spicy dish with sweet overtones.

Caribbean flavorings prevail throughout Florida, including a variety of curries and jerk seasoning. Foods reflecting the Caribbean influence like fried plantains, guava, and foofoo (cornmeal mush containing okra) hail from various islands and are served commonly.

Another contribution from the cuisine of the islands, beans paired with rice, shows up often. Each island specialty features their favorite bean or pea like black turtle beans from Cuba, red beans from Nicaragua, and pigeon peas from Haiti and the Bahamas. Because of the large number of immigrants coming from various islands, beans and rice became an intrinsic part of the cuisine of Florida.

Floridians throughout the state enjoy a wide variety of fritters. While hush puppies made from cornmeal reign in northern and central Florida, conch fritters are a staple in the Keys. From the Caribbean influence, salt cod fritters appear frequently, and the Cubans contributed *bollitos*, black-eyed pea fritters.

All sorts of fruits and vegetables flourish in Florida's long growing season, making this state a huge exporter of produce. After World War II, the development of frozen orange concentrate further strengthened the already thriving orange industry. Most of the citrus crop, including oranges, tangerines, lemons, limes, and grapefruits, prospers in central Florida from Ocala to Lake Okeechobee. From appetizers to desserts, citrus shows up in every segment of the menu. In addition, citrus often serves as the base for fish marinade. With mild, sweet-flavored fish like snapper or pompano, orange enhances the sweetness without overpowering the delicacy of the fish as a stronger citrus flavor like lemon might.

Strawberries flourish in the central region and are another important crop for Florida. Lying east of Tampa in central Florida, Plant City is known for its strawberry production.

Also known as swamp cabbage, hearts of palm are harvested from the sabal or cabbage palm. After peeling away branches of the palm, the smooth, white, moist core known as the heart of palm lies at the middle of the fibrous trunk. This firm, slightly crunchy center of the stalk is the prized ingredient used to prepare hearts of palm salad. The tube-shaped delicacy usually is cut into slices and eaten raw in salads. Heart of palm adds a slightly sweet taste and crunchy texture. Located off the western coast of Florida, the Island Hotel on Cedar Key prepared a renowned and very unusual hearts of palm salad. It consisted of salad greens and slices of hearts of palm combined with a unique dressing containing vanilla ice cream, peanut butter, and a few drops of green food coloring. Date pieces, fresh pineapple, and candied ginger topped this salad. Although it is usually served raw, some people cook hearts of palm. When cooked, the fresh hearts of palm are generally boiled with salt pork.

Coconut, the fruit of the palm tree, appears in all sorts of recipes throughout Florida. Like citrus, it shows up in every segment of the menu, from coconut-coated shrimp appetizers to countless coconut desserts. The fruit is prized for the meat of the coconut as well as the liquid contained in the coconut, known as coconut milk or coconut water.

Popular throughout Latin America, plantains belong to the banana family. Unlike bananas, plantains almost always are cooked before eating, usually by frying, baking, or boiling. Although both the green and ripe stage are cooked, ripe plantains possess a sweeter flavor. Many believe plantains cure stomach problems.

Cutting Mango from Seed
photo by David Murray and Jules Selmes
© Dorling Kindersley

Cutting Squares into Mango
photo by David Murray and Jules Selmes
© Dorling Kindersley

Extending Mango to Expose
Cut Fruit
photo by David Murray and Jules Selmes
© Dorling Kindersley

Cutting Mango Fruit into Bowl
photo by David Murray and Jules Selmes
© Dorling Kindersley

The mango is thought to be the oldest cultivated fruit. Some say that Buddha received an orchard of mango trees as a gift many centuries ago.

The first mango grew wild in the Himalayan Mountains. Now more than 1,000 varieties of mangos exist.

Developed around 1858, condensed milk became widely used after the Civil War in the devastated South because of the lack of fresh milk. It became incorporated in many recipes.

The Persian lime is a large green lime commonly seen in supermarkets, but Key limes are much smaller, yellow in color, and more acidic.

While Key limes are indigenous to the Florida Keys, Persian limes grew in Florida only after the Spanish brought them.

Although mangos arrived in Florida just before the Civil War, numerous mango varieties flourish in this state today. The smooth, sweet flesh of the mango fruit adds a velvety texture to salads or is wonderful eaten alone. Because the mango contains a large flat pit, cutting the fruit away from the seed can be tricky. The easiest method is to cut a slice of fruit from the long side, cutting as close to the seed as possible. Place the slice with the skin side down and score it into little squares or diamonds with a knife. To score it, first cut parallel lines about 1/2- to 3/4-inch apart through the fruit, then repeat the procedure, cutting another set of lines on the diagonal across the first set. Extend the skin backward so the scored fruit sticks up, making it easy to cut the fruit away from the skin with a knife or a spoon.

A cornucopia of tropical fruits and vegetables grows in southern Florida. In addition to mango, carambola (known as star fruit), papaya, and avocado grow well. Reportedly grown in Mexico as early as 8000 BC, avocados thrive in Florida. First planted south of Miami in 1833, Florida avocados differ from the California variety in both looks and flavor. Called alligator pears, the Florida avocado has a sweeter flavor than the Haas avocado, which grows in California. Also, the Florida avocado grows much larger than the Haas and has a distinctive smooth, bright green skin. Avocados appear frequently in salads or as the Mexican dish, *guacamole*. Many serve *guacamole* as a dip accompanied by taco chips or raw vegetables.

With long, hot, humid summers, salads and cold dishes often serve as the entrée in Florida dining. Mixed greens topped with boiled shrimp or grilled fish appears on menus in homes and restaurants.

A condiment enjoyed in the Keys, Old Sour consists of lime juice and salt fermented for months before using. Datil peppers are very hot chili peppers primarily grown in St. Augustine and Jacksonville. Peppers flavor numerous Florida dishes. On a sweet note, beekeepers produce lots of honey in Florida. The light, fragrant, orange blossom honey remains very popular.

Citrus is the basis for an assortment of desserts within this state. Key limes—small, tart, acid, yellow-skinned, intensely flavored limes native to Key West—form the foundation of the famous Key lime pie. Besides Key limes, this pie also contains eggs and condensed milk, a product used extensively because of the lack of cows throughout the Keys. Another popular dessert with ties to the island/Spanish influence, flan appears on menus throughout the state.

Produced in a number of Caribbean islands where sugarcane grew, rum became the basis for many alcoholic beverages in Florida. Because rums made in the early days were often harsh, people added readily available sugar and lime juice as flavoring. These ingredients make the daiquiri, which originated in Cuba.

Area	Weather	Topography	Foods
north Panhandle, Pensacola	cooler winters, hot and humid summers	forests, rolling hills, lakes, Apalachicola Bay in southwest, Gulf of Mexico on south, Atlantic on east	oysters, mackerel, grouper, mullet, snapper, fried fish, fried chicken, pork, ham, hock, salt pork, game, soybeans, peanuts, pecans, greens, okra, datil peppers, melons, grits, cornbread, hush puppies
central Orlando	warm, dry winters; hot, humid, rainy summers	Indian River, Ocala National Forest, Lake Okeechobee, flat terrain	shellfish, clams, oysters, freshwater fish, catfish, bass, perch, frogs, cattle, game, deer, rabbit, wild hogs, quail, wild turkey, duck, citrus fruits, oranges, lemons, limes, tangerines, grapefruits, strawberries, all sorts of fruits and vegetables, sugarcane
east Cape Canaveral, Daytona, Fort Lauderdale, West Palm Beach	warm, dry winters; hot, humid, rainy summers	Atlantic Ocean on east, flat terrain	snapper, grouper, pompano, shrimp, coconut, mango, hearts of palm
west Tampa, Sarasota, Fort Myers, Naples	warm, dry winters; hot, humid, rainy summers	Gulf of Mexico on west, flat terrain	mullet, grouper, snapper, shrimp, smoked fish, tomatoes, strawberries, mango, coconut, hearts of palm
south Miami, Keys	warm, dry winters; hot, humid, rainy summers; tropical climate	Atlantic on east, Gulf of Mexico to west, Everglades, Big Cypress Swamp, flat terrain	fish, seafood, stone crabs, lobster, shrimp, conch, turtle, ducks, alligator, frogs, tomatoes, avocados, plantains, Key limes, mango, bananas, guava, coconut, hearts of palm

REVIEW QUESTIONS

1. Discuss the Caribbean influence on Florida's cuisine and how it arrived in Florida.
2. How did citrus fruits arrive in Florida, what happened once they got there, and where in Florida is most of the citrus crop?
3. How does the climate affect the crops planted and the foods eaten in Florida?
4. Discuss the Spanish influence on the cuisine of Florida.
5. How are stone crabs harvested and why?
6. Name four fish frequently caught off Florida's coasts.
7. Discuss the different culinary influences on the north and south of Florida.

GLOSSARY

adobo—marinade for meats brought to Florida by the Cubans. In Spain, this marinade consisted of salt and vinegar. Adapting the marinade to their taste, Cubans changed the mixture to salt, garlic, cumin, oregano, and sour orange juice.

alcoporado—Spanish dish consisting of beef stew containing raisins, olives, and spicy flavorings

arepas—corn cakes from South America

arroz con carne—island dish of rice with meat

arroz con pollo—island dish of rice with chicken

barbacoa—Spanish word that became "barbecue," meaning cooked over an open fire

boliche—eye of beef stuffed with Cuban sausage or ham, green pepper, onions, and pimento-stuffed olives, and flavored with lime juice and cumin

bollitos—black-eyed pea fritters from the Islands

carambola—a tropical fruit also known as star fruit because of its star-shaped cross section when cut

en papillote—fish (or any food) encased in parchment paper, placed in a paper bag, or enveloped in aluminum foil, and then baked. The food steams in its own juices.

guacamole—avocado dip from Mexican influence

COCONUT SHRIMP

Coconut Shrimp
photo courtesy of McCormick Spices

To serve this delicious appetizer as an entrée, just double the portion size using 8 shrimps instead of 4 for each serving.

These shrimp can be sautéed or deep-fried.

NUMBER OF SERVINGS: 12
COOKING METHOD:
  Fry
SERVING SIZE:
  4 shrimp, about 3 oz
TOTAL YIELD:
  2 lbs, 6 oz

Wine Style: Light- to medium-bodied white wine such as Chenin Blanc, Sauvignon Blanc, or Blanc du Bois
Example: Blanc du Bois—Lake Ridge Winery and Vineyards, Clermont, FL. This wine mingles spicy flavor with an exciting bouquet. It is semidry, light, and elegant.

INGREDIENTS	WEIGHT	VOLUME
shrimp, jumbo (21/25), shells removed with tail shells intact, deveined, washed, dried	1 lb, 12 oz	
salt		1/2 teaspoon
pepper		1/2 teaspoon
lime juice	1 oz	2 tablespoons
eggs	6³/4 oz	4 each
water	1 oz	2 tablespoons
coconut, unsweetened, shredded	7 oz	2 cups
flour, all purpose	4¹/2 oz	1 cup
oil for frying	about 6 oz	about 3/4 cup
GARNISH:		
lemon or lime wedge		
Chinese duck sauce or sauce of choice		

1. Place shrimp in bowl. Sprinkle with salt, pepper, and lime juice; toss to mix. Refrigerate to marinate for 5 to 10 minutes while preparing breading station.
2. Mix eggs with water in shallow bowl. Place coconut in another shallow bowl or plate. Place flour in third shallow bowl or plate.
3. Dip shrimp in flour, shake off excess, dip in egg, then dip into coconut. Place shrimp on platter until all coated. Cover and refrigerate until needed.
4. Heat 1/4 inch (about 2 to 3 oz or 4 to 6 tablespoons) oil in skillet until hot.
5. Add shrimp; cook until golden brown, about 1 minute on each side.
6. Remove to pan lined with absorbent paper. Keep warm in oven until all fried.
7. Serve, garnished with lemon or lime wedge. Accompany with Chinese duck sauce or sauce of choice.

BOLLITOS

Bollitos
photo courtesy of the American Dry Bean Board

This fritter contains no flour, so people on a wheat-restricted diet can consume these.

These black-eyed pea fritters come from the prevalent Spanish/Cuban influence found in Florida. The original recipe for these fritters calls for the tedious, time consuming job of removing the skins or husks from the beans before processing them. Not removing the skins results in a fritter with a coarser texture.

Begin soaking the black-eyed peas the day before cooking.

Smooth textured and mild flavored, serve bollitos with salsa, tomato sauce, dill mustard mayonnaise, or the sauce of choice.

NUMBER OF SERVINGS: 10
COOKING METHOD:
  Deep-fry
SERVING SIZE:
  5 fritters
TOTAL YIELD:
  2 lbs, 5¹/2 oz batter
  50 fritters containing 3/4 oz batter each

Wine Style: Wide variety—Light- to medium-bodied red wine, Blush, or Rose
Example: Conquistador Blush—Rosa Fiorelli Winery, Bradenton, FL. This wine, made from Conquistador grapes plus other varieties, has a semisweet finish.

INGREDIENTS	WEIGHT	VOLUME
black-eyed peas, dried	12 oz	2 cups
onion, small dice	5 oz	1 medium
garlic, peeled	3 oz	12 large cloves
salt	1/4 oz	1 teaspoon
hot pepper sauce or fresh hot pepper, seeded, minced		1 teaspoon or 1 pepper or to taste
eggs	3½ oz	2 each
baking powder		pinch
oil for deep-frying		

1. Rinse peas. Place in container covered by water at least 2 inches over top of peas. Refrigerate overnight.

2. Drain; rub peas between palms of the hands or between thumb and index finger to remove skins (husks). Remove as much skin as possible.

3. Cover with water. Return to refrigerator for at least 3 hours.

4. Drain, remove remaining husks.

5. Place peas in bowl of food processor fitted with steel knife blade. Process until finely ground.

6. Add onion, garlic, salt, hot pepper, and eggs. Process until smooth paste. Transfer mixture to bowl.

7. Thoroughly chill batter. Add baking powder to batter; mix vigorously until very smooth.

8. Heat about 3 inches oil in pan to 375 degrees.

9. Drop ¾ oz (about 1 teaspoon) batter into oil. Do not add too many at once to maintain oil temperature. Fry about two minutes, until golden. Turn fritter; fry other side until golden.

10. Remove to pan lined with absorbent paper to drain. If necessary, keep warm in low oven until service. Serve hot fritters with salsa, tomato sauce, dill mustard mayonnaise, or sauce of choice.

FRESH CRACKED CONCH WITH VANILLA RUM SAUCE AND SPICY BLACK BEAN SALAD

Start soaking the black beans the day before cooking.

—Recipe by Mark Militello

NUMBER OF SERVINGS: 8
COOKING METHOD:
　Boil, Fry
SERVING SIZE:
　2 oz bean salad,
　1 oz vanilla rum sauce,
　3 oz conch
TOTAL YIELD:
　1 lb bean salad,
　3 cups vanilla rum sauce,
　1 lb, 8 oz conch

Wine Style: Light- to medium-bodied white wine, Pinot Gris, Gewürztraminer, or Sauvignon Blanc
Example: Gewürztraminer—Ridgeback Winery, Mt. Dora, FL. A dry, German-style white wine exhibiting overtones of melons and apples with a spicy finish.

INGREDIENTS	WEIGHT	VOLUME
BLACK BEAN SALAD:		
black beans, dried	3½ oz	½ cup
garlic clove, whole	¼ oz	2 cloves
red pepper, seeded, membrane removed, finely diced	12 oz	2 each
mango, peeled, seeded, finely diced	14 oz to 1 lb	2 each
green onions, thinly sliced	3 oz	6 each
scotch bonnet or habanero, seeded, membrane removed, minced		½ each
olive oil, extra virgin	3 oz	¼ cup + 2 tablespoons
lime juice, fresh	2 oz	¼ cup
cilantro, fresh, minced	½ oz	2 tablespoons
mint, fresh, minced	½ oz	2 tablespoons
red onion, minced	¾ oz	2 tablespoons
salt	as needed	
pepper	as needed	
sugar	to balance	
VANILLA RUM SAUCE:		
rum, white	4 oz	½ cup
rum, dark	4 oz	½ cup
lime juice	1 oz	2 tablespoons
sugar	2¾ oz	¼ cup + 2 tablespoons
shallot, minced	½ oz	2 small
vanilla bean		1 each
butter, unsalted, cut into pieces	1 lb	4 sticks or 2 cups
salt	as needed	
pepper	as needed	
CONCH:		
conch, removed from shell	2 to 3 lbs	8 to 10 each
salt	as needed	
pepper	as needed	
eggs, beaten	6¾ oz	4 each
milk	4 oz	½ cup
flour, all purpose	9 oz	2 cups
bread crumbs, freshly ground	9 oz	2 cups
butter, clarified	8 oz	1 cup
GARNISH:		
red pepper, fine dice	2 oz	
green onion, fine dice	2 oz	
lime, cut into wedges; slice down outsides of lime, top to bottom, avoiding pithy centers		8 each wedges

For Black Bean Salad:

1. The day before serving, cover beans with cold water and soak overnight.

2. Place beans in saucepan with garlic and water to cover. Bring to boil over high heat; reduce and simmer for 1 to 1½ hours or until tender.

3. Drain beans; rinse in cold water. Drain thoroughly; place in medium bowl.

4. Add red pepper, mango, green onions, scotch bonnet, olive oil, lime juice, cilantro, mint, red onion, salt, pepper, and sugar. Stir well to combine.

5. Correct seasonings. Cover and chill.

For Vanilla Rum Sauce:

1. Combine both rums, lime juice, sugar, and shallot in heavy saucepan.

2. Cut vanilla bean in half lengthwise and scrape seeds into rum mixture with point of knife.

3. Heat mixture to boiling, reduce heat, and continue cooking until reduced to 1½ oz (3 tablespoons) of liquid.

4. Reduce heat to medium; whisk in butter. Be careful not to allow to boil. Season with salt and pepper. Correct seasonings. Strain; keep warm until needed.

For Conch:

1. Cut conch on diagonal into ¼-inch slices. Place between sheets of plastic wrap and pound as thinly as possible using meat tenderizer. *(Conch is very tough!)* Season with salt and pepper.

2. Whisk eggs and milk in bowl. Place flour in shallow bowl. Place bread crumbs in another shallow bowl.

3. Just before serving, heat clarified butter in sauté pan. Following standard breading procedure, dip conch first in flour and shake to remove excess, then into egg, and finally into bread crumbs.

4. Fry conch until golden brown on each side. Blot conch on paper toweling to remove excess butter.

For Assembly:

1. Place 2 oz (about 2 tablespoons) bean salad in the center of each plate.

2. Spoon 3 pools (1 oz) of vanilla sauce around the salad. Place 3 slices conch between pools of sauce.

3. On each plate, sprinkle 1 teaspoon red pepper and green onion over sauce. Garnish each plate with wedge of lime.

—Copyright Mark Militello

Executive Chef & Restaurateur

Chef Mark Militello oversees four award-winning restaurants in southern Florida: Mark's Las Olas in Fort Lauderdale, Mark's Mizner Park in Boca Raton, Mark's South Beach at the Nash Hotel, and Mark's CityPlace in West Palm Beach. In 1988, he opened his first restaurant, and two years later, *Food and Wine* magazine named him one of the "Ten Best Chefs in America."

During the past decade, Militello has received some of the industry's most prestigious accolades including the James Beard Award for Best Regional Chef in the Southeast, a Distinguished Restaurant Award from *Conde Nast Traveler*, two Golden Dish Awards from *GQ* magazine, a DiRona 25 Top Restaurants in the Country Award, and *Nation's Restaurant News* Hall of Fame. Recently, *The New York Times* chose Militello for "The Chef," an eight-week series highlighting signature recipes.

Besides being featured in numerous magazines, he has appeared on cooking shows including *Julia Child's Cooking with the Master Chefs* TV series. Supporting many national and local charities and causes, Militello participates in national events like the Share Our Strength's Taste of the Nation and local causes like Jack and Jill Children's Foundation.

As a pre-med student at Marquette University in Milwaukee, Militello realized his love of cooking. After changing schools and careers, he obtained culinary degrees from Florida International University's School of Hospitality and Hotel Management and New York State University's Hotel and Culinary Program.

CONCH CHOWDER

NUMBER OF SERVINGS: 10
COOKING METHOD:
  Boil
SERVING SIZE:
  10 oz
TOTAL YIELD:
  6 lbs, 9$\frac{1}{2}$ oz

Conch Chowder
photo © Dorling Kindersley

INGREDIENTS	WEIGHT	VOLUME
conch, trimmed, minced	1 lb	
tomato paste	2 oz	3 tablespoons
lime juice	2 oz	1/4 cup
bacon or salt pork, diced	4 oz	
olive oil	up to 2 oz	up to 1/4 cup
onion, small dice	5 oz	1 cup
carrot, small dice	3 oz	1 large
celery, small dice	2 oz	1 large stalk
garlic, minced	1/2 oz	2 cloves
green pepper, seeded, diced	3 oz	1/2 cup
jalapeño pepper, seeded, minced	1/2 oz	1 medium
flour, all purpose	3 oz	6 tablespoons
water, hot	3 lbs	6 cups or 1 qt + 2 cups
tomatoes, peeled, diced	14 oz	1 each 14-oz can
potatoes, peeled, diced	10 oz	2 cups
sherry, dry	4 oz	1/2 cup
bay leaves		2 each
thyme		1/2 teaspoon
Worcestershire sauce	1 oz	2 tablespoons
salt	1/4 oz	1 teaspoon
black pepper		1/2 teaspoon
evaporated milk	12 oz	1 each 12-oz can
Tabasco or other hot sauce, *optional*		to taste

GARNISH:

parsley, minced

1. Pound conch with meat mallet, then cut into pieces and chop in food processor until minced, or put through fine blade of meat grinder.
2. Combine conch, tomato paste, and lime juice in bowl. Mix well; refrigerate to marinate for 1 hour.
3. Brown bacon or salt pork in stock pot until almost crisp. Add enough olive oil to pan to make 1/4 cup fat.
4. Add onion, carrot, celery, garlic, green pepper, and jalapeño. Cook over medium heat until vegetables begin to brown.
5. Stir in flour; cook for 1 or 2 minutes, until lightly browned.
6. Add water slowly, whisking constantly until mixture starts to thicken.
7. Add tomatoes, potatoes, sherry, conch mixture, bay leaves, thyme, Worcestershire sauce, salt, and pepper. Bring to boil, reduce heat, cover, and simmer until potatoes and conch are tender, about 1 hour.
8. Just before serving, add evaporated milk; bring to simmer. Correct seasonings, adding Tabasco sauce if desired.
9. Garnish with parsley, serve immediately.

HEARTS OF PALM SALAD

Chill plates in advance of service.

Cutting Sections of Orange from Membrane
photo by Jerry Young © Dorling Kindersley

Hearts of Palm
photo by Philip Dowell © Dorling Kindersley

Hearts of Palm Salad

NUMBER OF SERVINGS: 15
SERVING SIZE:
  5 oz
TOTAL YIELD:
  4 lbs, 11 oz

INGREDIENTS	WEIGHT	VOLUME
SALAD:		
oranges	2 lbs, 13 oz	6 each
salad greens, variety or mixture of choice, washed, torn into bite-sized pieces	1 lb, 1 oz	14 cups
red pepper, diced	7 oz	1 cup
green onion, trimmed, 1/4-inch slice; include about 5 inches of green top	3 oz	6 each
hearts of palm, sliced 1/4-inch thick	1 lb, 7 oz	4 cups
DRESSING:		
lime juice	8 oz	1 cup
orange juice (use reserved juice from peeling oranges for salad)	4 oz	1/2 cup
balsamic vinegar	1 oz	2 tablespoons
Dijon mustard	1/2 oz	2 teaspoons
sugar	3 3/4 oz	1/4 cup
olive oil	3 oz	6 tablespoons
tarragon, dried, crushed	1/4 oz	2 teaspoons
salt		1/2 teaspoon
pepper		1/2 teaspoon

For Salad:

1. Peel oranges over plate or bowl to catch any juice and reserve for dressing. Peel oranges, removing pith (white covering under orange zest) with sharp paring knife. To release orange segment from membrane, cut on each side of membrane to the middle of orange, staying as close to membrane as possible. Cover and refrigerate orange segments until needed.

2. Combine salad greens, red pepper, and green onion in bowl. Refrigerate until service.

For Dressing:

1. Combine all dressing ingredients in jar or bowl.

2. If using jar, shake vigorously. If using bowl, whisk briskly until well combined.

To Assemble:

1. Pour dressing over salad greens, using just enough to coat ingredients. Mix gently.

2. Correct seasonings. Place on serving plate, arranging orange segments and hearts of palm on top.

AVOCADO GRAPEFRUIT SALAD

Chill plates in advance of service.

Cutting on Side of Grapefruit Membrane

Removing Grapefruit Segments over Bowl to Catch Juices

Avocado Grapefruit Salad

NUMBER OF SERVINGS: 8
SERVING SIZE:
  about 6 1/2 oz
TOTAL YIELD:
  3 lbs, 6 oz
DRESSING:
  1 lb, 5 oz or 2 1/2 cups

INGREDIENTS	WEIGHT	VOLUME
SALAD:		
grapefruit	3 lbs, 8 oz	4 each
lettuce, romaine or variety of choice, washed, dried, torn into bite-sized pieces	8 oz romaine	8 large leaves romaine, 10 cups
avocados, peeled, pit removed, sliced from stem end to bottom	1 lb, 3½ oz	2 each
olives, kalamata or variety of choice	4 oz	24 each
DRESSING:		
grapefruit juice, reserved from sliced grapefruits	6 oz	¾ cup
olive oil	4½ oz	½ cup + 1 tablespoon
balsamic vinegar		2 teaspoons or to taste
sugar		1 teaspoon
salt	¼ oz	1 teaspoon
white pepper		¼ teaspoon
tarragon		1 teaspoon

For Salad:

1. Peel grapefruits over plate or bowl to catch any juice, and reserve for dressing. Peel grapefruits, removing pith (white part) with sharp paring knife. To remove membrane, cut on each side of membrane to the middle, staying as close to membrane as possible. Discard peel, pith, and membrane.

2. Place lettuce on salad plate.

3. Arrange grapefruit sections and avocado slices on top, alternating them in pinwheel design.

4. Place olives (3) on each salad. Drizzle about 1 oz (2 tablespoons) dressing over salad.

For Dressing:

1. Combine all dressing ingredients.

2. Shake vigorously or mix well with whisk until well combined.

3. Correct seasonings.

BOLICHE

Making Opening in Meat

Placing Stuffing in Meat

Making Cuts in Meat for Garlic Slivers

Inserting Garlic Slivers into Meat

Browning Meat

Slicing Meat

Boliche

Essentially a high-class pot roast, this recipe reflects Cuban influence.

If possible, begin this recipe the day before cooking so the roast can marinate overnight.

NUMBER OF SERVINGS: 13
COOKING METHOD:
  Braise
SERVING SIZE:
  5 oz
TOTAL YIELD:
  4 lbs, 2 oz meat

Wine Style: Medium- to full-bodied red wines such as Cabernet Sauvignon, Shiraz, or Zinfandel
Example: Castillo Red—San Sebastian Winery, St. Augustine, FL. This medium-dry red wine is delightful with a deep burgundy color and a hint of oak, as well as some spice.

INGREDIENTS	WEIGHT	VOLUME
STUFFING:		
bacon	1 lb	
chorizo or other spicy sausage, skinned, crumbled	6 oz	4 small
olives, whole pimento-stuffed	6 oz	2 each 3-oz jars
garlic, minced	1/2 oz	2 large cloves
tomato, peeled, seeded, diced, fresh or canned	12 oz	1 1/2 cups
MEAT:		
eye round roast, trimmed of fat	2 each 2 1/2 to 3 lbs	
garlic, slivered	1/2 oz	2 large cloves
olive oil	1 1/2 oz	3 tablespoons
onion, diced	1 lb	3 1/3 cups or 4 each medium
garlic, minced	1 oz	4 large cloves
carrots, peeled, cut in chunks	15 oz	4 medium
celery, sliced	8 oz	4 ribs
green pepper, diced	5 oz	1 cup
tomato, peeled, seeded, diced, fresh or canned	12 oz	1 1/2 cups
beef stock	1 lb	2 cups
dry red wine	12 oz	1 1/2 cups
bay leaf		4 each
cumin	1/2 oz	2 teaspoons
paprika	1/2 oz	5 teaspoons
oregano		1 teaspoon
lime juice	4 oz	1/2 cup or about 2 limes
potatoes, red, scrubbed	5 lb	26 small
salt	to taste	
pepper		1/2 teaspoon
GARNISH:		
parsley or cilantro, minced		

For Stuffing:

1. Cook bacon until crisp; drain on paper toweling. Crumble and place in bowl with *chorizo*.
2. Add olives, garlic (1/2 oz or 2 cloves), and tomato (12 oz or 1 1/2 cups).
3. Mix well, cover, and refrigerate until needed.

For Meat:

1. With boning knife or long thin knife, make 1-inch slit lengthways through center of meat (from end almost to other end) to create cavity for stuffing. Do not pierce through back end of roast. If needed, use sharpening steel to stretch cavity.
2. Fill cavity tightly with stuffing. Refrigerate and reserve any excess stuffing for later.
3. With point of knife, make incisions in meat and push garlic slivers into them. Cover and refrigerate several hours or preferably overnight.
4. Preheat oven to 250 degrees.
5. Heat olive oil in braising pan; brown roast on all sides to sear. Remove from pan.
6. Add onion to pan; sauté until translucent. Add garlic (1 oz or 4 large cloves), carrots, celery, and green pepper. Lightly sauté.
7. Add tomato (12 oz or 1 1/2 cups), beef stock, red wine, bay leaves, cumin, paprika, oregano, lime juice, and any reserved leftover stuffing that did not fit in the cavity. Return meat to pan, cover, bake for 2 hours, then raise oven temperature to 300 degrees.
8. Add potatoes. Cook until potatoes and meat are tender, about 45 minutes to 1 hour.
9. Remove meat to cutting board; allow to stand for about 10 minutes. Remove potatoes from pan, set aside. Skim fat from sauce.
10. Bring sauce to boil over medium heat. Reduce it to thicken slightly while scraping bottom of pan to release any baked scraps.
11. Add salt and pepper; correct seasonings.
12. Slice meat into approximately 1/4-inch slices. Arrange on platter or plate with potatoes; nap with sauce. Serve immediately, passing additional sauce. If desired, garnish with parsley or cilantro.

CHICKEN PILAU

Chicken Pilau
photo © Dorling Kindersley

A version of rice pilaf, this one-pot dish consisting of chicken, meat, and/or seafood cooked with rice can be spicy or not. From the Spanish influence, the traditional version contains datil pepper, a spicy pepper that grows in the South; however, other renditions served throughout the South omit the chili pepper.

Traditionally, this dish is served with chopped or shredded chicken mixed into the rice. More conducive for commercial foodservice, try preparing this dish with uncut boneless chicken breasts.

NUMBER OF SERVINGS: 10
COOKING METHOD:
 Braise
SERVING SIZE:
 12 oz
TOTAL YIELD:
 7 lbs, 14 oz

Wine Style: Wide Variety—medium-dry white wines, Semillon, Viognier, Pinot Blanc, Rose, or Grenache
Example: Seabreeze Horizon White—Seabreeze Winery, Panama City, FL. A remarkable delicate, dry muscadine blend that is fruity with a clean finish.

INGREDIENTS	WEIGHT	VOLUME
olive or vegetable oil	2½ oz	5 tablespoons
chicken breasts, boneless, cut into thirds across the grain, if desired	3 lbs, 12 oz	10 each 6-oz boneless chicken breasts
salt pork, small dice	4 oz	
onions, medium dice	1 lb, 8 oz	4 large
celery, medium dice	4 oz	2 ribs
green pepper, medium dice	7½ oz	1 each
garlic, minced	¾ oz	4 cloves
rice, long grain	1 lb, 13½ oz	4 cups
whole tomatoes, fresh or canned, diced	4 lbs	7 cups
chicken stock	4 lbs	2 qts or 8 cups
thyme	¼ oz	2 teaspoons
salt	¼ oz or to taste	1 teaspoon or to taste
pepper		1 teaspoon
chili pepper, datil or variety of choice, minced, seeded if desired		2 each or to taste

GARNISH:
hard-boiled egg, sliced
parsley, minced

1. Preheat oven to 350 degrees.
2. Heat oil on medium-high in ovenproof pan; sauté chicken just until browned. Remove chicken to plate; set aside until needed.
3. Add salt pork to pan; sauté until almost crisp. Add onions; sauté until softened, a few minutes.
4. Add celery, green pepper, and garlic. Cook another couple of minutes.
5. Add rice; stir until starting to brown. Add tomatoes, chicken stock, thyme, salt, pepper, and chili pepper; bring to boil.
6. Remove from heat, add chicken, cover, and bake about 45 minutes or until liquid is absorbed, rice is tender, and chicken is done.
7. Correct seasonings. Serve immediately, garnished with hard-boiled egg and parsley.

ZUCCHINI AND PROSCIUTTO-WRAPPED SNAPPER WITH SAFFRON, WHITEWATER CLAMS, AND FINGERLING POTATOES

—Recipe by Mark Militello

NUMBER OF SERVINGS: 8
COOKING METHOD:
  Bake
SERVING SIZE:
  6 oz
TOTAL YIELD:
  3 lbs

Wine Style: Medium- to full-bodied dry white wines, Blanc du Bois, or Chardonnay
Example: Blanc du Bois Dry—Rosa Fiorelli Winery, Bradenton, FL. This is a very dry white table wine with a spicy, unique finish.

INGREDIENTS	WEIGHT	VOLUME
OVEN-DRIED TOMATOES:		
plum tomatoes, peeled, seeded, cut in half	4 lbs	24 each whole
extra virgin olive oil	3 oz	6 tablespoons
sea salt	as needed	
black pepper	as needed	
extra virgin olive oil	8 oz	1 cup
POTATOES:		
fingerling potatoes, halved	1 lb, 8 oz	24 each whole
extra virgin olive oil	4 oz	1/2 cup
rosemary, fresh, chopped		1 teaspoon
salt	as needed	
pepper	as needed	
SNAPPER:		
snapper or other firm white fish fillets	2 to 3 lbs	16 each 2- to 3-oz pieces
salt	as needed	
pepper	as needed	
oven-dried tomato puree	8 oz	4 tablespoons
basil leaves		48 each
prosciutto ham, very thinly sliced	1 lb	16 slices
zucchini, cut into 1/8-inch slices lengthwise, avoid seedy centers	about 3 lbs, 8 oz to 4 lbs	about 4 large, 32 slices

For Oven-Dried Tomatoes:

1. Preheat oven to 275 degrees. Place cooling rack on baking sheet.
2. Coat tomato halves with 3 oz (6 tablespoons) olive oil; season with salt and pepper.
3. Arrange tomatoes in single layer on rack over baking sheet. Bake until dried and concentrated, about 2 1/2 hours.
4. Place dried tomatoes in bowl of food processor fitted with knife blade. With motor running, slowly drizzle 8 oz (1 cup) olive oil through feed tube. Run until tomatoes are pureed.

For Potatoes:

1. Preheat oven to 400 degrees. Coat potatoes with olive oil, season with rosemary, salt, and pepper.
2. Arrange in single layer on baking sheet. Roast until potatoes are tender on the inside and golden brown on outside, about 35 to 45 minutes.

For Snapper:

1. Season fish with salt and pepper. Spread one teaspoon oven-dried tomato puree on each piece of fish. Place a few basil leaves over tomato puree.
2. Wrap each piece of fish in prosciutto slice. *If necessary to cover fish, overlap two pieces of ham.*
3. Shingle zucchini slices to width of pieces of fish. Place fish, basil side down, in center and carefully enclose by folding one half over other. Trim zucchini slices if they extend past width of fish.

(Continued)

INGREDIENTS	WEIGHT	VOLUME
SAFFRON CLAM SAUCE:		
saffron threads, lightly toasted, ground		2 teaspoons
littleneck clams		24 each
chardonnay wine	1 lb, 8 oz	3 cups
light fish stock or clam juice	1 lb, 12 oz	3 1/2 cups
garlic, thinly sliced	2 oz	4 tablespoons
butter, cold	2 oz	4 tablespoons
parsley, Italian, minced	1/2 oz	1/2 cup
salt	as needed	
pepper	as needed	
olive oil	for frying	
cornmeal, fine, for dusting	2 3/4 oz	1/2 cup

For Saffron Clam Sauce:

1. Combine saffron, clams, wine, stock, and garlic in saucepan over high heat. Cover and cook until clams open. Length of time depends on freshness of clams.
2. Remove clams, place in bowl, and keep warm.
3. Over high heat, reduce broth by one-quarter, then whisk in cold butter and parsley.
4. Correct seasonings. Add salt and pepper, if needed.

To Finish:

1. Heat olive oil in a sauté pan over medium heat. Place cornmeal on plate or flat pan. Dust wrapped fish with cornmeal.
2. Sauté fish, unfolded zucchini side down, for 3 to 4 minutes on each side. Drain on absorbent toweling.
3. Ladle about 4 oz (depending on size of serving bowl) saffron clam sauce into individual serving bowl. Place fish in center. Arrange clams and potatoes around the fish. Serve.

—Copyright Mark Militello

RED SNAPPER FLORIDA STYLE

Red Snapper Florida Style

Found in every older Florida cookbook I read, this traditional Florida recipe could certainly be "jazzed up" by adding some minced jalapeño and/or white wine to the marinade.

NUMBER OF SERVINGS: 8
COOKING METHOD:
  Bake
SERVING SIZE:
  7 oz
TOTAL YIELD:
  3 lbs, 10 oz

Wine Style: Medium- to full-bodied dry white wines, Chardonnay, or Viognier
Example: Chardonnay—Dakotah Winery, Chiefland, FL. A dry white wine with a bright clean taste and medium to full body.

INGREDIENTS	WEIGHT	VOLUME
oranges	15 oz	2 medium
onion, minced	1 1/2 oz	1/4 cup
oil	1/2 oz	1 tablespoon
salt	1/4 oz	1 teaspoon
red snapper fillets	4 lbs	8 each 8-oz fillets
thyme		1 teaspoon
pepper		to taste
nutmeg		dash, to taste
GARNISH:		
parsley or cilantro, minced		

1. Wash oranges. Grate zest (do not include white pith just under orange zest as this is quite bitter). Juice oranges.
2. Combine orange juice, orange zest, onion, oil, and salt in baking dish large enough to hold fish. Mix well.
3. Place fish fillets in marinade; coat well. Refrigerate for at least 1 hour.
4. Preheat oven to 400 degrees.
5. Arrange fish skin side down in dish. Sprinkle with thyme, pepper, and nutmeg.
6. Place in oven; baste fish once or twice. Bake until fish is done and flakes easily, about 15 to 20 minutes. Cooking time depends on thickness of the fish.
7. Correct seasonings. If desired, garnish with parsley (traditional) or cilantro. Serve immediately.

GROUPER ENCRUSTED IN MACADAMIA NUTS

Grouper Encrusted in
Macadamia Nuts

*Since macadamia nuts are oily, grinding them with the bread crumbs prevents them
from turning into a paste.*

NUMBER OF SERVINGS: 9
COOKING METHOD:
  Fry
SERVING SIZE:
  4 oz salsa
TOTAL YIELD:
  2 lb, 6 oz salsa

Wine Style: Sauvignon Blanc, Riesling, Semillon, or blended dry
white wines
Example: Cuvee Blanc—Lake Ridge Winery and Vineyards,
Clermont, FL. A blended wine made with Suwannee,
Miss Blanc, and Blanc du Bois grapes. It has a nice balance
of fruit and oak, very clean flavors, and some crispness
balanced by good fruit flavors.

INGREDIENTS	WEIGHT	VOLUME
SALSA:		
pineapple, ripe, peeled, cored, medium dice	12 oz	2¹/₂ cups
mango, ripe, peeled, seeded, medium dice	9¹/₄ oz	1¹/₄ cups
cucumber, peeled, seeded, medium dice	7¹/₂ oz	1 large
jalapeño pepper, seeded, minced	³/₄ oz	1 large
red bell pepper, seeded, medium dice	1³/₄ oz	¹/₃ cup
red onion, peeled, medium dice	1³/₄ oz	¹/₃ cup
ginger, fresh, peeled, minced	¹/₂ oz	2¹/₂ teaspoons
brown sugar, packed	³/₄ oz	1 tablespoon + 1 teaspoon
lime juice	2 oz	¹/₄ cup
cilantro, minced	³/₄ oz	¹/₃ cup
salt	to taste	
pepper	to taste	

For Salsa:

1. Combine pineapple, mango, cucumber, jalapeño, red bell
   pepper, red onion, ginger, brown sugar, and lime juice in bowl.
   Mix gently to combine.
2. Add cilantro, salt, and pepper. Correct seasonings.
3. Cover and refrigerate until needed.

For Fish:

1. Sprinkle grouper lightly with salt and pepper.
2. Place nuts and bread crumbs in bowl of food processor fitted
   with steel blade. Pulse until finely ground. Transfer to plate.
3. Beat eggs in bowl with about 1 teaspoon water. Place flour on
   plate.
4. Dredge grouper with flour, dip into egg, and coat with nut mixture (standard breading procedure).
5. Heat oil in pan until about 350 degrees.
6. Pan fry grouper until crispy and golden brown on both sides.
   Remove and drain on absorbent paper. Keep warm in oven.
7. To serve, place salsa on plate; top with fish. If desired, garnish
   with red bell pepper, cilantro, and lime slice or wedge.

(Continued)

INGREDIENTS	WEIGHT	VOLUME
FISH:		
grouper filet, rinsed, dried, cut into 9 each 4-oz portions	2 lbs, 4 oz	
salt	to taste	
pepper	to taste	
macadamia nuts, coarsely ground	6³/₄ oz	1¹/₂ cups
bread crumbs	5³/₄ oz	1¹/₂ cups
eggs, beaten	8¹/₂ oz	5 each
flour, all purpose	3³/₄ oz	³/₄ cup
oil, for frying, about ³/₄ inch in pan, to cover grouper halfway	as needed	
GARNISH:		
red bell pepper, minced		
cilantro, minced		
lime slices or wedges		

POMPANO EN PAPILLOTE

Drawing Heart on Parchment Paper

photo by David Murray and Jules Selmes © Dorling Kindersley

Pleating Parchment Paper

photo by Jerry Young © Dorling Kindersley

Finishing the Enclosure

photo by David Murray and Jules Selmes © Dorling Kindersley

Pompano en Papillote

This classic French preparation often appears in Florida. Enclosing the fish in parchment paper actually steams it.

A mild tasting, flat fish, pompano is sometimes difficult to find. In the absence of pompano, substitute another mild, thin fish fillet. If parchment paper is unavailable, wrap the fish in aluminum foil instead.

NUMBER OF SERVINGS: 8
COOKING METHOD:
  Bake
SERVING SIZE:
  1 packet of fish with
  4 oz or ¹/₄ cup filling
TOTAL YIELD:
  2 lbs or 4 cups filling

Wine Style: Medium-dry white wines, Sauvignon Blanc, Pinot Gris, or Riesling
Example: Lake Emerald—Eden Winery, Alva, FL. This wine is dry with an undercurrent of ripe fruit.

INGREDIENTS	WEIGHT	VOLUME
parchment paper	8 sheets, 12 by 16 inches	
(Note: This is the size of half-sheet pan.)		
butter	4 oz	1/2 cup or 1 stick
flour, all purpose	1 1/2 oz	1/4 cup
scallions, chopped	1 oz	1/4 cup
parsley, minced	1 1/2 oz	1/4 cup
salt		1/2 teaspoon
white pepper		1/2 teaspoon
nutmeg		1/2 teaspoon
cayenne		1/8 teaspoon or to taste
heavy cream	8 oz	1 cup
white wine	4 oz	1/2 cup
dry sherry	1 oz	2 tablespoons
crab meat	6 1/2 oz	1 cup
shrimp, small to medium, peeled, deveined	8 oz	1 cup
pompano, rinsed	about 3 lbs	8 fillets

1. Fold sheets of parchment in half so each piece is 8 by 12 inches. Holding folded edge of paper, cut each sheet into half a heart, so it forms full heart when unfolded. Widest part of heart should include full width of paper. Do not cut across the fold. Place oven rack in top third of oven. Preheat oven to 400 degrees.

2. Melt butter in saucepan. Whisk in flour, scallions, and parsley. Cook about 4 minutes, whisking frequently.

3. Add salt, pepper, nutmeg, cayenne, cream, wine, and sherry. Heat gently until almost simmering, but do not boil.

4. Stir in crab and shrimp. Heat 3 to 4 minutes, stirring occasionally. Remove from heat.

5. Open parchment paper heart; place fish on right side of heart along fold line. Top fish with 4 oz (1/4 cup) filling.

6. Bring other half of heart over fish and align sides of paper. Starting at top of heart, crimp sides of paper together, creating tightly sealed package. Twist bottom point to seal tightly. *Note for left-handed people: after closing paper over fish, rotate heart halfway around so that wide top faces bottom of table, then crimp beginning at widest part of heart.*

7. Place completed packets on flat baking pan. Bake for 20 minutes. Parchment will brown.

8. Remove from oven, serve packet to each diner. Cut packet open at tableside, if possible. Be careful of escaping hot steam when first opening packet.

COLACHE

Colache contains three vegetables often used in Native American cooking: corn, squash, and tomatoes.

NUMBER OF SERVINGS: 13
COOKING METHOD:
  Braise
SERVING SIZE:
  5 oz
TOTAL YIELD:
  4 lbs, 3 1/2 oz

INGREDIENTS	WEIGHT	VOLUME
yellow summer squash, 1/8-inch slices	1 lb, 8 oz	
flour, all purpose	1 1/2 oz	3 tablespoons
olive oil	1 1/2 oz	3 tablespoons
onion, diced	2 oz	1/2 cup
garlic, minced	1/2 oz	2 large cloves
corn, cut off the cob	1 lb	2 3/4 cups or 4 ears
green pepper, seeded, diced	6 1/2 oz	1 medium
salt		1 1/2 teaspoons
black pepper		1/2 teaspoon
oregano		1 teaspoon
sugar		1/2 teaspoon
tomatoes, peeled, diced	15 oz	3 medium
capers	1 oz	2 tablespoons

1. Mix squash and flour together to coat well.

2. Heat oil in large pan until hot. Cook onion until translucent; add garlic.

3. Add squash, corn, green pepper, salt, pepper, oregano, and sugar. Mix well.

4. Cover pan. Simmer 20 minutes, stirring occasionally.

5. Add tomatoes. Simmer uncovered until mixture thickens, about 5 minutes.

6. Add capers. Correct seasonings. Serve immediately.

BROILED TOMATO

Broiled Tomato
photo by David Murray and Jules Selmes
© Dorling Kindersley

The baking time depends on the ripeness of the tomatoes. Obviously, ripe tomatoes need less time to bake.

NUMBER OF SERVINGS: 10
COOKING METHOD:
    Bake, Broil
SERVING SIZE:
    4 oz, ½ tomato with topping
TOTAL YIELD:
    2 lbs, 10 oz

INGREDIENTS	WEIGHT	VOLUME
tomatoes, washed, cut in half, core removed	2 lb, 8 oz	5 whole
bread crumbs, plain	2 oz	½ cup
Parmesan cheese	½ oz	2 tablespoons
basil		¼ teaspoon
tarragon		¼ teaspoon
rosemary		¼ teaspoon
thyme		¼ teaspoon
salt		¼ teaspoon
pepper		⅛ teaspoon

1. Place tomatoes with cut side up on baking sheet. If necessary, cut thin slice off bottom so tomatoes stand upright. Preheat oven to 375 degrees.
2. Combine bread crumbs, Parmesan cheese, basil, tarragon, rosemary, thyme, salt, and pepper.
3. Place ¼ oz (1 tablespoon) mixture on top of each tomato half. Bake for 12 to 15 minutes, to soften and heat tomatoes thoroughly.
4. Broil until lightly brown, about 1 to 3 minutes. Serve.

BLACK BEANS AND RICE

Black Beans and Rice

Begin soaking the black beans the day before serving, if possible.

While the number of servings might seem a lot for 14 oz of dried beans, the combination of beans and rice as a side dish requires more rice than beans. This dish also makes a good vegetarian entrée.

NUMBER OF SERVINGS: 19
COOKING METHOD:
    Boil
SERVING SIZE:
    3 oz beans + 4 oz rice
TOTAL YIELD:
    3 lbs, 10¾ oz beans

INGREDIENTS	WEIGHT	VOLUME
black beans, dried	14 oz	2 cups
water, as needed to cover beans	about 2 lbs, 8 oz	about 5 cups
olive oil	1/2 oz	1 tablespoon
onions, small dice	11 1/2 oz	3 medium
green peppers, seeded, small dice	7 1/2 oz	2 small
celery, small dice	2 1/2 oz	2 stalks
garlic, minced	3/4 oz	5 cloves
bay leaves		2 each
oregano		1 teaspoon
pepper		1/2 teaspoon
salt	1/2 oz	2 teaspoons
vinegar, cider or red wine	1 oz	2 tablespoons
rice, hot, cooked	4 lbs, 12 oz	14 1/4 cups

GARNISH:

green onions, sliced

egg, hard boiled, diced

1. Carefully wash beans, rinse, and place in large bowl or pot. Cover with water by at least 2 inches. Soak overnight.
2. Drain beans, again cover with water, bring to boil, reduce heat, cover, and simmer.
3. Meanwhile, heat oil in frying pan. Sauté onions, peppers, and celery about 5 minutes, until softened.
4. Add garlic, bay leaves, oregano, and pepper, and cook another 2 to 3 minutes.
5. Add vegetables to beans. Cook until beans are tender, about 2 hours.
6. Add salt and vinegar; correct seasonings. Serve 3 oz beans over or next to 4 oz rice. Garnish with green onions and hard-boiled egg, if desired.

SPOONBREAD

Spoonbread

This typical southern recipe would most likely appear in northern or central Florida.

NUMBER OF SERVINGS: 10
COOKING METHOD:
   Bake
SERVING SIZE:
   5 oz
TOTAL YIELD:
   3 lbs, 5 oz

INGREDIENTS	WEIGHT	VOLUME
cornmeal	8 1/2 oz	1 1/2 cups
flour, all purpose	3 1/2 oz	2/3 cup
salt	1/4 oz	1 teaspoon
sugar	1 oz	2 tablespoons
baking powder	1/2 oz	2 1/2 teaspoons
milk	1 lb, 12 oz	3 1/2 cups
eggs, separated	6 3/4 oz	4 each
butter, melted	3 oz	6 tablespoons
milk	5 1/2 oz	2/3 cup

1. Pan spray 2 each 1 1/2-quart soufflé dishes. Place rack in upper half of oven. Preheat oven to 350 degrees.
2. Sift cornmeal, flour, salt, sugar, and baking powder together in bowl. Make well into center of flour mixture. Set aside.
3. Mix egg yolks with 1 lb, 12 oz (3 3/4 cups) milk. Beat egg whites until stiff peaks.
4. Pour yolk mixture into well.
5. Place melted butter in 3-quart ovenproof pan. Swirl to coat pan; pour excess butter into yolk mixture. Quickly whisk, just to combine.
6. Fold in beaten egg whites. Pour into prepared dishes. Pour remaining 5 1/2 oz (2/3 cup) milk over top.
7. Bake for 45 minutes until puffed and brown. Serve immediately.

BAKED KEY LIME PIE

Baked Key Lime Pie

Originally, pie crust surrounded Key lime pie, but today, most versions come in a graham cracker crust. Also, while meringue tops most traditional recipes, many now serve Key lime pie crowned with whipped cream instead of meringue. This eliminates the problem of meringue "weeping" in the refrigerator or from the high humidity found in Florida. Either topping contrasts well with the tart lime filling.

NUMBER OF SERVINGS: 8
COOKING METHOD:
  Bake
SERVING SIZE:
  1 slice 1/8 of pie
TOTAL YIELD:
  1 each 9-inch pie

Although it varies from the traditional recipe for Key lime pie, a dash of cinnamon and nutmeg added to the filling creates a nice flavor component. Also, mix 1/4 teaspoon cinnamon with the graham cracker crumbs and sugar for the crust, then add the melted butter and form the crust.

INGREDIENTS	WEIGHT	VOLUME
CRUST:		
graham cracker crumbs	4 3/4 oz	1 cup
sugar	1/2 oz	1 tablespoon
butter, unsalted, melted	2 oz	4 tablespoons or 1/2 stick
FILLING:		
egg yolks	4 oz	6 each
sweetened condensed milk	1 lb, 5 oz	1 1/2 each 14-oz cans or 1 can plus 2/3 cup
Key lime juice, fresh or bottled	6 oz	3/4 cup
vanilla		1/2 teaspoon
egg whites, room temperature	4 oz	4 each
cream of tartar		1/8 teaspoon
sugar	2 3/4 oz	1/3 cup

For Crust:

1. Preheat oven to 350 degrees.
2. Place graham cracker crumbs, sugar, and melted butter in 9-inch pie tin.
3. Rub together until crumbs are thoroughly coated with butter, and evenly moist. Press firmly into even layer up sides and on bottom of pan.

For Filling:

1. Beat egg yolks and condensed milk about 3 minutes.
2. Add lime juice and vanilla. Mix and pour into prepared shell.
3. Bake for 12 minutes. Remove from oven and raise temperature to 400 degrees.
4. Meanwhile, whip egg whites and cream of tartar until foamy, then increase to high speed and continue beating until white. Slowly add sugar, a teaspoon at a time. Beat until stiff peaks.
5. Decoratively, spread or pipe meringue over baked filling. If spreading, form peaks by tapping meringue with flat side of icing spatula to raise peaks. If piping, use large star tip or tip of choice.
6. Return to oven for 5 minutes, until top browns slightly.
7. Remove from oven. Cool completely; refrigerate several hours before serving. Store pie in refrigerator.

UNBAKED KEY LIME PIE

For sanitation safety, prepare this unbaked version of Key lime pie with pasteurized eggs. It is unsafe to serve raw eggs that are not pasteurized. After preparation, this pie is stored in the freezer. It is much like ice cream in texture, so remove the pie from freezer and cut immediately for service; then return to the freezer for storage.

NUMBER OF SERVINGS: 8
SERVING SIZE:
   1 slice 1/8 of pie
TOTAL YIELD:
   1 each 9-inch pie

Unbaked Key Lime Pie
photo © Dorling Kindersley

INGREDIENTS	WEIGHT	VOLUME
CRUST:		
graham cracker crumbs	4 3/4 oz	1 cup
sugar	1/2 oz	1 tablespoon
butter, unsalted, melted	2 oz	4 tablespoons or 1/2 stick
FILLING:		
eggs, separated, room temperature	6 3/4 oz	4 each
cream of tartar		1/8 teaspoon
sweetened condensed milk	1 lb, 12 oz	2 each 14-oz cans
Key lime juice, fresh or bottled	6 oz	3/4 cup
vanilla		1/2 teaspoon
nutmeg		dash, to taste
GARNISH:		
whipped cream, sweetened		
nutmeg, *optional*		
lime peel strip, *optional*		

For Crust:

1. Preheat oven to 350 degrees.
2. Place graham cracker crumbs, sugar, and melted butter in 9-inch pie tin.
3. Rub together until crumbs are thoroughly coated with butter, and evenly moist. Press firmly into even layer up sides and on bottom of pan.
4. Bake for about 5 or 6 minutes, until starting to color. Remove from oven; cool completely.

For Filling:

1. Whip egg whites and cream of tartar until foamy, then increase to high speed and continue beating until stiff peaks. Set aside until needed.
2. Beat egg yolks until thick and light yellow in color.
3. Add condensed milk; beat well.
4. Add lime juice, vanilla, and nutmeg. Fold in beaten egg whites. Mix and pour into prepared shell.
5. Place in freezer until service. Garnish each slice with whipped cream and a dusting of nutmeg or lime peel. Store any remaining pie in freezer.

COCONUT CAKE

Coconut Cake
© 2008 Jupiterimages Corporation

While this recipe uses a white cake as the base for the coconut cake, many prefer a 1-2-3-4 cake recipe, which contains the whole egg and yields a heavier cake. In addition to putting coconut on the outside of the cake, some like to sprinkle coconut on the icing between the cake layers.

Coconut cake often appears at celebrations throughout the South.

NUMBER OF SERVINGS: 16
COOKING METHOD:
 Bake
SERVING SIZE:
 1 slice $^1/_{16}$ of cake
TOTAL YIELD:
 1 each 3-layer 9-inch cake

INGREDIENTS	WEIGHT	VOLUME
CAKE:		
butter, softened	for greasing pans	
flour	for dusting pans	
flour, all purpose, sifted	13 oz	3 cups
salt		$^1/_4$ teaspoon
baking powder	$^1/_2$ oz	1 tablespoon
butter, unsalted, softened	8 oz	2 sticks or 1 cup
sugar	14 oz	2 cups
milk	8 oz	1 cup
vanilla		1 teaspoon
egg whites, room temperature	8 oz	1 cup or 8 each
ICING:		
egg whites	3 oz	3 each
sugar	14 oz	2 cups
water	3 oz	6 tablespoons
corn syrup, white	$^1/_2$ oz	$1^1/_2$ teaspoons
vanilla		1 teaspoon
coconut, shredded or flaked	6 oz	2 cups

For Cake:

1. Grease or pan-spray 3 each 9-inch cake pans, then lightly flour or line with parchment paper. Place oven rack in middle of oven. Preheat oven to 350 degrees.

2. Sift together flour, salt, and baking powder, then sift them again. Set aside.

3. Cream butter with mixer; add sugar and beat until fluffy.

4. Add one-third of flour mixture to butter; mix together just to combine. Scrape sides of bowl. Add one-half of milk; mix together just to combine. Scrape sides of bowl. Add half of remaining flour; mix together just to combine. Scrape sides of bowl. Add remaining milk and vanilla; mix together just to combine. Add rest of flour; mix together just to combine. Scrape sides of bowl.

5. Beat egg whites until stiff peaks. Begin beating on medium-low speed until frothy, then mix on high.

6. Stir one-quarter of egg whites into batter, then fold in remaining egg whites.

7. Divide batter evenly between the three pans, smooth tops. Bake for 23 to 28 minutes, until knife inserted comes out almost clean and tops spring back when lightly touched.

8. Cool pans a few minutes, then turn over on cake racks and cool cakes completely.

For Icing:

1. Place egg whites, sugar, water, and corn syrup in bowl that fits on top of pan of gently boiling water (double boiler or *bain marie*).

2. Beat mixture with whisk or mixer on medium-low speed for about 7 minutes, until fluffy.

3. Add vanilla; beat to mix.

To Assemble:

1. Place one cake layer on cardboard round or plate. Spread about $^1/_4$ inch icing over layer.

(Continued)

2. Top with another layer, lining up cakes to level them if necessary. If they are uneven, align low side of first layer with high part of layer on top. Repeat, spreading icing on second layer. Top with final cake layer placed so top of cake faces down.

3. Spread icing smoothly over top and sides of cake.

4. Gently press coconut into sides of cake by holding coconut in hand and patting very gently into side of cake. If desired, cover 1-inch outer rim of top of cake or entire top with coconut.

5. Serve immediately or refrigerate until serving.

TROPICAL STICKY CARROT CAKE

—Recipe by Mark Militello

NUMBER OF SERVINGS: 12
COOKING METHOD:
　Bake, Boil
SERVING SIZE:
　1 each 3-inch cake
　1 oz sauce for each serving
TOTAL YIELD:
　12 each 3-inch cakes
　3 cups sauce

INGREDIENTS	WEIGHT	VOLUME
CAKE:		
dates, pitted	8 oz	
carrots, peeled, shredded	6 oz	about 3 each
coconut milk	1 lb, 4 oz	
vanilla bean, split, scraped	1 each	
flour, all purpose, unsifted	12 oz	about 2²/₃ cups
baking soda	³/₄ oz	1 tablespoon + 1 teaspoon
baking powder	¹/₄ oz	2 teaspoons
cinnamon		¹/₂ teaspoon
nutmeg		¹/₄ tsp
butter, unsalted	4 oz	1 stick or ¹/₂ cup
vanilla sugar	12 oz	
eggs	6³/₄ oz	4 each
RUM CARAMEL SAUCE:		
butter, unsalted	1 lb	2 cups or 4 sticks
light brown sugar	12 oz	2 cups
heavy cream	10 oz	1¹/₄ cups
dark rum, Meyer's or variety of choice	4 oz	¹/₂ cup
butterscotch liqueur, DeKuyper's Buttershots or variety of choice	2 oz	¹/₄ cup

For Cake:

1. Pan-spray 12 each 3-inch ramekins (6 oz capacity). Preheat oven to 325 degrees.

2. Place dates in bowl of food processor; pulse until finely chopped.

3. In saucepan, combine dates, carrots, coconut milk, and vanilla bean. Bring mixture to a boil; remove from heat. Set aside until needed. In a small bowl, combine flour, baking soda, baking powder and spices.

4. Using electric mixer fitted with paddle attachment, if available, cream butter and vanilla sugar until light and fluffy.

5. Add eggs one at a time, scraping bowl after each addition.

6. Using rubber spatula, fold flour mixture into butter mixture. Remove vanilla bean pod from date mixture; gently fold into flour/butter mixture.

7. Divide batter evenly among prepared ramekins. Place them on baking sheet; bake for 20 to 30 minutes, or until it springs back when lightly touched. *While baking, prepare rum caramel sauce.*

8. Cool about 10 minutes in ramekins. Serve warm, accompanied by Häagen-Dazs coconut ice cream or sorbet.

For Rum Caramel Sauce and Assembly:

1. Combine all ingredients for sauce in nonreactive saucepan.

2. Bring to boil, reduce heat, and simmer for 4 to 5 minutes. Keep warm until needed.

3. Place one cake on plate. Ladle 1 oz rum caramel sauce over and around cake.

—Copyright Mark Militello

6

Louisiana

OBJECTIVES

By the end of this chapter, you will be able to

- Discuss the different ethnic groups that contributed to Louisiana's cookery
- Describe similarities and differences in Cajun and Creole cookery
- Discuss the climate and topography of Louisiana and its impact on the cuisine
- Explain the importance of waterways and how they affected Louisiana's cookery
- Identify food products prevalent in Louisiana
- Prepare a variety of dishes indicative of Louisiana's cuisine

HISTORY

The cooking of Louisiana developed by blending culinary aspects from the French, Spanish, Africans, English, Native Americans, and Acadian French from eastern Canada over a period of 300 years. In the port city of New Orleans, the mixture of culinary heritages evolved into Creole cookery, known as food for aristocrats. Meanwhile, in the bayou (swampland) of southern Louisiana, the cookery developed to feed the poor people living off any foods they could hunt, fish, gather, or grow. This unique cookery of the bayou became Cajun cooking.

In 1699, immigrants from France arrived in southern Louisiana. They established the town of New Orleans in 1718. The Spanish gained control of the Louisiana territory from the French in 1762 and ruled this land until about 1800. At that time, the French again claimed the leadership. This back-and-forth governance between Spain and France ensured that each country contributed significant impact to the cuisine. In 1803, the United States annexed this area with the Louisiana Purchase.

When the women of New Orleans protested the lack of food ingredients from their native homelands, Governor Bienville enlisted the help of his housekeeper, Madame Langlois. She instructed the women about local ingredients and how to prepare them. In essence, Langlois established the first cooking school in the United States.

The term *Creole* came from the Spanish word *Criollo*, which referred to the people of European heritage living in New Orleans. Basically, Creole cooking combined elements from the culinary heritage of the upper-class French and Spanish immigrants with the ingredients available in Louisiana. Later, African slaves, Native Americans, and immigrants from the West Indies added their influence to the Creole cookery that formed in New Orleans. Since New Orleans ranked as a major trading port in the Gulf of Mexico, a wide range of foods from countries throughout the world passed through the port. This exposed the inhabitants to many new ingredients, dishes, and recipes. All of these influences played an important role in building the Creole cuisine.

In the early part of the seventeenth century, many people from France immigrated to Nova Scotia (known as Acadia) in eastern Canada. The French lost control of Nova Scotia to Britain in the early 1700s. During the middle 1700s, thousands of French-speaking Catholic Acadians left Nova Scotia in search of a place to live without persecution. That migration led many to Louisiana, where numerous people of French descent already lived. Known as *Cajuns*, a derivation of the word *Acadians*, these people melded their simple cooking style from Nova Scotia with their French heritage and the ingredients available in the bayous of their new home. Cajun cooking emerged.

From the Spanish influence, Louisiana cooks mixed meat and poultry in a single dish and added Mexican hot peppers to dishes. The Spanish also contributed beans and the frequent addition of rice into the cookery. Two traditional Louisiana dishes—red beans and rice and jambalaya, a mixed dish containing seafood, fish, sausage, meat, and/or poultry with seasonings and rice—developed from the Spanish influence.

While red beans reign as the legume of choice in New Orleans, Cajuns prefer white beans.

The French also left enormous impact on Louisiana's cookery. Their influence brought delicate combinations of flavors, many sauces, and a multitude of recipes including étouffée, stews, bisques, pralines, and beignets. In addition to island immigrants from Haiti and Martinique adding hot chili peppers to the cookery in New Orleans, Creole cooks adopted the unique herbs and seasonings they learned from the Choctaw Indians. Cooks gained many culinary traits from the African slaves who worked on the plantations. For example, they often cooked by deep-fat frying, braising, and cooking on a barbecue (grilling). In addition, they prepared foods in iron cooking pots and skillets and used many African food ingredients and flavorings like okra, sesame seeds, hot spices, and peppers.

With a multitude of indigenous plants and animals, Louisiana presented the settlers with an incredible bounty of sustenance. A wide variety of freshwater and saltwater fish and seafood lived in the ocean, bayous, rivers, and lakes, providing pompano, flounder, redfish, speckled and brook trout, shrimp, oysters, crab, crayfish, alligator, and turtle.

Copious amounts of game such as deer, rabbit, squirrel, wild turkey, geese, duck, quail, squab, pheasant, partridge, and more flourished here. Abundant fruits and vegetables thrived in this hot, humid, subtropical climate, and, with a year-round growing season, some fruits and vegetables were always in season.

Numerous other ethnic groups contributed to Louisiana's cuisine. Germans introduced brown mustard and sausages, and those sausages became Louisiana's famous *boudin* and *andouille* sausages, which still remain popular. Of course, Native Americans brought corn, hominy, cornmeal, and cornbread. The native Choctaw Indians taught the settlers to use filé powder, ground leaves of the sassafras tree, to season and thicken dishes. Muffuletta, the famous sandwich from New Orleans, originated from Italian influence. Prepared on a round loaf of Italian bread, this "meal in a sandwich" consists of an assortment of cheeses and cold cuts, including Italian salami and ham, with a flavorful olive salad condiment. Many say the olive salad "makes" the sandwich. Although there are countless recipes, olive salad contains green olives, pimentos, garlic, celery, vinegar, olive oil, and seasonings.

Muffuletta
photo by Greg Ward © Rough Guides

In 1803, Thomas Jefferson orchestrated the purchase of the Louisiana territory for 15 million dollars. Because of the accessible transportation created by the Mississippi River running through the state and into the Gulf of Mexico, this area thrived. Not surprisingly, the Mississippi River played a crucial role in Louisiana's history and livelihood in the early years. While the Gulf of Mexico connected Louisiana with many far-away places, the Mississippi River linked Louisiana with much of the continental United States. Between these two waterways, Louisiana became a major transportation center and mecca for trade.

To gain control of the Mississippi River and its accessible transportation, many Civil War battles were fought in Louisiana. The state sustained huge losses as a result of that war. Like the rest of the South, Louisiana emerged from the Civil War devastated and bankrupt.

TOPOGRAPHY AND CLIMATE

Hot, humid, subtropical climate determines much of what grows in Louisiana. With a very long growing season and abundant rainfall, a cornucopia of fruits and vegetables flourish here. As a result, rice, sugarcane, okra, tomatoes, eggplant, sweet potatoes, chili peppers, bell peppers, soybeans, strawberries, oranges, figs, peaches, and much more thrive. In fact, most vegetables grow somewhere in this state.

Arkansas borders Louisiana on the north, Mississippi and the Gulf of Mexico lie to the east, the Gulf of Mexico forms its southern border, and Texas joins it on the west. Consisting of low-lying land, Louisiana's highest elevation measures 535 feet. With bays, inlets, islands, and jagged bits of land jutting into the Gulf of Mexico, Louisiana contains miles and miles of coastline. Several rivers, including the Mississippi River, flow through Louisiana and empty into the Gulf. Lying at sea level, the area near the Gulf of Mexico floods periodically. Of course, the Gulf yields plentiful seafood. The many bayous found in Louisiana provide a home for a wide range of fish, shellfish, birds, and other animals, including crayfish, shrimp, oysters, clams, crabs, redfish, catfish, bass, ducks, quail, alligators, and turtles.

The Mississippi River forms much of the eastern boundary separating Louisiana from Mississippi. While plains and ridges form the landscape away from the river, flooding deposited rich, fertile land around this river, creating the flat land called delta. Encompassing about 13,000 square miles, the delta area contains silt, alluvial soil, and extremely fertile farmland.

The southwestern part of the state consists of prairie. Because numerous cattle graze here, residents in this region consume many beef dishes. Pork ranks as the favorite meat in the rest of the state. Rolling hills make up part of the north where poultry farms flourish, producing many chickens and other poultry. Most of the southern part of the state contains lowlands, marshes, and bayous. Cajun country reigns in the southern and southwestern regions of Louisiana. Covering about half of the state, forests teem with game.

Ingredients and foods commonly used throughout the cuisine of Louisiana include

- shellfish, including shrimp, crayfish, oysters, crabs, and clams
- fish, including redfish, catfish, pompano, bass, trout, flounder, and red snapper
- pork and pork products, including smoked ham, tasso, ham hocks, ham bones, pigs' knuckles, fatback, and salt pork
- sausages, including *andouille* and *boudin*
- alligator, turtle, and frogs' legs
- ducks, geese, chicken, wild turkey, squab, pheasant, partridge, and quail
- game, including deer, rabbit, and squirrel
- rice
- scallions, onions, and garlic
- bell peppers and chili peppers
- okra, eggplant, all sorts of squash, mirliton (chayote squash), corn, tomatoes, and beans
- sweet potatoes
- figs, strawberries, oranges, and peaches
- pecans
- filé
- sugarcane

COOKING METHODS

Braising, frying, and boiling commonly appear in Louisiana's cookery. The long, slow cooking of braising created the soups, stews, and one-pot dishes like gumbo, jambalaya, and étouffée. Although it is prevalent in both Cajun and Creole cooking, Cajun cookery, in particular, features braised dishes made with any available ingredients obtained from hunting, fishing, or the garden.

Deep-fried, pan-fried, and sautéed items, including fritters, croquettes, fish, seafood, chicken, and beignets, are served very often. With plenty of lard rendered from hogs, abundant fat was available for frying a wide range of foods.

Still today, boiled seafood graces many tables in Louisiana. Large family gatherings or parties often center on boiling pots of crayfish, shrimp, or crab. After draining the cooked seafood, cooks place the seafood directly on the table, and everyone peels and eats. Following the typical southern tradition, vegetables boiled until soft and limp with some sort of smoked pork flavoring like bacon, bacon grease, ham bone, or ham hocks are still favorites.

Cooking *en papillote*, literally "in an envelope," involves tightly enclosing the food in parchment paper, which steams the contents. Pompano, a flat fish caught from the Gulf of Mexico, is often prepared using this cooking technique.

Cooks learned about cast iron pots from the African slaves. Used both for frying and for the long, slow cooking of one-pot dishes, thick cast iron pots and skillets conduct heat well and evenly. Many in Louisiana still prefer cast iron cookware.

In Louisiana's hot climate, smoking, pickling, and canning were crucial to preserve meat, seafood, and produce in the days before refrigeration. From the Native Americans, the settlers learned two techniques to preserve foods: smoking the foods and drying them in the sun. As in the Southern states, butchering hogs usually occurred in the cooler months. After butchering, the early settlers smoked, salted, made sausages, or otherwise preserved all excess parts of the hog. A Cajun specialty, *tasso*, highly spiced smoked pork, flavors numerous dishes.

REGIONS

While people of English and American descent practicing the Protestant religion dominated the northern part of the state, individuals of French and Spanish heritage and the Catholic faith populated the majority of the south. Of course, the food found in each region reflected the inhabitants' culinary background.

Situated in the southeastern part of the state, New Orleans was established by the French around the beginning of the eighteenth century. Lake Pontchartrain lies on the northern side of the city, Lake Borgne and the waters leading to the Gulf are situated to the east and southeast, and the Mississippi River flows on the western side of the city. The numerous bodies of water played an intrinsic part in the life of New Orleans residents. Besides yielding a wealth of fish and seafood, the waterways provided transportation. As a major port city, New Orleans received many foreign food items from ships docking there. Residents also had access to a wide assortment of produce, game, fowl, fish, and seafood from the bayous. With all of these resources for obtaining foods, added to the influences from the many ethnic groups who settled here, the cookery of New Orleans developed into an opulent cuisine. Even today, eating and dining receive great importance and attention in this city. A few of the many dishes that originated in New Orleans include shrimp rémoulade, oysters Rockefeller, baked oysters on the half-shell covered with a spinach mixture, and bananas foster. Subsequently, cuisines throughout the United States adopted many of these dishes from New Orleans.

Lying west and southwest of New Orleans, the bayous seem like a totally different country. Countless waterways including the Atchafalaya River, streams, and ponds crisscross this low-lying land, creating marshes and swamps filled with all sorts of fish, shellfish, turtles, alligators, and birds. Cajun cooking began in the bayous, and it still flourishes there. Whether turtle, frogs' legs, duck, fish, crawfish, or game, any available ingredients entered one large iron pot and emerged as a flavorful, spicy Cajun dish.

Because the swampland and crisscrossing waterways of the bayous created difficult travel, the resulting isolation led to little sharing of recipes. Every Cajun dish has countless

Because Catholics abstained from eating meat on Fridays and holy days, meatless dishes abound in Louisiana's cuisine. The abundance of fish, seafood, and vegetables made it easy to create meatless meals.

The original recipe for oysters Rockefeller came from Antoine's Restaurant in New Orleans. The owner's son wanted to create an oyster dish to replace snails, and he covered oysters on the shell with a rich, green-colored sauce. Some say customers proclaimed the dish was as rich as Rockefeller, so he named the dish oysters Rockefeller after the richest man at that time, John D. Rockefeller. Controversy still rages over the ingredients in the green sauce. Some claim spinach creates the topping while others attribute the color to watercress or other greens. The sauce recipe remains a closely guarded secret of Antoine's Restaurant.

CAJUN TRAITS AND DISHES

- spicy from generous use of hot peppers
- cook in one pot
- start with brown or dark brown *roux*
- braise any available ingredients in large iron pot—the ingredient list depending on foods obtained from fishing, hunting, gathering, and the garden
- gumbo
- jambalaya
- bisque
- étouffée
- crayfish
- rice
- dirty rice
- stuffed eggplant, mirliton, squash, or other vegetables
- white beans

CREOLE TRAITS AND DISHES

- generous amount of herbs and spices, but not overpowering
- wide variety of sauces reflecting European heritage
- cook with extensive assortment of ingredients
- shrimp rémoulade
- oysters Rockefeller
- gumbo
- pompano *en papillote*
- *grillades* (braised round steak)
- red beans
- *beignets*
- bananas foster

SIMILARITIES OF CAJUN AND CREOLE COOKERY

- start many dishes by sautéing onions, celery, and sweet bell peppers
- thicken dishes with a *roux*
- dishes accompanied by rice
- abundance of fish and shellfish
- many braised dishes, including soups and stews
- cook in iron pots

The holy trinity is a variation of the French *mirepoix,* which consists of diced onion, celery, and carrot.

---

variations served in different areas of the bayous. As a result, every community created its own unique blend of Cajun cookery, and every community treasures its own particular (and different) rendition of each dish.

CHARACTERISTICS OF THE CUISINE

Although they have some similarities, Creole and Cajun cookery are two distinct and different styles of cooking. Resulting in a subtle yet very flavorful cuisine, Creole cooking contains a generous amount of herbs and spices without being overpowering. Creole cooks are known for utilizing any leftover foods, whether cooked or uncooked. Leftovers often become croquettes. To tenderize tough cuts of meat, Creoles use wine (an acidic ingredient) for at least part of the liquid in the recipe and simmer it until tender. Reflecting their European heritage, a wider variety of sauces appear in Creole cookery than in Cajun. Some say that Creole cooking developed when Native American herbs and foods merged with French and Spanish cookery. As more and more ethnic groups moved into New Orleans, their culinary heritages added to the evolving Creole cuisine.

The typical New Orleans resident planted a garden containing herbs and produce reflecting the gardener's culinary heritage. In addition to the harvest from the garden, lots of foods were available because of New Orleans' port. As a result, Creole dishes exhibited a wide variety of ingredients. In contrast, Cajun dishes used whatever the people caught from the waterways, hunted, found growing wild, or grew in their own gardens.

Many people confuse the spiciness of Cajun and Creole dishes. While Cajun cookery exhibits spicy flavor from the liberal use of hot chili peppers, Creoles prepare flavorful but not overly spicy dishes. Creole dishes usually contain sweet bell peppers instead of the hot chilies that the Cajuns favor.

Harkening from the French influence, *roux* forms the basis of many sauces throughout Louisiana. To make a *roux,* cook equal weights of flour and fat until it becomes the desired color of white, blonde, brown, or dark brown. Unlike the lightly colored *roux* typically used in French cookery, many Louisiana recipes require a darker *roux* to produce a sauce with a dark color and a strong, nutty flavor. Traditional Louisiana cookery requires cooking the *roux* very slowly until it reaches the desired color. With its great conductivity and even heating, the iron pot is excellent for this. Creole cooks often prepared *roux* with butter, but Cajun cooks had no butter. Instead they used oil, duck fat, or any available fat.

Having moved from Nova Scotia to this new land filled with swamps, marsh, fish, shellfish, frogs, turtles, alligators, wild birds, and game, the Cajuns developed a cuisine of their own. Besides cooking whatever was available, they extended many dishes with rice. Hunting and fishing provided most of the protein portion of the diet, and the meal revolved around whatever settlers brought home after hunting and fishing. As a result, they cooked game in many guises and served it at numerous meals. In order to utilize all parts of the animal, Cajuns prepared many varieties of sausages. As a result, sausage often joined other meats, fish, shellfish, and/or fowl in the cooking pot. Most Cajun dishes feature full-bodied spicy sauces to flavor the bland rice that accompanied them.

Dishes typically begin with the famous flavoring triumvirate of Cajun and Creole cooking, known as the holy trinity: onions, celery, and sweet bell peppers. As in Creole cooking, the thickening comes from a *roux,* but Cajuns prefer a brown or dark brown *roux* to give a rich, full-bodied flavor to the sauce. While hot chili peppers frequently flavor Cajun dishes, their recipes also often include bay leaves, thyme, and filé powder.

Since filé powder becomes gummy as it cooks, remove the pot from heat at the end of cooking, add the filé, cover, and allow the dish to sit about five minutes before serving.

With a huge variety of pepper sauces available in Louisiana, most adamantly claim their favorite variety is the best. Making pepper sauce on Avery Island, Louisiana, since 1868, the McIlhenny family named their sauce "Tabasco" since they made the sauce from tabasco peppers. Apparently, the Trappey family feuded with the McIlhennys for control of the Tabasco trademark, but the Trappeys lost. They still sell their hot pepper sauce under their own name.

Louisiana ranks as the crayfish capital of the world.

Soft-shell crabs are very popular in Louisiana and often appear on menus.

With a wide variety of hot peppers growing in Louisiana, the cookery incorporates fresh peppers, dried peppers, and pepper sauce. Still a popular condiment, pepper sauce is actually hot peppers preserved with salt and vinegar to pickle the peppers. Besides the amount of ingredients and the types of peppers used in the mixture, aging creates remarkable differences in the pepper sauce. Like wine or balsamic vinegar, both the length of time and the container (type of barrel) used in aging affect the flavor of the sauce.

With rivers, lakes, swamps, marshes, bayous, and the Gulf of Mexico, a wealth of shellfish and fish from fresh water, brackish water (a mixture of fresh water and salt water), and salt water dominate the recipes and meals found throughout Louisiana. Oysters, crayfish, shrimp, and crab provide the base for many dishes. An oyster po' boy is a submarine roll filled with fried oysters. Oysters Rockefeller, oysters casino, oysters Bienville, oysters Rossignac, and oyster stew, as well as raw oysters on the half-shell, frequent menus. Both freshwater and saltwater seafood and fish create significant revenue for the state. Louisiana boasts it produces more shrimp and crayfish than any other state. Commercial catfish and crayfish farms thrive here.

Cooked in a variety of ways, commonly consumed fish include catfish, trout, bass, pompano, red snapper, and redfish. A type of drum fish, redfish flourished in Louisiana waters. In the 1980s, Chef Paul Prodhomme made blackened redfish, and Cajun cooking became famous. To prepare blackened fish, Prodhomme dredged the fish in a very highly spiced, peppery coating containing pepper, cayenne pepper, salt, paprika, garlic powder, onion powder, oregano, and thyme. After dredging, he fried the fish in butter in an *extremely* hot cast iron skillet. Because this high-heat frying creates intense fumes, frying outside is recommended unless there is a powerful exhaust system. (The grill works well.) Due to the extreme popularity of this dish after Prodhomme introduced it, the population of redfish plummeted because of overfishing. Limits were established on the redfish catch, and the population rose. Redfish is no longer in danger of extinction.

Stews and soups play an important part in Louisiana's cookery. Using any available scraps of foods or bones, soups ranging from turtle soup and gumbo to classic consommé and court bouillon to bisques and cream soups remain popular. Oyster and artichoke soup is another favorite. Either used alone or combined with meat, sausage, or vegetables, seafood provides the base for many soups and stews.

Displaying its roots, gumbo derives its name from the West African word for okra, *guingombo*. Both Cajuns and Creoles prepare this soup/stew by beginning with a *roux* and then incorporating seafood, pork, chicken, or whatever is available. They thicken gumbo by cooking okra with the soup or adding filé powder at the end. Many say that in the early days, they used okra from the garden in the summer when it was available and filé powder in the winter. Regardless of the choice of thickener, rice always accompanies this soup. The rice is added to each bowl of soup rather than adding it to the pot of gumbo. While the Creole version begins with a blonde *roux*, the Cajun rendition starts with a very dark *roux* and *tasso*, a spicy, smoked ham that contributes to its robust flavor. Like gumbo, many of the traditional Cajun and Creole soups

Soft-Shell Crab Po' Boy

Often served during Lent and other religious days requiring abstinence from meat, gumbo z'herbes contains seven greens and no meat.

Typically, families throughout Louisiana ate red beans and rice on Mondays, the "wash day." The slow-cooking pot of beans on the back of the stove transformed itself into dinner while the cook washed the week's laundry. They used the ham bone left over from the weekend to flavor the beans.

According to statistics, residents of Louisiana consume about 70 pounds of rice each year, which ranks as the highest rice consumption of any state.

In French, *café au lait* means "coffee with milk." *Café au lait* combines strong coffee with scalded milk.

are heavy and full-bodied. A small bowl of the hearty soups functions as a soup course while a larger portion easily serves as an entrée.

Resembling the Spanish dish *paella*, jambalaya derives its name from the Spanish and French words for ham. Like *paella*, jambalaya combines rice with all sorts of meats, poultry, and/or seafood. In fact, many of Louisiana's famous dishes revolved around ways to use all parts of the animal and stretch any available food supplies. For example, the wide assortment of sausages is made from leftover organ meats and other less desirable parts. Plentiful in the bayou, crayfish replaced shrimp for the poor man.

Another dish embedded in Louisiana's cuisine, *étouffée* literally means "smothered." *Étouffée* begins with the "holy trinity" of vegetables—onion, celery, and green pepper—in a *roux* with shrimp or crayfish. The finished dish is served over hot rice.

Still an important crop in Louisiana, rice was first planted in the swamps of Louisiana by French explorers in 1718. The rice flourished and soon became an intrinsic part of the cuisine. Beans and rice continues as a popular combination, whether red beans and rice or hoppin' John, a combination of cowpeas or black-eyed peas with rice. In each of these dishes, the beans cook with a ham bone, pig's knuckle, fatback, or some other pork flavoring. Rice, usually cooked separately, is piled on the plate and surrounded with the beans. To use excess food products, the Cajuns created dirty rice by cooking chicken livers and gizzards with seasoned rice. Today, Louisiana ranks third among the states in rice production with only California and Arkansas producing more.

Breakfast or brunch remains an important meal in Louisiana. New Orleans restaurants feature a variety of egg dishes, and many consist of poached eggs combined with vegetables, seafood, or meat, then topped with a sauce. For example, eggs Sardou pairs poached eggs with artichoke bottoms, creamed spinach, and hollandaise sauce. Cooks also prepare poached eggs topped with crabmeat and a cream sauce, poached eggs with tomato and Canadian bacon cloaked with a wine sauce and hollandaise, or whatever combination the cook creates. Another well known breakfast entrée, *pain perdu* translates as "lost bread." It is simply French toast prepared with stale French or Italian bread. *Grillades*, braised round steak similar to Swiss steak, is served with grits for breakfast.

The vegetable garden growing at most homes provided the family with a wide array of produce. Eggplant, green beans, tomatoes, squash, okra, sweet potatoes, corn, mild and hot peppers, scallions, onions, mirlitons (chayote squash), and much more filled out the meals. Stuffed vegetables still appear often.

As in Florida, salads provide a cool entrée in the hot, humid climate found in Louisiana. Salad possibilities abound with the wealth of available fresh produce. Bean salads, potato salads, salads containing meat, poultry, and/or seafood, gelatin salads, and many more grace picnics and dining tables throughout the state.

An important item at any picnic and most family gatherings, potato salad accompanies all sorts of dishes and many meals in Louisiana. The ubiquitous potato salad shows up with fried chicken and fish as well as with dishes containing rice, like gumbo. Also widely consumed, sweet potatoes frequently appear on menus, both as a side dish and as dessert. With the typical Southern fondness for sweets, sweet potato preparations for side dishes often include plenty of sugar. Desserts made with sweet potatoes include sweet potato pie and sweet potato pudding.

Although the choice of breads varies with the region, bread accompanies most meals. Following Southern tradition, cornbread or biscuits commonly appear in the northern part of the state. People in southern Louisiana prefer French bread. A specialty served with *café au lait* or strong coffee, *beignets* consist of deep-fried pieces of square dough that are dusted with a thick coating of confectioners' sugar before serving. Throughout the countryside, people eat another deep-fried dough confection called *oreilles de cochon*, which means "pigs' ears." They dip the fried *oreilles de cochon* in cooked cane sugar syrup before serving.

With many pecan trees growing throughout Louisiana, pecans join the ingredient list for all sorts of dishes ranging from appetizers to desserts. Often, ground pecans replace flour in a dessert or as the breading used to coat food items before frying. Besides an assortment of cakes, cookies, and candies containing pecans, dessert menus often feature pecan pie or fig and pecan pie.

The Creoles adapted pralines from their native homeland to Louisiana, creating a cloyingly sweet candy quite different from the European version of pralines. Pecans replaced the almonds used in European recipes, and brown sugar substituted for the white sugar. Some versions add cream to the recipe, which totally changes the texture from the original praline found in Europe.

Because plenty of sugarcane grew in Louisiana in the early days and today, the local affinity for sweets and desserts is not surprising. Exhibiting the same frugality with food ingredients in desserts as in entrées, cooks use leftover ingredients in some of the favorite confections like bread pudding. With countless variations, bread pudding uses pieces of day-old bread baked in a rich egg and milk mixture flavored with bourbon, vanilla, and spices. Bread pudding is often accompanied by a sauce, such as whiskey, bourbon, or rum sauce or nonalcoholic custard or lemon sauce.

Another simple, yet elegant dessert that is usually prepared tableside, bananas foster originated at Brennan's Restaurant in New Orleans. To prepare this creation, melted butter and brown sugar are cooked until syrupy, and bananas are added, quickly followed by rum and/or other liqueur, which is flambéed. For serving, the hot bananas and syrup are accompanied by vanilla ice cream.

King cake is a pastry served during Carnival season, which lasts from January 6 (Twelfth Night or King's Day) through Mardi Gras (the day before Lent begins). This confection consists of cake made from brioche or a similar rich coffeecake type of dough with a bean or small plastic baby (representing the baby Jesus) baked into it.

King Cake

Traditionally, the cake is baked in an oval shape and is frosted with white icing decorated with purple, green, and yellow sugar sprinkles. According to folklore, whoever finds the baby in his or her piece of cake receives a year of good luck. Some say that person hosts the next party or buys the next King cake.

Because coffee was scarce in the early days, many in Louisiana extended coffee with chicory. Today, strong coffee containing chicory remains a Louisiana signature. After-dinner coffees flavored with liquor, sugar, orange rind, lemon rind, or other flavorings often finish a meal. Still a popular ending for a special dinner, *café brûlot* contains brandy, orange liqueur, and sugar.

(Continued)
the day before the beginning of Lent. Around 1700, the early French settlers in Louisiana first celebrated this holiday. By the middle of the nineteenth century, the festivities reached the current status of intense partying, numerous parades with floats, hordes of people dressed in costumes, and lots of eating and drinking throughout the city of New Orleans.

Known as a party town, New Orleans is the birthplace of a number of cocktails. A druggist with an apothecary in the French Quarter, Antoine Peychaud invented the cocktail when preparing his first Sazerac cocktail in the early 1800s. Also responsible for creating bitters, the company still produces Peychaud bitters. Combining his mixture of brandy or cognac, sugar, and bitters to cure the aches of customers who came to his pharmacy, Peychaud mixed his concoction in an egg cup, called *coquetier* in French. Before long, the word *coquetier* became the word "cocktail," and the Sazerac cocktail was born. In the late 1800s, Henry Ramos created the first Gin Fizz. Another well-known drink, the Hurricane cocktail was invented during World War II at Pat O'Brien's in the French Quarter. Tasting like fruit punch, this cocktail combines rum, juice, and other flavorings.

Area	Weather	Topography	Foods
Louisiana Arkansas to north, Mississippi and Gulf of Mexico to east, Gulf of Mexico to south, Texas to west	hot, humid, wet, summers; warm winters; subtropical	north: rolling hills south: lowlands, bayou (swamps), marsh, coast, bays, inlets, islands; forests cover half of state; Mississippi River flows north to south and forms part of eastern border; Mississippi Delta in south; rich, fertile farmland in Delta southwest: prairie	seafood, fish, crayfish, crabs, shrimp, oysters, pompano, catfish, bass, flounder, trout, red snapper, redfish, alligator, turtle, frogs, chicken, game, deer, rabbit, squirrel, ducks, wild turkey, geese, pheasant, quail, partridge, sausage, *tasso, boudin, andouille,* beans, rice, sugarcane, fruits and vegetables, tomatoes, mild and hot peppers, okra, corn, hominy, cornmeal, grits, eggplant, green beans, squash, onions, mirlitons, sweet potatoes, soybeans, garlic, filé, bay leaves, figs, peaches, strawberries, pecans, chicory

REVIEW QUESTIONS

1. Describe the climate and terrain found in Louisiana and how they affected the cuisine.
2. Discuss the immigrants who migrated to New Orleans and the evolution of Creole cookery.
3. Discuss the history of the immigrants and the development of Cajun cookery.
4. What are the similarities and differences in Creole and Cajun cookery?
5. Discuss the importance of braising in Louisiana cooking and name at least three braised dishes.
6. How did the waterways affect the cuisine?

GLOSSARY

alluvial—rich, fertile land deposited around rivers as a result of flooding; excellent soil for crops

bayou—swamps found in Louisiana

beignets—deep-fried pieces of bread dough, dusted with a thick coating of confectioners' sugar before serving

brackish water—a mixture of fresh water and salt water

café brûlot—hot coffee drink containing strong coffee flavored with brandy, orange liqueur, and sugar

en papillote—literally "in an envelope," this cooking technique involves tightly enclosing the food in parchment paper or other wrapper, which actually steams the contents inside the parchment envelope

étouffée—literally means "smothered"; the dish begins with sautéing the "holy trinity" of vegetables—onion, celery, and green pepper—in a *roux* with shrimp or crayfish

filé powder—spice made from the ground leaves of the sassafras tree that frequently appears in Cajun cooking; first used by the Choctaw Indians; flavors as well as thickens the dish

grillades—braised round steak similar to Swiss steak, usually served at breakfast and accompanied by grits

gumbo—from the West African word for okra, *guingombo*, this soup/stew begins with a *roux*, then incorporates seafood, pork, chicken, or whatever is available, thickened with either okra (African) or filé powder (Choctaw Indians) added at the end, and served with rice

gumbo z'herbes—meatless version of gumbo containing seven greens and no meat, often served during Lent

jambalaya—name from the Spanish and French words for ham, dish resembles the Spanish dish *paella*. Jambalaya combines rice and seasonings with all sorts of meats, poultry, and/or seafood.

oreilles de cochon—fried dough dipped in sugar syrup, served throughout the countryside in Louisiana; literally means "pigs' ears"

pepper sauce—pickled peppers preserved with salt and vinegar; type of peppers, amount of aging time, and type of container used in aging create differences in the flavor of the sauce

pralines—cloyingly sweet candy containing pecans and brown sugar; some versions add cream; derived from European version of praline, which consists of almonds and white sugar

roux—basis for a thickening made by sautéing equal parts of fat and flour, from French cookery; cooked to different colors from white to brown depending on desired flavor and color outcome

tasso—spicy, smoked ham; Cajun specialty used to flavor many dishes

OYSTERS ROCKEFELLER

Oysters Rockefeller

Although countless variations on this recipe exist and controversy prevails over what makes the topping green, we know the dish originated at Antoine's Restaurant in New Orleans.

NUMBER OF SERVINGS: 8
COOKING METHOD:
  Sauté, Bake
SERVING SIZE:
  6 oysters
TOTAL YIELD:
  48 oysters
SPINACH TOPPING:
  3 lbs, 1/2 oz

Wine Style: Sparkling wine; crisp, dry Riesling; or mild Chardonnay
Example: Esperanza—Feliciana Cellars Winery, Jackson, LA. This is a crisp, bubbly sparkling wine.

INGREDIENTS	WEIGHT	VOLUME
butter	8 oz	2 sticks or 1 cup
green onions, sliced	2½ oz	1 cup
celery, medium dice	5 oz	1 cup
fennel, medium dice	5 oz	1 cup
garlic, chopped	1 oz	8 small cloves
spinach, defrosted	2 lbs, 8 oz	4 each 10-oz packages
parsley, sprigs without stems	2 oz	1 cup
Pernod or anise-flavored liqueur	5½ oz	⅔ cup
salt	¼ oz	1 teaspoon
celery salt	¼ oz	1 teaspoon
pepper		1 teaspoon
Worcestershire sauce	2 oz	¼ cup
cayenne		¼ teaspoon or to taste
anchovies, flat fillets	1 oz	8 each
oysters, scrubbed, opened on the half shell		48 each
bread crumbs	4¾ oz	1 cup
butter, melted	2 oz	4 tablespoons
rock salt		

1. Preheat oven to 450 degrees.
2. Melt 8 oz (2 sticks or 1 cup) butter in pan. Sauté green onions, celery, fennel, garlic, spinach, and parsley for 4 to 5 minutes.
3. Add Pernod, salt, celery salt, pepper, Worcestershire sauce, cayenne, and anchovies.
4. Transfer to bowl of food processor fitted with steel knife; process until smooth. Correct seasonings.
5. Place oysters on baking pans. Top each oyster with 1 oz (1¾ tablespoons) spinach mixture to cover oyster. *Amount of topping will vary based on size of oyster.*
6. Sprinkle lightly with bread crumbs; dot with melted butter.
7. Bake for 10 minutes, until bubbly. Serve on bed of rock salt.

SHRIMP RÉMOULADE

Shrimp Rémoulade

Some serve the shrimp separately from the sauce like a shrimp cocktail; others coat the shrimp with the rémoulade sauce and then serve.

NUMBER OF SERVINGS: 14
COOKING METHOD:
 Boil
SERVING SIZE:
 4 oz shrimp +
  1½ oz sauce
TOTAL YIELD:
 1 lb, 6 oz sauce

Wine Style: White hybrid wines such as Blanc du Bois, light fruity Pinot Blanc, Chardonnay, or White Zinfandel
Example: Blanc du Bois—Landry Vineyards, Folsom, LA. Developed for the South, this hybrid bursts forth with a clean, crisp flavor.

INGREDIENTS	WEIGHT	VOLUME
SAUCE:		
vinegar, white	2 oz	1/4 cup
mustard, Creole or Dijon	5 oz	1/2 cup
mayonnaise	4 1/2 oz	1/2 cup
horseradish, prepared	3 oz	1/4 cup
catsup	3 oz	1/4 cup
celery, minced	2 1/2 oz	1/2 cup
anchovy, minced	1/2 oz	2 filets
garlic, minced	1/2 oz	2 large cloves
paprika	1/4 oz	2 teaspoons
hot pepper sauce		1/2 teaspoon
salt	1/4 oz	1 teaspoon
pepper		1 teaspoon
olive oil	1 oz	2 tablespoons
green onions, sliced	1 1/2 oz	1/2 cup
parsley, minced	1 oz	1/4 cup
shrimp, boiled, shelled, deveined	3 lbs, 8 oz	
lettuce leaves or field greens, for plating		

For Sauce:

1. In nonreactive bowl, combine vinegar, mustard, mayonnaise, horseradish, catsup, celery, anchovy, garlic, paprika, hot pepper sauce, salt, and pepper.
2. Slowly whisk in olive oil until mixture is well blended. Stir in green onion and parsley.
3. Correct seasonings. Cover and chill until needed.

For Assembly:

1. Gently mix shrimp and rémoulade sauce in nonreactive bowl.
2. Cover and chill at least 4 hours.
3. Serve on lettuce leaf or bed of greens.

CORN AND CRAB BISQUE

Corn and Crab Bisque

If reheating bisque, do not boil or it might curdle.

NUMBER OF SERVINGS: 13
COOKING METHOD:
  Sauté, Boil
SERVING SIZE:
  6 oz
TOTAL YIELD:
  4 lbs, 14 1/4 oz

INGREDIENTS	WEIGHT	VOLUME
oil	2 oz	1/4 cup
flour, all purpose	2 1/4 oz	1/2 cup
onions, small dice	2 1/2 oz	1/2 cup
celery, small dice	2 1/2 oz	1/2 cup
corn, removed from cob	6 3/4 oz	2 each ears or 1 1/3 cups
garlic, minced	1/4 oz	2 cloves
fish stock, hot	1 lb	2 cups
half-and-half	2 lbs	1 qt
salt		1/2 teaspoon
white pepper		1/2 teaspoon
thyme, dried		1/4 teaspoon
basil		1/4 teaspoon
hot pepper sauce		1 teaspoon
bay leaf		1 each
sherry, dry	1 oz	2 tablespoons
Worcestershire sauce		1 teaspoon
crabmeat, lump, picked over to remove shells and cartilage	1 lb	
green onions, sliced	1 1/4 oz	1/2 cup
parsley, minced		1 tablespoon

1. Heat oil in large pot over medium heat, whisk in flour, and cook a few minutes until light blonde color.
2. Add onions, celery, corn, and garlic. Sauté 4 to 5 minutes, until vegetables soften.
3. Slowly whisk in stock, then whisk in half-and-half, salt, pepper, thyme, basil, hot pepper sauce, bay leaf, sherry, and Worcestershire sauce.
4. Bring to boil, reduce heat, and simmer 25 minutes.
5. Add crabmeat; heat for another 5 minutes. Add green onions and parsley; mix well.
6. Correct seasonings; remove bay leaf. Serve immediately.

DUCK AND SAUSAGE GUMBO

Duck and Sausage Gumbo
photo courtesy of National Pork Board

Some serve gumbo as a soup; others call it a stew. Remember: this is a hearty dish, so if served as soup, make it an appropriately small serving.

NUMBER OF SERVINGS: 10
COOKING METHOD:
  Braise
SERVING SIZE:
  12 oz
TOTAL YIELD:
  7 lbs, 13 1/2 oz

INGREDIENTS	WEIGHT	VOLUME
andouille sausage, sliced ½-inch thick on bias	1 lb	
flour, all purpose	2¼ oz	½ cup
salt	½ oz	2 teaspoons
pepper		½ teaspoon
paprika		2 teaspoons
thyme		1 teaspoon
cayenne		¼ teaspoon
duck, trimmed of all fat, each cut into eight pieces, washed	6 lb, 15 oz	2 each
oil	up to 4 oz	up to ½ cup
butter	2 oz	4 tablespoons
flour, all purpose	1½ oz	6 tablespoons
onion, small dice	10 oz	2 medium or 2 cups
green pepper, small dice	6½ oz	1⅓ cups
celery, small dice	5 oz	1 cup
garlic, minced	½ oz	4 small cloves
duck or chicken stock, hot	3 lbs	6 cups
hot pepper sauce		2 teaspoons
cayenne		¼ teaspoon
scallions, sliced	2 oz	⅔ cup
filé powder		2 teaspoons

ACCOMPANIMENTS:

rice, cooked, hot	2 lb, 6 oz	

1. Brown sausage in large braiser or skillet over medium-low heat. Remove sausage from pan; set aside.
2. Combine 2¼ oz (½ cup) flour, salt, pepper, paprika, thyme, and cayenne in bowl. Dredge duck pieces in flour mixture.
3. Meanwhile, add enough oil to fat remaining from sausage in braiser to make 4 oz (½ cup). Heat fat and fry duck pieces until well browned, about 5 to 7 minutes. Remove duck, place on absorbent paper, and set aside.
4. Melt butter in braiser; add 1½ oz (6 tablespoons) flour. Stir constantly until dark *roux*, about 5 minutes.
5. Add onion; cook until soft, about 4 to 5 minutes. Then add green pepper, celery, and garlic. Cook another 2 to 3 minutes.
6. Slowly whisk in hot stock. Add duck and sausage; season with hot pepper sauce and cayenne. Bring to boil, reduce heat, and cover. Simmer for about 1 hour, until duck is tender.
7. Skim off as much fat from top of pan as possible. Remove from heat; add scallions and filé powder. Correct seasonings.
8. Place about 3¾ oz (¾ cup) rice into soup bowl, ladle about 12 oz gumbo over rice.

POTATO SALAD

Potato Salad

Potatoes will absorb the seasonings, so taste and correct seasonings after chilling.

NUMBER OF SERVINGS: 15
COOKING METHOD:
  Boil
SERVING SIZE:
  4 oz
TOTAL YIELD:
  3 lbs, 13 oz

INGREDIENTS	WEIGHT	VOLUME
potatoes, all purpose, boiled until just tender, cooled	3 lbs	about 8 medium
eggs, hard cooked, chopped	6³/₄ oz	4 each
celery, small dice	2¹/₂ oz	¹/₂ cup
green onion, sliced	1¹/₂ oz	¹/₂ cup
green pepper, small dice	1³/₄ oz	¹/₃ cup
pickle relish	1¹/₂ oz	2 tablespoons
olives stuffed with pimento, chopped	1¹/₄ oz	¹/₄ cup
mayonnaise	4 oz	¹/₂ cup
mustard, Creole or Dijon	¹/₂ oz	1 teaspoon
white vinegar	1 oz	2 tablespoons
salt		1¹/₂ teaspoons
pepper, white or black		1 teaspoon
hot pepper sauce		1 teaspoon

1. Peel potatoes; cut into 1-inch cubes. Place in large nonreactive bowl.
2. Place remaining ingredients in bowl with potatoes. Mix gently, being careful not to break potatoes.
3. Correct seasonings. Serve immediately or cover and chill until serving time. If chilling, correct seasonings again before serving.

GRILLADES

Cooking Grillades

This recipe resembles traditional Swiss steak so much that it could be called Creole Swiss steak. If preparing this recipe with veal, check the meat for tenderness after one hour instead of two. Traditionally, grillades are served for brunch or lunch accompanied by grits or cheese grits, but some prefer grillades with rice or wide egg noodles instead.

NUMBER OF SERVINGS: 12
COOKING METHOD:
  Braise
SERVING SIZE:
  8¹/₂ oz
  (4³/₄ oz meat + 3³/₄ oz
    sauce)
TOTAL YIELD:
  7 lbs, 14 oz

Wine Style: Rich Merlot, Zinfandel, or Cabernet Sauvignon
Example: Zinfandel—Pontchartrain Vineyards, Bush, LA. A medium-bodied Zinfandel with light garnet color. Its soft plummy fruit gives way to a burst of spice.

INGREDIENTS	WEIGHT	VOLUME
round steak, beef or veal, trimmed of fat, pounded until 1/2 inch thick, cut into 12 pieces 5 to 6 ounces each	4 lbs	
flour, all purpose	4 1/2 oz	1 cup
bacon grease or oil	4 oz	1/2 cup
butter	4 oz	1/2 cup
onions, small dice	10 oz	2 cups
green pepper, small dice	10 oz	2 cups
celery, small dice	5 oz	1 cup
garlic, minced	1 oz	4 large cloves
tomatoes, chopped, fresh or canned	1 lb, 10 oz	3 cups
basil		1 teaspoon
thyme		1 teaspoon
salt	1/2 oz	2 teaspoons
pepper		1/2 teaspoon
bay leaves		4 each
beef or veal stock, hot	1 lb	2 cups
red wine, dry	8 oz	1 cup
hot pepper sauce		1 tablespoon + 1 teaspoon
Worcestershire sauce	1 oz	2 tablespoons
green onions, sliced, white and green	2 1/2 oz	1 cup
parsley, minced	1/2 oz	1/4 cup

1. Dredge meat with half of the flour (2 1/4 oz or 1/2 cup). Heat grease in braiser; sauté meat on both sides until brown. Remove meat to plate and reserve.
2. Melt butter in braiser. Whisk in remaining flour (2 1/4 oz or 1/2 cup) and continue whisking for 4 to 5 minutes, until brown.
3. Add onions; cook 5 minutes. Add green pepper, celery, and garlic; cook another 2 minutes.
4. Add tomatoes, basil, thyme, salt, pepper, bay leaves, stock, wine, hot pepper sauce, and Worcestershire sauce.
5. Return meat to pan, bring to simmer, cover, and cook about 2 hours (for beef) or 1 hour (for veal) until very tender.
6. Remove bay leaves. Stir in green onions and parsley. Correct seasonings. Serve with grits or starch of choice.

CHICKEN, HAM, AND SHRIMP JAMBALAYA

Chicken, Ham, and Shrimp Jambalaya
photo by Ian O'Leary © Dorling Kindersley

NUMBER OF SERVINGS: 12
COOKING METHOD:
   Braise
SERVING SIZE:
   12 oz
TOTAL YIELD:
   9 lbs, 10 1/4 oz

Wine Style: Full-bodied Chardonnay, medium-bodied red wines, rich fruity Pinot Noir, or Zinfandel
Example: Rouge Militaire—Pontchartrain Vineyards, Bush, LA. This wine has ruby red and deep garnet color with hints of spice and plum fruit.

INGREDIENTS	WEIGHT	VOLUME
flour, all purpose	1¼ oz	¼ cup
paprika		1 teaspoon
cayenne		⅛ teaspoon
salt	¼ oz	1 teaspoon
pepper		¼ teaspoon
chicken breasts, boneless, 1-inch cubes	1 lb, 8 oz	
butter	2 oz	4 tablespoons or ¼ cup
smoked ham, ½-inch cubes	1 lb	
onion, small dice	12½ oz	2 medium or 2½ cups
green pepper, small dice	7½ oz	1 large or 1½ cups
celery, small dice	3¾ oz	2 stalks or ¾ cup
garlic, minced	¾ oz	5 small cloves
tomatoes, canned, chopped	1 lb, 12 oz	1 each 28-oz can
chicken stock	1 lb, 8 oz	3 cups
tomato paste	1½ oz	2 tablespoons
scallions, sliced	1¼ oz	½ cup
shrimp, peeled and deveined	2 lb	
parsley, minced	¼ oz	2 tablespoons
hot pepper sauce		1 teaspoon
thyme		½ teaspoon
rice	1 lb, ¼ oz	2½ cups
cloves, ground		⅛ teaspoon

1. Combine flour, paprika, cayenne, salt, and pepper. Dredge chicken in flour mixture, shaking off excess flour.
2. Melt 1 oz (2 tablespoons) butter in skillet, brown chicken, remove from pan, and reserve.
3. Add remaining 1 oz (2 tablespoons) butter to skillet, sauté ham until lightly browned, remove, and reserve.
4. Sauté onion, green pepper, celery, and garlic in skillet for 4 to 5 minutes, until tender.
5. Add tomatoes, chicken stock, and reserved chicken and ham. Cook about 25 minutes over medium heat.
6. Add tomato paste, scallions, shrimp, parsley, hot pepper sauce, thyme, rice, and cloves. Cover and simmer about 20 minutes, until rice absorbs excess liquid.
7. Correct seasonings; serve.

SHRIMP CREOLE

Shrimp Creole
© 2008 Jupiterimages Corporation

NUMBER OF SERVINGS: 8
COOKING METHOD:
   Sauté, Boil
SERVING SIZE:
   8 oz Shrimp Creole +
   3¾ oz (¾ cup) cooked rice
TOTAL YIELD:
   4 lbs, 6¼ oz

Wine Style: Soft, fruity Chenin Blanc, Pinot Gris, or Viognier
Example: Creole Blanc—Pontchartrain Vineyards, Bush, LA. This is a rich, complex wine based primarily on the Viognier grape with excellent overall balance and a medium-long finish.

INGREDIENTS	WEIGHT	VOLUME
oil	1 oz	2 tablespoons
flour, all purpose	3/4 oz	3 tablespoons
onion, small dice	5 oz	1 cup
garlic, minced	1/4 oz	2 cloves
celery, small dice	2 1/2 oz	1/2 cup
green pepper, small dice	2 1/2 oz	1/2 cup
tomato sauce	6 oz	
tomato paste	6 oz	
tomatoes, canned, drained, large dice	4 1/4 oz	1/2 cup
water	1 lb	2 cups
sherry, dry	2 oz	1/4 cup
Worcestershire sauce	1/2 oz	1 tablespoon
hot pepper sauce	1 oz	2 tablespoons
bay leaf		1 each
salt		1/4 teaspoon
pepper		1/4 teaspoon
basil		1/2 teaspoon
paprika		1/2 teaspoon
shrimp, medium, peeled and deveined	2 lbs	
scallions, sliced	1 1/2 oz	1/2 cup
parsley, minced	1/4 oz	2 tablespoons

ACCOMPANIMENT:

rice, cooked, hot	1 lb, 14 oz	

1. Heat oil in skillet. Whisk in flour and stir constantly for 5 to 6 minutes, until brown *roux*.
2. Add onions; cook another 5 minutes. Add garlic, celery, and green pepper; sauté for 2 more minutes.
3. Add tomato sauce, tomato paste, tomatoes, water, sherry, Worcestershire sauce, hot pepper sauce, bay leaf, salt, pepper, basil, and paprika.
4. Bring to boil, reduce heat, and cover. Let mixture simmer for 10 minutes.
5. Add shrimp; cook another 8 minutes. Add scallions and parsley; cook 2 more minutes.
6. Correct seasonings. Serve over rice using about 3 3/4 oz (3/4 cup) for each serving.

CRAWFISH ÉTOUFFÉE

Crawfish Étouffée

If desired, substitute shrimp for the crawfish.

NUMBER OF SERVINGS: 9
COOKING METHOD:
   Braise
SERVING SIZE:
   8 oz or 1 cup
TOTAL YIELD:
   4 lbs, 12 1/4 oz

Wine Style: Soft, fruity Gewürztraminer, semi-dry white wines, Riesling, Semillon, or White Zinfandel
Example: Mardi Gras Gold—Feliciana Cellars Winery, Jackson, LA. This is an off-dry, flavorful, and fruity wine.

INGREDIENTS	WEIGHT	VOLUME
butter or oil	1 oz	2 tablespoons
onion, small dice	5 oz	1 cup
celery, small dice	5 oz	1 cup
green pepper, small dice	5 oz	1 cup
garlic, minced	1/4 oz	2 large cloves
flour, all purpose	1/2 oz	2 tablespoons
crawfish tails, shells removed	2 lbs	
seafood stock, hot	1 lb, 4 oz	2 1/2 cups
tomatoes, fresh or canned, diced	1 lb	
salt		1/2 teaspoon
pepper		1/2 teaspoon
cayenne		1/8 teaspoon
basil		1 teaspoon
thyme		1 teaspoon
Worcestershire sauce	1/2 oz	1 tablespoon
green onions, sliced	2 1/2 oz	1 cup
parsley, minced	1/4 oz	2 tablespoons
ACCOMPANIMENT:		
rice, cooked, hot	2 lbs, 4 oz	

1. Heat butter or oil in large pot over medium heat. Sauté onions, celery, green pepper, and garlic for 4 minutes, until onion softens.
2. Add flour. Cook 3 to 4 minutes, whisking constantly, until *roux* begins to darken.
3. Add crawfish tails, slowly whisk in stock, then add tomatoes.
4. Stir in salt, pepper, cayenne, basil, thyme, and Worcestershire sauce. Simmer uncovered for 20 minutes.
5. Add green onions and parsley; correct seasonings.
6. To serve, place about 4 oz (3/4 cup) rice in center of bowl, ladle 8 oz (1 cup) étouffée around rice.

BLACKENED REDFISH

Blackened Redfish

Cast iron is the usual choice for the skillet when blackening fish. Many say the pan cannot be too hot!

Blackening creates a large amount of smoke. If the exhaust system in the kitchen is not very strong, consider cooking outside on a grill.

NUMBER OF SERVINGS: 8
COOKING METHOD:
  Sauté
SERVING SIZE:
  1 fillet, about 5 1/4 oz
TOTAL YIELD:
  2 lbs, 11 1/4 oz

Wine Style: Gewürztraminer, Chenin Blanc, White Zinfandel, or Rose

Example: Zydeco Rose—Pontchartrain Vineyards, Bush, LA. This wine is bright, rich, full-bodied, and sophisticated.

INGREDIENTS	WEIGHT	VOLUME
SEASONING:		
paprika	1/4 oz	**1 tablespoon**
salt	1 1/2 oz	**2 tablespoons**
onion powder		**1 teaspoon**
garlic powder		**1 teaspoon**
cayenne		**1 teaspoon**
black pepper		**1 teaspoon**
thyme		**1/2 teaspoon**
oregano		**1/2 teaspoon**
basil		**1/2 teaspoon**
redfish or other boneless fillets of flat fish (about 5 3/4 oz each), washed	about 2 lb, 14 oz	
butter, melted	8 oz	**1 cup or 2 sticks**
GARNISH:		
lemon wedges		
melted butter		

1. Combine all seasonings together in small bowl.
2. Preheat cast iron skillet over high heat at least 10 minutes until extremely hot. White ash may form in skillet.
3. Dip fish in butter, then sprinkle both sides of fish with seasoning mixture, patting the seasonings on fish. Use about 1/4 oz (2 teaspoons) on each fillet.
4. Place 1 or 2 fillets in skillet and sauté about 1 1/2 minutes. Place 1 teaspoon butter over each fillet, turn fish, and cook another 1 1/2 minutes. Cooking time will vary depending on thickness of fish.
5. Continue cooking fillets, keeping them warm in low oven until all are cooked. Serve accompanied by lemon wedges and additional melted butter.

EGGPLANT WITH SHRIMP

In Louisiana, mirliton, also known as chayote squash, often replaces the eggplant in this dish. If preparing this dish with mirliton, boil the whole mirliton until soft. Remove flesh from shell, leaving 1/4 inch, and place mixture into mirliton shell instead of ovenproof dish. Divide bread crumb and cheddar topping evenly over mirlitons, and then bake in shell.

NUMBER OF SERVINGS: 13
COOKING METHOD:
  Boil, Sauté, Bake
SERVING SIZE:
  4 oz
TOTAL YIELD:
  3 lbs, 4 oz

INGREDIENTS	WEIGHT	VOLUME
eggplant	2 lb, 5 oz	**1 large or 2 medium**
butter	3/4 oz	**1 1/2 tablespoons**
onion, small dice	5 oz	**1 cup or 1 large**
celery, small dice	1 1/4 oz	**1/4 cup**
garlic, minced	1/4 oz	**2 large cloves**
green onions, chopped	1 oz	**1/3 cup**
shrimp, small or medium, peeled, deveined	10 oz	
bread crumbs	3 3/4 oz	**1 cup**
egg	1 3/4 oz	**1 each**
parsley, minced	1/2 oz	**1/4 cup**
salt		**1/2 teaspoon or to taste**
cayenne		**1/8 teaspoon or to taste**
cheddar cheese, grated	4 oz	

1. Peel eggplant; cut into 2-inch pieces. Boil in salted water until soft, about 7 minutes. Drain well, purée in food processor, and reserve.
2. Pan-spray ovenproof dish. Preheat oven to 350 degrees.
3. Melt butter in skillet. Sauté onion, celery, garlic, and green onions until tender, about 4 to 5 minutes.
4. Add eggplant to skillet; cook about 3 minutes. Add shrimp and cook for 2 minutes, just until they begin to turn pink.
5. Remove from heat. Add 3 oz (3/4 cup) bread crumbs, egg, parsley, salt, and cayenne. Stir well. Correct seasonings.
6. Place eggplant mixture into prepared dish, sprinkle with remaining bread crumbs, and top with cheddar cheese. Bake for 30 minutes, until mixture is hot and cheese begins to brown.
7. Serve immediately.

MAQUE CHOUX

NUMBER OF SERVINGS: 14
COOKING METHOD:
 Sauté, Boil
SERVING SIZE:
 4 oz
TOTAL YIELD:
 3 lbs, 9 oz

Maque Choux

INGREDIENTS	WEIGHT	VOLUME
butter	1/2 oz	1 tablespoon
onion, small dice	3³/4 oz	1 medium or 3/4 cup
green pepper, small dice	3³/4 oz	3/4 cup
celery, small dice	2¹/2 oz	1 large stalk or 1/2 cup
garlic, minced	1/4 oz	2 large cloves
corn, removed from cob or frozen	1 lb, 6 oz	4 cups
tomatoes, fresh, peeled, and seeded, or canned, chopped	1 lb, 12¹/2 oz	3 cups
milk	4 oz	1/2 cup
salt		1/2 teaspoon
pepper		1/4 teaspoon
sugar	1/4 oz	1 teaspoon
paprika		1/2 teaspoon
hot pepper sauce		1/2 teaspoon or to taste

1. Melt butter in saucepan over medium heat. Add onions, peppers, and celery; sauté until softened, about 5 minutes.

2. Add remaining ingredients, bring to simmer, and cook until corn is tender, about 10 to 15 minutes.

3. Correct seasonings; serve.

GREEN BEANS WITH NEW POTATOES

Traditionally in the South, the beans and potatoes cook about 45 minutes to one hour, until very soft. If that result is desired, lengthen cooking time in this recipe.

If desired, substitute stock for the water in this recipe and adjust the salt, adding it to taste.

NUMBER OF SERVINGS: 10
COOKING METHOD:
 Boil
SERVING SIZE:
 4 oz
TOTAL YIELD:
 2 lbs, 8¹/4 oz

INGREDIENTS	WEIGHT	VOLUME
bacon, large dice	7 oz	7 slices
onion, small dice	5 oz	1 medium or 1 cup
garlic, minced	1/4 oz	1 large clove
green beans, fresh, stems removed	1 lb	
water	8 oz	1 cup
red new potatoes, scrubbed, cut into quarters	1 lb, 1/2 oz	5 medium
salt		1/2 teaspoon
black pepper		1/4 teaspoon
cayenne pepper		1/8 teaspoon

1. Sauté bacon until crisp in pot over medium heat. Remove bacon from pot.
2. Add onion and garlic. Sauté about 4 to 5 minutes, until onion softens.
3. Add green beans, water, potatoes, salt, pepper, cayenne, and reserved bacon. Mix gently to combine.
4. Bring to boil, cover, and reduce heat to simmer. Cook about 20 to 25 minutes, until potatoes are tender.
5. Correct seasonings; serve.

SWEET POTATOES WITH PECANS

NUMBER OF SERVINGS: 11
COOKING METHOD:
  Boil, Bake
SERVING SIZE:
  4 oz
TOTAL YIELD:
  2 lbs, 13 oz

INGREDIENTS	WEIGHT	VOLUME
sweet potatoes, scrubbed	2 lb, 2 oz	2 large or 3 medium
evaporated milk	5 oz	2/3 cup
brown sugar, firmly packed	2 1/4 oz	1/4 cup
butter, melted	2 oz	4 tablespoons or 1/2 stick
egg	1 3/4 oz	1 each
vanilla		1 1/2 teaspoons
salt		1/2 teaspoon
TOPPING:		
butter	2 oz	4 tablespoons or 1/2 stick
brown sugar, firmly packed	2 3/4 oz	5 tablespoons
flour, all purpose	1 oz	1/4 cup
pecans, chopped	2 oz	1/2 cup

1. Boil sweet potatoes in salted water until tender, 35 to 45 minutes. Drain, cool until they can be handled, peel, and cut into 1-inch pieces. Place pieces in mixing bowl fitted with paddle beater, if available.
2. Pan-spray ovenproof dish. Preheat oven to 350 degrees.
3. Add milk, brown sugar, butter, egg, vanilla, and salt. Beat until well mixed and fluffy. Correct seasonings.
4. Transfer mixture into prepared dish.

For Topping:
1. Melt butter in saucepan. Stir in brown sugar and flour; stir until combined.
2. Add pecans; mix to combine.
3. Sprinkle pecan mixture evenly over sweet potato mixture.
4. Bake for 30 to 35 minutes. Serve.

CORNBREAD

Testing Cornbread
photo by David Murray and Jules Selmes
© Dorling Kindersley

Cornbread
photo courtesy of Land O' Lakes, Inc.

NUMBER OF SERVINGS: 8
COOKING METHOD:
 Bake
SERVING SIZE:
 1/8 wedge of pie
TOTAL YIELD:
 1 each 9- or 10-inch pie

INGREDIENTS	WEIGHT	VOLUME
butter	2 oz	4 tablespoons or 1/4 cup
cornmeal	7 3/4 oz	1 1/2 cups
flour, all purpose	4 1/2 oz	1 cup
sugar	1/2 oz	1 tablespoon
baking powder	1/2 oz	1 tablespoon
baking soda		3/4 teaspoon
salt		3/4 teaspoon
buttermilk	12 1/4 oz	1 1/2 cups
eggs	5 oz	3 each

1. Place oven rack in center of oven. Preheat oven to 425 degrees. Place butter in pie pan; put pan in oven until butter melts.
2. Place cornmeal in bowl. Sift flour, sugar, baking powder, baking soda, and salt into bowl with cornmeal. Make well in center of ingredients.
3. Mix buttermilk and eggs together. Pour into well in dry ingredients.
4. Pour in butter from pie pan. Do not scrape pan with spatula so coating of butter remains.
5. Quickly mix with fork until just combined. Some lumps may remain.
6. Pour into hot prepared pan. Bake for 22 to 28 minutes, until golden brown and knife comes out almost clean.
7. Cut into wedges and serve, accompanied by butter.

BEIGNETS

Beignets
photo by Renee M. (Cordona) Hood

Usually, beignets and strong coffee or chicory coffee go together. Really bits of deep-fried bread, beignets are the famous doughnuts dusted with confectioners' sugar served at Café du Monde in the French Quarter in New Orleans.

NUMBER OF SERVINGS:
 13 or 9
COOKING METHOD:
 Deep-fry
SERVING SIZE:
 3 or 4 beignets
TOTAL YIELD:
 36 beignets
DOUGH:
 1 lb, 10 1/2 oz

INGREDIENTS	WEIGHT	VOLUME
water, warm (*not hot*)	2 oz	1/4 cup
yeast, granulated, dry	1/4 oz	1 tablespoon
milk	4 oz	1/2 cup
sugar	1 1/4 oz	3 tablespoons
butter	1 1/2 oz	3 tablespoons
flour, all purpose	about 13 oz	about 2 1/2 cups
salt	1/4 oz	1 teaspoon
egg	1 3/4 oz	1 each
oil, for frying		
confectioners' sugar, for dusting		

1. Place water in large nonreactive bowl. Sprinkle yeast over it. Stir with nonreactive spoon; set aside for a few minutes to hydrate until foamy.
2. Meanwhile, heat milk, sugar, and butter until milk is warm and butter partially melts. Remove from heat; let sit until lukewarm and butter melts.
3. Combine flour and salt. Set aside.
4. Add lukewarm milk mixture to yeast; stir to mix.
5. Add egg to milk mixture, mix well, then add flour mixture. Mix with mixer or by hand for 1 minute.
6. Knead thoroughly until smooth and elastic, adding extra flour only if needed to prevent dough from sticking; dough should remain soft. Return to bowl, cover, and let rise for 1 to 1 1/2 hours, until doubled.
7. Punch down, cover, and let rise for another 30 minutes, until almost doubled.
8. Punch down; roll dough to 1/2-inch thickness. Cut out rectangles about 1 inch by 2 inches. Place on greased or parchment covered baking pan, cover, and rise about 1 hour, until puffy.
9. Heat oil to 375 degrees for deep-frying. Place a few beignets in oil; too many at one time will cool oil temperature too much. Fry about 1 or 2 minutes on each side until golden brown. Remove from oil, drain, place on absorbent paper, and keep warm until service.
10. At time of service, generously dust beignets with confectioners' sugar.

BREAD PUDDING WITH WHISKEY SAUCE

Bread Pudding with Whiskey Sauce

If desired, substitute bourbon or brandy for the whiskey in the sauce. To accompany with a sauce containing no alcohol, top with lemon sauce.

NUMBER OF SERVINGS: 9
COOKING METHOD:
  Bake, Boil
SERVING SIZE:
  4 3/4 oz or
  1/9 of 9- by 13-inch pan
  1 1/4 oz or 2 tablespoons sauce
TOTAL YIELD:
  2 lbs, 12 oz bread pudding
  13 1/4 oz or 1 1/2 cups sauce

INGREDIENTS	WEIGHT	VOLUME
PUDDING:		
French or Italian bread cubes, day old	7¹/₂ oz	6 cups
milk	1 lb, 8 oz	3 cups
butter, melted	2 oz	¹/₄ cup or 4 tablespoons
eggs	5 oz	3 each
sugar	10 oz	1¹/₄ cups
cinnamon		¹/₂ teaspoon
nutmeg		¹/₂ teaspoon
vanilla	¹/₂ oz	1 tablespoon
raisins	2³/₄ oz	¹/₂ cup
SAUCE:		
butter	4 oz	1 stick or ¹/₂ cup
sugar	7¹/₂ oz	1 cup
egg	1³/₄ oz	1 each
whiskey	2 oz	¹/₄ cup

For Pudding:

1. Combine bread and milk in bowl. Refrigerate for about 1 hour until milk is absorbed, stirring 3 or 4 times.

2. Meanwhile, place melted butter in 9- by 13-inch pan. Swirl pan to coat with butter. (This coats pan with butter, and later the butter is poured from this pan into pudding mixture.)

3. Place oven rack in center of oven. Preheat oven to 350 degrees.

4. Whisk or mix eggs and sugar until thickened and light yellow in color.

5. Add egg mixture, cinnamon, nutmeg, vanilla, raisins, and butter from 9- by 13-inch pan to bread mixture. Mix well.

6. Pour into prepared pan. Bake about 50 minutes to 1 hour, until lightly browned and knife inserted comes out almost clean.

For Sauce:

1. Melt butter in top of double boiler.

2. Add sugar and egg. Whisk over gently simmering water until sugar dissolves and sauce is proper temperature.

3. Remove from heat; add whiskey.

To Serve:

1. Cut bread pudding into serving size. If it has cooled, heat in oven until warm, if desired.

2. Top with 1¹/₄ oz (2 tablespoons) warm whiskey sauce. Serve immediately.

BANANAS FOSTER

Caramelizing Sugar in Skillet
photo by David Murray © Dorling Kindersley

Flaming Bananas Foster
photo by Greg Ward © Rough Guides

Bananas Foster
photo by Greg Ward © Rough Guides

NUMBER OF SERVINGS: 2
COOKING METHOD:
 Sauté
SERVING SIZE:
 6 oz (1 banana + sauce)
TOTAL YIELD:
 12 oz

For a show-stopping dessert, this classic New Orleans confection is almost always flambéed at tableside.

Be careful when pouring alcohol near a flame since it ignites easily. For safety, always pour the desired amount of alcohol from a bowl or cup instead of from the bottle because the flame could travel up the pouring alcohol and ignite the entire bottle.

INGREDIENTS	WEIGHT	VOLUME
butter, unsalted	1 oz	2 tablespoons
brown sugar	3/4 oz	2 tablespoons
banana liqueur	1/2 oz	1 tablespoon
banana, peeled, sliced in half and then lengthwise or sliced as desired	9 1/2 oz	2 each
rum, preferably dark	1 oz	2 tablespoons
vanilla ice cream		

GARNISH:

cinnamon, *optional*

1. Melt butter in pan suitable for flaming. Add brown sugar; stir until well blended.
2. Add banana liqueur; stir well.
3. Add bananas; stir gently until completely coated with sauce.
4. Remove from heat. Carefully pour rum into front of pan, return to heat, and tilt pan forward to ignite rum. Baste bananas with sauce.
5. When flames go out, serve one banana (4 pieces) and sauce over vanilla ice cream. Dust with cinnamon, if desired. Serve immediately.

Midwestern States

OBJECTIVES

By the end of this chapter, you will be able to

- Discuss the groups of people who settled in the Midwest, why they came there, and how their heritages impacted the cuisine
- Discuss the role of the Native Americans in the cookery of the Midwest
- Explain how the topography and climate affected the crops and the cuisine in the Midwest
- Identify food products prevalent in the Midwest
- Prepare a variety of dishes indicative of the cuisine of the Midwest

States included in the Midwest:

- Michigan
- Wisconsin
- Minnesota
- Ohio
- Indiana
- Illinois
- Iowa
- Missouri

HISTORY

Before Europeans settled in Michigan, Wisconsin, and Minnesota, tribes of Ojibwa, Sauks, Potawatomi, Winnebagos, Menominee, Oneida, Sioux, Chippewa, Ottawa, Iroquois, and more inhabited the area. The Native Americans living in the northern states that bordered the Great Lakes depended on wild rice instead of the ubiquitous corn found in most other states. Wild rice flourishes in the area around the Great Lakes. Because it grows in water like rice, settlers erroneously called it "rice." Actually, wild rice is an aquatic grass, not a grain. Indigenous to the United States, wild rice and cranberries quickly became part of the settlers' diet. The settlers also feasted on the bounty of fish swimming in the Great Lakes. The Native Americans helped the settlers survive in this new land. They taught them to smoke and dry fish for the winter, gather cranberries, prepare wild rice, and make *pemmican* for the winter by pounding dried venison, dried berries, and fat into patties. The many forests yielded plenty of wild mushrooms, many varieties of berries, and a multitude of wild fowl and game including ducks, partridge, geese, wild turkey, pigeon, squab, bear, moose, elk, rabbit, and deer. Despite its cold climate, the northern section of the Midwest supplied the early inhabitants with abundant food.

In the 1620s, numerous French trappers and fur traders came to upper Michigan, Wisconsin, and Minnesota to hunt. These trappers ate the meat and sold the furs from the animals they caught. Many of the French trappers and traders permanently settled in this area.

Basically, two different groups of immigrants moved to the Midwest. The first group consisted of settlers leaving New England, the Middle Atlantic States, or the South, who traveled west in search of available land in the 1700s. From these people, the cuisine of the Midwest combined elements representing the cookery of each of these regions with strong emphasis on the German influence found in Pennsylvania and New York. The second wave of settlers to the Midwest came from Europe seeking freedom from religious or political persecution, escape from famine or starvation, or simply a better life.

During the 1800s, the next influx of immigrants arrived from Scandinavia, Germany, Holland, Eastern Europe, the British Isles, and other countries. Each group of immigrants brought the recipes and culinary heritage from their homeland, and those merged with the existing cuisine of the Midwest.

Linking the eastern and western United States, the Erie Canal opened in 1825. Before long, a huge number of travelers chose the northern route for their westward journey. Finding fertile plains around Lakes Huron, Michigan, and Superior, many immigrants decided to stop their western migration and settle in this area. Even though the Erie Canal was located in the Middle Atlantic region, it exerted an enormous effect on the Midwest. During the five years after the canal opened, the population of Illinois more than doubled.

In search of more land, numerous settlers, including Amish, Mennonites, and Germans, left western Pennsylvania. They traveled along the Ohio River and settled in the Midwest. Meanwhile, French settlements developed along the Mississippi, Wabash, and Missouri Rivers in Missouri, Illinois, and Indiana. These settlers introduced French influence into the cookery where they settled. Although many of the French settlers came from Canada, they still seasoned with fresh herbs and prepared classic French dishes.

Collecting Wild Rice

The Germans found Milwaukee, Wisconsin, an ideal place for operating breweries. To make beer, they needed a river and a climate cold enough to form ice on the river. In Milwaukee, they discovered a place with three rivers converging and harsh enough winters to produce plenty of ice. Soon, Joseph Schlitz, Frederick Miller, and Fred Pabst settled in this city and opened breweries, and Milwaukee became known as the "beer capital." Also of German descent, Eberhard Anheuser and Adolphus Busch each started a brewery in St. Louis, Missouri, a city situated on the Mississippi River.

In the early days, meat was packed in salt for preserving. The "packing in salt" accounts for the name "packing house." At that time, cooks used salt pork in many recipes for flavoring.

Typically, immigrants adapted their native recipes and cooking techniques to the foods and conditions available in their new homeland. For example, those who traveled and/or settled along the rivers in many areas consumed catfish. Although the fish was unknown to them before coming to the Midwest, they quickly adopted the readily available catfish into their diet.

Finding cold climate like that in their homeland, many Germans migrated to Wisconsin. Today, half of the population of Wisconsin claims German ancestry. Wanting to duplicate their life in Germany, these immigrants hunted, raised dairy cattle, and produced beer and fine cheeses. Although the French and English dominated the population of Milwaukee in the early days, that changed with the opening of the Erie Canal in 1825. Many Germans arrived at that time. Almost 25 years later, the next wave of immigrants arrived in Milwaukee. Most of those newcomers came from Scandinavia, Eastern Europe, and Germany.

Seeking areas with cold northern climates near water that resembled their homeland, many Scandinavians migrated to the states around the Great Lakes. This area proved a perfect fit for the Scandinavians, with northern Michigan and Minnesota attracting many immigrants from Finland. Wisconsin and Iowa (which does not border water but has the cold climate) drew many Swedes. Of course, each group brought their culinary traditions with them to their adopted land. As a result, *lutefisk*, dried, salted cod treated with lye, became an important part of Christmas dinner and church suppers held in the fall.

Between 1870 and 1900, Michigan prospered, economic opportunity soared, and its population doubled. The railroads connected to Michigan, allowing travel by rail in addition to the already established waterways. Because of the excellent accessibility, the lumber business thrived and industry boomed. Immigrants flocked to this land of opportunity.

By the early 1900s, droves of immigrants from Norway, Finland, Czechoslovakia, Germany, Russia, and Eastern Europe moved to Michigan, Wisconsin, and Minnesota for work in factories, mills, logging camps, mines, and the railroad. Each ethnic group added to the existing cuisine. To provide food and housing for these immigrant workers, many boardinghouses opened.

Located in the southern tier of the Midwest, Cincinnati, Ohio, attracted thousands of immigrants from Germany in the 1830s and 1840s. These immigrants built breweries, made sausage, and cooked the dishes from their homeland. Situated on the Ohio River, the city had easy access by boat. When the railroad connected Cincinnati with much of the East and South, pigs and pork became big business. Before long, Cincinnati became a major pork-processing center with feedlots, slaughterhouses, meatpacking facilities, and plenty of available jobs. Because of its accessible transportation, this booming city became the first major meatpacking city. Of course, pork ranked as the meat of choice.

Chicago grew into a large, vibrant city for several reasons. Railroads from the East, West, and Southwest transected there. In addition, Chicago's location at the southern end of Lake Michigan ensured easy transportation through the waterways. With many stockyards and slaughtering houses, scads of job opportunities, and excellent quality beef, Chicago became a magnet for immigrants and well known for serving steak and potatoes.

In addition to attracting immigrants from all nationalities, Chicago drew many people living in rural areas who wanted to change from farming to city living. Because of its location in the Midwest, many farmers from the Midwest and Plains relocated here. Chicago was the closest large city with job opportunities in several booming industries. Even if they spoke no English, a job in a factory, packing house, or refinery awaited the immigrants and relocating farmers. This city formed into a melting pot of ethnicity.

Since the immigrants moved into neighborhoods that had attracted others from their homeland, the children often grew up speaking only their parents' native language and no

English. Culinary traditions from their former home prevailed until later generations adopted American customs. At that time, the two heritages blended. Chicago claims the biggest Polish community in the United States. Many Polish foods like *pierogis*, a small filled turnover or dumpling; *kielbasa*, Polish sausage; and *bigos*, a stew containing a variety of meats and sauerkraut, are readily available in Chicago. Like New York, San Francisco, and other melting pots, Chicago offers representation from almost every ethnic group.

After the end of the Vietnam War in the middle 1970s, many Asian immigrants settled in the Midwest. Like all immigrants, they brought their culinary traditions and recipes with them. Wherever these people settled, they introduced stir-fries, Asian vegetables, rice, and Asian noodles into the cuisine.

TOPOGRAPHY AND CLIMATE

The Midwest region includes much of the central portion of the United States. Providing excellent farmland, flat, dark, fertile soil lies in this region. Lakes, streams, and rivers traverse the Midwest, and they yield plenty of fish. Bluffs, valleys, and rolling hills often surround these waterways. Glaciers once covered a portion of the Midwest, and their retreat formed many lakes and fertile plains. In fact, the melting glaciers left more than 15,000 lakes in Wisconsin!

When the first settlers arrived in Iowa and Missouri, they found soil covered with tough grasses. After the difficult job of removing the grasses, they found fertile soil that proved excellent for growing all kinds of crops.

Since abundant wildlife including game and birds inhabited the forests, plains, and wetlands, hunting and trapping supplied plentiful food for the early settlers. In addition, the many maple trees in the Great Lakes area yielded sap for making maple syrup.

Situated in the northern tier of the Midwest, Michigan lies farthest to the east, Wisconsin borders Michigan on the west, and Minnesota is situated west of Wisconsin. Directly south of these three states, Ohio lies most east, Indiana is to the west of Ohio, Illinois is west of Indiana, and Iowa lies to the west of Illinois. Missouri is situated to the south of Iowa.

The Midwest borders four of the five Great Lakes. Lake Michigan is positioned between Michigan and Wisconsin, Lake Superior lies to the north of Michigan and Wisconsin, Lake Erie is situated to Ohio's north and Michigan's southeast, and Lake Huron borders Michigan on the east. An abundance of fish like whitefish, sturgeon, herring, smelt, bass, perch, and trout enticed many immigrants to settle near the Great Lakes. Because the water moderates the winter temperatures, grapes and other fruits thrive in the land near these lakes. As a result, wine is produced in several of the states lying next to the Great Lakes, including Ohio and Michigan.

Starting in Minnesota, the Mississippi River flows down the western boundary of Wisconsin and Illinois before cutting through the Midwest, and turning to the south. The Ohio River forms the southern boundary of the Midwest, creating the southern border of Ohio, Indiana, and Illinois. The Ohio River flows into the Mississippi River on the eastern side of Missouri. Another tributary of the Mississippi River, the Missouri River starts in Montana and eventually flows through Missouri before joining the Mississippi near St. Louis. Often, rivers form the boundary that separates one state from another. Surrounding the rivers, fertile valleys provide excellent farmland throughout the Midwest.

Bountiful fish swim in Michigan's 11,000 lakes, streams, and rivers. With more than 3,200 miles of coastline, Michigan contains more shoreline than any state except Alaska.

A five-mile bridge over the Strait of Mackinac connects Michigan's Upper Peninsula to the Lower Peninsula. Although the western half of the Upper Peninsula contains rugged hills and forests, the eastern half and the entire Lower Peninsula consists of plains, hills, and fertile farmland. Long, very cold winters and cool summers reign in the northern portion, while the south experiences cold winters and warm summers. Because of the harsh climate, most of Michigan's agriculture grows in the southern half of the Lower Peninsula.

Extensive forests throughout the Midwest provided a bounty of game, berries, mushrooms, and nuts for the settlers as well as plenty of fur-bearing animals for the fur trappers. Today, forests cover half of the land in both Michigan and Wisconsin.

Rich, fertile soil found in the central, eastern, and southern portions of Wisconsin lured numerous pioneers who started farms. In the beginning, they planted wheat to make their own breads. Because the wheat thrived, they soon produced enough wheat to export. With a multitude of fruits and vegetables flourishing in the fertile farmland, canning facilities for processing the bountiful crops into canned goods were built. Processing plants still operate in this area today.

Gently rolling plains, forests, valleys, some swamps, and thousands of lakes make up the terrain of Minnesota. Northwestern Minnesota contains rich soil and the fertile Red River Valley where grains, particularly wheat, potatoes, and sugar beets thrive. Farmers in southern and western Minnesota raise hogs, dairy cattle, turkeys, eggs, corn, soybeans, and beets. As in nearby states, the forests yield game, mushrooms, and berries. The waterways provide bass, pike, walleye, trout, whitefish, and carp.

Known as the Corn Belt, Ohio, Indiana, Illinois, and Iowa supply much of the corn used as feed for cattle and hogs. Consisting of flat or gently rolling terrain and fertile farmland, this area yields a wide range of crops including all sorts of fruits and vegetables. The hot, humid summers found in central and southern Ohio, Indiana, Illinois, and Missouri provide excellent conditions for the growth of a variety of produce. Since Midwestern farmers raise lots of pigs, pork frequently appears on menus in restaurants and homes.

The retreating glaciers greatly impacted the terrain of Ohio. Plains, lowlands, fertile farmland, and some sandy soil supporting the growth of fruits and vegetables like grapes, tomatoes, corn, and cucumbers describes the land in the north near the Great Lakes. While plateaus, hills, valleys, and forests lie in the east, rolling hills and plains make up the south of Ohio. In the western part of the state, plains made of very fertile farmland yield excellent crops. An abundance of corn and soybeans provides feed for the cattle, hogs, sheep, and chickens.

Although the northern section of Indiana consists of sand dunes near the Great Lakes, fertile farmland describes the rest of the state. Corn, soybeans, hogs, and cattle flourish in Indiana's humid, warm summers and cool winters. Many rivers and lakes yield catfish, bass, and pike while the forests abound with deer and rabbits. The fertile plains of the central portion support plentiful crops of corn, soybeans, fruits, and vegetables, as well as lots of cattle. In the south, the land turns into hills, forests, and some lowlands where popcorn, blueberries, and apples thrive.

Fertile plains make up most of the land found in Illinois with some forests and rolling hills breaking the flat landscape. Deer, rabbits, wild turkey, pheasant, and quail thrive in the forests and on some of the plains. Forming the western boundary of Illinois, the Mississippi River separates Illinois from Iowa and Missouri.

In contrast to eastern Iowa's gently rolling hills and valleys, the western part of the state resembles the flat terrain of the Plains. When the glaciers melted, they created a number of lakes and exposed incredibly rich soil. That soil is prized, fertile farmland. Abundant corn and soybeans in addition to hogs thrive on farms throughout this state. In fact, Iowa is well known for raising high quality hogs. Minnesota is situated to the north of Iowa, the Mississippi River forms the eastern boundary separating Iowa from Wisconsin and Illinois, Missouri lies to the south, and Nebraska and South Dakota border on the west.

In general, the states in the Midwest experience tornadoes like the Plains states. In the early days, each farm had a root cellar dug into the ground for storing fruits and vegetables for the winter. When tornadoes and bad storms rolled through, families took shelter in these underground bunkers.

Lying south of Iowa, Missouri neighbors Illinois, Kentucky, and Tennessee on its east, Arkansas on its south, and Nebraska, Kansas, and Oklahoma to the west. Surrounded by fertile farmland, the Mississippi River creates the eastern border. The Missouri River flows through the state.

The northern part of Missouri contains rolling plains, streams, and fertile soil yielding acres of corn and soybeans. In the southeast, the Ozark Mountains and fertile farmland support the growth of crops like soybeans and rice. Southern Missouri consists of forests, plateaus, low mountains, hills, valleys, streams, and lakes. Strawberries and many other crops thrive in the south. Deer and quail populate the forests while trout, bass, and catfish fill the waters. Flat plains where corn and other grains grow define the western section. Missouri experiences mild climate with cool winters and hot summers.

Ingredients and foods commonly used throughout the cuisine of the Midwest include

- hogs, cattle, and poultry
- game, including deer, rabbit, squirrel, bear, turkey, dove, quail, pheasant, partridge, and duck
- freshwater fish, including perch, bass, trout, salmon, whitefish, smelt, bluegill, walleye, pike, and catfish
- dairy products, including cheeses, butter, and milk
- wheat, corn, and soybeans
- wild rice
- cranberries
- wild mushrooms and berries
- wide assortment of vegetables, including asparagus, many varieties of beans, carrots, beets, corn, celery, and potatoes
- many fruits, including apples, cherries, plums, grapes, blueberries, and strawberries
- nuts, including black walnuts, pecans, and hazelnuts
- honey
- wine and beer

COOKING METHODS

In order to retain the pure, unmasked flavor of freshly caught fish, cooks in the Midwest preferred simple cooking methods like steaming, grilling, or frying. In the early days, boiling proved a fast and easy cooking technique for fish.

Stews and braised meats remain popular throughout the Midwest. With plenty of deer throughout the forests and cattle on the farms, braising served as an often-used cooking method. Because venison contains less fat than beef, braising helped to tenderize venison's lean meat. When dairy cows stopped producing milk, the farmers butchered them. These older cows yielded lean, tough meat that became tender with the long, slow cooking of braising. Midwestern cooks still prepare stews and pot roast from any fibrous or tough cut of meat like round or chuck steak. To prepare these braised dishes, cooks dredge the meat in flour, brown it in fat, and then add vegetables and the cooking liquid of choice. With a tight lid on the pot, the meat simmers over low heat until becoming tender.

Early residents transformed any scraps of excess beef and/or pork into sausage or ground meat. Ethnic specialties like stuffed cabbage rolls from Eastern Europe, meatloaf, and Swedish meatballs used meat from trimmings and tough cuts. In the early days, people minced cooked meat. When the meat grinder became available during the Industrial Revolution, people could grind raw meat. Whether they used leftover cooked or raw meat, the early inhabitants wasted nothing.

The abundance of clay in the soil allowed Midwesterners to cook foods in clay. To prepare this, they packed clay around the foods and then cooked them in the embers of the fire. After cooking, they cracked the hardened clay and removed it. In essence, the food steamed inside the clay enclosure.

In the pioneers' day, all sorts of foods boiled in a pot over an open fire. Today, Midwestern cooks often boil vegetables and simply season them with butter, salt, and pepper.

The Native Americans taught the settlers to dry any available foods for the winter. This preservation of foods was particularly crucial to survive the harsh winters found in the northern sections of the Midwest. In addition to meat and fish, settlers dried fruits, vegetables, and mushrooms. When ready to use the dried foods, they rehydrated them by braising or simmering. Made from dried beef or venison, jerky served as a staple during the lean times.

With the ocean far away, salt was expensive in the Midwest. As a result, people usually preserved foods by smoking or drying rather than salting. From whitefish caught in the Great Lakes to various parts from the pigs raised on farms, people in the Midwest smoked any excess food. A smokehouse where they smoked and preserved hams, bacon, sausages, fish, cheeses, and more stood behind the main house on many farms. People living in the Midwest also pickled and canned many foods.

STATES

A bounty of freshwater fish from lakes and rivers as well as game, wild mushrooms, and berries from the many forests provided abundant sustenance for the people who immigrated to Michigan. Plentiful deer, bear, rabbits, squirrel, bullfrogs, and all sorts of birds including ducks, geese, grouse, wild turkey, dove, quail, partridge, and pheasant inhabited the forests and plains. A highly prized wild mushroom, morels emerge in the spring. Even today, people hunt for morels and other mushrooms. In fact, many treat the places where the morels grow as closely guarded secrets.

Derived from the French Canadian word for bouillon, hunters in the forested areas prepared *booyaw*, a stew comprising any available game, salt pork, onions, potatoes, and carrots. Although venison usually dominated this stew, cooks added rabbit, squirrel, possum, and/or woodchuck when available.

With the opening of the Erie Canal, myriad settlers from the eastern United States as well as Germany, Holland, the British Isles, and Ireland began moving into Michigan. Many settled in Detroit. British immigrants introduced the Cornish pasty, which proved an ideal lunch for the men working in the mines in northern Michigan. The traditional pasty consisted of diced beef, potatoes, and carrots encased in pastry dough and then baked. Some innovative cooks in this area prepared a unique pasty by placing a savory filling at one end of the dough and a sweet apple filling at the other end. This provided the miners with a self-contained meal—an entrée and dessert baked in one pastry shell.

Most of Michigan's cherry crop grows near Lake Michigan. The lake moderates the temperature, tempering the cold spring weather that otherwise would damage the budding trees.

In 1866, Seventh Day Adventists established the Battle Creek Sanitarium in Battle Creek, Michigan. The Seventh Day Adventists are a religious sect whose members follow a vegetarian diet. At the age of 24, Dr. John Kellogg came to work at the Battle Creek Sanitarium in 1876. He followed a holistic approach to medicine and advocated a low-calorie vegetarian diet, plenty of fiber and whole grains, and the importance of exercising. During his 62 years at the sanitarium, Kellogg and his brother invented the first processed cereals when they developed precooked flake cereals. They made corn flakes, wheat flakes, rice flakes, and cereal that combined several grains. In essence, Kellogg introduced cold cereal for breakfast. His brother, W. K. Kellogg, founded the food company bearing his name to produce their cereal.

When C. W. Post was a patient of Dr. Kellogg at the Battle Creek Sanitarium, he became interested in producing healthy foods. In 1895, he began the Postum Cereal Company, where he made Postum cereal beverage and later Grape Nuts. Eventually, the Postum Cereal Company became General Foods.

A cheesemaker of Swiss descent living in Wisconsin, John Jossi first created brick cheese in 1877 by squeezing Limburger curd between two bricks.

Attracted by the cold, harsh winters, mild summers, and miles of coastline that resembled their Nordic homeland, many Scandinavians settled in Michigan. They brought a fondness for herring, rye breads, and Danish pastry. The Dutch arrived next, introducing their culinary treasures like smoked and salted fish and Dutch pastries. The next group consisted of Eastern Europeans and Germans, who came with sausages, noodles, dumplings, and their culinary traditions.

The southern part of Michigan became prime farmland where the settlers planted fields of wheat and grazed herds of dairy cows on the prairie grasses. Soon butter, cheese, and milk production flourished. Today, agriculture thrives in Michigan. Asparagus, many varieties of beans, carrots, beets, corn, celery, potatoes, and fruits like apples, cherries, pears, peaches, plums, and blueberries are cultivated here. Growing bountiful crops of beans, Michigan exports them all over the country. Grapes thrive in southwestern Michigan, while cranberries flourish in the swampy areas. Michigan is known for honey.

Settlers from Normandy brought cherry seeds from their French home to plant in Michigan. The cherry trees thrived, and today, Michigan produces huge crops of tart cherries that supply about 70 percent of the world's tart cherries.

Jobs in the lumber industry in Michigan's north lured many immigrants to Michigan in the 1870s. When Henry Ford began mass-producing automobiles in the early 1900s in Detroit, the population exploded again. Seeking work in factories, people came from Poland, Greece, the Middle East, and Russia. Today, Michigan boasts a huge Middle Eastern population. In fact, Detroit claims the largest number of people from the Middle East of any city in North America. As a result, all sorts of Middle Eastern ingredients and dishes are available and served here.

Numerous German immigrants settled in Wisconsin, leaving a pronounced effect on the cuisine. Their menus included sausages, schnitzel, Sauerbraten, sauerkraut, and beer. Milwaukee became well known for sausages and breweries. The beer styles produced in Milwaukee reflected the English and German heritage of the immigrants who settled there. Meanwhile, the Scandinavians brought herring and pastries, the British came with cookies and cakes for tea, and people from Eastern Europe arrived with dumplings, noodles, and poppy seeds. As a result, the cuisine of Wisconsin became a fusion of the cookery from these countries, tempered with influences from the Native American cuisine.

A cornucopia of produce flourishes in Wisconsin. Cranberries, cherries, beans, corn, carrots, cabbage, and beets are just a few of the many fruits and vegetables grown here.

When the Swiss arrived, dairy production increased greatly. Wisconsin became known for producing many types of excellent quality cheeses. Today, large and small dairies operate throughout the state. A variety of cheeses including cheddar, Colby, brick, and muenster, in addition to many classic European cheeses like Brie, Romano, provolone, blue, Camembert, mozzarella, and gorgonzola are produced in the many dairies. Wisconsin claims the invention of two cheeses made by pressing the curds under a brick: mild flavored, yellow-colored Colby and mild flavored, white brick cheese. Today, Wisconsin claims a 20 billion dollar dairy industry producing more than two billion pounds of cheese each year. Northwestern Wisconsin contains the best dairy land in the state.

With plenty of dairy products, ice cream production became another important industry in Wisconsin. Also, the abundance of milk led to raising milk-fed veal. As a result, veal dishes appear commonly on menus throughout the state.

Minnesota attracted immigrants from Germany, Scandinavia, and Eastern Europe who settled throughout the state. They planted wheat, made bratwurst and other sausages,

Colby cheese came from Colby, Wisconsin, around the turn of the century. Although similar to cheddar, Colby tastes milder and has a softer texture.

The first ice cream sundae was created in an ice cream parlor in Wisconsin when a customer asked for some chocolate syrup over ice cream. Soon, customers tried a variety of toppings, including nuts and other condiments, and the sundae became a permanent ice cream confection.

Established in the 1800s, the goal of the Settlement House was to help immigrants become familiar with customs, foods, and the ways of their new country, the United States. Elizabeth Kander wrote *The Settlement Cookbook* to provide printed instructions for the immigrants taking cooking classes at the Milwaukee Settlement House. Besides covering very basic recipes and classic American recipes, this book contained many German and German Jewish recipes that reflected the heritage of the majority of the immigrants seeking help. The first *Settlement Cookbook* was published in 1901.

In 1869, Charles Pillsbury moved to Minneapolis and started a flour mill. Pillsbury's business prospered and the company bearing his name still exists. Since the highest grade of flour was marked with three Xs, Pillsbury marked his flour with four Xs and started the expression "Pillsbury's Best."

When dairy farms emerged throughout the states of the Midwest, milk and cheese production began. Borden's Dairy is located in Ohio.

pickled green cabbage into sauerkraut, grew red cabbage, baked hard-crusted breads and rolls from the wheat, and prepared many other dishes from their native homelands. Reflecting the culinary identity of the settlers, these dishes still frequent menus in restaurants and in homes throughout Minnesota.

The mills in Minneapolis, Minnesota, flourished using power generated from the falls situated on the Mississippi River. Soon, Minneapolis became a thriving milling center where grain was traded as well as milled.

Another important crop in Minnesota, wild rice flourishes in shallow lakes. After draining the lakes containing wild rice, commercial growers gather the seeds of this aquatic grass.

Cranberries are another lucrative crop for Minnesota. To harvest cranberries, farmers flood the bog in which the berries grow and then collect the floating cranberries.

Dairy farms throughout Minnesota yield excellent butter and cheese. Minnesota ranks just behind Wisconsin in dairy production. Also, the rich soil found in northwestern Minnesota yields a multitude of grains, sugar beets for making sugar, and potatoes.

With their ethnic traits permeating the cookery, the majority of Minnesota's population claims Scandinavian or German ancestry. In particular, a huge Finnish population still resides here. The Germans prepared hearty foods like sausages, breads, dumplings, beer, and German pastries. Meanwhile, Scandinavians contributed meatballs, cod dishes, herring, soups, Scandinavian breads and pastries, beer, *aquavit* (the clear liquor made from potatoes or grain flavored with caraway seeds), and the smörgåsbord. With plenty of work opportunities, the many immigrants found work in agriculture, in the iron mines of the north, or for lumber companies.

Today, Minnesota farmers raise hogs; dairy cattle for milk, butter, and cheese; turkeys; eggs; corn; soybeans; wheat; and beets. The majority of the agriculture grows in the southern part of the state.

Thanks to Johnny Appleseed, apples played a major role in the diet of the pioneers. Particularly prevalent in Michigan and Ohio, apples combine with corn and pork in numerous dishes.

As they migrated to the west, Shakers settled in several locations in Ohio. Establishing their homes near Lake Erie provided easy access to plenty of fish for food. The Shakers also set up communities near Dayton and Cincinnati. Remnants of their cookery still appear in these cities as well as in many areas throughout the Midwest.

Immigrants flocked to large cities like Cleveland, Akron, Toledo, Youngstown, Columbus, and Cincinnati for jobs in distilleries, breweries, industry, mills, and plants. Emigrating from Germany, Poland, Hungary, and Italy, they lived in ethnic enclaves within the cities. Of course, each group brought the recipes from their homeland, and those recipes penetrated into Ohio's cuisine. Goulash and the use of paprika in numerous dishes still prevail from the Hungarian influence.

Located in northern Ohio on Lake Erie, Cleveland attracted many immigrants from Slovenia. In fact, Cleveland claims a larger Slovenian population than any other city outside of Slovenia.

Besides being known for its German food, Cincinnati conjures up visions of chili for many. Served over spaghetti, this chili stems from the prominent Greek and Bulgarian influence found in this city. Depending how it is ordered, the beef chili is served over spaghetti and crowned with one topping or a combination of cheddar cheese, onions, and/or beans.

By the 1860s, railroads provided access to Indiana. This allowed easy transportation to the East for the sheep, hogs, corn, and wheat from this state. Many immigrants moved to Indiana, and each group prepared their ethnic specialties. Hungarians cooked veal

While hot dogs remain an icon of American food, the condiments of choice for hot dogs vary depending on the location. Hot dogs in Cincinnati often receive a topping of chili, onions, and cheese. New Yorkers want their hot dogs nestled under sauerkraut. People in Chicago prefer their "red hots" adorned with pickle, mustard, relish, onions, and maybe even more condiments. On the subject of condiments, prepared mustard first debuted at the 1904 World's Fair in St. Louis.

Scientists have developed hybrid strains of corn with high moisture content within the kernel. Because the corn pops when the water within the kernel turns to steam, these hybrids yield excellent-popping popcorn. A number of companies producing popcorn are located in Indiana.

Around 1875, both Phillip Armour and Gustavus Swift made fortunes with pork processing in Chicago. Although Swift designed a refrigerated rail car in 1885, the railroad companies refused to buy refrigerated cars for transporting the butchered meat to the East. In spite of them, Armour and Swift bought their own refrigerated rail cars and arranged for the railroad companies to transport their cars filled with meat. As a result, Armour was the first to ship dressed (processed) meat instead of living livestock to destinations. Railroad executives quickly realized the financial benefit of transporting meat instead of livestock and soon purchased their own refrigerated cars.

In the 1880s, the popular Red Delicious apple was developed in Iowa.

paprikash, veal in a sauce containing paprika, and the Swiss immigrants made cheeses. Pioneers transformed the indigenous persimmon into persimmon pudding.

With pork reigning as the meat of choice in Indiana, settlers created plenty of sausage by using all parts of the hog. Also, duck served as an important protein source. Located in Milford, Indiana, Maple Leaf Farms raises and exports ducks throughout the United States.

With dark, fertile soil conducive for growing crops, 75 percent of the land in Illinois supports agriculture. Cold winters and long hot summers provide a long growing season. Farmers grow a bounty of fruits, vegetables, and grains like corn, soybeans, wheat, cabbage, beans, asparagus, and apples. They raise cattle, hogs, and dairy cows. Brought to the area by German immigrants, horseradish thrives here. Providing food for the early settlers, flocks of ducks and geese migrate to or through Illinois. In addition, the rivers and lakes yield catfish, pike, bass, carp, and more.

When the herds of buffalo and bountiful game that the pioneers found roaming the Midwest dwindled, beef and pork replaced them as the meat of choice. Since ranchers raised countless herds of cattle in the Midwest, Texas, and the Plains states, they transported the cattle to Chicago for slaughter and processing. Reigning as the largest city in Illinois, Chicago's location in the central part of the country facilitated Chicago's growth as a meat-processing hub.

Because of the many factories and industries providing ample opportunity for employment, hordes of immigrants settled in Chicago. This city developed into a huge melting pot.

On their western migration from Pennsylvania, many Amish and Mennonites settled in Ohio, Indiana, Kansas, Missouri, and Minnesota. Others made southeastern Iowa their home. Lying in fertile, rolling farmland, the seven villages making up the Amana Colonies in Iowa became home to a large community of Amish and Mennonites. Like their brethren in Pennsylvania, the Amish and Mennonite cooks embraced simple, hearty food. Much of that food reflected their ancestry from Germany, Switzerland, and Alsace-Lorraine. Noodles, dumplings, lots of pork, sausages, sweet and sour foods, and pies filled their tables. Living on farms, they began their day with a hearty breakfast. The main meal of the day, served midday, consisted of meat, potatoes, perhaps dumplings or noodles, vegetables, bread, and dessert.

The early European immigrants who settled in Iowa mostly came from Germany and Scandinavia. In the beginning, they found few foods to cook, so they relied on a diet of pork, potatoes, and bread. Since the fertile soil yielded excellent crops and supported all sorts of livestock, they soon prepared bratwurst, Sauerbraten, vegetables, rye breads, and Scandinavian pastries. Significant numbers of Dutch and Czech immigrants moved to Iowa, where they still celebrate their heritage with foods from their native land. Specialties like fritters, doughnuts, and split pea soup commonly appear in the Dutch communities, while the Czechs prefer goulash, sauerkraut, dumplings, and *kolache*, sweet yeast rolls filled with prune or apricot filling, poppy seeds, or cheese. Similar to Danish pastry, *kolache* contain much less butter.

Ninety-three percent of the land in Iowa is farmland. The incredibly fertile soil supports a bounty of corn, high quality pork, beef cattle, dairy cattle, milk, soybeans, oats, corn, cucumbers, onions, beans, potatoes, cabbage, and apples. With many beekeepers throughout the state, half of the honey sold in the United States is claimed to come from Iowa. Quail, pheasants, and partridges flourish on the open farmland. Ducks and geese fly through Iowa as they migrate.

In 1920, a member of the Maytag family (of washing machine fame) started a dairy farm in Newton, Iowa. Eventually, they made cheese and produced the well-known blue cheese called Iowa Maytag.

Many from Virginia, Kentucky, and other states in the South migrated west to Missouri. They cooked typical Southern fare like fried chicken, biscuits, and greens. Meanwhile, the French Canadians who settled in Missouri prepared French dishes like crêpes and pea soup. Specialties including sausages, herring, and cheesecake appeared in the many areas where Germans settled.

Situated on the Mississippi River halfway between New Orleans and the northern territories, St. Louis began as a trading post in 1722. Almost 100 years later, many steamboats traveled through this city, establishing it as a transportation center and a city with culinary influences from a number of ethnic groups. After the Civil War, many freed slaves made their home in St. Louis. Of course, each group arrived with its culinary heritage.

In 1837, Germans began a settlement on the banks of the Missouri River in Hermann, Missouri. The site reminded the settlers of the Rhine River area, so they planted grapes to produce wine. Hermann developed into a major wine-producing area in the United States.

Today, Kansas City, Missouri, is known for its unique barbecue. To prepare this barbecue, cooks begin by slowly smoking beef brisket or any tough cut of meat until tender over a fire, usually of hickory or oak wood. They thinly slice the cooked tender meat, pile it on a slice of bread, and cover it with the famous Kansas City barbecue sauce. Many top that concoction with another slice of bread, ham, more barbecue sauce, dill pickles, and finally a third slice of bread.

Agriculture remains an important part of Missouri's economy. Beef cattle, hogs, turkeys, corn, wheat, soybeans, apples, grapes, peaches, and the distinctively flavored black walnuts flourish here. Missouri claims to produce more black walnuts than any other state. Pecan trees and bees producing honey also thrive in this state.

> **Looking for a high-protein food for patients, a St. Louis doctor developed peanut butter in 1890.**

> **Many foods first made their debut at the St. Louis World's Fair in 1904. Some were ice cream served in a cone, hot dogs in a bun accompanied by prepared mustard, peanut butter, and tea bags. Although already in existence, iced tea became popular at the St. Louis World's Fair.**

> **One difference exists between Kansas City barbecue and the barbecue found in the rest of the Midwest. For Kansas City barbecue, the meat smokes slowly over wood. Outside of Kansas City, most grill the meat and baste it with sauce.**

CHARACTERISTICS OF THE CUISINE

The foods we call "comfort foods" dominate the cooking of the Midwest. Described as sturdy, plain, and hearty, some of the comfort foods include meat loaf, pot pie, pork chops, creamed chicken, egg noodles, dumplings, a wide range of potato dishes, green beans, fruit pies, and cobblers.

Typical of the westward migration that eventually moved settlers across the United States, many of the early pioneers to the Midwest came from areas lying to the east. Those settling in Ohio immediately planted wheat and corn for grinding into flour to make breads, noodles, and dumplings. Since the early days, corn and pork filled the diet of inhabitants of Indiana, Illinois, and Iowa.

When people of German descent arrived in the Midwest, they made sausages, sauerkraut, breads, beer, and wine. Eastern Europeans brought stuffed cabbage and numerous dishes flavored with paprika, poppy seeds, and fruit sauces to their new land. Wherever Swedish immigrants settled, their impact on the cuisine still appears. It shows up in dishes like pickled herring, pickled beets, yellow pea soup, crêpe-like pancakes, wonderful pastries and breads, and dill flavoring paired with many foods. By adopting foods and cooking techniques from their new land, each ethnic group linked their culinary heritage with the cuisine of their new home.

Cattle and hogs thrived throughout this region. They provided plenty of meat for meals and an abundance of scraps for the incredible variety of sausages produced in the

Midwest. In early days, each ethnic group prepared the sausages from their native land. Whether the sausages contained beef, veal, pork, or a combination of meats, the choice of spices and flavoring and the sausage style reflected their German, Scandinavian, Czech, Bohemian, Polish, Italian, Russian, or Ukrainian heritage. The wide range of preparations yielded smoked, cured, dried, or fresh sausages.

With so much milk available from the many dairies, milk-fed veal is often consumed. Veal dishes from Germany and Eastern Europe like Hungarian goulash and *Wiener Schnitzel*, a breaded and fried veal cutlet, appear frequently.

From the early days, venison served as a versatile and important source of protein. While each ethnic group prepared dishes from its homeland, cooks often substituted readily available venison for the customary meats used in the original recipes. As a result, German immigrants replaced the beef in Sauerbraten with venison, and Italians and Swedish settlers prepared sausages using venison combined with the spices that defined their native cuisines.

In addition to obtaining plentiful freshwater fish such as whitefish, lake trout, sturgeon, salmon, perch, pike, bass, smelt, bluegill, walleye, and catfish from the Great Lakes, as well as other lakes, streams, and rivers throughout the Midwest, the early residents stocked their pantries with dried salt cod imported from the East. Dried salt cod needed no refrigeration and provided food for the lean times. Each ethnic group prepared the salt cod according to their culinary heritage. Many still serve salt cod dishes as part of their traditional Christmas Eve or Christmas dinner.

The many forests yielded game, nuts, and produce like fiddlehead ferns, berries, and numerous types of wild mushrooms. These foods played an important part in the diet of the early inhabitants. Joining the scraps from hogs and cows, any undesirable parts from the game went into sausages.

All types of nuts thrive throughout the Midwest. Black walnut trees flourish in Missouri, Iowa, Wisconsin, and Minnesota. Often used in baked goods in earlier times, black walnuts possess a unique, pungent, earthy flavor. Because their hard shells make these nuts difficult to shell, the availability of black walnuts decreased greatly compared to their popularity in the early days of the Midwest. Large quantities of pecans come from Missouri.

Known for dairy and cheese production, the Dairy Belt encompasses parts of Michigan, Wisconsin, Minnesota, Ohio, and Indiana. Farmers of German, Swiss, French, and Italian descent create excellent American and European varieties of cheeses as well as butter for cooking and baking from the herds of dairy cattle, sheep, and goats.

From pickles to pickled herring to *Sauerbraten* (marinated beef in a sweet and sour sauce), the large German population throughout the Midwest consumed a variety of sour and sweet and sour foods. Sweet and sour sauces appeared frequently with vinegar supplying the sour and any type of sugar providing the sweet.

Each ethnic group planted the beans of their culinary past. Scandinavians grew yellow peas and brown beans, Italians planted cannellini and fava beans, and the French preferred flageolets and navy beans. Making their way into soups, salads, and entrées, these beans became part of the diet in each area.

Soups and stews rank as favorite dishes in this part of the country. From clear to cream soups served both hot and cold, a wide range of soups remains popular. Another well-liked dish of the settlers in the Midwest, potpie often featured stew topped with dumplings instead of pastry crust.

By the early 1900s, most wheat farmers in the Midwest planted spring wheat. The abundant crop provided the essential ingredient for breads, noodles, dumplings, pancakes,

As in many parts of the country, farmers' markets operate every spring, summer, and fall in locations throughout the Midwest. Numerous cities like Indianapolis established permanent structures to house their farmers' markets. Besides featuring fresh fruits, vegetables, and nuts, many sell meats, fish, sausages, cheeses and other dairy products, baked items, and even crafts!

CHEESES PRODUCED IN THE MIDWEST

Asiago—Italian cheese; hard texture; somewhat sharp

Blue—Maytag blue first produced in Newton, Iowa, in 1920s; crumbly texture; strong, pungent flavor, blue veins run through the cheese

Brick—developed in Wisconsin in 1877; semihard texture; mild, nutty, spicy, sweet flavor

Brie—French cheese; soft texture; usually mild flavor depending on degree of ripening

Camembert—French cheese; soft texture; mild, salty flavor

Cheddar—one of the oldest cheeses produced in the United States; firm texture; ranges from mild to extra sharp flavor depending on the aging time

Colby—developed in 1885 in Wisconsin; firm texture; mild flavor

Gouda—Dutch cheese produced in Minnesota; buttery firm texture; mild flavor; sometimes smoked for flavoring

Muenster—good melting cheese; soft texture; mild flavor

Provolone—Italian cheese; semihard texture; mild but flavorful; all purpose cheese

Romano—Italian cheese similar to Parmesan; hard texture; full flavored

Swiss—hard to semihard cheese; mild, nutty, distinctive flavor; contains holes

---

pie dough, and all sorts of pastries. Scandinavians baked aromatic limpa rye bread containing rye flour, caraway, anise, and fennel.

Besides serving as everyday food, special yeast breads and rolls marked holidays. People from each ethnic group prepared their own traditional Christmas bread. For example, the Czechs baked *houska*, the Germans prepared *Stollen*, the Austrians made *Vanocka*, *Julekage* for the Norwegians, and *Julbrød* for the Swedish. Each group preferred their own spices and flavorings. Scandinavian breads and pastries often contained almonds, almond extract, and cardamom, while the Germans flavored with anise and nutmeg.

Menus throughout the Midwest feature starches like noodles, dumplings, and potatoes. *Spätzel*, a cross between a noodle and a dumpling, as well as dumplings made from potatoes, flour, and/or bread remain popular.

All sorts of fruits flourish in the Midwest. Cherries, apricots, plums, and apples grow in the many orchards throughout the countryside. Berries such as blueberries, strawberries, blackberries, raspberries, and cranberries proliferate here.

Apple trees grow throughout the Midwest with each state producing varieties that thrive in the climate and soil of that area. Also, persimmons grow in parts of the Midwest. These fruits are quite sour and astringent if not ripe, so the settlers initially rejected them. Later, settlers recognized the excellence of persimmons baked into puddings, cakes, and breads. They also dried this fruit and ate it without cooking. Many think persimmons are best when picked from the ground after they fall from the trees. Actually the fruit just needs to ripen until soft. There are two varieties of persimmons: the larger Asian variety that is commercially grown and the smaller American variety. The American variety is described as sweet and very fragrant. Some say it tastes like a date.

From the Scandinavian, German, and Dutch heritage, many people in the Midwest, particularly in the states of Michigan, Wisconsin, Minnesota, and Iowa, adopted the custom of serving coffee in the late afternoon. They often invited friends for coffee and always served one or more sweet confections with the coffee. Women stocked their kitchens with cookies, coffeecake, pound cake, or some type of pastry for unexpected guests.

Generally, women reserved one day each week for baking breads, pies, and other pastries. Regardless of the season, early settlers in the Midwest prepared pies. When fresh or dried fruits were not available, sugar or nut pies filled the larder. The season determined the type of pie. Spring brought strawberries and rhubarb; early summer yielded blueberries, raspberries, and cherries; late summer delivered peaches; and the fall was laden with pumpkins, apples, pears, and nuts. In addition, settlers served cream, custard, chocolate, and meringue-topped pies.

Throughout the rural areas of the Midwest, breakfast meant a hearty meal. A typical breakfast might consist of a stack of pancakes, two or three eggs, bacon, and some type of bread. Because farming required hard physical work, many meals included meat and potatoes.

Apples yielded both hard and nonalcoholic cider for the early settlers. With breweries and microbreweries in numerous cities, beer continues as big business in the Midwest. Native grapes yielded wine in the early days, but later, imported French grapevines produced American/French hybrid grapes for the wine. Much of the early wine production took place in northern Ohio. Michigan, Ohio, and Missouri produce wine today.

Area	Weather	Topography	Foods
Michigan Lake Superior and Canada to north, Lake Huron to east, Ohio and Indiana to south, Lake Michigan and Wisconsin to west	cold winters, cool summers in north; cold winters, warm summers in south	more than 11,000 lakes, streams, rivers, coastline, forests, fertile valleys, hills, plains, swamps, fertile farmland Upper Peninsula east: plains, hills, fertile farmland Upper Peninsula west: rugged hills, forests Lower Peninsula: plains, hills, fertile farmland	fish, bass, perch, lake trout, salmon, white-fish, walleye, herring, sturgeon, smelts, pike, bluegill, game, deer, ducks, geese, turkey, grouse, pheasant, dairy cattle, sheep, goats, cheese, butter, milk, wheat, many varieties of beans, asparagus, morels, wild mushrooms, wild rice, celery, beets, corn, carrots, potatoes, cherries, apples, pears, plums, peaches, cranber-ries, blueberries, grapes, many vegetables and fruits, maple syrup, honey, wine
Wisconsin Lake Superior, Canada, and Michigan to north; Lake Michigan and Michigan to east; Illinois and Iowa to south; Iowa and Minnesota to west	long, cold winters; mild summers	more than 15,000 lakes, forests, rivers, fertile valleys, Mississippi River, rich fertile soil	fish, perch, trout, herring, whitefish, smelt, bass, perch, sturgeon, game, hogs, sausages, veal, dairy cattle, sheep, goats, milk, cheeses, butter, wheat, wild rice, mushrooms, many fruits and vegetables, peas, carrots, beans, corn, cabbage, beets, cherries, cranberries, black walnuts, maple syrup, beer
Minnesota Canada to north, Wisconsin to east, Iowa to south, North and South Dakota to west	long, cold winters; mild summers	rolling plains, lakes, forests, valleys, fertile farmland, swamps, Mississippi River, Red River in northwest, rich soil, Lake Superior to northeast	fish, perch, trout, herring, smelts, stur-geon, walleye, pike, whitefish, carp, bass, game, hogs, sausages, turkey, sheep, goats, dairy cattle, eggs, butter, milk, cheeses, soybeans, grains, wheat, corn, mushrooms, wild rice, sugar beets, red cabbage, cabbage, potatoes, berries, cranberries, black walnuts, hazelnuts
Ohio Lake Erie and Michigan to north, Pennsylvania and West Virginia to east, Kentucky and West Virginia to south, Indiana to west	cold winters; hot, humid summers	fertile farmland and valleys, flat or gently rolling terrain, forests, Ohio River north: plains, fertile farmland, lowlands east: plateaus, valleys, forests south: rolling hills, plains west: fertile farmland	hogs, beef, chicken, sheep, goats, white-fish, sturgeon, bass, pike, smelt, catfish, dairy cattle, milk, cheeses, soybeans, corn, wheat, many fruits and vegetables, cucum-bers, tomatoes, apples, grapes, wine, beer
Indiana Michigan to north, Ohio to east, Kentucky to south, Illinois to west	cool winters; hot, humid summers	fertile farmland, hills, valleys, flat in north, gently rolling in south, forests, Ohio River, Mississippi River north: flat, sand dunes central: fertile plains south: hills, forests, lowlands	hogs, sausage, beef, duck, game, rabbits, deer, fish, catfish, pike, bass, sheep, goats, dairy cattle, wheat, corn, soybeans, many fruits and vegetables, apples, blue-berries, persimmons, popcorn
Illinois Wisconsin to north, Indiana and Kentucky to east, Kentucky to south, Missouri and Iowa to west	cold winters; hot, humid summers	flat or gently rolling plains, valleys, hills, fertile farmland, Mississippi River, forests, Ohio River	hogs, cattle, dairy, game, deer, rabbits, quail, turkey, pheasant, ducks, geese, bass, pike, catfish, carp, wheat, corn, soybeans, beans, cabbage, asparagus, horseradish, apples, many fruits and vegetables
Iowa Minnesota to north, Wisconsin and Illinois to east, Missouri to south, South Dakota and Nebraska to west	cold winters, mild to hot summers	fertile farmland, flat or gently rolling plains in east, flat in west, forests, fertile valleys, Mississippi River, Missouri River	hogs, beef, sausages, game, quail, pheas-ant, partridges, ducks, geese, dairy cattle, cheeses, Maytag blue cheese, milk, corn, soybeans, oats, cucumbers, onions, beans, potatoes, mushrooms, cabbage, many fruits and vegetables, apples, honey, black walnuts
Missouri Iowa to north; Illinois, Kentucky, and Tennessee to east; Arkansas to south; Nebraska, Kansas, and Oklahoma to west	cool winters; hot, humid summers	forests, lakes, hills, fertile valleys, plains, rich farmland, low mountains, Mississippi River, Missouri River north: rolling plains, streams, fertile soil southeast: Ozark Mountains, fertile farmland south: forests, hills, plateaus, valleys, low mountains, lakes, streams west: flat plains	beef cattle, hogs, game, deer, quail, turkey, fish, catfish, trout, bass, wheat, corn, soybeans, rice, grains, fruits and vegetables, mushrooms, strawberries, apples, peaches, grapes, wine, honey, pecans, black walnuts

1. Discuss the waterways found in the Midwest, including how they impacted the area and contributed to the cuisine.
2. Why did Chicago grow into such a large city? How did this affect the cuisine of Chicago?
3. Why did the Midwesterners make so much sausage? Why did they produce such a wide variety of sausages?
4. Discuss the Dairy Belt, including the states in it, how it developed, and the products that come from there.
5. Why did so many breweries start in the Midwest?
6. Define wild rice and describe the method for harvesting it.

aquavit—clear liquor made from potatoes or grain flavored with caraway seeds, served in Scandinavia

bigos—stew containing a variety of meats and sauerkraut originating in Poland

booyaw—stew comprising any game available, salt pork, onions, potatoes, and carrots, commonly served in the numerous forested areas of Michigan. The name derived from the French Canadian word for bouillon.

kielbasa—Polish sausage

kolache—sweet yeast rolls filled with fruit, poppy seeds, or cheese; similar to Danish pastry, but containing much less butter

limpa rye bread—aromatic bread of Scandinavian heritage containing rye flour, caraway, anise, and fennel

lutefisk—dried, salted cod treated with lye; became an intrinsic part of Christmas dinner and church suppers in the fall in Scandinavian communities

pemmican—patty consisting of pounded dried venison, dried berries, and fat; made by Ojibwa tribe to preserve food for the winter

pierogis—a small filled turnover or dumpling from Poland

Sauerbraten—marinated beef in a sweet and sour sauce; German dish

Spätzel—a cross between a noodle and a dumpling prepared in Germany

veal paprikash—Hungarian dish featuring veal in a sauce containing paprika

Wiener Schnitzel—breaded and fried veal cutlet served in Germany

Wurst—German word for sausages

SWEDISH MEATBALLS

This versatile dish functions as hors d'oeuvre at a cocktail party, a first course, or an entrée served over egg noodles.

NUMBER OF SERVINGS: 9
COOKING METHOD:
  Sauté, Braise
SERVING SIZE:
  4¾ oz, 2 meatballs with sauce
TOTAL YIELD:
  2 lbs, 14¾ oz total
SAUCE:
  1 lb, 5½ oz
RAW MEAT MIXTURE:
  1 lb, 14 oz

Wine Style: Wide variety—Pinot Blanc; Chardonnay; soft, fruity red wines; Beaujolais; or soft Merlot
Example: Ruby Nouveau—Wollersheim Winery, Prairie du Sal, WI. This wine is young and fruity, made using traditional Beaujolais methods.

Swedish Meatballs
© 2008 Jupiterimages Corporation

INGREDIENTS	WEIGHT	VOLUME
MEATBALLS:		
ground beef, lean	1 lb	
ground pork	8 oz	
bread crumbs	2 oz	½ cup
milk	2 oz	¼ cup
egg	1¾ oz	1 each
cardamom		¼ teaspoon
nutmeg		¼ teaspoon
allspice		⅛ teaspoon
ginger		⅛ teaspoon
salt		½ teaspoon
pepper		¼ teaspoon
butter or oil	2 oz	¼ cup or 4 tablespoons
SAUCE:		
butter or drippings	1½ oz	3 tablespoons
onion, minced	2½ oz	½ cup or 1 small
flour, all purpose	1½ oz	¼ cup
beef stock, hot	1 lb	2 cups
salt		¼ teaspoon
pepper		¼ teaspoon
sour cream	4¼ oz	½ cup

For Meatballs:

1. Combine beef, pork, bread crumbs, milk, egg, cardamom, nutmeg, allspice, ginger, salt, and pepper in bowl. Mix gently to combine well.

2. With moistened hands, shape into balls of desired size (about 1½-oz meat mixture for 1½-inch meatball). Cover and refrigerate until needed.

3. Heat butter or oil (2 oz or ¼ cup) in skillet over medium heat.

4. Add meatballs; sauté until browned on all sides. If necessary, sauté meatballs in batches to avoid crowding.

5. Remove to platter lined with absorbent paper. Keep warm in low oven for immediate service or cool, cover, and refrigerate until needed.

For Sauce:

1. Heat butter or drippings (1½ oz or 3 tablespoons) in pan. Add onion and sauté until softened, about 5 minutes.

2. Sprinkle flour over mixture; whisk about 2 minutes. Whisking constantly, gradually add beef stock, a little at a time into flour.

3. Bring to boil; reduce heat and simmer about 10 minutes, until thickened.

4. Add salt, pepper, and sour cream. Correct seasonings.

5. Strain sauce to remove onion and any lumps.

6. Pour sauce over meatballs or add meatballs to sauce. Cook over low heat until meatballs are hot. Serve immediately.

WILD RICE STUFFED MUSHROOMS

These serve well as either a first course or an hors d'oeuvre.

NUMBER OF SERVINGS:
  9 as appetizer
  36 individual mushrooms
COOKING METHOD:
  Bake
SERVING SIZE:
  4¼ oz, 4 stuffed mushrooms
TOTAL YIELD:
  1 lb, 8 oz filling

Wine Style: Light- to medium-bodied Pinot Gris, dry Riesling, dry Sherry, or soft, fruity red wine
Example: Lake Michigan Shore Dry Riesling—Tabor Hill Winery, Buchanan, MI. This Riesling has melon and apple aromas with a nice light oak finish.

Wild Rice Stuffed Mushrooms
photo by David Murray and Jules Selmes
© Dorling Kindersley

INGREDIENTS	WEIGHT	VOLUME
WILD RICE:		
water	1 lb	2 cups
salt		½ teaspoon
wild rice	3½ oz	½ cup
MUSHROOMS:		
mushrooms, large white	2 lb, 1¾ oz	36 each
butter	3 oz	6 tablespoons
garlic, minced	¾ oz	6 large cloves
wild rice, cooked,	8¼ oz	1½ cups
from above		
sour cream	13 oz	1½ cups
salt		¾ teaspoon
pepper		¾ teaspoon
rosemary, crushed		1½ teaspoons
Parmesan cheese	2¼ oz	6 tablespoons

For Wild Rice:

1. Combine water, salt, and rice in saucepan. Bring to boil.
2. Cover, reduce heat, and simmer about 35 minutes, until rice is tender.
3. Set aside until needed.

For Mushrooms:

1. Pan-spray baking dish. Preheat oven to 400 degrees.
2. Wash mushrooms, remove stems, and reserve.
3. Place mushroom caps in prepared baking dish with stem side facing up. Bake until partially cooked, 8 to 10 minutes.
4. Chop mushroom stems into small dice. Melt butter in skillet over medium heat; add mushroom stems and garlic. Cook for 3 to 4 minutes.
5. Add wild rice, sour cream, salt, pepper, and rosemary. Stirring constantly, bring to boil, and cook until thickened. Correct seasonings.
6. Fill mushroom caps with ½ oz filling (about 1½ to 2 teaspoons; amount of filling depends on size of mushrooms). Filling should mound in caps.
7. Sprinkle with Parmesan cheese. Bake 10 to 15 minutes, until hot. Serve immediately.

CHEDDAR CHEESE BEER SOUP

Adding Cheese to Soup
photo by David Murray and Jules Selmes
© Dorling Kindersley

Cheddar Cheese Beer Soup

This recipe produces a thick, rich soup. If desired, thin soup with additional chicken soup or beer. Leftover soup makes a great cheese sauce for broccoli, asparagus, cauliflower, and other vegetables.

NUMBER OF SERVINGS: 8
COOKING METHOD:
  Sauté, Boil
SERVING SIZE:
  7 oz
TOTAL YIELD:
  3 lbs, 13 oz

INGREDIENTS	WEIGHT	VOLUME
butter	1¹/₂ oz	3 tablespoons
onion, medium dice	6¹/₂ oz	1 large
celery, medium dice	2¹/₄ oz	1 stalk
carrot, medium dice	6¹/₂ oz	2 medium
flour, all purpose	1 oz	3 tablespoons
chicken stock, hot	1 lb, 8 oz	3 cups
potatoes, peeled, medium dice	9¹/₂ oz	2 medium
beer, amber or dark	12 oz	1 each 12-oz bottle or can
cream cheese	3 oz	
nutmeg		¹/₄ teaspoon
cayenne pepper		¹/₈ teaspoon
black pepper		¹/₄ teaspoon
dry mustard		¹/₄ teaspoon
Worcestershire sauce	¹/₄ oz	¹/₂ tablespoon
salt		¹/₈ teaspoon
cheddar cheese, sharp, grated	12 oz	3 cups

GARNISH:

cheddar cheese, sharp, grated, or fried cheddar cheese cubes

paprika and/or minced parsley

1. Melt butter in large pan over medium heat. Add onions, celery, and carrots. Sauté until tender, about 6 to 8 minutes.

2. Whisk in flour; cook about 1 minute. Whisk in chicken stock slowly, adding a little at a time.

3. Add potatoes and beer; bring to boil. Reduce heat, cover, and simmer about 20 minutes until potatoes are tender.

4. Place mixture in bowl of food processor; process to puree.

5. Return to pan. Add cream cheese, nutmeg, cayenne, black pepper, dry mustard, Worcestershire sauce, and salt.

6. Bring to simmer, add cheddar cheese, and stir gently until melted. Do *not* allow soup to boil.

7. Correct seasonings. Serve immediately, garnished with additional cheese and a sprinkling of paprika.

CINCINNATI CHILI

Cincinnati's famous chili recipes are based on Greek and Bulgarian cooking influences, resulting in an incredibly aromatic dish with a complex flavor palate. Don't be confused; this chili veers far from the typical chili found in the Southwest. Customers order Cincinnati chili five ways: one is plain; two-way adds spaghetti under the chili; three-way consists of two-way topped with grated cheese; four-way means three-way with diced onions; five-way combines the previous additions with beans.

Note: The flavor of the chili improves after reheating, so this dish benefits by being prepared a day in advance.

NUMBER OF SERVINGS: 9
COOKING METHOD:
  Braise
SERVING SIZE:
  7 oz chili with no accompaniments
TOTAL YIELD:
  3 lbs, 15 oz

Cincinnati Chili
photo courtesy of Land O' Lakes, Inc.

INGREDIENTS	WEIGHT	VOLUME
beef, ground	2 lbs	
onion, small dice	10³/₄ oz	2 medium
garlic, minced	³/₄ oz	3 large cloves
tomato puree	1 lb, 12 oz	2 cups or 1 each 28-oz can
water	1 lb	2 cups
chocolate, unsweetened	¹/₂ oz	
bay leaf		1 each
chili powder	¹/₂ oz	2 tablespoons
cumin, ground	¹/₄ oz	1 teaspoon
coriander, ground		¹/₄ teaspoon
turmeric		¹/₂ teaspoon
cardamom, ground		¹/₄ teaspoon
cinnamon	¹/₄ oz	1 teaspoon
allspice, ground		¹/₂ teaspoon
cloves, ground		¹/₄ teaspoon
cayenne pepper, ground		¹/₄ teaspoon
black pepper		1 teaspoon
Worcestershire sauce		2 teaspoons
salt	¹/₄ oz	1 teaspoon

ACCOMPANIMENTS:

spaghetti, cooked	12 oz	
onion, minced	5¹/₄ oz	1 medium
cheddar cheese, grated	8 oz	2 cups
kidney beans	1 lb	2 cups or 1 each 16-oz can

1. Heat pan over medium heat, add beef, onion, and garlic. Sauté until lightly browned, breaking any large clumps of meat. Drain excess fat and discard.

2. Add tomato puree and water; bring to boil.

3. Add remaining ingredients, mix to combine, cover pan, lower heat, and simmer at least 45 minutes to an hour, stirring occasionally.

4. Correct seasonings; serve hot with accompaniments of choice.

THREE BEAN SALAD

Three Bean Salad

If possible, prepare this salad the day before serving.

Any combination of three beans works. Some replace the yellow beans with garbanzo beans.

NUMBER OF SERVINGS: 8
SERVING SIZE:
  4 oz
TOTAL YIELD:
  2 lbs, 2 oz

INGREDIENTS	WEIGHT	VOLUME
green beans, cut, canned, drained, or fresh cooked	8 oz	1 each 14^1/$_2$-oz can
yellow beans, canned, drained, or fresh cooked	8 oz	1 each 14^1/$_2$-oz can
kidney beans, drained	9^1/$_2$ oz	1 each 15-oz can
red pepper, cored, seeded, medium dice	3 oz	^{1}/$_2$ each or ^{1}/$_2$ cup
green onions, sliced thinly	1^1/$_4$ oz	^{1}/$_2$ cup or 2 each
parsley, fresh, minced		1 tablespoon
DRESSING:		
red wine vinegar	2^3/$_4$ oz	^{1}/$_3$ cup
prepared mustard		2 teaspoons
garlic powder		^{1}/$_4$ teaspoon
parsley, fresh, minced		1 tablespoon
oregano		^{1}/$_2$ teaspoon
thyme		^{1}/$_2$ teaspoon
paprika		^{1}/$_2$ teaspoon
basil		^{1}/$_2$ teaspoon
sugar		^{1}/$_2$ teaspoon
salt		1^1/$_2$ teaspoons
pepper		^{1}/$_4$ teaspoon
olive oil	4 oz	^{1}/$_2$ cup

1. Combine green beans, yellow beans, kidney beans, red pepper, green onions, and parsley (1 tablespoon) in bowl.

2. Prepare dressing by placing vinegar, mustard, garlic powder, parsley (1 tablespoon), oregano, thyme, paprika, basil, sugar, salt, and pepper in nonreactive bowl (or bowl of food processor fitted with knife blade).

3. Slowly whisk in olive oil (or add very slowly through feed tube) until dressing emulsifies (thickens).

4. Pour over beans; toss gently to coat. Correct seasonings.

5. Cover and refrigerate overnight, gently tossing occasionally. Correct seasonings again. Serve.

MARINATED ASPARAGUS SALAD

Peeling Asparagus
photo by David Murray © Dorling Kindersley

Chill plates for this salad.

NUMBER OF SERVINGS: 8
COOKING METHOD:
  Boil
SERVING SIZE:
  4 oz asparagus,
  1 oz red pepper, ½ oz red onion,
  1¼ oz lettuce

INGREDIENTS	WEIGHT	VOLUME
VINAIGRETTE:		
olive oil	**4 oz**	**½ cup**
sesame oil		**2 teaspoons**
balsamic vinegar	**2 oz**	**¼ cup**
salt		**½ teaspoon**
pepper		**½ teaspoon**
tarragon		**1 teaspoon**
garlic, minced	**1 oz**	**4 large cloves**
asparagus, peeled, trimmed of woody ends, cooked until *al dente,* still crisp, cut in half on bias	**2 lbs**	
lettuce leaves, washed	**10 oz**	
red pepper, medium dice	**8 oz**	**1½ cups**
red onion, sliced thinly	**4 oz**	**1 medium**

For Vinaigrette:
1. Whisk olive oil, sesame oil, and vinegar together.
2. Add seasonings; whisk thoroughly.

To Marinate:
1. Place asparagus in flat dish; cover with vinaigrette. Turn to coat.
2. Cover and refrigerate to marinate at least 2 to 3 hours or overnight.

To Assemble:
1. Place 1¼ oz lettuce on each chilled plate.
2. Top with 4 oz marinated asparagus. Decoratively place 1 oz red pepper and ½ oz onion slices on top of asparagus.
3. Drizzle with extra vinaigrette, if desired. Serve.

GRILLED BRATWURST IN BEER WITH ONIONS

Caramelized Onions
photo courtesy of National Onion Association

Grilled Bratwurst in Beer with Onions
photo courtesy of National Pork Board

NUMBER OF SERVINGS: 8
COOKING METHOD:
  Boil, Sauté, Grill
SERVING SIZE:
  2 each bratwurst
  2¾ oz onions
TOTAL YIELD:
  1 lb, 6½ oz onions

Wine Style: Full-bodied red wines, Merlot, Shiraz, Cabernet Sauvignon, or Zinfandel
Example: Big Stuff Red—Botham Vineyards, Barneveid, WI. This estate-grown semidry wine is fruit-filled with an explosion of flavor.

INGREDIENTS	WEIGHT	VOLUME
bratwurst, fresh, about 3 oz each	3 lbs	16 each
beer	1 lb, 8 oz	2 each 12-oz bottle
peppercorns, whole		16 each
ONIONS:		
butter	2 oz	4 tablespoons or ½ stick
onion, thinly sliced	1 lb, 15 oz	4 large
caraway seeds	¼ oz	1 tablespoon
brown sugar	2 oz	¼ cup
vinegar	2 oz	¼ cup
catsup	1½ oz	2 tablespoons
Worcestershire sauce		2 teaspoons
salt	¼ oz	1 teaspoon
ACCOMPANIMENTS:		
hot dog rolls		16 each
mustard, whole-grain, Dijon, or variety of choice		

1. Combine bratwurst, beer, and peppercorns in pan. Bring to boil, reduce heat, and simmer for 15 minutes, until bratwurst is done and no longer pink.
2. Remove bratwurst, strain liquid, and reserve. Discard peppercorns.

For Onions:
1. Melt butter in skillet over medium heat. Add onion; sauté for 10 minutes, stirring frequently, until soft and lightly browned.
2. Add caraway seeds; cook for 3 more minutes.
3. Add brown sugar, vinegar, catsup, Worcestershire sauce, salt, and reserved liquid from cooking bratwurst.
4. Bring to boil, reduce heat, and simmer until liquid evaporates and onion is glazed.

Finish:
1. Preheat grill.
2. Grill bratwurst about 7 minutes until golden brown, turning frequently.
3. Place bratwurst into roll; top with mustard and onions. Serve.

STUFFED PORK CHOPS

Stuffed Pork Chops

Instead of placing stuffing on top, a pocket can be cut into the side of the chop and stuffing placed inside of the pocket. Be sure to check internal temperature of stuffing with this method to ensure safety. If stuffing pocket, less than 3 oz of stuffing will fit inside, but it can cascade to the outside if desired.

Note: Watch the temperature of the meat closely. Lean pork chops become dry if over-cooked.

NUMBER OF SERVINGS: 10
COOKING METHOD:
  Bake
SERVING SIZE:
  1 chop with 3 oz stuffing
TOTAL YIELD:
  5 lbs, 6¼ oz

Wine Style: Fruity, medium-bodied Viognier, Gewürztraminer, medium-bodied red wines, or light Shiraz
Example: Summerset Red—Summerset Winery, Indianola, IA. A blend of French-American hybrids and other varietals, this wine is aged in French oak with a very smooth yet spicy finish.

INGREDIENTS	WEIGHT	VOLUME
STUFFING:		
oil	1 oz	2 tablespoons
onion, thinly sliced	6³/4 oz	1 large
apple, peeled, cored, small dice	7¹/2 oz	2 medium
cornbread, coarsely crumbled	8¹/4 oz	3 cups
corn kernels	3³/4 oz	³/4 cup
celery, small dice	3³/4 oz	³/4 cup
red pepper, small dice	3³/4 oz	³/4 cup
sage		³/4 teaspoon
thyme		³/4 teaspoon
salt		³/4 teaspoon
pepper		¹/2 teaspoon
butter, melted	3 oz	6 tablespoons or ³/4 stick
egg, beaten	5 oz	3 each
pork chops, boneless, center cut, 1¹/4-inch thick	4 lbs, 6 oz	10 each 7-oz chops

1. Heat oil in skillet over medium heat. Add onion; sauté for 4 minutes to begin caramelizing.

2. Add apple. Continue cooking 8 to 10 minutes, until caramelized onions and apples are soft and lightly browned.

3. Place onions and apples in bowl, add cornbread, corn, celery, red pepper, sage, thyme, salt, pepper, butter, and egg. Mix gently to combine. Correct seasonings.

4. Preheat oven to 350 degrees. Place pork chops in baking dish or sheet pan.

5. Mound 3 oz (¹/3 cup) stuffing on top of each chop.

6. Bake, covered, for 15 minutes. Uncover; bake another 10 to 15 minutes, until done and proper temperature on meat thermometer. Serve immediately.

HAMBURGERS STUFFED WITH MAYTAG BLUE CHEESE

Hamburger Stuffed with Maytag Blue Cheese

NUMBER OF SERVINGS: 10
COOKING METHOD:
  Grill
SERVING SIZE:
  5 oz raw beef stuffed with
  ³/4 oz blue cheese
TOTAL YIELD:
  3 lbs, 6½ oz raw beef

Wine Style: Wide variety—Pinot Blanc, Chardonnay, Rose, Merlot, or Cabernet Sauvignon
Example: Cabernet Sauvignon—Eagle City Winery, Iowa Falls, IA. This rich, medium-bodied, moderately oaked wine exhibits distinct flavors of tea, berries, and herbs.

INGREDIENTS	WEIGHT	VOLUME
beef, ground	3 lbs	
Worcestershire sauce	1/2 oz	1 tablespoon
catsup	2 1/2 oz	1/4 cup
salt	1/4 oz	1 teaspoon
pepper		1 teaspoon
egg	3 1/2 oz	2 each
Maytag blue cheese	7 1/2 oz	

ACCOMPANIMENTS:

hamburger rolls		10 each
catsup		
mustard		
relish		
onions, diced or sliced, raw or sautéed		

1. Mix ground beef, Worcestershire sauce, catsup, salt, pepper, and egg in bowl.
2. Weigh 5 oz beef mixture for each patty. Divide into halves and pat each half into 3- to 3½-inch disk.
3. Place ¾ oz crumbled blue cheese in center of half the patties.
4. Top with remaining patties, seal edges well to encase cheese.
5. Preheat grill.
6. Grill hamburgers on both sides until desired internal temperature.
7. Serve on hamburger rolls with accompaniments of choice.

SMOTHERED CHICKEN

Smothered Chicken

NUMBER OF SERVINGS: 8
COOKING METHOD:
  Braise
SERVING SIZE:
  ¼ chicken
  14¼ oz chicken with sauce
TOTAL YIELD:
  12 lbs, 11½ oz

Wine Style: Light- to medium-bodied Chenin Blanc, Sauvignon Blanc, Chardonnay, or Rose
Example: Chardonnay—Ferrante Winery, Harpersfield Township, OH. This wine has melon, pear, and vanilla aromas, medium acid with a long finish, and buttery flavors.

INGREDIENTS	WEIGHT	VOLUME
oil	4 oz or as needed	1/2 cup or as needed
chicken, whole cut into quarters *or* whole split bone-in breasts	about 6 lbs, 3 oz	2 whole fryers
onion, medium dice	14 oz	2 large or 2 2/3 cups
garlic, minced	1/2 oz	4 large cloves
celery, medium dice	8 oz	1 1/2 cups or 4 stalks
carrot, medium dice	8 oz	1 1/2 cups or 2 large
mushrooms, button, sliced	1 lb	
flour, all purpose	8 oz	1 1/2 cups
chicken stock, hot	5 lbs	2 qt + 2 cups or 10 cups
sherry, dry	4 oz	1/2 cup
paprika		1 teaspoon
salt	1/4 oz or to taste	1 teaspoon or to taste
pepper		1 teaspoon

1. Preheat oven to 350 degrees.
2. Heat oil in large ovenproof skillet or braising pan until hot. Add chicken and brown on both sides. Remove from pan.
3. Sauté onion, garlic, celery, carrot, and mushrooms for about 5 minutes, until almost tender.
4. Stir in flour; cook about 2 minutes until *roux* is blonde.
5. Slowly whisk in hot chicken stock, sherry, paprika, salt, and pepper. Bring to boil.
6. Place in oven; cook about 1½ hours, until chicken is done.

PLANKED WHITEFISH

Planked Whitefish

To prepare this dish, fish is cooked directly on a hardwood plank, usually oak or maple. The wood cannot be treated, so be careful about buying a board from a home supply store.

For a dramatic presentation, serve fish on the plank. If desired, frame fish with a border of piped duchess potatoes.

NUMBER OF SERVINGS: 9
COOKING METHOD:
  Bake, Broil
SERVING SIZE:
  6½ oz
TOTAL YIELD:
  3 lbs, 12 oz

Wine Style: Light- to medium-bodied Riesling, Chardonnay, Seyval Blanc, or Rose
Example: Seyval Blanc—Alexis Bailly Vineyard, Hastings, MN. This dry, crisp wine is well balanced with fruit and has a bright, clean finish.

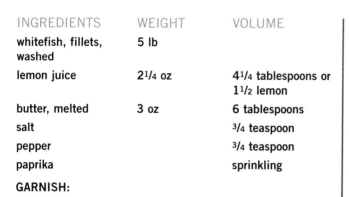

INGREDIENTS	WEIGHT	VOLUME
whitefish, fillets, washed	5 lb	
lemon juice	2 1/4 oz	4 1/4 tablespoons or 1 1/2 lemon
butter, melted	3 oz	6 tablespoons
salt		3/4 teaspoon
pepper		3/4 teaspoon
paprika		sprinkling

GARNISH:
lemon wedges or slices
tartar sauce or sauce of choice

1. Soak plank(s) in warm water for at least 5 minutes. Preheat oven to 400 degrees.
2. Place fish fillets on plank(s), brush with lemon juice, then brush with butter, and season with salt, pepper, and a sprinkling of paprika.
3. Bake 8 to 10 minutes, then broil for 6 to 10 minutes, depending on thickness of fish, until fish is flaky and thoroughly cooked.
4. Serve immediately, accompanied by lemon and sauce of choice.

CHICAGO DEEP-DISH PIZZA

Chicago Deep-Dish Pizza

For a spicy filling, use hot Italian sausage or add crushed red pepper flakes to filling mixture.

If desired, fill this deep-dish pizza with ingredients like mushrooms, spinach, or olives.

NUMBER OF SERVINGS: 8
COOKING METHOD:
  Sauté, Bake
SERVING SIZE:
  ¼ pie
TOTAL YIELD:
  2 each 12-inch pies
  8 lbs, 5½ oz total weight
  3 lbs dough

Wine Style: Zinfandel, Shiraz, Chambourcin, Sangiovese, or Merlot
Example: Chambourcin—Fox Valley Winery, Oswego, IL. This wine features the aromas of bing cherries and ripe plums with a soft oak flavor.

For Crust:

1. Sprinkle sugar and yeast over 4 oz (½ cup) warm water in small bowl; stir to mix well. Set aside until yeast bubbles, a few minutes.
2. Meanwhile, place about 1 lb, 7 oz (5 cups) flour, cornmeal, semolina, salt, olive oil, and remaining water (12 oz or 1½ cups) in large bowl. Mix well.
3. Add yeast mixture; mix well.
4. Knead on counter, adding more flour if necessary, until dough is smooth and elastic, about 6 to 8 minutes.
5. Return to bowl; cover; let rise in warm place until doubled, about 1½ hours.

For Assembly:

1. Sauté sausage and onion until sausage is done and onion is tender. Drain well.
2. Add pizza sauce to sausage mixture; refrigerate until needed.
3. Grease 2 each 12-inch pans. When dough has risen, punch down; divide in half for each pan. Place oven rack in middle of oven. Preheat oven to 500 degrees.
4. For each pan, use about two-thirds of dough (about 15 oz) for bottom crust. Roll dough into circle about 15 inches in diameter. With fingertips, pat into pan and up sides about 2 inches.
5. Sprinkle 5¼ oz (1½ cups) mozzarella cheese over bottom crust.
6. Place sausage mixture evenly over cheese, top with tomato pieces, then sprinkle oregano and basil over filling. Place pepperoni evenly over filling.
7. Sprinkle Parmesan cheese and remaining mozzarella over filling.
8. Roll out dough for top crust in circle. Place over filling, seal edge of top dough to bottom crust well by firmly crimping doughs together. With sharp knife, cut 2 or 3 slits about 1 to 1½ inches long into top crust to allow steam to escape.
9. Bake for 10 minutes; lower heat to 375 degrees. Continue baking for 20 minutes, until crust is golden.
10. Remove from oven; cool in pan for about 5 minutes. Slice and serve immediately.

INGREDIENTS	WEIGHT	VOLUME
CRUST:		
sugar	¼ oz	2 teaspoons
yeast, dry, granulated	½ oz	4 teaspoons
water, warm	1 lb	2 cups
flour, all purpose	1 lb, 7 oz to 1 lb, 11 oz	5 to 6 cups
cornmeal	2½ oz	½ cup
semolina	3 oz	½ cup
salt	½ oz	2 teaspoons
olive oil	2 oz	¼ cup
FILLING:		
sausage, sweet Italian, bulk	2 lbs	
onion, small dice	8 oz	1½ cups or 2 medium
pizza or spaghetti sauce	1 lb	2 cups
mozzarella cheese, grated	1 lb, 8 oz	7 cups
tomatoes, whole plum, drained, chopped	1 lb, 2½ oz	2 cups
oregano		2 teaspoons
basil		2 teaspoons
pepperoni, thinly sliced	4 oz	
Parmesan cheese, grated	2 oz	½ cup

GREEN BEANS WITH DILL

If available, substitute fresh dill for the dried using double the amount of fresh as dried.

NUMBER OF SERVINGS: 9
COOKING METHOD:
  Boil, Sauté
SERVING SIZE:
  4 oz
TOTAL YIELD:
  2 lbs, 4 oz

INGREDIENTS	WEIGHT	VOLUME
water	5 lbs or as needed	2 qts + 2 cups
salt		1/2 teaspoon
green beans, trimmed, ends and strings removed	2 lbs, 2 oz	
oil	1 oz	2 tablespoons
onions, sliced thinly	12 oz	3 medium
butter	1 oz	2 tablespoons
dill, dried		4 teaspoons
salt		1/2 teaspoon
pepper		1/2 teaspoon

1. Place water and salt (1/2 teaspoon) in large pot. Bring to boil, add green beans, and cook until tender, about 5 to 6 minutes.
2. Drain beans in colander; rinse immediately with cold water to stop the cooking. Set aside until needed.
3. Heat oil in saucepan over medium-low heat; add onions. Sauté, stirring occasionally until onions caramelize, about 15 minutes.
4. Heat butter in pan; add beans, caramelized onions, dill, salt, and pepper.
5. Sauté until beans are thoroughly hot and desired tenderness.
6. Correct seasonings; serve immediately.

CAULIFLOWER WITH WALNUTS

NUMBER OF SERVINGS: 14
COOKING METHOD:
  Boil, Sauté
SERVING SIZE:
  4 oz
TOTAL YIELD:
  3 lb, 9½ oz

INGREDIENTS	WEIGHT	VOLUME
cauliflower, cut into florets	3 lb	2 heads
butter	4 oz	8 tablespoons or 1 stick
walnuts, chopped	8 oz	2 cups
salt	to taste	
pepper	to taste	

1. Boil cauliflower in 1 inch of water for 8 to 12 minutes, until tender. Drain and reserve.
2. Melt butter over medium heat, add walnuts, and sauté for 7 to 10 minutes, until golden.
3. Add cauliflower; heat thoroughly. Add salt and pepper.
4. Correct seasonings. Serve.

FRIED CORN

With many hogs and acres and acres of corn, this dish is a natural from Iowa.

NUMBER OF SERVINGS: 10
COOKING METHOD:
  Sauté
SERVING SIZE:
  4 oz
TOTAL YIELD:
  2 lbs, 9 oz

INGREDIENTS	WEIGHT	VOLUME
bacon	8 oz	8 slices
onion, small dice	7 oz	1 1/3 cups or 1 each large
corn, fresh, removed from cob	2 lbs, 1 oz	6 cups
red pepper, small dice	2 1/2 oz	1/2 cup
salt		1/2 teaspoon
pepper		1/2 teaspoon
marjoram		1/2 teaspoon

1. Fry bacon in skillet until crisp. Remove from skillet, drain well, and chop. Set aside until needed.
2. Add onion, corn, and red pepper to skillet. Stir to mix and coat well.
3. Add salt, pepper, and marjoram.
4. Cover; cook until corn is tender, about 6 minutes.
5. Correct seasonings; top with bacon crumbles. Serve immediately.

WILD RICE PILAF

NUMBER OF SERVINGS: 15
COOKING METHOD:
   Sauté, Boil
SERVING SIZE:
   4 oz
TOTAL YIELD:
   3 lbs, 12 oz

Wild Rice Pilaf

INGREDIENTS	WEIGHT	VOLUME
olive oil	1 oz	2 tablespoons
onion, small dice	11 1/2 oz	2 large
wild rice	14 1/2 oz	2 cups
chicken stock	3 lbs	1 qt + 2 cups
pepper		1/2 teaspoon
salt	as needed, depending on saltiness of stock	

1. Heat olive oil in pan. Add onion and sauté until soft and translucent, stirring often.
2. Add wild rice. Continue sautéing a few minutes, stirring frequently.
3. Add stock and pepper, bring to boil, cover, reduce heat, and simmer for 55 minutes.
4. Turn off heat; leave pan covered for 5 minutes.
5. Check rice to be sure liquid is absorbed. If liquid remains, heat a few more minutes.
6. Correct seasonings. Serve immediately.

POPOVERS

Basically, popovers bake much like a cream puff. They puff up and create a hollow center. Serve these right away because they deflate!

Although ingredients for popovers vary little, the cooking directions differ dramatically. Some cooks place the pans of popover batter in a cold oven; others heat the muffin tin in the 450-degree oven and then pour the batter in the pan and bake the popovers in the preheated oven. While some bake them at 450 or 425 degrees, still others bake at 350 degrees.

NUMBER OF SERVINGS: 12
COOKING METHOD:
   Bake
SERVING SIZE:
   2 each
TOTAL YIELD:
   2 lbs, 1½ oz (4 cups) batter

Popovers
photo courtesy of Land O' Lakes, Inc.

INGREDIENTS	WEIGHT	VOLUME
flour, all purpose, sifted	8 oz	2 cups
salt	1/4 oz	1 teaspoon
eggs, beaten	6 3/4 oz	4 each
milk	1 lb	2 cups
butter, melted	2 oz	1/4 cup or 4 tablespoons

1. Pan-spray or butter muffin tins. Preheat oven to 450 degrees.
2. Sift flour and salt in bowl. Make well in center.
3. Mix eggs, milk, and butter together. Pour into well; mix with fork just until incorporated. Lumps will remain in batter. Do not overmix.
4. Pour into prepared tins, using 1 1/4 oz filling to fill each cup two-thirds full. *The weight of filling varies with the size of cup in muffin tin.*
5. Bake for 15 minutes. Lower temperature to 350 degrees; bake another 15 minutes. Remove from oven.
6. If desired, pierce each popover to allow steam to escape. Serve immediately, accompanied by butter and jam or honey.

BUTTERSCOTCH BLACK WALNUT BARS

Butterscotch Black Walnut Bars

Black walnut trees flourish in Missouri.

NUMBER OF SERVINGS:
  15 each 2 1/2- by 3-inch
  48 each 1 1/2- by 1 1/2-inch
COOKING METHOD:
  Bake
TOTAL YIELD:
  1 each 9- by 13-inch pan

INGREDIENTS	WEIGHT	VOLUME
butter, unsalted, cut into pieces	8 oz	2 sticks or 1 cup
brown sugar, firmly packed	7 1/2 oz	1 cup
butterscotch chips	1 lb, 1 3/4 oz	3 cups
eggs	8 1/2 oz	5 each
vanilla		2 teaspoons
flour, all purpose, unsifted	7 1/2 oz	1 1/2 cups
salt		1/4 teaspoon
black walnuts	4 1/2 oz	1 cup

GARNISH:
confectioners' sugar

1. Grease or pan-spray 9- by 13-inch baking pan. Move rack to center of oven. Preheat oven to 350 degrees.
2. Heat butter and brown sugar in saucepan over medium heat, stirring frequently with wooden spoon until mixture is very hot.
3. Place butterscotch chips in bowl of food processor fitted with knife blade. Pulse until finely chopped.
4. With motor running, pour the hot butter mixture through the feed tube and process until butterscotch is melted. Scrape bowl of processor as needed.
5. With motor running, add eggs, one at a time, through feed tube. Then add vanilla. Process until well mixed, about 15 seconds.
6. Add flour and salt; process until combined, about 5 seconds.
7. Scrape sides of bowl. Add nuts. Pulse about 8 or 10 times to chop and mix them into batter.
8. Place batter into prepared pan. Smooth top, if necessary. Bake until knife comes out almost clean, about 28 to 32 minutes. Do not overbake. Remove from oven.
9. Cool completely. Lightly dust top with confectioners' sugar by sifting through sieve over top. Cut into desired size.

CHERRY GOAT CHEESE STRUDEL

Cherry Goat Cheese Strudel

Although unusual, this recipe combines the cherries and the dairy products so prevalent in Michigan to create a confection with both sweet and savory overtones. To lessen the goat cheese flavor, replace half of the goat cheese with cream cheese.

NUMBER OF SERVINGS: 12
COOKING METHOD:
  Bake
SERVING SIZE:
  2-inch slice
TOTAL YIELD:
  2 each 12-inch strudels

INGREDIENTS	WEIGHT	VOLUME
goat cheese	1 lb, 8 oz	
sugar	5 oz	2/3 cup
cinnamon		1 1/2 teaspoons
egg yolks	2 3/4 oz	4 each
cherries, tart, canned, drained	1 lb, 4 1/2 oz	2 each 14 1/2-oz cans
phyllo dough	about 8 oz	12 or 14 sheets
butter, unsalted, melted	about 5 oz	about 10 tablespoons (1 stick + 2 tablespoons)
sugar	about 3 oz	about 6 tablespoons

1. Place goat cheese, 5 oz (2/3 cup) sugar, cinnamon, and egg yolks in bowl. Mix with mixer to combine thoroughly.

2. Gently stir in cherries, being careful not to smash cherries. Reserve.

3. Cover baking pan with parchment paper. Place oven rack in center of oven. Preheat oven to 375 degrees.

4. Lay stack of phyllo sheets on table. Keep unused phyllo dough covered with damp towel to prevent drying out. Move one sheet of phyllo to work surface. With pastry brush, gently brush lightly with melted butter. Sprinkle lightly with sugar.

5. Repeat using 5 or 6 more sheets, stacking each directly on top of the one below.

6. About one-third of the way from top edge of dough, place one-half of goat cheese mixture in a log running the length of the dough, stopping about 2 inches from each side.

7. Fold side edges over filling, then fold top edge over filling, and roll to encase dough.

8. Place strudel on prepared pan with seam side down. Brush outside with melted butter. Sprinkle with sugar. Repeat layering phyllo dough and rolling around remaining filling to make another strudel. Place on prepared pan, brush with butter, and sprinkle with sugar.

9. Bake for 25 to 30 minutes, until golden. Remove from oven; cool. Serve warm or at room temperature.

LEMON MERINGUE PIE

Lemon Meringue Pie
photo courtesy of Land O' Lakes, Inc

For pie dough recipe, see recipe for pie dough with pumpkin pie in Chapter 2 or use any pie dough recipe desired.

This pie shell requires about 12 oz of pie dough, so use a ball of dough weighing at least 13 oz.

As a rule, meringue-topped pies do not keep well. Because it is less likely to "weep" or become wet, Italian meringue tops this pie.

Brushing the bottom of the pie shell with egg white helps create a barrier to prevent the crust from becoming soggy.

NUMBER OF SERVINGS: 8
COOKING METHOD:
  Bake
SERVING SIZE:
  ⅛ of 9-inch pie
TOTAL YIELD:
  1 each 9-inch pie

INGREDIENTS	WEIGHT	VOLUME
pie dough	about 12 oz	
egg white, reserved from filling	1 oz	1 each
FILLING:		
cornstarch	2¼ oz	½ cup
water, cold	1 lb	2 cups
sugar	8¾ oz	1¼ cups
egg yolks	4 oz	6 each
salt		¼ teaspoon
lemon juice	4 oz	½ cup, about 3 to 4 each
lemon rind, finely grated	¾ oz	2 tablespoons
butter, unsalted	1½ oz	3 tablespoons
MERINGUE:		
cream of tartar		¼ teaspoon
water		1 teaspoon
sugar	4½ oz	⅔ cup
water	1 oz	2 tablespoons
egg whites, room temperature, reserved from filling	4 oz	4 each

For Pie Shell:

1. Place ball of dough on table. With rolling pin, hit ball to flatten into disk about one inch thick. Lightly flour table and rolling pin, if needed.

2. Roll dough, from middle to sides, releasing dough from table with icing spatula every few rolls. Turn dough one-quarter turn to keep dough even and roll into circle until desired thickness.

3. Release dough from table with spatula. Fold gently in half. Lift and move dough to 9-inch pie pan. Position dough over pan so it covers pan when unfolded.

4. Press dough into pan. Flute edges or cut dough flush with top outside edge of pan. Stick bottom with tines of fork about six times scattered around bottom crust to prevent bubbling when baking blind (with no filling inside).

5. Thoroughly chill dough in pan in refrigerator or freezer.

6. Place oven rack in bottom half of oven. Preheat oven to 400 degrees.

7. Weight pie shell by lining inside of dough with aluminum foil placed with shiny side down *or* parchment paper filled with dried beans or rice for weight. Make sure foil or paper reaches into corner seams where sides and bottom join.

8. Bake until dough sets, about 5 to 10 minutes. Remove foil or paper and weights, brush bottom lightly with egg white, return to oven, and bake until golden.

9. Cool completely.

For Filling:

1. Whisk cornstarch and water in nonreactive saucepan. Add sugar and whisk over medium-low heat until mixture thickens, about 5 to 10 minutes.

2. Meanwhile, beat egg yolks and salt with fork to break up. Continually whisking, add hot cornstarch mixture to eggs very slowly, to temper eggs.

(Continued)

For Meringue:

1. Mix cream of tartar with 1 teaspoon water; set aside until needed. Place oven rack in upper third of oven. Preheat oven to 400 degrees.

2. Mix sugar and 1 oz (2 tablespoons) water in small saucepan just to moisten.

3. Meanwhile, beat egg whites with mixer using whisk attachment, if available. Begin on low speed until frothy, then increase to high.

4. Cover saucepan containing sugar and boil on high heat for a couple of minutes, until sugar dissolves and condensation washes sugar crystals from side of pan.

5. Remove lid, add cream of tartar mixture, and cook without stirring until 248 degrees, firm ball stage. Slowly pour sugar syrup into beating egg whites with mixer running on medium speed.

6. Continue beating until room temperature, about 5 minutes.

To Finish:

1. Transfer lemon filling into baked pie shell.

2. Top with meringue. Either spread it with a flexible-bladed spatula (icing spatula) or pipe meringue on top with pastry bag and star tip or tip of choice. If spreading with spatula, form peaks in meringue by tapping meringue with flat part of spatula.

3. Bake until nicely browned, about 4 minutes.

4. Cool, then refrigerate a few hours, until service.

5. To serve, cut with clean knife.

PERSIMMON PUDDING

Persimmon Pudding

To reheat persimmon pudding, wrap it in foil and heat in preheated 300-degree oven for about 15 minutes.

NUMBER OF SERVINGS: 12
COOKING METHOD:
  Bake
SERVING SIZE:
  4½ oz piece, ¹⁄₁₂ of pan
TOTAL YIELD:
  3 lbs, 6¼ oz

INGREDIENTS	WEIGHT	VOLUME
raisins	5½ oz	1 cup
brandy	4 oz	½ cup
flour, all purpose, unsifted	7¼ oz	1½ cups
baking powder		1 teaspoon
baking soda	¼ oz	1 teaspoon
salt		¼ teaspoon
cinnamon	¼ oz	2 teaspoons
nutmeg		¼ teaspoon
cloves		⅛ teaspoon
ginger	¼ oz	1 teaspoon
allspice		¼ teaspoon
persimmon pulp, frozen or from very ripe persimmons	1 lb, 2 oz	2 cups
sugar	7½ oz	1 cup
half-and-half	12 oz	1½ cups
eggs	3½ oz	2 each
butter, melted	2 oz	4 tablespoons or ½ stick
walnuts, chopped	4½ oz	1 cup

ACCOMPANIMENTS:

ice cream *or*

custard sauce *or*

whipped cream, slightly sweetened, flavored with brandy

1. Soak raisins with brandy for several hours. If time is limited, heat raisins and brandy in microwave and allow to sit as long as possible.

2. Grease or pan-spray 9- by 13-inch baking pan. Preheat oven to 350 degrees.

3. Sift together flour, baking powder, baking soda, salt, cinnamon, nutmeg, cloves, ginger, and allspice. Set aside until needed.

4. In large bowl, combine persimmon pulp, sugar, half-and-half, eggs, butter, and brandy from raisins. Mix well.

5. Sift half of dry mixture over wet ingredients; gently combine. Sift remaining dry ingredients over wet ingredients and combine. Do not mix too much, but be careful to avoid pockets of flour mixture in dough.

6. Fold in walnuts and raisins. Pour into prepared pan. Bake for 55 minutes to 1 hour, until knife inserted comes out almost clean.

7. Remove from oven. Serve warm accompanied by ice cream, custard sauce, or whipped cream.

8

Plains States

OBJECTIVES

By the end of this chapter, you will be able to

- Discuss the role of the buffalo for the Native Americans and the settlers
- Describe the conditions that made life on the Plains difficult for the settlers
- Explain issues that encouraged people to move to the Plains states
- Identify food products prevalent in the Plains states
- Prepare a variety of dishes indicative of the cuisine of the Plains states

States included in the Plains:

- North Dakota
- South Dakota
- Nebraska
- Kansas
- Oklahoma

HISTORY

While archaeologists conclude that Native Americans migrated from Alaska to North Dakota more than 10,000 years before the arrival of the Europeans, other Native American tribes moved to the Plains states from areas lying in the East. Some Native Americans sought life in the Plains, but most fled to the west in search of freedom, unoccupied land, and to escape the white man's invasion of their lands. Contrary to the Native Americans in the East who lived primarily through agriculture, for these tribes the buffalo became the center of their survival in the Plains. Many of these nomadic tribes moved constantly, following the herds of buffalo throughout the Plains.

The mainstay of the diet for the Native Americans living in the Plains consisted of buffalo and corn, augmented by game, wild vegetables, fruits, berries, squash, beans, and wild rice where it grew. When buffalo was scarce, the Native Americans hunted game such as deer and rabbit. They dried any excess food for two reasons. First, drying food made it more compact and easier for the nomadic tribes to carry with them. Second, the dried foods provided sustenance through the long winter months, drought, and other lean times when fresh food was not available. Like those in New England, the Native Americans in the Plains made *pemmican*, a combination of pounded dried berries and jerky. The jerky was made from buffalo on the Plains. To prepare jerky, thin slices of the meat dried in the sun for days. Later, mass-produced salt simplified the process, since dipping the meat in a salt solution expedited the drying and helped keep the flies away.

Unfortunately, the white man almost obliterated the buffalo that once roamed so freely through the Plains. For the Native Americans, the flesh of the buffalo provided meat and fat, the hide and fur became clothing and blankets, bones were transformed into tools and other utensils, and the dried manure fueled the fire. For the white man, this animal supplied meat when they needed it, but the only other valued parts of the buffalo were the fur and the tongues for selling. They slaughtered countless buffalo, removed the tongues and fur, and then left the rest of the buffalo to rot. Soon the herds of buffalo dwindled, and the Native Americans lost the source of their survival. The buffalo almost vanished.

Thomas Jefferson sent Meriwether Lewis and William Clark to explore the lands included in the Louisiana Purchase of 1803. From 1804 to 1806, Lewis and Clark trekked through the Plains and the West, carefully documenting and mapping their exploration. Lewis and Clark had three goals for their expedition: to look for passage to the Pacific Ocean, assess the Native Americans, and establish trade with them. They began their journey of more than 8,000 miles at the mouth of the Missouri River in St. Louis. The expedition finally ended at the Columbia River and the Pacific Ocean in Oregon.

Numerous Scandinavian immigrants settled in North and South Dakota in the 1850s, but the influx of settlers into the Plains began when the Homestead Act became law. Passed in 1862, the first Homestead Act granted 160 acres of free land to homesteaders who paid a minimal filing fee, promised to live on the homestead for five years, and claimed intent to become a citizen of the United States (if not already a citizen). The Homestead Act enticed hundreds of thousands of pioneers to move west into the sparsely inhabited territories.

In 1863, the first settler, Daniel Freeman, claimed free land in Nebraska through the Homestead Act. Hordes of settlers from Germany, Scandinavia, and Bohemia immigrated to Nebraska and Kansas, bringing recipes, foods, and the culinary traditions from their native lands. Subsequent groups of people established homesteads in North and South Dakota and Oklahoma. Homestead Acts passed in later years encouraged expansion into all of the western territories.

Buffalo meat contains more protein and less fat than beef.

By 1910, only 254 buffalo remained. Fortunately, ranchers throughout the Plains and the West started raising buffalo, and the number of these animals has increased dramatically.

By 1900, six hundred thousand homesteaders had filed claims for 80 million acres of land in the Plains and West.

While making the journey to the West in search of gold, numerous pioneers traveled along the Platte River in Nebraska. Having endured a long and arduous journey just to reach this point, many gave up their quest for gold and settled in Nebraska.

As a result of the Homestead Act, the population of Kansas increased tenfold between 1865 and 1880. In addition to freed slaves, immigrants from around the world relocated to Kansas to farm. Around the same time, groups of Mennonites moved to Kansas in search of religious freedom and farmland. They brought strong German and Russian culinary influence. Ensuring transportation for crops and people, several railroad lines crisscrossed the state.

Later versions of the Homestead Act lured Norwegian, Swedish, Irish, Polish, German, Czechoslovakian, Austrian, and Bohemian immigrants to North Dakota, South Dakota, Nebraska, and Iowa. Even today, the Scandinavian, Eastern European, and Germanic influence on the cuisine in these states remains strong. Yellow pea soup, pickled herring, pickled beets, crêpe-like pancakes, lingonberry and currant sauces, breads, pastries, and dill flavoring reflect the Scandinavian presence throughout the Plains. The Norwegians reproduced favorite dishes like *lutefisk*, dried fish (usually cod) soaked in lye or potash; *lefse*, a thin potato pancake made from mashed potatoes; and *rømmegrøt*, porridge. Eastern Europeans prepared numerous varieties of strudels, both sweet and savory. Immigrants from Bohemia (part of the Czech Republic today) and Czechoslovakia favored winter vegetables like cabbage, carrots, parsnips, and potatoes; seasoning with caraway seeds, poppy seeds, and nutmeg; sweet and sour flavorings; and all sorts of dumplings. Their culinary traits remain in the cuisines of North and South Dakota, Nebraska, and Kansas.

After pushing the Native Americans out of the Southeast in the 1820s, the settlers designated Oklahoma as "Indian Territory." After deciding Oklahoma was barren, useless land, the settlers forced many Native American tribes to relocate there. The tides turned in 1889 when Oklahoma opened to homesteaders. Once again, the Native Americans lost their land! People from the eastern United States as well as immigrants from Germany, Africa, the British Isles, Spain, Italy, Mexico, Poland, and other Eastern European countries moved into Oklahoma. Each group brought their culinary heritage, which mixed with the existing cuisine and that of the Native Americans.

To transport cattle from the ranches of Texas to the feedlots and slaughterhouses of Chicago, cowboys sometimes drove as many as two or three thousand head of the cattle through Oklahoma and Kansas, where they caught a train bound for Chicago. Cattle drives became a way of life for many working on the ranches, particularly from 1866 (shortly after the Civil War ended) until 1885. Many cowboys worked on these long drives, and all of those workers needed to eat. An entire way of cooking developed for these traveling ranchhands, but this way of life ended when the railroad connected to Texas. The railroad eliminated the need to transport the cattle on foot to northern destinations for shipment. Now they could load the cattle into trains in Texas and unload them in Chicago, Kansas City, Omaha, or another stop on the rail line.

During the time of the cattle drives, cooking on the road (or trail) involved preparing three meals each day over an open fire for all the cowboys. A revered member of the group of cowboys on the trail, the cook, called "cookie," wielded a lot of power. The cook controlled all the food and meals for many hungry men, but cooking on the trail was a hard job with long hours. Responsibilities of the cook included finding fuel for the fire and keeping the fire going, in addition to planning and cooking three meals each day. Cooks carried everything they needed, such as sourdough for leavening bread, flour, cornmeal, meat, bacon, beans, coffee, rice, dried fruits, and canned vegetables. Since they were moving cattle, they often ate beef, the available meat. In fact, they cooked all edible parts of the cow and frequently added the organs to the pot of simmering stew. In addition, the pot of stew often contained dumplings. Sourdough biscuits accompanied most meals. Any game or fish caught during their journey augmented their diet, while beans, chili, potatoes, biscuits, and cornmeal dishes rounded out the menu on the trail.

Two major routes to the west cut through the Plains states: the Santa Fe Trail and the Oregon-California Trail. Sometimes used for transporting cattle, the Santa Fe Trail went from Santa Fe, New Mexico, through Kansas to Independence, Missouri. On the other hand, 300,000 settlers moved to the west on the heavily traveled Oregon-California Trail, also called the Overland Trail, between 1840 and 1860. Beginning in Kansas City, Missouri, the trail moved westward through Kansas, Nebraska, Wyoming, and Idaho. At that point, travelers turned north to continue their journey to Oregon and Washington, or south through Nevada to California. The entire trip took four to six months. Most of the settlers traveled in a covered wagon—sometimes called a prairie schooner—that protected their belongings. Usually 20 or 25 groups of people banded together and drove their wagons westward, forming "wagon trains." The food staples on the wagon trains consisted of some type of bread or biscuit, beans and/or bacon, maybe dried apples, and coffee. Like the cowboys moving herds of cattle on the trail, these westward-bound travelers consumed any foods that they fished, hunted, or found growing along their journey.

Cooking took place over an open fire, but finding fuel for the fire often presented a significant problem on the Plains. In the absence of firewood, they burned dried grasses or buffalo chips (dried buffalo manure). Cooks worked very hard, often cooking until midnight. Besides cooking, they baked both sweet and savory pies as well as bread.

TOPOGRAPHY AND CLIMATE

Five states lying just west of the Midwest compose the Plains states. Geographically stacked on top of each other from north to south, they are North Dakota to the far north bordering Canada, South Dakota to its south, Nebraska lying south of South Dakota, followed by Kansas and Oklahoma.

When the first pioneers moved west into the Plains, they discovered a difficult land for survival. Although herds of buffalo roamed the prairie, the terrain consisted of treeless, flat plains covered with tough grasses. In addition, dry conditions prevailed. With little to stop the wind, it howled across the Plains. In the winter, the wind often whipped the falling snow into a blizzard. The absence of trees to provide wood for fuel created significant hardship for the settlers. With nothing to fuel a fire, they resorted to burning dried buffalo or cow manure, dried grasses, or corncobs. Finding a land void of trees, many of the immigrants settled close to rivers where a few trees grew and the waterways yielded fish. Buffalo, deer, antelope, prairie dogs, jackrabbits, coyotes, and foxes roamed the land. Eagles and hawks soared through the sky, while pheasant, quail, dove, and wild turkey thrived in the prairies of the Dakotas, Nebraska, and Kansas. With little growing except the prairie grasses, monotony described the diet here. The abundant wild berries, greens, and nuts prevalent in regions lying to the east did not grow in the Plains states. Furthermore, the effects of the unpredictable and sometime treacherous weather often left the early settlers facing little or no food and starvation.

After the formidable task of removing the tough grasses, the flat terrain revealed fertile soil well suited for growing corn, wheat, and oats, in addition to vegetables and fruits. The remaining grasslands proved excellent for grazing cattle. Today, Kansas, Nebraska, and North and South Dakota make the area known as the Wheat Belt.

Hot, dry summers and cold, harsh winters dominate the Plains states. In addition, tornadoes, blizzards, droughts, and dust storms sometimes occur here. Nicknamed the Dust

Removing the tough prairie grasses, with their long, deep roots, proved an extremely difficult job for the settlers. Even a team of oxen pulling a plow made slow work of churning the soil where these grasses grew. That changed in 1847, when John Deere invented the steel plow. With this plow, farmers could turn the ground holding the tough grasses, and the life of the farmer in the Plains became much easier.

When farming equipment first became available, most farmers in the Plains could not afford to purchase it. As a result, farmers shared equipment and helped each other during harvest. As many as 50 men gathered to bring in the harvest at a farm, and the women assembled in the kitchen at that farm to prepare three meals a day for the 50 hungry workers. With this cooperative spirit, they reaped the grain from each farm, sharing their time, many meals, and recipes with each other.

The worst of the destruction in the Dust Bowl took place between 1935 and 1938. About 40 dust storms occurred in 1935 alone.

Instituting irrigation and conservation measures throughout the Plains alleviated the problem of dust storms. Although the winds still roar across the Plains, the soil does not become so dry that the winds carry it away.

Bowl, the states of Colorado, Kansas, New Mexico, Oklahoma, and Texas experienced a huge number of intense dust storms during the 1930s. Two conditions existed that made this area susceptible to the incredible devastation caused by the countless dust storms that occurred during that decade. First, the Plains states had seven years of drought. Second, homesteaders altered the land by removing the grasses. The long roots of the natural grasses anchored the soil. After stripping the Plains of most of its natural grasses, the settlers planted wheat and grazed too many herds of cattle. The shorter roots of the wheat and the overgrazing of the remaining grasses by the cattle left the parched dry land with little protection against the vicious series of wind and dust storms that swept across the flat land. With the wheat crop just starting to grow in the spring of 1934, accounts state that one major storm actually ripped about 318 metric tons of soil from this area. Reports state that some of that soil was deposited as far away as the East Coast! Many farmers lost everything they owned and bankruptcies ran rampant. Displaying the pioneer spirit that created the United States, many farmers continued their westward migration, moving to California to find better living conditions for themselves and their families.

Containing thick forests, the Turtle Mountains form North Dakota's northern border with Canada. Minnesota borders North Dakota on the east, South Dakota neighbors to the south, and Montana lies to the west. Surrounded by fertile valleys, the Red River creates the eastern border with Minnesota. Huge wheat fields dominate the flat, fertile farmland of the east, and herds of beef cattle graze there. The central section contains rolling hills, streams, lakes, and valleys. With buttes, steep hills, deep gorges, and unusual, dramatic rock formations, the dry and rocky area called the Badlands lies in the western part of North Dakota. Long, harsh, frigid winters prevail throughout North Dakota.

Starting in the northwest, the Missouri River flows through the center of the state to the southeast. The Red and Missouri Rivers, along with lakes, streams, and other rivers, supply enough water for irrigation. In addition, they yield a bounty of fish, including catfish, perch, trout, bass, walleye, and pike. These waterways also attract ducks and other waterfowl.

South Dakota lies south of North Dakota, Minnesota and Iowa are situated to its east, Nebraska borders South Dakota's southern side, and Montana and Wyoming lie on its west. The Missouri River runs from north to south through the center of the state. Hot, dry summers and cold winters define the climate. Although periodic droughts plagued South Dakota throughout its history, irrigation from the rivers, lakes, and streams helps the farmers to minimize the effects of the droughts.

The eastern portion of South Dakota consists of prairie, fertile farmland, hills, and lakes. Many farms with livestock and crops flourish in the east. Consisting of forests, canyons, and rock formations, the low-lying Black Hills are situated in the western part of the state along with the Badlands, rolling plains, canyons, valleys, hills, and buttes. Large livestock ranches cover much of the west.

Nebraska lies south of South Dakota with Iowa and Missouri to its east, Kansas and Colorado to the south, and Colorado and Wyoming situated to the west. The dry climate and frequent droughts presented significant hardship for the early farmers. Today, crops thrive due to irrigation from the rivers and the large underground water table that lies under about one-third of Nebraska. The Missouri River forms the northeastern and the eastern boundary with South Dakota, Iowa, and Missouri. The Platte River flows across the state from the west to the east.

Also consisting of flat plains with few trees, Nebraska presented the early settlers with an additional challenge: no wood to build homes or to fuel their fires or cook stoves. As a result, the settlers built houses of sod and burned anything available to fuel the fire. Later, they imported wood for building from states east of the Plains.

Farmland covers 95 percent of the land in Nebraska, with most of the crops growing in the fertile soil found in the eastern side of the state. In addition to hogs, wheat, corn, soybeans, and other grains and crops thrive here. The land in the east consists of plateaus, hills, valleys, rivers, and streams. With sandy soil and much drier conditions, the western part of Nebraska provides grasslands for grazing a bounty of cattle. Wheat grows well in the western part of the state, but most other crops fare better in the eastern half. Plains, prairie, sand dunes, grasslands, and some hills and streams make up the western part of Nebraska.

Kansas lies at the heart of the contiguous United States. Nebraska borders Kansas on its north, Missouri lies to the east, Oklahoma to the south, and Colorado is on the west. The Kansas terrain consists of rolling plains that gain elevation in the western part of the state and grasslands that provide excellent grazing for the many herds of cattle. Wheat, corn, soybeans, and hogs flourish on the farms throughout the state.

Oklahoma is situated south of Kansas and Colorado. Arkansas and Missouri lie east of Oklahoma, Texas to the south, and Texas and New Mexico to the west. Flat plains and low hills describe most of Oklahoma's terrain, although fertile farmland, grasslands, rivers, valleys, forests, hills, and low mountains dominate the terrain in the southern region. The Red River forms the border with Texas in the south, and the Arkansas River flows through the northeast.

Ingredients and foods commonly used throughout the cuisine of the Plains include

- beef, including steaks, stews, pot roast, and more
- pork, salt pork, bacon, sausages, and other pork products
- game, buffalo, and deer
- chicken, duck, quail, and pheasant
- barbecued foods
- catfish, bass, walleye, pike, perch, and trout
- corn and soybeans
- wheat, barley, rye, oats, and other grains
- sunflowers
- cold weather vegetables, including carrots, potatoes, parsnips, turnips, rutabagas, cabbage, and salsify (called oyster plant)
- sugar beets
- apples, berries, and rhubarb
- honey

COOKING METHODS

Boiling vegetables with a ham hock, pig's foot, or piece of salt pork reigned as the usual treatment for hearty vegetables like cabbage and greens. With plenty of lard available from the many hogs, frying served as a frequent cooking technique. Both pan-frying and deep-frying appeared often throughout the Plains states.

When cowboys moved herds of cattle from Texas to Chicago (or anywhere in between), the most common cooking methods included grilling, one-pot cookery (boiling and braising), and frying in a pan over the open fire. The cooks prepared long-simmering (braised) dishes like pot roast and stews. A pot of beans often cooked over the fire. Wasting as little meat as possible, stews incorporated offal like the heart, tongue, stomach, intestines, brains, sweetbreads, and other organs. Rendered beef fat provided the fat for cooking on the trail.

Even managing to bake over the open fire, cowboys baked biscuits and cornbread in a Dutch oven, a cast iron kettle and lid made with or without three legs to elevate it from the embers in the fire. By placing the pot directly into the embers and putting embers or coals on top of the lid, heat from the top and bottom baked the contents of the Dutch oven. Another advantage of these pots was that the thick cast iron kettles and skillets conducted heat evenly.

Initial preservation methods included salting, smoking, pickling, and drying any excess meat, fish, or produce. For use in the winter, settlers dried any extra fruits and vegetables such as apples, peaches, rhubarb, and more. In 1858, the invention of the glass canning jar opened the way for the canning of garden produce. This invention made preserving food for the winter months much easier.

STATES

Ethnic enclaves developed throughout the Plains states. Many Polish and German immigrants settled in Kansas. Groups of Germans, Czechs, and Bohemians adopted Nebraska as their home. Meanwhile, Scandinavians relocated to Nebraska, Kansas, and both North and South Dakota. Oklahoma and Kansas attracted large numbers of Italians. Wherever they settled, the culinary heritage from each ethnic group melded with the foods and cookery already there. For example, the Bohemians who settled in Nebraska, the Dakotas, and other parts of the Plains introduced *kolache*, sweet yeast rolls with a filling of apricot, prune, other fruits, poppy seeds, or cheese. Soon, people throughout the Plains made *kolache*.

During the 1870s, large numbers of immigrants finally started moving into North and South Dakota. At that time, the railroad came through North Dakota, which helped to persuade many settlers from Germany, Norway, and Russia to relocate. Besides the newly available railway transportation, the cold climate that resembled that of their native country attracted these immigrants to the Dakotas.

Located on the eastern border of North Dakota, the Red River and the fertile valleys surrounding it drew many immigrants. Most planted wheat, North Dakota's most important crop. They also grew sunflowers, rye, flax (for seeds), barley, and sugar beets. In addition, the Scandinavian, Irish, and German settlers planted potatoes that soon became a regular part of the diet. They raised bees for honey.

When they found gold in the Black Hills of South Dakota in the 1870s, thousands of immigrants, including Norwegians, Germans, and Russians, as well as settlers from states to the east flooded into South Dakota. Providing food for the early settlers, deer, elk, buffalo, catfish, pike, trout, walleye, bass, and perch naturally inhabited the forests, plains, and waterways of South Dakota. The settlers soon imported hogs, which survived on anything available, including the tough natural grasses. As a result, hogs served as the basis for the diet of the early prospectors and settlers. The most common meal consisted of beans with salt pork or bacon accompanied by cornbread. Even today, pork remains a favorite in South Dakota.

By the late 1870s, settlers in South Dakota raised cattle for their personal consumption and to sell. Soon, many immigrants from Scotland purchased cattle and ranches, and

Because of the Homestead Act, the population of North Dakota grew from fewer than 2,500 to more than 190,000 people between 1870 and 1890.

The central point of the United States, including Hawaii and Alaska, lies in western South Dakota.

Numerous famous people from the "Old West," including Calamity Jane, Sitting Bull, Wild Bill Hickok, and George Custer, played a part in South Dakota's history.

they imported Scottish breeds of cattle like Angus and Herefords. Cattle became big business in South Dakota, with much of the cattle raised in the western half of the state.

The many Scandinavian immigrants contributed much to the cuisine here. They served foods like herring; headcheese, a sausage made from all the meat removed from the head of the pig or cow; rutabagas; and the vegetable dish combining peas and mushrooms.

Originally imported from China, pheasants still roam the countryside. Farmers in South Dakota raise cattle for beef, hogs, sheep, wheat, corn, soybeans, and sunflowers.

Early pioneers in Nebraska fared about the same as those in Kansas. After six or seven years, the settlers replaced their worn, leaking sod houses with log cabins. The wood houses became a possibility only when they could transport wood from the northern Great Lakes area or the East. Although great numbers of buffalo grazed on the grasslands, the early pioneers did not use these animals as did the Native Americans, who relied on them for food, clothing, and shelter. Gardens thrived around each of the settlers' houses. They preserved any excess food for the harsh winter. Hogs roamed the farms, providing pork and lard. Smoking, salting, and preparing sausages ensured food for the winter months, with ham serving as a mainstay.

In the late 1940s, Duncan Hines developed cake mixes in Nebraska.

Immigrants from Switzerland, Scandinavia, and Czechoslovakia joined Americans from the East in their western migration to settle in Nebraska. Bringing the recipes and culinary traditions from their native lands, each of these groups impacted the cuisine of Nebraska. Today, corn, wheat, and soybeans thrive in Nebraska, and the abundant land feeds cattle destined for slaughter.

The wild indigenous fruits and vegetables prevalent in the eastern states did not grow in Kansas. With little meat available, the early pioneers in Kansas ate meagerly. Pancakes with gravy and/or sorghum often served as the entrée.

Straddling the border of Kansas and Missouri, residents of Kansas City boast that they prepare the finest barbecue in the United States. The history of Kansas barbecue began in the 1860s and 1870s. When cowboys from Texas or any of the Plains states moved livestock to the major cities for slaughter, they traveled through Kansas. Readily available beef dominated the diet, and the slow-cooked barbecue made use of the tougher cuts of meat. Barbecue became very popular. To prepare barbecue, cooks first place the meat in a marinade or apply a rub. Next, the meat is cooked slowly over a fire made of the wood of choice. The smoke from the fire permeates and flavors the meat. The marinade or rub, slow cooking, and smoke flavoring create the famous barbecue of Kansas City. Today, any meat, poultry, fish, or shellfish is fair game for barbecue.

The possibility of a job in the factories or meatpacking facilities in Omaha or Kansas City drew many immigrants. This led to influence from Italians, Polish, Czechoslovakians, Bohemians, Serbians, and other ethnic groups showing up in the cookery in these cities. With many stockyards and meatpacking houses, Omaha, Nebraska, remains known for high quality beef, particularly steaks. Because of the large number of Italians living in Omaha, a dish of spaghetti typically accompanies a steak dinner here.

In the 1860s, Abilene, Kansas, emerged as the rail junction for the cattle transportation through the Midwest. Cowboys drove herds of cattle from Texas to Abilene, where the cattle waited in cattle yards before being shipped to destinations like Chicago for slaughter.

Wichita, Kansas, claims to be the home of the first hamburger chain in the United States. Still popular today, White Castle Restaurants started in 1921.

In the 1870s, numerous Mennonites from Russia settled in Kansas. They came with two important things: their German and Russian culinary heritage and the seeds of Turkish wheat. The Turkish wheat flourished in Kansas and changed the lives of farmers in this area forever. Because its harvest occurred in the early summer before heat, droughts, and/or insects could ruin the crop, winter wheat had a huge advantage over other varieties.

Because of its location, Oklahoma displays remnants of cookery from the South, Midwest, Southwest, and the Plains. Oklahoma attracted immigrants from Germany, Czechoslovakia, Bohemia, Italy, Poland, and Mexico. In later years, numerous immigrants from Southeast Asia chose to settle there. Also, many African Americans moved to this state. All of these ethnic groups came with recipes from their homeland, which became part of Oklahoma's cookery. Traditional favorite dishes in Oklahoma include fried chicken, chicken-fried steak, pot roast, mashed potatoes, pies, and cobblers.

The warm, dry climate found in Oklahoma proved conducive for growing wheat as well as grazing herds of cattle on the grasslands. In some of the regions with more water, corn, soybeans, spinach, carrots, beans, peanuts, peaches, watermelons, and pecans thrive.

CHARACTERISTICS OF THE CUISINE

Today, the majority of the livestock and grain raised in this country comes from the Plains states and a few of the states in the Midwest, Southwest, and West. Called the breadbasket of the United States, this area is known as the country's heartland.

Hearty and simple describes the food that dominates the states of the Plains. Steaks, stews, and roasts appear frequently. The food reflects the straightforward, hardworking people who settled this area and created farmland from soil covered in tough prairie grasses.

Because the hog was so adaptable, pork played a large role in the diet in the early days. Hogs could survive by foraging in the Plains. They even ate the tough prairie grasses. As a result, the early settlers relied on hogs or game for their meat. After the disappearance of the buffalo, ranchers grazed herds of cattle on the grasslands, and beef became the meat of choice.

Most farmers in the Plains raised chickens for eggs and meat. Fried chicken accompanied by green beans cooked slowly with a ham hock or a piece of country ham served as the usual Sunday dinner.

Although the Plains are known for wheat production, the early pioneers in this region did not experience good results with their wheat crops. Initially, pioneers planted a variety of spring wheat, but its fall harvest rarely survived the frequent summer droughts and/or insect infestations. When the Russian Mennonites planted red winter wheat seeds, the wheat flourished. Planted in the fall and harvested in June, this type of wheat thrives through the winters found in Kansas and Nebraska. Because of the long, harsh winters of North and South Dakota, the winter wheat failed in those states. Instead, settlers planted spring wheat in the spring and reaped it in the fall.

In the absence of wheat during the early years, the pioneers replaced flour with corn and cornmeal. Cornbread, corncakes, and all sorts of dishes containing corn filled the diet of these early settlers. Later, the abundance of wheat allowed the preparation of breads, pancakes, and desserts made with wheat flour.

Root cellars played a significant part in survival over the winter. The settlers planted a variety of winter vegetables such as carrots, potatoes, parsnips, turnips, salsify (called oyster plant), and cabbage in their gardens. They stored any excess produce in their root cellars. Soups, stews, and other dishes prepared from these ingredients filled many meals throughout the winter.

Vegetable gardens yielded a bounty of produce that loaded the tables in the summer. Any excess was dried or canned for use during the winter. A multitude of vegetables such as peas, beans, beets, corn, onions, tomatoes, and much more thrived here. With a bounty

Seen quite frequently in areas where the cowboys herded their cattle, chicken-fried steak is made from round steak or another tough cut of beef. After thoroughly pounding the meat, cooks bread and fry it like fried chicken. Chicken-fried steak, accompanied by mashed potatoes and gravy, still appears on menus at many down-home restaurants throughout the Plains.

of wild greens available for gathering, as well as a variety of greens such as Swiss chard, mustard greens, collard greens, and turnip greens planted in the garden, greens functioned as a staple in the diet of the early settlers in the Plains. Greens grew easily and thrived into the late fall, making them an ideal addition to the vegetable garden. Flavored with a piece of pork or salt pork, one type or a combination of greens often graced the dining table.

Throughout the Plains states, pioneers planted apples, pears, plums, apricots, cherries, peaches, rhubarb, and numerous varieties of berries. Besides drying them for use in the winter, they transformed the produce into jams, pies, cobblers, cakes, and other desserts.

Feasting on fields of clover and wildflowers, bees produce several types of honey throughout this region. Probably the most common type of honey today, clover yields a light colored, sweet honey. On the other hand, wildflower honey is a dark amber color and tastes stronger but less sweet. North and South Dakota, in particular, produce lots of honey.

Indigenous to the Plains, sunflowers, corn, and pumpkins provided the pioneers with sustenance. Acres and acres of sunflowers thrive in North Dakota, South Dakota, and Kansas. The sunflower harvest yields two products: oil that is processed alone or blended with other types of oil and the actual sunflower seeds.

As in the Midwest, starches like potatoes, noodles, and/or dumplings in addition to biscuits or cornbread accompanied most meals in the Plains. The early settlers prepared and baked pies one day each week throughout the seasons. In the absence of fresh or dried fruits, sugar or nut pies filled the larder. The season determined the type of fruit available to fill the pie. Reflecting the culinary heritage, all sorts of Scandinavian and Czech or Bohemian pastries, including saffron cakes, *kolache*, poppy seed cakes, and many kinds of cookies remain popular throughout this region.

Providing fruit for stewing or baking into pies, cobblers, cakes, crunches, and more, the prolific patch of perennial rhubarb came up every spring near many homes. Whether made with rhubarb alone or in combination with strawberries, pie ranked as the favorite rhubarb dessert.

Area	Weather	Topography	Foods
North Dakota Canada to north, Minnesota to east, South Dakota to south, Montana to west	long, harsh winters; hot, dry summers; windy	north: forests, Turtle Mountains east: fertile farmland, Red River Valley, flat central: rolling hills, streams, lakes, valleys west: Badlands, rock formations, buttes, Missouri River, lakes, streams, rivers	beef cattle, hogs, game, pheasants, deer, ducks, catfish, perch, trout, walleye, bass, pike, wheat, barley, rye, sunflowers for oil and seeds, flaxseeds, sugar beets, potatoes, honey
South Dakota North Dakota to north, Minnesota and Iowa to east, Nebraska to south, Montana and Wyoming to west	long, harsh winters; hot, dry summers; windy	east: prairie, hills, fertile farmland, lakes west: Black Hills, forests, canyons, rock formations, Badlands, rolling plains, hills, valleys, buttes north to south: Missouri River	beef cattle, hogs, sausage, sheep, chickens, game, deer, buffalo, elk, pheasant, pike, catfish, trout, walleye, bass, perch, wheat, soybeans, corn, peas, rutabagas, sunflowers, honey
Nebraska South Dakota to north, Iowa and Missouri to east, Kansas and Colorado to south, Wyoming and Colorado to west	cold winters; hot, dry summers; windy	east: fertile farmland, plateau, hills, valleys, Missouri River, rivers, streams west: drier, plains, grasslands, sandy soil, dunes, prairie, streams, some hills, Platt River west to east	cattle, hogs, sausages, game, deer, pheasant, quail, doves, wild turkey, chickens, wheat, corn, soybeans, grains
Kansas Nebraska to north, Missouri to east, Oklahoma to south, Colorado to west	cold winters; hot, dry summers; windy	rolling plains gaining elevation toward the west; grasslands; rivers	cattle, hogs, barbecue, quail, pheasant, doves, wild turkey, chickens, wheat, corn, soybeans
Oklahoma Kansas and Colorado to north, Missouri and Arkansas to east, Texas to south, Texas and New Mexico to west	cool winters; hot, dry summers; dry climate	flat plains, low hills, fertile farmland, grasslands, rivers, valleys, forests, hills, Red River in south, Arkansas River in northeast	cattle, hogs, chickens, wheat, corn, soybeans, spinach, beans, carrots, peanuts, watermelon, peaches, pecans

1. Discuss the role of the buffalo to the Native Americans and the settlers.
2. How does buffalo meat differ from beef?
3. Describe the terrain found by the settlers arriving in the Plains, what they did to the land, and the results of their actions.
4. Why is this area called the Dust Bowl?
5. What were the Homestead Acts and what was their impact on the states of the Plains?
6. Discuss the history of planting wheat in the Plains.

cookie—nickname for the cook who prepared all the meals while traveling with the cowboys herding cattle on the trail

Dutch oven—a cast iron kettle with a lid and with or without three legs to elevate it from the embers of the fire, used by early settlers and cowboys for cooking and baking in an open fire

headcheese—sausage made from all the remaining meat on the head of the pig or cow

jerky—dried and salted preserved meat, prepared from buffalo by Native Americans in the Plains states

kolache—sweet yeast rolls filled with apricot, prune, poppy seeds, or cheese filling; similar to Danish pastry, but made with less butter

lefse—Norwegian traditional thin potato pancake made from mashed potatoes

lutefisk—Norwegian specialty of salted cod soaked in lye or potash

pemmican—dried and salted meat mixed with fat and berries, prepared from buffalo by Native Americans in the Plains states

prairie schooner—covered wagon used by settlers to protect their belongings

rømmegrøt—Norwegian porridge

TOURTIÈRE
Meat and Potato Pie

Tourtière
photo courtesy of CanolaInfo

Of French Canadian origin, tourtière serves as a first course or entrée. In northern regions near Canada, this meat and potato pie graced the Christmas Eve table. The name of this pie derives from "tourte," the pot used to bake this dish.

NUMBER OF SERVINGS: 8
COOKING METHOD:
    Boil, Sauté, Bake
SERVING SIZE:
    about 5¾ oz, wedge ⅛ pie
TOTAL YIELD:
    1 each 9-inch pie

Wine Style: Wide variety—Sauvignon Blanc, Viognier, Rose, medium-bodied red wines, or Zinfandel
Example: Pasque—Valiant Vineyards, Vermillion, SD. This wine achieves an excellent balance between sugar and acidity, with overtones of berries and the pleasing aroma of cut grass.

> **Use recipe of choice, follow recipe for pie dough with pumpkin pie in Chapter 2, or use chicken pot pie crust recipe in Chapter 3.**

INGREDIENTS	WEIGHT	VOLUME
pastry for 2-crust pie		
potato, peeled, cut into 2-inch cubes	6¼ oz	2 medium
butter	½ oz	1 tablespoon
onion, small dice	3¾ oz	¾ cup
garlic, minced	¼ oz	1 large clove
ground beef, pork, and veal, mixed	1 lb	
beef stock or water	8 oz	1 cup
bread crumbs	2¼ oz	½ cup
salt	¼ oz	1 teaspoon
pepper		¼ teaspoon
sage		⅛ teaspoon
nutmeg		⅛ teaspoon
cinnamon		¼ teaspoon
thyme		⅛ teaspoon
savory		¼ teaspoon
oregano		¼ teaspoon
cloves		⅛ teaspoon
parley, minced	¼ oz	1 tablespoon

1. Line pie pan with pastry dough. Chill thoroughly.
2. Place potatoes in saucepan, cover with water, bring to boil, and cook for about 10 minutes, until potatoes are tender.
3. Drain water from potatoes, then mash potatoes. Set aside until needed.
4. Melt butter in pan over medium heat. Sauté onion and garlic for 2 to 3 minutes.
5. Add meat; sauté about 10 minutes, until cooked. Drain off excess fat; return to heat. Add stock, bread crumbs, reserved mashed potatoes, salt, pepper, sage, nutmeg, cinnamon, thyme, savory, oregano, cloves, and parsley. Mix. Correct seasonings. Remove from heat to cool.
6. Position rack in lower portion of oven. Preheat oven to 400 degrees.
7. Place meat mixture in pastry-lined pan. Roll out pastry dough for top crust; place over pie. Flute edges to seal tightly. Make a few slits in the top so steam can escape.
8. Bake for 30 minutes, until golden brown. If edges become too brown, cover loosely with aluminum foil. Cut into wedges and serve.

BIEROCKS

Bierocks

Bierocks make a great luncheon entrée. To prepare an entrée portion, double the size of dough and filling. Roll the 4¹/₂-oz dough into 8- by 12-inch rectangle and fill with 3 oz of filling.

NUMBER OF SERVINGS: 14
COOKING METHOD:
  Sauté, Bake
SERVING SIZE:
  1 bierock containing 1½ oz
    (¼ cup) meat and 2¼ oz
    dough
TOTAL YIELD:
  1 lbs, 7¾ oz meat
  2 lb, 8½ oz dough

Wine Style: Soft, light to medium reds; Grenache; or red hybrids such as Chambourcin
Example: Tailgate Red—Holy-Field Winery, Basehor, KS. Made in an off-dry style, this wine is a blend of St. Vincent, Chambourcin, and Cynthiana grapes.

INGREDIENTS	WEIGHT	VOLUME
DOUGH:		
water, lukewarm, about 106 degrees	2 oz	¼ cup
yeast, dry, granulated		¾ teaspoon
milk	9 oz	1 cup + 2 tablespoons
butter	3 oz	6 tablespoons
sugar	2 oz	¼ cup
salt		¼ teaspoon
egg, beaten	1¾ oz	1 each
egg yolk	¾ oz	1 each
flour, all purpose	1 lb to 1 lb, 2 oz	3¾ to 4 cups
FILLING:		
ground beef	1 lb	
cabbage, cored, large dice	8 oz	2 cups or ⅓ medium head
onion, small dice	5 oz	1 cup
garlic, minced	½ oz	2 large cloves
caraway seeds		1 teaspoon
salt	¼ oz	1 teaspoon
pepper		½ teaspoon
water	as needed for brushing dough	

For Dough:

1. Place water in small bowl, sprinkle yeast over it, mix, and set aside to hydrate until foamy, about 5 minutes.
2. Heat milk and butter in saucepan until butter melts. Transfer to mixing bowl; set aside until lukewarm.
3. Add sugar, salt, egg, and egg yolk to milk mixture. Mix in yeast mixture.
4. Mix in flour, one cup at a time, until soft dough. Knead by hand or mixer with dough hook until smooth and elastic.
5. Cover; let rise for 30 minutes. Punch down dough, cover, and let it rise for another 20 minutes.

For Filling:

1. Brown beef in skillet over medium heat. Drain fat.
2. Add cabbage, onion, garlic, caraway seeds, salt, and pepper. Sauté until cabbage and onions soften, about 5 minutes. Correct seasonings.
3. Remove from heat and reserve.

To Assemble:

1. Grease baking sheets or cover with parchment paper. Preheat oven to 350 degrees.
2. Scale dough into 2¼-oz pieces. Lightly flour table; roll each piece into rectangle about 8- by 6-inches. Brush edges of dough with water.
3. Place 1½ oz (¼ cup) filling in center of dough. Fold top and bottom of dough to meet; seal tightly. Fold sides up and press tightly to seal.
4. Place bierocks, seam side down, on prepared baking sheet. Let rise for 10 to 15 minutes.
5. Bake until brown, about 15 minutes. Serve.

BUFFALO CHILI

NUMBER OF SERVINGS: 13
COOKING METHOD:
  Braise
SERVING SIZE:
  8 oz
TOTAL YIELD:
  6 lbs, 9 oz

Buffalo Chili
photo courtesy of Land O' Lakes, Inc.

INGREDIENTS	WEIGHT	VOLUME
bacon, chopped	4 oz	4 strips
vegetable oil		1 teaspoon
onions, small dice	10 oz	2 cups
garlic, minced	1 oz	4 large cloves
green pepper, small dice	10 oz	2 cups
celery, small dice	4 oz	2/3 cup
buffalo, ground	2 lbs	
dark beer	1 lb	2 cups
tomatoes, canned, chopped	2 lbs	
tomato paste	2¹/₂ oz	¹/₄ cup
water	8 oz	1 cup
thyme		¹/₂ teaspoon
rosemary		¹/₂ teaspoon
bay leaves		2 each
chili powder	1¹/₂ oz	¹/₄ cup
cumin	¹/₄ oz	2 teaspoons
salt	¹/₂ oz	2 teaspoons
black pepper		1 teaspoon
kidney beans, canned, drained	18¹/₂ oz	2 each 15-oz cans

1. Sauté bacon in large pot until crisp, about 5 minutes. Remove bacon from pan; reserve.

2. Add vegetable oil to pot; heat. Add onions and garlic; cook about 3 minutes, until onion begins to soften.

3. Add green pepper and celery; cook another 3 minutes.

4. Add buffalo, stir to break up any large clumps, and cook until browned.

5. Add reserved bacon, beer, tomatoes, tomato paste, water, thyme, rosemary, bay leaves, chili powder, cumin, salt, and pepper. Stir to mix well. Bring to boil, reduce heat, and cook for 1¹/₂ hours, stirring occasionally. Skim any excess fat that floats to top of mixture.

6. Add kidney beans; cook another 10 minutes to thoroughly heat. Correct seasonings. Serve.

VEGETABLE BARLEY SOUP

Vegetable Barley Soup
photo courtesy of Paul Poplis Photography

Use vegetable stock in this recipe to create a vegan dish.

NUMBER OF SERVINGS: 12
COOKING METHOD:
  Boil
SERVING SIZE:
  8 oz
TOTAL YIELD:
  6 lbs, 4½ oz

INGREDIENTS	WEIGHT	VOLUME
butter	1 oz	2 tablespoons
onion, small dice	5 oz	1 medium or 1 cup
carrot, small dice	2½ oz	2 small or ½ cup
celery, small dice	2½ oz	1 stalk or ½ cup
garlic, minced	½ oz	2 large cloves
barley	4 oz	½ cup
chicken or beef stock, warm	4 lbs	2 quarts
turnip, medium dice	4¾ oz	1 cup
potato, medium dice	6½ oz	1 cup
tomatoes, chopped	8¾ oz	1 cup
green beans, stems removed, cut into 1½-inch lengths	8¼ oz	1¼ cups
corn, removed from cob or frozen	4¾ oz	1 cup
peas	4¼ oz	1 cup
parsley, minced	½ oz	3 tablespoons
salt		½ teaspoon
pepper		¼ teaspoon

1. Melt butter in large pot. Add onion, carrot, celery, garlic, and barley. Cook, stirring occasionally, about 7 minutes, until vegetables soften.

2. Add stock, cover and bring to boil, reduce heat, and simmer for 35 minutes.

3. Add turnip, potato, tomatoes, green beans, and corn if using fresh. Cover and simmer another 30 minutes. If using frozen corn, cook 15 minutes, then add frozen corn, cover, and return to simmer for additional 15 minutes.

4. Add peas, parsley, salt, and pepper. Heat thoroughly. Correct seasonings. Serve.

PICKLED BEETS

Recipes abound for pickled beets, and the spices included in the recipe reflect its ethnic origin. While some contain little sugar, others taste intensely sweet and sour. Also, while some recipes include lots of spices, others have none.

NUMBER OF SERVINGS: 9
COOKING METHOD:
  Boil
SERVING SIZE:
  4 oz, 6 small beets
TOTAL YIELD:
  4 lbs, 7½ oz

Pickled Beets
photo by Ian O'Leary © Dorling Kindersley

INGREDIENTS	WEIGHT	VOLUME
cider vinegar	1 lb	2 cups
water or juice from boiling beets	8 oz	1 cup
sugar	15 oz	2 cups
salt		½ teaspoon
cloves, whole	¼ oz	1 teaspoon
allspice	¼ oz	1 teaspoon
cinnamon	¼ oz	1 teaspoon
peppercorns	¼ oz	1 teaspoon
onions, sliced thinly	5 oz	2 small or 1 medium
beets, cooked, drained, skins removed after cooking, if fresh	2 lb, 6 oz	56 small or 4 each 15-oz cans

1. Combine vinegar, water, sugar, salt, cloves, allspice, cinnamon, peppercorns, and onions in saucepan.
2. Bring to boil; reduce heat and simmer until onions are tender, about 5 to 10 minutes.
3. Place beets in jar or nonreactive bowl. Pour vinegar mixture over beets.
4. Cool, cover, and refrigerate at least overnight. Serve as salad, in combination with other salads, as a side dish, as accompaniment to sandwich, or as desired.

CHUCKWAGON STEW

Chuckwagon Stew

NUMBER OF SERVINGS: 8
COOKING METHOD:
 Braise
SERVING SIZE:
 11 oz
TOTAL YIELD:
 5 lbs, 14¼ oz

Wine Style: Medium- to full-bodied dry red wines, Cabernet Sauvignon, Shiraz, or Zinfandel
Example: Cabernet Sauvignon—Smoky Hill Vineyards and Winery, Salina, KS. This wine is a deep purple color with up-front berry flavor and intense tannins that give way to a smooth, spicy finish.

INGREDIENTS	WEIGHT	VOLUME
bacon, chopped	2½ oz	2 strips
flour, all purpose	¾ oz	3 tablespoons
salt	¼ oz	1 teaspoon
pepper		½ teaspoon
thyme		1 teaspoon
oregano		1 teaspoon
stew beef, chuck or bottom round, 1½-inch cubes, washed, dried	2 lbs	
oil	as needed	
onion, small dice	4 oz	¾ cup
garlic, minced	¼ oz	2 cloves
strong coffee	12 oz	1½ cups
catsup	2¼ oz	3 tablespoons
molasses	1½ oz	2 tablespoons
Worcestershire sauce	1 oz	2 tablespoons
beer	8 oz	1 cup
onions, small boiling, peeled	10¼ oz	12 each
water	10 oz	1¼ cups
red potatoes, scrubbed, quartered	1 lb, 4 oz	4 medium
carrots, peeled, cut into 1½-inch lengths	7 oz	4 medium
corn kernels	5 oz	1 cup
flour, all purpose	¾ oz	3 tablespoons

1. Cook bacon in heavy pot over medium heat until crisp. Remove bacon, leaving fat in pot; reserve bacon pieces.

2. Mix ¾ oz (3 tablespoons) flour, salt, pepper, thyme, and oregano in bowl. Coat meat with flour mixture.

3. Brown beef in batches in pot with bacon fat over medium heat. Add oil as necessary to avoid sticking.

4. Remove meat as it browns and reserve with bacon.

5. Adding oil if necessary, add onion and garlic, then sauté for 2 to 3 minutes until onion begins to soften.

6. Stir in coffee, catsup, molasses, Worcestershire sauce, and beer. Deglaze by scraping all bits from bottom of pan.

7. Add reserved beef and bacon, bring to boil, reduce heat, and simmer for 1 hour, stirring occasionally.

8. Add boiling onions and 8 oz (1 cup) water. Cover and simmer 20 to 30 minutes, until onions begin to soften. Add potatoes and carrots; simmer another 30 minutes until tender. Add corn.

9. Blend ¾ oz (3 tablespoons) flour with 2 oz (¼ cup) water; stir until smooth. Add this to stew. Cook and stir until mixture thickens. Correct seasonings. Serve accompanied by biscuits.

CHICKEN-FRIED STEAK WITH CREAM GRAVY

Chicken-Fried Steak

NUMBER OF SERVINGS: 12
COOKING METHOD:
   Fry
Serving Size:
   6 oz
Total Yield:
   12 each 6-oz portions
   Gravy: 1 lb, 1¼ oz or 2 cups

Wine Style: Medium- to full-bodied reds, Cabernet Sauvignon, Merlot, or Zinfandel
Example: Rodeo Red—Cabin Creek Vineyard and Winery, Big Cabin, OK. This wine is a big, full-bodied Cabernet with a smooth finish.

INGREDIENTS	WEIGHT	VOLUME
flour, all purpose	9 oz	2 cups
salt	½ oz	2 teaspoons
pepper		1 teaspoon
eggs	6¾ oz	4 each
milk	2 oz	¼ cup
fat, as needed for frying	at least 1 lb	at least 2 cups
round steak, ½ inch thick, cut into 6-oz portions, then pounded until ¼ inch thick	4 lbs, 8 oz	12 each 6-oz portions
GRAVY:		
whole milk	1 lb, 2 oz	2¼ cups
salt		½ teaspoon
pepper		¼ teaspoon
hot pepper sauce		½ teaspoon

For Meat:

1. Combine flour, salt, and pepper on plate or shallow bowl; set aside. Beat eggs with milk in bowl; set aside until needed.
2. Heat fat in large skillet until hot, about 350 degrees.
3. Dredge meat in flour mixture, then dip meat into egg wash, and dredge again with flour. Continue until all meat is coated.
4. Fry meat in fat until lightly brown on both sides.
5. Remove meat from skillet; keep warm in low oven.

For Gravy:

1. Pour off all fat, leaving brown bits in skillet.
2. Deglaze pan with milk, scraping all brown bits into gravy. Let thicken slightly.
3. Season with salt, pepper, and hot pepper sauce. Correct seasonings. Serve over meat accompanied by mashed potatoes.

CHICKEN AND DUMPLINGS

Chicken and Dumplings

If desired, instead of rolling dumpling dough, drop dough from a teaspoon into the simmering stock. Dropped dumplings need to cook about 15 minutes.

NUMBER OF SERVINGS: 15
COOKING METHOD:
   Boil
SERVING SIZE:
   11 oz
TOTAL YIELD:
   10 lbs, 15½ oz

Wine Style: Soft, dry, fruity whites; Vignoles; Pinot Gris; or Pinot Blanc
Example: Nebraska White—James Arthur Vineyards and Winery, Raymond, NE. This wine is a blend of Vignoles, Lacrosse, and Seyval Blanc grapes with a crisp, dry flavor.

INGREDIENTS	WEIGHT	VOLUME
chicken, fryer, washed, cut into pieces	5 lb, 8 oz	2 each
onion, large dice	10 oz	2 medium or 2 cups
celery, large dice	10 oz	4 stalks or 2 cups
carrots, peeled, sliced 1/2 inch thick	14 oz	4 each or 2 2/3 cups
salt	1/2 oz	2 teaspoons
pepper		1 teaspoon
bay leaves		2 each
water	about 5 lbs	about 10 cups
water	as needed to form paste	
flour, all purpose	4 1/2 oz	1 cup
DUMPLINGS:		
flour, all purpose	1 lb, 1/2 oz	4 cups
baking soda	1/4 oz	1 teaspoon
salt	1/4 oz	1 teaspoon
butter, cold, cut into pieces	3 oz	6 tablespoons
buttermilk	12 oz	1 1/2 cups

1. Place chicken, onion, celery, carrots, salt, pepper, and bay leaves in large pot. Cover with water (about 5 lbs or 10 cups).
2. Bring to boil, reduce heat, cover, and simmer for 1 1/2 to 2 hours to make chicken stock.
3. Remove chicken from pot, remove meat from bones, discard skin and bones of chicken, and cut meat into bite-sized pieces. Reserve.
4. Skim fat and any foam from top of stock. Mix just enough water into 4 1/2 oz (1 cup) flour to make paste.
5. Bring stock containing vegetables to simmer. Slowly whisk in flour slurry (paste). Return chicken to pot. Correct seasonings.

To Make Dumplings:

1. Combine flour, baking soda, and salt in bowl.
2. With pastry blender, two knives, or food processor, cut in butter until size of peas.
3. Quickly stir in buttermilk just to incorporate.
4. Roll dough to 1/4-inch thick. Cut into 3- by 1/2-inch strips.

To Finish:

1. Drop dumplings into simmering stock. Cover.
2. Cook 8 to 10 minutes, until dumplings are cooked.

PARMESAN AND HERB CRUSTED PERCH

Parmesan and Herb Crusted Perch

NUMBER OF SERVINGS: 9
COOKING METHOD:
  Broil
SERVING SIZE:
  5 oz
TOTAL YIELD:
  3 lbs, 1/2 oz

Wine Style: Light- to medium-bodied Riesling, Chardonnay, or Rose

Example: Reserve Chardonnay—Tidal School Vineyards, Drumright, OK. This wine has subtle citrus and butter flavors with a classic oak finish.

INGREDIENTS	WEIGHT	VOLUME
Parmesan cheese, grated	1½ oz	6 tablespoons
mayonnaise	7 oz	⅔ cup
horseradish	2½ oz	¼ cup
Dijon mustard	1 oz	2 tablespoons
dill	¼ oz	2 teaspoons
basil	¼ oz	2 teaspoons
oregano		1 teaspoon
paprika		1 teaspoon
pepper		½ teaspoon
perch fillets, washed	2 lb, 8 oz	

GARNISH:

lemon wedges

1. Pan-spray baking sheet. Place fish on baking sheet. Adjust rack about 6 inches from heat source. Preheat broiler.
2. Combine Parmesan cheese, mayonnaise, horseradish, mustard, dill, basil, oregano, paprika, and pepper. Spread cheese mixture evenly over fish.
3. Broil for about 10 minutes per inch of thickness of fish, until done.
4. Serve immediately, garnished with lemon.

CREAMED CABBAGE

NUMBER OF SERVINGS: 10
COOKING METHOD:
  Boil, Bake
SERVING SIZE:
  4 oz
TOTAL YIELD:
  2 lbs, 10¼ oz

INGREDIENTS	WEIGHT	VOLUME
cabbage, cored, grated	1 lb, 4 oz	1 each small
green pepper, small dice	5¾ oz	1 each small
water	1 lb	2 cups
butter	1½ oz	3 tablespoons
flour, all purpose	¾ oz	3 tablespoons
milk, hot	4 oz	½ cup
nutmeg		¼ teaspoon
salt	¼ oz	1 teaspoon
white pepper		½ teaspoon
cheddar cheese, grated	2 oz	½ cup
bread crumbs, toasted	2¼ oz	½ cup

1. Place cabbage, green pepper, and water in pot, bring to boil, simmer for 5 minutes, drain, and reserve. Preheat oven to 350 degrees.
2. Melt butter in same pot over low heat, whisk in flour, and continue whisking for 2 to 3 minutes, until white *roux*.
3. Slowly whisk in milk, a little at a time. Continue whisking and cooking until lightly thickened, about 3 to 5 minutes.
4. Whisk in nutmeg, salt, pepper, and 1 oz (¼ cup) cheese.
5. Add reserved cabbage mixture; cook for 5 minutes. Correct seasonings.
6. Transfer to ovenproof dish. Top with remaining 1 oz (¼ cup) cheese and bread crumbs.
7. Bake, uncovered, for 5 minutes, until bubbling and top is lightly browned. Serve immediately.

GLAZED TURNIPS

NUMBER OF SERVINGS: 9
COOKING METHOD:
   Boil, Sauté
SERVING SIZE:
   4 oz
TOTAL YIELD:
   2 lbs, 6 oz

INGREDIENTS	WEIGHT	VOLUME
turnips, peeled, cut into 1/2-inch slices	3 lbs	
butter	3 oz	6 tablespoons
sugar	1 1/2 oz	3 tablespoons
onion, small dice	8 1/4 oz	2 medium
salt		1 1/2 teaspoons
pepper		3/4 teaspoon

1. Steam or parboil turnips until almost half tender, about 4 minutes.
2. Melt butter with sugar in skillet over medium-high heat.
3. Add turnips and onions. Stir frequently, reduce heat to medium-low, and allow them to caramelize.
4. Cook until tender and lightly browned. Season with salt and pepper.
5. Correct seasonings; serve immediately.

CORN PUDDING

If fresh corn is not in season, substitute frozen corn. If desired, increase sugar to 2 teaspoons for frozen corn.

NUMBER OF SERVINGS: 8
COOKING METHOD:
   Bake
SERVING SIZE:
   4 oz
TOTAL YIELD:
   2 lbs, 1 oz

Corn Pudding
photo © Dorling Kindersley

INGREDIENTS	WEIGHT	VOLUME
corn, fresh, removed from cob, scraping to obtain milk from cob	1 lb, 4 3/4 oz	3 1/3 cups
eggs, beaten	3 1/2 oz	2 each
butter, melted	1 oz	2 tablespoons
milk	8 oz	1 cup
flour, all purpose		1 1/2 teaspoons
sugar		1 teaspoon
salt	1/4 oz	1 teaspoon
pepper		1/4 teaspoon
TOPPING:		
butter, unsalted, melted	1 oz	2 tablespoons
bread crumbs	2 oz	1/2 cup

1. Pan-spray 2-quart ovenproof dish. Preheat oven to 350 degrees.
2. Combine corn, eggs, 1 oz (2 tablespoons) melted butter, milk, flour, sugar, salt, and pepper in bowl. Correct seasonings.
3. Pour into prepared dish.

For Topping:

1. Mix 1 oz (2 tablespoons) melted butter and bread crumbs together.
2. Sprinkle over corn mixture. Bake for about 45 minutes, until firm.
3. Remove from oven; serve immediately.

SCALLOPED POTATOES

Scalloped Potatoes
photo by Clive Streeter © Dorling
Kindersley

NUMBER OF SERVINGS: 9
COOKING METHOD:
  Bake
SERVING SIZE:
  4 oz
TOTAL YIELD:
  2 lbs, 4 oz

INGREDIENTS	WEIGHT	VOLUME
potatoes, peeled, sliced 1/8 inch thick	2 lb, 15 oz	8 medium
cheddar cheese, grated	10 oz	3 cups
onion, minced	8 1/2 oz	1 1/2 cups
salt	1/4 oz	1 teaspoon
black pepper		1/2 teaspoon
butter, melted	2 oz	4 tablespoons, 1/2 stick, or 1/4 cup
half-and-half	1 lb	2 cups
paprika	for sprinkling	

1. Pan-spray ovenproof 3-qt dish. Preheat oven to 350 degrees.
2. Place thin layer potatoes on bottom of dish. Top with light sprinkling of cheese, onion, salt, and pepper. Drizzle lightly with butter.
3. Repeat layers until all ingredients are used except top layer of cheese.
4. Pour half-and-half over potatoes in dish. Top with last layer of cheese, sprinkle top with paprika, cover, and bake for 30 minutes.
5. Uncover; continue cooking 1 hour, 30 minutes to 1 hour, 45 minutes, until potatoes are tender, liquid is bubbling, and top is golden brown. Serve.

BUTTERMILK BISCUITS

Ball of Biscuit Dough
photo by David Murray © Dorling
Kindersley

Kneading Biscuit Dough
photo by David Murray © Dorling
Kindersley

Patting Dough for Biscuits
photo by David Murray © Dorling
Kindersley

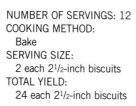

NUMBER OF SERVINGS: 12
COOKING METHOD:
  Bake
SERVING SIZE:
  2 each 2½-inch biscuits
TOTAL YIELD:
  24 each 2½-inch biscuits

Cutting Biscuits from Dough
photo by David Murray © Dorling Kindersley

Buttermilk Biscuits
photo courtesy of Land O' Lakes, Inc.

INGREDIENTS	WEIGHT	VOLUME
flour, all purpose, sifted	14 oz	3½ cups
baking powder	¾ oz	1 tablespoon + 1 teaspoon
baking soda	¼ oz	1 teaspoon
salt	¼ oz	1 teaspoon
sugar	¼ oz	2 teaspoons
butter, unsalted, cold, cut into pieces	6 oz	12 tablespoons or 1½ sticks
buttermilk	12 oz	1½ cups
flour, all purpose	as needed	

1. Place oven rack in center of oven. Preheat oven to 450 degrees.

2. Place flour, baking powder, baking soda, salt, and sugar in bowl of food processor with steel knife blade. Pulse a few times to mix. Without food processor, place mixture in bowl and mix.

3. Place cold butter pieces on top of flour mixture. Pulse to mix until size of peas. Without food processor, cut butter into flour mixture using 2 knives or pastry cutter until size of peas.

4. With machine running, pour buttermilk through feed tube. Pulse until mixed and dough comes together. Without food processor, make well in center of mixture, pour in buttermilk, and stir with fork until just combined.

5. Remove from processor. Place on lightly floured surface. Knead for about 30 seconds.

6. Pat into disk about ½ inch thick. Cut out using 2½-inch biscuit cutter or desired size.

7. Place on baking sheet; bake until golden brown, about 10 to 12 minutes. Serve with butter.

KOLACHE WITH PRUNE FILLING

Joining Corners of Kolache
photo by Jerry Young © Dorling Kindersley

These sweet rolls come from the Bohemian or Czechoslovakian heritage of many who settled in the Plains states. While prunes or apricots usually fill these pastries, some prefer a cottage cheese stuffing or other fillings.

Prepare filling while dough rises.

COOKING METHOD:
  Boil, Bake
TOTAL YIELD:
  24 each *kolache*
  2 lbs, 7½ oz dough
  1 lb, 3 oz filling

INGREDIENTS	WEIGHT	VOLUME
PRUNE FILLING:		
prunes, pitted	15 oz	
water	8 oz	1 cup
lemon rind, grated	¼ oz	2 teaspoons
sugar	½ oz	1 tablespoon
cinnamon		¼ teaspoon
nutmeg		¼ teaspoon
yeast, dry	¾ oz	1½ tablespoons
water, warm	4 oz	½ cup
milk	4 oz	½ cup
sugar	4 oz	½ cup
salt		½ teaspoon
butter	6 oz	¾ cup or 1½ sticks
flour, all purpose	1 lb, 4½ oz to 1 lb, 7½ oz	4 to 4½ cups
egg yolks	2¾ oz	4 each
lemon rind, grated		1 teaspoon
butter, melted for brushing *kolache* before baking		
GLAZE OPTIONAL:		
confectioners' sugar	4 oz	1 cup
lemon juice	½ oz	1 tablespoon
water		about 1 teaspoon

For Filling:

1. Place prunes and water in nonreactive pan. Stirring often, cook over medium heat until very soft, about 10 to 15 minutes. Remove from heat, add lemon rind and sugar, and cool slightly.

2. Place prunes in bowl of food processor fitted with knife blade. Add cinnamon and nutmeg; pulse until smooth puree.

For *Kolache*:

1. Sprinkle yeast over warm water in nonreactive bowl; let sit until hydrated and foamy.

2. Bring milk to boil over medium heat. Remove from heat; add sugar, salt, and butter. Stir to mix thoroughly until butter is almost melted. Set aside to cool until barely lukewarm.

3. Place 10¼ oz (2 cups flour) flour in mixing bowl; make well in center. Pour in yeast mixture, egg yolks, lemon rind, and milk mixture.

4. Beat with flat beater, if available, at medium speed for 5 minutes.

5. Stir in remaining 10¼ oz (2 cups flour), as needed to form soft dough. Knead about one minute.

6. Place in bowl, cover well with plastic wrap and/or towel, and let rise in warm place until doubled, about 1 to 1½ hours. Meanwhile, prepare filling.

7. Punch down, knead about 3 to 5 minutes. Divide dough in half. Cover one half well while working with other.

8. Briefly knead one of the halves until smooth; roll to ¼-inch thickness. Cut into 12 squares.

9. Place about ¾ oz (1 tablespoon) filling in center of square. Bring corners of dough together and pinch to seal. *Filling will show through the seams in dough.*

10. Cover and let rise until puffy, about 45 minutes. Meanwhile, preheat oven to 350 degrees.

11. Brush with melted butter. Bake for 12 to 15 minutes, until beginning to brown. Cool on rack.

12. If desired, drizzle with glaze.

(Continued)

Alternate Method for Forming *Kolache*:

1. After dough has risen (step 6), divide dough in half. Cover one half well while working with other. Briefly knead one of the halves until smooth; divide into 12 equal balls.

2. Flatten each ball into disk, place on baking sheet, cover, and let rise until puffy, about 45 minutes. Meanwhile, preheat oven to 350 degrees.

3. Make indentation in center of each disk; place ³/₄ oz (1 tablespoon) filling in indentation.

4. Brush with melted butter. Bake for 12 to 15 minutes, until beginning to brown. Cool on rack.

5. If desired, drizzle with glaze.

For Glaze:

1. Mix confectioners' sugar and lemon juice. Add water, a few drops at a time, until spreading consistency.

2. Let glaze rest for 5 to 10 minutes.

3. With fork, drizzle glaze on top of kolache.

RHUBARB PIE

Placing Butter over Rhubarb Filling
photo by David Murray © Dorling Kindersley

Cutting Lattice Strips
photo by David Murray © Dorling Kindersley

Placing Lattice Strips on Pie
photo by David Murray © Dorling Kindersley

Fluting Dough
photo by David Murray © Dorling Kindersley

Many call this rhubarb cream pie since the eggs cause a creamier filling. If desired, place a solid top crust over the rhubarb filling instead of topping it with a lattice crust.

The range of sugar is provided since some prefer a sweeter rhubarb pie than others.

NUMBER OF SERVINGS: 8
COOKING METHOD:
  Bake
SERVING SIZE:
  ¹/₈ pie
TOTAL YIELD:
  1 each 9-inch pie

INGREDIENTS	WEIGHT	VOLUME
pie dough	about 12 oz	
rhubarb, sliced 1/2-inch	1 lb, 61/4 oz	5 cups
sugar	131/4 to 141/4 oz	13/4 to 2 cups
flour, all purpose	11/4 oz	1/4 cup
salt		1/4 teaspoon
nutmeg		1/2 teaspoon
orange rind, grated	1/4 oz	2 teaspoons
eggs	31/2 oz	2 each
butter, unsalted	11/2 oz	3 tablespoons

To Roll Dough:

1. Place ball of dough on table. With rolling pin, hit ball to flatten into disk about one inch thick. Lightly flour table and rolling pin, if needed.

2. Roll dough from middle to sides, releasing dough from table with icing spatula every few rolls. Turn dough one-quarter turn to keep dough even and roll into circle until desired thickness.

3. Release from table with spatula. Fold gently in half. Lift and move dough to pan. Position dough over pan so it covers pan when unfolded.

4. Press dough into pan. Cut dough flush with top outside edge of pan or leave overhang of dough if fluting edge.

5. Chill for one hour before baking, if possible. While chilling, prepare filling.

To Finish Pie:

1. Mix rhubarb, sugar, flour, salt, nutmeg, orange rind, and eggs in bowl. Set aside at least 10 minutes or until needed.

2. Meanwhile, place oven rack in bottom half of oven. Preheat oven to 425 degrees.

3. Place filling into pie pan lined with chilled dough. Distribute small pieces of butter over filling.

4. Roll out remaining dough. Cut into strips about 1/2 inch wide for lattice top.

5. Place strips across top of pie about 3/4 inch apart. Then rotate pie one-quarter turn and lay strips across top going in the opposite direction, or lay them at an angle across the bottom strips.

6. Seal edges of lattice strips with bottom crust by pressing evenly around edge of pie with the tines of a fork. If overhang of dough was left, flute edges.

7. Bake in preheated oven for 10 minutes. Reduce heat to 350 degrees and bake another 30 to 40 minutes, until crust is golden brown and filling bubbles.

8. Remove from oven; cool on rack to room temperature. Serve.

BUTTERMILK POUNDCAKE

Buttermilk Poundcake
photo courtesy of Land O' Lakes, Inc.

Serve this cake plain or with fresh berries and/or ice cream.

This portion is fairly large, but the cake is not too rich so the portion size works for a dessert served in a restaurant. Depending on the type of food service establishment, a smaller portion might be desired.

NUMBER OF SERVINGS: 10
COOKING METHOD:
  Bake
SERVING SIZE:
  3 each 1-inch slices
TOTAL YIELD:
  1 each 10-inch cake

INGREDIENTS	WEIGHT	VOLUME
PAN PREPARATION:		
pan spray or butter		
flour		
CAKE:		
flour, all purpose, unsifted	8½ oz	2 cups
baking powder	¼ oz	1½ teaspoons
baking soda		¼ teaspoon
salt		½ teaspoon
mace		¼ teaspoon
butter, unsalted, softened	8 oz	1 cup or 2 sticks
sugar	14¼ oz	2 cups
eggs	6¾ oz	4 each
buttermilk	5 oz	⅔ cup
vanilla		1 teaspoon
GARNISH:		
confectioners' sugar, sifted		

1. Pan-spray or grease 10-inch tube pan or Bundt pan. Dust lightly with flour, shaking out any excess. Position rack in center of oven. Preheat oven to 350 degrees.

2. Sift together flour, baking powder, baking soda, salt, and mace. Set aside until needed.

3. Cream butter and sugar in mixer until light and fluffy using flat beater, if available.

4. Add egg yolks, one at a time, beating well after each addition. Reserve whites in separate bowl.

5. Add ⅓ of flour mixture; beat on lowest speed just to incorporate.

6. Add half of buttermilk and vanilla; mix just to incorporate.

7. Repeat procedure with remaining ingredients: half of remaining flour, remaining buttermilk, then remaining flour. After each addition, mix just to incorporate. *Over-mixing the batter could result in tough batter or uneven texture.*

8. Pour into prepared pan; smooth top. Bake for 45 to 55 minutes, until top of cake springs back when gently touched and knife inserted into cake comes out clean.

9. Remove from oven, let rest in pan 4 or 5 minutes, then invert on wire rack. Cool completely. Dust top with sifted confectioners' sugar. Serve.

9

Southwestern States

OBJECTIVES

By the end of this chapter, you will be able to

- Discuss the role of the Native Americans, Spanish, and Mexicans in the development of the cuisine of the Southwest
- Discuss the impact of the railroad on the Southwest and how that affected the cookery
- Explain the effects of topography and climate on the cookery of the Southwest
- Identify food products prevalent in the Southwest
- Prepare a variety of dishes indicative of the cuisine of the Southwest

States included in the Southwest:
- Texas
- New Mexico
- Arizona

HISTORY

The Anasazi tribe, whose name means "Ancient Ones," inhabited the Colorado Plateau until the 1400s. At that time, they divided into numerous individual tribes including Zuñi, Hopi, and Papago. Called cliff dwellers, the Anasazi lived in caves in the cliffs as well as in adobe homes they built near those cliffs. They actually constructed some of the adobe homes against canyon walls. Some of those adobe buildings connected to caves, and the Anasazi used the caves as rooms. Forerunners of the high-rise building, some of their living quarters stood four stories tall.

Known as innovative people, the Anasazi planted crops, irrigated their land, hunted game, gathered wild plants and herbs, and cooked foods in woven baskets and pottery that they created. As early as AD 500, they planted corn, beans, and squash together. The large leaves of the squash plant shaded the area, helping to retain moisture in the soil while the corn and bean seeds germinated. When all three plants grew, the later-germinating beans climbed the corn stalk for support, and the corn plant provided some shade for the squash.

The Anasazi later became the Pueblos. Meanwhile, the Athabascans, who lived in southwestern, western, and northern Arizona, divided into the Apache and Navajo tribes. Another tribe that inhabited southern Arizona, the Pimas, irrigated their lands from the Gila and Salt Rivers.

The culinary history of the Southwest combines influences from the Native Americans, the Spanish, and the Mexicans. About 50 years before the English landed in Jamestown, the Spanish entered the Southwest from Mexico. Since the majority of these settlers went to New Mexico, that state exhibits much stronger Spanish influence than Arizona. In New Mexico, the Spanish found oases where crops could grow. Because they discovered more arid land in Arizona, most of the Spanish chose to settle in New Mexico.

Introducing both Mexican and Spanish foods to the Southwest, the Spanish brought Mexican foods like tortillas, wheat, chili peppers, tomatoes, *tomatillos*, avocados, squash, potatoes, cinnamon, and chocolate. From their own heritage, the Spanish contributed olives, garlic, rice, lamb, pork, and the spicy sausage *chorizo*, as well as fruits such as peaches, apricots, various citrus fruits, and grapes for making wine. In addition to Mexican and Spanish contributions, the Native American triumvirate of corn, beans, and squash became an important part of the cookery of the Southwest. The culinary mingling of the Spanish, Mexicans, and Native Americans plus the culinary heritage of later immigrants moving into the area created the cuisine of the Southwest.

Evidence shows Native Americans inhabited parts of New Mexico 10,000 years ago. More than 2,000 years ago, the Anasazi lived in the Four Corners region, a large area of high plateau where four states—Arizona, New Mexico, Colorado, and Utah—join. The Anasazi built and lived in villages of adobe huts called pueblos. Rather than relying solely on hunting, they planted gardens and gathered wild foods. The Anasazi planted beans, corn, squash, and other vegetables; gathered indigenous foods such as cacti, berries, seeds, nuts, and greens; and hunted animals like rabbit, turkey, and deer. When the Anasazi killed a deer, a communal feast took place. Considered the most advanced of all the Native Americans, the Anasazi developed methods of irrigation for their crops. They also constructed dwellings where many people lived that resemble apartment buildings.

Corn served as a mainstay in the Anasazi diet, and they developed and planted seven different varieties of corn in their gardens. Besides providing food, corn assumed a paramount role in the spiritual part of their lives. For example, to thank the gods for their bounty, they sprinkled cornmeal over a slain deer. As a symbol of fertility and to bless and protect their home, a cornstalk hung at the doorway to the house. Corn even appeared in the traditional Pueblo wedding ceremony. Besides filling a major part of the Native American diet, corn still plays a large role in the cuisine of the Southwest.

Anthropologists believe Native Americans in the Southwest began cultivating beans in the fifth century. Although they developed many varieties, the most important were red, white, blue, yellow, black, and pinto. To the Native Americans, these six types represented directions: north, south, east, west, zenith (above), and nadir (below).

In addition to corn and beans, the Native Americans consumed numerous types of squash, pumpkins, peas, pine nuts, wild fruits and berries, fish, and all sorts of animals, including turkey, deer, elk, rabbit, sheep, and buffalo. To prepare for the winter, they dried any excess produce and meat.

In 1540, Spanish explorer Francisco Coronado entered the Southwest from Mexico. The Spanish brought sheep, cattle, and horses to the area. Soon, Spanish priests came and began developing outposts in the fertile valley around the Rio Grande River. They built missions, irrigated to transform the barren land into fertile farmland, raised animals as well as crops of fruits and vegetables, and converted many of the Native Americans to Catholicism. Before long, mutton, lamb, beef, and wheat became an important part of the cuisine here. In 1598, the Spanish gained control over the Pueblos. Spanish rule lasted more than 75 years until the Pueblos revolted in 1680.

Also dwelling in the Southwest, Navajos survived by hunting and trapping. The Navajos inhabiting the mountains hunted elk, mountain lion, deer, and mountain sheep, while those living at lower elevations sought deer, rabbit, fox, wild turkey, and antelope. The Pueblos taught the Navajos about agriculture and gardening.

In 1775, the Spanish settled in the area now known as Tucson, Arizona. Before long, the Mexican, Spanish, and Native American heritages merged, and the town of Tucson developed its own culinary identity.

Spain ruled Texas from the early 1500s until 1821. The Mexicans then gained control for a short time until Texas achieved independence in 1836. At that time, the eastern portion of Texas consisted of seaports and plantations, while the western section remained undeveloped. Many Southerners relocated to Texas in the early 1800s. Moving from Alabama and Mississippi, some owners of cotton plantations came with their slaves and established plantations in the eastern portion of Texas. Settled by Moses Austin and his son Stephen in 1839 along the Colorado River, Austin became the capital of Texas.

When the Mexican American War ended in 1848, many settlers made their way to the Southwest. While some passed through the Southwest on their way to California in search of gold, others came looking for available land and a better life. They brought cattle, but cattle required constant herding to find enough grazing in this area of sparse grasslands. As a result, cowboys found work here. They tended the herds and moved them to the stockyards for slaughtering.

Actually, jobs herding cattle from Texas to Kansas lasted only about 20 years, from 1865 to 1885. After that time, the completed railroad eliminated the need for the cowboys to transport the cattle on the trail. During those 20 years, cowboys handled a tough job. They moved as many as 3,000 head of cattle on the 700-mile long trails, traveling only 10 or 15 miles each day. The journey from Texas to Kansas took several months. Known as the "chuck wagon," one of the wagons served as a portable kitchen. The chuck wagon contained cabinets for storing the foods as well as a board that unfolded to function as a worktable for the cook. Typical foods prepared on the trail included fried or barbecued meat, game, fish, beans, chili, a variety of cornmeal dishes, hash brown potatoes, and biscuits.

With the invention of barbed wire in the 1870s, the cowboys' work changed drastically. Repairing fences and caring for sick animals replaced rounding up stray cattle. Ranchers began breeding cattle to create superior breeds around this time. They worked to develop disease-resistant varieties and cattle that could withstand drought better. When the railroad finally crossed Texas in the 1880s, two benefits occurred: the cattle drives ceased and more settlers and immigrants moved to Texas. At the beginning of the twentieth century, jobs in the gas and oil industries enticed more people to move to Texas.

> Cowboys learned most of their skills like riding and roping cattle from the Mexican *vaqueros*. The cowboys even adopted the attire of the *vaqueros*, chaps and a wide-brimmed hat.

TOPOGRAPHY AND CLIMATE

Sharing a border with Mexico, the Southwest exhibits strong Mexican influence on its cookery. Besides flavoring many foods with chili peppers and cumin, residents of the Southwest serve tamales, burritos, enchiladas, *chiles rellenos*, beans, and many other Mexican dishes.

Mountains, desert, semiarid land, plains, mesas, canyons, and gorges characterize much of the terrain of the Southwest. Although dramatic and starkly beautiful, the topography created difficult travel and intense isolation for the early settlers throughout this region. While the vegetation in many arid areas consisted of cacti, yucca, sagebrush, and mesquite, other areas contained water. The land with access to water supported diverse agriculture. Trout and bass swam in the rivers, streams, and lakes found in inland areas of the Southwest. Although the Pueblos were a friendly group and helped the early settlers survive, other Native Americans resented the white man's intrusion on their land. As a result, settlers in some areas fought continual battles with Native Americans.

For the settlers, water or the lack of it posed a major problem. After rebuilding canals that ancient Native American tribes built long ago, they irrigated a little of the land. Unfortunately, the irrigation efforts proved too meager to make a significant difference. Dry, cracked streams and riverbeds filled and overflowed in the spring when the snow melted in the mountains. Later, those streams and rivers became dry again. Ultimately, water ranked as the critical factor in crop production throughout much of the Southwest until the government began building dams to control the water in the 1930s. With the building of dams and the subsequent ability to irrigate, growing crops became much easier as well as more reliable. This enticed many people to move to the previously arid areas of the Southwest. In addition to the usual crops of corn, beans, squash, chilies, and tomatoes, the new residents planted a multitude of fruits and vegetables.

Oklahoma lies to the north of Texas; the Gulf of Mexico, Louisiana, Arkansas, and Oklahoma lie on the east; Mexico neighbors on the south; and New Mexico and Mexico are situated to the west. Although the expansive plains were too arid for planting crops, they proved excellent for grazing livestock on the grasses that flourished there. On the mountains and arid plains without enough grasses to support cattle, the settlers raised sheep and goats.

Truly a land of topographical diversity, the huge state of Texas contains a variety of terrains, including rivers, lakes, coastline, sandy beaches, rolling hills, rugged hills, gorges, grasslands, fertile farmland, extensive plains, plateaus, arid land, mountains, and islands. Cattle is the one commonality that flourishes throughout the state. Today, ranches and farms occupy three-fourths of the land in Texas, with two-thirds of those devoted to raising cattle.

An extension of the Plains, the Panhandle of northern Texas endures cold winters and hot summers. Copious amounts of wheat grow here, and dairy products come from the northeastern area.

The eastern section consists of rolling hills, rivers, some forests, and humid weather. Flat plains form the coastline at the Gulf of Mexico. A bounty of fish and seafood come from the Gulf, including shrimp, oysters, crabs, snapper, flounder, grouper, redfish, drum, and mackerel. Game flourishes in the forests, and there are many chicken farms in the east.

The central portion of Texas experiences mild winters and hot summers. Rolling and rugged hills, forests, and fertile farmland make up this region. A multitude of hogs thrive in the central region and the Panhandle. Many people characterize the west and central regions as cowboy country. Ample game, especially deer and wild turkey, inhabit the forests of the east and central regions as well as the plains in the west.

In the south, the Rio Grande River forms the more than 800-mile border between Texas and Mexico. Like the climate in southern Florida, this area experiences subtropical conditions with hot, humid weather. The fertile farmland in the valleys surrounding the Rio Grande River yields a cornucopia of fruits and vegetables like cantaloupes, peaches, and citrus fruits as well as plenty of rice and abundant pecans. With strong influence from Mexico apparent in the cooking, the so-called "Tex-Mex" cookery originated here.

Arid plains characterize drought-prone western Texas. Covered with sparse grasses and almost no trees, this plateau receives little rainfall and has very low humidity. Western Texas also contains high plains with some grasslands, dramatic gorges, intermittent mountains extending from the Rocky Mountains, and some irrigated farmland. Cattle, sheep, and goats thrive in this dry region.

Colorado lies to the north of New Mexico, Texas and a corner of Oklahoma border on New Mexico's east, Mexico and Texas are to the south, and Arizona is situated to the west. The dramatic landscape found in New Mexico includes expansive plateaus, mountains, cliffs, and huge rock formations. Running north to south through the central portion of this state, the Rio Grande River is surrounded by valleys of fertile farmland. Before the settlers arrived, the Pueblos settled along the banks of the Rio Grande and used the flooding of the river for irrigation. Because the difficult terrain found in much of New Mexico created significant isolation, few settlers ventured into this land in the beginning.

North-central New Mexico contains the Rio Grande Valley, an area characterized by a valley floor that lies at an elevation of six to seven thousand feet. Snow-capped mountains dot the mountain ranges that run through this region.

Land near the Texas Panhandle in the eastern portion of New Mexico reflects the flat plains found throughout the Plains states. In fact, the eastern third of the state consists of plains and high plateau where cattle and sheep graze. Southern New Mexico contains a large basin formed around the Rio Grande River as it travels south. Scattered mountains complete the landscape in the south and the west.

Since New Mexico receives very limited rainfall, the Rio Grande and the other rivers that flow through the state provide much-needed water for the inhabitants and for irrigation. Cutting through New Mexico from north to south, the Rio Grande serves as a major source of water. Southern New Mexico receives much less rainfall than the north.

Supplying plenty of game, forests stand on one-quarter of the land in New Mexico. Chili peppers and pecans grow well throughout much of the state.

Utah lies north of Arizona, New Mexico borders on the east, Mexico is on the south, and California and Nevada are to the west. Hot summers, warm winters, little rainfall, and low humidity describe the climatic conditions of Arizona, although the mountainous areas experience much cooler weather. In the many areas classified as desert, the temperature plummets as soon as the sun goes down. Even when the days are blistering hot in the desert, it cools off drastically at night. More than half of the land in Arizona consists of plateaus and mountains where cattle and sheep roam. In the early days, Native Americans feasted on the abundant game, such as deer, antelope, and buffalo.

The Colorado River flows through northwestern Arizona and cuts through the bottom of the deep, wide chasm known as the Grand Canyon. Forming Arizona's western border with Nevada and California, this river winds through the northern part of the state before turning south.

Encompassing almost half of the state, the Colorado Plateau lies in the north. Plateaus with some mountains and canyons make up this area. Rugged mountains and valleys lie just south of the Colorado Plateau. The southern portion of the state displays a variety of terrains including mountains, fertile valleys supported by irrigation, and some desert land almost devoid of vegetation.

Running from central Arizona to western New Mexico, a ridge of volcanic mountains show remnants of geological upheaval in the past. The eruptions left a rocky landscape with dramatic features like the red soil and rocks of Sedona in central Arizona and the pastel rocks of the Datil Mountains. Mountains and canyons describe the northern half of the state while the Sonoran Desert dominates the southern half with arid land, hot summers, and mild winters.

In the 1860s, settlers revived the irrigation ditches in the Salt River Valley originally constructed by the Hohokam Indians about two thousand years before. As a result, irrigation transformed this once-desert, arid land that supported only cacti and other succulents into soil suitable for planting. Soon crops of dates, citrus fruits, and pecans prospered, and the town of Phoenix emerged.

The region known as the Four Corners lies where northwestern New Mexico, northeastern Arizona, southeastern Utah, and southwestern Colorado touch. This rugged country that includes some of the Colorado Plateau contains mesa, plains, plateau, canyons, gorges, valleys, cliffs, and extinct volcanoes.

Ingredients and foods commonly used throughout the cuisine of the Southwest include

- pork, beef, lamb, goats, and game, including deer and turkey
- fish and seafood, including shrimp, oysters, snapper, flounder, grouper, redfish, trout, and mackerel
- corn and cornmeal
- beans and peas
- squash, pumpkins, and tomatoes
- tortillas
- rice and wheat
- many varieties of chili peppers
- onions and garlic
- cantaloupes, peaches, citrus fruits, dates, and figs
- cumin, oregano, and cilantro
- pine nuts, pecans, and pistachios

COOKING METHODS

Incorporating many dried food items, slow-cooking soups and stews often simmered over a fire. Braising and boiling effectively rehydrated and tenderized dried meats and dried beans as well as tenderizing tough cuts of fresh meat. In addition to dried foods, Native Americans and settlers added any available fresh foods to the pot.

Native Americans prepared beans by a variety of methods, including braising, boiling, and frying. Beans served as a major part of their diet and were even added to salads.

Squash remains a mainstay in the Southwest. Preparations include boiling, baking, braising, mashing, stuffing, broiling, and grilling.

Fried foods appear often, including Indian fry bread, all sorts of meats and vegetables, and even desserts. From the Mexican and Spanish influence, fried pastries like *sopaipillas* and *buñuelos* remain favorites.

Hornos, dome-shaped ovens made of stone and adobe, became popular after the Spanish introduced wheat in the Southwest. To heat these ovens, cooks burned wood until it turned to ash. After removing the ash, they baked

Horno
photo by Francesca Yorke © Dorling Kindersley

254   Chapter 9

the bread in the hot oven. They still use *hornos* to bake breads and pastries at pueblos (communities of Native Americans located throughout the Southwest that often have adobe buildings) and in the back yards of many Native American homes.

The technique of pickling foods in an acid mixture, *escabeche* came to the Southwest through the Spanish, who learned this procedure from the Moors. Initially used to prevent spoilage, this technique pickled cooked meat or fish by covering it with an acid liquid (vinegar, citrus juice, or a combination) flavored with herbs and spices. Usually, the meat or fish was fried before pickling. Although not a typical food to use when preparing *escabeche*, some cooks now offer raw vegetables *escabeche* (marinated in an herb- or spice-flavored acidic liquid) on menus in the Southwest.

Barbecue (grilling) remains a popular cooking method throughout this region. Texans show particular fondness for outdoor parties or gatherings serving grilled foods. Originally, the first step to prepare the barbecue was digging a pit and filling the pit with wood, usually mesquite, pecan, hickory, or other aromatic varieties. Foods were then cooked over the fire or in the pit of smoldering embers. Like the Native Americans preparing a New England clambake, Texans wrapped the meats with leaves and/or covered them with wet cloth before placing them in the smoldering pit. Wrapping the foods actually steamed them. Later, the popular barbecue meant grilling meats instead of steaming them in a pit. In the early days, settlers cooked lamb, beef, goat, or buffalo.

Containing spices and flavorings like cumin, onions, garlic, tomatoes, and chili peppers, the sauce for barbecue reflects strong Mexican influence. As an alternative to slathering the meat with sauce, some prefer a dry rub or paste made of a combination of spices applied to the meat before cooking.

Cowboys driving cattle over the open range also cooked over the fire. They built an open fire in a trench, so that the coals remained hot and protected while the pot buried in the embers cooked. Although grilling and one-pot cookery were frequent cooking methods, cowboys often fried foods, also. They fried by placing the skillet directly over the open fire. In order to cook biscuits, they suspended a Dutch oven over the fire or buried it in the embers to bake.

Beans, beef, and biscuits in one form or another composed the majority of meals on the range. Beginning their journey with a crock of sourdough starter, cooks on the trail had leavening for biscuits, breads, and pancakes. The cooks used all parts of the cow, including the fat, which they rendered into tallow. In addition, all of the organs joined any other available ingredients in the pot. Regardless of the ingredients, stews ranked high on the cowboys' menu.

Typical of Native Americans all over the United States, Native Americans and settlers in the Southwest preserved any extra meat and produce for the lean times. The desert conditions found in this region greatly impacted the cookery. For example, because of the arid climate, drying in the sun was the most common and practical method for preserving foods. Strips of dried meat became jerky. Settlers dried corn, beans, all sorts of peppers, pumpkin strips, and apple slices for easy storage and later use. Jerky was eaten in its dried state or cooked in stew. Even today, braided bouquets of green

Ristra
photo by Francesca Yorke © Dorling Kindersley

chilies, called *ristras*, hang in front of houses in the fall. While the chilies are still green when picked and strung to dry, they soon ripen to red. People then pluck the chilies from the *ristra* when needed for cooking.

STATES

Texas is the second largest state in the United States; only Alaska contains more land. Abundant game roaming in many parts of Texas provided meat for the early settlers as well as today's inhabitants.

With acres and acres of wide-open land, Texas proved an excellent place for raising cattle. Because the slaughtering facilities were situated in Chicago and the trains did not travel to Texas, cowboys transported the livestock in cattle drives to Kansas and Missouri, where they loaded them into railcars for shipping to Chicago. Descendants of cattle that the Spanish raised in the Southwest, the longhorn steers yielded tough, stringy meat. In the 1800s, cattlemen began breeding longhorns with Herefords from England to produce the American Hereford, a large steer with tender meat.

Because of its proximity to states with widely different culinary characteristics, Texas displays distinct culinary traits from each of its bordering regions. For example, bountiful cattle thrive in the north of Texas, and the cookery of that region resembles the characteristic cookery found in the Plains. Foods and recipes from eastern Texas reflect strong impact from neighboring Louisiana with typical Southern, Cajun, and/or Creole cooking. Cooks here serve gumbos, okra, rice dishes, biscuits, crawfish, and other fish and seafood from the Gulf of Mexico. The tropical southern sections of the state that border Mexico exhibit pronounced Mexican traits in the use of chili peppers, tortillas, and salsa. The cookery found in the western part of the state is much like New Mexico's, with prominent Native American overtones and extensive use of chilies. Beef, beans, and corn dominate the cuisine of western Texas.

A favorite throughout the South, black-eyed peas grow well in southeastern Texas. Grapefruit, figs, cantaloupes, and many other melons, as well as a cornucopia of fruits and vegetables thrive in eastern Texas.

The Gulf of Mexico yields a bounty of shellfish and fish that often appears in recipes throughout this area. Whether cooked in beer with hot chilies or deep-fried, a multitude of shrimp dishes remain popular and frequent menus at homes and restaurants.

The central and southern sections of Texas became divided into huge ranches for raising great numbers of cattle. Of course, the plentiful beef became the meat of choice. Barbecued meat; Tex-Mex cookery with lots of chili peppers, cumin, and other spices; and chili reign supreme in these areas. In countless combinations, corn, beans, chili peppers, tomatoes, and squash define Tex-Mex cooking.

The cookery of central Texas reflects the culinary background of settlers from Germany, Poland, and Eastern Europe. Pork, dumplings, and potatoes are served often.

Although the Spanish certainly impacted the cuisine found in Texas, the Mexican influence remains much stronger. Mostly, this results from the many miles of border shared by Texas and Mexico.

The first written mention of chili appeared in the 1820s and cited chili made by poor people in San Antonio in southern Texas. Today, thousands of chili variations abound throughout Texas and every other state. In addition, San Antonio claims to be the home of chili powder, a mixture of spices traditionally added to chili and other dishes.

The fiery *chiletepin* pepper grows wild in Texas, and the Native Americans used this pepper as a flavoring even before the Spanish arrived. In addition, the popular jalapeño pepper flavors many dishes.

Texas ranks second in pecan production. Only Georgia grows more pecans. As a result, pecans show up in all sorts of recipes, from appetizers to breads and desserts.

New Mexico's cookery exhibits heavy influence from the Native American and Spanish cuisines with additional impact from the Mexicans. Spanish missionaries migrated north from Mexico and built missions in New Mexico. In addition to the Native American's crops of corn, squash, and beans, the missionaries planted tomatoes, avocados, sweet potatoes, citrus fruit, wheat, peaches, apples, and grapes for wine. Prior to the Spanish missionaries, most meat came from hunting. By raising cattle and chickens, the missionaries greatly increased the amount of available meat. Soon, Spanish and Mexican culinary traits joined the existing cookery of the southwestern Native Americans. The resulting cuisine married these three culinary heritages to form the cuisine of New Mexico.

Today, New Mexico contains orchards producing abundant apples, peaches, apricots, plums, and citrus fruits. Wheat production surpasses corn, chilies abound, and the grapes yield wines.

In addition to abundant pecan trees, pine trees yielding pine nuts, also called pignoli or piñons, thrive in New Mexico. As a result, nuts appear in a wide range of dishes.

Atole, cornmeal porridge, remains a traditional New Mexican dish. Even today, sick people eat this version of New Mexico's comfort food.

Although Arizona shows some impact from Mexican and Spanish cookery, it exhibits much less of their influence than found in New Mexico's cuisine. As a result, the cookery of Arizona uses fewer chilies than the rest of the Southwest. While Arizona attracted some Spanish missionaries, few Spanish settlers actually moved there. The most significant Mexican influence found in Arizona comes from the state of Sonora in the north of Mexico. Sonora boasts huge cattle and wheat production and remains the only Mexican state where the people prefer beef to pork and wheat tortillas to corn tortillas. Most people in Arizona also choose beef over pork and wheat over corn tortillas.

Until the 1850s, few settlers chose to make Arizona their home. Most of Arizona's early settlers came from the eastern parts of the United States hoping to find fortune by raising cattle or mining silver, copper, or gold. The mining prospects attracted immigrants from Eastern Europe and the British Isles. Because these prospectors found few ingredients available from their native cookery, they had a minimum impact on the cuisine.

When Mormons from Utah settled in Arizona, they established successful farms by irrigating. Today, much of Arizona's best farmland lies in irrigated portions of the Sonoran Desert near Phoenix. A wealth of crops including lettuce, cantaloupes, citrus fruits, and many more fruits and vegetables thrive in the long growing season found here. Irrigated farmland in other parts of the state produces figs, dates, corn, chilies, jicama, *tomatillos*, pecans, and pistachios.

CHARACTERISTICS OF THE CUISINE

Some describe the food of the Southwest as food of the sun. Four major foods dominate the cookery: corn in numerous forms, many types of beans, a variety of squashes, and a wide assortment of chili peppers. Mexican influence on Southwestern food appears strongly. From the beans and chili peppers to the burritos, enchiladas, tamales, and *chili rellenos*, Mexican ingredients and dishes permeate menus in homes as well as restaurants.

With ample land for grazing, cattle thrived in the Southwest. Sheep and goats roamed in mountainous areas and the semi-arid regions with insufficient grasses to sustain cattle. Many Navajos and Basque shepherds raised sheep. Goat meat, lamb, and goat cheese became part of the diet of the Southwest. Pigs roamed freely and flourished. Providing food for the inhabitants, game like wild pigs, deer, rabbits, and quail wandered many parts of the Southwest.

Developed out of the need to extend the small amounts of meat, *chili con carne*, meat chili, originated in Texas in the early 1800s. At that time, the dish consisted of lots of chili peppers and whatever meat was available—pork, beef, or lamb. Although many use ground meat, purists of Texas chili insist on diced meat. In fact, some say authentic *chili con carne* consists of browned chunks of beef cooked with chilies and seasonings like cumin, oregano, garlic, chili powder, paprika, cayenne pepper, onions, and more as desired and then thickened with cornmeal. Traditionally, many add cornmeal at the end of cooking to thicken the chili and absorb the grease released from the meat. Basically, chili reflects the marriage of European stew with Mexican sauces. In 1893 at the Columbian Exposition in Chicago, chili came to national attention when people at the Texas booth offered chili samples.

Ordering chili in New Mexico produces a totally different dish. Cooks there start with green chili sauce and add other ingredients like beans, hominy, meat, onions, and/or potatoes.

For the early settlers in the Southwest, soups and stews used the many dried food items, and many of the soups and stews show marked Mexican influence. Often referred to as soup, *posole* is actually more like stew. While there are countless variations of *posole*, all contain hominy, pork, and chili peppers. This stew appears frequently in the cooler mountainous areas of the Southwest. Traditionally, menus on Christmas Eve and New Year's Eve include *posole*.

Appearing in many forms, corn shows up constantly. Recipes including corn, cornmeal, and other corn products abound. These recipes include cornbread, hominy, tortillas, tamales, and many more. Corn varieties grow in several colors, yielding blue, white, and yellow corn and cornmeal.

Along with corn and beans, the ubiquitous squash frequents menus throughout the Southwest. Pumpkin, acorn squash, butternut, patty pan, yellow summer squash, zucchini, and more appear in numerous preparations. Called mirliton in Louisiana, chayote adds crisp texture that many compare to water chestnuts. Although chayote is usually cooked, it is sometimes served raw. The New Mexican squash dish *calabacitas* consists of sautéed zucchini mixed with corn, flavorings, and/or other ingredients.

From the times before the European settlers arrived, Native Americans valued the pumpkin for its food value both in the pulp and the seeds. Wasting nothing, the Native Americans hollowed the pumpkin shell to serve as a cooking vessel for soups and stews. Widely available throughout the Southwest, *pepitas* are pumpkin seeds. They appear in a variety of forms – raw or roasted, salted or unsalted, hulled or not hulled. Today, *pepitas* frequently show up as a snack, garnish, or as part of a dish or sauce.

Another vegetable, jicama (pronounce the *j* as an *h*) appears often in Southwestern cookery. Many describe its taste and texture as similar to water chestnuts. After this large root vegetable is peeled, its crisp texture and mild flavor adds crunch to any dish. Often incorporated into salads, jicama is served raw or cooked.

Residents of the Southwest feature all sorts of beans in their diet. "Ranchero style" means cooking beans with bacon, onions, tomatoes, and chilies. The pinto bean reigned as the most common bean cooked on the trail when the cowboys herded cattle. That bean remains a favorite for refried beans, called *frijoles refritos* in Mexico. Although people

Americans translate *frijoles refritos* as refried beans, but the actual translation is "overly fried beans." This refers to frying the beans very well, until they form a paste. They are not fried twice.

When the diner orders "Christmas" in New Mexico, it means to crown the entrée with both green and red chili sauces.

In Mexico, a tortilla wrapped around any type of filling takes the place of a sandwich. This version of Mexico's sandwich became the prototype for today's "wrap." To create a wrap, take any flat bread like a tortilla or the flat breads commonly served in the Middle East and Africa and wrap it around the filling of choice.

disagree on recipes for refried beans, preparation of refried beans involves sautéing onion and garlic in lard, adding the pinto beans, and cooking until quite soft.

Traced from the Aztecs close to five centuries ago, tamales consist of a filling wrapped in cornhusks and then cooked in the fire (which steamed the filling). Many now cook popular tamales in a steamer, but whether steamed or baked, the tamale filling steams inside the husk. Filling possibilities include meat, cheese, vegetables, or fruit.

Enchiladas are another popular dish from the Mexican heritage. To prepare them, coat corn tortillas with chili sauce and briefly fry the tortilla before rolling it around any variety of fillings. Before serving the enchilada, pour some chili sauce over it. In New Mexico, enchiladas commonly appear stacked instead of rolled. For this preparation, cooks sandwich the filling between two corn tortillas and top the enchilada with chili sauce made from green or red chilies.

Many traditional Mexican dishes show up on Tex-Mex menus, although they greatly differ from the original versions served in Mexico. One of the big differences between Tex-Mex and Mexican cookery is that Tex-Mex incorporates more meat and cheese into the dishes. Some Tex-Mex specialties include

burrito—flour tortillas wrapped around any desired filling

chalupa—flat, fried tortilla shells topped with any assortment of meat, beans, cheese, vegetables, and/or condiments

chili rellenos—poblano peppers stuffed with cheese or meat, dipped in batter, and deep-fried

chimichangas—deep-fried burritos

fajitas—any type of grilled meat, poultry, or occasionally seafood cut into strips and served with warm tortillas for wrapping. In earlier times, cooks marinated tough cuts of meat before grilling for fajitas. Even when using tender cuts of meat, today they frequently marinate the meat for additional flavor. Onions and peppers often are cooked with the meat.

huevos rancheros—fried eggs placed on top of a tortilla and covered with salsa; served accompanied by beans on the side

quesadillas—tortillas filled with cheese and/or other fillings, folded in half, and then fried

taco—filling placed in a deep-fried, folded-almost-in-half tortilla shell

Two basic types of cheeses appear in Southwestern cookery. The first, melting cheeses, contribute texture as well as mild flavor to any dish. The second, hard cheeses, generally possess strong flavors and often are grated over dishes to add a pungent flavor just before serving.

The bread of Mexico, (both wheat and corn tortillas) plays an important role in Texas, Tex-Mex cuisine, and throughout the Southwest. Even from the time of the Pueblos, tortillas served as the most common type of bread in this area. Preparing tortillas from ground corn, Pueblo women cooked them on a hot baking stone. The popular enchilada developed when someone wrapped a corn tortilla around beans.

Cultivated and prized by the Hopi Indians, blue cornmeal appears often in the cooking and baking of the Southwest. A traditional bread prepared by the Hopis, *piki* blends blue cornmeal and water to form a thin batter that they cook on a hot stone. After removing the very thin bread from the stone, they roll it into a tubular shape. Some say the bread tastes like a large sheet of corn flakes.

Another favorite bread, *sopaipillas* consist of dough that transforms into golden brown, puffed, air-filled pockets when deep-fried. Some fill the *sopaipilla* with meat, vegetables,

CHILI PEPPERS COMMONLY USED IN THE SOUTHWEST

Anaheim—mild to slightly hot, often used for stuffing; also called California green chilies

Ancho—mild to slightly hot, dried poblano pepper

Cayenne—hot

Chiletepin—very hot, small round pepper; native to Texas

Chipotles—medium to hot, smoked and dried jalapeños

Jalapeños—medium to hot; called *escabeche* when pickled in vinegar

Pasilla—mild to slightly hot, dried Anaheim chilies; also called New Mexico chilies

Pequín—very hot

Poblano—mild to slightly hot; often used for *chili rellenos*

Sante Fe Grande—fairly hot to very hot; used pickled or fresh in a range of dishes including salsas, salads, and vegetable dishes

Serrano—fairly hot to hot; used fresh or pickled in many dishes

and/or cheese and serve it as an entrée. Others serve them the way biscuits are served in the South, placing a basket of *sopaipillas* and a jar of honey on the table to accompany meals. Still others serve them for dessert with honey, syrup, cinnamon and sugar, confectioners' sugar, ice cream, or any combination.

Similar to *sopaipillas*, Indian frybread is very simple bread dough leavened with baking powder, kneaded, and deep-fried. After forming the disk for frying, cooks insert a small hole in the center of each disk. Originally, they placed a stick through the hole to lower the bread into the hot fat. Now, the tradition continues, and they say the hole allows the bread to puff. The resulting bread resembles a cross between a thick tortilla and a *sopaipilla*. Native Americans used frybread as the base for building a taco-type entrée.

As in Mexican cookery, sauces and stews are thickend with ground nuts and seeds instead of flour and cornstarch in the Southwest. Dried corn added to stews also functions as a thickener. Either raw or roasted, indigenous pumpkin seeds and pine nuts appear in numerous recipes. From the Native Americans, the settlers learned uses for the pungent pine nuts or piñon nuts that come from the cones of the pine trees that thrive throughout the Southwest. These small nuts show up in both savory and sweet dishes. Also growing throughout the Southwest, pecans appear in many recipes.

Wild sage flavors many dishes. Another often-used seasoning, cilantro is included in a wide range of dishes, salsa, and sauces. In addition, many Southwestern dishes contain garlic, onions, oregano, cumin, and chili peppers.

Countless varieties of salsa exist; only the imagination limits the possibilities. Any assortment of vegetables, fruits, herbs, and/or spices can become a salsa. Ranging from mild to very hot, salsas contain very different levels of spice and chili peppers. The Mexican word *picante* means hot in terms of spice, not temperature. While the tomato usually provides the basis for red salsa, *tomatillos* give the foundation for green salsa. A bowl of salsa often replaces salt and pepper on the table for many inhabitants of the Southwest.

Guacamole, a dip based on avocado, functions as another popular dip or condiment. Often used as an appetizer with chips or vegetables, guacamole frequently accompanies an entrée. Because the smooth, buttery texture and flavor of avocadoes complements the spicy hot chili peppers, cooks frequently garnish dishes with diced avocado or guacamole.

Ranging widely in the amount of heat they contain, hundreds of varieties of chili peppers permeate the cookery of the Southwest. Introduced by Mexicans about 400 years ago, today chilies appear in all sorts of dishes, from the very simple to the most complex. Due to differences in soil and growing conditions, an individual pepper might contain more or less heat than another of the same type. In fact, two chilies from the same plant can vary in their hotness. As a result, tasting a dish while adding peppers is crucial! Generally, the smaller varieties of peppers are the hottest. Because of the great differences in the flavor of peppers and the amount of heat they contain, many recipes require several types of peppers to create their particular flavor profile. Although immature chilies are green, mature chilies turn red or orange as they ripen.

Besides making it easier to remove the tough outer skin, charring peppers over a flame adds a roasted flavor to the dish. To remove the skin, immediately place hot, well-charred peppers in a tightly closed bag to steam for about 20 minutes. At that point, remove the peel of the pepper, cut the pepper into strips, dice it, or leave it whole for stuffing. If stuffing, cut a slit into the side of the pepper only large enough to allow removal of seeds and membranes and then pack the inside of the pepper with any desired filling.

Anaheim Chili
photo by Roger Phillips © Dorling Kindersley

Cayenne Peppers
photo by Dave King © Dorling Kindersley

Ancho Chili
photo by Roger Phillips © Dorling Kindersley

Jalapeño Peppers

Pasilla Pepper
photo by Philip Dowell © Dorling Kindersley

Poblano Peppers
photo © Culinary Institute of America

Serrano Peppers
photo by David Murray © Dorling Kindersley

Chipotle Peppers
photo by Dave King © Dorling Kindersley

Dried Pequín Peppers

Prickly Pear Cactus

After the thorns are removed, some varieties of cacti provide food in the arid Southwest. The prickly pear cactus is valued for its water-filled paddles (*nopales*) as well as its fruit. When eaten raw, the *nopales* add crunchy texture. If cooked, *nopales* are usually boiled. People in the Southwest often make prickly pears into jelly, candy, or some confection.

As in Mexico, people of the Southwest prepare flan and a variety of custards for dessert. Other favorite sweet endings include all sorts of puddings made from cornmeal, rice, pumpkin, and bread as well as fried pastry confections like *sopaipillas* and *buñuelos*. Generally, desserts in the Southwest tend to be cloyingly sweet, and many recipes contain ingredients like dried fruits and honey. Rather than serving a sweet dessert, many meals end with fresh fruit.

Tequila and beer remain popular alcoholic beverages throughout the Southwest. Made from the agave cactus, tequila is a clear liquor incorporated into a variety of beverages as well as marinades and sauces. While the list of drinks containing tequila is long, the margarita stands at the top of the list. Although they come in all kinds of flavors and combinations, the traditional margarita contains tequila, orange liqueur, and lime juice. Margaritas are served either frozen or over ice in a glass rimmed with salt.

Nopales

Prickly Pear

photo by Roger Phillips © Dorling Kindersley

Area	Weather	Topography	Foods
Texas north	hot summers, cold winters	borders Oklahoma; plains	cattle, hogs, dairy, wheat
east	hot summers, warm winters, high humidity	borders Gulf of Mexico, Louisiana, Arkansas, Oklahoma; coastline, flat plains, rolling hills, rivers, forests, islands, fertile farmland, some mountains	shrimp, oysters, crawfish, crabs, snapper, flounder, grouper, redfish, mackerel, drum, cattle, chicken, game, wild turkey, deer, gumbos, corn, beans, black-eyed peas, okra, tomatoes, chili peppers, avocado, pumpkin seeds, rice, tortillas, salsa, biscuits, fruits and vegetables, figs, melons, cantaloupes, citrus fruit
south	hot summers, warm winters, high humidity	borders Mexico, Rio Grande River and Valley; fertile farmland	cattle, chili, Tex-Mex cookery, barbecue, beans, tomatoes, squash, chili peppers, pumpkin seeds, avocado, rice, corn, tortillas, salsa, cumin, fruits and vegetables, figs, citrus fruits, grapefruits, cantaloupes, peaches, pecans
west	hot summers, warm winters, low humidity, little rainfall	borders Mexico and New Mexico; plains, plateaus, dry, arid grasslands, some mountains	cattle, sheep, goats, game, deer, wild turkey, beans, corn, chili peppers
central	hot summers, mild winters	rolling and rugged hills, forests, fertile farmland	cattle, hogs, game, wild turkey, deer, chili, barbecue, beans, tomatoes, chili peppers, pumpkin seeds, avocado, cumin, Tex-Mex cookery
New Mexico Colorado to north, Texas and Oklahoma to east, Mexico and Texas to south, Arizona to west	hot summers, cool winters, low humidity, low rainfall especially in south	mountains, canyons, cliffs, gorges, forests, valleys; Rio Grande River and Valley runs north to south; plains, fertile farmland, mesa, plateau, Colorado Plateau in north and east, desert in south	cattle, sheep, game, pork, chickens, *posole*, beans, corn, squash, avocado, red and green chili peppers, wheat, sweet potatoes, pumpkin seeds, tomatoes, sage, marjoram, cilantro, apples, peaches, apricots, plums, grapes, citrus fruits, pecans, pine nuts, wine
Arizona Utah to north, New Mexico to east, Mexico to south, California and Nevada to west	hot summers, warm winters, low humidity, little rainfall, cooler in mountains	plateaus, valleys, mountains, canyons, desert; Colorado River flows through northwest forming western boundary; Colorado Plateau in north, Sonoran Desert and irrigated farmland in south	cattle, sheep, game, deer, trout, bass, wheat, tortillas, fruits and vegetables, beans, corn, chili peppers, tomatoes, lettuce, avocados, *tomatillos*, jicama, sweet potatoes, cilantro, salsa, pumpkin seeds, citrus fruits, dates, figs, pecans, pistachios

REVIEW QUESTIONS

1. Discuss the Native Americans who settled in the Southwest, including how they lived, their diet, and their effect on the cuisine.
2. Discuss the topography and climate of the Southwest and how that affected the cuisine.
3. Explain the role of the Spanish and Mexicans in the development of the Southwest and how that impacted the cuisine.
4. What is an enchilada and how does it differ in Arizona and New Mexico?
5. Name and describe at least five dishes commonly served in the Southwest.
6. Describe the role of corn in the diet of inhabitants of the Southwest. Define *posole, chicos,* and *masa harina.*

atole—cornmeal porridge, a traditional New Mexican dish

calabacitas—dish featuring sautéed zucchini, usually with corn, flavorings, and/or other ingredients

chicos—whole dried corn kernels

chili rellenos—poblano peppers stuffed with cheese or meat, battered, and deep-fried

chorizo—spicy sausage of Spanish origin

escabeche—preserving technique of pickling cooked foods in an acid mixture flavored with herbs and spices, often used in early days in the Southwest to prevent cooked meat or fish from spoiling

hominy—dried corn cooked with slaked lime

hornos—dome-shaped ovens made of stone and adobe

huevos rancheros—breakfast dish consisting of a tortilla topped with fried eggs covered with salsa and accompanied by beans on the side

masa—ground hominy, used in preparation of tortillas

pepitas—pumpkin seeds, used as a snack, garnish, or part of a dish

picante—"hot" in terms of spice, not temperature

pine nuts—nuts harvested from cones from pine trees, also called pignoli or piñons

posole—dried whole corn kernels treated with slaked lime to remove the husks; soup or stew containing hominy (*posole*), pork, and chili peppers

pueblos—communities where Native Americans live throughout the Southwest; they often contain adobe houses and/or buildings as well as *hornos*

quesadillas—tortillas filled with cheese or other items, folded in half, and then fried

salsa—uncooked condiment usually containing tomatoes and/or *tomatillos*, peppers, and herbs

sopaipillas—dough that puffs into golden brown, air-filled pockets when deep-fried

Tex-Mex cookery—a variation of Mexican cooking prepared in Texas; incorporates more meat and cheese into the dishes than Mexican cookery

CHICKEN QUESADILLA

Chicken Quesadilla

Quesadillas come in any variety and flavor combination imaginable, including meat, poultry, seafood, or vegetarian. Myriad accompaniments are served with quesadillas: sour cream, guacamole, diced tomato, avocado, lettuce, onion or scallion, minced peppers, any type of salsa, cheeses, and/or any sauce.

NUMBER OF SERVINGS: 1
COOKING METHOD:
    Grill or Bake
SERVING SIZE:
    1 each 8-inch tortilla
TOTAL YIELD:
    5³/4 oz each

Wine Style: Soft and fruity Sauvignon Blanc, Pinot Blanc, or light red wines
Example: Fume Blanc—Sonita Vineyards, Elgin, AZ. This wine is 100% Sauvignon Blanc, completely dry, and with a slight flinty character.

INGREDIENTS	WEIGHT	VOLUME
tortilla, flour	**1 each 8-inch**	
salsa, hot or choice	**1¹/2 oz**	**2 tablespoons**
green chili pepper strips	**¹/4 oz**	**1 teaspoon**
chicken, grilled, cut into ¹/2-inch strips		**1 oz**
cheese, Monterey Jack or variety of choice, shredded	**1 oz**	**3¹/2 tablespoons**

POSSIBLE ACCOMPANIMENTS:

avocado, diced *or* guacamole

tomato, diced

lettuce, shredded

scallion, sliced

chili pepper, hot, medium, or mild, minced

sour cream

salsa

sauce of choice

1. Spread salsa over half of tortilla.
2. Top salsa half evenly with remaining ingredients. Fold empty tortilla half over filled side.
3. On griddle, brown each side over medium heat until tortilla is golden brown and cheese melts. *Note: Some prefer to bake tortillas in a 375-degree oven or grill them until golden brown and the cheese melts.*
4. Remove from heat, cut into thirds. Serve immediately with accompaniments of choice.

CHILES RELLENOS

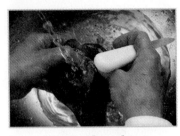

Removing Seeds and Veins from Peeled Pepper

Filling Pepper

Coating Rellenos with Batter

Chili Rellenos

Serve one relleno for an appetizer portion and two for an entrée.

Note: Depending on the size of the pepper, fill with 1½ to 2 oz cheese. When testing this recipe, the poblanos were fairly small and they held 1½ oz cheese.

NUMBER OF SERVINGS: 12
COOKING METHOD:
  Grill, Deep-fry
SERVING SIZE:
  1 filled pepper
TOTAL YIELD:
  3 lbs, 8 oz

Wine Style: Soft and fruity Gewürztraminer, Chenin Blanc, Sauvignon Blanc, Zinfandel, or Merlot
Example: Gewürztraminer—Llano Estacado Winery, Lubbock, TX. This wine is made in the classic German style with a spicy flavor and a balance between the sugar and acidity.

INGREDIENTS	WEIGHT	VOLUME
poblano peppers	2 lbs, 6 oz, depending on size	12 each
cheese, Monterey jack or variety of choice	1 lb, 2 oz to 1 lb, 8 oz	
BATTER:		
flour, all purpose	as needed, for dusting	
eggs	10 oz	6 each
salt		¼ teaspoon
oil	for deep-frying	
ACCOMPANIMENTS:		
sour cream		
salsa		

For Peppers:

1. Char peppers on grill or over flame of burner until blackened and blistered, but not soft.
2. Place in bag, seal, and wait about 15 to 20 minutes.
3. Remove from bag, peel skin from peppers. Be careful not to cut peppers.
4. Make slit on one side of pepper just large enough to remove seeds and ribs. Rinse with cold water; set aside until needed.

For Chile Preparation:

1. Stuff pepper with 1½ oz cheese, depending on size of pepper. Close tightly, using toothpicks to fasten.
2. Place flour on plate. Dredge peppers in flour; set aside.
3. Whip egg whites until stiff peaks.
4. Add salt and yolks, one at a time, until mixed.

For Assembly:

1. Heat about 1 inch oil in pan for deep-frying or use deep-fryer.
2. Place pepper in batter; turn to coat.
3. Gently place pepper into hot oil; fry until golden brown on all sides.
4. Remove from oil; drain well on paper toweling. Remove toothpicks.
5. Serve immediately, accompanied by salsa, sour cream, and/or condiments of choice.

SALSA FRESCA

Salsa Fresca
photo © Culinary Institute of America

Serve with chips as an appetizer or use as an accompanying sauce for many Mexican-inspired dishes.

NUMBER OF SERVINGS: 8
SERVING SIZE:
  2 oz or ¼ cup
TOTAL YIELD:
  1 lb, 2 oz or 2 cups

INGREDIENTS	WEIGHT	VOLUME
tomatoes, peeled, diced	1 lb	2 large
chilies, serrano, minced, seeds and membranes removed, if desired	¼ oz or to taste	1 or 2 each or to taste
cilantro, leaves, fresh, minced		1 tablespoon
onion, white, minced	2 oz	⅓ cup or ½ small
lime juice, fresh		2 teaspoons
salt		½ teaspoon

1. Mix all ingredients in bowl.
2. Correct seasonings. Serve with tortilla chips or as a condiment with any desired dish.

TORTILLA SOUP

Tortilla Soup

NUMBER OF SERVINGS: 13
COOKING METHOD:
  Sauté, Boil
SERVING SIZE:
  8 oz
TOTAL YIELD:
  6 lbs, 14 oz

INGREDIENTS	WEIGHT	VOLUME
oil or lard	1 oz	2 tablespoons
onion, small dice	1 lb	2 large
garlic, peeled, minced	1 oz	4 large cloves
green chilies, mild, chopped	8 oz	2 each 4-oz cans or 1 each 8-oz can
tomato, fresh or canned, peeled, seeded, diced	1 lb, 13 oz	1 each 29-oz can
chicken stock, hot	4 lbs	2 qts or 8 cups
jalapeño pepper, seeded, deveined, minced	1½ oz	¼ cup
chili powder	½ oz	2 teaspoons
cumin	¼ oz	2 teaspoons
oregano	¼ oz	2 teaspoons
lime juice, fresh	2 oz	¼ cup
chicken breasts, cooked, diced	1 lb	4 cups or 2 full breasts
tortillas, corn, 6-inch, cut into ½-inch strips	12 each	
oil or lard, for frying tortillas	as needed	
GARNISH:		
Monterey jack cheese, grated	13 oz	
cilantro, minced		
jalapeño or serrano peppers, minced		
avocado, diced or sliced		
lime juice, fresh		

1. Heat oil in skillet. Sauté onion and garlic about 3 or 4 minutes, until tender.
2. Add green chilies, tomatoes, chicken stock, jalapeño peppers, chili powder, cumin, oregano, lime juice, and chicken.
3. Bring to boil, reduce heat, and simmer for 20 to 25 minutes.
4. Meanwhile, fry tortilla strips until golden brown in oil or lard heated to 375 degrees.
5. Remove from skillet; drain on paper toweling.
6. Correct seasonings of soup.

Assembly:

1. Place some fried tortilla strips (about ¾ oz) in bottom of soup bowl.
2. Fill bowl with hot soup.
3. Top with about 1 oz Monterey jack cheese and a sprinkling of cilantro.
4. Serve immediately, accompanied by bowls of optional garnishes, if desired.

CHILI

Chili

Serve chili as soup or an entrée. The 8-oz portion represents a bowl of chili, not a cup. This traditional Texas recipe for "a bowl of red" contains no beans. Originally, this dish consisted of diced meat cooked with chilies.

If hot chili powder is not available, add 1 teaspoon of cayenne pepper or 2 teaspoons of minced jalapeño pepper.

NUMBER OF SERVINGS: 13
COOKING METHOD:
  Braise
SERVING SIZE:
  8 oz
TOTAL YIELD:
  6 lbs, 9 oz

INGREDIENTS	WEIGHT	VOLUME
oil	½ oz	1 tablespoon
beef, bottom round or chuck, trimmed of all fat, ½-inch dice	4 lbs, 7 oz	
onion, medium dice	1 lb, 1 oz	2 large
garlic, minced	1½ oz	8 cloves
beef stock	2 lbs	1 qt or 4 cups
tomatoes, chopped, drained of liquid	2 lbs, 3½ oz	2 each 28-oz cans
beer	1 lb, 8 oz	2 each 12-oz cans or bottles
hot chili powder	1½ oz	¼ cup or 4 tablespoons
oregano	½ oz	¼ cup
cumin	1 oz	¼ cup
salt	½ oz	2 teaspoons

1. Heat oil in large pan over medium heat. Sauté meat in batches, removing each batch as browned. Pour off all but one tablespoon fat.
2. Add onion; sauté for 3 minutes. Add garlic and sauté another 2 minutes.
3. Return meat to pan. Add stock, tomatoes, and beer. Bring to boil; reduce heat. Skim any foam or scum that rises to top.
4. Add chili powder, oregano, cumin, and salt. Cover and simmer for 2½ hours. Remove cover and cook another 30 minutes, until meat is tender.
5. Correct seasonings. Add more stock or water, if too thick. Serve immediately or cool, cover, and refrigerate. Reheat for later service.

GUACAMOLE

Twisting Avocado Halves
photo by David Murray and Jules Selmes © Dorling Kindersley

Removing Pit from Avocado
photo by David Murray and Jules Selmes © Dorling Kindersley

Spooning Pulp from Skin
photo by David Murray and Jules Selmes © Dorling Kindersley

Mashing Avocado Pulp
photo © Dorling Kindersley

Adding Lime Juice to Avocado Mixture
photo by David Murray and Jules Selmes © Dorling Kindersley

Guacamole

Guacamole darkens with exposure to air, so if not serving immediately, cover tightly to avoid oxidation. Many insert the avocado pit into the dip, saying it helps prevent the guacamole from darkening.

NUMBER OF SERVINGS: 10
SERVING SIZE:
  2 oz or 1/4 cup
TOTAL YIELD:
  1 lb, 4 oz or 2 1/2 cups

INGREDIENTS	WEIGHT	VOLUME
avocado, peeled, seeded	12 1/2 oz	2 medium
onion, white, minced	3/4 oz	2 tablespoons
chilies, serrano, seeded if desired, minced	1/2 oz or to taste	1 or 2 each or to taste
cilantro, leaves, fresh, minced	1/4 oz	2 tablespoons
lime juice, fresh		2 teaspoons
tomato, peeled, seeded, chopped	6 oz	1 medium
salt		1/2 teaspoon

1. Place avocado in bowl. Mash with fork against side of bowl until chunky paste.

2. Add remaining ingredients; mix well.

3. Serve immediately, accompanied by tortilla chips or warm tortillas, as part of a salad, or as a condiment with another dish. If not serving immediately, place avocado pit into dip and cover tightly with film wrap to prevent it from turning brown (oxidation).

JICAMA SALAD

Jicama

Jicama Salad

NUMBER OF SERVINGS: 17
SERVING SIZE:
  4 oz
TOTAL YIELD:
  4 lbs, 4 3/4 oz total
DRESSING:
  13 1/2 oz, 1 2/3 cups

INGREDIENTS	WEIGHT	VOLUME
DRESSING:		
garlic	1/4 oz	1 large clove
white vinegar	2 3/4 oz	1/3 cup
orange juice (reserved from oranges)	2 oz	1/4 cup
anise seed		1 teaspoon
honey	3 3/4 oz	5 tablespoons
salt	1/4 oz	1 teaspoon
white pepper		1/2 teaspoon
chili powder, hot		3/4 teaspoon
cayenne pepper		1/4 teaspoon
cumin		3/4 teaspoon
oil, olive or variety of choice	6 oz	3/4 cup
SALAD:		
oranges, seedless, peeled, pith and membrane removed	15 3/4 oz	4 large
jicama, peeled of outside and inner fibrous part, julienne	12 oz	1 small
lettuce, mixture of romaine and red leaf, torn into pieces, or spring mix	1 lb	
red peppers, julienne	9 1/2 oz	2 each
avocado, peeled, cut into 1/2-inch cube	4 1/4 oz	1 each
green onions, sliced	1 1/4 oz	4 each
cilantro, minced	1/2 oz	1/4 cup

For Dressing:

1. Chop garlic in food processor or blender.
2. Add vinegar, orange juice, anise seed, honey, salt, white pepper, chili powder, cayenne pepper, and cumin. Process until smooth (anise seeds are pulverized).
3. Slowly add oil through feed tube of food processor. Run machine until mixture thickens and emulsifies.
4. Refrigerate until needed.

For Salad:

1. Peel orange over bowl to catch juices. With sharp paring knife, peel oranges, removing pith. To remove membrane, cut on each side of membrane to middle, staying as close to membrane as possible. (Refer to "Cutting Sections of Orange from Membrane" photo on page 142 in Chapter 5, Florida.)
2. To peel jicama, use sharp knife to remove brown skin and woody, fibrous part under skin. Cut into julienne.
3. Place lettuce in bowl. Top with oranges, jicama, red pepper, avocado, green onions, and cilantro.
4. Add dressing; toss thoroughly to coat well. Serve immediately.

POSOLE

Posole

A traditional Native American dish served on New Year's Day and feast days, this hominy and pork stew symbolizes promises of good luck.

Begin soaking the posole the night before cooking. If using hominy instead of posole (corn treated with slaked lime, then dried), use half the amount of stock and cook for only 1 to 1 1/2 hours, until pork is tender. Substitute 2 to 3 each 14-ounce cans of hominy for the 2 cups of posole.

NUMBER OF SERVINGS: 8
COOKING METHOD:
  Boil
SERVING SIZE:
  8 oz
TOTAL YIELD:
  4 lbs, 4 1/2 oz

Wine Style: Grenache, soft Shiraz, or Zinfandel
Example: Primitivo—La Vina Winery, La Union, NM. A cousin of Zinfandel, this wine is fruity with medium tannins, spice, and pepper flavor.

INGREDIENTS	WEIGHT	VOLUME
posole	11 ½ oz	2 cups
water	1 lb, 8 oz	3 cups
oil or lard	½ oz	1 tablespoon
onion, medium dice	5¾ oz	1¼ cups or 1 large
garlic, minced	½ oz	3 cloves
pork, boneless, 1-inch cubes, lean, trimmed of fat	1 lb, 8 oz	
chicken stock	3 lbs	1 qt + 2 cups or 6 cups
oregano		1 teaspoon
cumin		½ teaspoon
cloves		½ teaspoon
bay leaf		1 each
green chilies, chopped	4 oz	1 each 4-oz can

GARNISH:

jalapeño pepper, seeded, deveined, minced, *optional*

1. Soak posole in water for at least 6 hours or overnight.
2. Heat oil over medium heat in saucepan. Sauté onion, garlic, and pork until pork browns.
3. Add stock and posole. Bring to boil, reduce heat, and simmer uncovered for 30 minutes. Periodically, skim to remove foam.
4. Add oregano, cumin, cloves, and bay leaf. Cover and simmer for about 2 hours, stirring occasionally.
5. Add green chilies. Cover and cook another hour, until posole is tender but still a bit chewy and pork is tender.
6. Remove bay leaf and correct seasonings. Serve, accompanied by minced jalapeño peppers.

GREEN CHILI SAUCE

Green Chili Sauce
photo by David Murray © Dorling Kindersley

Use this as a sauce over enchiladas, burritos, or anything else, or use the green chili sauce as the basis for green chili stew.

TOTAL YIELD:
  2 lbs, 11 oz, 5¼ cups
COOKING METHOD:
  Sauté, Boil

INGREDIENTS	WEIGHT	VOLUME
tomatillos, husks removed	12 oz	about 7 or 8 each, depending on size
oil	3/4 oz	1 1/2 tablespoons
onion, small dice	6 oz	1 large
garlic, minced	3/4 oz	3 large cloves
flour, all purpose	3/4 oz	3 tablespoons
cumin, ground		1 1/2 teaspoons
pepper		3/4 teaspoon
chicken stock, hot	1 lb, 2 oz	2 1/4 cups
oregano		1 1/2 teaspoons
jalapeño pepper, seeds and ribs removed, minced	1/2 oz	1 1/2 teaspoons
green chiles, diced	12 oz	3 each 4-oz can
salt	to taste	

1. Boil *tomatillos* for 8 to 10 minutes. Cool slightly. Remove skin; chop coarsely.
2. Heat oil over medium heat. Add onions and garlic, stir, cover pot, and cook over low heat until softened, 4 to 5 minutes.
3. Turn heat to medium. Add flour, cumin, and pepper. Stirring constantly, cook for 2 minutes.
4. Slowly whish in hot stock. Add remaining ingredients, bring to boil, reduce heat, and simmer for 30 minutes, until slightly thickened.
5. Correct seasonings. Use immediately or cool and store covered in refrigerator.

GREEN CHILI CHICKEN ENCHILADAS

Green Chili Chicken Enchiladas

To eliminate moving the enchiladas after baking, many bake them directly on an oven-proof serving plate.

If desired, use 8- or 10-inch enchiladas and provide two for each serving.

NUMBER OF SERVINGS: 8
COOKING METHOD:
    Bake
SERVING SIZE:
    3 each 6-inch corn tortillas each containing 2 1/4 oz filling
TOTAL YIELD:
    Filling: 3 lbs, 11 oz
    24 each 6-inch enchiladas

Wine Style: Wide variety—Pinot Grigio, Sauvignon Blanc, Grenache, medium-bodied reds, Merlot, or Zinfandel
Example: Redondo Red—Ponderosa Valley Vineyard and Winery, Ponderosa, NM. A perfect accompaniment to spicy Southwestern food, this wine is made in the style of a French Vin Ordinaire.

INGREDIENTS	WEIGHT	VOLUME
FILLING:		
chicken, cooked, shredded or cut into 1-inch pieces	1 lb, 13 oz	5^1/$_3$ cups
cheese, Monterey jack or cheddar, grated	8 oz	2^2/$_3$ cups
green chili sauce, *recipe above*	12 oz	1^1/$_3$ cups
sour cream	8^1/$_2$ oz	1 cup
tortillas, corn	24 each 6-inch	
green chili sauce, *recipe above*	as needed for dipping tortillas	
ASSEMBLY:		
green chili sauce, *recipe above*	1 lb, 1 oz	2 cups
cheese, Monterey jack or cheddar, grated	5^1/$_4$ oz	1^1/$_2$ cups

ACCOMPANIMENTS *OPTIONAL:*

beans

rice

onion, minced

tomatoes, chopped

lettuce, shredded

1. Pan-spray baking dish or sheet pan. Preheat oven to 350 degrees.

2. Mix all filling ingredients together in bowl: chicken, 8 oz or 2^2/$_3$ cups cheese, 12 oz or 1^1/$_3$ cups green chili sauce, and sour cream.

3. Dip both sides of each tortilla in green chili sauce.

4. Place 2^1/$_4$ oz filling (3 tablespoons) in line down tortilla about one-third of the way from the edge. Roll tortilla around filling.

5. Place enchilada seam side down, in prepared dish. Repeat with remaining enchiladas. Pour 1 lb, 1 oz green chili sauce (2 cups) evenly over enchiladas. Sprinkle 5^1/$_4$ oz cheese (1^1/$_2$ cups) over enchiladas.

6. Bake until cheese melts and enchiladas are thoroughly heated. Serve immediately, accompanied by beans, rice, onion, tomatoes, and lettuce, if desired.

CHICKEN WITH PUMPKIN SEED SAUCE

Serve warm tortillas with this dish to scoop up all the sauce.

Chicken with Pumpkin Seed Sauce

NUMBER OF SERVINGS: 8
COOKING METHOD:
  Braise
SERVING SIZE:
  7^1/$_2$ oz
TOTAL YIELD:
  5 lbs, 7 oz

Wine Style: Soft and fruity Riesling, Chenin Blanc, Viognier, Rose, or Grenache
Example: Viognier—Fall Creek Vineyards, Tow, TX. This is an elegant wine that exudes the taste of ripe peaches and grapefruits with a crisp, refreshing finish.

INGREDIENTS	WEIGHT	VOLUME
almonds	4¹/₂ oz	³/₄ cup
pumpkin seeds, hulled	6 oz	1 cup + 2 tablespoons
cumin		³/₄ teaspoon
onion, medium dice	7 oz	1 large
garlic, minced	³/₄ oz	3 large cloves
green chilies	6 oz	
chili powder	¹/₂ oz	1¹/₂ tablespoons
cilantro, minced	³/₄ oz	¹/₄ cup + 2 table-spoons or 6 table-spoons
chicken stock	1 lb, 8 oz	3 cups
lime juice	³/₄ oz	1¹/₂ tablespoons
olive oil	³/₄ oz	1¹/₂ tablespoons
chicken breasts, boneless, skinless, cut in half	3 lbs	8 each 6-oz breasts

1. Heat frying pan. Add almonds and pumpkin seeds; shake pan to keep them moving. Toast until lightly browned. Pour into bowl of food processor fitted with knife attachment.
2. Add cumin, onion, garlic, green chilies, chili powder, cilantro, chicken stock, and lime juice to bowl of food processor. Blend until smooth.
3. Heat olive oil in large skillet; brown chicken breasts on both sides.
4. Pour paste from food processor into pan with chicken.
5. Bring to boil, lower heat and simmer, uncovered, until chicken is done and sauce thickens, about 25 minutes.
6. Correct seasonings, serve immediately.

PORK TENDERLOIN WITH ANCHO AND PASILLA CHILIES

Pork Tenderloin with Ancho
and Pasilla Chilies
photo courtesy of National Pork Board

NUMBER OF SERVINGS: 10
COOKING METHOD:
  Bake
SERVING SIZE:
  6 oz
TOTAL YIELD:
  3 lbs, 14¹/₂ oz

Wine Style: Wide variety—soft, fruity Sauvignon Blanc, Pinot Blanc, Pinot Noir, Zinfandel, or Merlot
Example: Pinot Noir Reserve—Bell Mountain Vineyards, Fredericksburg, TX. This wine has a rich, brick red color with aromas of raspberry and violets.

INGREDIENTS	WEIGHT	VOLUME
ancho chilies	2 oz	4 each
pasilla chilies	1 oz	2 each
garlic, peeled	1 oz	6 cloves
honey	4 oz	¹/₄ cup + 2 tablespoons or 6 tablespoons
molasses	1¹/₂ oz	2 tablespoons
paprika	¹/₂ oz	1 tablespoon
chili powder	¹/₄ to ¹/₂ oz	1 tablespoon
salt	¹/₄ oz	1 teaspoon
pork tenderloin, trimmed	4 lbs, 4 oz	

1. Soak chilies in water to cover for 20 minutes. Preheat oven to 425 degrees.
2. Drain chilies; remove stems. Place chilies in bowl of food processor fitted with steel knife blade.
3. Add garlic, honey, molasses, paprika, chili powder, and salt. Process until smooth paste.
4. Rub chili paste over pork; place in baking dish.
5. Bake for 27 to 29 minutes, until proper internal temperature. If desired, slice into thin diagonal slices; fan on plate. Serve immediately.

TEXAS BARBECUED SHRIMP

Texas Barbecued Shrimp

Serve this sweet/spicy dish as an entrée or an appetizer. Use half the portion size for an appetizer.

NUMBER OF SERVINGS: 15
COOKING METHOD:
    Sauté, Boil
SERVING SIZE:
    8 oz
TOTAL YIELD:
    7 lbs, 14 oz

Wine Style: Soft, fruity, and light Pinot Grigio, Chardonnay, White Zinfandel, or light Pinot Noir
Example: Reserve Chardonnay—Cap Rock Winery, Lubbock, TX. This wine has notes of floral, butter, and oak combined with the flavors of green apple, pear, vanilla, and citrus.

INGREDIENTS	WEIGHT	VOLUME
butter	2¹/₂ oz	5 tablespoons
onion, small dice	15 oz	2 large
garlic, minced	1 oz	6 cloves
white vinegar	8 oz	1 cup
balsamic vinegar	4 oz	¹/₂ cup
water	8 oz	1 cup
white wine, dry	8 oz	1 cup
catsup	10 oz	1 cup
Worcestershire sauce	2 oz	¹/₄ cup
lime juice	4 oz	¹/₂ cup or about 2 each
dry mustard	¹/₂ oz	1 tablespoon
hot chili powder	³/₄ oz	2 tablespoons
if using mild or medium chili powder, add ¹/₄ teaspoon cayenne		
brown sugar, firmly packed	12 oz	1¹/₂ cups
bay leaf		2 each
pepper		1 teaspoon
salt	¹/₄ oz	1 teaspoon
cilantro, minced	¹/₂ oz	¹/₄ cup
shrimp, medium, peeled and deveined	4 lbs, 1¹/₂ oz	

1. Melt butter in large skillet over medium heat. Add onion and garlic; sauté until softened, about 5 minutes.

2. Add both vinegars, water, wine, catsup, Worcestershire sauce, and lime juice. Simmer 15 to 20 minutes. Skim any foam from top.

3. Add mustard, chili powder, brown sugar, bay leaf, pepper, salt, and cilantro. Simmer another 10 to 15 minutes.

4. Add shrimp; cook in sauce until shrimp are opaque and thoroughly cooked, about 5 to 8 minutes. Do not overcook or shrimp will become tough and rubbery.

5. Correct seasonings. Serve immediately with rice or tortillas.

CALABACITAS

Calabacitas

All types of squash are popular throughout the Southwest. Some prepare this dish with a combination of zucchini and yellow summer squash.

NUMBER OF SERVINGS: 11
COOKING METHOD:
  Boil
SERVING SIZE:
  4 oz
TOTAL YIELD:
  2 lbs, 12 oz

INGREDIENTS	WEIGHT	VOLUME
olive oil	1/2 oz	1 tablespoon
onion, small dice	2 1/2 oz	1/2 cup
garlic, minced	1/2 oz	2 large cloves
zucchini, medium dice	1 lb, 11 1/4 oz	2 medium
corn kernels, fresh or frozen	4 3/4 oz	1 cup
tomato, peeled, seeded, diced	5 oz	3/4 cup
green chilies, chopped	4 oz	1 each 4-oz can
cilantro, minced		1 tablespoon
salt		1 1/2 teaspoons
pepper		1 teaspoon
cheese, Monterey jack or variety of choice, grated	2 oz	1/2 cup

1. Heat oil in pan. Sauté onion and garlic over medium heat for 3 minutes.

2. Add zucchini and corn if using fresh, not frozen. Cook 3 to 4 minutes, until zucchini starts to become tender.

3. Add tomato, corn if frozen, green chilies, cilantro, salt, and pepper. Cook until thoroughly heated.

4. Correct seasonings. Transfer to serving dish; sprinkle with cheese. Serve immediately.

REFRIED BEANS

Refried Beans
photo by Clive Streeter © Dorling Kindersley

Variations: Some cooks add chorizo sausage, onions, garlic, green chilies, cheese, or any other desired ingredients to refried beans. To prepare with any of these additions except for cheese, sauté the ingredients first, then add the beans. Sprinkle cheese over beans after frying.

NUMBER OF SERVINGS: 10
COOKING METHOD:
  Sauté
SERVING SIZE:
  4 oz
TOTAL YIELD:
  2 lbs, 8 1/2 oz

INGREDIENTS	WEIGHT	VOLUME
oil or lard	2 oz	1/4 cup
beans, pinto or variety of choice, cooked, with some broth, or canned	2 lbs, 12½ oz	4 each 15½-oz cans
salt	1/4 oz	1 teaspoon
pepper		1 teaspoon
cumin	1/4 oz	2 teaspoons

1. Heat oil in heavy pan over medium to medium-low heat.
2. Add beans, salt, pepper, and cumin to pan; mash well with spoon or spatula.
3. Continue mashing and stirring constantly. Sauté until purée starts to dry out. If necessary, add cooking liquid or water, but beans should be dry at end of cooking.
4. Serve, accompanied by salsa and/or cheese, if desired.

SOUTHWESTERN CORNBREAD

Southwestern Cornbread
photo courtesy of Land O' Lakes, Inc.

This bread is delicious when first baked, but it does not keep extremely well. Reheat by sprinkling bread with a few drops of water, wrapping tightly in aluminum foil, and baking in oven for a few minutes, until hot.

NUMBER OF SERVINGS: 12
COOKING METHOD:
  Bake
SERVING SIZE:
  1 wedge, 1/12 pie
TOTAL YIELD:
  1 each 9-inch pie

INGREDIENTS	WEIGHT	VOLUME
lemon juice	1/2 oz	1 tablespoon
milk	8 oz	1 cup
flour, all purpose, unsifted	4¾ oz	1 cup
cornmeal	5¼ oz	1 cup
baking powder	1/4 oz	2 teaspoons
baking soda		1/2 teaspoon
salt		1/4 teaspoon
butter, melted	3 oz	6 tablespoons
egg	1¾ oz	1 each
jalapeño, minced, canned or fresh	1/4 oz	2 teaspoons
corn, chopped	4½ oz	1 cup
cheese, Monterey jack, mild cheddar, or variety of choice, grated	3 oz	3/4 cup

1. Grease or pan-spray 9-inch pie tin. Mix lemon juice with milk, set aside until needed. Preheat oven to 425 degrees.
2. Place flour, cornmeal, baking powder, baking soda, and salt in bowl of food processor. Pulse to combine.
3. Combine milk mixture, butter, and egg in bowl. With processor running, pour liquid mixture through feed tube. Pulse just until combined.
4. Stir jalapeño and corn into mixture. Pour half of batter into prepared pan.
5. Sprinkle cheese over batter. Place remaining batter over cheese.
6. Bake for 23 to 26 minutes, until knife inserted comes out almost clean.
7. Cool slightly. Serve immediately, accompanied by butter.

INDIAN FRYBREAD

Indian Frybread

Serve this bread accompanied with honey.

This dough holds well when refrigerated overnight. Just make sure it is wrapped tightly.

NUMBER OF SERVINGS: 15
COOKING METHOD:
  Fry
SERVING SIZE:
  1 piece, 2-oz dough
TOTAL YIELD:
  1 lb, 15 oz

INGREDIENTS	WEIGHT	VOLUME
flour, all purpose, unsifted	1 lb, 2 oz	4 cups
baking powder	1/2 oz	2 tablespoons
salt	1/4 oz	1 teaspoon
shortening, butter, or lard, cut in half	1/2 oz	1 tablespoon
water, cold	10 3/4 oz	1 1/3 cups
oil, shortening, or lard for frying	as needed	

1. Place flour, baking powder, and salt in bowl of food processor fitted with steel knife blade. Pulse to mix.

2. Place shortening, butter, or lard on top of flour mixture. Pulse to mix until size of peas.

3. With machine running, add water through feed tube. Pulse to mix until dough comes together into ball.

4. Remove dough from bowl. Add a little water if too stiff; add a little flour if too loose. Knead for a few minutes, until dough is smooth, soft, and pliable but not sticky.

5. Cover dough and allow to rest for 30 to 40 minutes.

6. Heat one inch of fat in skillet until hot but not smoking, about 360 to 375 degrees.

7. Form 2-oz piece of dough into ball. Lightly flour hands and table, if sticking. Roll dough into circle about 6 to 7 inches in diameter. With finger, make small hole in center of disk (about 1/2-inch circle).

8. Place disk into hot fat. Fry until golden, turn with tongs, and fry other side until golden. Remove from fat; drain on paper toweling. Repeat with remaining dough, frying one at a time.

9. Keep hot in warm oven or serve immediately.

SOPAIPILLAS

Sopaipillas
photo courtesy of National Honey Board

NUMBER OF SERVINGS: 12
COOKING METHOD:
  Deep-fry
SERVING SIZE:
  3 each 3- by 2-inch pieces
TOTAL YIELD:
  1 lb, 15 1/2 oz dough,
  36 each 3- by 2-inch pieces

INGREDIENTS	WEIGHT	VOLUME
flour, all purpose	1 lb, 3½ oz	4 cups
baking powder	½ oz	1 tablespoon + 1 teaspoon
salt	¼ oz	1 teaspoon
shortening	1½ oz	3 tablespoons
water, warm	10¾ oz	1⅓ cups
oil for frying	as needed	
TOPPING:		
cinnamon	½ oz	1 tablespoon + 1 teaspoon
sugar	4 oz	½ cup
honey		

1. Place flour, baking powder, and salt in bowl of food processor. Pulse to mix.
2. Place shortening on top of mixture. Pulse to cut in, until the size of peas.
3. Remove from processor; stir in water with fork. Briefly knead until it forms smooth ball, cover, and refrigerate 30 minutes.
4. Divide dough in half. Roll each piece into 9- by 12-inch rectangle. Cut each rectangle into pieces 3 by 2 inches (18 pieces).
5. Heat oil until 400 degrees. Fry dough pieces about 1 or 2 minutes on each side, until puffed and golden. Do not fry too many pieces at once to maintain temperature of oil. Remove to absorbent paper to drain.
6. Mix cinnamon and sugar together. Serve *sopaipillas* topped with plenty of the cinnamon sugar mixture and drizzled with honey. Alternately, serve honey on the side so diners can apply the desired amount.

PECAN PIE

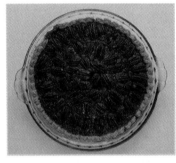

Pecan Pie

photo by Barnabas Kindersley © Dorling Kindersley

This recipe produces a pecan pie with more filling than the usual. As a result, the pie needs a bit longer to cook and the top will need to be tented with aluminum foil to protect the crust from becoming too brown.

NUMBER OF SERVINGS:
  8 to 12
COOKING METHOD:
  Bake
SERVING SIZE:
  1 wedge ⅛ or 1/12 of pie
TOTAL YIELD:
  2 lbs, 14¼ oz, 1 each 9-inch pie

INGREDIENTS	WEIGHT	VOLUME
pastry dough for single crust	about 10 oz	
For pie dough recipe, see recipe for pie dough with pumpkin pie in Chapter 2 or use recipe of choice.		
eggs	6¾ oz	4 each
sugar	6¼ oz	¾ cup
corn syrup, light	1 lb, 1¼ oz	1½ cups
butter, unsalted, melted	2½ oz	5 tablespoons
salt		¼ teaspoon
vanilla		1 teaspoon
pecans, halves or pieces	9¼ oz	2 cups

1. Line pie pan with pastry dough; crimp edges. Place pie in freezer for ½ to 1 hour.
2. Place rack at lowest level in oven; preheat oven to 400 degrees. Remove pie from freezer, line inside of pie shell with aluminum foil with shiny side down (to prevent dough from buckling). Make sure foil reaches into all "corner" seams (where sides and bottom of pan join).
3. Bake for 8 to 10 minutes. Remove from oven, remove foil, and cool on rack.
4. Raise oven temperature to 450 degrees. Place eggs and sugar in mixing bowl. Whisk lightly to combine.
5. Add corn syrup, butter, salt, and vanilla. Whisk to combine well.
6. Place pecans in bottom of pie shell. Pour liquid mixture over nuts.
7. Bake for 5 minutes. Reduce heat to 350 degrees. Bake another 40 to 50 minutes, until filling is almost firm in center. *Cover loosely with aluminum foil when pie/crust is almost desired color.*
8. Refrigerate to cool thoroughly to set filling before cutting.

10

Mountain States

OBJECTIVES

By the end of this chapter, you will be able to

- Discuss the slow development of the Mountain States
- Explain how the topography affected the cookery of the Mountain States
- Discuss why the Mormons settled in the Mountain States and their impact on the land and the cuisine
- Identify protein sources prevalent in the Mountain States
- Prepare a variety of dishes indicative of the cuisine of the Mountain States

States included in the Mountain States:

- Montana
- Idaho
- Wyoming
- Colorado
- Utah
- Nevada

HISTORY

Anasazi tribes who settled in the Southwest also established communities as far north as the mountains of Colorado and Utah. Like those who inhabited the Southwest, these Anasazi built their homes into the sides of mountains, irrigated the land, and planted crops. According to archaeologists, the Anasazi lived here from about 1300 until 1500. Around that time, severe drought gripped the area and the buffalo vanished.

Following the herds of buffalo and the food sources available in the different seasons, nomadic tribes of Native Americans roamed the plains and mountainous areas of the West. They survived on the foods they hunted, fished, and gathered: wild game and fish such as buffalo, moose, elk, bear, deer, antelope, rabbit, trout, berries, mushrooms, and other wild plants.

When Lewis and Clark explored the western half of the United States in the early nineteenth century, they reported the rich bounty of wildlife and fur-bearing animals living throughout the West. The lure of hunting, trapping, and obtaining furs enticed some hearty French and English pioneers to the mountains. Called "Mountain Men," these early trappers and fur traders lived a solitary life, surviving on the incredible abundance of game. Most slept on the ground or in a teepee and ate what they caught or gathered. Any money they needed came from the furs they sold. Although they lived a simple life, the Mountain Men made a significant contribution to the settling of this country by finding passes through the mountains and developing the foundation of the Oregon Trail.

> During the early 1800s, beaver hats for men were quite fashionable, which created a huge market for beaver skins. When the beaver hat went out of style in the 1830s, the market for beavers dwindled drastically. This severely cut the trappers' livelihood.

Since the Rocky Mountains created difficult passage for settlers traveling to the West, the influx of people into this region happened very slowly until the middle of the 1800s. With the discovery of gold in 1849, the sparse population of the West swelled dramatically. Enchanted by the possibility of finding gold and becoming rich, many settlers traveled to California. Others came to the West in search of available land. Reports claim that more than 500,000 people traveled the 2,000-mile Oregon Trail on their westward migration during the 25-year period beginning in the early 1840s. Most of these travelers continued their journey through the mountainous states and settled in California or Oregon.

Traveling through the West proved an arduous voyage. In fact, one out of ten people died while making this trip. Contrary to popular belief, most travelers did not die at the hands of the Native Americans. Illness, disease, or accidents caused the majority of deaths.

Since horses needed more to eat than the tough prairie grasses and mules had a mean disposition, most of those traveling in the West relied on oxen. The disadvantage of oxen was that they moved very slowly, only two miles per hour. At that speed, it required at least six months of traveling from five in the morning until six o'clock at night to complete the journey through the West. While the wagon trains started the trek well stocked with provisions, the food soon dwindled, leaving the cooks with meager rations like dried beans, salt pork, and cornmeal to prepare into three meals each day. Depending on whether cornmeal or wheat flour was available, the cooks made either cornbread or hardtack. A mixture of flour and water, hardtack served as the indestructible bread in times of need. Although this incredibly hard bread often needed dipping in liquid to soften it enough to chew, hardtack sustained trips across the ocean and the United States without spoiling.

Difficult terrain characterized by mountains and flat, arid plains; bad weather including rain, dust storms, and blizzards; lack of food and provisions; and the fear of Native American attacks made this an extremely hard and challenging trip. On their way to California, some of the settlers gave up, deciding to stop and settle in the Mountain States. Becoming farmers or merchants, they provided services, food, and provisions for others making the grueling journey farther west.

Prosperous Fort Laramie, Wyoming, served as an important stop along the Oregon-California Trail (also called the Overland Trail). In this prairie town, the travelers purchased all kinds of foods and provisions. They also traded their tired animals for fresh ones to complete their trip.

After the frantic quest for gold lessened in California in the middle 1800s, settlers made their way back to the Mountain States in search of land or gold. One by one, a number of the western states became the next site of discovered gold and/or silver. Each discovery brought waves of prospectors carrying their pick axes and the dream of striking it rich. Although the majority of the settlers came from other regions of the United States, some immigrated from Europe, Asia, and Latin America. Regardless of their native homeland, all of the settlers and prospectors searched for gold and a better life. Cuisines from all over the world impacted the cookery of the West.

Hotels, taverns, and boarding houses opened to serve food and provide lodging to the masses of people moving west in pursuit of gold. The quality of the food and the menus varied greatly from one establishment to the next, depending on the skills of the cook and the affluence of the area. Making the journey to the West easier, the stagecoach traveled through Denver, Santa Fe, and Salt Lake City by 1865. With the completion of the railroad in 1869, people no longer needed to make the difficult trek to the West in a covered wagon.

Springing up throughout the West, mining camps displayed the same diverse culinary standards that applied to hotels, taverns, and boarding houses. While some inhabitants received beans and bacon three times a day, others enjoyed varied menus of well-prepared foods.

Work in the mines attracted many Italian, English, Cornish, Irish, and Scandinavian immigrants. Meanwhile, numerous Chinese and Japanese moved to the West to work on the railroad. Each of the different culinary backgrounds melded with the existing cookery of the area to create a unique cuisine.

By the middle of the 1800s, the Spanish brought sheep into the United States. Soon the herds spread from New Mexico and Arizona into the western states. Sometimes more sheep than cattle grazed in the West. At other times, the cattle greatly outnumbered the sheep.

Immigrating to the Mountain States from the Pyrenees Mountains in Spain and France, many Basque shepherds raised sheep in this mountainous land. Mainly settling in Nevada and Idaho, these men were accustomed to the isolation of herding sheep in the mountains. Because of the isolation, their native culinary traditions changed little, and they left significant impact on the cookery in the areas where they settled. A fondness for mutton, fish, salt cod, cured ham, *chorizo* (a spicy Spanish sausage), olive oil, garlic, onions, parsley, tomatoes, and sweet red peppers permeated Basque cooking. While tending their flocks, the shepherds baked thick-crusted bread in a cast iron Dutch oven. After the bread baked, they used the same pot to cook one-pot meals like lamb stew or beans flavored with *chorizo*.

To escape persecution for their religious beliefs, Mormons led by Brigham Young left Illinois in 1846 in search of a new home with religious freedom. After one year of traveling west, Mormons became the first permanent group of white settlers to settle in Utah. They established their home in Salt Lake Valley, the valley surrounding the Great Salt Lake. Finding arid land with sagebrush growing, the Mormons irrigated the land using the streams from the surrounding mountains. Through irrigation, they transformed the dry, barren land into lush farmland. Today, at least 70 percent of the residents of Utah claim to be Mormons, and the headquarters of the Mormon religion are located in Salt Lake City.

Bringing many travelers through the state of Wyoming, all three of the major trails leading to the West crossed through the mountains at the South Pass in Wyoming. After traveling through the pass, the Oregon Trail turned northwest toward the Pacific Northwest while the California Trail and the Mormon Trail continued to the southwest. The Mormon Trail led into Utah, and those traveling the California Trail traveled through Utah and Nevada before reaching California. With tall mountains in the west and dry plains in the east, the rugged terrain did not encourage many settlers to stop and make Wyoming their home.

Between 1846 and 1861, more than 70,000 Mormons traveled along the Mormon Trail from Illinois to Utah.

Brigham Young started over 350 communities in Canada, Mexico, and many western states including Idaho, Wyoming, Colorado, New Mexico, Arizona, Nevada, California, and Utah.

On May 10, 1869, workers finished the transcontinental railroad connecting the East to the West. Bringing enormous culinary impact, the completed railroad allowed the shipping of foods across the country as well as providing people with much easier travel between cities throughout the United States. Now seasonal foods could be shipped to locations where those same foods were out of season or did not grow at all. Erasing many culinary boundaries, the railroad increased the availability of products and the sharing of recipes from coast to coast. As a result, the melting pot grew larger.

With the Homestead Acts of 1909, 1912, and 1916, many settlers moved into the sparsely populated western states, lured by the promise of free land. Even though the Homestead Acts enticed numerous inhabitants to move to the West, the population of many of these states remains very low.

TOPOGRAPHY AND CLIMATE

The Mountain States contain incredibly diverse topography such as snow-capped mountains, forests, plains, plateaus, streams, lakes, rivers, canyons, lush valleys, and desert. Known for the "big sky," the stark terrain exhibits miles and miles of unobstructed views of the sky. The West is a land of contrasts. Cactus, sagebrush, desert, and dramatic rock formations form the landscape in some areas, while the snowy peaks of the Rocky Mountains loom in others. The severe blizzards that sometimes raged across the Plains also posed a grave threat to the settlers in the Mountain States. With howling winds and blinding snow, those blizzards eliminated many people and countless head of cattle.

Although much of this region suffers from lack of rainfall, the early residents created viable farmland by irrigating from the existing rivers and streams. Cattle grazed on the extensive areas of dry grassy land that formed the plains and plateaus, while sheep flourished in the high elevations. With irrigation, crops thrived.

The word "Montana" came from the Spanish word for mountainous. Montana contains valleys, forests, and many cold-water lakes remaining from the glaciers. While the Rocky Mountains tower in the western section of the state, eastern Montana consists of expansive plains and rolling hills. Although the intense canyons and high ridges discouraged settlers from coming to Montana for many years, the lure of gold mines and instant wealth finally drew settlers to this area.

Cold winters and cool summers describe the climate of Montana, but the elevation determines the climate in many regions. The Continental Divide runs through this state. Rivers on the western side of the Continental Divide flow into the Pacific Ocean, and those on the eastern side run toward the Atlantic Ocean.

Montana lies south of Canada with North and South Dakota to its east, Wyoming and Idaho bordering on the south, and Idaho on its west. The Missouri River begins in southwestern Montana, and the Columbia River flows through the western part of the state.

Canada lies north of Idaho, Montana and Wyoming are situated to Idaho's east, Nevada to its south, and Oregon and Washington to the west. The Salmon River runs through the central portion of the state, and the Snake River flows in the southern part. Idaho contains mountains, forests, valleys, canyons, rivers, many lakes, and plateaus. Because of warm winds from the Pacific Ocean and mountains in the north blocking the cold Canadian winds, Idaho's climate stays warmer than other states lying so far north.

Mountains and forests dominate the terrain in northern Idaho. Herds of sheep graze in the mountains. Providing fertile farmland for crops like peas and wheat, valleys and plateaus lie between the mountains. Plateau makes up the southern part of the state. Because of irrigation, much of southern Idaho is fertile farmland. In addition, many cattle feed on the grasses found in the plains of central and southern Idaho.

Wyoming is situated with Montana to its north, South Dakota and Nebraska lie to the east, Colorado and Utah border on the south, and Utah and Idaho are on the west. Three distinct types of terrain compose this state: mountains, plateaus, and plains.

Several mountain ranges that are part of the Rocky Mountains rise in the west and run from north to south through Wyoming. Known as basins, flat plateaus lie between the mountains. With limited rainfall and almost void of trees, these dry basins are covered with grasses that support grazing cattle. Also functioning as prime grazing land for a bounty of cattle and sheep, endless, dry plains covered with grasses make up the eastern portion of the state. In fact, 50 percent of Wyoming's land is used for grazing. With irrigation, settlers transformed some of the arid plains into fertile farmland. The Black Hills are located in the northeastern part of the state and continue into South Dakota.

Wyoming experiences a sunny, dry climate with cold winters and warm summers. Of course, colder weather prevails at the higher elevations. Yielding plenty of game, forests cover much of the mountains.

Three major rivers begin in the mountains—the Columbia, Missouri, and Colorado Rivers. Besides carving canyons in the hills and mountains, these rivers with all their tributaries supply water for the state. Hundreds of lakes dot the mountainous areas. Wyoming is known for beautiful scenery and parks, with both Yellowstone National Park and Grand Teton National Park lying within its borders. In addition, the Continental Divide runs through Wyoming from the northwest to the south central region.

Wyoming and Nebraska border Colorado to the north, Kansas lies on its east, Oklahoma and New Mexico to the south, and Utah on its west. Mountains actually run through the center of Colorado with plateaus, valleys, and mesas (flat-topped hills) lying in the west. Claiming more tall peaks than any other state, Colorado contains more than 50 peaks that tower at 14,000 feet or above. The Continental Divide runs through the Rocky Mountains. The plains of eastern Colorado support a bounty of cattle as well as crops. Actually comprising two-fifths of the state, the plains consist of arid land. Irrigation changed this once-dry soil into rich farmland.

Yielding abundant game like elk, moose, deer, bear, rabbit, quail, dove, and turkey, extensive forests grow in Colorado. Numerous streams and lakes flow, particularly in the mountainous western and central regions. The cold mountain streams in these areas teem with several varieties of trout, bluegill, and other fish. The Colorado River runs through the west, and the Rio Grande River starts in the mountains of Colorado. Cool summers and cold winters prevail here.

Idaho and Wyoming lie north of Utah, Wyoming and Colorado to the east, Arizona is situated to the south, and Nevada borders on the west. Like much of the West, Utah boasts a varied terrain, including mountains, canyons, valleys, forests, lakes, rivers, and desert. Depending on elevation, the climate varies greatly.

About one-third of the land in Utah qualifies as desert. Although western Utah ranks as one of the driest areas in the United States, productive farmland emerged from much of this barren land with irrigation from the lakes and rivers.

Lakes and canyons formed by glaciers mark the landscape, particularly near the Uinta and Wasatch Mountain Ranges. Rising in the northeastern part of the state, these two ranges are part of the Rocky Mountains. The forests found in and around the mountains

In 1872, the United States government established Yellowstone National Park as the first national park.

provide a habitat for plenty of game, such as deer, elk, and moose, which supplied food for the early pioneers. Wind and rain eroded rocks, creating dramatic formations of arches and natural bridges throughout Utah.

Containing salt water and ranking as the largest natural lake in the United States west of the Mississippi River, the Great Salt Lake lies in northwestern Utah. The fertile valleys around the Great Salt Lake support abundant agriculture and dairy farms producing plentiful milk.

Extensive plateaus with canyons and valleys cover southern and eastern Utah. The Colorado River and Green River flow through the east, providing water for irrigation. In the days of the early inhabitants, the waterways and the plateaus yielded a multitude of buffalo, quail, ducks, geese, and fish.

A land of great diversity, Nevada's terrain consists of arid land with jagged rock formations, high mountains, valleys, canyons, forests, streams, lakes, and desert. Because Nevada receives less annual precipitation than any other state, land for farming requires irrigation. Oregon and Idaho lie to the north of Nevada, Utah and Arizona to the east, Arizona and California border on the south, and California is situated to its west.

While plateaus dominate the northeast, the south and west contain mountains and lakes. The terrain in the rest of Nevada consists of mountains, plateaus, and arid desert land.

The Sierra Nevada Mountains rise in western Nevada. When they discovered gold there in 1859, droves of people moved to Nevada. The early settlers found food in the bountiful game of deer, rabbits, quail, and doves. Also, the streams, rivers, and lakes teemed with trout, catfish, and bass. Pine trees yielding pine nuts thrived in many of the dry regions of Utah and Nevada, supplying another source of food for the early settlers.

Nevada's climate varies greatly depending on the elevation of the region. Generally, low humidity, dry conditions, and limited rainfall prevail. Long cold winters and short hot summers reign in the northern portion and the mountainous areas, the west experiences short mild winters and short hot summers, and the south receives mild winters and long hot summers.

Ingredients and foods commonly used throughout the cuisine of the Mountain States include

- beef and lamb
- game, including buffalo, deer, elk, moose, antelope, and rabbit
- quail, duck, and geese
- trout, bass, catfish, bluegill, and whitefish
- milk and dairy products
- potatoes
- wheat, barley, and corn
- sugar beets
- lentils, peas, and beans
- onions
- apples and berries
- pine nuts

COOKING METHODS

With shepherds herding sheep and cowboys on the trail driving cattle, grilling and one-pot cookery established early roots throughout this region. Traditionally, cowboys gathered around the fire built near the chuck wagon for the serving of meals. Since they relied on the open fire to cook, the primary cooking methods used in those early days were grilling, boiling, and braising (slow cooking in liquid). As a result, cowboys ate lots of soups and stews. To bake bread on the trail, they buried a cast iron pot filled with bread dough in the embers of the fire. This produced bread surrounded by a very thick, hard crust.

The many sheep grazing in the mountains ensured plenty of lamb and mutton to eat. Shish kabob, barbecued lamb, and baked, grilled, or broiled lamb were served, as well as stew made by braising the tougher cuts.

Preparation of trout caught from the mountain streams included pan-frying the fresh fish in a skillet or placing a stick through the trout and grilling it over the open fire. The latter method imparts a distinctly smoky taste to the fish.

In the pioneer days, drying any excess meat, fish, fruits, and vegetables increased the possibility of survival through the long winter months. In the arid climate, settlers preserved by drying and smoking foods. Jerky remains a favorite in the West. As in other regions of the United States, the Native Americans prepared *pemmican*, dried meat pounded with berries as a staple for the winter. When salt was available, they salted many foods to preserve them.

STATES

The discovery of gold attracted many immigrants to Montana in the latter half of the 1800s. Germans, British, Irish, Italians, Scandinavians, Yugoslavians, and more came for work as miners. Each group brought their native recipes and culinary traditions to their new homeland.

Since great numbers of cattle thrived on the grasslands of eastern Montana and sheep flourished in the mountains of the west, residents consumed ample amounts of beef and lamb. The valleys proved an excellent environment for raising dairy cattle. The settlers found trout swimming in the many cold streams and plenty of game such as deer, elk, moose, bison, geese, duck, and pheasant roaming here. The bounty of game added significantly to the diet of the early settlers.

By the 1870s, ranchers in Wyoming and Montana expanded their herds. This expansion was at least partly due to the invention of barbed wire, which allowed the cowboys to fence the herds. The days of chasing and rounding up wandering cattle ended.

In the beginning of the twentieth century, farmers started growing wheat in the plains of eastern Montana. Sugar beets, barley, potatoes, and oats also flourished here. Immigrants from Russia, Scandinavia, Germany, Ireland, and Eastern Europe came to this region to farm. They each contributed bits from their culinary heritage to the cookery already found there.

In 1805, Lewis and Clark explored Idaho. Early settlers in Idaho feasted on the bounty of elk, deer, antelope, buffalo, pheasant, partridge, ducks, trout, whitefish, and salmon. Still today, many varieties of trout thrive in the numerous mountain streams. In addition, bass, sturgeon, and more swim in the rivers and streams.

Belonging to several ethnic backgrounds, including Scandinavian, Swiss, and British, Mormons began to settle in Idaho in the late 1850s. As in Utah, the Mormons turned dry land into fertile farmland with irrigation. The combination of rich soil and ample sources of water resulted in productive farms for the Mormons and the other settlers who made Idaho their home.

In 1860, the discovery of gold in Idaho brought an influx of prospectors with hopes of striking it rich. Soon, Irish, Cornish, English, Welsh, Finnish, French Canadian, Hispanic, and Chinese immigrants flooded into this state. By 1870, one-quarter of the inhabitants of Idaho were of Chinese descent. Although most of the Chinese came for mining jobs or work on the railroad, some turned to vegetable farming. As in their homeland, they terraced the mountainsides and farmed the land. Around 1880, many Japanese from Hawaii and Japan immigrated here to work on the railroad. Also seeking new opportunity in Idaho, Basque shepherds left Spain and France to tend sheep here in the late 1800s. Today, Idaho claims a large population with Basque heritage. Of course, each ethnic group impacted the existing cookery of Idaho.

While the north of Idaho mainly consists of grazing land for cattle and sheep, fields in the northwest yield abundant lentils, dried beans, barley, and wheat. Initially, farmland near the Snake River in the south supported agriculture. With irrigation, crops like potatoes, broccoli, sugar beets, asparagus, and blueberries thrive throughout the southern portion of the state.

Now a huge crop for Idaho, the first potatoes were planted in 1836. In 1872, Russet Burbank developed the famous Idaho russet potato. One of the most widely known varieties of potatoes, the russet has a high starch content, which makes it excellent for baking or mashing. Because of its low moisture content, the potato stores well in the proper cool, dark conditions.

Well known for high quality potatoes, Idaho produces many varieties for export. The warm summer days and the cool nights, combined with the volcanic soil, yield bountiful crops. Today, Idaho ranks as the top producing state for potatoes.

In the early 1800s, numerous trappers and traders inhabited Wyoming. After the trappers left, immigrants from many countries, including France, Germany, Greece, Spain, and China, came to Wyoming. The settlers' cattle and sheep grazed on the lush grasses found here. The perpetual battle between men who raise cattle and those who raise sheep raged in Wyoming. The cattlemen claimed the sheep destroyed the grass and felt they should not be allowed to graze there. Of course, the men raising sheep vehemently disagreed.

In the late nineteenth century, a rancher decided to graze cattle and sheep on the same land. Although this was quite a revolutionary idea at that time, sheep and cattle coexisted on the high plains of Wyoming. Of course, both lamb and beef frequently appear on menus throughout this state.

With moose, elk, bear, deer, partridge, duck, wild turkeys, pheasants, and trout thriving here, the early settlers found plenty of food. When the Mormons came to Wyoming, they developed communities and planted crops like they had in other areas they settled. Today, sugar beets, corn, wheat, barley, beans, and potatoes grow well here.

In 1858, settlers first came to Denver, Colorado. A year later, the gold craze struck, and the town grew into a city of great wealth. To accommodate the newly rich inhabitants, opulent hotels and restaurants opened.

Settlers moved into Colorado late; in fact, wagon trains of settlers still arrived there in the late 1870s. Throughout the West, prospectors quit mining and turned to farming and ranching when they finally realized it brought more lucrative results. Soon, sugar beets became an important crop in Colorado. The success of the sugar beet crops lured Russian, German, and Mexican immigrants to this area to farm and/or harvest the crops. These immigrants came with their native recipes. Soon stuffed cabbage leaves, tamales, German sausages, Sauerbraten, mole, dumplings, flan, and German pastries joined the cookery of Colorado.

Moscow, Idaho, claims the title of the Pinto Capital of the United States. In fact, all sorts of dried peas and beans come from Idaho.

The basis for the intense hatred between cattlemen (cowboys) and sheep-raising men (shepherds) developed from the different ways the two animals graze. Cattlemen claimed the sheep ate the grasses down to the roots, which killed the grass. Because cows did not eat the grass to such a short level, it grew back. With this reasoning, cattlemen believed sheep should not be allowed to graze on their land.

Because of the booming cattle business, Cheyenne, Wyoming, became an extremely wealthy town in the 1870s. In fact, Cheyenne claimed the richest population per capita of any town in the United States around that time.

Wyoming ranks as the least populated state in the United States.

The origin of the Western sandwich remains a mystery. Also called Denver sandwich, this egg sandwich features an omelet containing ham, onions, and red or green peppers between two slices of toast. Some say a chuck wagon cook invented this sandwich as a way to use rancid eggs and that the onions were added to mask the taste of the spoiled eggs. Others
(Continued)

(Continued)
claim a pioneer woman or Basque immigrant first made this sandwich. Still others believe Chinese workers who came to Colorado to work on the railroad created it. According to legend, the workers needed a way to take their traditional egg fu yung for lunch. To remedy this problem, they put the egg fu yung between two slices of bread. Regardless of which version is true, the Western sandwich was born.

Herds of sheep and cattle graze on the slopes of the mountains and on the plains in Colorado. Consequently, Colorado produces more lamb than any other state, and it ranks high in production and consumption of beef and veal. In addition to cattle and sheep ranches, today, a number of buffalo ranches flourish throughout this state. Fruit orchards and crops of cantaloupes, peaches, apples, potatoes, lettuce, barley, and more grow in the fertile mountain valleys. Wheat and corn thrive in the dry plains, while potatoes, sugar beets, and an assortment of vegetables flourish on the irrigated farmland found in the east. The hot, dry southwest is known for production of pinto beans. Fruits and plentiful game come from the mountainous, western part of the state.

The fact that their favorite cake recipes did not rise correctly in their new home baffled the early settlers. Finally, they realized the effect of high altitude on baking and adjusted their recipes to compensate for it.

In the beginning, Utah contained so much arid desert that only a few Native Americans lived there. Their diet consisted of the beans, corn, and squash that they planted and the wild berries, plants, seeds, and nuts that they gathered.

After enduring religious persecution in their settlements to the east, the Mormons moved to the Salt Lake Valley in 1847 and began farming. Carrying seeds and saplings to plant, the Mormons arrived in their new homeland. They proceeded to plant and irrigate, which successfully transformed desert land into fertile farmland. Although the early years proved difficult because of lack of food, the Mormons not only survived, but also created a prosperous homeland through hard work and perseverance. The Mormons brought culinary influences from the Germans and Scandinavians who had converted to their faith. Dishes like sweet and sour red cabbage, fruit soups, and Scandinavian cookies permeated their cookery. Before long, the Mormons expanded their settlements and moved into other states of the Southwest and West. Around the same time, prospectors surged into Utah with hopes of striking it rich in mining.

Because of irrigation, Utah produces a bounty of crops. All sorts of vegetables, fruits, and berries thrive here, with raspberries remaining a favorite. Potatoes, wheat, barley, corn, pears, peaches, and apples flourish. Farmers raise cattle and turkeys as well as a bounty of dairy products. Like most of the western states, sheep graze in the mountainous areas.

Since most of Nevada consisted of desert, few settlers came until the discovery of gold and silver in the Comstock Lode in Virginia City in 1859. Reports state that 17,000 miners flooded into Nevada within one year! According to history, that productive strike created numerous wealthy men and actually helped President Lincoln finance the Civil War. Mormons also moved into the region near the Sierra Nevada Mountains in the western part of the state.

The mountains of Nevada provided extensive areas for grazing livestock. Many Basque men immigrated for jobs as shepherds in the 1870s. As a result, beef, lamb, and occasionally mutton dominated menus. Due to the arid conditions, crop production remained secondary to raising livestock. With the help of irrigation, growing fruits turned into a prosperous venture by the beginning of the twentieth century. In fact, farmers planted all sorts of orchards, potatoes, wheat, onions, and grapes for wine.

While Mormon cooking with its German and Scandinavian roots remains strong, the cuisine of Nevada also reflects traces from the cookery of Mexicans, Spanish, British, Dutch, and Native Americans. Dishes include plenty of lamb or beef in addition to dried fruits from the Mormon cookery and chilies from the cuisine of the nearby Southwest.

Located in southern Nevada near California and Arizona, Las Vegas was named from Spanish words meaning "the meadows." Now a large, bustling, vibrant city, Las Vegas features all the culinary traits of a melting pot, with Mexican food served as commonly as cheese blintzes.

CHARACTERISTICS OF THE CUISINE

Hearty food describes the cookery of the West. Stews, soups, and dishes using produce from the summer gardens as well as meat from available cattle, sheep, and game fill menus here.

Beef retains first place as the meat of choice in this former bastion of cowboy country. Ranches still dominate much of the flat lands. Beef stews, grilled steaks, and dishes involving all cuts of beef appear on menus in homes and restaurants. Sheep graze on the grasses found on the open ranges and especially in the mountains in all of these states. In fact, most of the lamb raised in the United States comes from the mountainous states of the West. With a bounty of game including elk, moose, deer, rabbits, and much more roaming the forests and plenty of fish like perch, whitefish, pike, arctic char, and many varieties of trout inhabiting the cold mountain streams and lakes, hunting and fishing remain popular and play a significant role in the cuisine throughout the Mountain States.

The cuisine of the West reflects strong impact from the Native Americans who inhabited the land before the arrival of European and Asian immigrants, settlers from more eastern regions of the United States, and Mexicans. The prominent Native American influence results from a couple of issues. First, the settlers kept pushing the Native Americans farther west as they took over their lands. This led to a larger population of Native Americans in the West. Second, fewer settlers moved to the Mountain States than most other regions in the United States. With both of these factors, a higher proportion of people with Native American heritage live in this region.

Basque men from the Pyrenees in Spain and France made a significant impact on the cuisine of the Mountain States. These shepherds lived solitary lives for long stretches of time with their herds in the mountains. This isolation kept their culinary traits from being diluted with other influences. Characteristics of Basque cookery include the use of plenty of garlic, lamb, beef, and spicy sausages like *chorizo*. Easily cooked in a single pot over a fire while the shepherd tended the herds of sheep, lamb stew still appears commonly. To serve this population, many Basque restaurants, hotels, and boarding houses opened. In a Basque restaurant, diners typically sit together at long tables and eat their meals family style.

A wide variety of wild mushrooms and berries flourish in the forests, which added to the diet of the early settlers. In addition, the pine forests yield pine nuts. All of these indigenous foods commonly appear in many dishes throughout the West.

With plenty of cold weather, soups dominate menus. Split peas, lentils, and many other beans in soups regularly fill the menus at homes and restaurants. In addition, numerous grains flourish throughout this region. Barley, wheat, and corn grow well and play an important part in the cuisine. Root vegetables such as potatoes, parsnips, carrots, and more thrived in this cool climate and filled root cellars for consumption throughout the winter. Even today, root vegetables serve as the foundation for soups, salads, the vegetables in stews, or as a side dish.

Area	Weather	Topography	Foods
Montana Canada to north, North and South Dakota to east, Wyoming and Idaho to south, Idaho to west	cold winters, cool summers	plains, mountains, valleys, forests, glacial lakes, hills, Continental Divide, canyons east: plains and rolling hills southwest: Missouri River west: Rocky Mountains, Columbia River	cattle, beef, dairy, sheep, lamb, game, deer, elk, moose, bison, geese, duck, pheasant, trout, wheat, barley, oats, sugar beets, potatoes
Idaho Canada to north, Montana and Wyoming to east, Nevada to south, Oregon and Washington to west	cold winters, cool summers, tempered by warm ocean winds and mountains blocking cold; more temperate than most states that far north	mountains, forests, valleys, canyons, many lakes, rivers, plateaus, fertile farmland north: forests, mountains, valleys, fertile farmland, plateaus central: Salmon River, plains south: plateau, Snake River, plains	beef, cattle, lamb, sheep, game, elk, deer, pheasant, partridge, duck, trout, bass, whitefish, salmon, sturgeon, wheat, potatoes, barley, dried peas and beans, lentils, sugar beets, broccoli, asparagus, blueberries
Wyoming Montana to north, South Dakota and Nebraska to east, Colorado and Utah to south, Utah and Idaho to west	sunny, dry climate; cold winters, warm summers; colder at higher elevations	mountains, plateaus, plains, forests, hills, canyons, many lakes northeast: Black Hills east: dry plains, grasses, fertile farmland with irrigation west: Rocky Mountains running north to south; flat plateaus; forest; Columbia, Missouri, and Colorado Rivers flow through state; Continental Divide	beef, cattle, sheep, lamb, game, moose, elk, bear, deer, partridge, duck, wild turkey, pheasant, trout, wheat, corn, barley, sugar beets, beans, potatoes
Colorado Wyoming and Nebraska to north, Kansas to east, Oklahoma and New Mexico to south, Utah to west	cold winters, cool summers	east: arid plains, fertile farmland with irrigation central: Rocky Mountains, forests, streams, rivers, lakes, plateaus, valleys, Continental Divide; Rio Grande River starts in mountains west: plateaus, forests, mesas, valleys, Colorado River	beef, cattle, veal, game, beaver, buffalo, elk, moose, deer, quail, dove, wild turkey, sheep, lamb, fish, trout, bluegill, wheat, corn, barley, beans, sugar beets, potatoes, many fruits and vegetables, lettuce, cantaloupes, peaches, apples, fruit orchards
Utah Idaho and Wyoming to north, Wyoming and Colorado to east, Arizona to south, Nevada to west	cold winters, cool summers, hot summers in desert	mountains, canyons, valleys, forests, lakes, rivers, desert northeast: Rocky Mountains, lakes, canyons, forests northwest: Great Salt Lake, fertile valleys east and south: valleys, canyons, plateaus east: Colorado River and Green River west: irrigated farmland, desert	cattle, beef, dairy, milk, lamb, sheep, turkey, game, deer, elk, moose, buffalo, quail, duck, geese, wheat, barley, beans, corn, potatoes, many fruits and vegetables, pears, peaches, apples, raspberries, many berries, pine nuts
Nevada Oregon and Idaho to north, Utah and Arizona to east, Arizona and California to south, California to west	dry, low humidity, limited rainfall north and mountains: long cold winters, short hot summers south: short mild winters, long hot summers west: short mild winters, short hot summers	mountains, valleys, canyons, forests, streams, lakes, desert, plateaus, irrigated farmland northeast: plateaus south and west: mountains, lakes west: Sierra Nevada Mountains rest of state: desert, plateaus, mountains	cattle, beef, sheep, lamb, mutton, game, deer, rabbits, quail, doves, trout, catfish, bass, potatoes, wheat, onions, fruit orchards, dried fruits, grapes, wine, pine nuts

1. Discuss factors that dissuaded settlers from moving to the Mountain States and what caused that to change.
2. Why did settlers raise sheep in this region? Discuss the relationship between cowboys and shepherds and the reasons for this relationship.
3. Discuss the Mormons' settlement of Utah, why they left the Midwest, and how they transformed the land.
4. Describe the general topography of this region and what animals and crops flourish there.
5. What is the Continental Divide?
6. Discuss the history of the potato in Idaho and why it grows well in that state.

chorizo—a spicy Spanish sausage
hardtack—mixture of flour and water that served as an indestructible, hard bread; used on long voyages across land or sea because it did not spoil

mesas—flat-topped hills
pemmican—dried meat pounded with berries; a staple food for the winter months

SMOKED TROUT WITH HORSERADISH SAUCE

Smoked Trout with Horseradish Sauce

If a smoker is available, try smoking the fresh trout instead of purchasing it already smoked.

NUMBER OF SERVINGS: 14
SERVING SIZE:
 1 oz (2 tablespoons) sauce
 2 oz smoked trout
TOTAL YIELD:
 14½ oz sauce
 1 lb, 12 oz smoked trout

Wine Style: Light- to medium-bodied Sauvignon Blanc, Chardonnay, Rose, or light Merlot
Example: Sauvignon Blanc—Ste. Chapelle Winery, Caldwell, ID. This fresh, crisp-flavored wine develops ripe melon and spicy, herbal notes.

INGREDIENTS	WEIGHT	VOLUME
sour cream	13½ oz	1½ cups
horseradish, prepared	2¼ oz	3 tablespoons
mustard, prepared	½ oz	2 tablespoons
garlic, minced	¼ oz	1 large clove
vinegar, white	½ oz	1 tablespoon
salt		½ teaspoon
white pepper		¼ teaspoon
smoked trout fillets	1 lb, 12 oz	14 each 2-oz pieces

GARNISH:
chives, minced or left in long strands

1. Whisk sour cream, horseradish, mustard, garlic, vinegar, salt, and pepper together in bowl. Correct seasonings. Cover and refrigerate until needed.
2. Place 2 oz smoked trout on plate; nap with 1 oz (2 tablespoons) horseradish sauce. Garnish with chives and serve.

POTATO SKINS WITH ELK SAUSAGE AND GOAT CHEESE

Removing Pulp from Potato
photo by David Murray and Jules Selmes
© Dorling Kindersley

If elk sausage is unavailable, substitute another type of game sausage or sausage of choice.

Potato Skins with Elk Sausage and Goat Cheese

NUMBER OF SERVINGS: 12
COOKING METHOD:
  Sauté, Bake
SERVING SIZE:
  1 potato (4 each quarters)
TOTAL YIELD:
  4 lbs, 6 oz

Wine Style: Merlot, Cabernet Sauvignon, Zinfandel, or Shiraz
Example: Cabernet Sauvignon—Mission Mountain Winery, Dayton, MT. This wine is dark and smooth with great balance of fruit and oak.

INGREDIENTS	WEIGHT	VOLUME
baking potatoes, russets, scrubbed	5 lb, 8 1/2 oz	12 each medium to large
oil	1 oz	2 tablespoons
salt	for sprinkling	
elk sausage, bulk, sautéed until browned	1 lb	
green and red peppers, small dice	10 oz	2 cups
pepper	for sprinkling	
goat cheese	10 oz	
green onions, sliced, green part only	1 oz	6 each
paprika	for sprinkling	
GARNISH:		
sour cream		

1. Preheat oven to 450 degrees.
2. Coat potatoes with oil; cut in half lengthwise. Place cut side down on parchment-lined baking sheet; sprinkle with salt.
3. Bake about 20 minutes, until done. Remove from oven; cool.
4. Using spoon, remove most of potato flesh, leaving about 1/4 inch flesh remaining around skin. Place skins cut side up on baking sheet.
5. Distribute sausage evenly over 24 potato halves, top with green and red peppers, sprinkle lightly with pepper, then top with crumbled goat cheese.
6. Return to oven; bake about 10 minutes, until hot and cheese softens.
7. Remove from oven. Divide green onions evenly over potatoes, sprinkle with paprika. Cut in half lengthwise, if desired. Serve 4 quarters or 2 halves, garnished with sour cream.

WILD MUSHROOM SOUP

Wild Mushroom Soup
photo by Clive Streeter © Dorling Kindersley

Use any desired assortment of wild mushrooms.

NUMBER OF SERVINGS: 13
COOKING METHOD:
　Boil
SERVING SIZE:
　8 oz
TOTAL YIELD:
　6 lbs, 8½ oz

INGREDIENTS	WEIGHT	VOLUME
butter	4 oz	½ cup, 8 table-spoons, or 1 stick
onions, small dice	12½ oz	2½ cups or 2 large
garlic, minced	1 oz	4 large cloves
wild mushrooms, cleaned, coarsely chopped, varieties of choice	4 lbs	
flour, all purpose	2¼ oz	½ cup
chicken stock, hot	3 lbs	6 cups
white wine	8 oz	1 cup
bay leaves		2 each
salt	¼ oz	1 teaspoon
pepper		1 teaspoon
nutmeg		1 teaspoon
heavy cream	4 oz	½ cup

GARNISH:

parsley, minced and/or chives

1. Melt butter in large pot over medium heat. Add onions and garlic; sauté 3 to 4 minutes until onions soften.

2. Add mushrooms; sauté until tender and releasing liquid, about 5 to 6 minutes.

3. Sprinkle in flour and stir until smooth paste. Slowly stir in hot stock. Add wine, bay leaves, salt, pepper, and nutmeg. Bring to simmer for 25 minutes.

4. Add cream; correct seasonings. Heat thoroughly, but do not boil. Serve, garnished with parsley and/or chives.

SPLIT PEA SOUP

Adding Split Peas to Pot

Adding Croutons to Split Pea Soup

NUMBER OF SERVINGS: 8
COOKING METHOD:
　Boil, Sauté
SERVING SIZE:
　8 oz
TOTAL YIELD:
　4 lbs, 2½ oz

INGREDIENTS	WEIGHT	VOLUME
ham hock, smoked, cooked	10 oz	
water	4 lbs	2 qts
split peas, rinsed	1 lb	2 cups
butter	1/2 oz	1 tablespoon
onion, small dice	4 oz	1 medium or 3/4 cup
carrot, small dice	4 oz	1 large or 3/4 cup
celery, small dice	2 1/2 oz	1 rib or 1/2 cup
bay leaf		1 each
marjoram		1/4 teaspoon
sage		1/4 teaspoon
salt		1 1/4 teaspoons
pepper		3/4 teaspoon

GARNISH:

croutons, *if desired*

1. Place ham hock, water, and split peas in pot. Stirring occasionally, cover and cook for 1 hour.
2. Remove ham hock; cut meat from bone into small pieces. Reserve meat.
3. Purée split peas and their liquid in food processor fitted with steel knife.
4. Meanwhile, melt butter in pot. Sauté onions, carrots, and celery for 5 minutes. Add split pea purée, reserved ham, bay leaf, marjoram, sage, salt, and pepper.
5. Bring uncovered pot to simmer. Cook until desired thickness, about 30 minutes. If too thick, add a little water. If too thin, cook a little longer to reduce. Correct seasonings. Serve, garnished with croutons, if desired.

SPINACH SALAD WITH HORSERADISH DRESSING

Chill plates in advance for this salad.

NUMBER OF SERVINGS: 11
SERVING SIZE:
  2 3/4 oz
TOTAL YIELD:
  2 lbs, 1/4 oz total
  11 1/4 oz dressing
  1 lb, 5 oz salad

INGREDIENTS	WEIGHT	VOLUME
DRESSING		
balsamic vinegar	4 1/2 oz	1/2 cup + 1 tablespoon
dry mustard		3/4 teaspoon
garlic, minced	1/4 to 1/2 oz	3 small cloves
paprika		3/4 teaspoon
oregano		3/4 teaspoon
thyme		3/4 teaspoon
basil		3/4 teaspoon
salt		3/4 teaspoon
pepper		3/4 teaspoon
olive oil	9 oz	1 cup + 2 tablespoons
horseradish	3 oz	3/4 cup
SALAD		
baby spinach, washed, stems removed	12 oz	12 cups
green onions, sliced, white and green	3 oz	6 each
radishes, cleaned, washed, sliced	6 oz	9 large

For Dressing:

1. Whisk together vinegar, mustard, garlic, paprika, oregano, thyme, basil, salt, and pepper in nonreactive bowl. Alternately, mix these ingredients in bowl of food processor fitted with knife blade.
2. Slowly whisk in olive oil to form emulsion (mixture thickens). Alternately, slowly add olive oil through food tube; continue processing until mixture emulsifies (thickens). Stir in horseradish.
3. Correct seasonings. Cover and refrigerate until needed.

For Salad:

1. Combine spinach, green onions, and radishes in large bowl.
2. Pour dressing over and toss gently to coat.
3. Arrange on chilled salad plate, making sure that some radishes and onions are on top of spinach. Serve.

VEGETABLE SALAD WITH PINE NUTS

Vegetable Salad with Pine Nuts

Chill plates in advance for this salad.

NUMBER OF SERVINGS: 8
COOKING METHOD:
  Boil
SERVING SIZE:
  5 oz vegetable, 1 oz lettuce
TOTAL YIELD:
  2 lbs, 11¼ oz vegetable

INGREDIENTS	WEIGHT	VOLUME
potatoes, cooked until done but still firm, large dice	5½ oz	1 cup
cucumber, peeled, seeded, large dice	5 oz	1 cup
carrots, peeled, large dice	3¼ oz	¾ cup
green pepper, large dice	3½ oz	¾ cup
red pepper, large dice	3½ oz	¾ cup
tomato *concasse*	7½ oz	1½ cups
red onion, thinly sliced	2¾ oz	¾ cup
green beans, stemmed, cut into ¾- to 1-inch strips	3¼ oz	¾ cup
mayonnaise	8¾ oz	1 cup
basil	¼ oz	1 tablespoon
celery seed		½ teaspoon
cumin		¼ teaspoon
salt	¼ oz	1 teaspoon
pepper		½ teaspoon
romaine leaves	8 oz	
pine nuts	2½ oz	½ cup

1. In bowl, gently combine potatoes, cucumber, carrots, green pepper, red pepper, tomato, red onion, green beans, mayonnaise, basil, celery seed, cumin, salt, and pepper.

2. Correct seasonings. Cover and refrigerate to chill thoroughly.

3. Place romaine on chilled plate. Place 5 oz vegetable mixture on top. Sprinkle with pine nuts. Serve.

STUFFED TROUT

Stuffed Trout

Preparation of this recipe used trout with the head and tail intact; therefore, the weight reflects this. If serving trout without head and tail, the weights of the serving size, total yield, and trout will differ.

NUMBER OF SERVINGS: 8
COOKING METHOD:
  Bake
SERVING SIZE:
  1 lb, 4 oz
TOTAL YIELD:
  10 lbs, 4 oz

Wine Style: Soft and fruity Riesling, Pinot Blanc, Pinot Gris, or Rose
Example: Pinot Gris—Sawtooth Winery, Nampa, ID. This wine has aromas of peach and pear that lead the way to crisp acidity.

INGREDIENTS	WEIGHT	VOLUME
butter	2 oz	4 tablespoons or ½ stick
onions, small dice	6¾ oz	1⅓ cups
celery, small dice	6¾ oz	1⅓ cups
green pepper, small dice	5 oz	1 cup
mushrooms, small dice	10 oz	2⅔ cups
bread, soft, cut into 1-inch cubes	15 oz	12 slices
thyme		1½ teaspoons
rosemary		1½ teaspoons
dill		1½ teaspoons
pine nuts, lightly toasted	2½ oz	½ cup
salt		¼ teaspoon or to taste
pepper		¼ teaspoon
chicken stock	1 lb	2 cups
trout, bones removed, head and tail left on *if desired*, rinsed	7 lb, 2 oz	8 each
butter, melted	4 oz or as needed	½ cup or 1 stick or as needed

GARNISH:
lemon wedges or slices

1. Melt 2 oz (4 tablespoons) butter in skillet over medium heat. Add onions, celery, green pepper, and mushrooms. Sauté until softened, about 3 to 5 minutes.
2. Remove onion mixture from pan; place into large bowl.
3. Add bread, thyme, rosemary, dill, pine nuts, salt, pepper, and chicken stock to onion mixture. Stir to moisten evenly. Correct seasonings.
4. Pan-spray or place parchment paper on ovenproof dish or sheet pan. Preheat oven to 400 degrees.
5. Divide stuffing equally and fill cavity of each fish with stuffing. Securely close fish with toothpicks or butchers' twine to encase stuffing.
6. Brush both sides of fish with melted butter, place in prepared pan, and bake for about 15 minutes, until fish is done and flakes.
7. Serve immediately, accompanied by lemon.

BASQUE SHEPHERD'S PIE

*For easier service, bake this stew in individual ovenproof dishes.
Lamb replaces the beef usually seen in recipes for shepherd's pie.*

NUMBER OF SERVINGS: 8
COOKING METHOD:
   Braise, Bake
SERVING SIZE:
   10 oz
TOTAL YIELD:
   5 lbs, 5½ oz

Wine Style: Soft and fruity Chenin Blanc, Rose, Pinot Noir, or Merlot
Example: Pinot Noir—Castle Creek Winery at Red Cliff Resort, Moab, UT. This is a smooth, sumptuous wine with hints of cherry.

Basque Shepherd's Pie
photo courtesy of Paul Poplis Photography

INGREDIENTS	WEIGHT	VOLUME
olive oil	2 oz	¼ cup
lamb, lean, cut into 1½- to 2-inch cubes	1 lb, 8 oz	
onion, large dice	5¼ oz	1 cup
carrots, large dice	5¼ oz	1 cup
celery, sliced ¼ inch on bias	2¾ oz	½ cup
garlic, minced	½ oz	3 cloves
green pepper, large dice	2¾ oz	½ cup
red pepper, large dice	2¾ oz	½ cup
flour, all purpose	½ oz	2 tablespoons
stock, lamb or beef, hot	8 oz	1 cup
red wine	8 oz	1 cup
tomato sauce	8 oz	¾ cup
tomato paste	¾ oz	1 tablespoon
tomatoes, canned or fresh, peeled, chopped	8 oz	1 cup
paprika	½ oz	2 tablespoons
salt		½ teaspoon
marjoram		½ teaspoon
thyme		½ teaspoon
dill		½ teaspoon
oregano		½ teaspoon
rosemary		½ teaspoon
pepper		½ teaspoon
bay leaf		1 each
peas	4½ oz	1 cup
corn	4½ oz	1 cup
potato, mashed	1 lb, 7¾ oz	about 4 large
cheddar cheese, grated	2 oz	⅔ cup

1. Heat olive oil in large pot over medium-high heat. Add lamb and sauté until brown on all sides. Remove lamb and reserve.

2. Reduce heat to medium. Add onion, carrot, celery, garlic, and green and red peppers to pot and sauté for 7 to 10 minutes, until soft.

3. Stir in flour and cook, stirring constantly, for 1 to 2 minutes.

4. Slowly whisk in hot stock, then add wine, tomato sauce, tomato paste, and tomatoes.

5. Return lamb with juices that drained from it to pot. Add all seasonings, stir, bring to boil, reduce heat, cover, and simmer for 40 minutes.

6. Remove cover and simmer for another 40 minutes, to slightly thicken sauce. Meanwhile, preheat oven to 400 degrees.

7. Add peas and corn; correct seasonings. Transfer mixture to ovenproof dish. Cover top of dish evenly with mashed potatoes. Sprinkle with cheese.

8. Bake for 20 minutes; place under broiler for 1 or 2 minutes to brown. Serve.

MARINATED GRILLED LEG OF LAMB

Allow at least eight hours for lamb to marinate.

NUMBER OF SERVINGS: 10
COOKING METHOD:
  Grill
SERVING SIZE:
  5 oz
TOTAL YIELD:
  3 lbs, 6½ oz

Wine Style: Full-bodied reds, Cabernet Sauvignon, Syrah, or Zinfandel
Example: Syrah—Creekside Cellars, Evergreen, CO. This distinctive, deep-colored Syrah exhibits sweet blackberries, black currants, and plums with a hint of smoke and pepper at the finish.

Marinated Grilled Leg of Lamb

photo by David Murray and Jules Selmes
© Dorling Kindersley

INGREDIENTS	WEIGHT	VOLUME
leg of lamb, boneless, butterflied	4 lb, 12 oz	
olive oil	4 oz	½ cup
red wine	4 oz	½ cup
oregano		1 tablespoon + 1 teaspoon
garlic, minced	¾ oz	4 large cloves
bay leaf, crumbled		2 each
thyme		1 teaspoon
rosemary		1 teaspoon
paprika		1 teaspoon
salt	¼ oz	1 teaspoon
pepper		½ teaspoon

1. Place lamb in nonreactive bowl with fat side down.
2. In separate bowl, mix oil, wine, oregano, garlic, bay leaf, thyme, rosemary, and paprika.
3. Pour liquid mixture over lamb. Cover and refrigerate for at least 8 hours, preferably overnight. Turn lamb at least twice.
4. Preheat grill. Remove lamb from marinade; drain. Sprinkle both sides of meat with salt and pepper.
5. Place lamb on section of grill with indirect heat so it cooks slowly. Depending on the amount of heat and the thickness of the meat, cook about 12 to 15 minutes on each side, until done and proper internal temperature.
6. Remove from grill; cover and let rest about 10 minutes before slicing. Slice thinly across grain and serve.

COLORADO LAMB DUET: HORSERADISH CRUSTED RACK OF LAMB & OSSO BUCCO WITH TOASTED FARRO & BARLEY RISOTTO, CAPONATA, NICOISE OLIVE LAMB JUS

—Recipe by Todd Slossberg

Purchase farro in a health food store and sambal oolek chili paste in an Asian market.

NUMBER OF SERVINGS: 12
COOKING METHOD:
 Boil, Braise, Bake, Fry
SERVING SIZE:
 2 each chops
 1 osso bucco
 4 oz farro and barley risotto
 2 slices fried eggplant
 1 oz (1/4 cup) caponata
 2 1/2 oz lamb jus
TOTAL YIELD:
 about 10 lbs rack of lamb
 about 4 lbs osso bucco
 3 lbs farro and barley risotto
 24 slices fried eggplant
 1 lb caponata
 2 lbs lamb jus

Wine Style: Medium- to full-bodied white wines, Sauvignon Blanc, rich fruity reds, Merlot, Shiraz, or Cabernet Franc
Example: Rabbits Ears Red—Steamboat Springs Cellars, Steamboat Springs, CO. This wine is named for the pass leading into Steamboat Springs. A dry, complex and full-bodied wine, it is a hearty blend of Cabernet Franc and Merlot.

INGREDIENTS	WEIGHT	VOLUME
LAMB OSSO BUCCO:		
oil	as needed	
lamb shanks, cut osso bucco style, washed	8 lbs	12 each
salt	as needed	
pepper	as needed	
onion, yellow, medium dice	11 oz	approximately 2 cups
carrot, peeled, medium dice	12 oz	approximately 2 cups
celery, medium dice	9 1/4 oz	approximately 2 cups
garlic cloves, crushed	2 1/4 oz	1/4 cup
thyme sprigs		6 each
parsley, minced	2 oz	1 cup
bay leaf		2 each
black peppercorns		16 each
tomato paste	12 oz	1 cup
red wine	1 lb	2 cups
dry sherry	8 oz	1 cup
chicken stock	3 lbs	1 qt + 2 cups or 6 cups
beef stock	3 lbs	1 qt + 2 cups or 6 cups

For Lamb Osso Bucco:

1. Place thin coating of oil in large ovenproof pot; heat over medium heat. Season lamb shanks with salt and pepper.

2. Place shanks in hot pan. Sauté until caramelized (browned) on all sides. Remove shanks from pan; set aside until needed. Preheat oven to 300 degrees.

3. Add onion, carrot, celery, and garlic to pan. Sauté over medium heat until caramelized. Add thyme, parsley, bay leaf, peppercorns, and tomato paste; cook 2 minutes.

4. Add wine and sherry, deglaze by scraping bottom of pan to release all bits. Continue cooking until liquid reduces by half.

5. Return lamb shanks to pan; add chicken and beef stocks. Return to simmer, cover, and place in oven for 2 hours, until very tender.

6. Remove lamb shanks, strain cooking liquid, and discard vegetables. Reserve liquid for lamb jus. Hold lamb in cooking liquid until ready to serve.

For Lamb Jus:

1. Place wine in medium saucepan. Cook over medium heat until reduced to 4 oz (1/2 cup).

2. Add braising liquid from lamb shanks, bring to boil, reduce heat, and simmer until liquid is reduced by half and has thick consistency. While it cooks, remove scum from surface. Add rosemary sprigs for last five minutes of cooking.

3. Strain and reserve until service.

(Continued)

INGREDIENTS	WEIGHT	VOLUME
LAMB JUS:		
port wine	2 lbs	1 qt or 4 cups
osso bucco braising liquid	6 lbs	3 qts or 12 cups
rosemary sprigs		4 each
EGGPLANT CAPONATA:		
olive oil, extra virgin	as needed	
eggplant, peeled, seeded, 1/2-inch dice	14 oz	8 cups
white onion, minced	10 oz	2 cups
celery, minced	5 oz	1 cup
tomato puree	7 oz	1/2 cup
tomatoes, seeded, 1/4-inch dice	3 lbs	6 cups
tomato paste	3 oz	1/4 cup
salt	1 oz	1 tablespoon + 1 teaspoon
chili paste, *sambal oolek*	1/2 oz	1 tablespoon + 1 teaspoon
FARRO & BARLEY RISOTTO:		
farro	1 lb	2 cups
barley	1 lb	2 cups
olive oil	as needed	
carrot, small dice	5 oz	1 cup
celery, small dice	5 oz	1 cup
leek, small dice	5 oz	1 cup
chicken stock	1 lb	2 cups
heavy cream	1 lb	2 cups
parsley, fresh, minced	4 oz	2 cups
parmesan cheese, grated	10 oz	2 cups
salt	as needed	
pepper	as needed	
BREADED FRIED EGGPLANT:		
bread crumbs	1 3/4 oz	1/2 cup
parmesan cheese, grated	2 1/2 oz	1/2 cup
flour, all purpose	2 1/2 oz	1/2 cup
eggs, beaten	3 1/2 oz	2 each
eggplant, peeled, cut into 2-inch rounds, 1/4-inch thick	1 lb, 8 oz	24 each rounds
olive oil	4 oz	1/2 cup
salt	as needed	
pepper	as needed	
HORSERADISH HERB CRUST:		
bread crumbs, plain	15 oz	4 cups
horseradish, fresh, grated	4 oz	1 cup
parsley, fresh, minced	1 oz	1/2 cup
thyme, fresh, minced	1 oz	1/4 cup
rosemary, fresh, minced	1 oz	1/4 cup

For Eggplant Caponata:

1. Place large pan over medium-high heat; add olive oil to coat bottom of pan.

2. Add eggplant to hot oil. Stirring often, cook until soft and browned. Remove eggplant from pan; cool.

3. Still over medium-high heat, coat bottom of pan with oil. Add onion and celery; sauté until soft and translucent.

4. Add tomato puree, tomatoes, tomato paste, salt, chili paste, and cooked eggplant to pan. Reduce heat to simmer and cook for 15 minutes, until thick consistency.

5. Correct seasonings; serve at room temperature.

For the Farro Barley Risotto:

1. Bring two (2) pots of salted water to boil.

2. Add farro to one pot; barley to other. Return to simmer, reduce heat, cover, and cook until tender, about 20 minutes for both farro and barley.

3. Drain excess water and cool. Set aside until needed.

4. Heat just a coating of olive oil in pan over medium heat. Add carrot, celery, and leek; sauté until softened, about 5 minutes.

5. Add farro and barley; cook for 1 minute. Add stock and heavy cream; continue cooking over medium heat until liquid thickens.

6. Stir in parsley and parmesan cheese; season lightly with salt and pepper. Correct seasonings. Risotto should be somewhat thick with creamy texture.

For Fried Breaded Eggplant:

1. Combine bread crumbs and cheese in bowl. Place flour on plate or bowl. Place egg in bowl.

2. Dip each eggplant round in flour, coat with egg, then dredge in bread crumb mixture. Repeat with all eggplant rounds.

3. Heat olive oil in nonstick pan over medium heat. Add eggplant rounds and fry until golden brown on each side.

4. Season with salt and pepper; reserve until ready to assemble.

For Horseradish Herb Crust:

1. Combine all ingredients together in bowl. Mix thoroughly.

2. Set aside until needed.

For Rack of Lamb:

1. Preheat oven to 350 degrees. Season lamb racks with salt and pepper. Cover bottom of large skillet with thin layer of olive oil. Heat until hot.

2. Add lamb, sear each side until caramelized (lightly browned), remove from pan, and cool slightly.

3. Brush lamb lightly with Dijon mustard; coat with horseradish herb crust. Place on ovenproof pan.

4. Bake until desired internal temperature; about 20 minutes yields medium rare.

(Continued)

INGREDIENTS	WEIGHT	VOLUME
RACK OF LAMB:		
Colorado lamb racks, trimmed of excess fat	12 lbs	6 each
salt	as needed	
pepper	as needed	
olive oil	as needed	
Dijon mustard	4½ oz	½ cup
nicoise olives, pitted	12 oz	2 cups
rosemary sprigs		

For Assembly:

1. Allow rack of lamb to rest for 5 minutes; slice into one-bone chops
2. Place 4 oz (¾ cup) risotto in center of each plate. Place 2 chops and 1 piece of osso bucco on top of risotto on each plate.
3. Place 1 oz (¼ cup) eggplant caponata between 2 slices of fried eggplant. Place that on top of osso bucco.
4. Add olives to hot lamb jus. Spoon 2½ oz lamb jus over osso bucco and chops.
5. Garnish with rosemary sprigs if desired. Serve immediately.

TODD SLOSSBERG
Executive Chef

While traveling in Europe with his uncle at the age of 15, Todd Slossberg began aspiring to become a chef. Dining in many wonderful restaurants, he realized that "chefs are not just preparers of food, but shapers of experience and creators of lingering memories." With memories of dining in three-star Michelin restaurants on that life-forming trip, he says "I am still intrigued by food's power over the senses."

After high school, Slossberg enrolled in the Culinary Institute of America, where he graduated with honors. In 1988, he moved to Aspen, Colorado, to work at the Hotel Jerome, and, after seven years, he became the executive chef operating four restaurants and the catering for the hotel. Pursuing a new direction in his career, Slossberg started his own restaurant and catering firm, Crave Kitchen and Catering in 2005.

Known for his use of seasonal ingredients, Slossberg crafts dishes exhibiting a robust quality that complements Aspen's rugged yet sophisticated locale. "I strive to create dishes that enhance the high quality of the ingredients I use. I work at accentuating their flavors, not masking them with heavy sauces or overwrought presentations." Slossberg appreciates and enjoys the creative process. "I beg, borrow, and steal from lots of different influences and then massage them into my own style." Furthermore, he finds great satisfaction in the challenging and rewarding parts of cooking, such as "tasting a flavor or seeing a presentation somewhere and then building upon it to develop something that people crave." Developing his unique style is part of why he has received two nominations by the James Beard Foundation for "Best Chef in the Southwest."

BRAISED BEEF SHORT RIBS

Braised Beef Short Ribs
photo courtesy of Paul Poplis Photography

NUMBER OF SERVINGS: 8
COOKING METHOD:
  Braise
SERVING SIZE:
  15 oz
TOTAL YIELD:
  7 lbs, 10¾ oz

Wine Style: Full-bodied reds, Cabernet Sauvignon, Shiraz, or Zinfandel
Example: Cabernet Sauvignon—Reeder Mesa Vineyards, Whitewater, CO. This wine has aromas of black cherries enhanced by vanilla flavors.

INGREDIENTS	WEIGHT	VOLUME
beef short ribs, washed	4 lbs, 12 oz	
flour, all purpose	3/4 oz	3 tablespoons
oil	1 1/2 oz	3 tablespoons
onion, sliced thinly	6 1/4 oz	1 1/4 cups
garlic, minced	1/2 oz	2 large cloves
beef stock, hot	8 oz	1 cup
beer	12 oz	1 each 12-oz bottle or can
red wine	4 oz	1/2 cup
water	4 oz	1/2 cup
tomato paste		1 teaspoon
carrots, 1-inch pieces, cut on bias	6 oz	1 1/4 cups or 2 each
potatoes, Yukon gold or variety of choice, peeled, 1-inch pieces	1 lb, 1 oz	2 large
parsnips, peeled, 1-inch pieces	7 oz	1 1/2 cups or 1 large
leeks, washed well, white and light green parts, 1/2-inch slices	3 oz	3/4 cup or 1 each
celery, 1/2-inch slices, cut on bias	4 1/2 oz	1 cup
turnip, peeled, 3/4-inch piece	5 3/4 oz	1 cup or 1 large
tomatoes, chopped	7 1/4 oz	1 cup
salt	1/4 oz	1 teaspoon
pepper		1/2 teaspoon
rosemary		1/2 teaspoon
thyme		1/2 teaspoon

GARNISH:

parsley, minced

1. Preheat oven to 350 degrees. Sprinkle ribs with flour.

2. Heat 1 oz (2 tablespoons) oil over medium heat in ovenproof pan.

3. Brown ribs on each side. Add onions and garlic; cook 2 minutes. Add beef stock, beer, wine, and water; deglaze by scraping bottom with spoon to release any clinging bits.

4. Add tomato paste, cover, and place in oven for 1 hour and 30 minutes.

5. Meanwhile, in skillet, heat remaining 1/2 oz (1 tablespoon) oil. Add carrots, potatoes, parsnips, leeks, celery, and turnips. Sauté for 7 minutes. Reserve.

6. Remove ribs from oven. Drain fat from pan, add sautéed vegetables, tomatoes, salt, pepper, rosemary, thyme, and additional braising liquid (stock, beer, and/or wine) as needed to make about 1 inch of liquid.

7. Cover, return to oven, and cook another 45 minutes. Correct seasonings. Serve meat surrounded by vegetables. If desired, sprinkle with parsley.

VEAL MEDALLIONS WITH MUSHROOMS AND CREAM

Veal Medallions with
Mushrooms and Cream

NUMBER OF SERVINGS: 8
COOKING METHOD:
  Sauté, Bake
SERVING SIZE:
  6 oz
TOTAL YIELD:
  3 lbs, 2 oz

Wine Style: Wide variety—enjoy with wine of your own choice such as Pinot Blanc, Chardonnay, Grenache, or Pinot Noir

Example: Chardonnay—Pahrump Valley Winery, Pahrump, NV. This is a dry, fruity wine that maintains a delicate balance of fruit and oak.

INGREDIENTS	WEIGHT	VOLUME
veal medallions, 1/4-inch thick, lightly pounded	1 lb, 10 oz	
flour, all purpose	1 oz	1/4 cup
butter	4 oz	1/2 cup or 1 stick
onions, small dice	5 oz	1 cup
garlic, minced	1/2 oz	2 large cloves
mushrooms, thinly sliced	12 oz	
brandy	4 oz	1/2 cup
chicken stock	8 oz	1 cup
heavy cream	8 oz	1 cup
salt		1/2 teaspoon
pepper		1/4 teaspoon
nutmeg		1/2 teaspoon
dill, fresh, minced	1/4 oz	1 tablespoon
Swiss cheese, thinly sliced	5 oz	

GARNISH:

dill sprigs

1. Dust veal lightly with flour. Melt 3 oz (6 tablespoons) butter in pan over medium heat. Lightly brown veal on both sides. Place in ovenproof dish in single layer. Preheat oven to 350 degrees.

2. Melt remaining 1 oz (2 tablespoons) butter in pan. Add onions, garlic, and mushrooms. Sauté until softened, about 3 to 4 minutes.

3. Add brandy. Carefully light with match to burn off alcohol. Add stock and cream. Deglaze pan by scraping all bits from bottom of pan.

4. Add salt, pepper, nutmeg, and dill. Stir until slightly thickened. Correct seasonings. Pour over veal.

5. Place cheese over veal. Bake about 5 minutes, until cheese melts and begins to brown.

6. Serve, garnished with sprigs of dill.

BRUSSEL SPROUTS WITH SAGE AND CREAM

Cutting "X" in Brussels Sprouts

photo by Dave King © Dorling Kindersley

NUMBER OF SERVINGS: 9
COOKING METHOD:
  Braise
SERVING SIZE:
  4 oz
TOTAL YIELD:
  2 lbs, 6¾ oz

INGREDIENTS	WEIGHT	VOLUME
butter	4 oz	½ cup or 1 stick
onion, small dice	5 oz	1 cup or 1 medium
garlic, minced	¼ oz	2 cloves
Brussels sprouts, fresh, washed, trimmed, "X" cut into bottom of stem	2 lbs	
dry white wine	4 oz	½ cup
water	2 oz	¼ cup
Dijon mustard	1¼ oz	2 tablespoons
sage		1 teaspoon
salt		½ teaspoon
pepper		¼ teaspoon
cream	2½ oz	5 tablespoons
parmesan cheese	¾ oz	3 tablespoons

1. Melt butter in pan over medium heat. Add onion, garlic, and Brussels sprouts. Sauté for 3 to 4 minutes, stirring occasionally.
2. Add wine and water. Cover and cook until Brussels sprouts are tender, about 8 to 10 minutes. Add more water if necessary.
3. Add mustard, sage, salt, pepper, and cream. Thoroughly heat to thicken so it coats Brussels sprouts.
4. Sprinkle with parmesan cheese. Correct seasonings. Serve.

CORN FRITTERS

Corn Fritters
photo by Clive Streeter & Patrick McLeavy
© Dorling Kindersley

NUMBER OF SERVINGS: 8
COOKING METHOD:
 Fry
SERVING SIZE:
 ¾ oz raw batter each fritter,
 4 each fritters
TOTAL YIELD:
 1 lb, 10¼ oz, 34 each fritters

INGREDIENTS	WEIGHT	VOLUME
corn, fresh or frozen, removed from cob	15 oz	3 cups
eggs, separated	5 oz	3 each
flour, all purpose	2½ oz	½ cup + 1 tablespoon
salt		¾ teaspoon
pepper		¼ teaspoon
nutmeg		¼ teaspoon
milk	3 oz	6 tablespoons
oil, for frying		

1. Combine corn and egg yolks in bowl. Add flour, salt, pepper, and nutmeg; mix to combine. Stir in milk.
2. Beat egg whites until stiff peaks form; fold into corn mixture.
3. Meanwhile, heat ¼ inch oil in skillet until hot, about 375 degrees.
4. Place ¾ oz (1 tablespoon) batter into hot fat. Fry until golden, about 2 or 3 minutes. Turn; fry other side. Remove from oil; drain on absorbent toweling.
5. Serve hot.

BAKED STUFFED POTATOES

Baked Stuffed Potatoes

photo courtesy of the Idaho Potato Commission

NUMBER OF SERVINGS: 12
COOKING METHOD:
  Bake
SERVING SIZE:
  1 potato
TOTAL YIELD:
  6 lb, 6½ oz total
  4 lb, 4½ oz filling

INGREDIENTS	WEIGHT	VOLUME
baking potatoes, scrubbed, washed	5 lb, 13 oz	12 each about 7 to 8 oz each
butter, softened	4 oz	½ cup, 8 tablespoons, or 1 stick
cream cheese, softened	10 oz	
sour cream	9 oz	1 cup
cheddar cheese, sharp, grated	10 oz	3 cups
salt	½ oz	2 teaspoons
white pepper		1 teaspoon

1. Preheat oven to 350 degrees. Stick potatoes all over with fork.
2. Bake potatoes for 45 to 55 minutes, until soft. Remove from oven; cool just until potatoes can be handled.
3. Raise oven temperature to 400 degrees.
4. Cut ¼-inch-thick slice (about 1 to 1½ inches wide) off top of potato. Remove potato pulp with spoon, leaving ¼-inch shell. Reserve shells for later; place pulp into bowl of mixer.
5. With paddle attachment on mixer at low speed, beat in butter, cream cheese, sour cream, one-half of cheddar cheese (5 oz or 1½ cups), salt, and pepper. Mix until smooth.
6. Dividing mixture evenly, spoon or pipe potato filling into shells. Mound filling well above top of potato.
7. Sprinkle remaining cheese evenly over potatoes. Bake for 15 to 20 minutes, until filling is hot and top is golden. Serve immediately.

SOURDOUGH BISCUITS

Sourdough Biscuits

photo courtesy of Land O' Lakes, Inc.

The sourdough must be started a number of days ahead of using it. Be sure to use very clean equipment—sourdough is actually wild yeasts collected from the atmosphere, so be careful to avoid foreign bacteria. To replenish starter after using, add flour and water, cover, and allow to sit in warm place overnight. Refrigerate excess starter, but "feed" it every week or two with more water and flour.

Note: Sourdough can be temperamental. If blackish water appears on the surface of the starter, stir it back in or pour it off and add fresh flour and water. If pink water appears, discard starter and start over.

NUMBER:
  25 each 2½-inch biscuits
COOKING METHOD:
  Bake
SERVING SIZE:
  2¼ oz dough per biscuit
TOTAL YIELD:
  3 lbs, 10 oz

INGREDIENTS	WEIGHT	VOLUME
SOURDOUGH STARTER:		
yogurt, plain, containing active culture	5 oz	1/2 cup
flour, all purpose, unbleached	2 oz	1/2 cup
sugar		1 teaspoon
water, filtered, warm	4 oz	1/2 cup
flour, all purpose, unbleached	2 oz	1/2 cup
water, filtered, warm	4 oz	1/2 cup
BISCUITS:		
sourdough starter	1 lb, 2 oz	2 cups
buttermilk	8 oz	1 cup
flour, all purpose, unbleached, sifted	1 lb, 8 oz	5 1/2 cups
baking powder	1/4 oz	2 teaspoons
baking soda	1/4 oz	1 teaspoon
salt	1/2 oz	2 teaspoons
butter, unsalted, cold, cut into pieces	8 oz	1 cup or 2 sticks

For Starter:

1. Using wooden or plastic spoon, stir yogurt, 2 oz (1/2 cup) flour, sugar, and 4 oz (1/2 cup) water together in nonreactive bowl. Cover loosely with towel and place in warm spot for 2 to 4 days, until bubbly.

2. Stir in 2 oz (1/2 cup) flour and 4 oz (1/2 cup) water. Cover and place in warm spot for overnight or one day. Use or refrigerate tightly covered until needed.

3. Replenish starter with 2 oz (1/2 cup) flour and 4 oz (1/2 cup) water after using or every one or two weeks.

For Biscuits:

1. Mix sourdough starter and buttermilk in nonreactive bowl. Set aside until needed.

2. Sift flour, baking powder, baking soda, and salt in bowl of food processor fitted with steel knife blade. Pulse a few times to mix. Without food processor, sift mixture in bowl and mix.

3. Place cold butter pieces on top of flour mixture. Pulse to mix until size of peas. Without food processor, cut butter into flour mixture using 2 knives, pastry cutter, or fingertips.

4. Transfer mixture to bowl, make well (or indentation) in center of flour, pour starter mixture into well, and stir quickly with fork just to incorporate.

5. Remove from bowl; knead on lightly floured surface for about 30 seconds.

6. Pat into disk about 1/2 inch thick. Cut out disks using 2 1/2-inch biscuit cutter or desired size.

7. Place on baking sheet, cover loosely, and allow to rise in warm place for about 45 minutes to an hour. Meanwhile, place oven rack in center of oven. Preheat oven to 425 degrees.

8. Bake until golden brown, about 15 to 20 minutes. Serve warm with butter, honey, and/or jam.

SPICE CAKE WITH CARAMEL ICING

The flavor of this cake actually improves on the second day because the spices blend together.

NUMBER OF SERVINGS:
12 or 16
COOKING METHOD:
Bake, Boil
SERVING SIZE:
1/12 or 1 1/16 of 8-inch cake
TOTAL YIELD:
1 each 3-layer 8-inch cake
CAKE BATTER:
2 lbs, 14 1/4 oz
ICING:
1 lb, 9 oz (2 cups)

INGREDIENTS	WEIGHT	VOLUME
CAKE:		
cake flour, sifted	10 oz	2½ cups
baking powder	¼ oz	1 tablespoon
salt		¼ teaspoon
cocoa	¼ oz	1 tablespoon
cinnamon		1 teaspoon
nutmeg		1 teaspoon
allspice		1 teaspoon
cloves		¼ teaspoon
butter, unsalted, softened	8 oz	1 cup or 2 sticks
sugar	15¼ oz	2 cups
eggs, separated	6¾ oz	4 each
vanilla		2 teaspoons
milk	6 oz	¾ cup
CARAMEL ICING:		
dark brown sugar, firmly packed	1 lb, 2¾ oz	2½ cups
half-and-half	12 oz	1½ cups
butter, unsalted	2½ oz	5 tablespoons
vanilla		1 teaspoon
GARNISH:		
toasted nut pieces, *optional*		

For Cake:

1. Sift flour, baking powder, salt, cocoa, cinnamon, nutmeg, allspice, and cloves together in bowl. Set aside until needed. Grease and flour 3 each 8-inch cake pans. Preheat oven to 350 degrees.
2. Cream butter and sugar with mixer until light and fluffy.
3. Add egg yolks, one at a time, mixing well after each addition. Add vanilla and mix.
4. Sift one-third of flour mixture over butter/sugar mixture. Mix just to incorporate.
5. Add half of milk; mix just to incorporate.
6. Sift half of remaining flour over mixture; mix just to incorporate.
7. Add remaining milk; mix to incorporate, then sift rest of flour over it; mix just to incorporate.
8. Whip egg whites until firm peaks. Stir one-quarter of whites into batter, then gently fold in remaining whites in two batches.
9. Divide batter evenly between prepared cake pans (15 oz per pan). Bake for 20 to 25 minutes until done, top springs back, and cake pulls free from sides of pan.
10. Remove from pans. Cool completely on racks.

For Icing:

1. Combine brown sugar and half-and-half in saucepan. Bring to boil, cover, and cook over medium-high heat for 3 minutes.
2. Remove cover. Wash down any sugar crystals from sides of pan with pastry brush dipped in cold water. Cook until 238 degrees.
3. Remove pan from heat; add butter and vanilla. Stir until butter melts and incorporates into mixture.
4. Cool until lukewarm; beat thoroughly until spreading consistency.

Assembly:

1. Place cake layer on flat platter. Top with thin layer of caramel icing.
2. Top with another cake layer, spread with icing.
3. Place remaining cake layer on top with the bottom of the cake layer facing up. Spread icing smoothly over sides and top.
4. If desired for decoration, press toasted nut pieces into icing on sides of cake. Store cake at room temperature.

APPLE DUMPLINGS

To speed the chilling time for the pastry dough, flatten dough wrapped in plastic wrap into 1-inch disk and place in freezer about one-half hour. Allow raisins to soak in rum at least an hour or gently heat raisins and rum in saucepan or microwave to plump them.

Note: To reheat apple dumplings, place in 350-degree oven for about 15 minutes, until thoroughly warmed.

NUMBER OF SERVINGS: 8
COOKING METHOD:
  Bake
SERVING SIZE:
  1 apple
TOTAL YIELD:
  5 lbs, 15 1/2 oz total weight
  2 lbs, 2 oz uncooked pastry
  dough

Apple Dumpling
photo courtesy of McCormick Spices

INGREDIENTS	WEIGHT	VOLUME
PASTRY:		
flour, all purpose, unsifted	1 lb	3 1/2 cups
salt		3/4 teaspoon
sugar	1/4 oz	1 teaspoon
butter, unsalted, cold, cut into pieces	12 oz	3 sticks or 1 1/2 cups
water, cold	about 5 1/2 oz	about 2/3 cup
FILLING:		
raisins	3 oz	6 tablespoons
rum	4 oz	1/2 cup
butter, unsalted, softened	3 oz	6 tablespoons or 3/4 stick
brown sugar	2 oz	1/4 cup
nutmeg		1/2 teaspoon
SYRUP:		
water	as needed	
dark brown sugar	13 oz	2 cups
lemon juice		2 teaspoons
butter, unsalted	2 oz	4 tablespoons or 1/2 stick
apples, peeled, cored	2 lb, 7 1/2 oz	8 medium

For Pastry:

1. Place flour, salt, and sugar in bowl of food processor. Pulse to combine.
2. Place butter pieces over flour; pulse to mix until size of peas.
3. With machine running, pour cold water through feed tube. Pulse just until dough comes together.
4. Remove from processor. Knead once or twice if necessary to stick together. Place in plastic wrap; refrigerate until cold, at least an hour.

For Filling:

1. Soak raisins in rum at least one hour.
2. Combine butter, brown sugar, and nutmeg until well mixed. Set aside until needed.

For Syrup:

1. Drain rum from raisins and add water to make 1 lb or 2 cups.
2. Place water/rum, brown sugar, lemon juice, and butter in saucepan over medium heat. Bring to boil and let boil gently for 5 minutes.
3. Remove from heat; set aside until needed.

For Assembly:

1. Pan-spray baking pan large enough to hold dough-wrapped apples.
2. Divide dough into 8 even pieces (4 oz each). Roll each piece of dough thinly, about 1/4 inch thick, into square.
3. Place apple in center of square. Brush water around edge of dough.
4. Stuff each apple core with one-eighth of raisins, then fill remaining core with one-eighth of butter/brown sugar/nutmeg mixture.
5. Bring corners of dough to top, gently stretching dough so ends meet. Firmly join all seams so apple is completely covered. Place all wrapped apples on prepared pan.

(Continued)

INGREDIENTS	WEIGHT	VOLUME
GARNISH:		
ice cream, *optional*		
cream swirled into syrup surrounding apple, *optional*		

6. Cover and refrigerate at least 30 minutes to firm dough. Meanwhile, place rack in middle or slightly above center of oven. Preheat oven to 400 degrees.

7. Brush apples generously with syrup. Bake for 10 minutes. Remove from oven, lower heat to 350 degrees, and baste apples with syrup.

8. Basting every 10 minutes, bake another 35 minutes, until apples are tender. During last basting, pour remaining syrup over apples.

9. Remove from oven; cool at least 10 minutes. Serve apple surrounded by syrup. If desired, accompany with ice cream or a little cream swirled in the surrounding syrup.

11

Pacific Northwest, Alaska, and Hawaii

OBJECTIVES

By the end of this chapter, you will be able to

- Discuss the groups of people who settled the Pacific Northwest, Alaska, and Hawaii, why they came to these areas, and how their heritage impacted the cuisine
- Explain the climate and topography of these regions and how that influences what grows there
- Discuss the impact of the sugar plantations on Hawaii and how that affected the cookery
- Identify food products prevalent in the Pacific Northwest, Alaska, and Hawaii
- Prepare a variety of dishes indicative of the cuisine of the Pacific Northwest, Alaska, and Hawaii

States included in the Pacific Northwest, Alaska, and Hawaii:

- Washington
- Oregon
- Alaska
- Hawaii

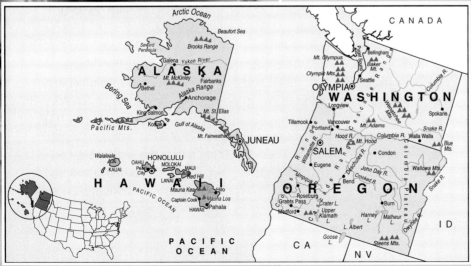

HISTORY

Archaeologists say Asia connected to Alaska, forming one huge landmass, thousands of years ago. According to their findings, the first inhabitants of Alaska, Washington, and Oregon actually trekked from Russia about 25,000 years ago. Archaeologists believe that three distinct groups came from Siberia to North America: Inuits (Eskimos), Indians, and Aleuts, who settled in Alaska. In the early days, fish (especially salmon), seafood, and wild berries provided much of the diet for people who lived near the coast. They dried excess fish for the lean months and made jerky, substituting fish for the traditional beef used in other regions. Meanwhile, the people living in the interior areas of the Pacific Northwest relied on caribou, elk, deer, and other game to sustain them.

While searching for a passage connecting the Atlantic to the Pacific, Englishman George Vancouver explored the coast of North America from Mexico to southern Alaska. In 1792, he discovered the Puget Sound in Washington and named it for one of his officers, Peter Puget. When settlers arrived at the Puget Sound many years later, they found a waterway that teemed with a staggering number of fish. To their amazement, the Native Americans stood at the shore picking up the fish and shellfish stranded by the receding tide. Rather than fishing, the astounded settlers only needed to wade into the waters and grab or spear their food. Copious amounts of oysters, salmon, sturgeon, geese, ducks, and more thrived along this coastline. Early residents also feasted on halibut, whale, herring, sole, flounder, clams, crabs, and mussels. As their preferred method of cooking the catch, they butterflied the fish, mounted it between sticks of wood fashioned like a spit, and roasted the fish over a fire.

Besides the rich bounty of fish and seafood, indigenous fruits and vegetables such as wild berries and greens thrived here. In addition, the many forests yielded plenty of game and wild mushrooms. The Pacific Northwest contained such a wealth of food that the Native Americans did not plant crops.

Forests of cedar, fir, and spruce provided materials for the Native Americans to build homes and make tools. Abundant game, including deer, elk, bear, goats, and pheasant, supplied meat as well as fur and hides for clothing.

In 1804, Lewis and Clark explored the Pacific Northwest. This was the last unsettled region in the what is now the contiguous United States. White settlers did not arrive in the Pacific Northwest until the 1800s. Although they all moved to the Northwest to find great wealth, those early settlers belonged to two distinctly different groups. They were either trappers and traders who hunted and sold furs or prospectors searching for gold. With many forests containing plenty of animals, fur-trading companies soon became established in the Northwest.

Traveling the 2,000-mile-long Oregon Trail from the Missouri River to Oregon required six to eight months. The settlers began this grueling journey in the late winter or early spring so that the cattle had grasses for grazing when crossing the Plains, and they reached Oregon before winter. These travelers ate repetitive meals made from staples of beans, salt pork, cornmeal, sourdough starter, and flour. They augmented their diet with fruits, vegetables, and/or berries gathered along the way and any game or fish they caught.

In the nineteenth century, droves of settlers arrived. Most of them settled in Oregon, where the Oregon Trail ended. In the process of building farms, the settlers cut down countless trees and eliminated much of the game. They also introduced smallpox and measles to the Northwest, which killed many of the Native Americans. In 1848, the United States government established the Oregon Territory. Five years later, they created the

Washington Territory. By 1860, the land belonged to the white settlers with the remaining Native Americans living on reservations.

The Donation Land Law of 1850 lured many settlers into Oregon. Under that law, any citizen over 21 years of age received 320 acres of land in exchange for living on that land for four years. Because of the Donation Land Law, many made Oregon their new home. Later, the law was extended to include California and Washington, which enticed many to relocate to those states.

Still more settlers claimed land as a result of the Homestead Acts of 1862. Around this time, immigrants came to the Oregon Territory from Ireland, the British Isles, Scandinavia, Poland, Austria, Germany, and Czechoslovakia. Later, attracted by work on the railroad, Chinese, Japanese, and Italian immigrants arrived. Each ethnic group brought their culinary heritage to their new land, and those customs and recipes combined with the existing cuisine.

To escape political upheaval, famine, and other bad conditions, many Chinese left their homeland in the middle 1800s. While many immigrated to California and the Pacific Northwest to work on the railroad or prospect for gold, others moved to Hawaii to work on the sugar plantations. As a result, the cuisine in the Northwest and Hawaii displays prominent Chinese influence.

The completion of the railroad in 1883 brought another influx of settlers to Washington. They began to irrigate the arid land in the eastern part of the state in 1890, and fertile farmland emerged. As a result, farmers and ranchers came to plant crops, raise livestock, and establish a new home in Washington.

Named for the Indian chief See-alth, the city of Seattle began as a lumber town. With the discovery of gold in the Yukon in the late 1800s, Seattle changed into a bustling port city. Started in 1907, Pike's Market in Seattle is the oldest continually running farmers' market in America. Today, Pike's Market covers seven acres, and vendors sell all types of fish, shellfish, produce, and much more.

Fueling dreams of becoming rich, the Gold Rush drew hordes of fortune seekers to Oregon, Washington, and Alaska. As in other areas of the country, boarding houses opened to provide food and shelter. Some of the boarding house menus consisted of beans and bacon for three meals a day, while others featured elaborate meals. Depending on the skill of the cook and the location of the boarding house, the quality of the food varied greatly. Most of the time, the boarders ate together and the food was served "family style" from large platters and bowls placed on the table or on the sideboard.

Long after the Gold Rush and the Homestead Acts lured people to this area, three booming industries in the Northwest continued to attract immigrants: fishing, lumber, and agriculture. These three industries still flourish today.

In 1784, Russian fur trappers established their first permanent Alaska settlement on Kodiak Island, which lies to the south of Alaska. After ruling Alaska for less than 100 years, Russia sold this huge land to the United States for $7,200,000 in 1867. Strong Russian impact on the cuisine remains obvious with dishes like beef stroganoff and kasha (buckwheat groats).

With the discovery of gold in 1896, Alaska's population exploded. The number of residents doubled in less than a decade, and more than 63,500 people lived in Alaska by 1900. As in the states of the Pacific Northwest, prospectors and settlers came to this new land with bacon, salt pork, flour, and their prized sourdough starter.

During the 1960s and 1970s, people moved to Alaska to work in the oil industry. In recent years, others relocated there because of Alaska's low population and/or its image as the last frontier. Although the Homestead Act expired in 1976 for all areas of the United States except Alaska, it continued to draw inhabitants to Alaska until 1986, when it ended.

Chinese men accounted for 80 percent of the workers on the railroad.

The expression "boarding house reach" developed because huge platters of food placed in the center of the dining table in the boarding houses were too heavy and awkward to lift and pass. As a result, the diner needed to reach over and remove his portion directly from the platter. Since this violated traditional good manners, diners excused this behavior by labeling it the boarding house reach.

Kodiak Island ranks as the second-largest island in the United States. The largest is the island of Hawaii.

Paying $7,200,000 for Alaska meant the United States purchased this state for about two cents per acre.

According to archaeologists, the Polynesians traveled to Hawaii in large seafaring canoes between AD 300 and 600. They discovered a tropical paradise with fertile volcanic soil, mountains, valleys, and forests. Surrounded by ocean that contained more than 100 types of fish and seafood as well as many varieties of seaweed, the Polynesians found no grains or dairy products in Hawaii. Their diet revolved around the bounty from the ocean as well as the fruits and vegetables that grew on these tropical islands.

Although no game existed on the islands at this time, the Polynesians brought pigs, chickens, and dogs. These early settlers also introduced sugarcane, coconuts, bananas, breadfruit, sweet potatoes, and taro. Prepared from pounded taro root, *poi* served as the only starch accompanying the cornucopia of fish, seafood, seaweed, fruits, and vegetables that sustained these early inhabitants. Besides functioning as a major food, the sacred taro plant became part of the spiritual lore of the early Hawaiians.

Searching for a connection between the Atlantic and Pacific Oceans in 1778, James Cook was the first Englishman to visit the Hawaiian Islands, which he called the Sandwich Islands. Cook brought pigs and goats to the islands, which the natives let run freely. A few years later, another English seaman, George Vancouver, introduced cows and a bull to the islands. Around 1786, trading ships from a variety of countries including Britain, France, and Russia stopped in the Hawaiian Islands while transporting furs from the Pacific Northwest to China. Unfortunately, those sailors introduced contagious diseases to the isolated Hawaiian Islands, and many natives became ill and died. As a result, the native population fell from about 300,000 in 1778 to 57,000 in 1866. In addition to ships carrying European sailors, whalers and missionaries from New England immigrated to Hawaii, bringing their foods and customs. Before long, whaling became Hawaii's major industry.

In 1813, the Spanish planted the first pineapples in Hawaii. With the arrival of one thousand pineapples from Jamaica in 1885, commercial planting of pineapples began. Pineapple growing and processing remains important business in Hawaii.

Beginning in the 1820s, Portuguese whaling ships came to Hawaii. A number of Portuguese men left the ships and made Hawaii their home. They found work in farming, raising dairy cattle, and raising cattle for meat.

Commercial production of sugarcane began in 1835. The sugarcane thrived in Hawaii, but this labor-intensive crop required many workers. Soon, growers needed to find cheap laborers.

In 1852, they began importing Chinese laborers to work on the sugar plantations. Like the African slaves brought to the South, the Chinese came with their culinary traditions and recipes. The cookery of Hawaii gained strong Chinese influence with the addition of rice accompanying meals; vegetables such as bamboo shoots, snow peas, and bean sprouts; new flavorings, including ginger; tea; and cooking methods, including stir-frying and steaming, typically used in China's cookery. Later, many other groups of immigrants, including Japanese, Samoans, Filipinos, Koreans, Southeast Asians, Russians, English, French, Spanish, Portuguese, Puerto Ricans, and more, found their way to the Hawaiian Islands. Most of these immigrants worked on plantations. Each group brought their culinary heritage with them, and they adapted their native dishes to the food ingredients available in this new land. Attracting immigrants from around the world, Hawaii became another of the great melting pots in this country.

Japanese laborers arrived in 1868 to toil in the sugar plantations. Their culinary influence contributed the use of soy products, including soybeans, tofu (soybean curd), shoyu (soy sauce), and miso (soybean paste). They also introduced teriyaki, sashimi (raw fish), saimin (Japanese noodle soup), tempura (fish, seafood, and vegetables coated with a light batter and then deep-fried), and extensive use of seaweed, pickled vegetables, sticky rice,

Today, the northern portion of the island of Hawaii contains the huge Parker Ranch, where descendants of those original cattle thrive.

The pineapple is indigenous to South America.

Until the 1820s, Hawaii had no written history. Instead, Hawaiians passed their history from generation to generation by telling stories and facts.

noodles, and rice wine. The Japanese shared several culinary traits with the Chinese. They consumed little meat, extended the small amount of meat in their diets with lots of vegetables, cut foods into small, uniform pieces for cooking quickly and evenly, and often stir-fried dishes. Reflecting Asian influence, fish sauce still flavors many dishes, and pork reigns as the meat of preference.

Attracted by the ocean, work as fishermen, and work on plantations, many Portuguese arrived in 1878. They brought their native cookery, including spicy foods and sausages like *linguica*, bean and other soups, seasoning with garlic and vinegar, sweetened breads, numerous egg-based desserts, and a fondness for cod, tuna, beans, and fried foods. Around the turn of the century, Puerto Ricans came to labor on the sugar plantations. They brought their substantial soups and stews in addition to Spanish-influenced meat turnovers.

About 1903, the Koreans arrived with their hot and spicy cookery featuring *kim chee* (fermented cabbage), garlic, hot peppers, sesame oil, and a preference for beef. The last of the laborers imported to work the plantations, Filipinos followed a few years later. The cookery found in the Philippines exhibits pronounced Spanish, Malaysian, and Chinese influences. Filipinos prepared adobo stews and soups flavored with garlic, onion, vinegar, and tomatoes.

In more recent years, many groups fleeing their native lands sought refuge and a better life in the Hawaiian Islands. For political reasons and/or the hope of more opportunity for their children, many Koreans immigrated during the 1970s.

Around the end of the Vietnamese War in the middle 1970s, many people from Vietnam, Thailand, and Laos immigrated to Hawaii. In many neighborhoods, lemongrass and fish sauce serve as common flavorings.

Like the immigrants settling on the continental United States, each ethnic group brought its culinary heritage and traditions to the new homeland. Those culinary traits melded with Hawaii's existing cookery to form a new, unique cuisine.

TOPOGRAPHY AND CLIMATE

Truly a land of contrasts, the Pacific Northwest contains a wide variety of climates, terrains, and topography. Miles of coastline, mountains, glaciers, rivers, valleys, forests, desert, and volcanoes are found within this region.

The Pacific Ocean borders on the west of the Pacific Northwest, providing a wealth of fish and seafood. Running from southern Alaska to northern California, the rugged coastline consists of 1,500 miles of rocky beaches, numerous islands, bays, and inlets. An incredible diversity of fish, seafood, and birds including ducks and geese live near the coast. Game like deer and elk inhabit the forested areas along the coast.

Although the Pacific Northwest lies relatively far north, warm currents from Japan temper the coastal waters. These currents keep temperatures moderate in the areas near the coast. With a long growing season, fertile soil, plentiful rain, and damp, foggy conditions near the coasts, this region produces a multitude of crops. A wide variety of fruits, berries, and vegetables thrive here.

Extensive forests in the Northwest gave rise to the lucrative logging industry for the early inhabitants. Covering much of the land in this region, the forests yielded abundant game, all sorts of mushrooms, ferns, and wild berries. Prized by the Native Americans, fiddlehead fern shoots appear in the spring. They remain a popular steamed or sautéed vegetable. For those living in Alaska, the caribou provided another source of protein.

Canada lies to the north of Washington, Idaho to its east, Oregon to the south, and the Pacific Ocean borders on the west. Washington's diverse topography includes mountains, valleys, volcanoes, forests, plains, lowlands, islands, coastline, bays, inlets, rivers, streams, and lakes. Because the state lies so far north, the winter brings very short days while summer days last as long as 18 hours.

Several mountain ranges rise in various areas of Washington. The Olympic Mountains stand in the northwest, the Rocky Mountains (called the Columbia Mountains in Washington) loom in the northeast, the Cascades dominate the central portion, and the Coast Range runs through the southwest. Receiving plenty of water from melting snows, many lakes and streams in the mountains provide water for crops and irrigation. Encompassing half of the land of Washington, forests cover the mountains except for those tall enough to rise above the tree line. Deer, pheasants, quail, ducks, geese, trout, shad, and bass thrive in the forests and streams found in the mountains.

Western Washington and the Puget Sound are situated between the Olympic Mountains on the west and the Cascade Mountains of the central region. This area consists of lowlands, plains, valleys, and coastline with many inlets and bays. The Puget Sound is the best known inlet, slicing from north to south in northwestern Washington. Because the Puget Sound provided excellent access and transportation, many ports, including the cities of Seattle and Tacoma, developed here.

Many visitors come to the Puget Sound to watch or hunt Canada geese, ducks, and a number of other fowl that pass through this area while migrating. Although fish and seafood, including oysters, crab, and mussels, live in the Puget Sound, consuming these fish and seafood raises safety concerns because of contamination by pollutants. One unusual, large shellfish found here, the geoduck clam, sometimes grows as large as nine pounds. The majority of geoducks harvested are about two pounds. Like most large clams, the tough geoducks require fine chopping and are often used in chowder or hash.

Consisting of almost 800 islands, the San Juan Islands lie in the Puget Sound and the Strait of Georgia. These islands receive about half the amount of rainfall as Washington's mainland. The seafood in this area includes herring, salmon, crabs, clams, oysters, mussels, and much more.

The Cascade Range runs north to south from Washington to California through the center of the state. Finding similar terrain to their native Pyrenees Mountains, numerous men from the mountainous Basque region between Spain and France immigrated to the Pacific Northwest to raise sheep. As in the Mountain States, traces of Basque cookery penetrated the cuisine throughout the Northwest. The Cascade Mountains create a rain shadow effect, causing the western side to receive ample amounts of rain, while little rain falls east of the mountains. Fertile valleys lie west of the mountains. Fruit orchards and a wealth of fruits, vegetables, and grains like wheat proliferate in this temperate climate of cool winters and cool summers. In fact, this land ranks as some of the best farmland in the United States.

Miles and miles of flat, dry land dominates the terrain east of the Cascades. Numerous cattle and sheep graze here. Hot, dry summers and cold winters prevail. Irrigation transformed this land into incredibly fertile farmland, particularly the Yakima Valley in the south central region. Apples, cherries, pears, asparagus, mint, hops, grapes, grains, and more grow in the fertile volcanic soil of the Yakima Valley. More plains make up the southeast.

Creating the border between Washington and Oregon, the Columbia River stretches for 700 miles through Washington. With 1,200 miles of waterways, the

Mount Rainier stands over 14,000 feet above sea level.

The San Juan Islands consist of more than 700 islands. With many islands and inlets, the Puget Sound encompasses 561 square miles and many miles of coastline. The water in the Puget Sound measures an average depth of 400 feet!

Olympia Oysters

Columbia River runs through Canada, Washington, and Oregon before flowing into the Pacific Ocean. Until the latter half of the nineteenth century, when more than 400 dams were built on the Columbia River and its tributaries, these waterways provided good of transportation as well as a home for fish like sturgeon, wild crawfish, and especially salmon, which traveled this river to spawn. Now, fish hatcheries dominate the area. Numerous canneries for processing salmon operate near the banks of this river. In addition, the Columbia River system serves as an important source of water for irrigating the dry valleys and plains in eastern Washington.

Situated at the southwestern coast of Washington, the Willapa Bay contains abundant oysters. More than half of the oysters found in Washington live in the Willapa Bay. Although most of them are farm-raised now, wild oysters remained plentiful until the latter part of the 1800s. During the middle 1800s, countless Willapa Bay oysters were shipped to San Francisco, but overfishing caused the number of oysters in the Willapa Bay to decline drastically. With the completion of the railroad, merchants began to transport oysters from the East coast to San Francisco. Besides oysters, this area is known for clams and cranberries.

Basically, three types of oysters are harvested in Washington for commercial use: the Pacific oyster, the European flat oyster, and the prized Olympia oyster. Because the commercial fisheries concentrate on producing larger, faster-growing varieties of oysters, the tiny, slow-growing Olympia oyster is difficult to obtain.

Olympia oyster—small, about 1/2 to 1 inch; requires three years to reach size of a quarter

Pacific oyster—about 2 1/2 to 7 inches; from Japan

European flat oyster—about 3 to 4 inches; some people describe their flavor as sweet while others say this type has a salty flavor; originally from Europe; grown in small quantities

Pacific Oysters
photo by Philip Dowell © Dorling Kindersley

European Flat Oysters

Throughout the Northwest, many people serve oyster stew on Christmas Eve.

PROMINENT PEAR VARIETIES OF THE HOOD RIVER VALLEY

Anjou—good eating, not good cooking, thin skinned; stores well in cold conditions

Bartlett—good cooking; does not store well

Bosc—brown skin, coarse texture; good for eating fresh and cooking

Comice—smooth texture; does not ship well

PROMINENT APPLE VARIETIES OF THE HOOD RIVER VALLEY

Newtown Pippin

Red Delicious

Washington lies north of Oregon, Idaho is situated to its east, Nevada and California to the south, and the Pacific Ocean borders on the west. As in Washington, the Cascade Mountains run through central Oregon, dividing the state into the moist, rainy, temperate western portion and the dry plains and plateaus of the east. Oregon's topography consists of mountains, valleys, coastline, forests, lakes, rivers, canyons, plateau, and desert.

On the far western side of the state, the Coast Range Mountains, valleys, and cliffs form the border at the Pacific Ocean. Abundant fish and seafood, including crab, shrimp, scallops, lingcod, black cod, rockfish, and squid, come from the Pacific. The Cascade Mountains dominate the central area. Moving toward the east, the land turns into lowlands and valleys around the Willamette River. Extremely fertile soil coupled with a great climate for agriculture creates prized farmland in the Willamette Valley. Plateaus, canyons, mountains, and the Snake River make up the eastern section. Forming the border between Oregon and Idaho, the Snake River now supports a flourishing business in farm-raised trout.

More valuable farmland lies in the Hood River Valley that is situated near Mount Hood and the Columbia River. Copious amounts of pears and apples come from this fertile valley.

When settlers discovered the Tillamook Bay along the northern shore of Oregon, they found a land with mild climate, thick grasses, and fertile meadows. The Tillamook Bay region proved excellent for grazing dairy cattle that yielded plenty of milk. Today, this area is known for cheese production, especially cheddar. Because they aged the cheddar for two years instead of the usual six or seven months, the early cheesemakers in Tillamook created a sharp, full-flavored cheese with a softer texture than the cheddars produced in the East.

Portland is the largest city in Oregon. Situated where the Willamette and Columbia Rivers meet, Portland served as a transportation center in the early days.

Although very different in many respects, Alaska and Hawaii have some similarities. First, volcanoes played a large role in the creation of both landmasses. Second, both claim an abundance of fish and seafood that dominated the diet of inhabitants from the earliest settlers to the present. Incidentally, both Alaska and Hawaii became states in 1959.

Reigning as the largest state in the United States and spanning two time zones, Alaska is twice the size of Texas, the next largest state. With only 53 to 55 miles between the mainland of Alaska and Russia, Alaska lies closer to Asia than any other state in the United States. The Arctic Ocean borders Alaska on its north, Canada lies to the east, the Pacific Ocean is to the south, and the Arctic Ocean and the Bering Sea are to the west.

The diverse terrain of Alaska includes mountains, volcanoes, valleys, islands, coastline, glaciers, rivers, streams, and lakes. Bordered by water on three sides, the peninsula of Alaska is surrounded by a multitude of fish and seafood. With many inlets, channels, bays, and islands, Alaska claims almost 34,000 miles of coastline. In fact, Alaska has many more miles bordering oceans and seas than any other state. Alaska contains numerous tall mountains. Located in south-central Alaska, the tallest mountain in the United States, Mount McKinley, rises 20,320 feet above sea level.

The Pacific Coast Range run along the western coast and then curve through the south-central and southeastern portion of the state. Besides mountains, this western area consists of forests, volcanoes, fields of ice, lowlands, valleys, rivers, and some farmland. Rolling hills, lowlands, valleys, and several rivers compose the central region. The Aleutian Islands lie off the southwestern coast of Alaska. Kodiak Island is situated to the south. While the Rocky Mountains stand in the east, the Arctic Coastal Plain makes up the frigid north. The Arctic Coastal Plain contains plains with ground frozen up to 1,000 feet deep and tundra, cold land with a grassy covering but no trees.

Climates found in Alaska span the range from temperate rain forest to Arctic tundra. Because the warm Japanese currents affect the southern part of the state, the climate found in some of the valleys near the southern coast remains warmer and more temperate, especially in areas where mountains block the Arctic winds. Although the southern area experiences very cold winters and cool summers, the seasons are much less severe than the frigid winters of the northern and central regions. The upper third of Alaska lies within the Arctic Circle and consists of tundra, deep snow, fields of ice, glaciers, relentless cold, and two months of darkness in the winter.

Coming from Canada, the Yukon River flows east to west across Alaska. It is the longest river in Alaska and ends at the Bering Sea. A few areas, such as the Yukon River Basin in the southwest and the Matanuska Valley in the south-central region, are warm enough for growing crops and farming. In fact, about three-fourths of Alaska's agriculture comes from the Matanuska Valley. Farmers in this valley raise livestock for meat and dairy, including cattle, hogs, sheep, and chickens. They also grow cold-weather crops.

Alaska experiences a short, very intense, prolific summer growing season. Because many hours of sunlight define the summer, the crops develop large, flavorful fruits and vegetables. A wide range of berries, apples, and other fruits and vegetables flourish here.

Besides ranking as the most southern state, Hawaii is the only state not attached to the continent. Lying in the Pacific Ocean more than 2,000 miles west of California, the Hawaiian Islands resulted from millions of years of volcanic eruptions. This island chain stretches more than 1,500 miles, about the distance from New York to Denver. The Hawaiian Islands contain 132 islands, but most of them are too small for inhabitants. A large number of the islands are almost completely submerged under water with just a tip of land jutting above the surface. Although eight larger islands lie within this chain, most think of Hawaii as the six populated islands that attract visitors from around the world. Situated from north to south, those islands are Kauai, Oahu, Molokai, Maui, Lanai, and Hawaii. Since January 1983, Kilauea, a volcano on the southern end of the island of Hawaii, has spewed lava. This volcano continues to add mass to the island.

The Hawaiian Islands contain mountains, valleys, coastline, some flatlands, and fertile, black volcanic soil in a tropical climate. The combination of soil and climate yields a cornucopia of tropical fruits and vegetables. Hawaii's most important crop for export is sugarcane, which thrives on many of the islands.

Because trade winds moderate the temperatures, the thermometer usually remains in the 80s throughout the year. In addition, the temperature varies little between day and night. All of the Hawaiian Islands with mountains experience two distinctly different amounts of rainfall. Abundant rain falls on the eastern side of each island while the western portion, lying on the other side of the mountains, receives very little rain. These islands often display lush tropical growth as a result of the heavy rainfall on the eastern side while desert plants grow in the west.

Ingredients and foods commonly used throughout the cuisine of the Pacific Northwest, Alaska, and Hawaii include

- seafood, crab including and other varieties, clams, shrimp, scallops, octopus, mussels, and oysters (Pacific Northwest)
- fish, including many varieties of salmon and cod, sturgeon, bass, shad, halibut, tuna, flounder, sole, rockfish, trout, Pacific perch (Alaska and Pacific Northwest); ahi, mahi-mahi, and snapper (Hawaii)
- smoked fish

- beef, veal, and lamb (Pacific Northwest)
- duck, geese, quail, and pheasant
- game, including deer, caribou, elk, and moose (Alaska)
- dairy and cheeses (Pacific Northwest)
- tropical fruits and vegetables, including papaya, guava, pineapple, mango, coconut, many varieties of bananas, plantains, passion fruit, avocado, and taro (Hawaii)
- macadamia nuts (Hawaii) and hazelnuts (Pacific Northwest)
- fruits, including apples, pears, cherries, apricots, peaches, nectarines, and plums (Pacific Northwest)
- all sorts of berries, including blackberries, raspberries, strawberries, blueberries, dewberries, and huckleberries (Pacific Northwest and Alaska)
- vegetables, including asparagus, beans, spinach, broccoli, cauliflower, garlic, tomatoes, lettuce, peppers, potatoes, and onions
- fiddlehead ferns and wild mushrooms (Pacific Northwest and Alaska)
- beans and peas
- wheat, barley, oats, and corn (Pacific Northwest)
- sugarcane (Hawaii)
- grapes and wine (Pacific Northwest)
- coffee (Hawaii)

COOKING METHODS

With an incredible bounty of fresh fish and seafood available, residents of the Pacific Northwest, Alaska, and Hawaii use virtually all cooking methods, including steaming, poaching, boiling, grilling, broiling, baking, and frying, to cook fish and seafood. Simple cooking methods best preserve the natural flavors of fresh fish. Often, the fat content of the fish determines the cooking method. While cooks often broil or grill fish with a high fat content, fish with less fat benefit from steaming or poaching. Pickling, drying, or smoking fish and shellfish preserves it for later consumption.

People poach, bake, broil, grill, dry, or smoke salmon. Besides cooking salmon in a pit that functions as an oven (as explained later in this section), another popular cooking method entails splitting the whole salmon and spearing it on a stick that is stuck into the ground next to the fire. The salmon cooks in the heat radiating from the burning wood. After one side of the salmon cooks, the stick is rotated so the raw side faces the heat of the fire to continue cooking. In the early days, alderwood was the preferred wood for cooking.

Today, many cooks grill whole salmon in the Northwest. This method allows the flavor of the very fresh, high quality salmon to dominate. Choosing a salmon weighing about three and a half to four pounds, they stuff it or grill the salmon plain.

With a humid climate and plenty of wood available from the extensive forests in the Northwest, Native Americans and settlers smoked many foods to preserve them. Their stock of dried, smoked salmon enabled people to survive the winter. Like Native Americans in other regions, they also prepared pemmican. They substituted salmon for the buffalo or beef traditionally used in other regions. In addition, they smoked shellfish like oysters, clams, and mussels for sustenance during the lean months. They also dried any excess berries, fruits, and vegetables, as well as salted extra meat and fish.

The Native Americans used two methods of cooking that were actually techniques to barbecue. In the first method, they cooked fish or game on a wooden spit over an open fire, which grilled the food. The second procedure involved steaming the foods in an oven. Like Native Americans in other parts of the country, the tribes of the Northwest and the early Hawaiians created an underground oven, called *imu* in Hawaii. To cook in the underground oven, they dug a large pit, filled the bottom with stones, placed wood on top, and built a fire. When the fire burned down, they removed the ashes, leaving the red-hot stones. After placing seaweed over the hot stones, they put chunks of fish or other food items wrapped in leaves on top of the seaweed. They then covered the food with more seaweed, and covered the entire pit with gravel. As in the clambake of New England, the foods steamed inside the oven (*imu*).

In the early days, Hawaiians used a few basic cooking methods. Besides baking or steaming foods in an *imu*, they cooked by boiling and grilling over a fire. Hawaiians still often grill the fresh fish caught there.

The Chinese introduced stir-frying and steaming foods. These two techniques continue as frequently used cooking methods in Hawaii. When the Japanese arrived, they cooked foods by broiling, frying, steaming, and simmering. Like the Japanese, the Filipinos did not have ovens in their homeland, so they did not bake foods.

Because of the hot climate, early Hawaiians needed to preserve many foods in the days before refrigeration. With plenty of salt available from the ocean, they salted fish, seafood, and meats. The abundant sunshine allowed them to easily dry foods. Also, they fermented some foods.

STATES

With a mild climate and rich volcanic soil, both Oregon and Washington produce plenty of fruits. Countless varieties of apples and cherries as well as 95 percent of the pears grown in the United States come from the Pacific Northwest. Many types of pears thrive in the areas of Washington and Oregon that have cold winters and warm summers. In the central portion of both of these states, huge amounts of berries such as raspberries, strawberries, and blackberries flourish. A multitude of other fruits and vegetables like peaches, plums, melons, grapes, potatoes, onions, hot and mild peppers, asparagus, garlic, tomatoes, lettuce, and much more also grows here. In summary, Oregon and Washington yield a cornucopia of produce.

Throughout the Pacific Northwest, the many rivers, streams, lakes, and the Pacific Ocean abound with salmon, trout, bass, and sturgeon, tuna, cod, sole, halibut, ocean perch, flounder, rockfish, herring, shrimp, oysters, clams, mussels, and crab. Deer, elk, quail, pheasant, duck, squab, goose, grouse, and more game fill the forests.

Washington ranks as the largest apple-producing state in the United States. Red Delicious apples rank at the top of production followed by Golden Delicious, Granny Smith, Rome, and finally Newton apples. Situated in the heart of the apple-growing area, the Wenatchee Valley in central Washington contains many apple orchards. Cherries are another important crop in the Wenatchee Valley and several varieties thrive. Farmers in Washington also grow potatoes, carrots, dried beans and peas, corn, barley, wheat, and grapes.

Mild, sweet flavored Walla Walla onions thrive in the volcanic, sandy soil of the Walla Walla Valley in southeastern Washington near neighboring Idaho. Other types of onions, peas, grapes, and wheat also thrive in this valley. Lured by the fertile farmland, many Italian immigrants settled in the Walla Walla Valley, where they grew all sorts of fruits and vegetables. The valley around the Yakima River in south-central Washington yields prodigious amounts of produce. The Yakima Valley is known for apricots, cherries, pears, peaches, plums, apples, grapes, hops, numerous varieties of mint, early spring asparagus, and many other vegetables. Since hops is an integral ingredient for making beer, its availability led to numerous microbreweries opening throughout the Pacific Northwest. The hot, dry conditions found in both of these inland valleys (Walla Walla and Yakima Valleys) provide excellent growing conditions for a wide range of crops. By contrast, coastal areas remain cooler and more temperate. Numerous Japanese immigrated to the areas west of the Cascade Mountains to grow fruits, vegetables, and berries. Their culinary impact remains strong.

With rolling hills, hot summers, and volcanic soil, eastern Washington produces a bounty of peas, beans, lentils, wheat, oats, barley, and rapeseed that is pressed to extract its oil. Huge ranches of livestock and wheat dominate much of the region lying east of the Cascade Mountains. Lush northeastern Washington yields plenty of dried beans, dried peas, and wheat, especially lentils and soft wheat. While the eastern and northeastern sections of Washington support herds of beef cattle, dairy cattle thrive in areas near the Puget Sound in western Washington. As a result of the large dairy production, farmers also raise milk-fed veal. In addition, they make high quality cheeses from the milk of cows, sheep, and goats in western Washington and throughout much of the Pacific Northwest.

Although Washington's rapidly growing wine industry centers on the grapes grown in the hot, dry, sunny climate of the eastern side of the Cascade Mountains, some varieties thrive on the wet western side of the mountains. The Yakima Valley yields many varieties of grapes and significant wine production. With many wineries scattered throughout the state, a wide range of both red and white wines comes from Washington.

The largest city in the state, Seattle, lies in northwestern Washington nestled between the Puget Sound on its west and the Cascade Mountains on the east. Pike's Place Market, an open-air market in the center of the city, features hundreds of vendors selling seafood, fish, all sorts of produce, cheeses, baked goods, coffee, flowers, and more. Seattle's International District, the section of the city with a large concentration of Asian immigrants, contains stores and restaurants from many Asian countries, including China, Japan, Cambodia, Vietnam, Malaysia, and Thailand. With many immigrants from numerous countries in Asia, the food in Seattle as well as much of the Northwest exhibits prominent Asian overtones.

Like Washington, the cuisine of Oregon hinges on the very fresh ingredients featuring a wide array of fish, seafood, meats, cheeses, vegetables, fruits, and berries available throughout the state. Fertile farmland supports a bounty of crops and orchards producing numerous varieties of pears, cherries, apples, plums, peaches, nectarines, melons, berries, grapes, and wheat.

Due to the wet, temperate weather found in western Oregon, a wealth of fruits, vegetables, orchards, and dairy cattle flourish. Cranberries thrive on the southern coast of Oregon. The area lying to the east of the Cascades experiences cold, dry winters and hot, dry summers. Because of irrigation, cattle and crops like wheat, potatoes, and beets thrive there.

With productive dairy farms, many fine cheeses including cheddar (particularly Tillamook cheddar), Monterey Jack, Gouda, blue cheese, and goat cheeses are produced in this state. Named from a Native American word meaning "land of many waters," Tillamook Bay, located in northwestern Oregon, became the site of numerous dairy farms. Swiss and German settlers established the first dairy farms, and cattle

Supposedly, the famous Walla Walla onion came from Italian seeds planted by a Frenchman in the Walla Walla Valley around the beginning of the twentieth century.

Washington produces 30 percent of the asparagus grown in this country.

In 1971, Starbucks Coffee opened its first store in Pike's Place Market. Since then Starbucks has expanded into an international company with thousands of locations. With coffee remaining an extremely popular beverage in Seattle, carts or stores selling coffee and all sorts of coffee drinks stand on many street corners throughout the city.

Reigning as the most popular sweet cherry, the bing cherry was named for Chinese worker Ah Bing in an orchard in Oregon in 1875.

In 1858, settlers planted the first hazelnut tree in the Willamette Valley. Today, this valley claims to supply 99 percent of the hazelnuts for the United States.

flourished in the lush countryside. Without reliable transportation out of this area, the farmers began making cheese to prevent the milk from spoiling before they shipped it to its destination.

In addition to cattle, many sheep graze in the mountains of Oregon. Like other mountainous areas in the United States, Basque shepherds immigrated here for jobs tending the sheep. As a result, Basque culinary influence remains.

The Willamette Valley lies between the Coastal Mountains and the Cascades. Encompassing an area about 100 miles by 20 or 30 miles, this fertile land consists of prairie, grasslands, and forests. The rich farmland found here yields abundant pears, apples, cherries, peaches, raspberries, blackberries, blueberries, strawberries, grapes, lettuce, onions, broccoli, beans, corn, a variety of herbs, and hazelnuts. Farmers also raise dairy and beef cattle in this valley.

In the 1830s, settlers brought Spanish cattle from California to the Northwest. Settlers from New England, the South, and the Midwest began moving into the Willamette Valley in the 1840s and 1850s. Some of the settlers from New England named towns like Portland after towns and cities in the East. Meanwhile, Scandinavian and British immigrants relocated to the coastal areas of Oregon, where they supported themselves by fishing, hunting, farming, and working dairy farms. The Scandinavians introduced pickled herring, pickled beets, and other Scandinavian delicacies. Germans, Basques, Russians, Scandinavians, British, and people moving from other parts of the United States came with their culinary past, and before long, their native foods and recipes penetrated into the cookery of the Northwest.

Of the Asians who immigrated to the Northwest, the Chinese arrived first, followed by the Japanese and eventually Asians from every country. In addition, many French Canadians moved south from Canada into this region. Like all immigrants, they arrived with their culinary heritage, and eventually, the cookery of the Northwest incorporated all of these cuisines into its own.

Like the rest of the western United States, Alaska received an influx of immigrants seeking gold in the late 1800s. When they arrived in Alaska, the prospectors discovered a sparsely populated land with cold ocean waters containing varieties of salmon, cod, halibut, flounder, herring, pollock, clams, shrimp, scallops, and crab. Frigid lakes, rivers, and streams in Alaska teemed with trout and more. Today, Alaska's seafood industry generates more than one and one-half billion dollars each year.

In the areas warm enough to grow crops, including the Yukon River Basin and the Matanuska Valley, fruits and vegetables reach mammoth sizes. Cabbages can weigh 70 pounds and strawberries grow to the size of a fist. The success of agriculture hinges on the many hours of sunlight in the summer months in this northern location. While many areas receive as much as 20 hours of daylight in the summer, Point Barrow, on the extreme northern side of the state, experiences continuous sunlight from May 10 until August 2. Traditional cold-weather crops like potatoes, barley, turnips, beets, cabbage, and carrots thrive in the combination of cool soil and almost endless sunlight. These conditions produce excellent root vegetables with a sweeter flavor. In addition, all sorts of berries grow well, including strawberries, blueberries, raspberries, lingonberries, gooseberries, and more. Farmers raise livestock for meat and dairy.

Simple and hearty describe the cuisine of Alaska. With many hunters in the state and game still plentiful, people consume deer, caribou, moose, elk, reindeer, walrus, mountain sheep, mountain goat, grouse, goose, and duck. The forests yield a variety of mushrooms that appear in many dishes. Soups, stews, and braised or baked dishes like pot roast or roasted meats dominate winter menus. During the summers, gardens yield abundant fruits and vegetables that play an important role in the diet.

In addition to plentiful game, fish, seafood, and fowl, influence from the Eskimos helped mold the cuisine that developed in Alaska. Eskimos survived as hunters and fishermen, and their diet consisted of mammals from the sea such as seals and whales, fowl and game including caribou, and whatever berries and greens they gathered in the summer months. Using all parts of the animals, Eskimos used the fat or blubber for cooking oil or burned it to provide light. In terms of cooking techniques, they boiled or grilled over the fire. Also, they ate many foods raw or lightly cooked due to the scarcity of fuel for cooking. The Eskimos dried and smoked foods for use over the long, harsh winter.

Although close in miles, each of the Hawaiian Islands exhibits its own unique characteristics. The islands differ in terms of topography, climate, and agriculture.

While the tropical climate and gorgeous beaches found in the Hawaiian Islands make it a top vacation destination, visitors expected expensive, mediocre food until recently. Food was expensive because Hawaiians imported so many ingredients from far away—usually from the mainland of the United States, Asia, or Australia. As a result, frozen ingredients dominated recipes, but that has changed. Now, Hawaiian cooks and chefs take advantage of the cornucopia of fruits and vegetables, the incredible wealth of fish and seafood from the ocean, and the animals raised on the islands. Hawaii's cuisine blends a multitude of ethnic influences from around the globe. Many define Hawaii's cuisine as a fusion of the East and the West that highlights Hawaii's fresh ingredients and the culinary heritage of many people who settled or migrated there.

Surrounded by the Pacific Ocean, people throughout the Hawaiian Islands catch and consume large amounts of fish and seafood. Tuna (*ahi*), *mahi-mahi*, swordfish, snapper, crabs, squid, and countless other varieties swim in these waters. In addition, aquaculture of fish, shrimp, and oysters now serves as a significant source of revenue in Hawaii.

Adopted from the many Asian immigrants, vegetables became an intrinsic part of the diet throughout the Islands. This tropical climate supports the growth of avocados, papayas, passion fruit (*lilikoi* in Hawaiian), more than 70 varieties of bananas, plantains, breadfruit, guava, coconut, mango, pineapple, corn, beans, tomatoes, potatoes, sweet potatoes, numerous varieties of lettuce, onions, an array of Asian vegetables, coffee, and much more. Because of their great availability, large amounts of fruits and vegetables fill the typical Hawaiian diet. Farmland occupies 40 percent of the land in the Hawaiian Islands.

Historically, Hawaii supplied lots of sugar, pineapples, and macadamia nuts to the rest of the United States. Today, the sugar and pineapple industries are waning in Hawaii because it is cheaper to grow and produce these two products in other countries.

Like most tropical fruits, pineapples thrive in Hawaii's tropical climate. In the early twentieth century, James Dole planted extensive pineapple fields on Oahu, and they yielded high quality pineapples. To increase his production, Dole bought the island of Lanai and planted the entire island with pineapples. Since delicate pineapples did not make the journey to California well in those days, Dole opened a cannery in Honolulu for processing and canning pineapple.

Originally imported from Australia, the first macadamia tree was planted on the Big Island of Hawaii in 1882. That tree survived, and macadamia nuts soon became an important crop in Hawaii. Today, this state ranks as the leading producer, supplying 90 percent of the world's macadamia nuts.

With its high annual rainfall, Kauai reigns as the wettest of the islands. Dubbed the Garden Island, Kauai's lush landscape and abundance of flowers result from the

(Continued)

the gravel at the bottom of the river or stream. After hatching, the fish grow for a while in the freshwater river, and then they begin their journey toward the ocean. Before reaching the salt water, they spend some time in brackish water, i.e., a mixture of salt and fresh water. While in the brackish water, their bodies transition from freshwater to saltwater conditions. Finally, they swim to the ocean, where they live for one to five years, depending on the species of salmon. After their period of time in the ocean, they make their journey back to the river of their birth to spawn. Most varieties of salmon die after spawning, but a few species repeat the cycle and return to the ocean.

TYPES OF SALMON FROM THE PACIFIC NORTHWEST AND ALASKA

King or Chinook—15 to 30 pounds, high fat content, largest, red flesh
Coho or Silver—8 to 12 pounds, half the fat content of the king salmon, light colored flesh
Sockeye or Red—4 to 8 pounds, high fat content, very red flesh, flaky
Chum or keta—7 to 18 pounds, low fat content, coarse texture, used for canning
Humpback or pink—3 to 5 pounds, low fat content, fine texture, mild flavored

With a cool, moist climate, the many forests of the Northwest yield a wide variety of wild mushrooms. Incredibly, more than 3,000 types of mushrooms grow here! Many of them are exported to destinations in the United States, Europe, and Asia, particularly Japan. Obviously, the mushroom industry generates significant revenue for the Northwest.

ample rain. With 460 inches of rainfall each year, Mount Waialeale in the interior of Kauai is one of the wettest places in the world. Streams of water flowing down from Mount Waialeale created numerous canyons and waterfalls. Sugarcane thrives in Kauai's wet environment. In fact, Hawaii's first sugar plantation was planted on this island in 1835.

Bustling Honolulu, the largest city and capital of the Hawaiian Islands, lies on the island of Oahu. Throughout Hawaii's history, Honolulu served as a major seaport for the islands. Pearl Harbor Naval Station is located in Honolulu. Mountains stand on both sides of the island with a fertile valley lying between the mountains. Fields of sugarcane and pineapples thrive in the valley.

Known as the Valley Island, Maui claims the highest production of sugarcane and pineapples found on any of the islands. Maui contains two dormant volcanoes with valleys situated between the mountains. The world's largest dormant volcano, Mount Haleakala a stands on Maui.

Called the Big Island, the island of Hawaii is the largest island in the chain. Diverse terrain makes up this island. Currently, two active volcanoes spew lava on this island. One erupts periodically and the other continues to release molten lava, creating a spectacle of light visible in the night. On the eastern side of the island, the city of Hilo boasts abundant orchids and fields of sugarcane that thrive in its very wet, humid climate. Scrubby land dominated by herds of cattle, huge cattle ranches, and the famous Parker Ranch lies in the north. With 150,000 acres and more than 50,000 head of cattle, the Parker Ranch ranks as one of the largest privately owned ranches in the United States. Referred to as the "Kona side," the western portion of the island has many resorts and tourists taking advantage of the dry climate. Coffee and cattle thrive on the hillsides of the west. Mauna Kea, the highest peak in the state of Hawaii, consumes the central portion of this island. As a result of the rugged, mountainous terrain, few roads cross through the center. Most people travel from one side to the other by driving around the island.

Lanai is known as the Pineapple Island. In 1922, James Dole bought the island for 1.1 million dollars. At one time, pineapple plantations covered the entire island and 75 percent of the world's pineapples came from Lanai. In the 1980s, the pineapple industry declined. Now Lanai relies on tourism.

The luau, a traditional Hawaiian feast, features many dishes, singing, and dancing. A whole, stuffed pig cooked in a pit lined with ti or banana leaves usually serves as the central dish of the luau. Other traditional dishes include *lomi lomi* salmon (salted salmon dish containing tomatoes and scallions), *poke* (raw fish), poi, rice, and haupia (coconut pudding). The luau resembles the New England clambake.

Poke is a popular Hawaiian appetizer or snack. The Hawaiian word for "cut up," *poke* utilizes leftover fresh raw fish. This dish consists of cubes or slices of fresh raw fish mixed with salt, nuts, and seaweed.

CHARACTERISTICS OF THE CUISINE

Bordering Alaska, Washington, and Oregon, the cold waters of the Pacific Ocean as well as the many bays, inlets, and rivers of the Northwest provide a wealth of fish and shellfish. These many waterways support marine life from saltwater, freshwater, and brackish water. The fish and seafood include many types of salmon, black cod, lingcod, Pacific cod, herring, smelts, tuna, swordfish, Pacific perch, Dover sole, flounder, halibut, sturgeon,

SOME POPULAR MUSHROOMS VARIETIES EXPORTED FROM THE NORTHWEST

Cèpes
Chanterelle
Matsutake
Morel
Oyster
Porcini

Venison resembles beef but contains less fat. Cooks often make stew with venison because the braising tenderizes the meat. Adding fat helps avoid dry meat, so recipes frequently mix ground venison with sausage.

CHEESES OF THE PACIFIC NORTHWEST

Cheddar—Tillamook is a variety from Oregon; firm texture; ranges from mild to extra sharp flavor depending on the length of aging time
Monterey Jack—semisoft; moist; mild flavor
Goat cheese—numerous varieties
Gouda—semisoft; mild flavor; originally from Holland
Blue cheese—soft to semisoft; creamy, smooth texture; strong flavor; veins of blue running through the cheese

SOME APPLE VARIETIES OF THE NORTHWEST

Golden Delicious
Gravenstein
Jonathan
McIntosh
Newton Pippin
Northern Spy
Red Delicious
Rome Beauty
Winesap

whitefish, rockfish, trout, striped bass, shad, walleye, perch, octopus, several varieties of crab such as the Dungeness crab, clams, shrimp, mussels, scallops, and numerous types of oysters. The most coveted of the fish and seafood probably are the Dungeness crab, tiny Olympian oysters, razor clams, and chinook (also called king) salmon. Fish and seafood dominates menus in restaurants and homes throughout the Pacific Northwest and Alaska.

In the days before the white settlers arrived in the Pacific Northwest, salmon served as the main source of food for the Native Americans. They ate large amounts of fresh salmon and dried any excess for lean times. Playing a role similar to that of corn for Native Americans living in other parts of the country, salmon intertwined with the spiritual beliefs of the Native Americans in the Northwest. They believed the spirits of people came back as salmon to provide food for the tribes. After serving that mission, the salmon changed back into their spiritual form and returned to the ocean.

While the Northwest remains well known for high quality salmon, the number of wild, native salmon in this region has decreased sharply for several reasons. First, the building of dams in rivers halted the ability of the salmon to swim back upstream to spawn. Second, overfishing caused sharp drops in the salmon population. Finally, pollution of the waterways killed many salmon. Now, farm-raised salmon has developed into a huge industry, creating abundant salmon for export.

The many forests of the Northwest and Alaska provided all sorts of game and wild fowl for hunters and trappers as well as copious amounts of wild mushrooms, fiddlehead ferns, and berries. Many claim this region grows more wild mushrooms than any other location in the United States. As a result, game and all sorts of mushrooms often appear on menus.

Farmers and cheese makers prepare excellent cheeses, butter, and cream from the milk of the cows, goats, and sheep grazing in the Pacific Northwest. They produce many firm and semifirm cheeses, including gouda, cheddar, Colby, Monterey jack, and goat cheeses.

In the cool, damp climate of the Northwest, soups remain popular. Chowders, bisques, oyster stew, and lentil, split pea, and bean soups represent just a few of the possibilities.

A cornucopia of fruits and vegetables grow in the valleys of the Northwest. In the early days, cold-weather vegetables filled root cellars in both the Pacific Northwest and Alaska. People incorporate the abundant fruits and berries into a variety of desserts. Cobblers, pies, crisps, poached fruits, and other fruit desserts frequently grace tables throughout the Northwest.

Hawaii produces an incredible assortment of tropical and subtropical fruits and vegetables. Made from taro, *poi* remains popular among native Hawaiians.

The pupu platter, an assortment of hors d'oeuvres, starts many festive meals in Hawaii. A small grill, hibachi, or even a can of Sterno stands in the middle of the platter so guests can grill their own meat skewers or other items. The pupu tray features a variety of foods. It might include Japanese rumaki (chicken livers wrapped with bacon), chunks of pineapple, tiny Chinese barbecued spare ribs, and/or shrimp.

A carryover from the days of the pioneers and prospectors, baked goods leavened with sourdough remain very popular throughout the Pacific Northwest and Alaska. These include breads, biscuits, pancakes, waffles, cakes, and more.

In 1854, the first vineyard in the Northwest was planted in southern Oregon. Grapes flourished throughout the Northwest, and today, the vineyards in Washington and Oregon support a blossoming wine industry. Pinot Noir, Riesling, Chardonnay, and many more wines are produced in the Northwest.

Area	Weather	Topography	Foods
Washington Canada to north, Idaho to east, Oregon to south, Pacific Ocean to west	east: hot, dry, arid, sunny hot summers, cold winters west: temperate; cool summers; cool winters; rainy, foggy, damp	east: valleys, forests, plains, rolling hills, volcanic soil northeast: Columbia Mountains, lush center: Cascade Mountains run north to south; plains, fertile valleys, Walla Walla Valley in southeast; Yakima Valley in south central west: coastal mountains, fertile valleys northwest: Olympic Mountains Puget Sound coast: lowlands, fertile soil, forests, islands, inlets, bays, plains, valleys southeast: plains southwest coast: Willapa River divides Washington Bay, Coast Range, Columbia and Oregon	fish, seafood, salmon, trout, halibut, sturgeon, herring, sole, flounder, cod, smelts, Pacific perch, tuna, rockfish, shad, bass, walleye, crab, oysters, clams, mussels, shrimp, octopus, pheasant, geese, ducks, quail, game, deer, elk, cattle, veal, sheep, goats, dairy, cheese, milk, wheat, barley, oats, rapeseed, dried beans and peas, lentils, corn, carrots, onions, garlic, Walla Walla onion, peppers, mushrooms, tomatoes, lettuce, broccoli, asparagus, root vegetables, turnips, cabbage, potatoes, apples, pears, cherries, apricots, plums, peaches, melons, many berries, strawberries, cranberries, raspberries, blackberries, mint, herbs, grapes, wine, hops, beer, sourdough
Oregon Washington to north, Idaho to east, Nevada and California to south, Pacific Ocean to west	east: dry, hot summers; cold, dry winters west: moist, rainy, temperate, foggy, damp, cool summers, cool winters	east: dry plains, plateaus, canyons, mountains, Snake River center: Cascade Mountains, Willamette River, fertile valleys, lowlands, forests north central: Hood River Valley west: Coast Range Mountains, coast, valleys, cliffs, lakes, forests, Pacific Ocean, fertile soil, islands, bays, inlets, Tillamook Bay on north coast; lush; Columbia River divides Washington and Oregon	fish, shellfish, halibut, tuna, salmon, lingcod, black cod, trout, sturgeon, herring, sole, flounder, smelts, whitefish, rockfish, Pacific perch, shad, bass, walleye, squid, octopus, crab, clams, oysters, mussels, shrimp, scallops, geese, ducks, quail, pheasant, game, deer, elk, cattle, sheep, goats, dairy, cheese, carrots, wheat, onions, fiddlehead ferns, mushrooms, peppers, garlic, asparagus, tomatoes, beans, lettuce, broccoli, corn, root vegetables, potatoes, beets, apricots, apples, pears, cherries, peaches, nectarines, plums, melons, watermelon, many berries, blackberries, strawberries, cranberries, blueberries, raspberries, grapes, wine, herbs, hazelnuts, sourdough
Alaska Arctic Ocean to north, Canada to east, Pacific Ocean to south, Arctic Ocean and Bering Sea to west	north: frigid, tundra, relentless cold central: frigid winters south: valleys and coast with cold winters and cool summers, Japanese currents temper climate near ocean winter: many hours of darkness summer: many hours of sunlight	mountains, valleys, islands, coastline, volcanoes, lakes, glaciers, rivers, streams, bays, inlets, channels north: plains, tundra, grassy covering, no trees, Arctic Coastal Plain, fields of ice, glaciers in Arctic Circle central: lowlands, valleys, rolling hills, rivers east: Rocky Mountains south: Matanuska Valley southwest: Yukon River Basin, Kodiak Island to south, Aleutian Islands to southwest west: Pacific Mountains on coast, south central, and southeast; mountains, forests, volcanoes, fields of ice, rivers, valleys, lowlands, farmland; Yukon River flows across Alaska east to west	fish, seafood, salmon, cod, halibut, sturgeon, pollock, Pacific perch, flounder, herring, trout, crab, clams, shrimp, scallops, octopus, walrus, game, caribou, deer, moose, elk, mountain sheep, reindeer, mountain goats, duck, grouse, goose, quail, cattle, dairy, sheep, chicken, hogs, lamb, beef stroganoff, kasha, barley, fruits and vegetables, mushrooms, fiddlehead ferns, cabbage, root vegetables, potatoes, carrots, beets, turnips, apples, many berries, strawberries, blueberries, lingonberries, raspberries, gooseberries, sourdough
Hawaii in Pacific Ocean more than 2,000 miles west of California, 132 islands; 6 populated islands from north to south: Kauai, Oahu, Molokai, Lanai, Maui, Hawaii	tropical, trade winds keep temperature in 80s all year east of mountains: rainy, lush, tropical west of mountains: dry, desert conditions	islands, coast, volcanoes, mountains, valleys, flatlands, canyons, waterfalls, fertile volcanic soil	fish, seafood, swordfish, tuna, *ahi*, snapper, *mahi-mahi*, sea bass, mackerel, marlin, squid, crabs, shrimp, oysters, sashimi, seaweed, pork, cattle, beef, chickens, pigs, eggs, milk, sugarcane, corn, beans, tomatoes, lettuce, pineapples, coconuts, mango, bananas, guava, papaya, passion fruit, plantains, breadfruit, onions, snow peas, bamboo shoots, bean sprouts, avocados, taro, *poi*, rice, sweet potatoes, yams, potatoes, soybeans, tofu, miso, soy sauce, macadamia nuts, coffee

REVIEW QUESTIONS

1. Explain the importance, availability, and types of fish encountered by the settlers of the Pacific Northwest, Alaska, and Hawaii.
2. What role did salmon play in the culinary history and present of the Northwest? Include salmon's role for the Native Americans and the fate of salmon through the history of the region.
3. Discuss the influences of the Polynesians, Chinese, Japanese, Koreans, Portuguese, and Filipinos on Hawaii's cuisine.
4. Discuss the growing conditions in Alaska and the Pacific Northwest, including the differences between the eastern and western regions of the Northwest.
5. Define fusion cooking. Why is Hawaii a "natural" place for it?
6. Discuss cooking and preserving methods used for fish in the Pacific Northwest, Alaska, and Hawaii. Include reasons for choosing these particular methods.

GLOSSARY

a'u—marlin in Hawaiian

ahi—yellowfin tuna in Hawaiian

brackish water—a mixture of salt and fresh water

chinook—king salmon

geoduck—type of clam, some of which grow as large as nine pounds; however, most are harvested at two pounds; usually finely chopped and used in chowder or hash

hapu'upu'u—black sea bass in Hawaiian

haupia—coconut pudding popular in Hawaii

kajiki—Pacific blue marlin in Hawaiian

kasha—buckwheat groats common in Russia and Eastern Europe

kim chee—fermented cabbage commonly served in Korea

lilikoi—Hawaiian word for passion fruit

linguica—Portuguese spicy sausages

lomi lomi **salmon**—salted salmon dish from Hawaii containing raw salmon mixed with onions and tomatoes, served at luaus; *lomi* is Hawaiian word meaning "to work with fingers"

luau—a feast with many dishes, singing, and dancing celebrated in Hawaii with a central dish of whole, stuffed pig cooked in a pit lined with ti or banana leaves

mahi-mahi—dolphinfish in Hawaiian

miso—fermented soybean paste, common in Japanese cookery; available in places where many Japanese immigrants live

ono—relative of king mackerel in Hawaiian; also known as *wahoo*

opah—moonfish in Hawaiian

opakapaka—Hawaiian for pink snapper

poi—starchy paste made from pounded taro root; staple starch for many native Hawaiians

poke—Hawaiian word for "cut up," dish containing raw fish; consists of cubes or slices of fresh raw fish mixed with salt, nuts, and seaweed

pupu platter—platter featuring an assortment of hors d'oeuvres; starts many festive meals in Hawaii

rumaki—chicken livers wrapped with bacon; Japanese hors d'oeuvre

saimin—Japanese noodle soup served frequently in Hawaii

sashimi—raw fish commonly eaten in Japan and places with many Japanese immigrants

shoyu—soy sauce; common in Japanese cookery and places with many Japanese immigrants

tempura—deep-fried fish, seafood, and/or vegetables coated with a light batter; Japanese dish

tofu—soybean curd, commonly used in Japanese cookery

tundra—cold land with a grassy covering but no trees, found in northern Alaska and other areas with frigid weather

uku—Hawaiian for gray snapper

ulua—pompano in Hawaiian

wahoo—also known as *ono;* relative of king mackerel

SWEET ONION PIE

Slice of Sweet Onion Pie
photo by David Murray and Jules Selmes
© Dorling Kindersley

With a larger portion size, this dish makes a good luncheon entrée. Also, this can be prepared in individual tarts instead of serving a slice from one large pie.

NUMBER OF SERVINGS: 8
COOKING METHOD:
  Bake
SERVING SIZE:
  1 slice, 1/8 of pie
TOTAL YIELD:
  1 each 9-inch tart, 2 lbs, 6 oz

Wine Style: Light- to medium-bodied Riesling, Pinot Blanc, Sauvignon Blanc, or mild Chardonnay
Example: Riesling—Argyle Winery, Dundee, OR. This wine contains flavors of lime, fresh fruit, and spice.

INGREDIENTS	WEIGHT	VOLUME
FILLING:		
butter	1 oz	2 tablespoons
sweet onions, Walla Walla or variety of choice, medium dice	1 lb, 12 oz	3 medium
salt		3/4 teaspoon
pepper		1/4 teaspoon
caraway seeds	1/4 oz	1 1/2 teaspoons
flour, all purpose	1/4 oz	1 1/2 teaspoons
heavy cream, hot	4 oz	1/2 cup
Swiss cheese, grated	2 oz	1/2 cup
eggs, beaten lightly	3 1/2 oz	2 each
pie shell fitted into 9-inch pan		
use recipe of choice or recipe for pie dough with pumpkin pie in chapter 2		
egg white, beaten lightly	1 oz	1 each

1. Melt butter in skillet over low heat. Add onions and sauté until tender and lightly browned, about 20 to 25 minutes.
2. Place oven rack in lower part of oven. Preheat oven to 375 degrees.
3. Add salt, pepper, and caraway seeds to onions. Stir in flour, slowly whisk in cream, add cheese, and whisk until blended and cheese melts. Remove from heat.
4. Whisk small amount (about 2 tablespoons) of mixture into eggs to temper them.
5. Combine onion mixture with eggs; stir to combine.
6. Using pastry brush, lightly coat pie shell with egg white.
7. Pour onion mixture into pie shell. Bake for about 30 minutes, until knife inserted in center comes out clean. Cool slightly; serve warm.

HAWAIIAN CURRIED PORK DUMPLINGS

Hawaiian Curried Pork Dumplings
photo courtesy of American Egg Board

These dumplings function well as a passed hors'd oeuvre.

NUMBER OF SERVINGS: 13
COOKING METHOD:
  Deep-fry or Steam
SERVING SIZE:
  5 each dumplings
TOTAL YIELD:
  2 lb, 1/2 oz filling, 65 each dumplings

Wine Style: Light- to medium-bodied white wines such as Chenin Blanc, Sauvignon Blanc, Rose, light- to medium-bodied red wines, or Pinot Noir
Example: Symphony Dry—Volcano Winery, Volcano, HI. With a crisp dry flavor, this wine is a cross between Symphony and Muscat of Alexandria grapes

INGREDIENTS	WEIGHT	VOLUME
ground pork	1 lb	
celery, small dice	2½ oz	½ cup
green onions, tops and whites, sliced	5 oz	2 cups
pineapple, crushed	8 oz	1 cup
water chestnuts, small dice	4 oz	⅔ cup
curry powder	¼ oz	1 tablespoon + 1 teaspoon
cinnamon		½ teaspoon
ginger		½ teaspoon
salt	¼ oz	1 teaspoon
pepper		¼ teaspoon
won ton wrappers, 3- by 3-inch	1 lb	
water	as needed	
cooking oil for deep frying		

1. Cook pork and celery in skillet until meat is browned and celery is tender. Remove from heat.
2. Add onions, pineapple, water chestnuts, curry powder, cinnamon, ginger, salt, and pepper.
3. Lay won ton wrapper on counter; moisten edges with water. Place ½ oz (1 tablespoon) filling in center of wrapper. Bring four corners together at top and pinch together to seal.
4. Either deep-fry or steam won tons. To deep-fry: Heat oil in fryer to 375 degrees. Add won tons, a few at a time; fry until golden, about 1 or 2 minutes. To steam: Pan-spray bottom of steamer. Place won tons in steamer and cook 12 to 14 minutes, until done.
5. Serve immediately, accompanied by dipping sauce(s) of choice, if desired.

OYSTER STEW

Oyster Stew
photo © Dorling Kindersley

NUMBER OF SERVINGS: 9
COOKING METHOD:
   Sauté, Boil
SERVING SIZE:
   10 oz
TOTAL YIELD:
   6 lbs

INGREDIENTS	WEIGHT	VOLUME
butter	2 oz	4 tablespoons
onion, small dice	3 oz	1/2 cup + 1 tablespoon
celery, small dice	7 1/2 oz	1 1/2 cups
oysters, canned or fresh, with liquor	3 lbs	
heavy cream, warm	1 lb, 8 oz	3 cups
milk, warm	12 oz	1 1/2 cups
Worcestershire sauce	1/4 oz	1 1/2 teaspoons
seafood seasoning, Old Bay or seasoning of choice		3/4 teaspoon
salt		3/4 teaspoon
white pepper		1/4 teaspoon
hot pepper sauce	dash or to taste	
sherry (optional)	1 oz or to taste	2 tablespoons or to taste

GARNISH:

paprika

crackers

1. Heat butter in large pot over medium heat. Add onion and celery; sauté 3 to 4 minutes, until tender. Reduce heat to low.
2. Add oysters and their liquor. Heat until edges begin to curl, 1 to 2 minutes. Be careful not to overcook oysters or they will become tough.
3. Add remaining ingredients and cook until thoroughly heated. Do not boil or cream will curdle and oysters will toughen. Correct seasonings.
4. Serve immediately, garnished with a sprinkling of paprika and accompanied by crackers.

LENTIL SOUP

Lentil Soup
photo © Culinary Institute of America

If lentils are not soaked, just cook them about 30 minutes longer or until tender.

Some prefer using all stock and bacon bits instead of water and ham hock.

NUMBER OF SERVINGS: 11
COOKING METHOD:
  Boil
SERVING SIZE:
  8 oz
TOTAL YIELD:
  5 lbs, 13 oz

INGREDIENTS	WEIGHT	VOLUME
lentils	1 lb	2 cups
water	to cover	
water	2 lb, 8 oz	1 qt + 1 cup or 5 cups
chicken stock	2 lb, 8 oz	1 qt + 1 cup or 5 cups
smoked ham hock	8 oz	1 each
onion, small dice	5 oz	1 cup
celery, small dice	2½ oz	½ cup
carrots, small dice	3¾ oz	¾ cup
garlic, minced	¼ oz	2 cloves
bay leaf		1 each
hot pepper sauce		¼ teaspoon
Worcestershire sauce	½ oz	1 tablespoon
oregano		¼ teaspoon
thyme		¼ teaspoon
basil		¼ teaspoon
salt		½ teaspoon
pepper		¼ teaspoon

GARNISH:

croutons

1. Soak lentils in enough water to cover them for 4 hours or overnight.
2. Drain; place in large pot; add water and chicken stock (2 lb, 8 oz or 1 qt + 1 cup each) and ham hock. Bring to boil, reduce heat, and simmer, covered, for 2 hours.
3. Remove ham hock from pot. Cut meat from bone and dice. Add meat to lentils in pot.
4. Add remaining ingredients. Cover and cook additional 30 minutes, until lentils are tender.
5. Correct seasonings, remove bay leaf, and serve. If desired, garnish with croutons.

FIELD GREENS WITH PEAR, WALNUTS, AND BLUE CHEESE

Field Greens with Pear, Walnuts, and Blue Cheese

© 2008 Jupiterimages Corporation

This recipe yields more dressing than is needed.

Chill plates before placing salad on them for service.

Use any type of greens desired. A mixture containing bitter greens will accentuate the sweetness of the pear.

The size of the pears affects the number of slices obtained from each pear.

NUMBER OF SERVINGS: 9
SERVING SIZE:
  about 3½ oz total
  1 oz (1½ cups) lettuce
  1 oz (⅛ each) pear—3 slices
  ¼ oz (1 tablespoon) toasted walnuts
  ½ oz (1 tablespoon) blue cheese
  ¾ oz (1½ tablespoons) dressing
TOTAL YIELD:
  9 oz (about 1 cup) dressing

INGREDIENTS	WEIGHT	VOLUME
PEAR VINAIGRETTE:		
pear, ripe, core and stem removed	3½ oz	½ each
balsamic vinegar	2 oz	¼ cup
salt		¼ teaspoon
pepper		¼ teaspoon
nutmeg		¼ teaspoon
cayenne		pinch
olive oil	4 oz	½ cup
lettuce, field greens or mixture of choice	9 oz	13½ cups
pears, ripe, cored, sliced thinly (about 6 slices per quarter)	9 oz	about 1⅛ pears
walnut pieces, lightly toasted	2¼ oz	about ½ cup + 1 tablespoon
blue cheese crumbles	4½ oz	about ¾ cup + 1½ tablespoons

For Vinaigrette:

1. Place pear, vinegar, salt, pepper, nutmeg, and cayenne in bowl of food processor or blender. Purée ingredients.

2. Slowly add olive oil through feed tube and process until emulsified (thickened). Correct seasonings. Refrigerate until needed.

To Assemble:

1. Place lettuce in bowl. Add ¾ oz (1½ tablespoons) dressing per 1 oz (1½ cups) lettuce. Toss to coat leaves.

2. Place coated lettuce on chilled serving plate. Decoratively top with 1 oz (3 each) pear slices, ¼ oz (1 tablespoon) walnut pieces, and ½ oz (1½ tablespoons) blue cheese.

3. Serve immediately.

GREEN BEAN, TOMATO, AND ONION SALAD WITH DILL DRESSING

Green Bean, Tomato, and Onion Salad with Dill Dressing

Chill plates in advance for this salad.

NUMBER OF SERVINGS: 9
COOKING METHOD:
  Boil, Sauté
SERVING SIZE:
  per salad: 1¼ oz lettuce (1¼ cups),
  1½ oz green beans, 2 oz (2 wedges)
  tomatoes, ½ oz red onion,
    ¾ oz bacon crumbles,
    1½ oz (3 tablespoons)
    dressing
TOTAL YIELD:
  11¼ oz lettuce, 13½ oz green
  beans, 1 lb, 2 oz tomatoes,
    4½ oz red onions,
    7 oz bacon crumbles,
    14¼ oz dressing

INGREDIENTS	WEIGHT	VOLUME
DRESSING:		
oil	4¹/₂ oz	1 cup + 1 tablespoon
balsamic vinegar	1¹/₂ oz	3 tablespoons
lemon juice	¹/₄ oz	1¹/₂ teapoons
pepper		¹/₈ teaspoon
paprika		¹/₈ teaspoon
dry mustard		¹/₈ teaspoon
garlic, minced		1 small clove
dill weed		1¹/₂ teaspoons
salt		¹/₈ teaspoon
mayonnaise	6 oz	³/₄ cup
sour cream	1¹/₂ oz	3 tablespoons
salad greens, washed, bite-sized pieces	11¹/₄ oz	11¹/₄ cups
green beans, steamed until *al dente*	13¹/₂ oz	
tomatoes, cut into wedges	1 lb, 2 oz	3 medium
red onions, sliced thinly	4¹/₄ oz	1 medium
bacon crumbles, crisp	7 oz	
GARNISH:		
fresh dill, minced		

For Dressing:

1. Whisk together oil, vinegar, lemon juice, pepper, paprika, mustard, garlic, dill weed, and salt.

2. Whisk in mayonnaise and sour cream; correct seasonings. Cover and refrigerate until needed.

For Assembly:

1. Place 1¹/₄ oz lettuce in center of chilled plate. Top with 1¹/₂ oz green beans. Place wedge of tomato on either side of green beans. Sprinkle onion slices on top.

2. Pour 1¹/₂ oz (3 tablespoons) dressing over salad. Sprinkle ³/₄ oz bacon crumbles on top. If desired, sprinkle dill over top. Serve.

VENISON STEW

NUMBER OF SERVINGS: 11
COOKING METHOD:
 Braise
SERVING SIZE:
 9 oz
TOTAL YIELD:
 6 lbs, 5³/₄ oz

Wine Style: Medium- to full-bodied dry red wines, Pinot Noir, Merlot, Cabernet Sauvignon, or Shiraz
Example: Cabernet Sauvignon—Alaska Denali Winery, Anchorage, AK. This is a deep, full-bodied wine with intense aroma and flavor.

Venison Stew
photo courtesy of Land O' Lakes, Inc.

INGREDIENTS	WEIGHT	VOLUME
bacon, chopped	4 oz	4 slices
venison stew meat, cut into 1½-inch cubes	1 lb, 15 oz	
oil	½ oz	1 tablespoon
onion, small dice	6¼ oz	1 large or 1¼ cups
garlic, minced	¼ oz	2 cloves
flour, all purpose	¼ oz	1 tablespoon
beef stock, hot	8 oz	1 cup
red wine	8 oz	1 cup
tomatoes, canned, chopped	14 oz	1½ cups
bay leaf		2 each
thyme		1 teaspoon
cayenne		¼ teaspoon
carrots, peeled, cut into 1-inch pieces	7 oz	4 each
celery, cut into ½-inch slices	7 oz	2 stalks
potatoes, peeled, cut into 1-inch pieces	11 oz	3 medium
mushrooms, chopped	8 oz	
salt		½ teaspoon
pepper		¼ teaspoon

GARNISH:

parsley, minced

1. Sauté bacon over medium heat until crisp. Remove and reserve. Preheat oven to 350 degrees.
2. Brown venison on all sides in bacon fat; remove from pan and reserve. Drain off liquid and discard.
3. Heat oil in ovenproof pan over medium heat; sauté onion and garlic for 2 to 3 minutes. Stir in flour and cook another 2 minutes. Slowly whisk in stock and then wine. Deglaze pan, stirring constantly to release bits from bottom of pan.
4. Add tomatoes, bay leaves, thyme, cayenne, reserved bacon, and venison. Bring to simmer, cover, and cook in oven for 1 hour.
5. Add carrots, celery, and potatoes; bake another 30 minutes. Add mushrooms, salt, and pepper; bake another 30 minutes until meat and vegetables are tender.
6. Correct seasonings. Serve garnished with parsley.

HAWAIIAN PORK TERIYAKI WITH GRILLED PINEAPPLE

Hawaiian Pork Teriyaki with Grilled Pineapple

Some cooks like to prepare this marinade several days ahead and store in the refrigerator so the flavors develop.

NUMBER OF SERVINGS: 10
COOKING METHOD:
  Grill
SERVING SIZE:
  5 oz meat + 4 oz grilled pineapple
TOTAL YIELD:
  3 lbs, 6 oz meat
  1 lb, 11½ oz (3 ⅓ cups) marinade

Wine Style: Medium-bodied Merlot, Cabernet Sauvignon, or Syrah
Example: Ulupalakua Red—Tedeschi Vineyards, Ulupalakua, HI. This is a smooth, medium-dry wine made from Cabernet Sauvignon and Syrah grapes with ripe berry and spicy flavors.

INGREDIENTS	WEIGHT	VOLUME
TERIYAKI MARINADE:		
soy sauce	8 oz	1 cup
dry sherry	4 oz	½ cup
oil	1 oz	2 tablespoons
vinegar, rice or white	1 oz	2 tablespoons
ginger, fresh, peeled, minced	1 oz	2 tablespoons
garlic, minced	½ oz	4 cloves
brown sugar, lightly packed	6½ oz	1 cup
orange juice	2 oz	¼ cup
water	4 oz	½ cup
pork tenderloin, trimmed, peeled	4 lb, 5 oz	
pineapple, peeled, cored, sliced ½ inch thick	3 lb, 2 oz	10 slices

For Teriyaki Marinade:

1. Combine all marinade ingredients in saucepan. Heat to dissolve sugar.

2. Cool, cover, and store in refrigerator until needed.

For Cooking and Assembly:

1. Place pork in nonreactive pan; pour 1 lb (2 cups) teriyaki marinade over meat. Marinate, turning occasionally, at least 4 hours, preferably overnight.

2. Place pineapple slices in nonreactive pan; pour remaining marinade over them. Marinate for 3 hours, turning once.

3. Preheat grill. Grill pineapple slices about 3 to 4 minutes on each side. Remove from grill; keep warm in low oven.

4. Place pork on grill; cook about 5 minutes on each side, until desired internal temperature.

5. Slice meat on bias, about ½ to ¾ inch thick. Place pineapple slice on plate. Arrange pork slices attractively (fan the meat) on top of pineapple.

MUSHROOM STUFFED CHICKEN IN SOUR CREAM ALMOND SAUCE

Mushroom Stuffed Chicken
in Sour Cream Almond Sauce

NUMBER OF SERVINGS: 12
COOKING METHOD:
Sauté, Bake
SERVING SIZE:
1 breast filled with 1½ oz stuffing
TOTAL YIELD:
7 lbs, 6 oz

Wine Style: Medium- to full-bodied dry white wines, Viognier, Pinot Blanc, Chardonnay, or Rose
Example: Chardonnay, Vintage Selection—Williamette Valley Vineyards, Turner, OR. This wine is ripe and medium-bodied with vanilla and spicy flavors and a long finish.

INGREDIENTS	WEIGHT	VOLUME
STUFFING:		
olive oil	1/4 oz	1 1/2 teaspoons
mushrooms, wild, varieties of choice, washed, cleaned of dirt	1 lb, 6 1/2 oz	
onion, small dice	4 1/2 oz	1 medium
garlic, minced	3/4 oz	6 cloves
salt		1/2 teaspoon
thyme		1/2 teaspoon
pepper		1/4 teaspoon
chicken breasts, halved, boned, skinless, washed	4 lb, 6 oz	12 each
SAUCE:		
butter	2 oz	4 tablespoons
onion, small dice	5 1/2 oz	1 medium to large
garlic, minced	1/2 oz	2 large cloves
flour, all purpose	1 1/4 oz	1/4 cup
chicken stock, hot	1 lb, 8 oz	3 cups
dry sherry	3 oz	1/4 cup + 2 tablespoons
tomato paste	1 1/2 oz	2 tablespoons
almonds, blanched, finely chopped	2 oz	1/4 cup + 2 tablespoons
tarragon		2 teaspoons
salt		1/2 teaspoon
pepper		1/2 teaspoon
sour cream	13 1/2 oz	1 1/2 cups
Gruyère or any type Swiss cheese, grated	10 1/2 oz	1 cup

For Stuffing:

1. Heat oil in skillet over medium heat. Add mushrooms, onion, garlic, salt, thyme, and pepper. Sauté 5 to 7 minutes until vegetables are tender.

2. Set aside until needed.

To Assemble:

1. Wrap chicken breasts loosely with plastic wrap and pound with mallet until about 1/4 inch thick. Be careful not to tear chicken. Pan-spray baking sheet or line with parchment paper. Preheat oven to 350 degrees.

2. Place 1 1/2 oz stuffing in center of chicken breast. Fold top over stuffing; fold sides over stuffing-filled chicken. Continue by rolling breast toward bottom to form log-shaped roll.

3. Place seam side down in baking pan. Continue stuffing and folding remaining chicken breasts.

4. Bake for 20 minutes. While they bake, prepare the sauce.

For Sauce:

1. Melt butter in skillet over medium heat. Add onion and garlic; sauté for 3 to 4 minutes, until onion softens.

2. Add flour and continue cooking and stirring about 2 to 3 minutes until lightly colored.

3. Slowly whisk in chicken stock, then add sherry, tomato paste, almonds, tarragon, salt, and pepper. Cook until slightly thickened, about 3 to 5 minutes.

4. Stir in sour cream. Correct seasonings. Remove from heat; reserve.

To Finish:

1. Pour sauce over cooked chicken.

2. Sprinkle cheese evenly over chicken. Broil for about 4 to 5 minutes until bubbly and browned.

3. Serve, accompanied by wide noodles or starch of choice.

MARINATED GRILLED SALMON

Marinated Grilled Salmon

Allow three to four hours for the salmon to marinate.

If desired, alter amounts of the ingredients in the marinade to create a grilled fish with more spice or sweetness.

The total yield for this recipe gives 11 portions; however, it is difficult to exactly cut a 5-oz portion, so allowing 10 portions provides a margin for error. If increasing this recipe, do not forget to take this into account and adjust the number of servings!

NUMBER OF SERVINGS:
10–11
COOKING METHOD:
  Grill
SERVING SIZE:
  5 oz
TOTAL YIELD:
  3 lbs, 8 oz

Wine Style: Soft fruity Gewürztraminer, Riesling, soft Chardonnay, Rose, or Pinot Noir
Example: Chardonnay—Columbia Crest Winery, Paterson, WA. This wine shows lemon and honeydew aromas that continue through a soft, fruity finish with hints of oak.

INGREDIENTS	WEIGHT	VOLUME
MARINADE:		
soy sauce	2 oz	1/4 cup
sesame oil		1/8 teaspoon
vinegar, rice or white	1 1/2 oz	3 tablespoons
honey	1 1/4 oz	2 tablespoons
molasses	1 1/2 oz	2 tablespoons
water	2 oz	1/4 cup
ginger		1/4 teaspoon
wasabi paste	1/4 oz	1 teaspoon
salmon filets, washed, all bones removed, skin intact	5 lb	

1. Mix all marinade ingredients together in nonreactive bowl.
2. Add salmon; turn to coat. Cover and refrigerate to marinate for 3 to 4 hours, turning once or twice.
3. Preheat grill. Remove salmon from liquid; place on grill with skin side down. Cook until salmon is flaky, about 8 minutes per side depending on thickness of salmon. *Note:* Skin will come off when turning salmon.
4. Remove from grill. Serve.

HAZELNUT ENCRUSTED HALIBUT WITH OLIVE CAPER HAZELNUT SALSA

Toasted Hazelnuts Before Removing Skins

photo by Dave King © Dorling Kindersley

Hazelnut Encrusted Halibut with Olive Caper Hazelnut Salsa

Allow at least four hours to refrigerate salsa.

To lower costs, reduce amount of hazelnuts and replace with bread crumbs.

NUMBER OF SERVINGS: 12
COOKING METHOD:
  Bake
SERVING SIZE:
  5 oz fish
  1 1/2 oz (1/4 cup) salsa
TOTAL YIELD:
  4 lbs fish
  1 lb, 2 oz salsa

Wine Style: Pinot Grigio, Chardonnay, or light Pinot Noir
Example: Reserve Chardonnay—Chateau Ste. Michelle, Woodville, WA. This wine is rich and ripe with concentrated fruit flavors and aromas of pear, hazelnut, and spicy, toasty oak.

Spread hazelnuts on baking pan. Bake for 10 to 15 minutes at 350 degrees, stirring occasionally, until lightly brown and skins loosen. Remove from pan. Immediately place in clean kitchen towel, twist top to enclose tightly, and leave to steam until cooled. Still enclosed in towel, rub nuts to release skins, then remove nuts from towel and discard skins.

INGREDIENTS	WEIGHT	VOLUME
OLIVE CAPER HAZELNUT SALSA:		
olives, salad variety with pimentos, drained, chopped	13½ oz	
hazelnuts, skinned, toasted, chopped	2¼ oz	5½ tablespoons
onion, minced	2¼ oz	½ medium
parsley, chopped	¾ oz	⅓ cup
capers	1¾ oz	2¾ tablespoons
lemon juice	¼ oz	1½ teaspoons
olive oil	¾ oz	1½ tablespoons
oregano		1½ teaspoons
HALIBUT:		
hazelnuts, skinned, chopped	14¾ oz	
dill		1½ teaspoon
cayenne		¼ to ½ teaspoon, depending on taste
thyme		1½ teaspoons
salt		¾ teaspoon
pepper		¼ to ½ teaspoon, depending on taste
halibut fillets, washed	3 lb, 11 oz	
butter, melted	4 oz	½ cup or 1 stick
GARNISH:		
dill sprigs		

For Salsa:

1. Combine all ingredients in bowl.
2. Cover and refrigerate for at least four hours or overnight.

For Halibut:

1. Place oven rack in center of oven. Place parchment paper on baking sheet. Preheat oven to 425 degrees.
2. Mix hazelnuts, dill, cayenne, thyme, salt, and pepper together.
3. Dip fillets in butter, then roll in hazelnut mixture. Place on prepared pan.
4. Bake until nuts begin to brown and fish flakes, about 10 to 14 minutes per inch of thickness.
5. To serve, place 1½ oz (¼ cup) salsa on plate. Top with fish and garnish with sprigs of dill.

WOK CHARRED AHI WITH CHINESE CABBAGE SLAW AND DIPPING SAUCE

—Recipe by Peter Merriman

Cook this ahi to the desired internal temperature by testing with a meat thermometer. According to Chef Merriman, the traditional way of serving this tuna in Hawaii is to sear the outside leaving the inside sashimi (raw).

NUMBER OF SERVINGS: 12
COOKING METHOD:
  Fry
SERVING SIZE:
  6 oz ahi, 2 oz slaw,
  1⅓ oz dipping sauce
TOTAL YIELD:
  13 oz marinade, 1 lb,
    8 oz slaw,
  16 oz (2 cups) dipping sauce

Wine Style: Wide variety—Gewürztraminer, Pinot Gris, Pinot Grigio, Grenache, or Gamay
Example: Pinot Gris—Duck Pond Cellars, Dundee, OR. Barrel-fermented to give it more depth and structure, this wine has a nose of peach, vanilla, and lime.

INGREDIENTS	WEIGHT	VOLUME
CHINESE CABBAGE SLAW MIXTURE:		
won bok (Chinese cabbage), thinly sliced	12¹/₂ oz	4¹/₂ cups
mung bean sprouts	4¹/₂ oz	1¹/₂ cups
red onion, julienne	6 oz	1¹/₂ cups
cilantro, minced	1¹/₂ oz	¹/₂ cup
DIPPING SAUCE:		
wasabi, dry	1¹/₄ oz	2 tablespoons
water	1 oz	2 tablespoons
lemon juice	2³/₄ oz	¹/₃ cup
mirin	2³/₄ oz	¹/₃ cup
shoyu	8 oz	1 cup
MARINADE:		
butter, clarified	8 oz	1 cup
shallots, minced	2 oz	¹/₄ cup
ginger, fresh, minced	1 oz	2 tablespoons
garlic, minced	1 oz	4 large cloves
marjoram, fresh, minced		1 tablespoon
red chili flakes		¹/₂ teaspoon
salt and pepper mix*	¹/₄ oz	1 teaspoon
thyme, fresh, minced		1 tablespoon
cayenne		¹/₄ teaspoon
lemon juice	1 oz	2 tablespoons
ahi tuna, cut into pieces, sashimi cut block, 1¹/₂ by 1¹/₂ by 4 inches	4 lbs, 8 oz	

*Note: Use 6 parts salt to 1 part pepper

For Chinese Cabbage Slaw:

1. Mix all ingredients in bowl.
2. Cover and refrigerate until well chilled.

For Dipping Sauce:

1. Mix wasabi with water until well combined. Set aside until needed.
2. Combine lemon juice, mirin, and shoyu. In nonreactive bowl, add half of liquid and wasabi paste. Mix well until no lumps remain.
3. Add remaining liquid. Correct seasonings. Store until needed.

For Marinade and Ahi:

1. Mix all ingredients for marinade together. Chill. Preheat wok over high heat until very hot. If marinade is chilled, bring to room temperature before using, since butter will solidify.
2. Coat ahi with marinade by rolling each log of fish in marinade.
3. Place ahi in hot wok; sear on each side until desired internal temperature. Cooking about 1 minute on each side sears the outside but leaves inside very rare.
4. Remove ahi from pan; let rest about 30 seconds. Cut into ¹/₄-inch slices. Serve on bed of Chinese cabbage slaw (2 oz or ²/₃ cup) with dipping sauce (1¹/₃ oz) in ramekin on side.

—*Copyright Chef Peter Merriman*

PETER MERRIMAN
Executive Chef & Restaurateur

Called the Pied Piper of Hawaii Regional Cuisine by the *Los Angeles Times* and a Culinary Renaissance Man by the *New York Times*, Peter Merriman owns several restaurants on the Big Island of Hawaii and on Maui. In December 1988, Merriman and his wife, Vicki, opened their first restaurant, Merriman's, located in the Big Island's ranch country.

Merriman grew up in Pittsburgh, Pennsylvania, where his mother was a food writer and restaurant critic for the Pittsburgh *Post Gazette*. After graduating from the University of Pennsylvania with a degree in political science, Merriman enrolled in a three-year chef's apprentice program under the auspices of the American Culinary Federation. After his apprenticeship, he cooked in resort areas throughout the United States and Europe, including a summer when he learned much about wine while working in the Champagne vineyards of France. In 1983, Merriman accepted a position with the Mauna Lani Bay Hotel on the Big Island of Hawaii and became the executive chef at the age of 28.

Honored with numerous awards, including several James Beard Award nominations, his restaurant has received the prestigious "Hale Aina Award" as the Top Big Island Restaurant. In addition to running restaurants, Merriman was instrumental in organizing Hawaii Regional Cuisine, Inc., a nonprofit organization including eleven of Hawaii's leading chefs. Merriman serves as president of the group, which is dedicated to the advancement of contemporary Hawaiian cuisine and bringing together chefs and farmers. The group published a cookbook, *The New Cuisine of Hawaii,* in 1994.

Traveling throughout North America on various cooking endeavors, Merriman has participated in many benefit dinners in New York, Miami, Honolulu, and Los Angeles, and has made numerous appearances on television shows. In addition, he serves on the Board of Hawaii Health Foundation and as Regional Director of Food Choices 2000.

CREAMED SPINACH

Creamed Spinach
photo by Dave King © Dorling Kindersley

To prepare this recipe with fresh spinach, use almost double the amount of the frozen spinach. Because of its high moisture content, fresh spinach compacts and greatly decreases in volume when cooked. Be sure to remove stems and wash thoroughly before chopping. Blanche the fresh spinach lightly to remove excess water before adding to the cream sauce.

NUMBER OF SERVINGS: 11
COOKING METHOD:
  Braise
SERVING SIZE:
  4 oz
TOTAL YIELD:
  2 lbs, 12 oz

INGREDIENTS	WEIGHT	VOLUME
butter	1 oz	2 tablespoons
garlic, minced	1/4 oz	2 cloves
flour, all purpose	1/2 oz	2 tablespoons
cream, hot	6 oz	3/4 cup
milk, hot	4 oz	1/2 cup
nutmeg, grated		1 teaspoon
salt		1/2 teaspoon
pepper		1/4 teaspoon
spinach, frozen, chopped, drained well	1 lb, 12 oz	2 each 1-lb packages

1. Melt butter over medium heat in large saucepan. Add garlic; sauté until lightly brown, about 1 minute.
2. Reduce heat to low; whisk flour into butter. Continue whisking about 3 minutes, until blonde.
3. Slowly whisk in cream and milk; heat until thickened.
4. Whisk in nutmeg, salt, and pepper. Add spinach, heat thoroughly.
5. Correct seasonings. Serve.

GINGERED CARROTS, LEEKS, AND BEAN SPROUTS

NUMBER OF SERVINGS: 12
COOKING METHOD:
  Sauté, Steam
SERVING SIZE:
  4 oz
TOTAL YIELD:
  3 lbs, 3½ oz

INGREDIENTS	WEIGHT	VOLUME
butter	4 oz	½ cup, 1 stick, or 8 tablespoons
carrots, peeled, julienne	2 lb, 9 oz	8 large
leeks, washed, white and pale green julienne	9 oz	4 each
ginger, fresh, peeled, minced	½ oz	2 tablespoons
mung bean sprouts	11½ oz	4 cups
soy sauce	1 oz	2 tablespoons

1. Melt butter in large skillet over medium heat.
2. Add carrots, stir, and cover. Cook about 5 minutes, stirring occasionally, until starting to become tender.
3. Add leeks and ginger, cover and cook another 2 minutes.
4. Uncover; add bean sprouts and soy sauce. Heat thoroughly, until carrots are *al dente*, slightly crunchy.
5. Correct seasonings. Serve.

GRATIN OF POTATOES AND MUSHROOMS

NUMBER OF SERVINGS: 14
COOKING METHOD:
  Bake
SERVING SIZE:
  4 oz
TOTAL YIELD:
  3 lbs, 11¾ oz

INGREDIENTS	WEIGHT	VOLUME
potatoes, Yukon gold, peeled, sliced ⅛ inch thick	2 lb, 3¾ oz	
mushrooms, sliced ¼ inch thick	13¾ oz	
onion, small dice	3¾ oz	1 medium
salt	¼ oz	1 teaspoon
pepper		½ teaspoon
paprika		½ teaspoon
butter, melted	1 oz	2 tablespoons
sour cream	7 oz	¾ cup
Swiss cheese, grated	5 oz	

1. Grease or pan-spray 9- by 9- by 2-inch ovenproof dish. Preheat oven to 350 degrees.
2. Layer half of potato slices in prepared pan. Top with half of mushrooms, half of onions, half of salt, pepper, and paprika.
3. Drizzle half (½ oz or 1 tablespoon) butter over mixture. Spread sour cream over mixture.
4. Top with layer of remaining potatoes, remaining mushrooms, onions, salt, pepper, and paprika. Drizzle with remaining butter.
5. Cover and bake for 40 minutes. Uncover, place Swiss cheese over top in even layer, and continue baking uncovered for 30 to 40 minutes, until potatoes are tender. Serve.

SOURDOUGH FRENCH BREAD

Forming Loaf of French Bread
photo by Ian O'Leary © Dorling Kindersley

Tapping Bottom of French Bread
photo by David Murray and Jules Selmes © Dorling Kindersley

Sourdough French Bread
photo © Dorling Kindersley

Begin preparing sourdough starter several days or a week before needed. In addition, the sponge for this French bread needs to sit in a warm spot for about 12 hours before making bread.

Brushing loaves with water helps form crusty bread. The pan of water in oven while baking also creates steam, which makes more crust.

COOKING METHOD:
  Bake
TOTAL YIELD:
  3 lbs, 4 oz dough, 2 loaves

INGREDIENTS	WEIGHT	VOLUME
SOURDOUGH STARTER:		
yogurt, plain, containing active culture	5 oz	1/2 cup
flour, unbleached	2 1/2 oz	1/2 cup
sugar		1 teaspoon
water, filtered, warm	4 oz	1/2 cup
flour, unbleached	2 1/2 oz	1/2 cup
water, filtered, warm	4 oz	1/2 cup
SPONGE:		
sourdough starter	8 oz	1 cup
water, warm	8 oz	1 cup
flour, unbleached, bread	8 1/4 oz	1 1/2 cups
BREAD:		
water, warm	5 1/2 oz	2/3 cup
sugar	1/2 oz	1 tablespoon
yeast, dry, granulated	1/2 oz	1 tablespoon
flour, unbleached, bread	1 lb, 8 oz to 1 lb, 14 1/4 oz	4 1/2 to 5 1/2 cups
salt	1/2 oz	2 teaspoons
cornmeal, for sprinkling baking sheet		

For Starter:

1. Using wooden or plastic spoon, stir yogurt, 2 1/2 oz (1/2 cup) flour, sugar, and 4 oz (1/2 cup) water together in nonreactive bowl. Cover loosely with towel and place in warm spot for 2 to 4 days, until bubbly.

2. Stir in 2 1/2 oz (1/2 cup) flour and 4 oz (1/2 cup) water. Cover and place in warm spot for overnight or one day. Use or refrigerate tightly covered until needed.

3. Replenish starter with 2 1/2 oz (1/2 cup) flour and 4 oz (1/2 cup) water after using or every one or two weeks.

For Sponge:

1. Using wooden or plastic spoon, stir ingredients for sponge together in nonreactive bowl.

2. Cover loosely with plastic wrap or towel and place in warm spot overnight, until bubbly.

To Finish Bread:

1. Place 5 1/2 oz (2/3 cup) water in nonreactive bowl. With wooden or plastic spoon, stir in sugar, then yeast. Set aside for about 3 to 5 minutes, until yeast dissolves and expands.

2. Add sponge to yeast mixture. Add part of flour and salt. Stir, adding more flour until soft dough and ready to knead.

3. Adding just enough flour as needed to prevent sticking, knead for 7 to 10 minutes, until smooth and elastic dough. Cover; let rise until doubled, about 1 hour and 30 minutes.

(Continued)

4. Punch down; let rise again until doubled, about 45 minutes. Meanwhile, pan-spray baking sheet or line with parchment paper; sprinkle with cornmeal.

5. Punch down dough. Form into loaves using the following method: Divide dough in half (1 lb, 10 oz each). Roll into about 14- by 10-inch rectangle. Roll tightly from 14-inch side, pressing firmly together like rolling a jelly roll. Press and tuck ends under to hide seams. Place seam side down on prepared baking sheet. Cover and allow to rise until doubled, about 45 minutes.

6. While bread rises, place pan of hot water on lower rack in oven to create steam while baking. Preheat oven to 400 degrees.

7. Using sharp knife or razor blade, make 3 or 4 diagonal slits in top of bread. Brush loaves with cold water. Bake for 15 minutes. Remove from oven; again brush loaves with water. Return to oven. Bake another 15 to 20 minutes, until golden brown on top and bottom and loaves sound hollow when tapped. Remove from oven; cool on racks.

CHERRY FRITTERS

Cherry Fritters

This recipe features tart cherries in a sweet fritter batter. If it seems too tart, add more sugar to the batter. If desired, accompany these with cherry, vanilla, or cinnamon ice cream.

NUMBER OF SERVINGS: 11
COOKING METHOD:
   Deep-fry
SERVING SIZE:
   5 fritters
   1¼ oz for each fritter
TOTAL YIELD:
   57 fritters, 4 lbs, 8¼ oz batter

INGREDIENTS	WEIGHT	VOLUME
oil for frying		
flour, all purpose	12¾ oz	3 cups
baking powder	¾ oz	1½ tablespoons
sugar	6 oz	¾ cup
cinnamon	½ oz	2¼ teaspoons
nutmeg		¾ teaspoon
salt		¼ teaspoon
milk	12 oz	1½ cups
almond extract		¼ teaspoon
butter, melted	1½ oz	3 tablespoons
eggs, separated	10 oz	6 each
cherries, tart, pitted, well drained	1 lb, 13 ¼ oz	5¼ cups or 3 each 14½-oz cans
confectioners' sugar for dusting		

1. Heat oil for deep-frying to 370 degrees.

2. Sift flour, baking powder, sugar, cinnamon, nutmeg, and salt into bowl. Make well in center of mixture.

3. Mix milk, almond extract, butter, and egg yolks together. Pour into well in center. Stir quickly with fork just to combine.

4. Whip egg whites until soft peaks. Gently fold into mixture, a third at a time. Fold in cherries.

5. Drop 1¼ oz (amount on serving spoon) batter into hot oil. Fry 2 or 3 minutes until golden. Turn and fry other side until golden. Remove from oil, drain, place on absorbent paper, and keep warm in low oven while frying rest of batter. *Note: Watch temperature of oil. Do not add too many fritters at once because it may lower temperature of oil.*

6. Sift heavy coating of confectioners' sugar over fritters. Serve immediately, warm or at room temperature. If desired, accompany with cherry, cinnamon, or vanilla ice cream.

APPLE CRISP

Apple Crisp
photo courtesy of Land O' Lakes, Inc.

The choice of apples determines how long to bake this dessert. Test by sticking a knife into apple filling to make sure they are soft.

NUMBER OF SERVINGS: 9
COOKING METHOD:
  Bake
SERVING SIZE:
  6 oz
TOTAL YIELD:
  3 lbs, 7½ oz

INGREDIENTS	WEIGHT	VOLUME
FILLING:		
apples, variety of choice, peeled, cored, sliced medium thickness	2 lbs, 4 oz	6 large, about 8 cups
brown sugar, firmly packed	1½ oz	3 tablespoons
cinnamon		1 teaspoon
lemon juice	½ oz	1 tablespoon
raisins	1½ oz	¼ cup
TOPPING:		
flour, all purpose	3¾ oz	¾ cup
cinnamon		1 teaspoon
nutmeg		½ teaspoon
salt		¼ teaspoon
brown sugar, firmly packed	2 oz	¼ cup
sugar	1¾ oz	¼ cup
butter, unsalted, cold, cut into pieces	6 oz	¾ cup or 1½ sticks
oats, rolled	5 oz	1¼ cups

For Filling:

1. Gently mix apples, brown sugar, cinnamon, and lemon juice in bowl. Add raisins and mix to combine.

2. Place apples in ovenproof 2-quart dish. Preheat oven to 350 degrees.

To Finish:

1. Place flour, cinnamon, nutmeg, salt, brown sugar, and sugar in bowl of food processor fitted with knife blade. Pulse a few times to combine.

2. Place butter pieces on top of flour mixture. Pulse to cut into dough until the size of peas.

3. Mix oats into mixture by hand or with one or two pulses.

4. Sprinkle evenly over top of apples. Bake for 40 to 45 minutes, until apples are done and topping browns. If topping browns before apples are done, cover with aluminum foil and continue baking. Test softness of apples by inserting knife tip through topping and into apples.

5. Serve warm, accompanied by ice cream, cream, or caramel topping.

CHOCOLATE HAZELNUT TORTE

Glazing Hazelnut Torte
photo by Dave King © Dorling Kindersley

Slice of Hazelnut Torte
photo courtesy of Hazelnut Marketing Board

This recipe produces a very rich cake, but, if desired, cut the torte into 12 pieces instead of 16.

The accompanying ganache recipe yields more ganache than needed for this torte; however, pouring the ganache to coat the torte requires more than needed just to coat. Excess ganache stores well in the refrigerator.

NUMBER OF SERVINGS: 16
COOKING METHOD:
    Bake
SERVING SIZE:
    1 wedge 1/16 of torte
TOTAL YIELD:
    1 each 9-inch cake

INGREDIENTS	WEIGHT	VOLUME
TORTE:		
chocolate, bittersweet or semisweet, coarsely chopped	9 oz	1 1/3 cups
hazelnuts	10 1/2 oz	2 1/4 cups
flour, all purpose	2 1/2 oz	1/2 cup
butter, unsalted, softened	6 1/2 oz	1 stick + 5 tablespoons or 13 tablespoons
sugar	6 oz	3/4 cup
egg	11 3/4 oz	7 each
salt	pinch	
frangelica or hazelnut liqueur	1 oz	2 tablespoons
GANACHE:		
heavy cream	10 3/4 oz	1 1/3 cups
chocolate, bittersweet or semisweet, coarsely chopped	1 lb	2 2/3 cups
frangelica or hazelnut liqueur	1 oz	2 tablespoons
GARNISH:		
hazelnuts, toasted, skins removed, chopped or left whole		

For Torte:

1. Pan-spray 9-inch springform pan and cover bottom with parchment paper. Pan-spray parchment paper. Place oven rack in center of oven and preheat oven to 350 degrees.

2. Melt chocolate in double boiler over barely simmering water (*bain marie*) or in microwave at half power. Remove from heat, but leave pan over warm water until ready for use.

3. Meanwhile, spread hazelnuts on baking pan. Bake for 10 to 15 minutes, stirring occasionally, until lightly brown and skins loosen. Remove from pan. Immediately place in clean kitchen towel, twist top to enclose tightly, and leave to steam until cooled. Still enclosed in towel, rub nuts to release skins, then remove nuts from towel and discard skins.

4. Place hazelnuts and flour in bowl of food processor fitted with steel blade. Process until nuts are very finely ground but not oily.

5. Beat butter and half of sugar (3 oz or 1/2 cup) using flat beater, if available, until light and fluffy.

6. Slowly, add 3 1/2 oz (2 each) whole eggs and 3 1/2 oz (5 each) egg yolks, beating well after each addition. Beat in salt and frangelica.

7. Add melted chocolate to mixture and beat on low speed.

8. In separate bowl, whip egg whites with whisk attachment on medium speed until frothy. Turn to high speed and beat until soft peaks form. Continue beating, adding remaining 3 oz (1/4 cup) sugar by the tablespoon, mixing after each spoonful. Beat until egg whites form stiff peaks but are not dry.

(Continued)

9. With rubber spatula, stir about one-quarter of egg whites into chocolate mixture to lighten. Now quickly fold in half the egg whites, then half the nut mixture, the remaining egg whites, and the remaining nuts.

10. Pour into prepared pan; bake for 45 minutes. Reduce temperature to 325 degrees. Bake another 10 to 20 minutes, until torte springs back when lightly pressed in center and knife inserted into cake comes out almost clean.

11. Cool a few minutes on wire rack; remove rim of pan and cool completely. Wrap well and store in refrigerator until needed.

For Ganache:

1. Bring cream just to a boil. Remove from heat, add chocolate, and whisk until melted. Add frangelica.

2. Let sit until cooled. Mixture may be used right away or covered and refrigerated for later use.

Assembly:

1. Using a large serrated knife, slice torte evenly into thirds horizontally. Place top third with cut side up on cardboard round or serving plate.

2. Spread layer of ganache over surface; top with second cake layer. Press lightly, then top second cake with layer of ganache. Place third cake layer on top with cut side down. Press gently to level.

3. If using cardboard round or base the size of the cake, place on wire rack with sheet pan underneath to catch chocolate. Pour ganache over cake, smoothing top and sides with icing spatula. Repeat if needed, for smooth coating.

4. Decorate top with hazelnut pieces. *Suggestion:* Place 1½-inch rim of chopped hazelnuts around perimeter on top of cake.

5. Store torte in refrigerator. Remove from refrigerator to warm slightly before serving.

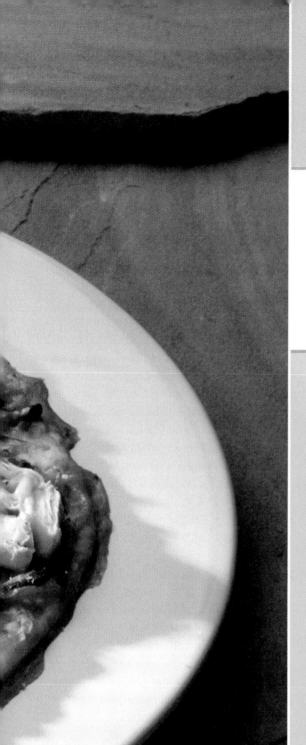

12
California

OBJECTIVES

By the end of this chapter, you will be able to

- Discuss the groups of people who settled in California, why they came, and how their heritage impacted the cuisine
- Discuss the influence of the Gold Rush and the railroad on the cookery of California
- Explain how the topography and climate affected the crops and the cuisine in California
- Identify food products prevalent in California
- Prepare a variety of dishes indicative of the cuisine of California

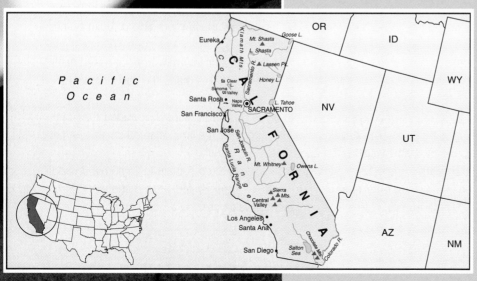

HISTORY

Prior to the arrival of the Franciscan friars, the Native Americans in California hunted game, fished if they were located near water, and gathered wild greens, seeds, and berries. In 1769, the first Europeans—Franciscan priests from Spain—arrived in California. Initially, they established a mission in San Diego to protect the lands claimed for Spain. They continued building missions and forts stretching from Texas to California. With about one day of traveling separating each of the missions, the Franciscan friars erected 21 missions nestled in the hills near the coast between San Diego in southern California and Sonoma, which lies northeast of San Francisco.

After building the missions, the friars established irrigation systems to transform the barren land into fertile farmland. They then planted a variety of crops at each of the missions. Depending on the climate in the particular location, they planted wheat, corn, squash, beans, chili peppers, *tomatillos*, tomatoes, sweet potatoes, avocados, pomegranates, citrus fruits, apricots, pears, grapes, figs, dates, olives, pistachios, and more. The friars raised cattle and hogs at the missions. Years later, towns and cities developed at the sites where these missions stood.

Among their many culinary contributions, the Franciscans receive credit for introducing winemaking to California. Initially, they planted grapes to make wine for religious uses. The grapes thrived. Later, influence from French and Italian winemakers improved the quality of the wine made in California. Today, wine remains a very important industry in this state. In addition to wine, the friars needed candles for the religious services and crackers for communion. To meet these needs, they imported bees for beeswax and planted wheat to make crackers.

When Mexico gained its freedom from Spain, the era of Spanish rule in California ended. From 1821 until 1848, the Mexicans controlled California. In 1850, California became a state in the United States.

Prior to 1848, two prominent groups moved into California: the Spanish, who migrated north from Mexico into California, and the Russians, who trekked from Russia to Alaska and then traveled south through the Pacific Northwest into California. The Spanish raised herds of cattle in sparsely populated California until the discovery of gold.

When gold was discovered at Sutter's Mill in 1848, life in California changed. Droves of prospectors from all over the United States and foreign countries flocked here. They arrived with dreams of finding gold and becoming rich. By the end of 1849, eighty thousand people had come to California in pursuit of gold. Reportedly, the population of California increased almost four times with the influx of people seeking gold.

The swarm of people moving to California during the Gold Rush differed from other westward migrations. Men without families flooded into California. Unlike the typical homesteaders who settled other areas of the United States, these men did not build homes, farms, and communities. They concentrated on seeking a fortune as opposed to caring for a family and creating a home. Since very few of these settlers grew crops or raised cattle, they needed to import much of the food from the East. This made the cost of food astronomical. Literally, many foods cost as much as gold.

By 1880, miners had either moved to other states to prospect or traded their picks for farming tools. Those who stayed in California irrigated the land, planted crops, and produced abundant grains, vegetables, and fruits.

In the middle to late 1800s, the Homestead Acts lured settlers to California. In addition to people moving from more eastern regions of the United States, immigrants from Ireland, Poland, Austria, Germany, and Czechoslovakia created a new home in this state.

Known as the father of California's viticulture, Agoston Haraszthy came from a wealthy winemaking family in Hungary. In 1840 at the age of 28, he immigrated to the United States. After purchasing land in Sonoma in 1857, he planted 25 acres of grapes for wine. Haraszthy started the Buena Vista Winery in Sonoma, which still operates today. In 1861, he traveled to Europe to learn the latest winemaking techniques. When he returned to California, Haraszthy brought over 100,000 grapevines. He introduced hundreds of different varieties of grapes that he obtained as roots and cuttings in Spain, France, Italy, Switzerland, and Germany. After disseminating these vines throughout the state, he adapted European methods of winemaking. Haraszthy made casks from the native redwoods. The wine industry in California blossomed.

Meanwhile, Mariano Vallejo settled in the Sonoma Valley. He built a home with a wine press, grew grapes, and made wine. In 1863, two of Vallejo's daughters married the sons of Agoston Haraszthy in a double wedding ceremony. This created the first of many marriages between families of winemakers.

Before the Gold Rush, many grizzly bears roamed California. The bears became almost extinct as more and more people moved into the state.

During the 1850s, Chinese immigrants flooded into California seeking work as laborers. Chinese food soon became common fare.

Partially due to the ability to irrigate the farmland, California's population grew during the early 1900s. Irrigation transformed barren, arid land into fertile farmland, dramatically increasing crop yields. As a result, many people relocated to California.

Another boost to California's population came with the completion of the Panama Canal in 1914. The creation of a passage that connected the Atlantic and Pacific Oceans meant that travelers from the east coast of the United States and from Europe no longer needed to sail around South America to reach California.

TOPOGRAPHY AND CLIMATE

With mountains and desert on much of its eastern border and the Pacific Ocean and mountain ranges forming a rugged coastline on its west, California experienced isolation from the rest of the United States in the early years. The first ships from the eastern part of the United States sailed to California in 1796, but those ships had to sail around Cape Horn at the southern end of South America to reach California. Besides being a very long voyage, the cold climate, frequent storms, and treacherous waters around Cape Horn ensured a difficult and dangerous trip. About thirty years later, travelers trekked across the country, crossed the mountains, and entered California. Because of the topographical barriers, it took the quest for gold in the middle 1800s to lure large numbers of settlers into California.

Ranked as the third largest state in area behind Alaska and Texas, today California claims the largest population of any of the fifty states. Oregon lies to the north of California, Nevada and Arizona to its east, Mexico to the south, and the Pacific Ocean forms its western border. While the Sierra Nevada Mountains run for 400 miles from north to south on the eastern side of California, mountains and steep cliffs line the coast of the Pacific Ocean, creating dramatic scenery along the coastline. The coastal mountain ranges vary in height, but in general, the tallest mountains dominate the north and they taper toward shorter elevations in the south.

Forests cover many of the slopes of the mountain ranges found throughout California. Dominating the terrain in the northwest, forests of huge redwoods and sequoias grow from the northern boundary to the center of the state. Many pine trees grow in the forests of the south. Although found primarily in the mountainous regions, forests actually cover 40 percent of California's land.

Numerous lakes, rivers, and streams dot the terrain in the mountains. Trout, salmon, bass, and more freshwater fish swim in these waterways. The Colorado River forms the border between California and Arizona. Situated near Nevada, mountains surround Lake Tahoe, which averages 1,000 feet deep.

Between the mountains on each side of the state, the interior consists of a huge expanse of valley. The Central Valley extends 450 miles from north to south in the center of the state and ranks as one of the premier agricultural areas in the United States. Providing water for crops, the Sacramento River flows through the northern section of the Central Valley, and the San Joaquin River runs through the south. Consequently, the northern region is known as the Sacramento Valley and the San Joaquin Valley lies in the south. Both the Sacramento Valley and the San Joaquin Valley experience hot, dry summers and wet, foggy winters. A multitude of fruits, vegetables, nuts, rice, wheat, cattle, and sheep flourish throughout the Central Valley.

California contains 840 miles of coastline along the Pacific Ocean. The cold waters of the Pacific yield a wealth of fish and shellfish. Of course, the warmer waters found in southern

California support the growth of different species from those found in the colder northern waters.

Mountains and deserts such as the Mojave Desert, the Colorado Desert, and Death Valley make up much of the southeast. This region covers 25 million acres, accounting for about 25 percent of California's land. Hot, dry climate reigns, but irrigated areas produce bountiful crops. The Coachella Valley is an example of barren land turned into fertile farmland by irrigation.

The climate in southern California remains warm throughout the year, but the northern half experiences winter. While the ocean moderates the temperature near the coast and eliminates extremes, many inland areas endure very hot summers. California's climate is described as two seasons: the rainy winter season and the dry summer. Much of the climate found in California resembles the Mediterranean climate with hot, dry summers and mild, rainy winters. As a result, olives, grapes, and other Mediterranean crops grow well here.

Until the late nineteenth century, most of the winemaking took place in southern California. After disease destroyed much of the grape crop in the south, growers planted grapes in the Sonoma Valley in northern California. Situated between ranges of hills, Napa Valley and Sonoma Valley, lying northeast of San Francisco, still support a prosperous wine industry today. The hot, dry summers and rainy, mild winters provide the ideal conditions for growing grapes. In fact, the climate in this area proved more favorable than the climate of southern California for growing the grape varieties found in Europe. Rivers running through these valleys create microclimates conducive to excellent wine production from specific grape varieties. Furthermore, the bay moderates the temperature for this entire area, ensuring mild winters.

Ingredients and foods commonly used throughout the cuisine of California include

- fish and seafood, including tuna, sole, swordfish, halibut, anchovies, oysters, several types of crab, including the prized Dungeness crab, and abalone
- cattle and sheep
- chicken and turkey
- dairy products, including many varieties of cheese
- vegetables, including artichokes, garlic, onions, broccoli, lettuce, spinach, celery, asparagus, cauliflower, avocados, mushrooms, peppers, Brussels sprouts, and much more
- fresh fruits, including dates, citrus fruits, apples, plums, peaches, nectarines, cherries, pears, kiwi, strawberries, apricots, and more
- dried fruits, including raisins, prunes, figs, and dates
- grapes and wine
- almonds, walnuts, and pistachios
- olives

COOKING METHODS

Californians used virtually every cooking method. Boiling, baking, grilling, braising, and frying all came into play with the incredible diversity of fruits, vegetables, grains, meats, fowl, fish, and seafood that grew in this state.

With plenty of beef and lamb, they often grilled and sautéed the tender cuts while braising tough cuts. The Spanish roasted meat over an open fire, so grilling appeared commonly. As in the Pacific Northwest, the Native Americans also cooked over the open fire. They speared fish with a stick and placed the stick in the ground near the fire. When the fish was cooked on one side, they rotated the stick to cook the other side. Today, cooking outdoors on a grill remains popular.

When the Chinese arrived in the 1850s, they introduced the technique of stir-frying, cooking small evenly chopped foods in a wok over high heat. They seasoned with soy sauce, ginger, and other flavorings. Californians quickly adopted Asian flavorings and the technique of stir-frying, and they became part of the cookery of California.

Californians often chose simple cooking techniques for fresh produce. Steamed or lightly sautéed vegetables appeared often. Of course, each of the ethnic groups brought their culinary heritage including recipes, food preferences, and cooking techniques.

REGIONS

Herds of cattle and sheep graze in northern California, and, as a result, numerous dairy products come from this area. Large and small cheese factories produce many varieties of cheeses, such as Monterey Jack, cheddar, numerous Mexican cheeses, feta, Brie, Camembert, and many more. Besides dairy, the northern coastal region yields pears, apples, and grapes for wine.

Lying northeast of San Francisco, the counties of Napa and Sonoma contain acres and acres of grapes and hundreds of wineries. Many say the wines produced in this region rival those from France.

Like New York, San Francisco grew around its port. Besides serving as a transportation center, the bay provided food to the early residents who found the waters abounding with fish and shellfish. While the bay contained abundant oysters in the early days, most oysters were depleted by 1851 because of overfishing.

San Francisco and New York City share another similarity. The water around both cities restricts the available land so the cities cannot spread. Bays surround San Francisco on three sides, and New York is an island. In both cities, bridges span the water to connect the city to the other side. As in New York, limited roadways make many San Francisco residents depend on public transportation.

Transforming this small town into a city, hordes of settlers, mostly men, moved to San Francisco in the 1840s in hopes of discovering gold and striking it rich. During the 1850s, more immigrants arrived to work on building the transcontinental railroad. Since many of the railroad workers emigrated from China, chow mein, egg fu yung, and chop suey became common fare. Still other immigrants like the Italians and Portuguese came to this area to work as fishermen.

With immigrants from France, Spain, Portugal, Germany, Italy, England, Ireland, Russia, Mexico, and other European and Asian countries moving into San Francisco, ethnic neighborhoods emerged, representing each country. While the cuisines from all of these ethnic groups melded to form the cuisine of San Francisco, the different nationalities remained separate in their own neighborhoods and communities. Today, Chinatown is still a bustling area filled with Asian stores, businesses, and restaurants. Chinatown houses a huge enclave of Asians and claims 30,000 residents. Situated just north of Chinatown, North Beach remains an Italian community filled with Italian shops, restaurants, and residents. San Francisco became one of the great melting pot cities of the United States.

Wanting to duplicate the intensely flavored tomato paste available in Italy, Tillie Lewis realized the problem was the type of tomatoes available in this new country. When Lewis began growing plum-shaped tomatoes in the San Francisco area in the 1930s, the quality of tomato paste improved dramatically.

Sourdough starter is a combination of wild yeasts collected from the air. The starter functions like the packaged yeast commonly used today to make bread and other baked goods rise. Unlike packaged yeast, sourdough starter imparts a pleasantly sour, tangy, distinctive taste to baked products like breads, biscuits, and pancakes. Today, bakers substitute sourdough starter for all or part of the baking yeast in a recipe.

To prepare sourdough starter, a combination of flour and water is placed in a warm environment, where it picks up wild yeasts from the atmosphere. The yeasts grow in the flour/water mixture, turning it into a leavening agent for baked goods.

In the 1880s, manufacturers produced the first commercial yeast. Before that time, people relied on sourdough starter for leavening all breads and baked goods. As a result, settlers moving west packed a jar of sourdough starter to use on their journey and in their new home.

Although the details change with different accounts, eleven-year-old Frank Epperson invented the Popsicle in 1905 in San Francisco. Apparently, Epperson left a glass of fruit juice with a stirrer in it outside on a cold night. The next morning, he discovered the frozen mixture. When he pulled out the stick, the frozen juice came with it. Eighteen years later, Epperson patented the Popsicle. During the Depression, he added a second wooden stick so that two children could share the sweet treat.

Boarding houses, hotels, and restaurants opened throughout San Francisco to accommodate the many immigrants and visitors. Since residents of boarding houses received meals in addition to lodging, these businesses flourished as a home for the many male immigrant workers.

By the 1890s, many wealthy and cultured people lived in San Francisco and patronized fine dining establishments. Today, both fine dining and ethnic restaurants thrive throughout the city, and San Francisco has restaurants representing almost every country or ethnic group.

When fishermen returned after fishing, they docked at the wharf and sold their catch directly to cooks, chefs, or anyone. The array of fresh fish and seafood included sole, abalone, crab, shrimp, red snapper, squid, salmon, and more. The San Francisco wharf developed into a thriving seafood center.

Several well-known dishes originated in San Francisco. Most believe Italians developed cioppino, a Mediterranean seafood soup or stew presumably named after *ciuppin*, a fish stew served in Genoa, Italy. Similar to the French *bouillabaisse*, cioppino consisted of the day's catch of fish and shellfish in a flavorful fish broth containing tomato, garlic, olive oil, and wine.

Many think that the finest sourdough bread comes from San Francisco. This is based on the theory that the air in San Francisco contains superior wild yeasts for sourdough starter. According to this theory, sourdough starter from San Francisco cannot be reproduced in any other location.

Opened in 1875 in San Francisco, the opulent seven-story Palace Hotel boasted four elevators to transport guests to the upper floors. Chefs at this elegant hotel created Green Goddess, a creamy salad dressing flavored with anchovies and green onions. They developed the recipe to commemorate a play by the same name that performed in San Francisco in the 1920s.

Italian confectioner Domingo Ghirardelli arrived in California in 1849 after living and working in Uruguay and Peru for about 12 years. With Peruvian cocoa beans, he started a business to manufacture chocolate. His chocolate business prospered. Around 1865, he or someone in his factory discovered that allowing the cocoa butter to drip from warm chocolate left the remains to process into ground chocolate. Known as the broma process, this resulted in separating the cocoa powder or residue from the fat, which began a production method that is still used today. In 1866, Ghiradelli's growing business imported 1,000 pounds of cocoa beans to make into chocolate. They imported 450,000 pounds in 1885! Needing more space, in 1893 Ghiradelli Chocolates moved into a brick building along the waterfront where the famous factory still stands. It reigns as the second oldest chocolate manufacturing business in the United States. (Founded in 1780, Bakers Chocolate in Massachusetts is the oldest.)

In 1906, a devastating earthquake struck San Francisco, causing 3,000 deaths and the destruction of 28,000 buildings. Citizens rebuilt the city, and soon San Francisco flourished again.

Situated south of San Francisco, the central coastal region including Monterey Bay yields a cornucopia of fruits and vegetables and is home to many wineries as well. Since this area rarely experiences a frost, a wide variety of produce grows throughout the year. Artichokes, spinach, mushrooms, Brussels sprouts, lettuce, celery, strawberries, apples, cherries, and grapes thrive here. The Monterey Bay area is known for a couple of other items. Abundant squid inhabit the waters in this bay. Also, Monterey Jack cheese, a soft cheese with a mild flavor, is well known from this area.

With the Cascades bordering on the north, the Sierra Nevadas on the east, the Tehachapi Mountains on the south, and the Central Range, Pacific Ocean, and bays lying to

Although the Spanish missionaries first made Monterey Jack cheese, Scottish dairy owner David Jacks popularized this cheese in the 1880s. He named the cheese for himself and the county where his dairy produced it. At some point, the *s* from Jacks was dropped, and the cheese became known as Monterey Jack.

The first large cannery for fruits opened in 1872 in San Jose. Dr. James Dawson and his son Thomas developed a metal can for holding the fruits. After filling the can with fruit, they soldered a metal lid on the can.

More than 90 percent of the nectarines in the United States come from the San Joaquin Valley.

With the help of irrigation, the entire central region consists of valleys that yield bountiful crops. The same is true of some of the former desert areas of southern California. Often, a small town revolves around the planting, cultivation, and harvesting of a single crop. Those towns frequently claim to be the "Whatever Fruit or Vegetable Capital" of the United States.

- Castroville lies along the central part of the coast and is known for production of artichokes. Watsonville, just north of Castroville, ranks as the Artichoke Capital of the United States.
- Acres of broccoli, lettuce, celery, cauliflower, and asparagus thrive in the Salinas Valley, lying inland (east) from Castroville.
- Gilroy claims to be the Garlic Capital.

the west, the central portion of the state contains the Central Valley. With irrigation, this series of valleys provides excellent farmland. Copious amounts of fruits and vegetables come from this entire section of fertile valleys. Each area grows the crops that thrive in the climate and soil found in that particular location. Also, dairy farms are productive in this region.

At the northern end of the Central Valley, the Sacramento Valley consists of fertile farmland and the Sacramento River. When the early settlers arrived, the Sacramento River contained abundant salmon. Apricots, honeydews, peaches, pears, apples, nectarines, plums, cherries, kiwi, grapes, tomatoes, avocados, sugar beets, corn, rice, oats, wheat, olives, pistachios, walnuts, almonds, and more now flourish in the Sacramento Valley.

Another area of prized farmland lies in the Salinas Valley in the central coastal portion of the Central Valley. This region includes Castroville and Watsonville, known for prolific production of numerous fruits and vegetables.

The San Joaquin Valley is located in the southern section of the Central Valley. In this valley, farmers grow a multitude of crops, including citrus fruits, peaches, nectarines, apricots, kiwi, plums, cherries, cantaloupes, melons, apples, figs, grapes, tomatoes, asparagus, onions, cucumbers, numerous varieties of dried beans, oats, wheat, walnuts, almonds, pistachios, and olives. Farmers raise dairy cattle, chicken for eggs and meat, lamb, beef, turkey, and bees for honey.

Unlike San Francisco, the huge city of Los Angeles sprawls for miles and miles in southwestern California. With the city lying close to Mexico, the cooking in this area exhibits pronounced Mexican influence. Since most ethnic groups are represented here, almost every type of food and cuisine flourishes in the melting pot of southern California. The entertainment industry and/or the beautiful weather and scenery attracted many "beautiful people" to this area. Healthy eating styles and fitness play a role in lifestyles for many. This impacts menus, too. Steaming and grilling often outrank frying, and many menus feature plenty of salads and low-calorie items.

With irrigation, the desert valleys of the southeastern region contain fertile soil and produce a wide range of agricultural products, such as citrus fruits, dates, avocados, melons, carrots, many types of lettuce, sugar beets, sweet potatoes, corn, wheat, dairy, and cattle. Located in the southeastern corner, the Imperial Valley yields a variety of fruits and vegetables with irrigation from the All American Canal. This canal contains waters from the Colorado River that flows along the border separating California from Arizona. The Imperial Valley also runs into neighboring northern Mexico.

In the 1890s, the first date palms were planted in southern California and Arizona in the hot, arid desert land near the Colorado River. An oasis lying 20 feet below sea level, the Coachella Valley in south-central California provided the perfect environment for this native fruit from the Middle East and northern Africa. By 1960, this valley contained over 5,000 acres of date trees. Today, the Coachella Valley yields huge crops of dates.

Situated in southeastern California, Death Valley remains almost uninhabitable desert. One part of Death Valley actually lies 282 feet below sea level. Soaring temperatures, mountains, valleys, and very little water make this region unfit for crops, farms, and towns.

The dry climate found in the hills north of San Diego proved excellent for growing avocado crops. In addition to avocados, the southern coastal area yields a multitude of lemons, oranges, strawberries, lettuce, and celery.

Less than 20 miles from the Mexican border, the port city of San Diego claims a very large Mexican population. The food here shows strong culinary influence from Mexico. Like the people in the Los Angeles area, inhabitants of San Diego are known for eating healthy and very fresh foods. Combining Mexican influence with fast food and healthy eating, fish tacos originated in San Diego.

CHARACTERISTICS OF THE CUISINE

With abundant land, diverse topography, and many climates stretching between the south and north of California, almost any plant and animal thrives somewhere in this large state. The incredible array of fresh foods provides chefs and cooks with excellent material to create recipes and dishes. Frequently, new cooking ideas or trends begin here and then spread to the rest of the United States.

While many describe California cooking as fresh, creative, and often daring, others say it is an easy, relaxed, laid-back cuisine. Regardless of how the cuisine is described, most agree that the emphasis remains on fresh, seasonal ingredients.

California remains a dichotomy of food styles. On the one hand, this state seems filled with people obsessed with eating "healthy" foods and staying fit. On the other hand, fast food hamburgers started in California. Today, menus are filled with items that fuse healthy foods with fast foods. The concept of healthy fast foods led to items like fish tacos, pizza topped with all sorts of fresh food items and often containing little or no cheese, and a wide range of salads.

To create fusion cuisine, some chefs combine (fuse) elements from two or more cuisines to create a different visual and taste sensation. For example, fusion might combine American cooking techniques with Asian ingredients and flavorings or use American ingredients with Asian cooking techniques and top it with a European sauce. Endless possibilities exist, restricted only by the imagination.

Many California residents prefer organically raised meats, fowl, fish, and produce. The goal of organic foods is to grow/raise/produce plants and animals as naturally as possible. That means not using chemical herbicides and pesticides. Many people who prefer organic foods have concerns about other issues with raising farm animals. They want farm animals that roam freely instead of spending their lives confined in cages or crowded into a small fenced area, eat feed grown without chemical herbicides and pesticides, and are not fed hormones or antibiotics. Many feel the use of chemical herbicides and pesticides, hormones, and antibiotics affects the health of consumers and environmental issues in our communities.

Although overfishing and/or pollution have diminished availability, the cold waters of the Pacific Ocean produce abundant fish and seafood. Many varieties of tuna, clams, and crabs (including Dungeness), oysters, scallops, mussels, swordfish, halibut, sole, mackerel, and anchovies provide a bounty of seafood for menus in homes and restaurants. With less availability of wild seafood, the market for farm-raised fish and shellfish continues to grow.

Complementing the available fish and seafood, California farmers raise plenty of meat and fowl. Turkey and chicken farms provide poultry, sheep thrive in the mountainous areas, and cattle ranches yield beef. Dairy farms flourish in many areas of the state. In 1993, California surpassed Wisconsin in dairy production to rank as the top dairy producer in the United States. As a result, dairy and cattle production account for significant revenue in California.

With the combination of fertile soil and a great climate, livestock and more than 350 varieties of crops flourish in California. The produce spans the range from cold weather to subtropical fruits and vegetables. Crops of carrots, tomatoes, celery, garlic, onions, avocados, broccoli, cauliflower, asparagus, mushrooms, lettuces, peppers, artichokes, melons, citrus fruits, strawberries, kiwi, peaches, pears, nectarines, apricots, plums, persimmons, guava, dates, figs, grapes, olives, almonds, pistachios, walnuts, and much more thrive in California.

- Lemon production brings significant revenue to southern California.
- Indio in the Coachella Valley calls itself the Date Capital of the United States.

In 1898, Emile Ortega began canning green chilies. Ortega's company grew into the largest cannery for Mexican foods in this country.

In 1906, the first hot fudge sundae was served at an ice cream parlor in Los Angeles.

With over one hundred varieties of dates flourishing in the Coachella Valley, the United States produces over 60 million pounds of dates each year.

Situated on the coast of the Pacific near Los Angeles, Santa Barbara claims to be the site of the first avocados grown in California. California currently grows 85 to 90 percent of the avocados in the United States, with Florida supplying the remainder.

In 1948, brothers Richard and Maurice McDonald developed the concept of a food restaurant with a very limited menu featuring hamburgers and quick food preparation. Their idea eliminated waitresses and tables inside the restaurant. Customers ordered their food at the counter and ate at tables outside or took the food with them. Their first McDonald's Restaurant with this concept opened in 1948 in San Bernardino, California. In 1954, they signed a franchise agreement with Ray Kroc, who later bought out the McDonald brothers. Kroc developed McDonald's into a major fast food corporation.

The soil and climate found in any given area determines which crops thrive there. As a result, individual fruits, vegetables, nuts, or grains became big business in various regions. Statistics show that California supplies more than 50 percent of the nation's fruits and vegetables and almost all of the artichokes, Brussels sprouts, kiwi, nectarines, olives, dates, figs, dried plums (prunes), almonds, pistachios, and walnuts consumed in the United States. Growing in a number of regions throughout the state, many different varieties of lettuce and grapes rank as two of California's most important crops. Grapes have a number of production uses. They are fermented and processed into wine, dried to create raisins, or consumed fresh.

The liberal use of fresh herbs and spices differentiate California's cookery from other parts of the United States. Residents commonly grow herbs and spices in their gardens, so adding them to a dish merely requires walking outside and picking them. Fresh garlic also flavors many dishes.

A wide variety of salads play a significant role in California's cuisine. Salads serving as an entrée appear on menus in homes and restaurants. Although Caesar salad was invented across the border in Tijuana, Mexico, Californians embraced this salad. It features romaine lettuce, croutons, and Parmesan cheese coated with a distinctive vinaigrette containing eggs and mashed anchovies. Invented in California, the Cobb salad consists of chopped lettuce topped with rows of chopped avocado, bacon, chicken, tomato, and hard-boiled egg.

Many Italians moved to California to raise crops of fruits and vegetables in the fertile valleys. As in their homeland, they planted grapes and made wine. Italian influence remains strong throughout California.

With Mexico situated to the south, Mexico's cuisine permeated California's cookery. The influence is particularly strong in southern California, which borders Mexico. Of course, the early Spanish who built missions through much of the state left Spanish culinary characteristics on California's cuisine.

One ethnic group often dominates the cookery in many small towns in California. For example, most inhabitants of Solange claim Danish ancestry. At the other end of the spectrum, San Francisco and Los Angeles contain ethnic neighborhoods of Italians, Chinese, Japanese, Mexicans, Russians, and many other nationalities.

Because California lies in the extreme western portion of the contiguous United States, more Asians crossed the Pacific Ocean to settle in California than in most other states. As a result, Japanese, Chinese, Philippine, Korean, Indonesian, Vietnamese, Thai, and other Asian immigrants made a strong culinary impact on the cuisine of California.

The Chinese exerted profound influence on California's cookery. While many immigrants came wanting employment in all sorts of fields, because of discrimination, the Chinese were only allowed to work menial jobs. Many worked in mines, on the railroad, or as cooks. This resulted in Chinese cooking techniques and ingredients permeating the cookery in the mining and railroad camps. Dried shrimp and fish flavored dishes and stir-fried foods were served often. Hot tea joined coffee as the beverage of choice. Chow mein, chop suey, and fortune cookies became normal fare in much of California. Like other immigrants, the Chinese adapted their cooking techniques and recipes to the ingredients available. In fact, chop suey was invented in America, and the name means "miscellaneous pieces" in Cantonese.

Agricultural opportunity attracted many Japanese immigrants. By 1920, Japanese farmed 450,000 acres in California. These immigrants introduced teriyaki, tempura, eel, and many soy products into California's cuisine. Adopted from the culinary heritage of all the Asian immigrants, rice became a staple.

California's own innovative cuisine is a combination of culinary traits from the cuisines of the immigrants, the cookery of the Native Americans, and the abundant fresh produce, grains, meat, fish, shellfish, and fowl available in this state. The cuisine continues to evolve.

Viticulture, the art of making wine, remains a flourishing industry in California. This industry began with the Franciscan fathers who prepared wine for religious purposes. They allowed the crushed grapes to ferment in vats or tubs, catching wild yeast from the atmosphere. Basically, the yeast changes the natural sugars from the grapes into carbon dioxide and alcohol. The carbon dioxide escapes into the atmosphere except in the case of sparkling wines, where the carbon dioxide bubbles are trapped and bottled with the wine. Through this process, the grape juice ferments and transforms into wine. Sealing the wine into bottles at the right time halts the fermentation process. As time went on, the winemaking process became both more scientific and more sophisticated. This led to the production of higher quality wine.

Until 1833, only the Spanish priests made wine. Around that time, European winemakers moved to California, and they brought cuttings of numerous grape varieties from their European vineyards. During the late nineteenth and early twentieth centuries, the new vineyards thrived under the guidance of people including Jacob and Frederick Beringer; Francis, Joseph, and Anton Korbel; William Hill; Charles Krug; Jacob and Annie Schram, and Thomas Rutherford. These names still mark vineyards and wineries that produce countless types of wine in California today.

As the nineteenth century closed, phylloxera, an insect that killed grapevines, invaded the vineyards. Through grafting, growers have developed disease resistant vines, but in spite of all efforts, the disease recurs periodically. Phylloxera remains a concern for winegrowers. During the Prohibition from 1919 to 1933, winemaking came to a standstill. In the 1960s, consumption of wine began to grow rapidly. While interest in wine continues to expand, the sophistication of customers has increased. Many advances have occurred in the winemaking process. Today, most winemakers study viticulture to learn the science of winemaking. They then combine scientific knowledge with the art of making wine.

Area	Weather	Topography	Foods
northern Oregon to north, Nevada to east, Pacific Ocean to west	cold, wet winters; cool, dry summers; foggy, hot summers in central area; more moderate near Pacific	mountains, forests, lakes, rivers in east; flat central area; mountains in west with forests, redwoods, sequoias, lakes, rivers, Pacific Ocean	cattle, sheep, dairy, cheese, tuna, sole, swordfish, halibut, anchovies, several types of crab including Dungeness, oysters, trout, salmon, bass, pears, apples, grapes, wine
central Nevada to east, Pacific Ocean to west	mild, wet, foggy winters; hot, dry summers; more moderate near Pacific and bays	fertile farmland, valleys, Cascade Mountains in north; Sierra Nevadas in east; Central Valley in center; Sacramento River in north central; San Joaquin River in south central; Tehachapi Mountains in south; Central Range, Pacific Ocean, and bays to west; forests, lakes, streams in mountains	beef, lamb, chicken, turkey, dairy, cheese, eggs, shellfish, fish, swordfish, red snapper, halibut, sole, salmon, tuna, bass, trout, squid, shrimp, crab, clams, abalone, rice, wheat, oats, dried beans, corn, olives, artichokes, lettuce, spinach, celery, Brussels sprouts, mushrooms, sugar beets, tomatoes, onions, garlic, avocados, asparagus, cucumbers, cauliflower, broccoli, apples, apricots, honeydews, cantaloupes, pears, plums, nectarines, peaches, citrus fruits, kiwi, cherries, strawberries, figs, prunes, raisins, grapes, wine, pistachios, walnuts, almonds, honey
south Arizona to east, Mexico to south, Pacific to west	mild, rainy winters; hot, dry summers; more moderate near Pacific	mountains and deserts, Mojave Desert, Colorado Desert, and Death Valley in east; Imperial Valley in southeast; Colorado River between California and Arizona; Coachella Valley in center; mountains and Pacific Ocean to west; forests, lakes, streams in mountains	beef, lamb, chicken, turkey, swordfish, tuna, halibut, sole, mackerel, anchovies, oysters, scallops, mussels, clams, crab, trout, salmon, bass, dairy, corn, wheat, avocados, many types of lettuce, celery, sweet potatoes, sugar beets, carrots, melons, strawberries, dates, citrus fruits, guava, persimmons, grapes

1. Discuss the topography and climate of California, what crops and/or animals flourish in the different regions, and how that affects the cookery.
2. Why did more Asians immigrate to California than to most other states? How did this impact the cuisine?
3. When did the Franciscan priests first arrive in California, why did they come there, and how did they affect California's cuisine?
4. How did San Francisco become a large melting pot city?
5. Describe the role of the Pacific Ocean in the settlement and cuisine of California.
6. Discuss the wine industry in California, including its history and an explanation of the winemaking process.

broma process—process that allows the cocoa butter to drip from warm chocolate; this resulted in separating the cocoa powder or residue from the fat, leaving the basis for ground chocolate; invented at Ghiradelli Chocolates in San Francisco

chop suey—stir-fried dish invented in America; the phrase means "miscellaneous pieces" in Cantonese

cioppino—seafood soup or stew, similar to French *bouillabaisse*, consisting of a variety of fish and shellfish in a flavorful fish broth containing tomato, garlic, olive oil, and wine; named after *ciuppin*, a fish stew served in Genoa, Italy

phylloxera—an insect that kills grapevines

sourdough starter—a combination of wild yeasts collected from the air that makes the bread and other baked goods rise; imparts a pleasantly sour, tangy, distinctive taste to breads, biscuits, and pancakes

stir-frying—cooking small, evenly chopped foods over high heat; cooking technique commonly used in China and throughout much of Asia

viticulture—the art of making wine

ARTICHOKE DIP

This dip might also be used to fill a salami coronet.

SERVING SIZE:
  2 crackers with 1½ oz
  dip, ¾ oz or 1 tablespoon
  per cracker
COOKING METHOD:
  Sauté
TOTAL YIELD:
  1 lb, 13 oz or 3½ cups

Wine Style: Wide variety—Pinot Grigio, Pinot Blanc, Sauvignon Blanc, White Zinfandel, or Grenache
Example: Sauvignon Blanc, Napa Valley—Beringer Blass Wine Estates, Napa, CA. This wine has vibrant acidity with concentrations of lime peel, fig, and green apple with a very long finish.

INGREDIENTS	WEIGHT	VOLUME
bacon	8 oz	8 slices
artichoke hearts, drained, chopped	1 lb, 1 oz	2 each 13¾ oz cans
onion, minced	1 oz	2 tablespoons
garlic, minced	¼ oz	1 large clove
lime juice	1 oz	2 tablespoons
mayonnaise	8½ oz	1 cup
Worcestershire sauce		1 teaspoon
cayenne pepper		⅛ teaspoon
salt		½ teaspoon
pepper		¼ teaspoon
oregano		1 teaspoon
parsley, fresh, minced		1 teaspoon
Parmesan cheese	½ oz	2 tablespoons
Dijon mustard		1 teaspoon

GARNISH:

paprika

1. Sauté bacon until crisp. Drain well and crumble.
2. Mix all ingredients together in bowl. Chill.
3. Place in mound on platter or in bowl. Sprinkle with paprika. Serve accompanied by crackers, tortilla chips, or raw vegetables.

CRAB LOUIE

Crab Louie

This functions well as a first course or entrée salad. Chill plates ahead of service.

NUMBER OF SERVINGS: 8
SERVING SIZE:
  2¼ oz (¼ cup) dressing
TOTAL YIELD:
  1 lbs, 2½ oz (2 cups)
  dressing

Wine Style: Sparkling wines, light and fruity Riesling, or Chardonnay
Example: S. Anderson Brut Sparkling Wine—Cliff Lede Vineyards, Yountville, CA. This wine is fresh and bright with a bouquet of candied ginger, biscuit, and peach, and flavors of lemon cream and citron balanced with a racy mineral finish.

INGREDIENTS	WEIGHT	VOLUME
DRESSING:		
mayonnaise	10¼ oz	1¼ cups
chili sauce	2¼ oz	¼ cup
horseradish, prepared	¼ oz	1 teaspoon
green onions, sliced ¼ inch thick	¾ oz	¼ cup
green pepper, small dice	1¼ oz	3 tablespoons
green olives, chopped	¾ oz	2 tablespoons
chives, minced	¼ oz	2 tablespoons
lemon juice		2 teaspoons
Worcestershire sauce		2 teaspoons
hot pepper sauce		¼ teaspoon
salt		½ teaspoon
heavy cream, cold	2¾ oz	⅓ cup
SALAD:		
lettuce, romaine or variety of choice, separated into leaves, washed	1 lb	1 large head
crabmeat, Dungeness or variety of choice, drained, all bits of shell and cartilage removed	2 lb	
avocado, sliced	10 oz	2 each
artichoke hearts, canned, quartered	8 oz	
tomatoes, fresh, cut into eighths	9 oz	2 each
eggs, hard cooked, quartered	6¾ oz	4 each
GARNISH:		
paprika		
chives		16 to 24 each

For Dressing:

1. In bowl, whisk together mayonnaise, chili sauce, horseradish, green onions, green pepper, olives, chives, lemon juice, Worcestershire sauce, hot pepper sauce, and salt.
2. In separate chilled bowl, whip cream until medium to stiff peaks form. Fold into mayonnaise mixture.
3. Cover and refrigerate until needed.

For Assembly:

1. Place 2 oz romaine or other lettuce on plate. Place 4 oz crab in center of plate.
2. Drizzle 2¼ oz (¼ cup) dressing over crab and lettuce.
3. Arrange 2 slices of avocado, 2 pieces of artichoke, 2 wedges of tomato, and 2 quarters of egg around the crab.
4. If desired, garnish with a sprinkling of paprika over crab and 2 or 3 chives standing in crabmeat.

PUMPKIN SOUP

NUMBER OF SERVINGS: 10
COOKING METHOD:
  Sauté, Boil
SERVING SIZE:
  8 oz
TOTAL YIELD:
  5 lbs, 1½ oz

Pumpkin Soup
photo © Dorling Kindersley

INGREDIENTS	WEIGHT	VOLUME
butter	2 oz	4 tablespoons
onion, medium dice	5¼ oz	1 cup or 1 large
carrot, peeled, medium dice	4 oz	⅔ cup or 2 small
garlic, minced	¼ oz	2 cloves
pumpkin, canned or fresh pureed	1 lb, 13 oz	1 each 29 oz can
chicken stock	2 lbs	1 qt or 4 cups
dry vermouth	8 oz	1 cup
sage		1½ teaspoons
nutmeg		1 teaspoon
salt		½ teaspoon
pepper		¼ teaspoon
heavy cream	4 oz	½ cup

GARNISH:

croutons

sage leaves

1. Melt butter in large pot over medium heat. Add onion, carrot, and garlic; sauté for 4 to 5 minutes.

2. Add pumpkin, chicken stock, vermouth, sage, nutmeg, salt, and pepper. Bring to simmer, cover and cook 15 minutes.

3. Transfer to bowl of food processor fitted with knife blade. Process until smooth.

4. Return to pot; add cream. Heat, but do not allow it to boil. Correct seasonings. Serve, garnished with croutons and sage leaves.

CHILLED AVOCADO SOUP

Chilled Avocado Soup
photo by David Murray and Jules Selmes
© Dorling Kindersley

Chill serving bowls before service.

NUMBER OF SERVINGS: 9
SERVING SIZE:
 8 oz
TOTAL YIELD:
 4 lbs, 12½ oz or 11 cups

INGREDIENTS	WEIGHT	VOLUME
avocado, peeled, pitted	1 lb, 1 oz	4 large
chicken stock	2 lbs	1 qt or 4 cups
lemon juice		1 tablespoon + 1 teaspoon
hot pepper sauce		½ teaspoon
sherry, dry	4 oz	½ cup
heavy cream	1 lb, 8 oz	3 cups
salt	¼ oz	1 teaspoon
pepper		½ teaspoon
nutmeg		1 teaspoon
GARNISH:		
sour cream		
cilantro, minced		

1. Place avocado, chicken stock, lemon juice, hot pepper sauce, sherry, cream, salt, pepper, and nutmeg in bowl of food processor.

2. Process until smooth. Chill thoroughly.

3. Correct seasonings. Serve, garnished with sour cream and cilantro.

BRIE SALAD WITH GRAPES, OLIVES, AND ALMONDS

Sliding Cheese onto Lettuce

Brie Salad with Grapes,
Olives, and Almonds

Basically, each portion of salad contains about 2½ leaves of romaine, ¾ oz (5 each) grapes, ¼ oz (2 teaspoons) olives, 2 tablespoons almonds, and 2 oz (2 good-sized slices) brie.

Chill plates ahead of service time.

NUMBER OF SERVINGS: 10
SERVING SIZE:
  2 oz brie
TOTAL YIELD:
  15 oz or 1¾ cups dressing

INGREDIENTS	WEIGHT	VOLUME
DRESSING:		
garlic, minced	½ oz	**2 large cloves**
balsamic vinegar	4 oz	**½ cup**
red wine vinegar	1 oz	**2 tablespoons**
basil		**2 teaspoons**
salt		**1½ teaspoons**
pepper		**¼ teaspoon**
olive oil	10¾ oz	**1⅓ cups**
SALAD:		
lettuce, romaine or variety of choice, washed, dried, torn into bite-sized pieces	1 lb, 6½ oz	**25 leaves of romaine**
grapes, red seedless, washed, cut in half	7½ oz	**50 grapes**
olives, kalamata, pitted, sliced	2½ oz	**6 tablespoons + 2 teaspoons**
almond slices, toasted	2 oz	**1¼ cups**
brie, sliced ¼ inch thick	1 lb, 4 oz	

For Dressing:

1. With food processor fitted with steel knife running, drop in garlic and process until chopped.
2. Add balsamic vinegar, red wine vinegar, basil, salt, and pepper. With food processor running, add oil very slowly through feed tube. Continue mixing until dressing emulsifies (thickens).
3. Correct seasonings. Cover and store in refrigerator until needed.

For Assembly:

1. Place lettuce, grapes, olives, and almonds in bowl.
2. Top with dressing; mix gently to coat each leaf.
3. Portion salad on chilled serving plates.
4. Lightly pan-spray microwave-safe plate. Place 2 oz brie on plate. Heat for about 15 to 25 seconds [depending on strength of microwave] until brie melts.
5. Using metal icing spatula to guide it, if necessary, slide brie from plate to top of salad. Serve immediately.

COBB SALAD

Cobb Salad

If cutting the avocado before service, mix it with a little lemon juice to prevent its turning brown.

Use any desired mixture of lettuces. Also, feel free to change the toppings. Those listed here are the traditional toppings for Cobb salad. Artichoke hearts, goat cheese, julienne beets, and/or chopped salami also make interesting toppings.

Chill plates prior to plating.

NUMBER OF SERVINGS: 10
COOKING METHOD:
   Boil
SERVING SIZE:
   About 13 oz total 5 oz lettuce with dressing, 3³/₄ oz chicken, ¹/₄ oz bacon, 1 oz avocado, 1 oz blue cheese, ³/₄ oz hard-boiled egg, 1 oz tomatoes
TOTAL YIELD:
   1 lbs, 7¹/₂ oz or 3 cups dressing

INGREDIENTS	WEIGHT	VOLUME
DRESSING:		
water	2 oz	¹/₄ cup
red wine vinegar	4 oz	¹/₂ cup
balsamic vinegar	2 oz	¹/₄ cup
sugar		1 teaspoon
lemon juice		2 teaspoons
Worcestershire sauce		1 tablespoon + 1 teaspoon
Dijon mustard		2 teaspoons
garlic, minced	¹/₂ oz	4 cloves
oregano		¹/₂ teaspoon
thyme		¹/₂ teaspoon
salt		¹/₂ teaspoon
pepper		¹/₂ teaspoon
olive oil	1 lb	2 cups
SALAD:		
lettuce, romaine, washed, dried, torn into pieces	15 oz	
lettuce, iceberg, washed, dried, torn into pieces	15 oz	
raddichio, washed, dried, torn into pieces	8 oz	
blue cheese, crumbled	10 oz	
tomatoes, chopped	10 oz	about 4 plum tomatoes
chicken breasts, grilled, sliced	2 lb, 6 oz	about 7 boneless half breasts
bacon, cooked, crumbles	3 oz	about 14 slices
avocados, Haas, peeled, pitted, cubed	10¹/₂ oz	3 each
eggs, hard-boiled, chopped	8¹/₂ oz	5 each

For Dressing:

1. Place water, red wine vinegar, balsamic vinegar, sugar, lemon juice, Worcestershire sauce, Dijon mustard, garlic, oregano, thyme, salt, and pepper in food processor fitted with knife blade. Mix to blend.

2. With machine running, slowly add oil through feed tube until all oil is added and mixture emulsifies (thickens). Set aside until needed.

For Salad:

1. Place all lettuces in bowl. Add 1 lb (2 cups) dressing; toss to coat lettuce leaves with dressing.

2. Place 5 oz coated lettuce on chilled plate. Arrange strips of blue cheese, tomatoes, chicken, bacon, avocado, and eggs on top of lettuce, with each item forming a row lying next to the other. *If desired, arrange ingredients over lettuce in wedge-shaped sections instead of rows.*

3. Drizzle ¹/₂ oz (1 tablespoon) of dressing over top of each salad. Serve.

CIOPPINO

A San Francisco favorite; use one variety or any desired assortment of seafood and fish for this dish. The weight of each serving depends on the fish and shellfish in it.

NUMBER OF SERVINGS: 11
COOKING METHOD:
    Sauté, Boil
SERVING SIZE:
    15 oz
TOTAL YIELD:
    11 lbs, 1½ oz

Wine Style: Soft and fruity Gewürztraminer, Riesling, Pinot Blanc, White Zinfandel, or Grenache
Example: Pinot Blanc Estate—Laetitia Vineyard and Winery, Arroyo Grande, CA. This is a full-flavored wine with melon and pear flavors layered with lemon, lime, and grapefruit.

Cioppino
photo by Andrew McKinney © Dorling Kindersley

INGREDIENTS	WEIGHT	VOLUME
olive oil	1 oz	2 tablespoons
onion, small dice	5¼ oz	1 large
leeks, white part only, sliced ¼ inch thick	3 oz	1 cup
mushrooms, sliced	2¾ oz	1 cup
red pepper, small dice	2½ oz	½ cup
carrots, peeled, sliced ¼-inch on bias	2¼ oz	½ cup
celery, sliced ¼ inch on bias	2 oz	½ cup
garlic, minced	¾ oz	4 cloves
tomatoes, canned with juice, chopped	1 lb, 12 oz	1 each 28-oz can
tomato paste	1½ oz	2 tablespoons
basil		½ teaspoon
oregano		½ teaspoon
thyme		½ teaspoon
fennel seeds, crushed or ground		½ teaspoon
crushed red pepper flakes		¼ teaspoon
bay leaf		2 each
fish stock	1 lb, 12 oz	3½ cups
white wine, dry	12 oz	1½ cups
salt		½ teaspoon
pepper		¼ teaspoon
clams, small, scrubbed	2 lb, 1 oz	24 each
halibut or haddock, cut into 2 inch pieces	1 lb, 3¼ oz	
whitefish, snapper, or sole, cut into 2 inch pieces	1 lb	
shrimp, peeled and deveined	1 lb, 9¼ oz	
crab claws or legs, cracked	15 oz	

1. Heat olive oil in stockpot over medium heat. Add onions, leeks, mushrooms, red pepper, carrots, celery, and garlic. Sauté about 7 to 8 minutes, until softened.

2. Add tomatoes, tomato paste, basil, oregano, thyme, fennel, red pepper flakes, and bay leaves. Cook about 3 to 4 minutes.

3. Add fish stock, white wine, salt, and pepper. Cover and simmer for 40 minutes.

4. Add clams; cook for 2 to 3 minutes.

5. Add haddock and whitefish; cook for 2 minutes. Add shrimp and crab; cook another 3 to 4 minutes.

6. Correct seasonings; remove bay leaves. Remove and discard any unopened clams. Serve, placing assortment of seafood and fish with plenty of sauce in each bowl. Accompany with French bread.

GRILLED GAME HENS WITH CABERNET SAUCE

Cutting Game Hen in Half
photo © Dorling Kindersley

NUMBER OF SERVINGS: 10
COOKING METHOD:
   Grill, Sauté, Boil
SERVING SIZE:
   1/2 game hen 2 oz sauce
   (3 to 4 tablespoons)
TOTAL YIELD:
   6 lb, 7 1/4 oz game hens
   1 lb, 5 3/4 oz (2 1/2 cups)
   Cabernet sauce

Wine Style: Soft, fruity Gewürztraminer, Viognier, Pinot Noir, or Cabernet Sauvignon
Example: Cabernet Sauvignon—Robert Mondavi Winery, Oakville, CA. This wine has rich, dense cassis and blackberry character interwoven with spice, vanilla, mineral, and cedar.

Grilled Game Hens with
Cabernet Sauce

INGREDIENTS	WEIGHT	VOLUME
Cornish game hens, cut in half, washed	7 lb, 1 3/4 oz	5 each
salt	1/4 oz	1 teaspoon
thyme		1 teaspoon
oregano		1 teaspoon
basil		1 teaspoon
nutmeg		1 teaspoon
pepper		1/2 teaspoon
olive oil	as needed for brushing	
CABERNET SAUCE:		
butter	2 1/4 oz	4 1/2 tablespoons
onion, small dice	3 3/4 oz	3/4 cup
carrots, sliced	4 1/2 oz	1 cup
celery, sliced	2 1/4 oz	1/2 cup
garlic, minced		3 cloves
flour, all purpose	2 1/4 oz	4 1/2 tablespoons
chicken stock, hot	12 oz	1 1/2 cups
cabernet sauvignon wine	1 lb, 8 oz	3 cups
thyme		3/4 teaspoon
oregano		3/4 teaspoon
basil		3/4 teaspoon
salt		3/4 teaspoon
pepper		1/4 teaspoon

1. Place game hens on flat pan. Combine salt, thyme, oregano, basil, nutmeg, and pepper.
2. Rub game hens evenly with seasoning mixture. Refrigerate until ready to grill.

For Cabernet Sauce:

1. Heat butter in pan over medium heat. Add onion, carrots, celery, and garlic. Sauté for 5 minutes.
2. Whisk in flour. Cook until blonde *roux*, about 3 minutes.
3. Slowly whisk in hot stock, then add cabernet. Add thyme, oregano, basil, salt, and pepper.
4. Bring to boil. Reduce heat and simmer until thickened, about 3 minutes.
5. Strain through sieve, correct seasonings, and keep warm until needed. If making ahead, cover and refrigerate until needed.

To Finish:

1. Preheat grill. Brush game hens lightly with olive oil. Place on grill, skin side down.
2. Grill until meat is thoroughly cooked and registers proper temperature on thermometer. Turn at least once during grilling.
3. Place on warm plate. Ladle or spoon 2 oz (almost 1/4 cup) of Cabernet sauce over each half hen.

LAMB SHANKS BRAISED IN RED WINE

Lamb Shanks Braised in Red Wine

photo courtesy of the American Lamb Board

NUMBER OF SERVINGS: 8
COOKING METHOD:
  Braise
SERVING SIZE:
  1 lb, 2³/₄ oz
    1 lamb shank with sauce
TOTAL YIELD:
  about 10 lb, 12¹/₂ oz
    8 lamb shanks with sauce

Wine Style: Medium- to full-bodied reds, Cabernet Sauvignon, Shiraz, or Zinfandel
Example: Zinfandel—Ravenswood Winery, Sonoma, CA. With muscular balance and berry fruit, this wine is deep, dark, full, and spicy with the complexity of its old-vine origins.

INGREDIENTS	WEIGHT	VOLUME
lamb shanks, washed	10 lbs	8 each lamb shanks
garlic, cut into slivers (about 8 slivers from each clove)	1 oz	4 large cloves
flour, all purpose	2¹/₄ oz	¹/₂ cup
oil	4 oz	¹/₂ cup
onion, large dice	8 oz	1¹/₂ cups or 2 each medium
garlic, minced	1 oz	4 large cloves
carrots, peeled, large dice	5¹/₂ oz	1 cup or 2 each
celery, large dice	5¹/₂ oz	1 cup or 2 stalks
mushrooms, washed, large dice	5 oz	1¹/₂ cups
flour, all purpose	1¹/₄ oz	¹/₄ cup
stock, beef or lamb, hot	1 lb	2 cups
red wine, dry like cabernet or zinfandel	1 lb	2 cups
balsamic vinegar	1 oz	2 tablespoons
tomato paste	1¹/₂ oz	2 tablespoons
tomatoes, chopped, canned	1 lb	2 cups
bay leaves		2 each
thyme		1 teaspoon
marjoram		1 teaspoon
rosemary		1 teaspoon
salt	¹/₄ oz	1 teaspoon
pepper		1 teaspoon

1. With boning knife, make four slits into meat evenly around lamb shank. Place sliver of garlic into each slit.
2. Dust each lamb shank with flour (using about ¼ oz or 1 table-spoon for each). Preheat oven to 350 degrees.
3. Heat oil in large braising pan; brown each lamb shank. Remove lamb shanks; add onion, garlic, carrots, celery, and mushrooms. Sauté 3 to 4 minutes until vegetables begin to soften.
4. Whisk in 1¼ oz (¼ cup) flour; heat for 2 minutes. Slowly whisk in hot stock, then add wine, vinegar, tomato paste, tomatoes, bay leaves, thyme, marjoram, rosemary, salt, and pepper.
5. Return lamb shanks to pan, bring to simmer, and correct seasonings. Cover, place in oven, and bake for 1 hour, 30 minutes.
6. Meanwhile, combine garlic, lemon and lime zest, and parsley in small bowl to make gremolada.
7. To serve, place lamb shank and some sauce on plate. Garnish with gremolada.

GREMOLADA:

	WEIGHT	VOLUME
garlic, minced	1/2 oz	2 large cloves
lemon zest, grated	3/4 oz	3 tablespoons
lime zest, grated	1/4 oz	1 tablespoon
parsley, fresh, minced	1/4 oz	3 tablespoons

MARINATED FLANK STEAK

Grilling Marinated Flank Steak

photo courtesy of the National Live Stock and Meat Board

Slicing Flank Steak

Start this the day before grilling to allow the meat to marinate overnight.

NUMBER OF SERVINGS: 9
COOKING METHOD:
  Grill
SERVING SIZE:
  5 oz
TOTAL YIELD:
  2 lbs, 15 1/4 oz

Wine Style: Wide variety—Gewürztraminer, White Zinfandel, Merlot, or Syrah
Example: Merlot—Kunde Estate Winery and Vineyards, Kenwood, CA. This wine is full-bodied with flavors of red currant, plum, cherry, black tea, vanilla, and caramel.

INGREDIENTS	WEIGHT	VOLUME
flank steak, trimmed of all fat	3 lbs, 6 1/4 oz	
MARINADE:		
olive oil	1/2 oz	1 tablespoon
sesame oil	1/2 oz	1 tablespoon
brown sugar, packed	1 oz	2 tablespoons
rice vinegar	1 oz	2 tablespoons
soy sauce	5 1/2 oz	2/3 cup
lemon juice	1/2 oz	1 tablespoon
dry sherry	2 3/4 oz	1/3 cup
hoisin sauce	1 oz	1 tablespoon
water	2 oz	1/4 cup
wasabi paste	1/4 oz	1 teaspoon
honey	3/4 oz	1 tablespoon
onion, minced	2 oz	1 small
garlic, minced	1/2 oz	2 large cloves
ginger, fresh, peeled, minced	3/4 oz	2 1/2-inch piece

1. With sharp knife, thinly score steak into checkerboard pattern on both sides of meat. Do not make incisions too deep. Place meat in nonreactive pan or bowl.

2. In separate bowl, combine all marinade ingredients and mix well.

3. Pour over steak, making sure to coat meat thoroughly on both sides. Cover and refrigerate at least 8 hours, preferably overnight. Turn at least once or twice while marinating.

4. Preheat grill. Grill steak over medium-hot fire until proper temperature, about 5 to 7 minutes per side, depending on thickness of meat.

5. Slice thinly across the grain on a bias. Serve immediately.

PIZZA WITH ARTICHOKE, CARAMELIZED ONION, AND GORGONZOLA

Pizza with Artichoke, Caramelized Onion, and Gorgonzola

Pizza dough can be prepared 1 day ahead and refrigerated. Also, this dough freezes well.

Only the imagination limits the toppings for these pizzas. Feel free to use any desired ingredients.

NUMBER OF SERVINGS: 8
COOKING METHOD:
   Sauté, Bake
SERVING SIZE:
   1 each 8-inch pizza
TOTAL YIELD:
   3 lb, 3 oz dough

Wine Style: Light- to medium-bodied Sauvignon Blanc, Chenin Blanc, White Pinot Noir, mild reds, Pinot Noir, Shiraz, or Zinfandel
Example: Pinot Noir—Bernardus Winery and Vineyard, Carmel Valley, CA. This wine has delicate notes of blueberry and plum that are rounded out with a touch of cinnamon.

INGREDIENTS	WEIGHT	VOLUME
PIZZA DOUGH:		
water, warm	12 oz + 3 oz	1½ cups + 6 tablespoons
sugar	¼ oz	1 tablespoon
yeast, granulated	½ oz	2 packages or 2 teaspoons
flour, all purpose	1 lb, 10 oz	6 cups
semolina flour	4½ oz	⅔ cup
salt	1 oz	1 tablespoon + 1 teaspoon
olive oil	1½ oz	3 tablespoons
cornmeal	for sprinkling baking sheets	
olive oil		2 tablespoons + 2 teaspoons
FILLING:		
olive oil		1 tablespoon + 1 teaspoon
onions, vidalia, sliced thinly	3 lb, 10 oz	6 large
olive oil	2 oz	¼ cup
mushrooms, portabello or variety of choice, sliced	1 lb, 2 oz	
Parmesan cheese, grated	7 oz	
artichoke hearts, sliced ½ inch thick	1 lb, 2 oz	

For Dough:

1. Place 3 oz (6 tablespoons) warm water in bowl. Add sugar and yeast; stir to dissolve. Let stand until foamy, about 5 minutes.
2. In large bowl, mix 1 lb (about 4 cups) flour, semolina, and salt.
3. Gradually mix in remaining 12 oz (1½ cups) water. Add oil; stir until well blended, about 2 minutes.
4. Fold in yeast mixture with rubber spatula.
5. Mix in 10 oz (about 2 cups) flour.
6. Knead on lightly floured surface until smooth and elastic, about 10 minutes. Add more flour if necessary.
7. Place dough in bowl, smooth side up. Cover with plastic wrap, allowing room to double. Let rise in warm area until doubled, about 1 hour.
8. Punch dough down.
9. Refrigerate, well covered with plastic wrap, until ready to use. At this point, the dough can be portioned, wrapped, and frozen for later use. If using right away, allow to rest 20 minutes at room temperature before punching down dough and proceeding.

To Assemble:

1. Place rack in lower third of oven and preheat oven to 375 degrees. Sprinkle cornmeal lightly on baking sheet.
2. Roll 6-oz dough into 8-inch round pizza crust. Place on prepared baking sheets.
3. Bake for about 5 minutes, to parbake and set crust. Remove from oven. Move rack to upper third of oven.
4. Meanwhile, heat 1 tablespoon + 1 teaspoon oil in skillet until warm. Add onions and stir occasionally. Cook over low heat for 30 to 40 minutes, until caramelized and golden brown.

gorgonzola cheese, crumbled	8 oz	
thyme		2 teaspoons
oregano		2 teaspoons
basil, fresh, shredded	1 oz	1/2 cup

5. In separate skillet, heat 2 oz (1/4 cup) oil over medium heat. Add mushrooms and sauté about 5 minutes, until they soften and release liquid.

6. Brush 1 teaspoon olive oil on each parbaked pizza dough.

7. Distribute one-eighth (about 2 1/2 oz) caramelized onions over each dough. Place one-eighth (about 2 oz) mushrooms over onions. Sprinkle one-eighth of Parmesan cheese over mushrooms, then top that with 2 1/4 oz artichokes on each pizza. Place 1 oz gorgonzola on top of each.

8. Sprinkle each pizza with 1/4 teaspoon of thyme and 1/4 teaspoon oregano. Bake for about 8 minutes, until crust is brown and cheese bubbles.

9. Remove from oven. Sprinkle each pizza with 1 tablespoon basil, cut into pieces, and serve.

ASIAN STYLE SUGAR SNAP PEAS

This recipe also works well for other vegetables like green beans or snow peas.

NUMBER OF SERVINGS: 9
COOKING METHOD:
  Braise
SERVING SIZE:
  4 oz
TOTAL YIELD:
  2 lbs, 4 oz

INGREDIENTS	WEIGHT	VOLUME
vegetable oil	1 oz	2 tablespoons
onion, small dice	7 1/2 oz	1 1/2 cups
garlic, minced	1/2 oz	4 cloves
sugar snap peas, strings removed	1 lb, 15 oz	
rice wine vinegar	1 oz	2 tablespoons
sesame oil		1/2 teaspoon
hoisin sauce	1 3/4 oz	2 tablespoons
soy sauce	1 oz	2 tablespoons
oyster sauce	1 1/2 oz	2 tablespoons
sherry, dry	1 oz	2 tablespoons
water	1 oz	2 tablespoons
pepper		1/4 teaspoon

1. Heat oil in pan. Add onion and garlic; sauté 3 minutes. Add sugar snap peas; sauté 5 to 6 minutes until they begin to soften.

2. Meanwhile, combine remaining ingredients in small bowl. Add to peas, cover, and cook for 3 to 5 minutes, until peas are *al dente*, tender but still crunchy.

3. Correct seasonings. Serve.

GRILLED VEGETABLES WITH GOAT CHEESE

Grilled Vegetables with Goat Cheese

Feel free to substitute any vegetables for the ones in this recipe.

If desired, brush vegetables with plain or infused oil before grilling.

This vegetable dish would make a great appetizer.

NUMBER OF SERVINGS: 12
COOKING METHOD:
   Grill
SERVING SIZE:
   5 oz with vegetable, cheese,
     and vinaigrette
TOTAL YIELD:
   6 oz (3/4 cup) vinaigrette

INGREDIENTS	WEIGHT	VOLUME
VINAIGRETTE:		
red wine vinegar	1 1/2 oz	3 tablespoons
balsamic vinegar	1/2 oz	1 tablespoon
basil		1 tablespoon
parsley, fresh, minced		1 tablespoon
oregano		1 tablespoon
salt		1/4 teaspoon
pepper		1/4 teaspoon
olive oil	4 oz	1/2 cup
eggplant, sliced 1/4 to 1/2 inch thick	12 1/2 oz	1 each
salt	as needed	
peppers, orange or red, cut in half, trimmed, seeded	12 1/2 oz	2 each
yellow squash, sliced on bias 1/2 inch thick	11 3/4 oz	2 each
sweet onion like Vidalia or Maui, peeled, sliced about 1/4 inch thick to yield 6 slices per onion	14 oz	2 each
portabella mushroom	8 1/4 oz	2 each
goat cheese	3 oz	

For Vinaigrette:

1. Place both vinegars, basil, parsley, oregano, salt, and pepper in bowl of food processor fitted with knife blade or bowl.

2. With food processor running, slowly add oil through feed tube. Continue mixing until dressing emulsifies (thickens). Alternately, slowly whisk in olive oil until it emulsifies (thickens). Set aside until needed.

For Vegetables and Assembly:

1. Layer eggplant slices in colander, sprinkling salt on each layer. Let sit in sink or over bowl for at least 30 minutes. Rinse, then dry slices.

2. Preheat grill. Grill vegetables until done.

3. If desired, remove skin from peppers by placing them in a sealed bag to steam for about 15 minutes after removing them from the grill. After steaming, the skin should peel off with help from a paring knife. Rinse in cold water. Cut each pepper half into thirds. Slice each portabella into 12 slices. Preheat oven to 250 degrees.

4. Assemble vegetables by placing eggplant slices on sheet pan or other ovenproof pan.

5. Top eggplant with onion slice, then piece of orange pepper, then yellow squash. Top with 2 slices of mushroom.

6. Bake vegetables for 3 to 5 minutes to warm.

7. Place vegetable stack on plate. Top with 1/4 oz (1 teaspoon) goat cheese and drizzle with 1/2 oz (1 tablespoon) vinaigrette. Serve.

ASPARAGUS RISOTTO

Asparagus Risotto
photo by David Murray and Jules Selmes
© Dorling Kindersley

For a creamier risotto, add 1 to 1½ oz (2 to 3 tablespoons) heavy cream to cooked risotto.

Serve risotto plain or add different types of ingredients, including vegetables, fish, seafood, poultry, or meat. When flavored with more substantial ingredients like duck and wild mushrooms, roasted corn and lobster, or scallops with peas, risotto functions as an entrée rather than a side dish.

NUMBER OF SERVINGS: 14
COOKING METHOD:
   Braise
SERVING SIZE:
   4 oz
TOTAL YIELD:
   3 lbs, 11¼ oz

INGREDIENTS	WEIGHT	VOLUME
olive oil	1½ oz	3 tablespoons
onion, small dice	5 oz	1 cup
garlic, minced	¼ oz	2 cloves
asparagus, peeled, trimmed, cut into 1-inch pieces, reserve tips	1 lb	3 cups
Arborio rice	11 oz	1½ cups
white wine, dry	4 oz	½ cup
chicken or vegetable stock, hot	2 lb, 8 oz	1 qt + 1 cup or 5 cups
Parmesan cheese, grated	2¼ oz	½ cup
salt, if needed		½ teaspoon
pepper		¼ teaspoon
parsley, fresh, minced		1 tablespoon

GARNISH:

parsley, minced

Parmesan cheese, grated

1. Heat 1 oz (2 tablespoons) olive oil over medium heat. Add onion and garlic; sauté for 2 minutes.

2. Add asparagus pieces except tips; sauté 2 minutes. Add rice; sauté another 2 minutes.

3. Stir in wine, then add stock, 4 oz (½ cup) at a time, stirring often, until stock is almost absorbed. Repeat process of adding 4 oz (½ cup) stock until all stock is used and rice is cooked. Add more or less stock, as needed until correct consistency. Risotto should be creamy, yet rice should not become mushy.

4. Meanwhile, heat remaining ½ oz (1 tablespoon) oil. Sauté asparagus tips until just *al dente*, cooked but still firm.

5. Stir asparagus, cheese, salt, pepper, and parsley into rice. Correct seasonings. Serve, sprinkled with additional parsley, if desired. Accompany with more Parmesan cheese.

DATE NUT BREAD

Date Nut Bread

photo by Martin Brigdale © Dorling
Kindersley

Many serve this bread with cream cheese instead of butter.

NUMBER OF SERVINGS: 9
COOKING METHOD:
   Bake
SERVING SIZE:
   2 each 1/2-inch slices
TOTAL YIELD:
   1 each 9- by 5-inch loaf

INGREDIENTS	WEIGHT	VOLUME
date pieces	10 oz	1 3/4 cups
boiling water	8 oz	1 cup
flour, all purpose, sifted	8 1/2 oz	2 cups
baking soda		2 teaspoons
salt		1/2 teaspoon
brown sugar, firmly packed	6 1/2 oz	1 cup
butter, melted	1 1/2 oz	3 tablespoons
eggs	3 1/2 oz	2 each
walnuts or variety of choice, chopped, toasted	3 1/2 oz	1 cup

1. Place dates in bowl; pour water over them. Let sit about 30 minutes, until lukewarm.

2. Sift flour, baking soda, and salt together in bowl. Make well in center of flour. Pan-spray 9- by 5-inch loaf pan. Place oven rack in center of oven. Preheat oven to 350 degrees.

3. Place brown sugar and butter in bowl. Mix to blend. Add eggs, one at a time, beating after each addition.

4. Pour sugar mixture into well in flour; stir briefly to blend.

5. Fold in date mixture, just to incorporate. Add nuts, stirring just to incorporate.

6. Pour batter into prepared pan. Bake for 55 to 60 minutes, until knife inserted in center of loaf comes out almost clean.

7. Let sit a few minutes, remove from pan, and cool completely on rack. Slice and serve with butter or cream cheese.

PEARS AND FIGS POACHED IN SPICY RED WINE

Pears and Figs Poached in
Spicy Red Wine

Allow at least several hours or overnight to marinate and chill the pears and figs.

The cooking time will depend on the ripeness of the pears. It is better to poach pears that are not too ripe and soft. To quickly and evenly core the pears, use a melon ball cutter to remove the core.

If desired, slice the pear half and fan the slices for plating.

To serve the whole pear instead of a half, peel the pear and remove core from the bottom but leave the pear whole. Poach by standing pears in simmering wine and then rotating them on all sides. Whole pears require a longer cooking time. Present whole pear standing on plate (cut off a little of bottom to provide flat surface for standing) in a pool of poaching liquid with figs around it.

NUMBER OF SERVINGS: 8
COOKING METHOD:
   Poach
SERVING SIZE:
   About 4$\frac{1}{4}$ oz, $\frac{1}{2}$ pear and
   3 figs
TOTAL YIELD:
   2 lbs, 2$\frac{1}{2}$ oz, 8 pear halves
   and 24 figs with sauce

INGREDIENTS	WEIGHT	VOLUME
red wine	750 ml	about 3 cups, 1 each 750 ml bottle
sugar	1$\frac{3}{4}$ oz	$\frac{1}{4}$ cup
cinnamon stick		1 each
cloves, whole		6 each
peppercorns		10 each
ginger		1 teaspoon
pears, variety of choice, peeled, cut in half, cored	1 lb, 9 oz	8 halves
figs, black mission or variety of choice	6$\frac{1}{4}$ oz	24 each

1. Place wine, sugar, cinnamon stick, cloves, peppercorns, and ginger in nonreactive pan. Bring to boil, reduce heat, cover, and simmer for 15 minutes.

2. Add pears and figs, cover, and simmer for 10 minutes. Gently turn pears to other side; poach another 5 to 10 minutes, until almost tender. *The length of cooking time depends on the type of pear and the ripeness of the fruit.*

3. Remove pears from liquid; set aside. Continue boiling wine about 10 minutes to reduce liquid by half.

4. Pour liquid over pears and figs. Refrigerate at least several hours or overnight.

5. Serve cold, placing a little poaching syrup on plate, then arranging fanned pear half and figs on top, or place pear half on plate surrounded by figs. If desired, accompany pear with some grated or crumbled cheese of choice or serve with custard sauce.

CHOCOLATE RASPBERRY DACQUOISE

Piping Meringue

Chocolate Raspberry Dacquoise

Meringue desserts are sensitive to humidity, so if preparing in a humid environment, definitely assemble on the day of service. The meringue and buttercream can be prepared ahead of time and frozen. Freeze the meringue, but if it is soggy when defrosted, recrisp by baking in a slow oven. Some bake the meringue the day before and store it in a turned-off oven since the pilot light keeps the humidity low. Buttercream can be prepared ahead and stored in the refrigerator or the freezer for longer storage. Allow buttercream to return to room temperature before beating with flat beater.

NUMBER OF SERVINGS: 12
COOKING METHOD:
 Bake
SERVING SIZE:
 1/12 of dacquoise
TOTAL YIELD:
 1 each 10-inch dacquoise
  buttercream: 1 lb, 5 oz
  (3 cups)

INGREDIENTS	WEIGHT	VOLUME
MERINGUE:		
almonds, blanched, finely ground	3 1/2 oz	3/4 cup
sugar	7 oz	1 cup
egg whites, room temperature	5 oz	5 each
FILLING:		
cream, whipping, cold	12 oz	1 1/2 cups
confectioners' sugar	1/2 oz	1 tablespoon
vanilla		1 teaspoon
raspberries, or berries of choice, washed, drained well	5 to 6 oz	1/2 pint
confectioners' sugar, for dusting top	about 3/4 oz	about 1 1/2 tablespoons
CHOCOLATE MERINGUE BUTTERCREAM:		
egg whites	3 oz	3 each
sugar	5 1/4 oz	3/4 cup
butter, unsalted, softened	6 oz	1 1/2 sticks or 3/4 cup

For Meringue:

1. Cut parchment paper to fit baking pan. Trace 2 each 10-inch circles on paper; place paper on baking pan with pencil (or ink) side down. Mix almonds with 1¾ oz (about ¼ cup) sugar; set aside until needed. Place baking rack in middle of oven. Preheat oven to 275 degrees.

2. Beat egg whites until frothy using mixer with whisk attachment at medium speed. Sprinkle with ½ oz (about 1 tablespoon) sugar.

3. Raise speed to high and slowly sprinkle in remaining sugar, ½ oz (1 tablespoon) at a time, beating well after each addition. Beat until stiff peaks.

4. Gently fold half of almond mixture into egg whites; repeat with remaining half.

5. Place half of mixture into each circle. Spread evenly with icing spatula.

6. Bake for about 1 hour, until crisp. If meringues begin to brown, lower oven temperature to 250 degrees. Remove; cool completely.

For Filling:

1. Whip cream until beginning to thicken (halfway thickened).

2. Sift confectioners' sugar over cream; add vanilla. Continue whisking until it holds peaks.

3. Refrigerate until needed.

(Continued)

brandy or other liquor	¹/₂ oz	1 tablespoon
chocolate, semisweet or bittersweet, melted, cooled	7 oz	1¹/₄ cups

For Buttercream:

1. Place egg whites and sugar in mixing bowl over pan of barely simmering water. Whisk constantly until sugar dissolves, mixture feels hot, and reaches 160 degrees.

2. Remove from bain marie (double boiler) and beat at high speed with whisk attachment until cooled to room temperature.

3. Lower mixer speed; add softened butter, ¹/₂ oz (1 tablespoon) at a time. Add brandy, beat until light and fluffy.

4. Add cooled chocolate, a little at a time. If room is warm and buttercream becomes too soft, refrigerate to firm. Excess buttercream can be refrigerated or frozen. Allow to come to room temperature before beating with flat beater, if available.

To Assemble:

1. Place one meringue layer on a serving plate. Spread thin layer of buttercream in 5-inch circle in center of meringue.

2. Using large star tip, pipe buttercream around perimeter of meringue about 1 inch from outside.

3. Pipe two more layers of buttercream on top of first one, to form wall of buttercream. Refrigerate after each layer to firm buttercream so it supports the next layer without sagging. Refrigerate to firm after third layer.

4. Place whipped cream to height three-quarters up wall of buttercream. Top with berries, then spread whipped cream on top of berries until level with buttercream.

5. Place other meringue on top. Sift heavy coating of confectioners' sugar over meringue. Decorate with buttercream and berries, if desired. *Tip: Buttercream will not stick to the confectioners' sugar. Using a finger, trace the design to be piped on the meringue to remove the confectioners' sugar, and then pipe buttercream.*

13

The Melting Pot

OBJECTIVES

By the end of this chapter, you will be able to

- Define the term *melting pot* and explain how it applies to the United States
- Discuss reasons immigrants moved from their native countries to the United States
- Define ethnic neighborhoods and discuss why they developed
- Discuss the waves of immigrants that entered the United States in various time periods and explain why each group came at that particular time
- Prepare a variety of dishes representing the cookery of the Melting Pot

The term "melting pot" refers to the blending of different ethnic groups to form one culture.

With a relatively small population of Native Americans, most people in the United States trace their ancestry to one or more other countries. From the time of the first settlements and continuing to the present, people from around the world immigrated to the United States to escape religious or political persecution, in search of economic opportunity, to avoid famine and starvation, and/or to find a better life for themselves and their families. Because the United States offered plenty of available jobs and free or inexpensive land to farm, this country attracted many who wanted to leave their native homeland. Coming from every continent, millions of people immigrated to this new land, and the population swelled. As a result, the United States developed as a nation of immigrants and became a melting pot of ethnic diversity. This melting pot constantly changes as people from varying ethnic backgrounds continue to immigrate here.

Several factors determined the characteristics of every region's cuisine. First, each area/region attracted people from different ethnic groups. Each group of immigrants came to their new land with recipes, traditions, and the culinary heritage from their homeland. Second, each area/region had its own type of soil, climate, topography, and growing conditions. These variants impacted the list of foods available in each area. Third, influence from the people already living in the region factored into the developing cuisine. Both old and new residents assimilated traits from each other's cookery. Although these issues molded the cuisine of each region, the cities defined as melting pots reflect particularly strong influence from the various ethnic groups who settled there.

When immigrants moved to this country, they arrived with their culinary heritage in tow. They prepared the recipes from their homeland, but when necessary, they replaced traditional foods with available ingredients. In neighborhoods and communities across the country, people shared dishes and recipes with their friends and neighbors. They adopted all that they liked from those dishes and added new recipes, ingredients, flavorings, and cooking techniques to their own cooking repertoire. Steadily, recipes changed and the cuisines began to mix together. Eventually, a new, distinctive cuisine developed in each neighborhood, community, town, city, and/or region.

Dishes served in the regions across the United States share similarities as well as distinct differences. For example, pot roast—braised beef—appears in every part of the country. Cooks in each region prepare their own versions using different seasonings and/or ingredients. For example, Yankee pot roast consists of braised beef and root vegetables simply seasoned. In New Orleans, cooks serve French-inspired pot roast called beef daube that uses flavorings of wine, stock, and herbs.

For a number of reasons, immigrants landed in the port cities and adopted them as their new home. First, these cities served as ports of entry. After making the journey to this new land, many arriving immigrants had neither money nor motivation to travel further. Second, these cities were situated on water, so they developed into transportation centers. With the ability to import and export products through the waterways, the port cities proved excellent locations for factories and industry. These businesses provided jobs for both skilled and unskilled workers. In essence, the port cities presented employment opportunities for poor and/or uneducated immigrants as well as people who spoke little or no English. After the long voyage to the United States and with good job possibilities awaiting them, many chose to stop their journey and establish a new home in the port towns and cities. Finally, these cities developed ethnic neighborhoods that provided a comfortable living environment for the new residents. For all of these reasons, a multitude of immigrants settled in the port towns. As more and more people moved there, these towns grew into large cities. Populated by immigrants from many countries, these port cities developed into ethnic melting pots.

Although immigrants do not necessarily settle in port cities today, large cities continue to draw many of the new residents. They move to large cities for the same reasons the early immigrants settled in the port cities. Large cities offer more job opportunities and have ethnic neighborhoods. Sometimes, friends or family from the native country already reside there. Today, more than half of the immigrants coming to this country settle in New York City, Chicago, Miami, Washington, D.C., Los Angeles, or San Francisco.

Many immigrants in the past spoke little or no English, so they chose to settle in neighborhoods or ghettos with people from their own ethnic background. In the ethnic neighborhoods, most people spoke their native language in both homes and businesses. Furthermore, most of the residents still prepared their native dishes and observed the traditions and customs from their homeland. Whether planting crops or importing foods, a larger ethnic group had an easier time accessing the foods needed to prepare traditional dishes. These factors helped the immigrants retain their culinary heritage, which left pronounced culinary influence on their new city. Finally, some settled in ghettos because of discrimination, which was often the case for Asian and African immigrants. For all of these reasons, many ethnic groups congregated in ghettos. As a result, most large cities have an area or neighborhood called "Chinatown," "Little Italy," or the "Greek section."

Although the process sometimes required a generation or more, the immigrants stopped speaking their native language, adopted the traditional clothing of their new land, and changed many of their customs. Eventually they became assimilated into the culture of the United States. Although many embraced American foods on a daily basis, they still served their traditional dishes during holidays and festivals. By passing the recipes from generation to generation, they preserved their culinary heritage. Mothers, mothers-in-law, and grandmothers taught their daughters to prepare the family's traditional favorites. In this way, recipes survived for many generations, and they still live in many families today.

When immigrants from different ethnic backgrounds married, the women learned to cook the traditional foods from their husbands' culinary past. Often taught by her mother-in-law, the wife added the foods from her husband's childhood to her cooking repertoire. As a result, children grew up with the cookery from two or more different ethnic backgrounds. For those children, these cuisines merged into one.

Immigrants created new dishes in the style of their native country, but they modified the recipes to incorporate American standards. Often, immigrants added extra meat and/or cheese to traditional dishes since Americans consume larger amounts of meat and cheese. For example, all but the wealthy Italians had limited quantities of meat in Italy. Although meat sauce contained some meat, there certainly was not enough to serve each person several meatballs. Similarly, Mexican food in this country features much more meat and cheese than its counterpart in Mexico. Another change from the original recipes occurred when cooks substituted ingredients based on the availability of products here. For example, Chinese immigrants invented chop suey in the United States. They prepared this stir-fried dish (Asian cooking technique) with available food ingredients. Even when preparing traditional dishes, the native cuisines fused with American cooking styles and ingredients. This led to Italian-American food, Tex-Mex, or Chinese-American.

While many immigrated to this country to escape conditions in their homelands, some people came to various areas of the country for specific jobs. For example, work in mines in the states near the Great Lakes lured many from the British Isles. In 1848, the discovery of gold brought hordes of prospectors from all over the United States, as well as countries around the world, to the West. Representing a third situation, many Basque men immigrated to the mountainous states of the West after receiving contracts for work raising sheep. Once the immigrants became accustomed to the area, they usually stayed. They remained in their new home even if the original job or reason for settling in that location ended. Future generations continued to reside in the area because they grew up there.

Leaving their families at home, men frequently came to the United States first. They wanted to check out this new land and establish a home before moving their families. According to plan, the men found work, earned money, and sent money home to their waiting families. When convinced that this would be a good move for his family, a man would send the funds for the family's journey to their new land.

Between 1820 and 1920, about 33 million people immigrated to the United States. Five million of them emigrated from Germany, over four million from both Italy and Ireland, over three million each from Great Britain, Austria, and Russia, and two million from both Canada and Scandinavia. In the two decades between 1900 and 1920, more than fourteen and one-half million people immigrated to the United States.

Situated just off the southern tip of Manhattan, Ellis Island was established as an immigration station on January 1, 1892. Ellis Island served as a major port of entry for people wishing to enter the United States on the eastern shore. In the early days, the purpose of this immigration station was to bar entry to people with diseases. Between its opening in 1892 and closing in 1954, over 12 million immigrants from myriad countries arrived on Ellis Island. The droves of immigrants passing through this port of entry dwindled around the time of World War I and in the 1920s, when Congress passed immigration laws that ended open immigration.

Located in the San Francisco Bay, Angel Island served as the counterpart of Ellis Island for immigrants crossing the Pacific Ocean. From 1910 to 1940, people from Australia, New Zealand, Mexico, Russia, Pacific Islands, and Asia entered the United States after stopping at Angel Island. Unlike Ellis Island, where people usually stayed for a few hours, people waited an average of two to three weeks on Angel Island before being allowed entry to this country. In some cases, people were detained for months or even a year. On Angel Island, immigrants underwent medical examinations and interrogations before they were allowed to enter the United States. They lived in barracks separating the men from the women. Although few immigrants from Ellis Island were denied admittance to this country, many were deported from Angel Island. Most of this treatment resulted from discrimination against the Chinese and other Asians.

Prior to 1880, the majority of the immigrants entering the United States came from western or northern Europe. The British settled most of the eastern shore including New England, the coastal regions of the Middle Atlantic States, and the South. Germans moved into Pennsylvania and much of the Midwest, the French settled in New Orleans, and the Spanish chose the Southwest and California. The states surrounding the Great Lakes, the Plains, and the Northwest attracted many Scandinavians.

Around 1880, droves of people immigrated from Southern and Eastern Europe, Mexico, and Asia. For a variety of reasons, Italians, Czechoslovakians, Hungarians, Serbians, Polish, Ukrainians, Russians, Romanians, Croatians, Balkans, and more sought refuge in the United States. The huge influx of Eastern Europeans lasted from 1880 until about 1914. Choosing to settle in areas with cold weather like their native countries, many moved to the East and the Midwest. In particular, immigrants from Eastern Europe established new homes in New York, Pennsylvania, New Jersey, and the states bordering the Great Lakes, including Ohio, Illinois, Michigan, Wisconsin, and Minnesota. Later, many of these people moved westward to obtain land in the Plains. Their culinary influence remains. Many people of Eastern European descent still live in New York City, Chicago, Detroit, Buffalo, Milwaukee, and Cleveland.

The exodus of immigrants from Eastern Europe included two distinct groups. First, in the late 1800s and early 1900s, poor farmers and laborers left parts of the Russian Empire to escape famine, bad economic conditions, and political unrest. At that time, the extensive Russian Empire encompassed Eastern Europe, parts of Asia, and even some of Western Europe. The second wave came when the socialists took control of Russia in

1917. At that time, the Empire collapsed and 30,000 people immigrated to the United States. In contrast to the immigrants who came at the turn of the century, this group mostly consisted of educated people with professions.

In 1880, three hundred thousand Italians lived in the United States. Most of them entered this country through New York. That number exploded to four million by 1920. While the majority settled in large cities like New York, Boston, Chicago, Detroit, Buffalo, Cleveland, and Milwaukee, eventually, Italians moved all over the country. They found work in agriculture or the trades from their homeland. In San Francisco, many worked as fishermen or on the docks.

Between 1880 and 1924, an estimated two and a half to three million Jewish immigrants left Eastern and Central Europe to escape religious persecution and find a better life in America. Because of the pogroms, organized persecution of an ethnic or religious group (in this case people of the Jewish faith), huge numbers of Jewish people fled from Eastern Europe. The next wave of Jewish refugees arrived in the 1930s and 1940s to escape from the Nazis and the atrocities of the Holocaust.

Like other immigrants, the Jewish people arrived with the culinary traditions from their homeland, but there was one difference. Although these people shared a religion, they did not necessarily have the same nationality. As a result of the significant culinary similarities and differences among Jewish immigrants, a melting pot of Jewish cookery developed. That melting pot combined the cooking traditions from many different countries with kosher dietary laws and influences from their new homeland. This gave birth to a new creation, Jewish-American cookery.

Of course, Jewish-American cookery reflected numerous distinct ethnicities. Strudel and stuffed cabbage came from the Hungarians and others from Central and Eastern Europe, borscht and blintzes from the Russians and Polish, and pastrami from the Romanians. Soon, Jewish immigrants opened delicatessens that featured all of these foods and more from the Jewish-American cuisine. Other regular items on the delicatessen menu included bagels (bread shaped like a doughnut, prepared by boiling first and then baking), lox (smoked salmon), numerous types of smoked fish, pickled herring in various sauces, corned beef, chopped liver, pickled tongue, rye bread, and an assortment of pickled vegetables, especially cucumbers and green tomatoes.

Regardless of the different foods and recipes from the immigrants' native homelands, several culinary traditions from their Jewish heritage remained the same. First, Jews observe the beginning of the Sabbath with a family meal on Friday night, and they celebrate other religious holidays with festive meals and/or specific foods. Whether from Poland, Russia, Germany, Spain, Argentina, Brazil, or Morocco, traditional foods reflecting their culinary heritage appear on each family's table for these special meals. Secondly, kashrut or kosher dietary laws apply to all Jewish people, regardless of nationality. The desire to maintain a kosher home resulted in a large number of Jewish immigrants staying in New York City. Even today, New York City's large Jewish population supports many kosher restaurants and businesses that close on Saturday, the Jewish Sabbath.

Of course, everyone did not settle in the large cities. Coming from the Pyrenees Mountains spanning the border of Spain and France, the Basques immigrated to this country with prearranged jobs as shepherds. They moved to the remote mountainous areas of the West where flocks of sheep thrived. While the men lived a solitary life in rugged country, their families inhabited the towns of the West and awaited the return of the men after months of tending their herds in the mountains. Basque cookery featured a variety of soups containing beans, potatoes, and/or grains, many stews filled with lamb, fish, or whatever was available, and numerous dishes incorporating dried salted cod. While garlic and onions flavored most Basque dishes, root vegetables filled the menus. Meals ended with cheese, not sweets.

TERMS FOR JEWISH IMMIGRANTS FROM DIFFERENT NATIONALITIES

Sephardic—Jewish people from the Iberian Peninsula (Spain and Portugal) as well as North Africa and the Middle East

Ashkenazi—originally from Germany; later also included those of Eastern European descent

SOME LAWS OF *KASHRUT*

- Separation of dairy products and meat products at each meal—one eats either a dairy meal or a meal containing meat; the two are never mixed
- Avoidance of pork and shellfish—animals used for meat must have cloven hooves and chew their cud; seafood must have a backbone, scales, and fins
- Specific methods of slaughtering animals used for meat in approved facilities
- Approved facilities for preparation of any kosher food

Greeks and Portuguese came for jobs connected with the sea. From the early days of settlers in this country, Portuguese settled in Cape Cod; Newport, Rhode Island; and other areas along the Atlantic to work as fishermen. In the 1800s, San Francisco and the Pacific Ocean enticed many Portuguese to move to the West. Wherever they settled, the Portuguese cooked a variety of soups and stews flavored with garlic. Their dishes often used plenty of fish, seafood, spicy sausages, and salted cod.

Many Greek immigrants settled in large cities like Chicago and New York City. In the early twentieth century, a number of Greeks moved to Tarpon Springs, Florida, to dive for sponges as they did in Greece. With more than 10 percent of the population in Tarpon Springs claiming Greek ancestry, numerous Greek restaurants still operate there. In addition to consuming lamb, fish, and seafood, the Greeks often use olive oil and lemon juice. These two ingredients appear in salad dressing, in marinades for meats and seafood, and as flavoring in many dishes.

Africans played a huge part in the development of the regional cuisines and the melting pots of the United States. Initially brought to this country against their will and forced to work as slaves, they settled wherever they were taken to live. Since many slaves worked as cooks for the families who owned them, they introduced many ingredients and recipes. Their influence became part of the cuisine found in every region. The development of "soul food" came from the African American slaves who prepared meals with any ingredients they received, regardless of the type of ingredients or how meager the quantity.

In the beginning, the slaves lived throughout the South and areas in the Middle Atlantic States and New England. After the Civil War, slaves received their freedom and could move. Searching for work led many to urban centers in the north, east, and eventually in the west. Although they were free, many former slaves could obtain only unskilled jobs in factories and industries. They settled in neighborhoods with other African Americans to establish communities and avoid discrimination. Eventually, the African Americans transitioned from a rural population to an urban one. Meanwhile, many chose to stay in the South and move to large cities or stay in rural areas. Today, more than 35 million African Americans live throughout the United States.

During the decade from 1890 to 1900, about 5,000 Syrian residents moved to the United States each year. Today, people from countries throughout the Middle East continue to immigrate. Reports claim that 500,000 Middle Eastern people moved to this country between 1994 and 2004. Drawn to large cities, many reside in Detroit, Washington, D.C., and New York City.

In the middle of the nineteenth century, China suffered from poor economic conditions. At that time, the possibility of discovering gold or finding work persuaded many Chinese to cross the Pacific and settle on the West Coast. Most of these Chinese immigrants were young men from rural areas. They wanted to earn money and send it home to their needy families. Unlike the Africans who came to the United States against their will, the Chinese were the first large group of a different race to voluntarily move to this country. Unfortunately, like the Africans, Chinese immigrants experienced fierce discrimination and persecution. By restricting job opportunities, this discrimination forced them into manual labor jobs such as building the railroad, digging canals for irrigation, doing laundry, or cooking. As cooks, the Chinese exposed Americans to the technique of stir-frying, introduced vegetables like bean sprouts, bok choy, and bamboo shoots, and cooked vegetables until still slightly crunchy rather than in the English style of boiling vegetables until very soft.

Many historians attribute much of the settling and success of California to the Chinese. Their manual labor built the railroads, constructed the vineyards, and excavated the caverns to store the wine, and they dug canals and waterways to irrigate much of the land. That irrigation literally transformed barren land into some of the most fertile and prolific farmland in the country. In spite of their many contributions, discrimination created intense hardship for the Asians. In addition, the government levied special taxes on the Chinese that provided additional revenue to the state.

After the completion of the railroad, many Chinese relocated to San Francisco. Chinatown, a neighborhood of Asian immigrants, developed because of the discrimination, especially after the Chinese Exclusion Act of 1882. Asian communities appeared in many large cities throughout this country, including San Francisco, Los Angeles, Seattle, Boston, Philadelphia, and New York City. Initially, Cantonese cooking dominated Chinese restaurants here, but regional Chinese cooking began to appear in restaurants around the 1940s.

In 1869, the first Japanese immigrants arrived with tea plants, silk cocoons, and mulberry trees. (The trees were vital for silk production because the larvae of silkworms eat the leaves of the mulberry tree). Coming from Hawaii, where they worked on plantations, many Japanese relocated to the United States in the late 1800s. While some settled in California and continued to work in agriculture, many eventually moved into Chinatowns in San Francisco, Los Angeles, Chicago, and New York City.

The history of immigration from Mexico began as a different story than that of other immigrants. During the middle 1800s, the United States gained control over some of Mexico's land, including Texas and California, as well as portions of New Mexico, Arizona, Colorado, Nevada, and Utah. At that time, the United States granted citizenship to Mexicans living in these areas.

In later years, Mexicans sought immigration into the United States for traditional reasons. Because of the weak economy and poor conditions in Mexico between 1910 and 1930, an estimated 400,000 Mexicans came to this country looking for jobs and a better life. Many found work in agriculture; however, the Depression and World War I ended most farming jobs for foreigners. As a result, large numbers of Mexicans left the rural areas to find jobs in industry and factories in urban centers. This migration to the cities caused the Mexican population in Los Angeles, San Antonio, Detroit, and Chicago to dramatically increase.

Around 1970, a distinct change occurred in immigration demographics. Since that time, the largest influx of immigrants into the United States comes from Mexico, Central America, the Caribbean Islands, or Asia rather than from Europe. As a result, the Hispanic population continues to increase rapidly, and the popularity and sales of goods with Hispanic roots keeps climbing. Beginning in 1996, sales of salsa surpassed catsup sales. Mexican restaurants appear in small towns and large cities. Reflecting current immigration trends, most large cities have ethnic pockets of Hispanics, African Americans, and Asians. The Hispanic section usually includes many Mexicans in addition to residents from Latin American countries. The Asian neighborhood contains Chinese and Japanese immigrants as well as people from the countries of Southeast Asia.

NEW YORK CITY

Referred to as "the melting pot that defines all melting pots," New York City served as the major debarkation port for immigrants from Europe in the early years. Since its beginning, the city lured wave after wave of residents from foreign countries. As in all melting pots, people from each ethnic group wanted to settle near each other, so, of course, ethnic neighborhoods sprung up throughout the city.

Although first settled by the Dutch, immigrants from every nationality eventually made their way to New York City. In the early 1800s, many English and Irish arrived and found work in factories. As in their native countries, they consumed ample amounts of oatmeal and potatoes.

After the 1820s, many Jewish immigrants came to New York in search of religious freedom, escape from persecution, and/or a better life. Opened by Eastern European Jews, the delicatessen was born in New York City. Delis featured foods reflecting Eastern European, German, and Jewish backgrounds. Many followed *kashrut* and served kosher foods. To accommodate the huge Jewish population, there are many kosher restaurants in New York City. Because *kashrut* forbids the mixing of meat and dairy foods, some restaurants serve only dairy or *parve* (neutral) dishes and no meat, while other restaurants serve only meat or *parve* (neutral) dishes and no dairy.

When crops died and famine swept through Ireland in the 1840s, droves of Irish immigrants flooded into New York City. Meanwhile, Germans fled to New York to escape the 1848 revolution in Germany. As the Irish and Germans improved their financial status in this new land, they moved into better neighborhoods. In their place, Eastern Europeans occupied their old ghettos.

At the turn of the century, thousands of Italians settled in the eastern side of New York City in the section still called Little Italy. Even today, Mulberry Street bustles with Italian restaurants and bakeries, while neighboring Canal Street is the main street running through Chinatown. A magnet for a variety of Asian groups, Chinatown continues to grow rapidly. Little Italy and Chinatown represent ethnic enclaves in Lower Manhattan. Russian, German, Polish, and Ukrainian neighborhoods are situated in the Lower East Side. Many African Americans and Puerto Ricans reside in Harlem. Basically, most ethnic populations created their own neighborhood somewhere in the city, and this results in the availability of all types of ethnic restaurants.

By 1900, as many Irish people lived in New York City as lived in Dublin, more Italians resided in New York City than any single city in Italy except for Rome, and New York City claimed more Polish residents than any city other than Warsaw. In addition, New York contained the largest Jewish population of any city in the world. Countless immigrants had arrived in New York City and made it their home, and the influx of immigrants did not stop.

The Puerto Rican population grew rapidly in the middle 1940s. In 1945, thirteen thousand Puerto Ricans lived in New York City. One year later, that number swelled to 50,000. Large Puerto Rican immigration continued until the 1950s. Because so many settled in northeastern Manhattan, that area became known as Spanish Harlem. This constant flood of residents brought new tastes and traditions to the existing melting pot that already simmered with ingredients from every nationality of the world.

CHICAGO

Another melting pot of ethnicity, Chicago attracted immigrants from all nationalities. In addition to new immigrants, people from rural areas in the Plains and Midwest who wanted to trade a life of farming for urban living moved to the largest city in close proximity, Chicago. They found work in one of Chicago's thriving industries. Even if they spoke no English, a job in a factory, packing house, steel mill, or refinery awaited the poor, hungry immigrants and relocating farmers. Like many foreigners settling in large cities, they moved into ethnic neighborhoods, and the children often grew up speaking only their parents' native language. Living in ghettos, these immigrants stayed segregated from the rest of the city. Because of this isolation, culinary traditions and dishes from their homeland prevailed until later generations began to adopt American customs and recipes, and the two worlds blended.

Situated at the southern end of Lake Michigan, location was at least partly responsible for Chicago's growth into a major city. In the middle 1830s, men from Ireland and

Germany found work in Chicago digging the canals that connected the waterways. By providing accessible transportation, those waterways transformed Chicago from a small town into a large, bustling city. In addition, railroads from the east, west, and southwest transected the country and connected in this city. Chicago served as the closest major transportation center to handle the herds of animals raised throughout the Southwest, Plains, and Midwest. As a result, industry developed to process livestock, and Chicago became the site of stockyards, slaughtering facilities, and meat processing plants. Because each of these required many laborers, immigrants found plenty of jobs. Eventually, countless immigrants from Poland, Greece, Italy, Ireland, Sweden, Slovakia, Germany, Mexico, China, Lithuania, and more countries settled in Chicago. Meanwhile, Jewish immigrants arrived in waves. They left Germany in the 1860s, Eastern Europe in the 1880s, Russia and Poland in the beginning of the twentieth century, and Germany and other European countries to escape Hitler in the 1930s and 1940s.

Each ethnic group established its own neighborhood and cooked from its culinary heritage. Regardless of their former nationality, the common thread running through all the ethnic groups was their desire to live a better life.

Throughout the twentieth century, so many Polish immigrants moved to Chicago that it developed one of the biggest Polish communities in the United States. Polish foods abound, evidenced by foods like pierogis, a filled turnover; kielbasa, Polish sausage; and bigos, stew containing a variety of meats and sauerkraut. In the meantime, a large Greek population established their own community. Lamb dishes and honey-soaked desserts appeared on menus in Greek restaurants and homes. Continuing their culinary traditions, the Hungarians cooked with lots of paprika, and the German immigrants ate sausages, pretzels, dumplings, and coffeecakes. Chicago claims the largest Swedish population of any city in the United States.

Chicago-style pizza, the deep-dish specialty of Italian origin, debuted in 1947. This substantial pizza consists of a thick layer of dough generously topped with mozzarella cheese, then crushed tomatoes, oregano, and other ingredients of choice. It is eaten with a knife and fork.

Today, Chicago's largest ethnic groups are the Polish, Irish, Germans, and Italians. Significant numbers of people from Greece, Russia, Ukraine, Scandinavia, India, China, Korea, and the Philippines live here, too. Hispanics make up the fastest growing ethnic group in Chicago. While most come from Mexico and Puerto Rico, smaller numbers immigrated from Cuba and other Latin American countries.

Many African Americans from the South moved to Chicago in search of jobs. Settling on the south side of the city, they lived in a ghetto and cooked typical southern food, especially "soul food" using all the parts of the animal no one else wanted. They also brought their love of music, and Chicago remains well known for blues and jazz.

SAN FRANCISCO

San Francisco developed its own unique cuisine from the culinary influence of a number of diverse groups. These included

- prospectors from every region of the United States and from countries around the world who came after the discovery of gold
- laborers from many nationalities who worked on the railroad, in factories, or in agriculture
- fishermen and those who worked on the docks
- Spanish missionaries who settled San Francisco
- fortunate ones who garnered great wealth from gold, silver, or other means and had plenty of money for fine dining

DISCRIMINATION AGAINST CHINESE

- Chinese children were not allowed to attend public schools, so the community established a Chinese School in 1859.
- The government levied special taxes on Asians.
- Asians could not vote.
- Asians could not marry non-Asians.
- Asians could not work for the government.
- Asians could not testify in court.
- Asians could not own property.

The cookery found here reflects culinary traces from various European countries as well as a wide range of Asian cuisines.

Enticed by the lure of gold and the promise of work in this new land, many immigrants from Asia and Europe arrived in San Francisco. Like Ellis Island in New York, Angel Island off the coast of San Francisco served as the point of entry for the multitude of immigrants coming to the western United States. Also as in New York, many immigrants decided to end their journey and establish their home in the city where they docked.

Escape from the droughts, floods, and civil war raging in China, coupled with the prospect of discovering gold, convinced many Chinese to immigrate in the 1840s. Because of discrimination, they were allowed only menial jobs that no one else wanted. As a result, they found work building the transcontinental railroad or digging canals for irrigation. With the completion of the railroad, many settled in San Francisco. By 1852, twenty thousand Chinese immigrants lived there. Meanwhile, a number of Japanese and other Asians immigrated to the San Francisco area because of the fertile fields throughout this region. Establishing a rural life for themselves, they came into San Francisco to buy goods and/or sell their produce. Because of discrimination and the need for a central location to buy and sell goods, Chinatown developed in the 1850s and 1860s. San Francisco's Chinatown ranks as the oldest Chinatown in the United States. It is the second largest, with only New York claiming a larger Chinatown. San Francisco contains the largest Chinese population of any city in the United States.

In 1869, the first Chinese restaurant opened in Chinatown. Called Canton, this restaurant set the tone for Chinese restaurants in America for the next one hundred years, when almost all Chinese restaurants reflected the cooking found in the province of Canton. Today, diners find Chinese restaurants representing all of the provinces of China.

In 1906, a strong earthquake shook bustling San Francisco. Although 3,000 people died and more than 28,000 buildings were destroyed, the residents overcame the huge destruction and rebuilt their city.

Since the grapevines brought by the Spanish missionaries flourished, many French and Italians settled in and around San Francisco, including Napa Valley and Sonoma Valley to the northeast of San Francisco. They planted vineyards, made wine, and prospered. Today, hundreds of wineries operate in this area, creating an important industry for California. The many Italians developed a large Italian neighborhood in San Francisco. Called North Beach, this neighborhood lies just north of Chinatown.

Living near some of the most prolific wine country of the United States, San Franciscans have access to an incredible range of wines from the nearby valleys of Napa and Sonoma counties. In addition, rich farmland lies to the east and southeast of San Francisco providing a cornucopia of fruits and vegetables. This wealth of fresh produce from the land as well as the bounty of fish and seafood from the Pacific Ocean and the bays provides excellent ingredients to prepare most dishes.

Today, statistics show that the population mix of San Francisco, San Jose, and Oakland contains 19 percent Hispanics and 17 percent Asians. In the city of San Francisco, 31 percent of the residents claim Asian ancestry.

HAWAII

With flourishing sugar and pineapple plantations, the plantation owners could not meet the demand for laborers with native Hawaiians. To fulfill their need for cheap labor, they actively recruited workers from many other ethnic groups. Consequently, successive waves of immigrants came to Hawaii, including 46,000 from China, 180,000 from Japan, 66,000 from the Philippines, and a number of Portuguese and Puerto Ricans. Between

1850 and 1898, more than 45,000 Chinese came to Hawaii with the hope of making plenty of money and returning home. In actuality, more than half of them did not return home, and they made Hawaii their home. Native Hawaiians accounted for 97 percent of Hawaii's population in 1853. Importing plantation workers caused the population of Hawaii to swell, and by 1923, native Hawaiians made up only 16 percent of the population. By the late 1930s, people from the Philippines constituted the largest ethnic group working on the plantations in Hawaii.

Around 1820, Portuguese began arriving on whaling ships. Many left the ships and stayed in Hawaii. They supported themselves by working in agriculture, on dairy farms, or on ranches. Between 1878 and 1899, almost 12,000 Portuguese relocated to Hawaii. Like the other groups, they contributed culinary remnants of their heritage to the cookery found in this state.

Today, many groups make up Hawaii's diverse population, including people from the mainland of the United States, native Hawaiians, Japanese, Chinese, Filipinos, Koreans, Thais, African Americans, Native Americans, Eskimos, Aleutians, Russians, Puerto Ricans, people from India, Samoans, and others from Asian and Pacific islands. This state is truly a melting pot, with no group claiming a clear majority of the population. Hawaii's cuisine shows strong culinary influence from the native Hawaiians and various Asian nationalities, as well as many other ethnic groups.

VARIOUS TOWNS AND CITIES

Boston

This port city attracted large numbers of Irish immigrants as well as many people from Italy and China. Thousands of Irish fleeing the Potato Famine of 1845 relocated to Boston. By 1855, approximately 50,000 Irish lived in this city. In the late 1800s, the many Italian immigrants in Boston established an Italian community called North End, located in the north end of the city. Today, more people in Boston claim Irish heritage than any other group. Italians rank as the second largest ethnic group.

Throughout its history, Jewish immigrants steadily came to Boston. Before 1869, the majority of the Jewish people in Boston claimed Portuguese or German ancestry. After 1869, they came from a variety of nations, including those in the Russian Empire like Russia and the countries of Eastern Europe, as well as Greece, Turkey, the Middle East, and Morocco. During the 1850s, the different groups began opening synagogues that represented their native countries.

Boston's thriving Chinatown came into existence in the latter part of the 1800s. From the late 1960s until the present, many Vietnamese immigrated to the United States. A large number of them chose to settle in Boston.

With African Americans making up 25 percent of its population, Boston contains a large African American section. Also typical of many cities throughout the United States, Boston is home to an influx of new Hispanic residents.

Detroit

Detroit had easy access to Lake Huron and Lake Erie by rivers and lakes. With the completion of the Erie Canal, waterways connected Detroit to the Atlantic Ocean. These waterways provided Detroit with great transportation and accessibility that attracted immigrants.

Henry Ford built the first automobile in Detroit in 1896 and established the Ford Motor Company in 1903. Jobs in the automobile industry lured many people to Detroit, which is nicknamed the Motor City.

CONTRIBUTIONS FROM ITALIAN IMMIGRANTS

- zucchini
- plum tomatoes
- fennel
- broccoli
- pizza
- lasagna
- antipasto
- espresso coffee

Note: European explorers discovered squash and tomatoes in South America and Central America and then took them to Europe. The Italians adopted these vegetables and incorporated them into their cuisine. Later, Italian immigrants brought dishes containing these ingredients to the United States.

CONTRIBUTIONS FROM JEWISH IMMIGRANTS

- delicatessens
- lox
- pastrami
- corned beef
- smoked and pickled fish
- matzo ball soup
- blintzes
- kosher dill pickles
- pickled green tomatoes
- bagels
- borscht

CONTRIBUTIONS FROM GERMAN IMMIGRANTS

- frankfurters (hot dogs)
- sausages
- pretzels
- dumplings
- coffeecakes

CONTRIBUTIONS FROM CENTRAL AND EASTERN EUROPEAN IMMIGRANTS

- dumplings
- noodles
- sauerkraut
- sausages
- stuffed cabbage
- strudel

CONTRIBUTIONS FROM HUNGARIAN IMMIGRANTS

- goulash
- paprika

CONTRIBUTIONS FROM POLISH IMMIGRANTS

- pierogis
- kielbasa
- borscht
- blintzes

CONTRIBUTIONS FROM GREEK IMMIGRANTS

- lamb dishes
- honey-soaked desserts

Besides large communities of African Americans, Mexicans, Latin Americans, Polish, Greeks, and people from India, Detroit contains the largest Middle Eastern population of any city in the United States. According to the 2000 census, African Americans make up 81.6 percent of Detroit's population.

San Antonio

Located near Mexico, San Antonio is home to a huge Mexican population. According to the 2000 census, 70 percent of San Antonio's population is Caucasian, 41 percent Mexican, and 58 percent claim Hispanic heritage. San Antonio contains the third largest urban Hispanic population in the United States. Only New York and Los Angeles have larger Hispanic populations (in number of people, not percentage of the population).

Miami

Statistics show that Miami ranks as the capital of the Cuban American and Latin American population in the United States, with Hispanics making up 60 percent of the city's population. Today, people from Cuba, Haiti, islands in the Caribbean, Central America, and South America constitute the majority of Miami's population.

Because of political turmoil in Cuba, many Cubans sought refuge here in the 1950s. After Castro came to power in 1959, another wave of Cubans fled to Miami. This group differed from the previous one because it contained a large number of highly educated people. Seventy-five percent of Miami's population reports they do not speak English at home, and 67 percent claim they do not speak English well. As a result, Spanish joins the English language in homes and businesses throughout the city.

New Orleans

This city is discussed in detail in Chapter 6 on Louisiana. Traits from the cuisines of France, Spain, Africa, the West Indies, and Native Americans melded to form the distinctive Creole cookery found here. As reported in the 2000 census, African Americans make up more than 65 percent of the population of New Orleans. Hurricane Katrina devastated the city in 2005, and the rebuilding and recovery continue.

Los Angeles

Although it ranks as the second largest city in the United States today, Los Angeles developed as another of the bustling port cities. At the beginning of the 1900s, this port supported shipbuilders, countless workers to unload ships, a huge commercial fishing industry, and numerous canneries to process the catch.

Many immigrants came to southern California for work in agriculture. Huge numbers of Mexicans crossed the border and settled in Los Angeles which is located close to Mexico. In fact, 20 percent of the Hispanics in the United States live in Los Angeles. Residents from Mexico, Central America, and the Philippines actually make up the majority of the population in Los Angeles. According to demographic studies, the population of Los Angeles, Orange, and Riverside consists of 38 percent Hispanics and 10 percent Asians. Orange County contains a large number of Vietnamese residents.

After the discovery of gold in 1848, Chinese immigrants began coming to Los Angeles. Only 200 Chinese lived in this city in 1870. Today, about 400,000 Chinese and many Japanese reside in Los Angeles. After the 1970s, Asian immigrants from China, the Philippines, Korea, Vietnam, India, and the smaller countries of Southeast Asia flocked into Los Angeles.

A huge, sprawling city, Los Angeles covers more than 465 square miles. In 2000, the population of Los Angeles was about 47 percent Caucasians, 11 percent African Americans, and 10 percent Asians. Forty-seven percent of the population claimed Hispanic heritage. Currently, the Hispanic and Asian populations demonstrate continual growth. Significant numbers of Mexicans, Filipinos, Thais, Japanese, Koreans, Israelis, Iranians, Armenians, and Hungarians live in Los Angeles.

REVIEW QUESTIONS

1. Discuss the ethnic makeup of most immigrants before 1880, after 1880, and from the 1970s. Also discuss where different nationalities settled.
2. Why did so many immigrants settle in the port cities?
3. Explain the importance of ethnic neighborhoods to the immigrants and how they preserved their culinary heritage.
4. Discuss the ethnic groups that settled in Hawaii and why they came there. What is Hawaii's ethnic population like now?
5. What made Jewish immigrants different from other groups of immigrants? Discuss foods associated with this group and their origin.
6. What makes the United States a melting pot, and how does this affect the cuisine?

GLOSSARY

bagels—bread shaped like a doughnut, prepared by boiling the bread and then baking it

bigos—Polish stew containing a variety of meats and sauerkraut

Chinatown—a neighborhood of Asian immigrants within a city, usually found in large cities

kashrut—Jewish dietary laws, kosher

kielbasa—Polish sausage

lox—smoked salmon

parve—foods categorized as neutral under Jewish dietary laws; neither milk nor meat foods

pierogis—a filled turnover served in Poland

pogroms—organized persecution of an ethnic group

SPRING ROLLS

Dipping Rice Paper in Water
photo by David Murray and Jules Selmes
© Dorling Kindersley

Wrapping Spring Rolls
photo by David Murray and Jules Selmes
© Dorling Kindersley

Spring Rolls
photo by David Murray and Jules Selmes
© Dorling Kindersley

NUMBER OF SERVINGS: 9
COOKING METHOD:
    Deep-fry
SERVING SIZE:
    2 spring rolls
    1½ oz filling per roll
TOTAL YIELD:
    1 lb, 12½ oz filling

Wine Style: Light- to medium-bodied Chenin Blanc, Riesling, Pinot Blanc, mild Chardonnay, or Rose
Example: Pacific Rim Dry Riesling—Bonny Doon Vineyard, Santa Cruz, CA. This wine is brilliant, crisp, racy, and floral with a creamy texture and suggestion of minerals in the finish.

INGREDIENTS	WEIGHT	VOLUME
FILLING:		
mushrooms, dried	³/₄ oz	6 each
cornstarch	¹/₄ oz	1 tablespoon
water	2³/₄ oz	¹/₃ cup
peanut oil	1 oz	2 tablespoons
pork, ground	10 oz	
shrimp, peeled, deveined, small dice	4 oz	
bean sprouts	5 oz	1 cup
bamboo shoots, julienne	2³/₄ oz	½ cup
napa cabbage, shredded	2³/₄ oz	1 cup
green onion, sliced	2¹/₂ oz	1 cup or 6 each
ginger, fresh, peeled, minced	¹/₄ oz	2 teaspoons
garlic, minced	¹/₄ oz	2 cloves
soy sauce	¹/₂ oz	1 tablespoon
salt	¹/₄ oz	1 teaspoon
pepper		¹/₄ teaspoon
sugar		1 teaspoon
sesame oil		1 teaspoon
spring roll wrappers		18 each
water	as needed	
oil	for frying	

For Filling:

1. Place mushrooms in bowl, cover with water, and let soak for 45 minutes. Drain; cut into small dice. Set aside until needed. Mix cornstarch and 2¾ oz (⅓ cup) water; set aside until needed.

2. Heat 1 oz (2 tablespoons) peanut oil in pan. Sauté pork over high heat until browned. Drain excess oil. Add shrimp; sauté until pink.

3. Add bean sprouts, bamboo shoots, cabbage, onion, ginger, garlic, and reserved mushrooms. Sauté for 1 to 2 minutes. Add soy sauce, salt, pepper, sugar, and sesame oil. Heat thoroughly.

4. Add cornstarch mixture; cook until thickened. Drain any excess liquid.

To Assemble:

1. Cover baking pan with parchment paper. Place each spring roll wrapper in water for about 1 minute until softened and pliable. Remove from water; place on counter.

2. About one-third of the way from bottom edge of wrapper, place 1½ oz (2 tablespoons) filling in log shape, stopping about 1 inch from each edge. Roll bottom over filling, fold in each side, then roll tightly toward top.

3. Place on prepared pan with seam on bottom. Let rest, covered with plastic wrap, until all are prepared.

4. Heat oil for deep-frying to 350 degrees. Add spring rolls, a few at a time, and fry about 4 minutes until crisp and brown. Remove to absorbent paper. Keep warm in low oven, if necessary.

5. Serve, accompanied by hot mustard, duck sauce, chili sauce, or soy sauce.

POTATO KNISHES

Potato Knishes

If chicken fat is unavailable, substitute cooking oil.

NUMBER OF SERVINGS: 11
COOKING METHOD:
    Sauté, Bake
SERVING SIZE:
    2 knishes, 3¼ oz each
TOTAL YIELD:
    1 lb, 6 oz dough
      2 lb, 15¼ oz filling

INGREDIENTS	WEIGHT	VOLUME
DOUGH:		
eggs	3½ oz	2 each
salt	¼ oz	1 teaspoon
baking powder		½ teaspoon
oil	1½ oz	3 tablespoons
cold water	4 oz	½ cup
flour, all purpose	about 13¼ oz	about 2½ cups
oil	for coating	
FILLING:		
rendered chicken fat, *schmaltz*	3 oz	6 tablespoons
onions, small dice	10 oz	2 cups or 2 large
potatoes, russets, peeled, cooked, mashed	2 lb	about 6 each
salt	½ oz	2 teaspoons
pepper		1 teaspoon
eggs, beaten	3½ oz	2 each
GLAZE:		
egg yolk	¾ oz	1 each
water		1 teaspoon
GARNISH:		
sour cream		
mustard		

For Dough:

1. Beat eggs with salt, baking powder, oil, and water in bowl.
2. Gradually add flour; mix with spoon until dry enough to knead. Knead for about 10 minutes, until smooth.
3. Lightly coat ball of dough with oil, place in bowl, cover, and let rest about 30 minutes while preparing filling.

For Filling:

1. Heat chicken fat over low heat, add onions, and slowly sauté until golden, about 20 minutes.
2. Place mashed potatoes in bowl; add onions with any remaining chicken fat, salt, pepper, and egg. Stir until combined.
3. Correct seasonings; reserve.

To Assemble:

1. Cover sheet pan with parchment paper. Lightly flour worktable for rolling dough. Preheat oven to 375 degrees.
2. Using one-quarter of dough, roll into 12- by 10-inch rectangle ⅛ inch thick. Cut into 5- by 4-inch rectangles. Place 2 oz (¼ cup) potato filling in center of each rectangle.
3. Fold opposite short sides into center, then fold opposite long sides over each other to form enclosed packet.
4. Place folded-side down on prepared sheet; adjust shape into neat rectangle.
5. Mix egg yolk and water together for glaze. Brush over each knish. Bake until slightly browned, about 30 to 35 minutes. Serve 2 per portion. If desired, garnish with sour cream or mustard.

BLACK BEAN SOUP

Black Bean Soup

Begin preparation for this soup the day before serving so beans soak overnight. If not enough time, place washed beans in pot, cover with water, bring to boil, remove from heat, and allow beans to sit for a couple of hours before proceeding with recipe.

NUMBER OF SERVINGS: 9
COOKING METHOD:
   Sauté, Boil
SERVING SIZE:
   8 oz bean soup + 2 oz (⅔ cup)
    cooked rice
TOTAL YIELD:
   4 lbs, 12¾ oz

INGREDIENTS	WEIGHT	VOLUME
black beans, dried	1 lb	
olive oil	1 oz	2 tablespoons
onion, small dice	7½ oz	1½ cups or 1 large
green pepper, small dice	7 oz	1⅓ cups or 1 large
garlic, minced	¾ oz	6 small cloves
ham hocks, washed	1 lb	2 each
white wine, dry	4 oz	½ cup
red wine vinegar	1 oz	2 tablespoons
bay leaves		3 each
black pepper		½ teaspoon
cumin		1 teaspoon
oregano		1 teaspoon
paprika		1 teaspoon
salt	½ oz	2 teaspoons
rice, cooked	1 lb, 2 oz	

GARNISH:

sour cream

green onions, sliced

1. Pick through beans to remove any debris, then wash them. Place beans in pot, cover with water (at least 1 inch above beans), refrigerate, and soak overnight.

2. Add water, if necessary, to cover beans. Heat olive oil in pan over medium heat; add onion, green pepper, garlic, and ham hocks. Sauté until vegetables become soft and ham hocks brown.

3. Add vegetables and ham hocks to beans; add wine, vinegar, bay leaves, pepper, cumin, oregano, and paprika. Bring to boil, reduce heat, and simmer 1½ to 2 hours, until beans are tender. Add salt.

4. Remove ham hocks from soup, remove meat from bones, cut into bite-sized pieces, and return meat to beans. Discard bones.

5. With slotted spoon, remove about 10 oz (about 1 cup) beans from pot, mash them, and return to soup for thicker consistency. Correct seasonings.

6. Heat thoroughly. Place 2 oz rice in each bowl, top with bean soup, and garnish with sour cream and green onions. Serve.

MEXICAN TOMATO SOUP

NUMBER OF SERVINGS: 12
COOKING METHOD:
  Boil
SERVING SIZE:
  8 oz
TOTAL YIELD:
  6 lbs, 5½ oz

Mexican Tomato Soup
photo courtesy of the Florida Tomato
Committee

INGREDIENTS	WEIGHT	VOLUME
oil	1 oz	2 tablespoons
onion, medium dice	6 oz	1¼ cups
garlic, minced	¾ oz	5 cloves
red pepper, medium dice	6 oz	1¼ cups
kidney beans, red, cooked	15½ oz	1²/3 cups or 1 each 15½-oz can
tomatoes, medium dice	1 lb, 1½ oz	2 cups
chicken or vegetable stock	2 lbs	1 qt or 4 cups
tomato paste	3 oz	¼ cup + 1 tablespoon or 5 tablespoons
corn	8 oz	2 cups
ancho chili, seeded, sliced ¹/16-inch thick	¼ oz	1 each
chili powder	¼ oz	1 teaspoon
cumin		1 teaspoon
oregano		1 teaspoon
salt	¼ oz	1 teaspoon
pepper		¼ teaspoon
tomatillos, husks removed, medium dice	6 oz	6 each
GARNISH:		
sour cream		
cheese, cheddar or jack, grated	3 oz	½ cup
cilantro, minced		

1. Heat oil in large pot over medium heat. Sauté onion, garlic, and red pepper until tender.

2. Purée beans and tomatoes in food processor; add to sautéed mixture.

3. Add stock, tomato paste, corn, ancho chili, chili powder, cumin, oregano, salt, and pepper. Simmer for about 35 to 40 minutes.

4. Add tomatillos; simmer another 10 minutes. Correct seasonings.

5. Serve, garnished with dollop of sour cream, ¼ oz (2 teaspoons) cheese, and sprinkling of cilantro.

THAI CUCUMBER SALAD

Thai Cucumber Salad

Allow at least two hours to marinate the cucumbers. Chill salad plates before plating.

NUMBER OF SERVINGS: 11
COOKING METHOD:
  Boil
SERVING SIZE:
  4 oz
TOTAL YIELD:
  2 lbs, 13 oz

INGREDIENTS	WEIGHT	VOLUME
sugar	1¹/₂ oz	3 tablespoons
salt	¹/₂ oz	2 teaspoons
vinegar, rice or white	4 oz	¹/₂ cup
white pepper		¹/₄ teaspoon
cucumber	2 lbs, 10 oz	4 each
red onion, thinly sliced	8¹/₂ oz	1 each
red pepper, seeds and membrane removed, julienne	4¹/₂ oz	1 medium

GARNISH:

lettuce leaves

cilantro, minced

1. Combine sugar, salt, vinegar, and pepper in nonreactive pan; heat until dissolved. Cool to room temperature.

2. Peel and remove seeds from cucumbers. Cut into julienne.

3. Place cucumber, onion, and red pepper in nonreactive bowl; add cooled marinade. Toss gently. Cover and refrigerate for 2 to 4 hours.

4. Correct seasonings. Arrange lettuce leaves on chilled salad plate. Top with 4 oz cucumber mixture. Drizzle with extra marinade, if desired. Garnish with sprinkling of cilantro. Serve.

GREEK SALAD

Greek Salad

Chill plates for salad in advance.

NUMBER OF SERVINGS: 8
SERVING SIZE:
  ¾ oz (1½ tablespoons)
    dressing
  8 oz salad
TOTAL YIELD:
  6½ oz dressing
    4 lbs salad

INGREDIENTS	WEIGHT	VOLUME
DRESSING:		
olive oil	4½ oz	½ cup + 1 tablespoon or 9 tablespoons
lemon juice, fresh	1½ oz	3 tablespoons
oregano	¼ oz	1 tablespoon
salt		½ teaspoon
pepper		¼ teaspoon
garlic, minced	¼ oz	2 cloves
SALAD:		
lettuce, romaine, torn into bite-sized pieces	15 oz	1 head
radish, sliced thinly	4 oz	about 6 each
cucumber, peeled, cut in half lengthwise, seeded, sliced ¼-inch thick	7 oz	1 small
green pepper, sliced	4 oz	½ each large
red onion, sliced thinly	3 oz	½ each large
tomatoes, cut into wedges	2 lb	2 large
green onions, sliced	2 oz	3 each
Greek olives	6¼ oz	1 cup
feta cheese, ½-inch cubes	8 oz	

For Dressing:

1. Whisk together oil, lemon juice, oregano, salt, pepper, and garlic. Correct seasonings.
2. Cover and refrigerate until needed.

For Salad:

1. Mix all salad ingredients together. Divide equally between 8 chilled plates, arranging salad ingredients attractively on each plate.
2. Drizzle ¾ oz (1½ tablespoons) salad dressing over each salad. Serve.

BIGOS
Polish Hunters Stew

Bigos

NUMBER OF SERVINGS: 10
COOKING METHOD:
  Braise
SERVING SIZE:
  8 oz
TOTAL YIELD:
  5 lbs, 4 oz

Wine Style: Medium- to full-bodied reds, Merlot, Pinot Noir, or red hybrid wines such as Chambourcin
Example: Chambourcin Reserve—Blue Sky Vineyard, Makanda, IL. This is a full-bodied dry red wine that is lightly oaked with hints of cherry, vanilla, and black currants.

INGREDIENTS	WEIGHT	VOLUME
bacon, cut into 1-inch pieces	6 oz	6 slices
onion, small dice	6³⁄4 oz	1¹⁄3 cups or 1 large
beef, boneless, trimmed, 1-inch cubes	12 oz	
pork, boneless, trimmed, 1-inch cubes	12 oz	
garlic, minced	¹⁄4 oz	1 large clove
kielbasa or other Polish sausage, cut into ¹⁄2-inch slices	12 oz	
cabbage, shredded	7 oz	2¹⁄2 cups or ¹⁄4 small head
mushrooms, fresh, washed, sliced	7 oz	2 cups
sauerkraut, drained	10 oz	2 cups
tomatoes, canned, cut in pieces	9 oz	1 cup
apple, peeled, cored, chopped	4³⁄4 oz	1 medium
bay leaf		1 each
paprika		1 teaspoon
beef stock	1 lb	2 cups
red wine	4 oz	¹⁄2 cup
salt		³⁄4 teaspoon
pepper		³⁄4 teaspoon

1. Place oven rack in middle of oven. Preheat oven to 325 degrees.
2. Cook bacon and onion in ovenproof pan over medium heat for 3 to 5 minutes.
3. Add beef and pork cubes; cook until browned.
4. Add remaining ingredients, stir to mix, cover, and bake for 2 hours. Meat should be very tender.
5. Remove bay leaf and correct seasonings. Serve immediately, accompanied by wide egg noodles, rice, or mashed potatoes, if desired.

LASAGNA

Pan of Lasagna

Piece of Lasagna

NUMBER OF SERVINGS: 12
COOKING METHOD:
   Sauté, Bake
SERVING SIZE:
   11 oz
TOTAL YIELD:
   8 lbs, 10½ oz

Wine Style: Light- to medium-bodied Pinot Grigio, Viognier, Rose, fruity reds, Sangiovese, or Pinot Noir
Example: Sangiovese, Alto Vineyards Dry Creek—Pedroncelli Winery and Vineyards, Geyserville, CA. This is a medium-bodied wine with cranberry and leather notes in the nose and on the palate.

INGREDIENTS	WEIGHT	VOLUME
lasagna noodles	12 oz	
olive oil	1 oz	2 tablespoons
onion, small dice	5 oz	1 cup
garlic, minced	¼ oz	2 cloves
ground beef	1 lb, 8 oz	
sweet Italian sausage, bulk	1 lb	
basil		1 tablespoon
oregano		1 tablespoon
bay leaf		1 each
salt	¼ oz	1 teaspoon
pepper		½ teaspoon
tomatoes, diced, fresh or canned	2 lb, 2 oz	1 qt or 4 cups
tomato paste	6 oz	1 each 6-oz can
sugar		1 teaspoon
red wine or water	6 oz	¾ cup
ricotta cheese	1 lb, 14 oz	
parsley, chopped	¼ oz	¼ cup
eggs, lightly beaten	3½ oz	2 each
Parmesan cheese, grated	1½ oz	½ cup
mozzarella cheese, shredded	12 oz	

1. Cook noodles in boiling water until *al dente*, cooked but still firm, about 10 minutes. Drain; coat lightly with olive oil.

2. In large pan over medium flame, heat remaining olive oil until hot. Add onion and garlic; sauté about 3 minutes.

3. Add ground beef and sausage; cook until no pink shows. Drain. Return pan to heat; add basil, oregano, bay leaf, salt, pepper, tomatoes, tomato paste, sugar, and wine. Cook for 15 to 20 minutes.

4. Meanwhile, combine ricotta, parsley, eggs, and Parmesan in bowl.

5. Preheat oven to 350 degrees. Coat bottom of 9- by 13-inch pan with thin layer of tomato/meat mixture.

6. Top with one-third of lasagna noodles, slightly overlapping noodles. Spread one-third of remaining meat mixture evenly over noodles. Spread half of ricotta cheese mixture over meat. Sprinkle with one-third of mozzarella.

7. Repeat procedure with another layer of overlapped noodles, meat, cheese, and mozzarella.

8. Top with remaining noodles, meat, and mozzarella.

9. Bake for 1 hour. Remove; let rest 15 or 20 minutes before cutting into portions. Serve.

LAMB VINDALOO

Lamb Vindaloo

Allot time to marinate the meat for 4 to 24 hours. The longer the meat marinates, the more flavor it will absorb from the seasoning paste.

NUMBER OF SERVINGS: 14
COOKING METHOD:
  Braise
SERVING SIZE:
  9 oz
TOTAL YIELD:
  8 lbs, 6 oz

Wine Style: Soft, fruity Pinot Blanc; Gewürztraminer; Chardonnay; rich, softer Merlots; Mourvedre; or Shiraz
Example: Mourvedre Ancient Vines—Cline Cellars, Sonoma, CA. This wine has dark plum, chocolate, eucalyptus, and exotic spice flavors.

INGREDIENTS	WEIGHT	VOLUME
paprika	3/4 oz	1 tablespoon + 1 teaspoon
cumin	1/2 oz	2 tablespoons
coriander, ground	1/2 oz	1 tablespoon + 1 teaspoon
cayenne		1/2 teaspoon
black pepper		1 teaspoon
turmeric	1/4 oz	2 teaspoons
mustard, ground	1/4 oz	2 teaspoons
cloves, ground		1 teaspoon
cinnamon		1 teaspoon
cardamom		1 teaspoon
cider vinegar	1 lb	2 cups
tamarind paste	5 1/2 oz	6 tablespoons
lamb, 3/4- to 1-inch cubes	4 lbs	
oil	1 1/2 oz	3 tablespoons
onion, thinly sliced	1 lb, 8 oz	4 large
garlic, minced	1 1/2 oz	8 cloves
ginger, minced	1/2 oz	1 tablespoon + 1 teaspoon
tomatoes, crushed	1 lb, 2 1/2 oz	2 cups
potatoes, peeled, 3/4-inch cubes	2 lbs	
water	1 lb	2 cups
GARNISH:		
cilantro, minced	1/2 oz	1/4 cup

1. Combine paprika, cumin, coriander, cayenne, black pepper, turmeric, mustard, cloves, cinnamon, cardamom, vinegar, and tamarind to form paste.

2. Rub lamb with paste; cover and marinate in refrigerator for 4 to 24 hours.

3. Heat oil in pan over medium heat; sauté onions 3 to 4 minutes. Add garlic and ginger; sauté until tender.

4. Add meat and marinade; sauté until brown. Add tomatoes, potatoes, and water. Bring to simmer, cover, and, stirring occasionally, cook for 30 to 40 minutes or until potatoes are done.

5. Correct seasonings. Serve, garnished with a sprinkling of cilantro.

JERK CHICKEN

Jerk Chicken
photo by Barnabas Kindersley © Dorling
Kindersley

Allow time to marinate the chicken for 4 hours or preferably overnight.

NUMBER OF SERVINGS: 8
COOKING METHOD:
    Bake, Grill
SERVING SIZE:
    about 9½ oz chicken
    (1 chicken breast) +
    2¼ oz marinade (¼ cup)
TOTAL YIELD:
    4 lbs, 12 oz chicken
    3 lbs, 9½ oz marinade
    (6½ cups)

Wine Style: Soft, fruity Gewürztraminer, Viognier, Rose, or Grenache
Example: Gewürztraminer—Glenora Wine Cellars, Dundee, NY. This wine has delicate floral and cinnamon spice aromas and flavors.

INGREDIENTS	WEIGHT	VOLUME
MARINADE:		
ginger, fresh, peeled, minced	1 oz	2 tablespoons
thyme	½ oz	2 tablespoons
allspice	½ oz	1 tablespoon
cinnamon	¼ oz	2 teaspoons
nutmeg	¼ oz	2 teaspoons
sage		2 teaspoons
cayenne	¼ oz	2 teaspoons
black pepper	¼ oz	2 teaspoons
salt	1½ oz	2 tablespoons
garlic, minced	½ oz	4 cloves
sugar	1 oz	2 tablespoons
olive oil	4 oz	½ cup
white vinegar	1 lb	2 cups
orange juice	10¾ oz	1⅓ cups
lime juice	4 oz	½ cup
soy sauce	4 oz	½ cup
onion, small dice	10 oz	2 cups or 2 medium
green onions, sliced	2½ oz	6 each
jalapeño, seeded, minced	1 oz	2 each
chicken breasts, bone-in, cut in half	6 lbs, 1 oz	4 whole

1. Combine ginger, thyme, allspice, cinnamon, nutmeg, sage, cayenne, black pepper, salt, garlic, and sugar in nonreactive bowl.

2. Whisk in olive oil, vinegar, orange juice, lime juice, and soy sauce. Add onion, green onions, and jalapeño. Mix well.

3. Place chicken in nonreactive baking dish. Pour 2 lbs, 7 oz (4½ cups) marinade over chicken, turn to coat, cover, and refrigerate at least 4 hours or overnight. Reserve 1 lb, 1¾ oz (2 cups) marinade for dipping sauce to accompany cooked chicken. Cover and store reserved marinade in refrigerator.

4. Preheat oven to 375 degrees. Bake chicken (still in marinade) for 30 minutes. Preheat grill.

5. Remove chicken from pan, place on grill, baste with marinade, and cook until chicken is done.

6. Serve chicken accompanied by heated reserved marinade (for dipping sauce).

LINGUINI WITH WHITE CLAM SAUCE

NUMBER OF SERVINGS: 12
COOKING METHOD:
  Boil, Braise
SERVING SIZE:
  4 oz clam sauce + 6 oz
  cooked linguini
TOTAL YIELD:
  3 lbs clam sauce

Wine Style: Light- to medium-bodied Riesling, Pinot Grigio, Sauvignon Blanc, mild Chardonnay, or light Sangiovese
Example: Pinot Grigio—Flora Springs Winery and Vineyards, St. Helena, CA. Rich and creamy, this Pinot Grigio has nicely balanced acids that smooth the sweetness to make it a clean and crisp wine.

Linguini with White Clam Sauce
photo courtesy of Poplis Paul Photography

INGREDIENTS	WEIGHT	VOLUME
linguini	2 lbs	
olive oil	8 oz	1 cup
garlic, minced	1¹/₂ oz	about 12 cloves
clams, minced with liquor	2 lbs, 7 oz	
white wine	4 oz	¹/₂ cup
oregano		2 teaspoons
salt		¹/₂ teaspoon
pepper		¹/₂ teaspoon
parsley, fresh, minced	2 oz	1 cup
GARNISH:		
clams, steamed	3 per serving	
parsley, minced		
Parmesan cheese		

1. Cook linguini *al dente*, until done but not soft. Rinse thoroughly with cold water; set aside until needed.

2. Heat olive oil in sauté pan over medium heat. Add garlic and cook until soft, being careful not to burn it.

3. Add clams and their liquor, wine, oregano, salt, and pepper. Heat thoroughly, about 2 minutes. Remove from heat; add parsley. Correct seasonings.

4. Heat linguini and place 6 oz into bowl; top with 4 oz sauce. Serve immediately, garnished with clams and parsley, accompanied by Parmesan cheese.

TOMATOES STUFFED WITH CORN, ZUCCHINI, AND ALMONDS

Tomatoes Stuffed with Corn, Zucchini, and Almonds

This recipe hails from South America.

NUMBER OF SERVINGS: 14
COOKING METHOD:
    Boil, Sauté, Bake
SERVING SIZE:
    1 each stuffed tomato
        Filling before cooking in
        each tomato: 1½ oz or 3
        tablespoons
TOTAL YIELD:
    14 each stuffed tomatoes
        Filling before cooking:
        1 lb, 5 oz

INGREDIENTS	WEIGHT	VOLUME
tomatoes	3 lbs, 8 oz	14 each
olive oil	½ oz	1 tablespoon
onion, small dice	5 oz	1 cup or 1 medium
zucchini, small dice	10 oz	2 cups or 2 medium
garlic, minced	½ oz	2 large cloves
corn	8½ oz	2 cups
almonds, chopped	3 oz	½ cup
jalapeño, seeds and ribs removed, minced	½ oz	1 each
salt		½ teaspoon
pepper		¼ teaspoon
cilantro, minced	¼ oz	2 tablespoons

1. Place tomatoes in boiling water for 30 seconds, remove from water, and remove skin when cool enough to handle. Using small spoon, remove core, pulp, and seeds. Be sure to leave thick shell, about ¼-inch. Preheat oven to 350 degrees.

2. Heat oil; sauté onion, zucchini, and garlic until softened, about 4 minutes.

3. Add corn, almonds, and jalapeño; heat another 2 minutes. Add salt, pepper, and cilantro; heat thoroughly.

4. Correct seasonings. Place 1½ oz (3 tablespoons) filling in each tomato, place on baking sheet, and bake for about 5 to 10 minutes, until thoroughly heated. Serve.

MUSHROOM GOULASH

This recipe comes from Eastern Europe.

NUMBER OF SERVINGS: 11
COOKING METHOD:
  Sauté
SERVING SIZE:
  4 oz
TOTAL YIELD:
  2 lbs, 12¾ oz

INGREDIENTS	WEIGHT	VOLUME
oil	1½ oz	3 tablespoons
onion, medium dice	5¾ oz	1 cup or 1 medium
green pepper, seeded, medium dice	5½ oz	1 cup or 1 medium
garlic, minced	¼ oz	2 cloves
mushrooms, button, washed, sliced thickly	12 oz	
mushrooms, wild, variety of choice, washed, sliced thickly	12 oz	
tomatoes, peeled, seeded, chopped	11½ oz	3 large
paprika	½ oz	2 tablespoons
salt	¼ oz	1 teaspoon
pepper		½ teaspoon
sour cream	2¼ oz	¼ cup

1. Heat oil in saucepan over medium-high heat; add onion and sauté for 3 to 4 minutes.

2. Add green pepper and garlic; sauté for 2 to 3 minutes. Add mushrooms; sauté for 2 to 3 minutes, until softened.

3. Add tomatoes; heat 2 to 3 minutes to heat thoroughly. Add paprika, salt, and pepper and cook another 3 to 4 minutes. Stir in sour cream.

4. Correct seasonings; serve.

POTATOES IN HORSERADISH CREAM SAUCE

Adding Horseradish to Cream Sauce

This recipe reflects its German heritage.

NUMBER OF SERVINGS: 10
COOKING METHOD:
  Bake
SERVING SIZE:
  5 oz
TOTAL YIELD:
  3 lbs, 6½ oz

Potatoes in Horseradish Cream Sauce

INGREDIENTS	WEIGHT	VOLUME
potatoes, variety of choice	2 lb, 1½ oz	about 8 medium
butter	1½ oz	3 tablespoons
onion, small dice	6¼ oz	1¼ cups or 1 large
flour, all purpose	¾ oz	3 tablespoons
milk, hot	1 lb, 4 oz	2½ cups
horseradish, ground	2 oz	3 tablespoons
salt	¼ oz	1 teaspoon
white pepper		½ teaspoon
GARNISH:		
paprika		
chives, minced		

1. Scrub potatoes. Cook in boiling water about 30 minutes, until tender. Cool until able to handle, then peel and slice into ¼-inch slices. Set aside until needed.

2. Melt butter in large pan over medium heat, add onion, and sauté until beginning to color, about 5 to 7 minutes.

3. Add flour; stir until blonde *roux*, just lightly colored. Slowly whisk in milk, whisking constantly and cooking until thickened.

4. Add horseradish, salt, and pepper. Add potatoes and heat thoroughly. Correct seasonings. Serve.

PORTUGUESE SWEET BREAD

COOKING METHOD:
   Bake
TOTAL YIELD: 4 lbs, ½ oz dough
   2 each 9-inch round loaves

Portuguese Sweet Bread

INGREDIENTS	WEIGHT	VOLUME
SPONGE:		
water, warm	**6 oz**	**3/4 cup**
sugar		**1 teaspoon**
yeast, dry, granulated	**1 oz**	**2 tablespoons**
flour, all purpose, unbleached	**2 3/4 oz**	**1/2 cup**
DOUGH:		
milk	**8 oz**	**1 cup**
butter	**4 oz**	**1/2 cup or 1 stick**
sugar	**5 3/4 oz**	**3/4 cup**
lemon zest, grated	**1/4 oz**	**2 teaspoons**
salt	**1/4 oz**	**1 teaspoon**
eggs, beaten	**5 oz**	**3 each**
flour, all purpose, unbleached	**1 lb, 15 1/4 oz to 2 lbs, 5 oz**	**6 to 7 cups**
EGG WASH:		
egg, beaten	**1 3/4 oz**	**1 each**

For Sponge:

1. Place water in large nonreactive bowl. Add sugar and yeast; stir with nonreactive spoon to dissolve.

2. Stir in flour. Cover and place in warm place to rise until mixture becomes bubbly, about 30 to 45 minutes.

For Dough:

1. Heat milk until warm; add butter, sugar, lemon zest, and salt. Stir until almost dissolved; cool to lukewarm.

2. Add eggs to milk and mix well. Stir milk mixture into sponge. Add flour, one cup at a time, until dough comes away from sides of bowl.

3. Remove from bowl. Knead until smooth, about 5 to 10 minutes, adding flour only as needed. Place in oiled bowl, cover with plastic wrap, and let rise in warm place until doubled, about 1½ hours. Meanwhile, pan-spray 2 each 9-inch round pans.

4. Punch dough down; divide into two equal pieces. Form each piece into coil or rope about 1¼ to 1½ inches in diameter. Starting in center of pan, coil rope of dough in circle to form snail shape. Press end under dough. Repeat with other piece of dough. Cover with plastic wrap and let rise until doubled, about 50 to 60 minutes. Meanwhile, preheat oven to 350 degrees.

5. Gently brush loaves with egg. Bake for about 30 minutes, until golden brown and loaves sound hollow when tapped on bottom. Cool completely on wire rack.

DOBOS TORTE

Dobos Torte
photo by Dave King © Dorling Kindersley

A traditional Hungarian pastry, Dobos torte consists of eight thin layers of cake sandwiched with chocolate buttercream, and the top layer is glazed with caramelized sugar. In this recipe, the torte is prepared as a rectangular cake, but many chefs bake round cake layers and prepare a round torte of 8 layers.

Instead of coating the top layer with caramelized sugar, some people decorate the Dobos torte by frosting all eight layers with a thin layer of buttercream, scoring the top into serving pieces, and decorating each slice with a piece of caramelized sugar. In this presentation traditionally the caramelized sugar is the same size as the top of the piece of torte and is positioned decoratively angled on top of the slice, propped up with a rosette of buttercream.

This recipe requires about 1 lb of buttercream, approximately 2 cups. Reserve remaining buttercream for another use; store in the refrigerator or freeze to preserve longer.

NUMBER OF SERVINGS: 8
COOKING METHOD:
  Bake, Boil
SERVING SIZE:
  2 each ¾-inch slices
TOTAL YIELD: 1 each 12- by
  4-inch torte
  Buttercream: 1 lb, 14¾ oz or
  4 cups
  Note: This recipe uses about
  half of the buttercream.

INGREDIENTS	WEIGHT	VOLUME
CAKE:		
flour, all purpose	1 oz	¼ cup
cornstarch	1 oz	3 tablespoons
eggs, separated	6¾ oz	4 each
salt		¼ teaspoon
sugar	2 oz	¼ cup
vanilla		1 teaspoon
CHOCOLATE BUTTERCREAM:		
cream of tartar		¼ teaspoon
water	2 oz	¼ cup + 1 teaspoon
sugar	7½ oz	1 cup
egg whites	3 oz	3 each
butter, unsalted, softened	8 oz	1 cup or 2 sticks
chocolate, semisweet, melted, cooled	15¾ oz	2½ cups
CARAMEL TOPPING:		
sugar	5¾ oz	¾ cup
water		1 teaspoon
lemon juice		1 teaspoon

For Cake:

1. Sift flour and cornstarch together in bowl. Set aside until needed. Line 2 each half-sheet pans (12 by 17 inches) with parchment paper. Grease well. Preheat oven to 350 degrees.

2. Beat egg whites and salt at medium speed with whisk attachment until foamy. Increase speed to high; whip until soft peaks. Slowly add sugar, a spoonful at a time, beating continuously until stiff peaks, about 4 to 5 minutes.

3. Meanwhile, whisk yolks and vanilla in large bowl by hand to combine. Stir in one-quarter of whites, then fold in rest of whites.

4. Sift half of flour mixture over eggs; fold in gently just to incorporate. Repeat with remaining flour mixture.

5. Divide batter between prepared pans; spread batter evenly. Place in oven and bake until lightly brown, about 10 to 15 minutes.

6. Remove from oven. Cut each cake into 4 each 12- by 4-inch pieces. Remove parchment paper; cool thoroughly.

For Buttercream:

1. Mix cream of tartar and 1 teaspoon water in small bowl; set aside until needed.

2. Place 5 oz (⅔ cup) sugar and 2 oz (¼ cup) water in small saucepan. Mix to combine.

3. Bring to boil, cover, and boil about one minute. Remove cover; wash down sides of pan with clean pastry brush dipped in cold water. Cook without stirring until thermometer registers 238 degrees.

4. Meanwhile, beat whites with whisk attachment if available, until soft peaks. Gradually beat in remaining 2½ oz (⅓ cup) sugar, a spoonful at a time, and continue beating until stiff peaks.

(Continued)

5. When sugar syrup reaches proper temperature, reduce mixer speed to low, and very slowly add syrup to egg whites, beating continually. After adding all sugar syrup, raise mixer to high speed and beat until room temperature.

6. Reduce speed to medium-low. Slowly add butter, a tablespoon at a time. Beat until fluffy.

7. Turn off mixer. Add three-quarters of chocolate; mix on low speed. Add remaining chocolate until desired color. Refrigerate while preparing caramel.

For Caramel:

1. Choose the most even and best-looking cake layer for top. Place cake layer on parchment paper and set aside until needed. Pan-spray serrated knife.

2. Combine sugar, water, and lemon juice in small saucepan. Mix to combine.

3. Bring to boil over medium-high heat. Do not stir, but swirl pan to mix sugar if it melts unevenly. Cook until medium brown, golden color.

4. Pour caramelized sugar evenly over cake layer, spreading if needed for smooth coating. With prepared knife, score into 16 each ¾-inch slices. Cut through excess caramel that overflowed cake layer for easy removal after caramel cools. Allow to cool.

To Assemble:

1. Reserve caramel-topped layer for later. Place one cake layer on serving plate or cardboard. Spread with thin layer of buttercream. Top with another cake layer, spread thinly with buttercream, and repeat with remaining five layers, ending with buttercream. If any cake layers break, piece them together.

2. Place caramel layer on top of buttercream to form top of cake. Frost sides of torte smoothly with buttercream.

3. Pipe decorative border around edge of torte where buttercream and caramel meet. If desired, apply more decoration to torte.

4. Refrigerate at least several hours. Remove from refrigerator to warm slightly before serving. Serve 2 each ¾-inch slices for each serving.

CHOCOLATE SOUFFLÉ

Wrapping Collar around
Soufflé Dish

photo by Jerry Young © Dorling Kindersley

Chocolate Soufflé
photo by David Murray © Dorling Kindersley

To allow the needed time to prepare soufflés, servers should take soufflé orders at the beginning of service. For an easy restaurant preparation, prepare cornstarch base ahead of time, and continue preparation at time of ordering.

Many cooks and chefs use smaller ramekins to bake individual soufflés or soufflés to serve two. Immediately before service, dust the hot soufflé in the ramekin with confectioners' sugar and place the hot ramekin on a larger plate. Reduce cooking time if preparing smaller ramekins.

Serve soufflés immediately because they begin deflating within a few minutes!

NUMBER OF SERVINGS: 12
COOKING METHOD:
Boil, Bake
SERVING SIZE:
⅙ of soufflé dish
TOTAL YIELD:
2 each 1½- to 2-quart
soufflé dishes

INGREDIENTS	WEIGHT	VOLUME
chocolate, bittersweet or semisweet, coarsely chopped	7 oz	1 cup
coffee, strong	2 oz	¼ cup
cornstarch	1½ oz	¼ cup + 1 tablespoon or 5 tablespoons
milk	12 oz	1½ cups
sugar	7½ oz	1 cup
butter, unsalted	1 oz	2 tablespoons
egg yolks	4 oz	6 each
brandy or liqueur of choice	2 oz	¼ cup
egg whites	10 oz	10 each
confectioners' sugar, for dusting		

1. Butter 2 each 1½- or 2-quart soufflé dishes. Coat lightly with granulated sugar: place some sugar in dish, then shake and roll dish to distribute sugar. Place collar of parchment paper or aluminum foil (with shiny side turned toward inside of dish) around upper rim of bowl to extend top of bowl about 2 or 3 inches. If needed, stabilize by tying with kitchen string. Pan-spray inside of collar. Place oven rack in center of oven and preheat to 375 degrees.

2. Melt chocolate and coffee over gently simmering water or in microwave at half power until melted. Set aside until needed.

3. Mix cornstarch with about 2¾ oz (⅓ cup) cold milk until smooth. Place in saucepan with remaining milk and about 6 oz (¾ cup) sugar. Whisking constantly, bring to boil, then remove from heat. Dot top with butter and set aside to cool.

4. When almost room temperature, thoroughly whisk in melted chocolate, egg yolks, and brandy. Whisk until smooth.

5. Beat egg whites until frothy. Turn mixer to high and continue beating, adding remaining sugar, one teaspoon at a time. Continue beating until egg whites are stiff.

6. Stir about ⅛ of whites into chocolate mixture. Gently fold in half of remaining whites; repeat with remaining whites.

7. Divide between prepared dishes. Bake for 40 to 45 minutes, until knife inserted into soufflé comes out almost clean.

8. Dust with confectioners' sugar; serve immediately.

GLOSSARY

a'u—marlin in Hawaiian

adobo—marinade for meats brought to Florida by the Cubans. In Spain, this marinade consisted of salt and vinegar. Adapting the marinade to their taste, Cubans changed the mixture to salt, garlic, cumin, oregano, and sour orange juice.

ahi—yellowfin tuna in Hawaiian

alcoporado—Spanish dish consisting of beef stew containing raisins, olives, and spicy flavorings

alluvial—rich, fertile land deposited around rivers as a result of flooding; excellent soil for crops

applejack—apple brandy

aquavit—clear liquor made from potatoes or grain flavored with caraway seeds; served in Scandinavia

arepas—corn cakes from South America

arroz con carne—island dish of rice with meat

arrozo con pollo—island dish of rice with chicken

ashcake—disk of cornmeal baked in the ashes of the fire

atole—cornmeal porridge; a traditional New Mexican dish

bagels—bread shaped like a doughnut; prepared by boiling the bread and then baking it

baked Alaska—originally called Alaska-Florida, the baked Alaska contains a core of ice cream placed on a foundation of cake, and then covered with meringue. The cake and meringue insulate the ice cream while the meringue quickly cooks in a very hot oven. Created at Delmonico's Restaurant in New York City, the baked Alaska was first served to celebrate the purchase of Alaska.

barbacoa—Spanish word that became the word *barbecue,* meaning cooked over an open fire

bayou—swamps found in Louisiana

beignets—deep-fried pieces of bread dough, dusted with a thick coating of confectioners' sugar before serving

benne—sesame seeds

bigos—stew containing a variety of meats and sauerkraut, originating in Poland

blintzes—cheese-filled crepês

boliche—eye of beef stuffed with Cuban sausage or ham, green pepper, onions, pimento-stuffed olives, and flavored with lime juice and cumin

bollitos—black-eyed pea fritters from the Islands

booyaw—stew made of any game available, salt pork, onions, potatoes, and carrots, commonly served in the numerous forested areas of Michigan. The name derived from the French Canadian word *bouillon.*

brackish water—a mixture of fresh and salt water

broma process—process that allows the cocoa butter to drip from warm chocolate; this resulted in separating the cocoa powder or residue from the fat, leaving the basis for ground chocolate; invented at Ghiradelli Chocolates in San Francisco

burgoo—a stew or thick soup containing a variety of meats, originally including squirrel, pork, beef, possum, chicken, or anything available in addition to vegetables and seasonings; a specialty of Kentucky

café brûlot—hot coffee drink containing strong coffee flavored with brandy, orange liqueur, and sugar

calabacitas—dish featuring sautéed zucchini, usually corn, flavorings, and/or other ingredients

carambola—a tropical fruit also known as star fruit because of its star-shaped cross section when cut

cassoulet—casserole of beans, various meats, and sausages; originated in France

chicken à la king—creamed chicken and vegetables served over toast points; created and served at Delmonico's Restaurant in New York City

chicos—whole dried corn kernels

chili rellenos—poblano peppers stuffed with cheese or meat, battered, and deep-fried

Chinatown—a neighborhood of Asian immigrants within a city; usually found in large cities

chinook—king salmon

chitterlings—pork intestines, part of "soul food" cookery

chop suey—stir-fried dish invented in America; the phrase means "miscellaneous pieces" in Cantonese

chorizo—spicy sausage of Spanish origin

cioppino—seafood soup or stew similar to French *bouillabaisse* consisting of a variety of fish and shellfish in a flavorful fish broth containing tomato, garlic, olive oil, and wine; named after *ciuppin,* a fish stew served in Genoa, Italy

cookie—nickname for the cook who prepared all the meals while traveling with the cowboys herding cattle on the trail

corn pone—bread made from cornmeal, baked in the fire but not covered with ashes

corned beef—cured spiced beef

crackling—pigs' skin fried until crisp; appears extensively in "soul food"

Dutch oven—a cast iron kettle with a lid and with or without three legs to elevate it from the embers of the fire; used by early settlers and cowboys for cooking and baking in an open fire

eggs Benedict—English muffins topped with Canadian bacon, poached eggs, and Hollandaise sauce; created and served at Delmonico's Restaurant in New York City

en papillote—literally "in an envelope," this cooking technique involves tightly enclosing the food in parchment paper or other wrapper, which steams the contents inside the parchment envelope

escabeche—preserving technique of pickling cooked foods in an acid mixture flavored with herbs and spices; often used in early days in the Southwest to prevent cooked meat or fish from spoiling

estuary—partially enclosed body of water that forms when fresh water sources meet with salt water

étouffée—literally means "smothered"; the dish begins with sautéing the "holy trinity" of vegetables—onion, celery, and green pepper—in a *roux* with shrimp or crayfish

filé powder—spice made from the ground leaves of the sassafras tree; frequently appears in Cajun cooking; first used by the Choctaw Indians; flavors as well as thickens the dish

foie gras—the enlarged liver from goose or duck; to enlarge the liver, the birds are fed large amounts of food

furkee—Indian word for turkey

gefilte fish—a fish dumpling

geoduck—type of clam that can grow as large as nine pounds; however, most are harvested at two pounds; usually finely chopped and used in chowder or hash

grillades—braised round steak similar to Swiss steak; usually served at breakfast and accompanied by grits

grits—ground dried hominy cooked like a cereal; accompanies eggs and sausage or bacon as a breakfast staple

guacamole—avocado dip from Mexican influence

gumbo—from the West African word for okra, *guingombo*, this soup/stew begins with a *roux*, then incorporates seafood, pork, chicken, or whatever is available, thick-

ened with either okra (African) or filé powder (Choctaw Indians) added at the end, and served with rice

gumbo z'herbes—meatless version of gumbo containing seven greens and no meat; often served during Lent

hapu'upu'u—black sea bass in Hawaiian

hardtack—mixture of flour and water that served as an indestructible, hard bread; used on long voyages across land or sea because it did not spoil

hasty pudding—cornmeal mush resembling English porridge topped with butter and maple syrup; often served for breakfast in colonial times

haupia—coconut pudding popular in Hawaii

headcheese—sausage made from all the remaining meat on the head of the pig or cow

hominy—corn product made by Native Americans by boiling corn with wood ashes until it swelled; the settlers made hominy by soaking corn in a lye solution, then removing it from the hulls, washing it, and boiling it until tender

hornos—dome-shaped ovens made of stone and adobe

huevos rancheros—breakfast dish consisting of a tortilla topped with fried eggs, covered with salsa, and accompanied by beans on the side

Huguenots—French Protestants; many immigrated to the New World in search of religious freedom

hush puppies—deep-fried balls of cornmeal mixed with onion; commonly served with fried fish

hutspot— meaning hodgepodge, a hearty Dutch stew made in colonial America containing cornmeal porridge, corned beef, and winter vegetables from the root cellar

Inuit—early group of people who migrated to North America, inhabited Alaska, and stayed in the cold northern areas near the Arctic Circle; known as Eskimos

jambalaya—name from the Spanish and French words for ham; dish resembles the Spanish dish *paella*. Jambalaya combines rice and seasonings with all sorts of meats, poultry, and/or seafood.

jerky—dried and salted preserved meat; prepared in the Plains states by Native Americans using buffalo

kajiki—Pacific blue marlin in Hawaiian

kasha—buckwheat groats common in Russia and Eastern Europe

kashrut—Jewish dietary laws, kosher

kielbasa—Polish sausage

kim chee—fermented cabbage commonly served in Korea

knishes—potato or meat-filled potato pastry

kolache—sweet yeast rolls filled with apricot, prune, poppy seeds, or cheese filling; similar to Danish pastry, but made with less butter

koolslaa—the Dutch word for coleslaw; this salad consisted of shredded cabbage and a dressing; often prepared in the winter months since cabbage stored well in a root cellar

kugel—noodle or potato pudding

latkes—potato pancakes

lefse—Norwegian traditional thin potato pancake made from mashed potatoes

lilikoi—Hawaiian word for passion fruit

limpa rye bread—aromatic bread of Scandinavian heritage containing rye flour, caraway, anise, and fennel

linguica—Portuguese spicy sausages

lobster Newburg—a rich mixture of lobster, cream, sherry, and eggs; created and served at Delmonico's Restaurant in New York City

lomi lomi salmon—a salted salmon dish from Hawaii containing raw salmon mixed with onions and tomatoes, served at luaus; *lomi* is Hawaiian word meaning "to work with fingers"

lox—smoked salmon

luau—a feast with many dishes, singing, and dancing, celebrated in Hawaii with a central dish of whole, stuffed pig cooked in a pit lined with ti or banana leaves

lutefisk—dried, salted cod treated with lye; became an intrinsic part of Christmas dinner and church suppers in the fall in Scandinavian communities

mahi-mahi—dolphinfish in Hawaiian

masa—ground hominy; used in preparation of tortillas

mesas—flat-topped hills

mincemeat—mixture made of meat, sugar, raisins, citron, suet, and any preferred dried fruits, candied fruit rinds, and spices; generally used as a filling for pie; stored well in a crock in a cool place like the root cellar

miso—soybean paste; common in Japanese cookery; available in places where many Japanese immigrants live

New England boiled dinner—one-pot dish consisting of corned beef boiled with an assortment of winter vegetables including cabbage, carrots, potatoes, and/or beets and parsnips

oenology—study of wines

olykoeks—oil cakes, prepared by the Dutch settlers in New York by dropping rolled balls of dough, "dough nuts," into hot fat. In the late 1700s, they shaped the dough into a circle and removed the center (creating a hole) to expedite the cooking, resulting in the modern doughnut.

ono—king mackerel in Hawaiian, also known as *wahoo*

opah—moonfish in Hawaiian

opakapaka—Hawaiian for pink snapper

oreilles de cochon—fried dough dipped in sugar syrup, served throughout the countryside in Louisiana; literally means pigs' ears

parve—foods categorized as neutral under Jewish dietary laws; neither milk nor meat foods

pearlash—a form of potash discovered as a leavening agent in the late 1700s; replaced by baking powder in the mid-1800s

pemmican—dried and salted meat mixed with fat and berries and placed in an animal casing, prepared from buffalo or venison by Native Americans in many regions, but made from salmon in the Northwest; a staple food for the winter months

pepitas—raw, unsalted, hulled pumpkin seeds; used as a snack, garnish, or part of a dish

pepper sauce—pickled peppers preserved with salt and vinegar; type of peppers, amount of aging time, and type of container used in aging create differences in the flavor of the sauce

phylloxera—a disease that kills grapevines by attacking their roots

picante—"hot" in terms of spice, not temperature

pierogi—Polish turnover filled with meat, cottage cheese, mushroom, potato, or sauerkraut

pine nuts—nuts harvested from cones from pine trees; also called pignoli or piñons

pogroms—organized persecution of an ethnic group

poi—starchy paste made from pounded taro root; staple starch for many native Hawaiians

poke—Hawaiian word for "cut up"; dish containing raw fish; consists of cubes or slices of fresh raw fish mixed with salt, nuts, and seaweed

posole—dried whole corn kernels treated with slaked lime to remove the husks; soup or stew containing hominy (*posole*), pork, and chili peppers

prairie schooner—covered wagon used by westbound settlers to protect their belongings

pralines—cloyingly sweet candy containing pecans and brown sugar; some versions add cream; derived from European version of praline, which consists of almonds and white sugar

pueblos—communities where Native Americans live throughout the Southwest; they often contain adobe houses and/or buildings as well as *hornos*

pupu platter—platter featuring an assortment of hors d'oeuvres; starts many festive meals in Hawaii

quesadillas—tortillas filled with cheese or other items, folded in half, and then fried

red flannel hash—dish made from chopping and frying leftover New England boiled dinner; red color of the dish came from the color of the beets

red-eyed gravy—popular sauce with country ham, prepared by adding coffee (or water) to the pan where the ham was fried and then reducing the liquid

Reuben—sautéed sandwich filled with corned beef, sauerkraut, Swiss cheese, and Thousand Island dressing

rivels—dough made from flour and eggs, resembling German *spaetzel,* which is a cross between a noodle and a dumpling

rømmegrøt—Norwegian porridge

roux—basis for a thickening made by sautéing equal parts of fat and flour; from French cookery; cooked to different colors from white to brown depending on desired flavor and color outcome

rumaki—chicken livers wrapped with bacon; Japanese hors d'oeuvre

saimin—Japanese noodle soup served frequently in Hawaii

salsa—uncooked condiment usually containing tomatoes and/or *tomatillos*, peppers, and herbs

samp—porridge prepared from cornmeal

sashimi—raw fish commonly eaten in Japan and places with many Japanese immigrants

Sauerbraten—marinated beef in a sweet and sour sauce; German dish

sauerkraut dumplings—dumplings cooked in sauerkraut

Schnitz un knepp—Pennsylvania Dutch dish consisting of smoked ham boiled with dried apples and topped with dumplings

scrod—young cod weighing less than two pounds

shoyu—soy sauce; common in Japanese cookery and places with many Japanese immigrants

sopaipillas—deep-fried dough that puffs into golden brown, air-filled pockets when fried; served in the Southwest

sourdough starter—a combination of wild yeasts collected from the air, which makes bread and other baked goods

rise and imparts a pleasantly sour, tangy, distinctive taste to breads, biscuits, and pancakes

souvlaki—Greek preparation of marinated lamb or chicken; usually served in pita bread and accompanied by sour cream, garlic, and mint sauce

Spätzel—a cross between a noodle and a dumpling; prepared in Germany

spider—a pan with three legs, which elevated it above the embers in the hearth

spoonbread—loose cornbread resembling a soufflé, eaten with a spoon; developed from porridge made from corn that the Native Americans ate; still served in the South

stir-frying—cooking small, evenly chopped foods over high heat; cooking technique commonly used in China and throughout much of Asia

tasso—spicy, smoked ham; Cajun specialty used to flavor many dishes

tempura—deep-fried fish, seafood, and/or vegetables coated with a light batter; from Japan

terrior—French word that refers to the soil, temperature, and climate of an area and how they affect the growing grapes and ultimately the wine

Tex-Mex cookery—a variation of Mexican cooking prepared in Texas; incorporates more meat and cheese into the dishes than Mexican cookery

tofu—soybean curd; commonly used in Japanese cookery

tourtiére—savory pie prepared by French Canadians

tundra—cold land with a grassy covering but no trees, found in northern Alaska and other areas with frigid weather

uku—Hawaiian for gray snapper

ulua—pompano in Hawaiian

veal *paprikash*—Hungarian dish featuring veal in a sauce containing paprika

viticulture—the art of making wine

wahoo—Hawaiian name for king mackerel, also known as *ono*

Wiener schnitzel—breaded and fried veal cutlet served in Germany

wurst—German word for sausages

BIBLIOGRAPHY

Adams, Jane, and Stewart, Jillian. *America and Its Cuisine*. New York: Mallard Press, 1990.

Adams, Marcia. *Cooking from Quilt Country: Hearty Recipes from Amish and Mennonite Kitchens*. New York: Clarkson N. Potter, 1989.

Adams, Marcia. *Heartland: The Best of the Old and New from Midwest Kitchens*. New York: Clarkson N. Potter, 1991.

Adams, Marcia. *New Recipes from Quilt Country: More Food & Folkways from the Amish & Mennonites*. New York: Clarkson N. Potter, 1997.

Anderson, Jean. *American Century Cookbook: The Most Popular Recipes of the 20th Century*. New York: Clarkson Potter Publishers, 1997.

Anderson, Jean. *The Grass Roots Cookbook*. New York: Times Books, 1977.

Andrews, Glenn. *Food from the Heartland: The Cooking of America's Midwest*. New York: Prentice Hall Press, 1991.

Arkell, Julie. *New World Wines: The Complete Guide*. London: Ward Lock, 1999.

Armstrong, Charlotte. *Charlotte's Table: Down Home Cooking from an Uptown Girl*. Hopewell, NJ: The Ecco Press, 1998.

Ash, John, and Goldstein, Sid. *American Game Cooking: A Contemporary Guide to Preparing Farm-Raised Game Birds and Meat*. Reading, MA: Aris Books, 1991.

Atkinson, Leland. *¡Cocina!: A Hands-on Guide to the Techniques of Southwestern Cooking*. Berkley, California: Ten Speed Press, 1996.

Balsey, Betsy, and the Food Staff of the Los Angeles Times. *The Los Angeles Times California Cookbook*. New York: Harry N. Abrams, 1981.

Bartlett, Virginia K. *Pickles and Pretzels: Pennsylvania's World of Food*. Pittsburgh, PA: University of Pittsburgh Press, 1980.

Bauer, Michael. *The Secrets of Success Cookbook: Signature Recipes and Insider Tips from San Francisco's Best Restaurants*. San Francisco: Chronicle Books, 2000.

Bauer, Michael, and Irwin, Fran. *The San Francisco Chronicle Cookbook*. San Francisco: Chronicle Books, 1997.

Bauer, Michael, and Irwin, Fran. *The San Francisco Chronicle Cookbook, Volume II*. San Francisco: Chronicle Books, 2001.

Beard, James. *James Beard's American Cookery*. Boston: Little, Brown & Company, 1972.

Berolzheimer, Ruth. *The United States Regional Cookbook*. USA: Halcyon House, 1947.

Bertolli, Paul, with Waters, Alice. *Chez Panisse Cooking*. New York: Random House, 1988.

Better Homes and Gardens Books. *Cajun Cooking*. Des Moines, IA: Meredith Corporation, 1987.

Birkby, Evelyn. *Up a Country Lane Cookbook*. Iowa City, IA: University of Iowa Press, 1993.

Blue, Anthony Dias. *American Wine: A Comprehensive Guide, Revised Edition*. New York: Harper & Row, 1988.

Bone, Eugenia. *At Mesa's Edge: Cooking and Ranching in Colorado's North Fork Valley*. New York: Houghton Mifflin, 2004.

Borghese, Anita. *Foods from Harvest Festivals and Folk Fairs*. New York: Thomas Y. Crowell, 1977.

Brack, Fred, and Bell, Tina. *Tastes of the Pacific Northwest: Traditional & Innovative Recipes from America's Newest Regional Cuisine*. New York: Doubleday, 1988.

Brennan, Ella, and Brennan, Dick. *The Commander's Palace New Orleans Cookbook*. New York: Clarkson Potter, 1984.

Brown, Dale, and the Editors of Time-Life Books. *American Cooking*. Alexandria, Virginia: Time-Life Books, 1968.

Brown, Sandy, and Young, Joyce LaFray. *Famous Florida! Restaurants & Recipes*. Altamonte Springs, FL: Winner Enterprises, 1988.

Bullock, Helen Duprey. *A National Treasury of Cookery: Recipes of the Westward Empire*. New York: Heirloom Publishing Company, 1967.

Butel, Jane. *Jane Butel's Tex-Mex Cookbook*. New York: Crown Publishers, 1980.

Callahan, Genevieve. *The California Cook Book*. New York: M. Barrows & Company, 1946.

Casey, Clyde. *New Mexico Cooking: Southwestern Flavors of the Past and Present*. Tucson, AZ: Fisher Books, 1994.

Casey, Kathy. *Pacific Northwest: The Beautiful Cookbook*. San Francisco: Collins Publishers, 1993.

Chavich, Cinda. *The Wild West Cookbook*. Toronto: Robert Rose, 1998.

Chiarello, Michael, and Fletcher, Janet Kessel. *Michael Chiarello's Casual Cooking Wine Country Recipes for Family and Friends—A Napastyle Cookbook*. San Francisco: Chronicle Books, 2002.

Chroman, Nathan. *The Treasury of American Wines*. New York: Rutledge–Crown Publishers, 1976.

Claiborne, Craig. *Craig Claiborne's Southern Cooking*. United States: Times Books, 1987.

Clayton, Bernard, Jr. *Bernard Clayton's Cooking Across America*. New York: Simon & Schuster, 1993.

Corum, Ann Kondo. *Ethnic Foods of Hawaii*. Honolulu: The Bess Press, 1983.

Cox, Beverly, and Jacobs, Martin. *Spirit of the Harvest: North American Indian Cooking*. New York: Stewart, Tabori & Chang, 1991.

Cox, Beverly, and Jacobs, Martin. *Spirit of the West: Cooking from Ranch House and Range*. New York: Artisan, 1996.

Culinary Arts Institute. *The Creole Cookbook*. Chicago: Book Production Industries, 1955.

D'Amico, Joan, and Drummond, Karen Eich. *The United States Cookbook: Fabulous Foods and Fascinating Facts from All 50 States*. New York: John Wiley & Sons, 2000.

Danforth, Randi, Feierabend, Peter, and Chassman, Gary. *Culinaria The United States: A Culinary Discovery*. New York: Konemann Publishers USA, 1998.

Davis, Frank. *Frank Davis Cooks Cajun, Creole, and Crescent City*. Gretna, LA: Pelican Publishing Company, 1994.

DeCherney, Nancy, DeCherney, John, Marshall, Deborah, and Brook, Susan. *The Fiddlehead Cookbook: Recipes from Alaska's Most Celebrated Restaurant and Bakery*. New York: St. Martin's Press, 1991.

DeMers, John. *Arnaud's Creole Cookbook*. New York: Simon & Schuster, 1988.

Dent, Huntley. *The Feast of Santa Fe*. New York: Simon & Schuster, 1985.

Dille, Carolyn, and Belsinger, Susan. *New Southwestern Cooking*. New York: Macmillan, 1985.

Doerper, John. *Eating Well: A Guide to Foods of the Pacific Northwest*. Seattle, WA: Pacific Search Press, 1984.

Dooley, Beth, and Watson, Lucia. *Savoring the Seasons of the Northern Heartland*. New York: Alfred A. Knopf, 1994.

Doré, Eula Mae, and Bienvenu, Marcelle R. *Eula Mae's Cajun Kitchen: Cooking Through the Seasons on Avery Island*. Boston: The Harvard Common Press, 2002.

Douglas, Tom, and Cross, Jackie. *Tom's Big Dinners: Big-Time Home Cooking for Family and Friends*. New York: HarperCollins, 2003.

Edge, John T. *A Gracious Plenty: Recipes and Recollections from the American South*. New York: G.P. Putnam's Sons, 1999.

Editors at Betty Crocker. *Betty Crocker's Southwest Cooking*. New York: Prentice Hall, 1989.

Editors of *American Heritage, the Magazine of History*. *The American Heritage Cookbook and Illustrated History of American Eating & Drinking*. New York: American Heritage Publishing Co., 1964.

Editors of Better Homes and Gardens Books. *Better Homes and Gardens Heritage Cook Book*. Des Moines, IA: Meredith Corporation, 1975.

Editors of Better Homes and Gardens Books. *75 Years of All-Time Favorites*. Des Moines, IA: Better Homes and Gardens Books, 1997.

Editors of *Cook's Illustrated*. *The Best Recipe: American Classics*. Brookline, MA: Boston Common Press, 2002.

Editors of Midwest Living Magazine. *Favorite Recipes from Great Midwestern Cooks*. Des Moines, IA: Meredith Corporation, 1992.

Editors of Saveur Magazine. *Saveur Cooks Authentic American*. San Francisco: Chronicle Books, 1998.

Editors of Time-Life Books. *Country Cooking: American Country*. Richmond, VA: Time-Life Books, 1989.

Elsah Landing Restaurant, Inc. *Elsah Landing Heartland Cooking*. St. Louis, MO: Sayers Communications Group, 1984.

Emmerling, Mary. *Mary Emmerling's American Country Cooking*. New York: Clarkson N. Potter, 1987.

Farmer, Fannie Merritt. *The Boston Cooking School Cookbook, Seventh Edition*. Boston: Little, Brown and Company, 1943.

Farmer, Fannie. *The Fannie Farmer Cookbook*. New York: Alfred A. Knopf, 1986.

Feibleman, Peter S., and the Editors of Time-Life Books. *American Cooking: Creole and Acadian*. New York: Time-Life Books, 1971.

Feibleman, Peter S., and the Editors of Time-Life Books. *Recipes American Cooking: Creole and Acadian*. New York: Time-Life Books, 1971.

Fertig, Judith M. *Prairie Home Cooking: 400 Recipes that Celebrate the Bountiful Harvests, Creative Cooks, and Comforting Foods of the American Heartland*. Boston: The Harvard Common Press, 1999.

Fichter, George S. *The Florida Cookbook*. Miami, FL: E. A. Seemann Publishing, 1973.

Flavor of New England. New York: Mallard Press. 1989.

Fobel, Jim. *Jim Fobel's Old-Fashioned Baking Book*. New York: Ballantine Books, 1987.

Folse, John D. *The Encyclopedia of Cajun & Creole Cuisine*. Donaldsonville, LA: The Encyclopedia Cookbook Committee, 1983.

Food Editors of Farm Journal. *Farm Journal's Homemade Breads*. New York: Galahad Books, 1985.

Fowler, Damon Lee. *Classical Southern Cooking: A Celebration of the Cuisine of the Old South*. New York: Crown Publishers, 1995.

Fussell, Betty. *I Hear America Cooking*. New York: Viking Penguin, 1986.

Gannon, Beverly, and Friedman, Bonnie. *The Hali'imaile General Store Cookbook: Home Cooking from Maui*. Berkeley, CA: Ten Speed Press, 2000.

Good, Phyllis Pellman. *The Best of Amish Cooking*. Intercourse, PA: Good Books, 2001.

Good, Phyllis Pellman, and Pellman, Rachel Thomas. *Amish and Mennonite Kitchens*. Intercourse, PA: Good Books, 1984.

Greenwald, Michelle. *The Magical Melting Pot: The All-Family Cookbook that Celebrates America's Diversity*. California: Cherry Press, 2003.

Haber, Barbara. *From Hardtack to Home Fries: An Uncommon History of American Cooks and Meals*. New York: The Free Press, 2002.

Hampton, Bob. *Jamba Maya: Marrying the Cuisines of Louisiana and Mexico*. Roswell, GA: Hampton Publishers, 1990.

Hechtlinger, Adelaide. *The Seasonal Hearth: The Woman at Home in Early America*. Woodstock, NY: The Overlook Press, 1977.

Henderson, Janice Wald. *The New Cuisine of Hawaii: Recipes from the Twelve Celebrated Chefs of Hawaii Regional Cuisine*. New York: Villard Books, 1994.

Hibben, Sheila. *American Regional Cookery*. Boston: Little, Brown and Company, 1946.

Hibler, Janie. *Dungeness Crabs and Blackberry Cobblers: The Northwest Heritage Cookbook*. New York: Alfred A. Knopf, 1991.

Jahoda, Gloria. *Florida: A Bicentennial History*. New York: W. W. Norton & Company, 1976.

Jambalaya: The Official Cookbook of the Louisiana World Exposition. New Orleans, LA: The Junior League of New Orleans Publications, 1983.

Jamison, Bill, and Jamison, Cheryl Alters. *American Home Cooking*. New York: Broadway Books, 1999.

Jamison, Cheryl Alters, and Jamison, Bill. *The Border Cookbook: Authentic Home Cooking of the American Southwest and Northern Mexico*. Boston: The Harvard Common Press, 1995.

Jenkins, Steven. *Cheese Primer*. New York: Workman Publishing, 1996.

Johnson, Betty. *The Complete Western Cookbook*. New York: A. S. Barnes and Company, 1964.

Jones, Evan. *American Food: The Gastronomic Story*. Woodstock, NY: The Overlook Press, 1990.

Jones, Judith, and Jones, Evan. *The L. L. Bean Book of New New England*. New York: Random House, 1987.

Jordan, Michele Anna. *California Home Cooking: American Cooking in the California Style*. Boston: The Harvard Common Press, 1997.

Josselin, Jean-Marie. *A Taste of Hawaii: New Cooking from the Crossroads of the Pacific*. New York: Stewart, Tabori & Chang, 1992.

Junior League of Denver. *Colorado Cache: A Goldmine of Recipes from the Junior League of Denver*. Denver, CO: The Junior League of Denver, 1978.

Junior League of Oakland–East Bay. *California Fresh Cookbook*. Oakland, CA: The Junior League of Oakland–East Bay, 1985.

Junior League of Pasadena, Inc. *California Heritage Continues*. Garden City, NY: Doubleday & Company, 1987.

Junior League of San Francisco. *San Francisco a la Carte*. Garden City, NY: Doubleday & Company, 1979.

Karousos, George, Ware, Bradley J., and Karousos, Theodore. *American Regional Cooking for 8 or 50*. New York: John Wiley & Sons, 1993.

Keegan, Marcia. *Pueblo & Navajo Cookery*. Dobbs Ferry, NY: Earth Books, 1977.

Kimball, Yeffe, and Anderson, Jean. *The Art of American Indian Cooking*. New York: Doubleday & Company, 1965.

Kirlin, Katherine S., and Kirlin, Thomas M. *Smithsonian Folklife Cookbook*. Washington, DC: Smithsonian Institution Press, 1991.

Kolpas, Norman, and Fenzl, Barbara Pool. *Southwest the Beautiful Cookbook*. San Francisco: Weldon Owen, 1994.

Koplan, Steven, Smith, Brian H., and Weiss, Michael A. *Exploring Wine: The Culinary Institute of America's Complete Guide to Wines of the World*. New York: Van Nostrand Reinhold, 1996.

Kotkin, Carole, and Martin, Kathy. *Mmmmiami: Tempting Tropical Tastes for Home Cooks Everywhere*. New York: Henry Holt and Company, 1998.

Lagasse, Emeril. *Prime Time Emeril*. New York: William Morrow and Company, 2001.

Laverick, Charles, Editor. *The Beverage Testing Institute's Buying Guide to Wines of North America*. New York: Sterling Publishing Company, 1999.

Lee, Hilde Gabriel. *Taste of the States: A Food History of America*. Charlottesville, VA: Howell Press, 1992.

Lemos, Charles. *Everybody's San Francisco Cookbook*. San Francisco: Good Life Publications, 1998.

Leonard, Jonathan Norton, and the Editors of Time-Life Books. *American Cooking: New England*. New York: Time-Life Books, 1970.

Leonard, Jonathan Norton, and the Editors of Time-Life Books. *American Cooking: The Great West*. New York: Time-Life Books, 1971.

Leonard, Jonathan Norton, and the Editors of Time-Life Books. *Recipes American Cooking: New England*. New York: Time-Life Books, 1970.

Leonard, Jonathan Norton, and the Editors of Time-Life Books. *Recipes American Cooking: The Great West*. New York: Time-Life Books, 1971.

Luchetti, Cathy. *Home on the Range: A Culinary History of the American West*. New York: Villard Books, 1993.

Lukins, Sheila. *USA Cookbook*. New York: Workman Publishing, 1997.

Lundy, Ronni. *Butter Beans to Blackberries: Recipes from the Southern Garden*. New York: North Point Press, 1999.

Malouf, Waldy, with Finn, Molly. *The Hudson River Valley Cookbook: A Leading American Chef Savors the Region's Bounty*. Boston: The Harvard Common Press, 1995.

Mandel, Abby. *Celebrating the Midwestern Table: Real Food for Real Times*. New York: Doubleday, 1996.

Marshall, Lillian Bertram. *Cooking Across the South*. Birmingham, AL: Oxmoor House, 1980.

McCullough, Fran, and Hamlin, Suzanne. *The Best American Recipes 1999*. New York: Houghton Mifflin Company, 1999.

McCullough, Frances, and Witt, Barbara. *Classic American Food Without Fuss*. New York: Villard, 1996.

McCully, Helen. *The American Heritage Cookbook*. United States: American Heritage Publishing Co., 1980.

McLaughlin, Michael. *The Manhattan Chili Co. Southwest American Cookbook*. New York: Crown Publishers, 1986.

Meredith Corporation. *Heritage of America Cookbook*. Des Moines, IA: Better Homes and Gardens Books, 1993.

Miller, Amy Bess, and Fuller, Persis. *The Best of Shaker Cooking*. New York: The Macmillan Company, 1970.

Miller, Mark, and Kiffin, Mark. *Coyote's Pantry: Southwest Seasonings and at Home Flavoring Techniques*. Berkeley, CA: Ten Speed Press, 1993.

Myhre, Helen, with Vold, Mona. *Farm Recipes and Food Secrets from the Norske Nook*. New York: Crown Publishers, 1993.

Neal, Bill. *Bill Neal's Southern Cooking*. Chapel Hill, NC: The University of North Carolina Press, 1985.

Nickerson, Jane. *Jane Nickerson's Florida Cookbook*. Gainesville, FL: University of Florida Press, 1973.

Nix, Janeth Johnson. *The Book of Regional Ameican Cooking. Southwest*. Los Angeles: HPBooks. 1993.

O'Connor, Hyla. *The Early American Cookbook*. Englewood Cliffs, NJ: Prentice-Hall, 1974.

Ojakangas, Beatrice. *The Book of Regional American Cooking: Heartland*. Los Angeles: HPBooks, 1993.

Olstein, Judi. *American Family Cooking: The Best of Regional Recipes*. New York: Exeter Books, 1984.

Patout, Alex. *Patout's Cajun Home Cooking*. New York: Random House, 1986.

Peyroux, Earl. *Gourmet Cooking by Earl Peyroux*. Pensacola, FL: Foote Printing Company, 1982.

Piercy, Caroline B., and Tolve, Arthur P. *The Shaker Cookbook: Recipes and Lore from the Valley of God's Pleasure*. Bowling Green, OH: Gabriel's Horn Publishing Co., 1984.

Politis, George. *Wild Game Cuisine*. Buffalo, NY: Firefly Books, 1996.

Price, B. Byron. *National Cowboy Hall of Fame Chuck Wagon Cookbook*. New York: Hearst Books, 1995.

Prudhomme, Paul. *Chef Paul Prudhomme's Louisiana Kitchen*. New York: William Morrow and Company, 1984.

Prudhomme, Paul. *Chef Paul Prudhomme's Seasoned America*. New York: William Morrow and Company, 1991.

Puck, Wolfgang. *Wolfgang Puck's Pizza, Pasta, and More!* New York: Random House, 2000.

Raichlen, Steven. *Miami Spice: The New Florida Cuisine*. New York: Workman Publishing, 1993.

Rebora, Giovanni. *Culture of the Fork: A Brief History of Food in Europe*. New York: Columbia University Press, 1998.

Riely, Elizabeth. *The Chef's Companion: A Concise Dictionary of Culinary Terms*. New York: Van Nostrand Reinhold, 1986.

Rodgers, Judy. *The Zuni Cafe Cookbook*. New York: W. W. Norton & Company, 2002.

Rombauer, Irma S., and Becker, Marion Rombauer. *Joy of Cooking*. Indianapolis, IN: Bobbs-Merrill Company, 1964.

Rosbottom, Betty. *American Favorites: New Renditions of the Recipes We Love*. Shelburne, VT: Chapters Publishing Ltd., 1996.

Rose, Peter G. *Foods of the Hudson: A Seasonal Sampling of the Region's Bounty*. Woodstock, NY: The Overlook Press, 1993.

Rosengarten, David. *It's All American Food: The Best Recipes for More Than 400 New American Classics*. New York: Little, Brown and Company, 2003.

Schroeder, Lisa Golden. *Sizzling Southwestern Cookery: From Margaritas to Fajitas to Sopaipillas*. New York: Meadowbrook Press, 1989.

Schulz, Phillip Stephen. *As American as Apple Pie*. New York: Simon & Schuster, 1990.

Shenton, James, Pellegrini, Angelo, Brown, Dale, Shenker, Israel, Wood, Peter, and the Editors of Time-Life Books. *American Cooking: The Melting Pot*. New York: Time-Life Books, 1971.

Shields, John. *The Chesapeake Bay Cookbook: Rediscovering the Pleasures of a Great Regional Cuisine*. Berkley, CA: Aris Books, 1990.

Showalter, Mary Emma. *Pennsylvania Dutch Cooking: A Mennonite Community Cookbook*. New York: Gramercy Books, 1978.

Sokolov, Raymond. *Fading Feast: A Compendium of Disappearing American Regional Foods*. New York: Farrar Straus Giroux, 1981.

Southern Living. *The Creole Cookbook*. United States: Oxmoor House, 1976.

Stamm, Sara B. B. *Favorite New England Recipes*. Camden, ME: Yankee Books, 1991.

Stanforth, Deirdre. *The New Orleans Restaurant Cookbook*. Garden City, NY: Doubleday & Company, 1967.

Stern, Jane, and Stern, Michael. *Jane and Michael Stern's Coast-to-Coast Real American Food*. New York: Alfred A. Knopf, 1986.

Stevenson, Tom. *The New Sotheby's Wine Encyclopedia*. New York: DK Publishing, 1997.

Tannahill, Reay. *Food in History*. New York: Crown Publishers, 1988.

Tawes, Helen Avalynne. *My Favorite Maryland Recipes*. New York: Random House, 1964.

The Art Institutes. *American Regional Cuisine*. New York: John Wiley & Sons, 2002.

The Creole Cottage and Catering. *Creole Cottage: A Collection of Recipes of the Creole Cottage*. Ruston, LA: The Creole Cottage, 1987.

Theriot, Jude W. *La Meilleure de la Louisiane: The Best of Louisiana*. Gretna, LA: Pelican Publishing Company, 1983.

Thibodaux Service League. *Louisiana Legacy: A Rich Tradition of Artistry with Food and Joy in Life*. Thibodaux, LA: The Thibodaux Service League, 1982.

Tirsch, Jessie. *A Taste of the Gulf Coast: The Art and Soul of Southern Cooking*. New York: Macmillan, 1997.

Toupin, Elizabeth Ahn. *Hawaii Cookbook & Backyard Luau*. New York: Silvermine Publishers, 1967.

Valenti, Tom, and Friedman, Andrew. *Tom Valenti's Soups, Stews, and One-Pot Meals*. New York: Scribner, 2003.

Villas, James. *My Mother's Southern Kitchen*. New York: Macmillan, 1994.

Voltz, Jeanne A. *The Flavor of the South: Delicacies and Staples of Southern Cuisine*. Avenel, NJ: Wing Books, 1993.

Voltz, Jeanne, and Stuart, Caroline. *The Florida Cookbook*. New York: Alfred A. Knopf, 1993.

Walter, Eugene, and the Editors of Time-Life Books. *American Cooking: Southern Style*. New York: Time-Life Books, 1971.

Warren, Mildred Evans. *The Art of Southern Cooking*. New York: Gramercy Publishing Company, 1981.

Webster's New World Dictionary of the American Language: College Edition. New York: The World Publishing Company, 1960.

Weir, Joanne. *Joanne Weir's More Cooking in the Wine Country.* New York: Simon & Schuster, 2001.

Weldon Owen Inc. *American Food: A Celebration.* San Francisco: CollinsPublishers, 1993.

White, Jasper. *Jasper White's Cooking from New England.* New York: Harper & Row, 1989.

Willan, Anne. *Cooking with Wine.* New York: Harry N. Abrams, 2001.

Williams, Jacqueline. *Wagon Wheel Kitchens: Food on the Oregon Trail.* Lawrence, KS: University Press of Kansas, 1993.

Williams, Sallie Y., and Cortner, Nancy G. *Down Home Feasts: The Native Cuisines of America's Gulf States.* Dallas, TX: Taylor Publishing Company, 1986.

Willis, Tyrone A. *Louisiana Creole and Cajun Cooking at Its Best.* Olathe, KS: Cookbook Publishers, 1991.

Wilson, José, and the Editors of Time-Life Books. *American Cooking: The Eastern Heartland.* New York: Time-Life Books, 1971.

Wilson, José, and the Editors of Time-Life Books. *Recipes American Cooking: The Eastern Heartland.* New York: Time-Life Books, 1971.

Wilson, Justin. *Justin Wilson's Easy Cookin'.* New York: William Morrow and Company, 1998.

Wilson, Justin, and Wilson, Jeannine Meeds. *Justin Wilson's Homegrown Louisiana Cookin'.* New York: Macmillan Company, 1990.

Woods, Marvin. *The New Low-Country Cooking.* New York: William Morrow, 2000.

World Book Encyclopedia. Chicago: World Book, 1999.

Wormser, Richard. *Southwest Cookery, or, at Home on the Range.* New York: Doubleday & Company, 1969.

Worthington, Diane Rossen. *The Cuisine of California.* Los Angeles: Jeremy P. Tarcher, 1983.

Young, Carrie, and Young, Felicia C. *Prairie Cooks: Glorified Rice, Three-day Buns, and Other Reminiscences.* Iowa City, IA: University of Iowa Press, 1993.

Zanger, Mark H. *The American Ethnic Cookbook for Students.* Phoenix, AZ: Oryx Press, 2001.

INDEX

A

Acorn Squash with Maple Syrup, 46
Ahi, Wok Charred with Chinese
    Cabbage Slaw and Dipping
    Sauce, 345
Ammann, Joseph, 63
Anchor Bar, 61
Anheuser, Eberhard, 189
Appetizers
    Artichoke Dip, 366
    Baked Stuffed Clams, 33
    Bierocks, 233
    Bollitos, 138
    Chicken Quesadilla, 267
    Chili Rellenos, 268
    Coconut Shrimp, 138
    Codfish Cakes, 33
    Crab Cakes, 71
    Crab Louie, 367
    Crisp Crab Cakes with Celeri
        and Fennel Slaw, 72
    Deviled Eggs, 109
    Foie Gras with Apples, 74
    Fresh Cracked Conch with
        Vanilla Rum Sauce and Spicy
        Black Bean Salad, 139
    Guacamole, 271
    Hawaiian Curried Pork
        Dumplings, 335
    Kentucky Catfish Spring Rolls
        with Asian Dipping Sauce, 110
    Oysters Rockefeller, 169
    Potato Knishes, 399
    Potato Skins with Elk Sausage
        and Goat Cheese, 297
    Salsa Fresca, 269
    Shrimp Rémoulade, 170
    Smoked Trout with Horseradish
        Sauce, 296
    Spring Rolls, 398
    Swedish Meatballs, 202
    Sweet Onion Pie, 335
    Tourtière, 232
    Wild Rice Stuffed Mushrooms, 203
Apple Cranberry Betty, 53
Apple Crisp, 351
Apple Dumplings, 313
Armour, Phillip, 196
Artichoke Dip, 366
Asian Style Sugar Snap Peas, 377
Asparagus Risotto, 379
Asparagus Salad, Marinated, 207
Austin, Moses, 251
Austin, Stephen, 251
Avocado Grapefruit Salad, 143
Avocado Soup, Chilled, 369

B

Baked Beans, 24, 28, 44
Baked Stuffed Potatoes, 310
Baker, Dr. James, 27

Baker, Walter, 14
Bananas Foster, 184
Barbecued Shrimp, 278
Barley Vegetable Soup, 235
Barq, Ed, 103
Basque Shepherd's Pie, 302
Bean Salad, Three Bean, 206
Bean Sprouts, Carrots, and Leeks,
    Gingered, 348
Bean, Black, Soup, 400
Beans, Refried, 279
Beard, James, xi
Beef
    Bierocks, 233
    Bigos, 404
    Boliche, 144
    Braised Beef Short Ribs, 306
    Chicken Fried Steak, 238
    Chili, 270
    Chuckwagon Stew, 237
    Cincinnati Chili, 205
    Grillades, 174
    Hamburgers Stuffed with
        Maytag Blue Cheese, 209
    Lasagna, 405
    Marinated Flank Steak, 375
    Mushroom Stuffed Meatloaf, 80
    New England Boiled Dinner, 39
    Swedish Meatballs, 202
    Tourtière, 232
    Yankee Pot Roast, 40
Beef on Weck, 61
Beet and Apple Salad, 38
Beets, Pickled, 236
Beignets, 182
Beringer, Frederick, 364
Beringer, Jacob, 364
Betty, Apple Cranberry, 53
Bibb, Jack, 105
Bierocks, 233
Bigos, 404
Bing, Ah, 328
Biscuits, Buttermilk, 242
Biscuits, Sourdough, 310
Black Bean Soup, 400
Black Beans and Rice, 152
Blackened Redfish, 178
Blaxton, William, 26
Blueberry Muffins, 48
Boliche, 144
Bollitos, 135, 138
Borden, Gail, 62
Boston Baked Beans, 44
Boston Brown Bread, 24, 28, 47
Boston Cream Pie, 30
Boston Tea Party, 6, 21
Bourbon, 102, 106
Braised Beef Short Ribs, 306
Bratwurst in Beer with Onions, 207
Breads
    Beignets, 182

Blueberry Muffins, 48
Boston Brown Bread, 47
Buttermilk Biscuits, 242
Cornbread, 182
Date Nut Bread, 380
Indian Frybread, 281
Popovers, 214
Portuguese Sweet Bread, 412
Sally Lunn, 121
Soft Pretzels, 85
Sourdough Biscuits, 310
Sourdough French Bread, 349
Southwestern Cornbread, 280
Spoonbread, 153
Bread Pudding with Whiskey
    Sauce, 183
Brie Salad with Grapes, Olives,
    and Almonds, 370
Brunswick Stew, 105, 115
Brussels Sprouts with Sage and
    Cream, 308
Buffalo Chili, 234
Bull, Ephraim, 29
Burbank, Russet, 292
Busch, Adolphus, 189
Buttermilk Poundcake, 246
Butterscotch Black Walnut Bars, 215

C

Cabbage, Creamed, 240
Calabacitas, 279
California recipes
    Artichoke Dip, 366
    Asian Style Sugar Snap Peas, 377
    Asparagus Risotto, 379
    Brie Salad with Grapes, Olives,
        and Almonds, 370
    Chilled Avocado Soup, 369
    Chocolate Raspberry Dacquoise,
        382
    Cioppino, 372
    Cobb Salad, 371
    Crab Louie, 367
    Date Nut Bread, 380
    Grilled Game Hens with
        Cabernet Sauce, 373
    Grilled Vegetables with Goat
        Cheese, 378
    Lamb Shanks Braised in Red
        Wine, 374
    Marinated Flank Steak, 375
    Pears and Figs Poached in
        Spicy Red Wine, 381
    Pizza with Artichoke,
        Caramelized Onion, and
        Gorgonzola, 376
    Pumpkin Soup, 368
Campbell, Joseph, 14, 63
Caramel Icing with Spice Cake, 311
Carrot Cake, Tropical Sticky, 157
Carrots and Peas, Glazed, 45

Carrots, Leeks, and Bean Sprouts,
    Gingered, 348
Carver, George Washington, 103
Cary, Kathy, 110, 111
Casserole, 15, 29
Cassoulet, 25
Cast iron cookware, 24, 163, 227
Catfish Spring Rolls with Asian
    Dipping Sauce, 110
Catfish, Fried, 118
Cauliflower with Walnuts, 213
Chapman, John. See Johnny
    Appleseed
Cheddar Cheese Beer Soup, 204
Cheese Grits, 121
Cheesecake, New York, 89
Cherry Fritters, 350
Cherry Goat Cheese Strudel, 216
Chicago Deep-Dish Pizza, 212
Chicken and Dumplings, 238
Chicken Corn Soup with Rivels, 74
Chicken Fried Steak, 238
Chicken Pilau, 146
Chicken Pot Pie, 78
Chicken Quesadilla, 267
Chicken with Pumpkin Seed
    Sauce, 276
Chicken, Ham, and Shrimp
    Jambalaya, 175
Chicken, Mushroom Stuffed in Sour
    Cream Almond Sauce, 342
Chicken, Smothered, 210
Child, Julia, xi, 15, 16
Chili, 270
Chili Rellenos, 268
Chili, Buffalo, 234
Chili, Cincinnati, 195, 205
Chilled Avocado Soup, 369
Chinese Exclusion Act, 391
Chocolate Chip Cookies, 52
Chocolate Hazelnut Torte, 352
Chocolate Raspberry Dacquoise,
    382
Chocolate Soufflé, 415
Chuckwagon Stew, 237
Cincinnati Chili, 195, 205
Cioppino, 372
Clam Chowder, 24, 34, 66
Clam Sauce, White with Linguini,
    408
Clambake, 5, 20, 23, 255, 327, 331
Clams, Baked Stuffed, 33
Clark, William, 10, 222, 286, 291,
    318
Cobb Salad, 371
Cobbler, Peach, 122
Coconut Cake, 156
Coconut Shrimp, 138
Cod Cake and Five Clam Chowder
    with Chorizo Aioli and Celery
    Salt, 35

Cod, Broiled Stuffed, 42
Codfish Cakes, 33
Colache, 151
Coleman, Mose, 102
Coleslaw, 113
Coleslaw, Creamy, 77
Colorado Lamb Duet: Horseradish Crusted Rack of Lamb & Osso Bucco with Toasted Farro & Barley Risotto, Caponata, Nicoise Olive Lamb Jus, 304
Columbus, Christopher, 5, 128, 135
Conch Chowder, 141
Conch with Vanilla Rum Sauce and Spicy Black Bean Salad, 139
Condiments
    Cranberry Relish, 39
Cook, James, 320
Cookies, Chocolate Chip, 52
Corn and Crab Bisque, 171
Corn Fritters, 309
Corn Pudding, 241
Corn, Fried, 213
Cornbread, 182
Cornbread, Southwestern, 280
Coronado, Francisco, 250
Country Captain Chicken, 105, 114
Country Ham, 65, 100, 104
Crab Bisque, 75
Crab Cakes, 71
Crab Cakes, Crisp with Celeri and Fennel Slaw, 72
Crab Louie, 367
Cracker cooking, 132
Cranberries, 22, 188
Cranberry Relish, 39
Crawfish Étouffée, 177
Creamed Spinach, 347
Creole, Shrimp, 176
Crisp, Apple, 351
Crow, James, 106
Cuban sandwich, 132
Cucumber Salad, Thai, 402
Curried Pork Dumplings, Hawaiian, 335

D
Dacquoise, Chocolate Raspberry, 382
Date Nut Bread, 380
Dawson, Dr. James, 361
Dawson, Thomas, 361
De León, Ponce, 128
Deep-Dish Pizza, Chicago, 212
Deere, John, 13, 224
Del-Monico, Giovanni, 67
Del-Monico, Pietro, 67
Delmonico's Restaurant, 67
Desserts
    Apple Cranberry Betty, 53
    Apple Crisp, 351
    Apple Dumplings, 313
    Baked Key Lime Pie, 154
    Bananas Foster, 184
    Beignets, 182

Bread Pudding with Whiskey Sauce, 183
    Buttermilk Poundcake, 246
    Butterscotch Black Walnut Bars, 215
    Cherry Fritters, 350
    Cherry Goat Cheese Strudel, 216
    Chocolate Chip Cookies, 52
    Chocolate Hazelnut Torte, 352
    Chocolate Raspberry Dacquoise, 382
    Chocolate Soufflé, 415
    Coconut Cake, 156
    Dobos Torte, 413
    Indian Pudding, 49
    Kolache with Prune Filling, 244
    Lemon Chess Pie, 124
    Lemon Meringue Pie, 217
    New York Cheesecake, 89
    Peach Cobbler, 122
    Pears and Figs Poached in Spicy Red Wine, 381
    Pecan Pie, 282
    Persimmon Pudding, 218
    Pie Dough, 51
    Pumpkin Pie, 50
    Rhubarb Pie, 245
    Shoofly Pie, 86
    Sopaipillas, 281
    Spice Cake with Caramel Icing, 311
    Strawberry Shortcake, 88
    Tropical Sticky Carrot Cake, 157
    Unbaked Key Lime Pie, 155
Deviled Eggs, 109
Diat, Louis, 68
Dip, Artichoke, 366
Disney, Walt, 129
Dobos Torte, 413
Dole, James, 330, 331
Donation Land Law, 319
Dorrance, Arthur, 63
Dorrance, John, 63
Duck and Sausage Gumbo, 172
Duck with Grapes, 79
Dumplings, Apple, 313
Dumplings, Hawaiian Curried Pork, 335

E
Eggplant with Shrimp, 179
Eggs, Deviled, 109
En Papillote, 131, 133, 150, 163
Enchiladas, Green Chili Chicken, 275
English, Todd, 35–37
Entrées:
    Barbecued Ribs, 117
    Basque Shepherd's Pie, 302
    Bigos, 404
    Blackened Redfish, 178
    Boliche, 144
    Braised Beef Short Ribs, 306
    Broiled Stuffed Cod, 42
    Brunswick Stew, 115

Chicago Deep-Dish Pizza, 212
    Chicken and Dumplings, 238
    Chicken Fried Steak, 238
    Chicken Pilau, 146
    Chicken Pot Pie, 78
    Chicken with Pumpkin Seed Sauce, 276
    Chicken, Ham, and Shrimp Jambalaya, 175
    Chuckwagon Stew, 237
    Cioppino, 372
    Cobb Salad, 371
    Colorado Lamb Duet: Horseradish Crusted Rack of Lamb & Osso Bucco with Toasted Farro & Barley Risotto, Caponata, Nicoise Olive Lamb Jus, 304
    Country Captain Chicken, 114
    Crab Cakes, 71
    Crawfish Étouffée, 177
    Duck and Sausage Gumbo, 172
    Duck with Grapes, 79
    Eggplant with Shrimp, 179
    Flounder Stuffed with Crabmeat, 82
    Fried Catfish, 118
    Green Chili Chicken Enchiladas, 275
    Grillades, 174
    Grilled Bratwurst in Beer with Onions, 207
    Grilled Game Hens with Cabernet Sauce, 373
    Grouper Encrusted in Macadamia Nuts, 149
    Hamburgers Stuffed with Maytag Blue Cheese, 209
    Hawaiian Pork Teriyaki with Grilled Pineapple, 341
    Hazelnut Encrusted Halibut with Olive Caper Hazelnut Salsa, 344
    Hot Brown, 118
    Jerk Chicken, 407
    Lamb Shanks Braised in Red Wine, 374
    Lamb Vindaloo, 406
    Lasagna, 405
    Linguini with White Clam Sauce, 408
    Marinated Flank Steak, 375
    Marinated Grilled Leg of Lamb, 303
    Marinated Grilled Salmon, 343
    Mushroom Stuffed Chicken in Sour Cream Almond Sauce, 342
    Mushroom Stuffed Meatloaf, 80
    New England Boiled Dinner, 39
    Oven Barbecued Pulled Pork, 116
    Parmesan and Herb Crusted Perch, 239
    Pizza with Artichoke, Caramelized Onion, and Gorgonzola, 376
    Planked Whitefish, 211

Pompano en Papillote, 150
    Pork Tenderloin with Ancho and Pasilla Chilies, 277
    Posole, 273
    Red Snapper Florida Style, 148
    Roast Turkey with Gravy, 41
    Scallops au Gratin, 43
    Schnitz und Knepp, 81
    Shrimp Creole, 176
    Smothered Chicken, 210
    Stuffed Pork Chops, 208
    Stuffed Trout, 301
    Texas Barbecued Shrimp, 278
    Veal Medallions with Mushrooms and Cream, 307
    Venison Stew, 340
    Yankee Pot Roast, 40
    Zucchini and Prosciutto Wrapped Snapper with Saffron, Whitewater Clams, and Fingerling Potatoes, 147
Epperson, Frank, 360
Erie Canal, 13, 188, 189, 193, 395
Erikson, Leif, x, xi
Estuary, 57, 58
Étouffée, Crawfish, 177
Exeter, Adam, 62
Exeter, John, 62

F
Field Greens with Pear, Walnuts, and Blue Cheese, 338
Figs and Pears Poached in Spicy Red Wine, 381
Filé, 104
Fish
    Blackened Redfish, 178
    Broiled Stuffed Cod, 42
    Cioppino, 372
    Codfish Cakes, 33
    Flounder Stuffed with Crabmeat, 82
    Fried Catfish, 118
    Grouper Encrusted in Macadamia Nuts, 149
    Hazelnut Encrusted Halibut with Olive Caper Hazelnut Salsa, 344
    Kentucky Catfish Spring Rolls with Asian Dipping Sauce, 110
    Marinated Grilled Salmon, 343
    Parmesan and Herb Crusted Perch, 239
    Planked Whitefish, 211
    Pompano en Papillote, 150
    Red Snapper Florida Style, 148
    Smoked Trout with Horseradish Sauce, 296
    Stuffed Trout, 301
    Wok Charred Ahi with Chinese Cabbage Slaw and Dipping Sauce, 345
    Zucchini and Prosciutto Wrapped Snapper with Saffron, Whitewater Clams, and Fingerling Potatoes, 147
Flank Steak, Marinated, 375

Florida recipes
  Avocado Grapefruit Salad, 143
  Baked Key Lime Pie, 154
  Black Beans and Rice, 152
  Boliche, 144
  Bollitos, 138
  Broiled Tomato, 152
  Chicken Pilau, 146
  Coconut Cake, 156
  Coconut Shrimp, 138
  Colache, 151
  Conch Chowder, 141
  Fresh Cracked Conch with
    Vanilla Rum Sauce and Spicy
    Black Bean Salad, 139
  Grouper Encrusted in
    Macadamia Nuts, 149
  Hearts of Palm Salad, 142
  Pompano en Papillote, 150
  Red Snapper Florida Style, 148
  Spoonbread, 153
  Tropical Sticky Carrot Cake, 157
  Unbaked Key Lime Pie, 155
  Zucchini and Prosciutto
    Wrapped Snapper with
    Saffron, Whitewater Clams,
    and Fingerling Potatoes, 147
Flounder Stuffed with Crabmeat, 82
Foie Gras with Apples, 74
Ford, Henry, 194, 395
Fournier, Chartes, xi
Frank, Dr. Konstantin, xi
Freeman, Daniel, 222
French Bread, Sourdough, 349
Fried Corn, 213
Fritters, Cherry, 350
Fritters, Corn, 309
Frybread, Indian, 281

G
Game
  Grilled Game Hens with
    Cabernet Sauce, 373
  Potato Skins with Elk Sausage
    and Goat Cheese, 297
  Venison Stew, 340
Georges Banks, 27
Ghirardelli, Domingo, 360
Gingered Carrots, Leeks, and
  Bean Sprouts, 348
Goat Cheese with Grilled
  Vegetables, 378
Goulash, Mushroom, 410
Grapefruit Avocado Salad, 143
Gratin of Potatoes and
  Mushrooms, 348
Greek Salad, 403
Green Bean, Tomato, and Onion
  Salad with Dill Dressing, 339
Green Beans with Dill, 213
Green Beans with Mustard Sauce,
  83
Green Beans with New Potatoes, 180
Green Chili Chicken Enchiladas, 275
Green Chili Sauce, 274
Greens, 119
Grillades, 174

Grilled Bratwurst in Beer with
  Onions, 207
Grilled Game Hens with Cabernet
  Sauce, 373
Grilled Vegetables with Goat
  Cheese, 378
Grits, Cheese, 121
Grouper Encrusted in Macadamia
  Nuts, 149
Guacamole, 271
Gumbo, 104
Gumbo, Duck and Sausage, 172

H
Halibut, Hazelnut Encrusted with
  Olive Caper Hazelnut Salsa,
  344
Hamburgers Stuffed with Maytag
  Blue Cheese, 209
Haraszthy, Agoston, xi, 356
Hasty Pudding, 29, 30
Hawaiian Curried Pork
  Dumplings, 335
Hawaiian Pork Teriyaki with
  Grilled Pineapple, 341
Hazelnut Chocolate Torte, 352
Hazelnut Encrusted Halibut with
  Olive Caper Hazelnut Salsa,
  344
Hearts of Palm Salad, 142
Heinz, Henry, 14, 64, 65
Hellman, Richard, 68
Herb Stuffing, 46
Hershey, Milton, 66
Hill, William, 364
Hines, Duncan, 228
Homestead Act, 12, 222–223,
  227, 288, 319, 356
Hominy, 8, 29, 105
Hoppin' John, 105, 120
Hot Brown, 118
Hudson, Henry, 60
Hush puppies, 105, 131, 135

I
Indian Frybread, 281
Indian Pudding, 30, 49
Industrial Revolution, 13, 14, 193

J
Jacks, David, 361
Jambalaya, Chicken, Ham, and
  Shrimp, 175
Jamestown, 5
Jefferson, Thomas, x, 9, 10, 95,
  101, 161, 222
Jerk Chicken, 407
Jicama Salad, 272
Johnny Appleseed, 30, 195, 199
Jossi, John, 194

K
Kale Soup, 25, 26
Kander, Elizabeth, 195
Kellogg, John, 194
Kellogg, William, 14, 194
Key Lime Pie, Baked, 154

Key Lime Pie, Unbaked, 155
Knishes, Potato, 399
Kolache with Prune Filling, 244
Korbel, Anton, 364
Korbel, Francis, 364
Korbel, Joseph, 364
Kroc, Ray, 362
Krug, Charles, 364

L
Lagasse, Emeril, xi
Lamb
  Basque Shepherd's Pie, 302
  Colorado Lamb Duet:
    Horseradish Crusted Rack of
    Lamb & Osso Bucco with
    Toasted Farro & Barley
    Risotto, Caponata, Nicoise
    Olive Lamb Jus, 304
  Lamb Shanks Braised in Red
    Wine, 374
  Lamb Vindaloo, 406
  Marinated Grilled Leg of Lamb,
    303
Lamb Duet: Horseradish Crusted
  Rack of Lamb & Osso Bucco
  with Toasted Farro & Barley
  Risotto, Caponata, Nicoise
  Olive Lamb Jus, 304
Lamb Shanks Braised in Red
  Wine, 374
Lamb Vindaloo, 406
Langlois, Madame, 160
Lasagna, 405
Leeks, Carrots, and Bean Sprouts,
  Gingered, 348
Leg of Lamb, Marinated Grilled, 303
Lemon Chess Pie, 124
Lemon Meringue Pie, 217
Lentil Soup, 337
Lewis, Meriwether, 10, 222, 286,
  291, 318
Lewis, Tillie, 359
Liederkranz Cheese, 66
Lincoln, Abraham, 12, 20, 293
Linguini with White Clam Sauce,
  408
Lost Colony, 94
Louisiana recipes
  Bananas Foster, 184
  Beignets, 182
  Blackened Redfish, 178
  Bread Pudding with Whiskey
    Sauce, 183
  Chicken, Ham, and Shrimp
    Jambalaya, 175
  Corn and Crab Bisque, 171
  Cornbread, 182
  Crawfish Étouffée, 177
  Duck and Sausage Gumbo, 172
  Eggplant with Shrimp, 179
  Green Beans with New
    Potatoes, 180
  Grillades, 174
  Maque Choux, 180
  Oysters Rockefeller, 169
  Potato Salad, 173

Shrimp Creole, 176
Shrimp Rémoulade, 170
Sweet Potatoes with Pecans, 181

M
Maple syrup, 7, 8, 28, 30, 62, 190
Maque Choux, 180
Marinated Asparagus Salad, 207
Marinated Flank Steak, 375
Marinated Grilled Leg of Lamb,
  303
Marinated Grilled Salmon, 343
Mason, John, 13
Mayflower, 5, 20
McDonald, Maurice, 362
McDonald, Richard, 362
McGrath, Ed, 57
Meatballs, Swedish, 202
Meatloaf, Mushroom Stuffed, 80
Melting Pot recipes
  Bigos, 404
  Black Bean Soup, 400
  Chocolate Soufflé, 415
  Dobos Torte, 413
  Greek Salad, 403
  Jerk Chicken, 407
  Lamb Vindaloo, 406
  Lasagna, 405
  Linguini with White Clam
    Sauce, 408
  Mexican Tomato Soup, 401
  Mushroom Goulash, 410
  Portuguese Sweet Bread, 412
  Potato Knishes, 399
  Potatoes in Horseradish Cream
    Sauce, 411
  Spring Rolls, 398
  Thai Cucumber Salad, 402
  Tomatoes Stuffed with Corn,
    Zucchini, and Almonds, 409
Merriman, Peter, 345–347
Mexican Tomato Soup, 401
Middle Atlantic recipes
  Amish Green Beans with
    Mustard Sauce, 83
  Chicken Corn Soup with Rivels,
    74
  Chicken Pot Pie, 78
  Crab Bisque, 75
  Crab Cakes, 71
  Creamy Coleslaw, 77
  Crisp Crab Cakes with Celeri
    and Fennel Slaw, 72
  Duck with Grapes, 79
  Flounder Stuffed with
    Crabmeat, 82
  Foie Gras with Apples, 74
  Mushroom Stuffed Meatloaf, 80
  New York Cheesecake, 89
  Noodles with a Crumb Topping,
    84
  Sauerkraut with Apples, 84
  Schnitz und Knepp, 81
  Shoofly Pie, 86
  Soft Pretzels, 85
  Strawberry Shortcake, 88
  Waldorf Salad, 76

Midwest recipes
  Butterscotch Black Walnut
    Bars, 215
  Cauliflower with Walnuts, 213
  Cheddar Cheese Beer Soup, 204
  Cherry Goat Cheese Strudel, 216
  Chicago Deep-Dish Pizza, 212
  Cincinnati Chili, 205
  Fried Corn, 213
  Green Beans with Dill, 213
  Grilled Bratwurst in Beer with
    Onions, 207
  Hamburgers Stuffed with
    Maytag Blue Cheese, 209
  Lemon Meringue Pie, 217
  Marinated Asparagus Salad,
    207
  Persimmon Pudding, 218
  Planked Whitefish, 211
  Popovers, 214
  Smothered Chicken, 210
  Stuffed Pork Chops, 208
  Swedish Meatballs, 202
  Three Bean Salad, 206
  Wild Rice Pilaf, 214
  Wild Rice Stuffed Mushrooms,
    203
Militello, Mark, 139–141, 147,
  148, 157
Miller, Frederick, 189
Mincemeat, 30
Mondavi, Robert, xi
Mountain States recipes
  Apple Dumplings, 313
  Baked Stuffed Potatoes, 310
  Basque Shepherd's Pie, 302
  Braised Beef Short Ribs, 306
  Brussels Sprouts with Sage and
    Cream, 308
  Colorado Lamb Duet: Horseradish
    Crusted Rack of Lamb & Osso
    Bucco with Toasted Farro &
    Barley Risotto, Caponata,
    Nicoise Olive Lamb Jus, 304
  Corn Fritters, 309
  Marinated Grilled Leg of Lamb,
    303
  Potato Skins with Elk Sausage
    and Goat Cheese, 297
  Smoked Trout with Horseradish
    Sauce, 296
  Sourdough Biscuits, 310
  Spice Cake with Caramel Icing,
    311
  Spinach Salad with Horseradish
    Dressing, 299
  Split Pea Soup, 298
  Stuffed Trout, 301
  Veal Medallions with
    Mushrooms and Cream, 307
  Vegetable Salad with Pine Nuts,
    300
  Wild Mushroom Soup, 298
Muffins, Blueberry, 48
Muffuletta, 161
Mushroom and Potato Gratin, 348
Mushroom Goulash, 410

Mushroom Soup, Wild, 298
Mushroom Stuffed Chicken in Sour
  Cream Almond Sauce, 342
Mushrooms, Wild Rice Stuffed,
  203

N
Natchez Trace, 96
New England Boiled Dinner, 24,
  25, 28, 39
New England recipes
  Acorn Squash with Maple
    Syrup, 46
  Apple Cranberry Betty, 53
  Baked Stuffed Clams, 33
  Beet and Apple Salad, 38
  Blueberry Muffins, 48
  Boston Baked Beans, 44
  Boston Brown Bread, 47
  Broiled Stuffed Cod, 42
  Chocolate Chip Cookies, 52
  Clam Chowder, 34
  Cod Cake and Five Clam
    Chowder with Chorizo Aioli
    and Celery Salt, 35
  Codfish Cakes, 33
  Cranberry Relish, 39
  Glazed Carrots and Peas, 45
  Herb Stuffing, 46
  Indian Pudding, 49
  New England Boiled Dinner, 39
  Pie Dough, 51
  Portuguese Sausage and Kale
    Soup, 37
  Pumpkin Pie, 50
  Roast Turkey with Gravy, 41
  Scallops au Gratin, 43
  Succotash, 44
  Yankee Pot Roast, 40
New York Cheesecake, 89
Noodles with a Crumb Topping, 84

O
Okra and Tomatoes, 120
Olivieri, Harry, 64
Olivieri, Pat, 64
Onion Pie, 335
Ortega, Emile, 362
Oyster roast, 66, 97, 98
Oyster Stew, 336
Oysters Rockefeller, 169

P
Pabst, Fred, 189
Pacific Northwest, Alaska, and
    Hawaii recipes
  Apple Crisp, 351
  Cherry Fritters, 350
  Chocolate Hazelnut Torte, 352
  Creamed Spinach, 347
  Field Greens with Pear,
    Walnuts, and Blue Cheese,
    338
  Gingered Carrots, Leeks, and
    Bean Sprouts, 348
  Gratin of Potatoes and
    Mushrooms, 348

Green Bean, Tomato, and
    Onion Salad with Dill
    Dressing, 339
  Hawaiian Curried Pork
    Dumplings, 335
  Hawaiian Pork Teriyaki with
    Grilled Pineapple, 341
  Hazelnut Encrusted Halibut
    with Olive Caper Hazelnut
    Salsa, 344
  Lentil Soup, 337
  Marinated Grilled Salmon, 343
  Mushroom Stuffed Chicken in
    Sour Cream Almond Sauce,
    342
  Oyster Stew, 336
  Sourdough French Bread, 349
  Sweet Onion Pie, 335
  Venison Stew, 340
  Wok Charred Ahi with Chinese
    Cabbage Slaw and Dipping
    Sauce, 345
Palmer, Charlie, 72, 73
Panama Canal, 357
Parke, Roy, 135
Parmesan and Herb Crusted
    Perch, 239
Peach Cobbler, 122
Peanut Soup, Creamy, 112
Pearlash, 29
Pears and Figs Poached in Spicy
    Red Wine, 381
Peas, Sugar Snap, Asian Style, 377
Pecan Pie, 282
Pemmican, 29, 188, 222, 291, 326
Penn, William, 62, 68
Perch, Parmesan and Herb
    Crusted, 239
Persimmon Pudding, 218
Peychaud, Antoine, 168
Philadelphia Pepper Pot, 63
Pickled Beets, 236
Pie
  Baked Key Lime Pie, 154
  Basque Shepherd's Pie, 302
  Lemon Chess, 124
  Lemon Meringue Pie, 217
  Pecan Pie, 282
  Pumpkin Pie, 50
  Rhubarb Pie, 245
  Shoofly Pie, 86
  Sweet Onion Pie, 335
  Unbaked Key Lime Pie, 155
Pie Dough, 51
Pilaf, Wild Rice, 214
Pilau, Chicken, 146
Pillsbury, Charles, 195
Pizza with Artichoke, Caramelized
    Onion, and Gorgonzola, 376
Pizza, Chicago Deep-Dish, 212
Plains States recipes
  Bierocks, 233
  Buffalo Chili, 234
  Buttermilk Biscuits, 242
  Buttermilk Poundcake, 246
  Chicken and Dumplings, 238
  Chicken Fried Steak, 238

Chuckwagon Stew, 237
  Corn Pudding, 241
  Creamed Cabbage, 240
  Glazed Turnips, 241
  Kolache with Prune Filling, 244
  Parmesan and Herb Crusted
    Perch, 239
  Pickled Beets, 236
  Rhubarb Pie, 245
  Scalloped Potatoes, 242
  Tourtière, 232
  Vegetable Barley Soup, 235
Planked Whitefish, 211
Pompano en Papillote, 150
Popovers, 214
Pork
  Barbecued Ribs, 117
  Bigos, 404
  Black Bean Soup, 400
  Chicago Deep-Dish Pizza, 212
  Chicken, Ham, and Shrimp
    Jambalaya, 175
  Duck and Sausage Gumbo, 172
  Grilled Bratwurst in Beer with
    Onions, 207
  Hawaiian Curried Pork
    Dumplings, 335
  Hawaiian Pork Teriyaki with
    Grilled Pineapple, 341
  Lasagna, 405
  Oven Barbecued Pulled Pork,
    116
  Pork Tenderloin with Ancho
    and Pasilla Chilies, 277
  Posole, 273
  Schnitz und Knepp, 81
  Split Pea Soup, 298
  Spring Rolls, 398
  Stuffed Pork Chops, 208
  Tourtière, 232
Pork Chops, Stuffed, 208
Pork Dumplings, Hawaiian
    Curried, 335
Pork Tenderloin with Ancho and
    Pasilla Chilies, 277
Pork Teriyaki with Grilled
    Pineapple, 341
Portuguese Sweet Bread, 412
Posole, 273
Post, Charles, 14, 194
Potato and Mushroom Gratin, 348
Potato Famine, 11, 21, 395
Potato Knishes, 399
Potato Salad, 173
Potato Skins with Elk Sausage
    and Goat Cheese, 297
Potatoes in Horseradish Cream
    Sauce, 411
Potatoes, Scalloped, 242
Poultry
  Brunswick Stew, 115
  Chicken and Dumplings, 238
  Chicken Pilau, 146
  Chicken Pot Pie, 78
  Chicken Quesadilla, 267
  Chicken with Pumpkin Seed
    Sauce, 276

Chicken, Ham, and Shrimp
  Jambalaya, 175
Country Captain Chicken, 114
Duck and Sausage Gumbo, 172
Duck with Grapes, 79
Green Chili Chicken
  Enchiladas, 275
Grilled Game Hens with
  Cabernet Sauce, 373
Hot Brown, 118
Jerk Chicken, 407
Mushroom Stuffed Chicken in
  Sour Cream Almond Sauce,
  342
Roast Turkey with Gravy, 41
Smothered Chicken, 210
Tortilla Soup, 269
Poundcake, Buttermilk, 246
Pretzels, Soft, 85
Prudomme, Paul, 165
Pudding, Corn, 241
Pudding, Indian, 30, 49
Pudding, Persimmon, 218
Puget, Peter, 318
Pulled Pork, Oven Barbecued, 116
Pumpkin Pie, 30, 50
Pumpkin Soup, 368

Q
Quesadilla, Chicken, 267

R
Ramos, Henry, 168
Ranhofer, Charles, 67
Rawlings, Marjorie Kinnan, 132
Red flannel hash, 28
Red Snapper, Florida Style, 148
Red-eyed gravy, 100
Redfish, Blackened, 178
Refried Beans, 279
Rellenos, Chili, 268
Removal Law, 129
Revolutionary War, 6, 21
Rhubarb Pie, 245
Ribs, Barbecued, 117
Risotto, Asparagus, 379
Roosevelt, Franklin, 391
Rumford, Count, 13
Rutherford, Thomas, 364

S
Salads
  Avocado Grapefruit Salad, 143
  Beet and Apple Salad, 38
  Brie Salad with Grapes, Olives,
    and Almonds, 370
  Cobb Salad, 371
  Coleslaw, 113
  Creamy Coleslaw, 77
  Field Greens with Pear, Walnuts,
    and Blue Cheese, 338
  Greek Salad, 403
  Green Bean, Tomato, and
    Onion Salad with Dill
    Dressing, 339
  Guacamole, 271
  Hearts of Palm Salad, 142

Jicama Salad, 272
Marinated Asparagus Salad, 207
Pickled Beets, 236
Potato Salad, 173
Spinach Salad with Horseradish
  Dressing, 299
Thai Cucumber Salad, 402
Three Bean Salad, 206
Vegetable Salad with Pine Nuts,
  300
Waldorf Salad, 76
Wilted Salad, 112
Sally Lunn, 105, 121
Salmon, Marinated Grilled, 343
Salsa Fresca, 269
Sauce, Green Chili, 274
Sauerkraut with Apples, 84
Sausage and Kale Soup,
  Portuguese, 37
Scalloped Potatoes, 242
Scallops au Gratin, 43
Schlitz, Joseph, 189
Schnitz und Knepp, 63, 81
Schram, Annie, 364
Schram, Jacob, 364
Scott, Walter, 68
Scrapple, 63
See-alth, Chief, 319
Serra, Father Junipero, xi
Shanks, Lamb Braised in Red
  Wine, 374
She-crab Soup, 104, 111
Shellfish
  Baked Stuffed Clams, 33
  Chicken, Ham, and Shrimp
    Jambalaya, 175
  Cioppino, 372
  Clam Chowder, 34
  Coconut Shrimp, 138
  Cod Cake and Five Clam
    Chowder with Chorizo Aioli
    and Celery Salt, 35
  Conch Chowder, 141
  Corn and Crab Bisque, 171
  Crab Cakes, 71
  Crab Louie, 367
  Crawfish Étouffée, 177
  Crisp Crab Cakes with Celeri
    and Fennel Slaw, 72
  Eggplant with Shrimp, 179
  Flounder Stuffed with
    Crabmeat, 82
  Fresh Cracked Conch with
    Vanilla Rum Sauce and Spicy
    Black Bean Salad, 139
  Linguini with White Clam
    Sauce, 408
  Oyster Stew, 336
  Oysters Rockefeller, 169
  Scallops au Gratin, 43
  She-crab Soup, 111
  Shrimp Creole, 176
  Shrimp Rémoulade, 170
  Spring Rolls, 398
  Texas Barbecued Shrimp, 278
Shepherd's Pie, Basque, 302
Shoofly Pie, 64, 86

Short Ribs, Beef, Braised, 306
Shrimp Creole, 176
Shrimp Rémoulade, 170
Shrimp with Eggplant, 179
Simmons, Amelia, 14, 27
Simons, Menno, 63
Slossberg, Todd, 304–306
Smoked Trout with Horseradish
  Sauce, 296
Smothered Chicken, 210
Snap Peas, Sugar, Asian Style, 377
Snapper, Red, Florida Style, 148
Snapper, Zucchini and Prosciutto
  Wrapped with Saffron,
  Whitewater Clams, and
  Fingerling Potatoes, 147
Sopaipillas, 281
Soufflé, Chocolate, 415
Soul food, 104, 132, 390, 393
Soup
  Black Bean Soup, 400
  Buffalo Chili, 234
  Cheddar Cheese Beer Soup, 204
  Chicken Corn Soup with Rivels,
    74
  Chili, 270
  Chilled Avocado Soup, 369
  Cincinnati Chili, 205
  Clam Chowder, 34
  Cod Cake and Five Clam
    Chowder with Chorizo Aioli
    and Celery Salt, 35
  Conch Chowder, 141
  Corn and Crab Bisque, 171
  Crab Bisque, 75
  Creamy Peanut Soup, 112
  Lentil Soup, 337
  Mexican Tomato Soup, 401
  Oyster Stew, 336
  Portuguese Sausage and Kale
    Soup, 37
  Pumpkin Soup, 368
  She-crab Soup, 111
  Split Pea Soup, 298
  Tortilla Soup, 269
  Vegetable Barley Soup, 235
  Wild Mushroom Soup, 298
Sourdough Biscuits, 310
Sourdough French Bread, 349
Southern recipes
  Barbecued Ribs, 117
  Brunswick Stew, 115
  Cheese Grits, 121
  Coleslaw, 113
  Country Captain Chicken, 114
  Creamy Peanut Soup, 112
  Deviled Eggs, 109
  Fried Catfish, 118
  Greens, 119
  Hoppin' John, 120
  Hot Brown, 118
  Kentucky Catfish Spring Rolls
    with Asian Dipping Sauce, 110
  Lemon Chess Pie, 124
  Okra and Tomatoes, 120
  Oven Barbecued Pulled Pork,
    116

Peach Cobbler, 122
Sally Lunn, 121
She-crab Soup, 111
Wilted Salad, 112
Southwest recipes
  Calabacitas, 279
  Chicken Quesadilla, 267
  Chicken with Pumpkin Seed
    Sauce, 276
  Chili, 270
  Chili Rellenos, 268
  Green Chili Chicken
    Enchiladas, 275
  Green Chili Sauce, 274
  Guacamole, 271
  Indian Frybread, 281
  Jicama Salad, 272
  Pecan Pie, 282
  Pork Tenderloin with Ancho
    and Pasilla Chilies, 277
  Posole, 273
  Refried Beans, 279
  Salsa Fresca, 269
  Sopaipillas, 281
  Southwestern Cornbread, 280
  Texas Barbecued Shrimp, 278
  Tortilla Soup, 269
Southwestern Cornbread, 280
Spice Cake with Caramel Icing, 311
Spinach Salad with Horseradish
  Dressing, 299
Spinach, Creamed, 347
Split Pea Soup, 298
Spoonbread, 153
Spring Rolls, 398
Spring Rolls, Catfish with Asian
  Dipping Sauce, 110
Spurrier, Steven, xi
Squanto, 20
Squash, Acorn, with Maple Syrup,
  46
St. Augustine, 5
Stamp Act, 6
Starches
  Asparagus Risotto, 379
  Baked Stuffed Potatoes, 310
  Black Beans and Rice, 152
  Cheese Grits, 121
  Gratin of Potatoes and
    Mushrooms, 348
  Green Beans with New
    Potatoes, 180
  Herb Stuffing, 46
  Hoppin' John, 120
  Noodles with a Crumb Topping,
    84
  Potatoes in Horseradish Cream
    Sauce, 411
  Refried Beans, 279
  Scalloped Potatoes, 242
  Sweet Potatoes with Pecans,
    181
  Wild Rice Pilaf, 214
Steak, Chicken Fried, 238
Steak, Marinated Flank, 375
Stew, Chuckwagon, 237
Stew, Venison, 340

Index **429**

Strawberry Shortcake, 88
Strudel, Cherry Goat Cheese, 216
Stuffed Pork Chops, 208
Stuffed Potatoes, Baked, 1310
Stuffed Trout, 301
Stuffing, Herb, 46
Succotash, 28, 44
Sugar Snap Peas, Asian Style, 377
Swedish Meatballs, 202
Sweet Bread, Portuguese, 412
Sweet Onion Pie, 335
Sweet Potatoes with Pecans, 181
Swift, Gustavus, 196

T
Tchelistcheff, André, xi
Texas Barbecued Shrimp, 278
Thai Cucumber Salad, 402
Thanksgiving, 8, 20, 29
Three Bean Salad, 206
Tomato Soup, Mexican, 401
Tomato, Broiled, 152
Tomatoes Stuffed with Corn,
    Zucchini, and Almonds, 409
Torte, Chocolate Hazelnut, 352
Torte, Dobos, 413
Tortilla Soup, 269
Tourtiére, 21, 232
Townsend Act, 6

Trout, Smoked with Horseradish
    Sauce, 296
Trout, Stuffed, 301
Truman, President Harry, 129
Tschirky, Oscar, 68
Turkey with Gravy, 41
Turnips, Glazed, 241

V
Vallejo, Mariano, 356
Vancouver, George, 318, 320
Veal Medallions with Mushrooms
    and Cream, 307
Vegetables
    Acorn Squash with Maple
        Syrup, 46
    Amish Green Beans with
        Mustard Sauce, 83
    Asian Style Sugar Snap Peas,
        377
    Black Beans and Rice, 152
    Boston Baked Beans, 44
    Broiled Tomato, 152
    Brussels Sprouts with Sage and
        Cream, 308
    Calabacitas, 279
    Cauliflower with Walnuts, 213
    Colache, 151
    Corn Fritters, 309

Corn Pudding, 241
Creamed Cabbage, 240
Creamed Spinach, 347
Fried Corn, 213
Gingered Carrots, Leeks, and
    Bean Sprouts, 348
Glazed Carrots and Peas, 45
Glazed Turnips, 241
Green Beans with Dill, 213
Green Beans with New
    Potatoes, 180
Greens, 119
Grilled Vegetables with Goat
    Cheese, 378
Hoppin' John, 120
Maque Choux, 180
Mushroom Goulash, 410
Okra and Tomatoes, 120
Refried Beans, 279
Sauerkraut with Apples, 84
Succotash, 44
Tomatoes Stuffed with Corn,
    Zucchini, and Almonds, 409
Vegetable Barley Soup, 235
Vegetable Salad with Pine Nuts,
    300
Venison Stew, 340
Vidalia onions, 102, 103
Vignes, Jean-Louis, xi

Vikings, 5
Vindaloo, Lamb, 406

W
Wagner, Philip, x, xi
Waldorf Salad, 68, 76
Washington, George, 95
Waters, Alice, xi
Western sandwich, 292
Whitefish, Planked, 211
Wild Mushroom Soup, 298
Wild rice, 8, 188, 195
Wild Rice Pilaf, 214
Wild Rice Stuffed Mushrooms, 203
Wilted Salad, 112
Wok Charred Ahi with Chinese
    Cabbage Slaw and Dipping
    Sauce, 345

Y
Yankee Pot Roast, 40
Ybor, Vincente, 132
Young, Brigham, 10, 287

Z
Zucchini and Prosciutto-Wrapped
    Snapper with Saffron,
    Whitewater Clams, and
    Fingerling Potatoes, 147